MANAGERIAL ECONOMICS

MANAGERIAL ECONOMICS

A Mathematical Approach

M. J. ALHABEEB
L. JOE MOFFITT
Isenberg School of Management
University of Massachusetts
Amherst, MA, USA

WILEY

A JOHN WILEY & SONS, INC., PUBLICATION

Cover Image: Heike Schenk Arena

Published by John Wiley & Sons, Inc., Hoboken, New Jersey
Published simultaneously in Canada

For general information on our other products and services or for technical support, please contact our Customer Care Department within the United States at (800) 762-2974, outside the United States at (317) 572-3993 or fax (317) 572-4002.

Wiley also publishes its books in a variety of electronic formats. Some content that appears in print may not be available in electronic formats. For more information about Wiley products, visit our web site at www.wiley.com.

Library of Congress Cataloging-in-Publication Data:

Alhabeeb, M. J., 1954–
  Managerial economics : a mathematical approach / M.J. Alhabeeb, L. Joe Moffitt.
    p. cm.
  Includes bibliographical references and index.
  ISBN 978-1-118-09136-4 (cloth)
1. Managerial economics. I. Moffitt, L. Joe. II. Title.
HD30.22.A39 2013
338.5024′658–dc23

                                              2012023746

Printed in the United States of America

ISBN: 9781118091364

10 9 8 7 6 5 4 3 2 1

Good management is the art of making problems so interesting and their solutions so constructive that everyone wants to get to work and deal with them.

Paul Hawken

The essence of mathematics is not to make simple things complicated, but to make complicated things simple.

S. Gudder

There was a young man from Trinity,
Who solved the square root of infinity.
While counting the digits,
He was seized by the fidgets,
Dropped science, and took up divinity.

Anonymous

To
Our Students
Our Families, and
The memory of our parents.

CONTENTS IN BRIEF

CONTENTS

UNIT III   MANAGERIAL DECISIONS AT THE FIRM LEVEL

PREFACE

We live in a competitive world. Competition, in all its forms, is the name of the game everywhere: across cultures, times, environments, and whether the economy is in boom or recession; it is particularly crucial in a free market economy. Business managers are among the few, at the forefront, who feel the brunt of having to compete in order to, first, secure their firm's survival and, second, insure a prosperous and progressive state of their business. The core of their performance is defined by their ability to make the best decisions they can and be capable of confronting increasingly complicated conditions and tangled circumstances, in their own market and beyond. Economic theory and other supporting fields have proved significantly useful in providing the required efficient tools to best understand and handle the decision-making process. Managerial economics is an application of microeconomics as it is bound with its supportive quantitative methods of mathematics and statistics, business sciences, and decision sciences, all in pursuit of recognizing and utilizing the optimal treatments of and solutions to managerial problems. The ultimate purpose is to maximize the firm's effectiveness and efficiency. This is one reason why the collective and integrative nature of the material in managerial economics perfectly reflects the interdisciplinary quality of managerial decisions and the structure of business firms as a unified whole of different, multifaceted, and multifunctional parts. All of these parts strive to work in sync for an ultimate collective goal.

This book is reasonably traditional in its scope and coverage, but it is different in its approach, as compared to the rest of the available books in the field. First, there is a central theme that encloses all the material together and serves as the spine that tightly holds the book's organization. The theme is decision making at four levels: the consumer, firm, market, and the future. They, along with the preliminary fundamentals, form the five major units of the book. Second, the approach is mathematical, to stress the problem-solving and analytical nature of the decisions, as the theoretical concepts are put to practice and testing. The book is written under the assumption that readers are familiar with micro- and macroeconomics, algebra, calculus, and statistics. However, Chapter 2 is dedicated to a general and brief review of selected mathematical and statistical topics to refresh the readers' memory. The exposition of material in this book is intended to strike a good balance between the theoretical and technical on the one hand, and practical on the other. The material is presented in a straightforward, right-to-the-point manner with no "fluff" or extra "fat," to avoid making it less relevant or heavy and boring. Concepts and models are presented in multilevel learning forms and styles to enhance the overall comprehension and to fit into the diverse learning patterns of all students. They are presented in an integrative combination of description, tabular analysis, mathematical and statistical expressions, geometrical representation, and diagrammatical illustration. A great number of numerical, step-by-step-solved, examples are given after each concept. Throughout the concepts and their examples, the emphasis is put on economic intuition rather than technical manipulation or mathematical proofs. With this level of exposure, we hope that the book would challenge and motivate three-fourths of the students in a standard class and lift them up to the level of the one-fourth already at the top. Our central objective is to help students comprehend, develop, and appreciate the ultimate connection between the descriptive concepts and their mathematical face, and be able to deal with the real and practical decisions they face every day at work and beyond, particularly in the matter of resource allocation that would lead to maximizing the benefit and minimizing the cost.

Each chapter ends up with a general summary, a list of key terms, a list of formulas used throughout the chapter, and review and exercise questions. The main intention behind this end-of-chapter material is to help students review the concepts, test their comprehension, and verify their ability to apply the theoretical models and realize their usability, as well as practice and develop their problem-solving skills.

The book is intended for the upper-level undergraduate and first-year graduate in business and economics majors, MBA, and other related majors such as industrial organization and engineering. It also serves as an excellent reference material for business managers, executives, and researchers. It covers material for more than one semester, but there is a degree of flexibility in the way this material has been organized so that an instructor can prioritize and choose what can efficiently fit into his or her own single semester agenda.

The book is organized into five units with a total of 14 chapters. The first unit presents the methodological preliminaries as an essential introduction to set the tone for the type of approach and the nature of analytical treatment in this book. It includes two chapters: Chapter 1 addresses the qualitative fundamentals, and Chapter 2 addresses the quantitative fundamentals in a brief review of selected mathematical and statistical topics. The second unit introduces the managerial decisions at the consumer level. It includes four chapters: Chapter 3 is on the theory of consumer choice, Chapter 4 on the theory of consumer demand, Chapter 5 on the empirical estimation of consumer demand, and Chapter 6 on the economic forecasting of consumer demand. The third unit discusses the managerial decisions at the firm level. It includes three chapters: Chapter 7 is on production theory, Chapter 8 on cost theory, and Chapter 9 on the empirical estimation and economic forecasting of cost and production. The fourth unit addresses the managerial decision at the market level. It consists of two chapters: Chapter 10 is on market structure and organization, and Chapter 11 on pricing practices, models, and policies. The fifth unit addresses the managerial decisions in the long run. It includes three chapters: Chapter 12 is on capital budgeting and investment project evaluation, Chapter 13 on risk analysis and decisions under uncertainty, and Chapter 14 on management consultants and information.

Every possible effort has been made to make the book error free, but we believe that there will always be some flaws and errors that may slip below the radar, despite our diligent attempt to perfect the work. All the flaws and errors remain our sole responsibility, and only great appreciation goes to those who lent their hands in the preparation of the book. Readers, particularly students and instructors, are invited to submit any error they may catch or suggestions they may have to improve the quality of this book for the next edition. We are indebted to our senior departmental secretary Peggy Cialek, who typed up the entire manuscript with exceptional patience and efficiency. We are also very grateful to our former student, now an architect to be, G. Marius De La Pena, who highly competently rendered all the graphs and diagrams, and to our former graduate student Don Hedeman for his continuous help and support. A special word of appreciation goes to our Wiley editor Susanne Steitz-Filler and associate editor Jackie Palmieri for their professional competency, understanding, and patience. Many thanks and appreciation also to our production editor Stephanie Loh and our project manager Baljinder Kaur for their remarkable punctuality and care. My deep appreciation also goes to our copy editors Asha Kumari and Ammu Ajith for thoroughly and meticulously checking the manuscript and giving smart and sensible editing suggestions. The author feels very lucky to have the help and support of his friends and international artists. Special thanks to the German artist Heike Schenk Arena, who provided the beautiful image of the book cover, and the British artist Sevina Yates for her follow-up and continuous support of the project.

M. J. Alhabeeb
Belchertown, MA
April 2012

UNIT I

METHODOLOGICAL PRELIMINARIES

1

QUALITATIVE FUNDAMENTALS

1.1 ECONOMIC THEORY AND MANAGERIAL ECONOMICS

The concept of **economic scarcity** epitomizes the paradox of the finite nature of resources and the infinite nature of human needs and wants. This inherent structural contradiction in our life is not only what characterizes our societies' natural and human resources in contrast to their needs, but also what stands as the very phenomenon that necessitates choices and, therefore, bears the responsibility for the existence of prices. It is also the best reason that signifies the concept of **opportunity cost**, which is one of the central premises in economic theory, where economists consider all costs as opportunity costs in the final analysis, for they are nothing more than the foregone opportunities of some other alternatives. The opportunity cost amplifies the economic notion that for any gain there has to be some loss, for any benefit there is some cost, and for any reward there is a sacrifice. It is because of this logic that economics has been described as the science to study and analyze human choices, subject to their constraints.

The **macroeconomics** side of the theory is concerned with the "whole" versus the "parts." It studies the entire economic system and considers the society's aggregate nationwide parameters such as national income and national debt, economic growth, fluctuation of interest and inflation rates, employment, national budget, and international trade. The other side of the theory is **microeconomics**, where the main focus is on the "parts," or the components and the comprising agents of that whole system. It considers the behavior of individuals, families, and firms as they seek to maximize their economic utility. Microeconomics considers consumers' optimization of their own utility, firms' maximization of their profits and minimization of cost, and all of what entails, such as economic efficiency, market structure, capital budgeting, production, distribution, marketing,

Managerial Economics: A Mathematical Approach, First Edition. M. J. Alhabeeb and L. Joe Moffitt.
© 2013 John Wiley & Sons, Inc. Published 2013 by John Wiley & Sons, Inc.

pricing, revenues, and sales. It is, therefore, the right domain and proper atmosphere to see where managerial economics stands, for it is how managers can function and make their business decisions.

Microeconomics is capable of identifying the nature of economic problems, understanding their logic, laying out their structure, and specifying their functions and conditions. However, since all of that cannot be done only verbally or in a qualitatively descriptive manner, there has been a growing need to quantify the ranges, estimate the parameters, analyze and assess the changes, and hence, the need to employ mathematical and statistical methods within microeconomics. **Managerial economics** is, therefore, an application of microeconomics and its supportive quantitative methods (drawn from mathematics and statistics) in the decision-making process for managers who are in pursuit of recognizing and utilizing the optimal treatments and solutions to managerial problems and issues in order to reach a certain level of efficiency in achieving the firm's objectives.

Managerial economics is concerned with both effectiveness and efficiency of the decisions made by managers and **management** teams regarding the economic function of the firm in its utilization of scarce resources. This multifaceted task includes organizational design, management strategies, finances and accounting of capital management, and economic analysis of production, distribution, marketing, pricing, consumer demands for output, controlling the supply of input, monitoring markets and reacting to competition. The major thrust in undertaking these functions is to identify the general and specific problems, analyze the opportunities, and evaluate the alternatives in preparation for making the final choices.

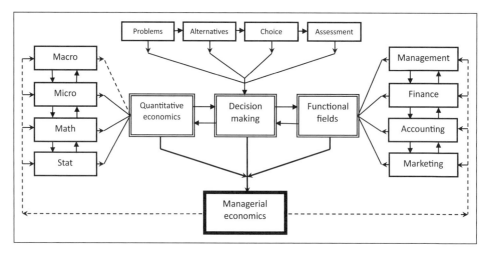

FIGURE 1.1

Figure 1.1 shows how managerial economics acquires its essential identity through the contributions of three components: (1) quantitative economics, (2) the scientific procedure of decision making, and (3) the related functional fields. Economic theory, especially microeconomics, provides the foundation for marginal analysis, theory of consumer choice, theory of the firm, industrial organization and behavior, and theory of public choice and policy. The quantitative approach would provide many technical tools such as numerical analysis, statistical estimation, mathematical optimization, econometrical **models**, forecasting procedures, game-theoretic scenarios and simulations, information system schemes, and linear programming. The **scientific approach** to decision making requires four sequenced and integrated steps:

1. Identifying and clearly defining the problems and their contexts, as well as setting clear and feasible objectives to deal with those problems.
2. Exploring all possible ranges of alternatives and their constraints, and evaluating them comparatively.
3. Deciding on the best choice among the deliberated alternatives.
4. Assessing the final choice as it is put to test in order to move to the next step, which is benefiting from the entire experience. This step also includes running some sensitivity analysis in which the chosen best alternative is examined against the possibility of changing the conditions and circumstances around it.

1.2   SOME METHODOLOGICAL FALLACIES

As stated earlier, managerial economics connects primarily to microeconomics because of its domain that is more relevant to managers and their business decisions. This does not mean a total disconnection from macroeconomics. It is more appropriate to say that the relevance of managerial economics to macroeconomics is not as certain and strong as it is to microeconomics. In some cases, there will be clear evidence of the connection, and in other cases, there would be none. Managers make many important decisions that may have implications for public policy and have to conform to state and federal rules and regulations, and abide by the local government codes. Also, many firm-specific decisions may be made in strong connection to macro parameters such as inflation and employment levels. The point here is that understanding the nature and level of connection with micro- or macroeconomics requires the problems in question to be well defined, their context to be well set, and the objectives to be correctly placed. Suffice it to say that borrowing the philosophical logic of size fallacies may help here. This fallacy is methodological in nature and is about the possibility of separating the "whole" from the "parts" (its components) and making them independent entities. Such entities may have their own characteristics, which may or may not be associated with each other. What has come to be known as the **fallacy of division** is about refuting the common logic that whatever is considered true of the "whole" is also true of the "parts." It is a fallacy because it is misleading. It may or may not be correct. Consider, for example, a well-known brand name of a product that has been dominating the market for a long time, and has acquired strong consumer loyalty. It is possible that one or more of its specific product lines may not live up to that whole good reputation and may fail in the market. On the other hand, the reversed fallacy is the **fallacy of composition**, which also refute the statement that whatever is true of the parts is also true of the whole because it may not necessarily be correct. Consider one or a few brilliant graduates who went on to become renowned scientists, poets, or artists, but their success and fame may not necessarily mean that the department or school they graduated from is as accomplished, successful, or famous as they are.

Another common methodological fallacy that should be well understood is the **fallacy of causation and correlation**. It simply refers to the fact that correlated events may not necessarily stand as causes for each other, since the correlation may only mean that they happen to occur at the same time or in the same place, but cause-and-effect relation requires a much deeper organic connection and more complicated structural ties. Consider, for example, that in inner large cities, there would be a high correlation between high-rise buildings and crime rates but, of course, it would seem preposterous to suggest that the existence of skyscrapers increases crime (!) or a high crime rate in inner cities motivates developers to build high-rise constructions (!!). A similar discussion would hold for the reverse statement that events known to be a cause or effect to each other may not necessarily be found correlated at certain circumstances such as in the case when they just happen to be there for different independent reasons. An example would be about the well-known fact that Lyme disease is caused by being bitten by a deer tick carrying the bacteria, but it is highly possible to find none or a weak correlation between being bitten by ticks and having the disease simply because it is estimated that the chances of contracting the disease after being bitten by a tick is only 1%.

Considering these fallacies, and going by the logic of serutinizing the generalized statements would eliminate the stereotypical conclusions and allow a more careful analysis. The connection of all elements in the economy and their intermingled relations are always there, but they occur in different degrees and priorities, which need to be tracked down and investigated. Consider, for instance, a macroeconomic decision by the federal or state government to increase taxes on consumption and its implications at micro levels on consumer demand on one hand and on the firm's managerial decisions on the other. Also consider the feedback of the firm's policies on consumers and the effects of both, firms and consumers, on the public policies in regard to inflation and employment.

1.3   PARADIGMS, MODELS, AND THE SCIENTIFIC METHOD

The overarching paradigm in economics pivots around three major assumptions on market participants, who are the main constituents in the economic activity (consumers, households, firms, and other economic agents). The first assumption is that they are goal-oriented, who tend to engage in a reasonably clear and purposeful participation, centered on the participants' own interest. The second assumption is that they have stable and well-defined preferences, which enable them to make rational choices that would ultimately maximize their gain, and to a certain degree, minimize their loss. The third assumption is that those participants operate in the reality of the scarce resources, which is exemplified by the resources' inability to satisfy all people's ever-increasing and changing needs and wants. In their own right, and as bold assertions as they are about the economic system, those assumptions serve as the foundation to build our economic models, which are supposed to depict the essential state of the economic system and the way it works. As basic and fundamental representation of reality, theoretical models are often simplistic, abstract, conditioned, and may very well seem unrealistic in their abstraction and intangible depiction. However, simplicity and abstraction are necessary characteristics to make models understandable, as well as make them subject to logical manipulation. Furthermore, such characteristics have to be reasonable and close enough to reality in order to be credible and capable of producing meaningful outcomes.

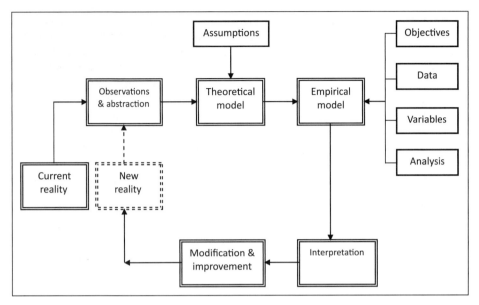

FIGURE 1.2

Figure 1.2 shows the flow of the scientific method by which observations on reality lead to theories and models, which may transfer to empirical models that can be tested, not only to validate the logic of the theoretical models but also to improve on them and take the improvements forward to modify the current realities, and create new realities so that the whole pattern would be repeated in a continuous cycle of progression.

By this **scientific process**, we would be sure to get an abstraction of reality that is objective, consistent, nonarbitrary, and reliable. It would make it possible to devise a set of testable hypotheses in order to explain, predict, and control that reality for

(a) achieving a higher performance in the current time;
(b) achieving the highest possible level of efficiency in a foreseeable future time. Relying on objectivity and nonarbitration as crucial characteristics of the scientific method is to prevent all sorts of possible personal, cultural, and spiritual beliefs from interfering with the interpretation of reality. It is also to allow the process to undergo evaluation in order to check for its degree of closeness to reality and eliminate the possibility of holding the "absolute" truth.

The quantitative approach to managerial economics, which may include optimization, statistical methods, geometrical depiction, game theory, and capital budgeting, is ultimately to derive optimal solutions to a wide variety of managerial problems. Proper solutions require the use of the scientific method to identify and quantify the changes among various important variables in the active domain of the business performance. The process would track down the interactions and recognize the major determinants and estimate their impact. Since the ultimate goal of any society is to reach the level of most efficient allocation of resources, the three classic **economizing** questions of what to produce, how much and how, and for whom, can effectively be answered with the help of economic theory and its quantitative models. It would remain true that the best models are those that can make good sense of a complex reality through an explanatory simplification and reliable prediction. The key to that is to construct positive and directional hypotheses that can be practically tested in order to delineate the map of causes and effects, determine how much and how crucial is the influence on each other, and predict what would happen to them under different circumstances. Beyond the practical benefits of the scientific process and the quantitative methods in the managerial world, the analytical approach in general is deemed to be crucial in modeling our thinking into more logical and structured patterns. It would help build higher conceptual mentalities and develop more critical thinking skills and fancier imagination, which would make it possible to creatively apply knowledge across boundaries of time and place and be better prepared for the real world beyond the present reality.

1.4   THE DESCRIPTIVE AND PRESCRIPTIVE TREATMENTS

The **descriptive approach** is concerned with positive economics. It is concerned with what was, is, and will be in actuality, with a certain degree of objectivity and regardless of any subjective positions. It considers the given conditions and circumstances, investigates any causes and effects, formulates theories and designs models, and predicts what might happen and what would change, and in what direction, all in a reasonable of neutrali. On the other hand, the **prescriptive approach** adopts a normative stand. It is based on subjective views and value judgment. It is all about "what ought to be" from a certain perspective. Outcomes, therefore, are deemed to be presented as good or bad. Economics is basically considered a descriptive and positive science. It is for this reason that economists have been for long taking a defensive stand against the charge that their analyses are often cold and heartless.

   Positive economic analyses of many contentious issues can appear to be harsh just because they are deliberately separated from any value judgment and sentimental consideration. Examples of these issues are rent control, minimum wage, welfare system, housing subsidies, comprehensive healthcare, and many more. Just like economics, managerial economics is essentially a positive science where managers are not suppose make their decisions on the basis of their sentiments. They are supposed to observe data and trends and use a scientific approach to predict consequences of their actions. The other dimension of their positive approach is that all decisions and actions can be tested empirically either by research or by plain experience. However, managerial economics does have its own prescriptive side too, especially when it comes to the issues in which managers and decision makers in general find themselves at a position in which they have to use their own value judgment and personal positions when only gut feelings can be the determinant.

1.5   THE PROFIT FUNCTION: ACCOUNTING VERSUS ECONOMICS

Seeking profit is a natural, human, and an essential self-interest motive. It is for this reason that making profit becomes a central characteristic of the for-profit firms in a free-market enterprise system. It can be stated further that, with bounded rationality and healthy conscience, making profits can elevate itself to be a virtue, especially if all standard business ethics are observed and honored. As firms pursue their self-interest, the mechanism of profit maximization works wonders for the efficient allocation of resources. It would constantly move resources toward the production of goods and services that are most valued and demanded by consumers. Other firms may leave less profitable projects and enter more lucrative markets, and eventually, the aggregate welfare is served. Under this consideration, profit would represent the society's reward for the greatest efficiency, while the lack of profit motive, especially if it translates itself into losses, would signal the lack of efficiency in the utilization of resources and result in an aggregate detriment to the society.

Conceptually, **profit** refers to the difference between the total cost of production and the total revenue brought by the sale of the products. While the total revenue is a clear-cut concept (referring to the dollar value of the product sold, as generated by multiplying the product market price by the quantity sold), the concept the total cost introduces the divergence between business profit and **economic profit**. In the business culture, the total cost consists of all the explicit or out-of-pocket expenditures on the major factors of production such as land, capital, and labor. However, the economists tend to think of the opportunity cost of all these resources and include their foregone value as an implicit part of the total cost. For example, according to the economist's view, the total cost would include the income the entrepreneur would have earned had he been hired by another firm or the return on land had it been utilized in a different project. Therefore, the **business profit** or the **accountant's profit** (π_a) would be different from the **economist's profit** (π_e) by

$$\pi_a = \text{TR} - \text{ETC},$$

$$\pi_e = \text{TR} - (\text{ETC} + \text{ITC}),$$

where the latter includes the implicit total cost (ITC) in addition to the explicit total cost (ETC), and TR is the total revenue. The business profit is a practical concept, especially for the purpose of calculating the book value, and considering the accounting and taxes, while the economist's concept of profit is important for a real understanding of the business decisions especially on investment, risk, and return.

1.6 ENTREPRENEURSHIP, MANAGEMENT, AND LEADERSHIP

Terms such as "entrepreneur" and "manager" or "owner-manager" are often used interchangeably, especially in the small business setting and entrepreneurship literature. For more accuracy, we can link these terms to the nature of activity of both entrepreneurship and management, as they are distinct phases of the production process. To a less extent, there has also been a certain mix-up between the management and leadership functions in the private and public administration process. Very early on, the French term **entrepreneur** meant the person who could organize and direct resources into a production process. At the start of the nineteenth century, Jean-Baptiste Say, a French economist and businessman, elaborated on the role of the entrepreneur in creating new values by simply knowing when and where to employ the economic resources and have them yield a higher return. In modern times, **entrepreneurship** is defined as the process of creating a new business by utilizing resources and taking them through the possible risk and bearing the responsibility for it. Accordingly, an entrepreneur is the person who has the vision for a business project and can start it up. That would be the individual who can assemble and combine the necessary economic resources for a project, employ them, and make a profit out of them. It takes a special personality with certain traits to become an efficient entrepreneur. Successful entrepreneurship requires the following:

- An ability to foresee the right opportunities and perceive their dynamics.
- A capacity to come up with innovative ideas that fit their time, place, and other circumstances.
- An attitude of courage, energy, and optimism to start up the project, go all the way with it, assume full responsibility for its ups and downs, and know and count for all risk involved.
- A spirit of commitment, flexibility, and tenacity, coupled with tolerance and ability and willingness to learn from mistakes.
- A natural talent for organizing the resources and utilizing them to achieve their highest yield.

The most important thing to realize here is that entrepreneurship is only the first phase of production, which is the innovative phase. This phase would end when the project can stand on its feet after starting production. Next, the project would enter the second phase of production and earning, which would need a different set of skills and a different process, and that would be the management phase. Here, the top performer is the manager and the required skills are managerial as opposed to entrepreneurial (Figure 1.3).

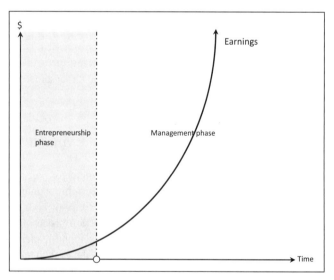

FIGURE 1.3

As for **management**, it is the effective and efficient use of resources to accomplish certain economic and administrative objectives for the managed unit. In the production phase and throughout the life of the project, management involves five integrative functions: planning, organizing, staffing, directing, and controlling. As for **leadership**, the focus is on the capacity and quality of making strategic decisions, oversee operations, and bring about changes. Leadership is not associated with a specific production phase. It can work anywhere and it may be required at all levels, any time, and under any circumstances.

SUMMARY

- The first unit of this book is dedicated to the fundamentals that would establish the approach and set the tone for the remaining four units. It is the springboard from which we leap, well equipped, to better understand the whole material on this subject matter.

- The unit includes two chapters. This first chapter is on the qualitative fundamentals. It started by defining economics and managerial economics and explained the link between them. It expanded the discussion to delineate the domains of micro- and macroeconomics and described the scientific approach to the process of decision making. In Section 1.2, the discussion moved to the most common methodological fallacies: the fallacy of division, which is about setting the logic that whatever might be considered correct on the "whole" may not necessarily be correct on the parts of that whole. The fallacy of composition would stand on the opposite side. Its logic suggests that whatever might be considered correct on the parts may not necessarily be correct on the whole. The third fallacy is of the causation and correlation. It refers to the fact that correlated events may not necessarily stand as causes for each other. The reason is that the correlation may only mean the events happen to occur at the same time, in same place, or under same circumstances, but the cause-and-effect relation requires a much deeper organic connection and more structural ties.

- More methodological clarification was presented in Section 1.3. The assumptions of the major paradigm in economic analysis were addressed, and they were all about the main economic players such as individual consumers, households, firms, and other constituents. Models were explained as basic and fundamental representation of reality, and the scientific method was presented in a descriptive and graphic way. It showed the flow from observations on reality to theoretical and, then, to empirical work that could be tested to either validate or refute the theoretical models.

- Positive and normative economics were discussed in terms of their descriptive and prescriptive approaches. The descriptive approach is concerned with what was, is, and will be in actuality with a certain degree of objectivity. The prescriptive approach is based on a subjective view and value judgment. It is more concerned with "what ought to be." Managerial economics basically belongs to the positive approach although it may have some sides of the normative approach too.

- Profit is reviewed from two perspectives: the economic and the accounting perspective. While profit is the difference between the total revenue and the total cost, it is the multifaceted concept of cost that would cause the difference between the accounting, or business, profit and the economic profit. The economists tend to think of the opportunity cost of all the resources as an implicit part of the total cost. Accountants are concerned with the explicit or out-of-pocket cost.

- Section 1.6 covered the concepts of entrepreneurship, management, and leadership. Entrepreneurship refers to the process of creating a new business by utilizing resources and taking them through the possible risk and bearing all the responsibilities of the task. The requirements of successful entrepreneurship are addressed, and management is distinguished from entrepreneurship not only by the nature of function but also by the timing of their effectiveness in the life of business projects. Management is defined as the effective and efficient use of resources to accomplish certain economic and administrative objectives for the managed unit, while leadership focuses on the capacity and quality of making strategic decisions, oversee operations, and being about changes.

KEY TERMS

economic scarcity	macroeconomics	microeconomics
opportunity cost	managerial economics	scientific approach
scientific process	methodological fallacies	fallacy of division
fallacy of composition	fallacy of causation and correlation	paradigm
model	economizing	descriptive approach
prescriptive approach	positive analysis	normative analysis
accounting profit	economic profit	entrepreneurship
management	leadership	

EXERCISES

1. What are the qualitative fundamentals and why are they important to know for the study of managerial economics?

2. How different is managerial economics from economics and how is it related to both microeconomics and macroeconomics?

3. What is opportunity cost? Is it one of the important considerations for economists?

4. List and explain the four major steps of the decision-making process according to the scientific approach.

5. What are the major methodological fallacies and why should we be concerned about them? Try to provide an example of each fallacy, especially something that you may have already contemplated in your daily life.

6. What is paradigm and how is it different from theory? Can you provide an example to set the two apart?

7. What is the scientific method and how is it different from the nonscientific methods? Why is it important for students to know this kind of material? Does it really have any significance in real life? If so, try to provide an example.

8. What is the descriptive approach? How is it different from the prescriptive approach and where would managerial economics stand?

9. Explain the concept of profit from both accounting and economic perspectives. What would make the two different from each other? Will this difference have any practical mix-up when it comes to the managerial decision making?

10. Explain the concepts of entrepreneurship, management, and leadership and set the link between an entrepreneur, a manager, and a CEO of a firm. How do the three work to set the firm and optimize its efficiency?

2

QUANTITATIVE FUNDAMENTALS

2.1 INTRODUCTION

The quantification of economic principles and analysis remains prominent even today, many decades after it began in earnest during the twentieth century. Inherently, the use of mathematics and statistics in economics encourages rigor and precision and is, therefore, appealing to economic theoreticians and practitioners alike. Even so, and often for different reasons, there are many naysayers, especially in the popular press (see, Jennings, 1994). However, this is not new, as the well-known quote by economist Kenneth Boulding explains: "Mathematics brought rigor to economics. Unfortunately, it also brought mortis." However, a quantitative approach to economics continues to flourish in spite of such criticisms. It is suggested that the use of quantitative methods in economics will continue, but the type of methods and the way they are applied may change in the future (e.g., Colander, 2000). We cannot be certain about what the future holds for quantitative economics, but we are certain that a number of fundamental quantitative methods will remain important in every managerial economist's toolkit even if there are some major changes in the way economics is taught and practiced in the years ahead. The mathematical and statistical fundamentals and terminology we emphasize in this chapter are used throughout the book. We focus on the fundamentals that we consider indispensable to rational application of economic principles under a robust set of circumstances, which will be an essential part of every managerial economist's training for years to come.

This chapter is intended as a refresher course on the basic mathematical and statistical tools that managerial economists use and, as already mentioned, will use in the foreseeable future. The refresher is intended, along with the rest of this book, to accommodate the aspirations of students who have fulfilled the prerequisites for an upper division managerial economics course and have done well in those prerequisites. We begin with the general notion of a **function** and follow that discussion with two specific functions, **logarithms**

Managerial Economics: A Mathematical Approach, First Edition. M. J. Alhabeeb and L. Joe Moffitt.
© 2013 John Wiley & Sons, Inc. Published 2013 by John Wiley & Sons, Inc.

and **exponents**, which we will use frequently. Then, we review some essentials of differential calculus along with multivariate and constrained optimization. **Probability** and statistical concepts along with a very important inference method, the method of **maximum likelihood**, are covered in the final sections of the chapter.

2.2   FUNCTIONS

Much of the mainstream economics depicts economic phenomena using the notion of a functional relationship between variables as described in mathematics. The key feature of a mathematical function is that it associates a unique value of one variable with every distinct value of other variables. An abstract example of a functional relationship, f, includes the association of a unique value of a variable, y, with every value of another variable, x_1. This relationship is often expressed as $y = f(x_1)$.

Similarly, $y = f(x_1, x_2, \ldots, x_n)$ expresses a relationship that associates a unique value of y with every distinct value of n variables $x_1, x_2, \ldots, x_n$. Figure 2.1 shows graphs of functions with $n = 1$ in panel (a) and $n = 2$ in panel (b). The key feature of a mathematical function is revealed in the graphs by a unique value of y appearing on the curve above each distinct value of x_1 in panel (a) and a unique value of y appearing on the surface above each distinct value of (x_1, x_2) in panel (b).

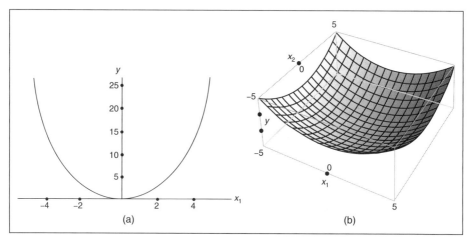

FIGURE 2.1

As already mentioned, economics abounds with functional relationships. For example, demand and supply relationships in a market can be depicted using functional relationships between quantity demanded, D, quantity supplied, S, quantity transacted, Q, and market price, P:

$$D = f(P),$$
$$S = g(P),$$
$$Q = D = S.$$

This economic model is graphed differently by mathematicians and economists as shown in Figure 2.2.

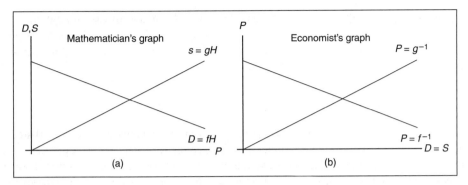

FIGURE 2.2

To examine the difference between the graphs shown in Figure 2.2 more specifically, suppose that the functional relationships are as follows:

$$D = 14 - 2P,$$
$$S = 2 + 4P,$$
$$Q = D = S.$$

The mathematician's graph shows these functional relationships as they are written above. The economist's graph shows

$$P = 7 - \tfrac{1}{2}D,$$

$$P = -\tfrac{1}{2} + \tfrac{1}{4}S,$$

where each relationship has been solved for P. Both graphs reveal $Q = D = S = 10$ and $P = 2$ as the solution to the model.

An important use of functional relationships in economic models is to predict the change in economic variables due to a change in one of the model's functional relationships. Figure 2.3 depicts a shift in the demand function from D_1 to D_2.

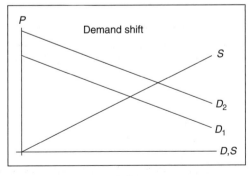

FIGURE 2.3

Now consider the algebra associated with the demand shift as depicted in Figure 2.3:

$$D = 14 - 2P + A,$$
$$S = 2 + 4P,$$
$$Q = D = S.$$

Changes in Q and P when the variable A changes from 0 to a number greater than 0 are of significant interest. This use of economic models to compare the changes in economic variables is known as **comparative statics analysis**. Note that comparative statics analysis can produce either qualitative or quantitative results, depending on how specific the economic model's functional relationships are.

2.3   EXPONENTS

Exponents are used throughout managerial economics and should be thoroughly understood. Both exponents and logarithms are examples of functions. We begin with definitions followed by examples to illustrate the definitions.

By definition, a^n, where a is the base (simply a number) and n is the exponent (for now, simply a nonnegative integer) is $a\,a\,a\,\ldots\,a$ (n times), that is, the product of a with itself n times.

Some examples that illustrate the definition of exponents are

$$a^5 = a\,a\,a\,a\,a,$$
$$a^1 = a,$$
$$\left(\frac{p}{q}\right)^5 = \left(\frac{p}{q}\right)\left(\frac{p}{q}\right)\left(\frac{p}{q}\right)\left(\frac{p}{q}\right)\left(\frac{p}{q}\right),$$
$$x^4 = x\,x\,x\,x,$$
$$(n+1)^3 = (n+1)(n+1)(n+1),$$
$$a^0 = 1 \text{ if } a \neq 0,$$
$$0^0 \text{ is undefined.}$$

Negative exponents are by definition $a^{-n} = \frac{1}{a^n}$. Some examples to illustrate this definition are as follows:

$$a^{-1} = \frac{1}{a},$$
$$8^{-3} = \frac{1}{8^3},$$
$$(x^2 + 5)^{-10} = \frac{1}{(x^2 + 5)^{10}},$$
$$(-10)^2 = (-10)(-10) = 100,$$
$$-10^2 = -(10 \times 10) = -100,$$

$$(2x)^{-1} = \frac{1}{2x},$$

$$2x^{-1} = \frac{2}{x}.$$

There are five general properties of exponents:

1. $a^n a^m = a^{n+m}$
2. $\frac{a^n}{a^m} = a^{n-m}$
3. $(a^n)^m = a^{nm}$
4. $(a\,b)^n = a^n b^n$
5. $\left(\frac{a}{b}\right)^n = \frac{a^n}{b^n}$

Some examples of these general properties are as follows:

$$a^3 a^2 = (a\,a\,a)\,(a\,a) = a^{3+2} = a^5,$$

$$\left(\frac{a^3}{a^2}\right) = \frac{aaa}{aa} = a^{3-2} = a,$$

$$(a^2)^3 = a^2\,a^2\,a^2 = a^{2+2+2} = a^6,$$

$$(a\,b)^3 = (a\,b)\,(a\,b)\,(a\,b) = a\,a\,a\,b\,b\,b = a^3\,b^3,$$

$$a^{-3}\,a^5 = a^{-3+5} = a^2,$$

$$(x\,y)^{-2} = x^{-2}\,y^{-2},$$

$$\left(\frac{a}{b}\right)^{-n} = \frac{a^{-n}}{b^{-n}} = \frac{b^n}{a^n}.$$

By definition, $a^{m/n} = $ the nth root of a^m.
Some examples of fractional exponents are as follows:

$$a^{1/2} = \sqrt{a} = \text{the square root of } a,$$

$$a^{3/2} = \text{the square root of } a^3,$$

$$10^{\frac{5}{3}} = \text{the cube root of } 10^5 = \text{the cube root of } 100{,}000 = (100{,}000)^{\frac{1}{3}}$$

$$= 46.42\ldots \text{since } (46.42\ldots)\,(46.42\ldots)\,(46.42\ldots) = 100{,}000,$$

$$4^{2.5} = 4^{\frac{5}{2}} = \text{the square root of } 4^5 = 32.$$

We will use exponents repeatedly, so you should ensure that you understand and can apply these definitions and properties.

2.4 LOGARITHMS AND THE NUMBER *e*

The natural logarithm, denoted by ln, is defined with reference to Figure 2.4—the graph of curve $1/t$ for $t > 0$. The function $\ln x_1$ is defined as the area under the curve between 1 and x_1 (shown as the shaded area). Hence, $\ln x_1$ is increasing on x_1 and is positive (negative) for x_1 greater (less) than one and is zero for x_1 equal to one. The value of x_1 that makes the area equal to 1 is the number e (a nonrepeating decimal number that is about 2.71). Moreover, the value of x_1 that makes the area equal to y is the number e^y, where y is a real number. Note that e^y is often written as $\exp(y)$.

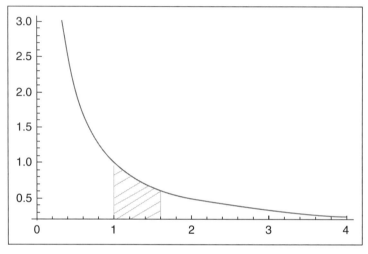

FIGURE 2.4

A remarkable property of function $\ln x_1$, which no other mathematical function has, is that the natural logarithm of the product of any two positive numbers is the sum of the natural logarithms of the two numbers, that is,

$$\ln x_1\, x_2 = \ln x_1 + \ln x_2 \text{ for all positive numbers } x_1 \text{ and } x_2.$$

This property of natural logarithm extends to the product of n positive numbers:

$$\ln \prod x_i = \sum \ln x_i \text{ for all } x_i > 0.$$

If one keeps the definition of logarithm in mind, there is no mystery associated with $\ln x_1$ or the number e.

2.5   DIFFERENTIAL CALCULUS

The **derivative** of a function is used in defining several basic economic concepts including elasticities and various "marginal" quantities. Derivatives can also be used to characterize critical values of a function such as a maximum. This section provides a brief review of the derivative of a function for its use in the later chapters.

The limit of a function, usually written as $\text{Lim}_{x_1 \to a} f(x_1)$, is defined as the number that the function $f(x_1)$ can be made arbitrarily close to by choosing the value of x_1 sufficiently close to a. The notion of a limit underlies differential (and integral) calculus. The derivative of a function $y = f(x_1)$ can be found directly from the definition of the derivative, $\text{Lim}_{h \to 0} [f(x_1 + h) - f(x_1)]/h$, and is usually written as dy/dx_1. The geometric interpretation of the derivative is: "A one unit move to the right along the x_1 axis will produce a change in $f(x_1)$ approximately equal to the derivative." Hence, the geometric interpretation of the derivative of $y = f(x_1)$ at a point is the slope of the tangent line to $f(x_1)$ at that point.

There are seven rules for finding the derivative of a function. Each rule along with an example is given below.

Differentiation rule 1: derivative of a constant

$$y = f(x_1) = a,$$

$$\frac{dy}{dx_1} = 0.$$

Example: $y = 3$

$$\frac{dy}{dx_1} = 0.$$

Differentiation rule 2: derivative of a function involving an exponent (power function)

$$y = x_1^b,$$

$$\frac{dy}{dx_1} = b\, x_1^{b-1}.$$

Example: $y = x_1^2$

$$\frac{dy}{dx_1} = 2x_1.$$

Differentiation rule 3: derivative of a constant times a function

$$y = af(x_1),$$

$$\frac{dy}{dx_1} = af'(x_1).$$

Example: $y = 3x_1$

$$\frac{dy}{dx_1} = 3.$$

Differentiation rule 4: derivative of the sum or difference of two functions

$$y = f(x_1) + g(x_1),$$
$$\frac{dy}{dx_1} = f'(x_1) + g'(x_1).$$

Example: $y = 10 + 5x_1 + 6x_1{}^2$

$$\frac{dy}{dx_1} = 5 + 12x_1.$$

Differentiation rule 5: derivative of the product of two functions

$$y = f(x_1)g(x_1),$$
$$\frac{dy}{dx_1} = f(x_1)g'(x_1) + g(x_1)f'(x_1).$$

Example: $y = (x_1{}^2 - 4)(x_1{}^2 + 2x_1 + 2)$

$$\frac{dy}{dx_1} = \left(x_1^2 - 4\right)(2x_1 + 2) + \left(x_1^2 + 2x_1 + 2\right)(2x_1).$$

Differentiation rule 6: derivative of the quotient of two functions

$$y = \frac{f(x_1)}{g(x_1)},$$
$$\frac{dy}{dx_1} = \frac{g(x_1)f'(x_1) - f(x_1)g'(x_1)}{(g(x_1))^2}.$$

Example: $y = \dfrac{x_1^2 - 3x_1}{x_1^2}$

$$\frac{dy}{dx_1} = \frac{x_1^2(2x_1 - 3) - \left(x_1^2 - 3x_1\right)(2x_1)}{\left(x_1^2\right)^2}.$$

Differentiation rule 7: derivative of a composite function (function of a function)

$$y = g(u),$$
$$u = f(x_1),$$

$$y = g(f(x_1)),$$

$$\frac{dy}{dx_1} = \left(\frac{dy}{du}\right)\left(\frac{du}{dx_1}\right).$$

Example: $y = u^2$

$$u = 2x_1 + 5,$$

$$y = (2x_1 + 5)^2,$$

$$\frac{dy}{dx_1} = (2u)(2),$$

$$= (2(2x_1 + 5))(2).$$

The derivative of the natural logarithm function, $y = \ln x_1$, and the derivative of the exponential function, $y = e^{x_1}$, are needed in the following chapters. The derivative of the natural logarithm, $y = \ln x_1$, is

$$\frac{dy}{dx_1} = \frac{1}{x_1}.$$

The derivative of the exponential function, $y = e^{x_1}$, is

$$\frac{dy}{dx_1} = e^{x_1}.$$

A derivative of a function is also a function that can often be differentiated. Derivatives of a derivative are referred to as higher order derivatives. For example, the second-order derivative of a function is

$$\frac{d}{dx_1}\left(\frac{dy}{dx_1}\right) = \frac{d^2y}{dx_1^2} = f''(x_1).$$

The seven differentiation rules are also used to find higher order derivatives. An example of higher order derivatives is given below. You should make sure that you can use these seven rules to reach the same results as shown in the example.

Example: $y = 10\,x_1^3 + 3\,x_1^2 - 5\,x_1 + 6$

$$\frac{dy}{dx_1} = 30x_1^2 + 6x_1 - 5,$$

$$\frac{d^2y}{dx_1^2} = 60x_1 + 6,$$

$$\frac{d^3y}{dx_1^3} = 60,$$

$$\frac{d^4y}{dx_1^4} = 0.$$

Derivatives of function $f(x_1, x_2, \ldots, x_n)$ are also found using the seven differentiation rules. The **partial derivative** of a function $y = f(x_1, x_2, \ldots, x_n)$ with respect to variable x_1 can be found directly from the definition of the derivative, $\text{Lim}_{h \to 0} [f(x_1 + h, x_2, \ldots, x_n) - f(x_1, x_2, \ldots, x_n)]/h$, and is usually written as $\partial y/\partial x_1$. Note that the partial derivative is the same as the derivative previously discussed with all variables other than x_1 treated as constants. The geometric interpretation of the partial derivative of f with respect to x_1 is: "A one unit move to the right along the x_1 axis will produce a change in $f(x_1, x_2, \ldots, x_n)$ approximately equal to the derivative." The geometric interpretation of the partial derivative of $y = f(x_1, x_2, \ldots, x_n)$ at a point is the slope of the tangent line to $f(x_1, x_2, \ldots, x_n)$ at that point with variables other than x_1 treated as constants. The partial derivative for variables other than x_1 is similarly defined and interpreted.

Example: $y = x_1 x_2$

$$\partial y/\partial x_1 = x_2,$$

$$\partial y/\partial x_2 = x_1.$$

2.6   MULTIVARIATE AND EQUALITY CONSTRAINED OPTIMIZATION

Maximization and **minimization** are widely used throughout microeconomics and statistics, and sometimes optimization is subject to constraints on the variable(s) of choice. In this section, the discussion and examples are limited to one or two decision variables; however, the techniques extend to more than two decision variables. A function, $f(x_1)$, can be maximized by choosing a value x_1^* so that $f(x_1^*) \geq f(x_1)$ for all possible values of x_1. Often, it may be possible to find x_1^* where the derivative of f with respect to x_1 is zero. Similarly, a maximization problem can be expressed as choosing values of variables x_1 and x_2 to make the value of the function, f, as large as possible, that is,

$$\text{Maximize } f(x_1, x_2).$$

The solution, for example, (x_1^*, x_2^*), can be characterized by $f(x_1^*, x_2^*) \geq f(x_1, x_2)$ for all values of x_1 and x_2. Frequently, derivatives are used to characterize the solution when the function f and the possible values of x_1 and x_2 permit differentiation. In such cases, the solution is necessarily a flat spot of the function and could be characterized by a zero value of the derivative of f with respect to x_1 and x_2:

$$\frac{\partial f}{\partial x_1} = 0,$$

$$\frac{\partial y}{\partial x_2} = 0.$$

Example: Maximize $f(x_1, x_2) = -5x_1^2 - 10x_2^2 + 50x_1 + 60x_2$

$$\frac{\partial f}{\partial x_1} = 50 - 10x_1 = 0,$$

$$\frac{\partial y}{\partial x_2} = 60 - 20x_2 = 0.$$

Solving these two equations gives $x_1^* = 5$ and $x_2^* = 3$ as the solution to the maximization problem.

In some cases, the choice variables, x_1 and x_2, in an optimization problem are constrained to satisfy an equation. The general equality constrained maximization problem with two choice variables and one equality constraint is

$$\text{Maximize } f(x_1, x_2),$$

$$\text{Subject to } g(x_1, x_2) = b.$$

We use the **Lagrangian method** for solving this equality constrained maximization problem. The method is based on introducing a new decision variable and forming a new function using it and the remaining parts of the maximization problem. The new function often possesses a "flat spot" for values of the decision variables that solve the constrained maximization problem. Hence, we can use derivatives to characterize the solution to the original problem.

The three steps that comprise the method for solving the general equality constrained maximization problem are described below.

First, form the **Lagrangian**, $L(x_1, x_2, \lambda)$, where

$$L(x_1, x_2, \lambda) = f(x_1, x_2) - \lambda[g(x_1, x_2) - b].$$

The variable λ in the Lagrangian is referred to as the **Lagrange multiplier**. x_1 and x_2 are the **decision variables**, $f(x_1, x_2)$ is the **objective function**, $g(x_1, x_2)$ is the **constraint function**, and b is the **constraint constant**.

Note that the Lagrangian should always be formed as

$$L(x_1, x_2, \lambda) = \text{Objective function} - \lambda(\text{Constraint function} - \text{Constraint constant}).$$

Second, set the derivatives of L with respect to the decision variables and the Lagrange multiplier equal to 0:

$$\frac{\partial L}{\partial x_1} = \frac{\partial f}{\partial x_1} - \lambda \frac{\partial g}{\partial x_1} = 0,$$

$$\frac{\partial L}{\partial x_2} = \frac{\partial f}{\partial x_2} - \lambda \frac{\partial g}{\partial x_2} = 0,$$

$$\frac{\partial L}{\partial \lambda} = b - g(x_1, x_2) = 0.$$

Third, solve these three equations for the optimal values of the decision variables and the Lagrange multiplier.

Example

$$\text{Maximize } x_1 + x_2,$$

$$\text{Subject to } x_1^2 + x_2^2 = 1.$$

The Lagrangian in this case is given by

$$L(x_1, x_2, \lambda) = x_1 + x_2 - \lambda \left[x_1^2 + x_2^2 - 1 \right].$$

The "flat spot" of the Lagrangian is indicated by

$$\frac{\partial L}{\partial x_1} = 1 - 2\lambda x_1 = 0,$$

$$\frac{\partial L}{\partial x_2} = 1 - 2\lambda x_2 = 0,$$

$$\frac{\partial L}{\partial \lambda} = 1 - x_1^2 - x_2^2 = 0.$$

The solution to these three equations is $(x_1, x_2, \lambda) = (2^{-0.5}, 2^{-.05}, 2^{-0.5})$.

In case the "flat spot" of the Lagrangian is a saddle point (defined below), it has special significance for the solution to the equality constrained optimization problem.

Let us consider the problem again:

$$\text{Maximize } f(x_1, x_2),$$

$$\text{Subject to } g(x_1, x_2) = b,$$

with Lagrangian given by

$$L(x_1, x_2, \lambda) = f(x_1, x_2) - \lambda[g(x_1, x_2) - b].$$

By definition, a saddle point of the Lagrangian, $(x_1^*, x_2^*, \lambda^*)$, satisfies

1. $L(x_1^*, x_2^*, \lambda^*) \leq L(x_1^*, x_2^*, \lambda)$ for all λ;
2. $L(x_1^*, x_2^*, \lambda^*) \geq L(x_1, x_2, \lambda^*)$ for all x, y.

Let us first focus on condition 1:

$$L\left(x_1^*, x_2^*, \lambda^*\right) \leq L\left(x_1^*, x_2^*, \lambda\right) \text{ for all } \lambda.$$

After writing the expression for the Lagrangian explicitly,

$$f\left(x_1^*, x_2^*\right) - \lambda^* \left[g\left(x_1^*, x_2^*\right) - b \right] \leq f\left(x_1^*, x_2^*\right) - \lambda \left[g\left(x_1^*, x_2^*\right) - b \right] \text{ for all } \lambda.$$

After eliminating $f(x_1^*, x_2^*)$ from both sides,

$$-\lambda^* \left[g\left(x_1^*, x_2^*\right) - b \right] \leq -\lambda \left[g\left(x_1^*, x_2^*\right) - b \right] \text{ for all } \lambda.$$

The last expression can be simplified as

$$(\lambda - \lambda^*) \left[g\left(x_1^*, x_2^*\right) - b \right] \leq 0 \text{ for all } \lambda,$$

which implies that

$$g\left(x_1^*, x_2^*\right) - b = 0.$$

Keeping the above result in mind, let us now focus on condition 2:

$$L\left(x_1^*, x_2^*, \lambda^*\right) \geq L\left(x_1, x_2, \lambda^*\right) \text{ for all } x, y.$$

Upon rewriting,

$$f\left(x_1^*, x_2^*\right) - \lambda^*\left[g\left(x_1^*, x_2^*\right) - b\right] \geq f(x, y) - \lambda^*[g(x, y) \text{ for all } b] \text{ for all } x, y.$$

This last expression can also be simplified by eliminating $-\lambda^*\left[g(x_1^*, x_2^*) - b\right]$ from the left-hand side, since analysis of condition 1 has already shown that $g(x_1^*, x_2^*) - b = 0$. The result is

$$f\left(x_1^*, x_2^*\right) \geq f(x, y) - \lambda^*[g(x, y) - b] \text{ for all } x, y.$$

Therefore, it must also be true that

$$f\left(x_1^*, x_2^*\right) \geq f(x, y) \text{ for all } x, y \text{ including those for which } g(x, y) = b.$$

The last expression implies that a saddle point of the Lagrangian solves the equality constrained optimization problem.

The derivatives of the Lagrangian can be interpreted in terms of some basic economic principles that you know from previous coursework. Suppose the problem is simplified to involve only a single choice variable:

$$\text{Maximize } f(x),$$

$$\text{Subject to } g(x) = b.$$

The Lagrangian is

$$L(x, \lambda) = f(x) - \lambda[g(x) - b].$$

A graph of the Lagrangian that applies to this problem is shown in Figure 2.5.

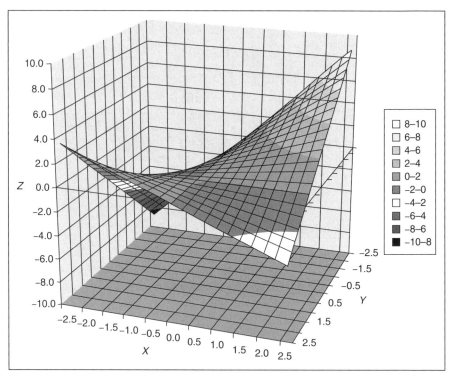

FIGURE 2.5

The marginal conditions associated with the Lagrangian are as follows:

$$f'(x) - \lambda g'(x) = 0,$$

$$b - g(x) = 0.$$

Let us focus on interpreting the first condition since the interpretation of the second condition is obvious. We envision a simple production problem where a single input is used to produce a single output and b units of input is employed. Suppose that x = output, $f(x)$ = value of output, λ = input value per unit, $g(x)$ = units of the input used, and b = units of input to be used. Then, the slope of the Lagrangian in the x-direction (the first condition) can be interpreted as involving familiar economic concepts. First note that, since x = output and input = $g(x)$, then $x = g^{-1}(\text{input})$, where g^{-1} is the inverse of function g and is also known as the total product (TP). So $dx/d\,\text{input} = d\,g^{-1}(\text{input})/d\,\text{input} = d\text{TP}/d\,\text{input}$ = marginal product (MP) of the input. In general, the derivative of a function's inverse is the reciprocal of the derivative of the function itself. With this in mind, note that $\text{MP} = d\,g^{-1}(\text{input})/dx = 1/g'(x)$. The latter implies that $g'(x)$ is $1/\text{MP}$. Looking at the first condition, we see that $\lambda\,g'(x) = \lambda/\text{MP}$. However, from your previous coursework in economic principles, you know that factor price/marginal product is marginal cost (MC). So the first condition can be interpreted as $f'(x) - \text{MC} = 0$. However, $f'(x)$ is marginal revenue (MR). Hence, the slope of the Lagrangian in the x-direction involves one of the most important elements of introductory microeconomics, that is, the slope is the difference between MR and MC.

The Lagrangian is specified so that in the λ-direction, the slope is the difference between the constraint function and the constraint constant ($g(x) - b)$). So this slope changes sign around the constraint. This means that the slope is zero along the constraint.

Therefore, the flat spot of the Lagrangian where the slopes in the λ- and x-directions are simultaneously zero is a significant point. At that point, the amount of output (x) and resource price (λ) are such that (1) the constraint is satisfied (zero slope in the λ-direction) and (2) MR = MC (zero slope in the x-direction). These conditions mean that the flat spot solves the equality constrained maximization problem. This is the essence of what is referred to as saddle point sufficiency.

The interpretation of the Lagrange multiplier can be derived as follows. Suppose that the equality constrained maximization problem

$$\text{Maximize } f(x_1, x_2),$$

$$\text{Subject to } g(x_1, x_2) = b,$$

is solved by (x_1^*, x_2^*). Note that, in general, x_1^* and x_2^* depend on b.

Assuming that $x_1^*(b)$ and $x_2^*(b)$ are differentiable functions of b, then the associated value of the objective function is also a function of b:

$$f^*(b) = f\left[x_1^*(b), x_2^*(b)\right].$$

The function, $f^*(b)$, is called the **value function** for the problem or the **indirect function**.

The Lagrange multiplier, λ, is the change in the value function due to an (one unit) increase in the constraint constant, b. Denote $\partial f/\partial x_1 = f_1$, $\partial f/\partial x_2 = f_2$, $\partial g/\partial x_1 = g_1$, and $\partial g/\partial x_2 = g_2$ and define the total differential of $f(x_1, x_2)$ to be $df = \partial f/\partial x_1 \, dx_1 + \partial f/\partial x_2 \, dx_2 = f_1 \, dx_1 + f_2 \, dx_2$.

Since $f^*(b) = f[x_1^*(b), x_2^*(b)]$,

$$df^*(b) = f_1\left[x_1^*(b), x_2^*(b)\right] dx_1^* + f_2\left[x_1^*(b), x_2^*(b)\right] dx_2^*.$$

From the necessary conditions for a maximum,

$$f_1\left(x_1^*, x_2^*\right) = \lambda \, g_1\left(x_1^*, x_2^*\right)$$

and

$$f_2\left(x_1^*, x_2^*\right) = \lambda \, g_2\left(x_1^*, x_2^*\right).$$

Substituting for $f_1(x_1^*, x_2^*)$ and $f_2(x_1^*, x_2^*)$ in the expression for $df^*(b)$ above gives

$$df^*(b) = \lambda \, g_1\left(x_1^*, x_2^*\right) dx_1^* + \lambda \, g_2\left(x_1^*, x_2^*\right) dx_2^*.$$

Also, since (x_1^*, x_2^*) satisfies the problem constraint,

$$g\left(x_1^*, x_2^*\right) = b$$

and

$$dg\left(x_1^*, x_2^*\right) = g_1\left(x_1^*, x_2^*\right) dx_1^* + g_2\left(x_1^*, x_2^*\right) dx_2^* = db.$$

Forming the ratio of $df^*(b)$ to db gives

$$\frac{df^*(b)}{db} = \lambda.$$

A value of the Lagrange multiplier that is consistent with this interpretation will always be obtained from solving for a critical point of the Lagrangian if the Lagrangian is formed as

$$L(x, \lambda) = \text{Objective function} - \lambda(\text{Constraint function} - \text{Constraint constant}).$$

Hence, the Lagrangian should always be formed this way.

Example

$$\text{Maximize } x_1 + x_2,$$

$$\text{Subject to } x_1^2 + x_2^2 = 1,$$

$$f^*(b) = f\left[x_1^*(b), x_2^*(b)\right]$$

$$= x_1^*(b) + x_2^*(b)$$

$$= \sqrt{\frac{b}{2}} + \sqrt{\frac{b}{2}}$$

$$= 2^{0.5} b^{0.5}.$$

Hence,

$$\frac{df^*(b)}{db} = 0.5 \, 2^{0.5} b^{-0.5}.$$

For $b = 1$,

$$\frac{df^*(b)}{db} = 2^{-0.5} = \lambda.$$

The working of the Lagrangian method can be described as the result of an equilibration process to further illustrate the forces behind the method. The method works because a critical point of the Lagrangian is seen as representing an equilibrium for a resource planner and a producer using price and quantity signaling, respectively.

In this discussion, an equilibrium is regarded as a state in which none of the parties to an exchange have an incentive to change their present decisions. This interpretation can be illustrated in a one good–one factor scenario.

We begin with the producer's problem, which is to select output, x, to maximize profit using an input purchased at price λ per unit from the resource planner. So the producer's problem is to

$$\text{Maximize } f(x) - \lambda\, g(x).$$

Note that $g(x)$ is the amount of resource used, λ is the resource price, and $f(x)$ is the value of the output. Also note that this problem has the same solution, x^*, as the following problem:

$$\text{Maximize } f(x) - \lambda\, g(x) + \lambda\, b,$$

since λb is a constant with respect to x.

The producer's objective function can be written as

$$f(x) - \lambda[g(x) - b].$$

So the producer's problem is equivalent to choosing x to maximize the Lagrangian by taking λ as given.

We now turn to the resource planner's problem, which is to select the resource price, λ, per unit of input to minimize the value of unused (overused) resources by taking x as given:

$$\text{Minimize } \lambda[b - g(x)],$$

where $g(x)$ is the amount of resource used and b is the planning goal for resource use.

Note that this problem has the same solution, λ^*, as the following problem:

$$\text{Minimize } \lambda[b - g(x)] + f(x),$$

since $f(x)$ is a constant for the resource planner.

The resource planner's objective function can be rewritten as

$$f(x) - \lambda[g(x) - b)].$$

So the resource planner's problem is equivalent to choosing λ to minimize the Lagrangian by taking x as given.

We now turn to an equilibration process that can occur with price and quantity signals from the resource planner and producer, respectively. The equilibration process begins with the resource planner specifying λ_1. The producer responds with x_1. In response, the resource planner selects λ_2. The producer then selects x_2, and so on.

Suppose λ_1 and x_1 are such that $b - g(x_1) < 0$. From the resource planner's perspective, there is oversupply of x at x_1 when the resource price is λ_1.

The resource planner sees that $\lambda_1\,[b - g(x_1)] < 0$ and raises λ_1 to λ_2 (note that a plus times minus is a minus and a minus is small).

The producer sees the higher resource price λ_2 and maximizes at x_2.

The equilibration process ends when λ^* and x^* are such that $b - g(x^*) = 0$. In this situation, $\lambda^*\,[b - g(x^*)] = 0$. So the resource planner has no incentive to change and sends the price signal λ^* again. The producer then has no incentive to change and sends the quantity signal x^* again.

At the equilibrium, (x^*, λ^*), the producer has solved Maximize $f(x) - \lambda^* [g(x) - b]$ by choosing $x = x^*$.

So $f(x^*) - \lambda^* [g(x^*) - b]$ is maximized at x^*. Also, $g(x^*) - b = 0$. So x^* maximizes $f(x)$ while satisfying $g(x^*) = b$. Hence, x^* solves the producer's problem. At the equilibrium, (x^*, λ^*), the resource planner has solved Minimize $f(x^*) - \lambda [g(x^*) - b]$ by choosing $\lambda = \lambda^*$.

Note that (x^*, λ^*) simultaneously solves Maximize $f(x) - \lambda [g(x) - b]$ and Minimize $f(x) - \lambda [g(x) - b]$. Hence, $L(x, \lambda)$ is simultaneously maximized over x and minimized over λ.

2.7   INEQUALITY CONSTRAINED OPTIMIZATION: LINEAR PROGRAMMING

Optimization with constraints can often involve inequalities rather than constraint equations. Decision variables may often be required to be nonnegative. The most popular model of optimization with such inequality constraints features a linear objective function and linear constraint functions as well. Optimization models of this form are known as linear programming models. A linear programming model may involve many decision variables and many inequality constraints; however, the form of the model when there are two decision variables and two inequality constraints reveals the characteristics of all linear programming models. In the following linear programming model, x_1 and x_2 are decision variables and the a, b, and c denote numbers:

$$\text{Maximize} \quad c_1 x_1 + c_2 x_2,$$

$$\text{Subject to } a_{11} x_1 + a_{12} x_2 \leq b_1,$$

$$a_{21} x_1 + a_{22} x_2 \leq b_2,$$

$$\text{where } x_1, x_2 \geq 0.$$

Linear programming models can be solved rapidly by computers even when the number of decision variables is large. For this reason, and for other reasons described in Chapter 7, linear programming models have been applied in many decision contexts.

2.8   SELECTED STATISTICAL CONCEPTS

The use of sample data to make inferences about uncertain circumstances is an important component of managerial decision making today. Marketing, production, and finance decisions are no exceptions in this regard. We anticipate that this practice will become far more sophisticated and important in the years ahead.

This section focuses on the statistical concepts that underlie the estimation by the method of maximum likelihood. **Maximum likelihood estimation (MLE)** is a cornerstone of statistics. MLE is an appealing estimation method because of its excellent statistical properties, its intuitiveness, and the fact that many other estimation techniques used by managerial economists can be shown as approximations to MLE. Anyone who aspires to do estimation with economic data needs to be familiar with MLE. It would be hard to overstate its importance for anyone who applies statistical analysis to economic data. In the following, the acronym MLE is used to denote both maximum likelihood estimation and maximum likelihood estimate—the precise meaning will always be clear from the context.

MLE is the most generally applicable estimation technique. It is applicable for estimation in every sub-area of managerial economics, including demand, production, cost, and forecasting. The MLE principle is that the best estimator of an unknown parameter is the value of the parameter that makes the sample data most likely. Concepts from statistics such as **random variables (rv)**, **probability (Pr)**, **probability density function (pdf)**, and **Likelihood (L)** must be understood to apply MLE. These concepts are reviewed here.

It is important to note at the outset that economic (and other) phenomena may actually be random or they may be simply so complicated and critically dependent on initial conditions that we cannot analyze them. Some classic statistics texts (e.g., Harald Cramer's *Mathematical Methods of Statistics*) include much more information on this issue than many modern texts do. Even so, you do not need to look far on the Internet today to find current discussions on this issue. Nevertheless, we treat economic phenomena as if they were random. With this perspective, consider the following interpretations of two important concepts, namely, random variable (rv) and probability (Pr).

We regard any variable whose value cannot always be determined exactly as a random variable (rv).

Probability (Pr) is the relative frequency with which the value of a random variable occurs in a sequence of many trials.

Note that neither random variable (rv) nor probability (Pr) can be defined in a manner that is both intuitively satisfying and rigorous; however, we can use the concepts effectively by treating their interpretations as if they were definitions.

Example

If we flip a coin twice, the number of heads resulting from the two flips can be regarded as a random variable. Note that we cannot predict exactly the number of heads beforehand.

We can talk about the probability of getting 0, 1, or 2 heads without being able to define precisely the term "probability."

Let us use notation to describe this example. Let X be a random variable, where X is the number of heads observed from flipping a coin twice: $X = 0$ or $X = 1$ or $X = 2$. Assuming that the flips are independent and the coin is fair, we define

$$\Pr[X = 0] = 1/4, \ \Pr[X = 1] = 1/2, \ \Pr[X = 2] = 1/4.$$

Note that "pdf" is a common acronym for "probability density function." The pdf relates the value of a random variable to the probability of that value. Here is its definition.

The probability density function (pdf) at a value of an *rv* is the relative frequency with which the value occurs in a sequence of many trials.

Example: Flipping a coin twice

Let $X =$ number of heads in two successive flips: $X = 0$ or $X = 1$ or $X = 2$.

$$\Pr[X = 0] = 1/4, \ \Pr[X = 1] = 1/2, \ \Pr[X = 2] = 1/4.$$

The pdf of X, called $f_X(x)$, is $f_X(0) = 1/4, f_X(1) = 1/2, f_X(2) = 1/4$.

Note that the pdf is indeed a function as described in Section 2.2. That a random variable X has a pdf $f_X(x)$ is usually written as

$$X \sim f_X(x).$$

Here $\sim$ means "is distributed as." So this is read as "X is distributed according to $f_X(x)$":

$$f_X(x) = 1/4, \ \text{if } x = 0; \quad 1/2, \ \text{if } x = 1; \quad 1/4, \ \text{if } x = 2; \quad 0, \ \text{otherwise.}$$

The normal probability density function is the most important example of a pdf.

Example: Normal probability density function

$$X \sim f_X(x),$$

where

$$f_X(x) = \frac{1}{\sqrt{2\pi\sigma^2}} \exp\left[\frac{1}{\sqrt{2\sigma^2}}(x - \mu)^2\right], \quad \text{where } \mu \text{ and } \sigma \text{ are parameters.}$$

Here X is said to be normally distributed with mean μ and standard deviation σ; this is often written as

$$X \sim N(\mu, \sigma).$$

Figure 2.6 shows (a) the standard normal ($\mu = 0$; $\sigma = 1$) probability density function, and (b) the normal probability density function with different values of the parameters ($\mu = 5$; $\sigma = 2$). Note that the new parameter values do not change the shape of the pdf but rather only shift it to the right and flatten it out.

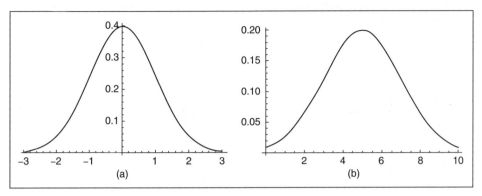

FIGURE 2.6

Recall, from your previous coursework, that the joint probability of n independent events is the product of the individual probabilities of those events.

Example: Flipping a fair coin

Let X = the outcome of flipping a fair coin (so X is either heads or tails, that is, either H or T for short). The pdf of X is $f_X(x) = 1/2$ if $X = H$; $1/2$ if $X = T$.

The data from a sequence of three coin flips are H–T–H.

The likelihood (joint probability) of these data is

$$L = f_X(H) \times f_X(T) \times f_X(H)$$
$$= (1/2) \times (1/2) \times (1/2)$$
$$= 1/8.$$

This means that if we replicated flipping a coin three times over and over again, then we would observe the sequence H–T–H in about 12% of the replications.

Example: Drawing numbers randomly from the standard normal pdf

Let X = the outcome of drawing a number from a normal pdf (so X is any real number). The pdf of X is

$$f_X(x) = \frac{1}{\sqrt{2\pi\sigma^2}} \exp\left[-\frac{1}{2\sigma^2}(x - \mu)^2\right].$$

The data from a sequence of three draws are (0.365725, –0.707673, –0.0657183).

The likelihood of this sample is

$$L = f_X(0.365725) \times f_X(-0.707673) \times f_X(-0.0657183)$$

$$= \frac{1}{\sqrt{2\pi\sigma^2}} \exp\left[-\frac{1}{2\sigma^2}(0.365725 - \mu)^2\right] \times \frac{1}{\sqrt{2\pi\sigma^2}} \exp\left[-\frac{1}{2\sigma^2}(-0.707673 - \mu)^2\right]$$

$$\times \frac{1}{\sqrt{2\pi\sigma^2}} \exp\left[-\frac{1}{2\sigma^2}(-0.0657183 - \mu)^2\right]$$

$$= \frac{1}{\sqrt{2\pi\sigma^2}} \exp\left[-\frac{1}{2\sigma^2}(0.365725 - \mu)^2 - \frac{1}{2\sigma^2}(-0.707673 - \mu)^2 \right.$$
$$\left. - \frac{1}{2\sigma^2}(-0.0657183 - \mu)^2\right].$$

Most of statistical inference is concerned with estimating an unknown parameter in a pdf where, of course, a parameter is an unknown constant. The pdf in the coin flipping example earlier involved no parameters because we assumed that the coin was "fair", that is, we assumed that the probability of getting "heads" was one-half. Had we not assumed that the coin was fair, but rather that $\Pr[X = H] = p$, then p would have been an unknown parameter in the pdf of X. For the previous example where $X \sim N(\mu, \sigma)$, μ and σ are parameters that characterize the pdf of X. Because of the widespread use of the normal pdf, much of statistics involves making inferences about population parameters such as μ and σ from data and using the inferred pdf to make predictions about the associated rv.

To perform MLE, it is necessary to know the pdf of the data (observed values of an rv), at least in form, though unknown parameters will often remain to be estimated. There are two definitions and three expectation rules that are very helpful in finding the pdf of an rv: The two definitions are as follows:

Definition: The average value of a random variable in a very large sample, denoted by $E(X)$, is called the expected value of the rv X.

Definition: The average distance of an rv from its expected value in a very large sample, denoted by SD(X), is called the standard deviation of the rv X: $SD(X) = \sqrt{E[(X - E(X))^2]}$.

The three expectation rules are as follows:

Expectation rule 1: If $E(X) = \mu$, then $E(a X) = a E(X) = a \mu$ for any constant a and any rv X.

Expectation rule 2: $E(X + Y) = E(X) + E(Y)$ for any rv X and Y.

Expectation rule 3: If $SD(X) = \sigma$, then $SD(a X) = a SD(X)$ for any constant a and any rv X.

Let us apply these definitions and expectation rules to the consumption function of macroeconomics, which is often illustrated with a linear function. Consider the consumption function from macroeconomics (C is consumption; Y is income; a and b are unknown parameters; and U is a random error):

$$C = a + bY + U, \text{ where it is assumed that } U : N(0, \sigma).$$

C is a random variable since we cannot predict its value exactly. The mean of the random error is assumed to be 0, that is, $E(U) = 0$. The standard deviation of U is

$$SD(U) = \sqrt{E[(U - E(U))^2]} = \sqrt{E(U^2)} = \sigma.$$

Let us find the expected value of C:

$$E(C) = E(a + bY + U)$$

$$= E(a) + E(bY) + E(U) \text{ (because of expectation rule 2)}$$

$$= a + bY + 0 \text{ (because a and bY are numbers (not rv) and } E(U) = 0 \text{ by assumption)}$$

$$= a + bY.$$

Let us find the standard deviation of C:

$$SD(C) = \sqrt{E[(C - E(C))^2]}$$

$$= \sqrt{E[(a + bY + U - a - bY)^2]}$$

$$= \sqrt{E(U^2)}$$

$$= \sigma.$$

Using the two definitions and the three expectation rules, we have found that the rv consumption, C, has expected value $a + bY$ and standard deviation σ.

Under the assumption of a normally distributed additive error, the pdf of C is

$$f_C(c) = \frac{1}{\sqrt{2\pi\sigma^2}} \exp\left[-\frac{1}{2\sigma^2}(c - a - by)^2\right],$$

where a, b, and σ are parameters to be estimated and lower-case letters c and y denote observed values of the rv C and Y, respectively.

Now let us find L for the case of the consumption function. The consumption function is again

$$C = a + bY + U, \text{ where it is assumed that } U \sim N(0, \sigma).$$

Suppose now that we have a data sample consisting of n observations on rv C_i, denoted by $(c_1, c_2, \ldots, c_n)$, and income variable Y_i, denoted by $(y_1, y_2, \ldots, y_n)$.

The pdf of each C_i (using the reasoning we used earlier) is

$$f_{C_i}(c_i) = \frac{1}{\sqrt{2\pi\sigma^2}} \exp\left[-\frac{1}{2\sigma^2}(c_i - a - by_i)^2\right].$$

The observations are assumed to be independent so the likelihood L (joint probability) is the product of the pdfs of the individual observations:

$$L = f_{C1}(c_1) \times f_{C2}(c_2) \times \cdots \times f_{Cn}(c_n) \text{ (a shorthand way to write this is } \prod f_{Ci}(c_i)).$$

Thus, L is just the product of the pdfs.

2.9 MAXIMUM LIKELIHOOD ESTIMATION

MLE is a general estimation technique (as previously mentioned, the most generally applicable estimation technique). It applies in many areas of estimation in managerial economics, including demand, production, cost, and forecasting. The MLE principle is that the best estimator of an unknown parameter is the value of the parameter that makes the sample data most likely.

To do MLE, recall the following problem. Suppose you have a sample of independent observations on a random variable and you believe that these observations occur with relative frequencies given by a pdf that has a parameter, μ. In other words, you have some data and you assume that these were drawn from a pdf with a known form, such as the normal, bell-shaped curve, but with an unknown parameter, μ. The method of maximum likelihood is based on forming the likelihood function (joint probability of the observations), L, from the pdf and then choosing as the estimate of the parameter μ the value that makes the observations most likely.

Example: Flipping a coin
Suppose that we flip a coin 50 times and get all heads. Our dataset consists of 50 observations, all of which are heads. The unknown parameter is the probability of heads, which we call, p.

The pdf of the outcome of a single flip, X, is $f_X(x) = p$; if $x =$ heads, $1 - p$; if $x =$ tails, 0; otherwise.

So the data we have are the result of 50 flips of the coin, x_i, $i = 1, 2, \ldots, 50$, which in this case is all heads:

$$L = \prod [f_{Xi}(x_i)] = \prod [f_{Xi}(\text{heads})] = \prod p = p^{50}.$$

Now let us apply the MLE principle. What value of p makes it most likely that we would observe the sample we have? The answer to this question is the maximum likelihood estimate of p.

To find the MLE, solve

$$\text{Maximize } L = p^{50},$$

where p, as any other probability, must be between 0 and 1, that is, $0 \le p \le 1$.

Example: X is an rv and it is assumed that $X \sim N(\mu, \sigma)$
Unknown parameters to be estimated are μ and σ.

Given a sample $x_1, x_2, \ldots, x_n$ of observations on X, the pdf associated with each sample observation is

$$f_X(x_i) = \frac{1}{\sqrt{2\pi\sigma^2}} \exp\left[-\frac{1}{2\sigma^2}(x_i - \mu)^2\right].$$

Assuming independent sampling, the likelihood of the sample data, $x_1, x_2, \ldots, x_n$, is

$$L = \prod [f_{Xi}(x_i)].$$

MLEs of μ and σ are the values of μ and σ that solve

$$\text{Maximize } L = \prod [f_{Xi}(x_i)].$$

Example: The consumption function from macroeconomics

$$C = a + bY + U, \text{ where it is assumed that } U \sim N(0, \sigma).$$

The parameters to be estimated are a, b, and σ.

Suppose now that we have a data sample consisting of n observations on the rv C_i, denoted by $(c_1, c_2, \ldots, c_n)$, and the income variable Y_i, denoted by $(y_1, y_2, \ldots, y_n)$.

The pdf associated with each C_i (using again the method we used earlier) is

$$f_{C_i}(c_i) = \frac{1}{\sqrt{2\pi\sigma^2}} \exp\left[-\frac{1}{2\sigma^2}(c_i - a - by_i)^2\right].$$

Assuming that the observations are independent, the likelihood, L, is

$$L = f_{C1}(c_1) \times f_{C2}(c_2) \times \cdots \times f_{Cn}(c_n) = \prod [f_{Ci}(c_i)].$$

MLEs of a, b, and σ are the values of a, b, and σ that solve

$$\text{Maximize } L = \prod [f_{C_i}(c_i)].$$

MLEs of parameters such as a, b, and σ will, of course, differ from sample to sample taken from the same population. As a result, the MLEs of population parameters are themselves rv with pdfs. Computerized statistical packages find the standard deviation of MLEs by studying the curvature of the likelihood function, L. The estimated standard errors reported by statistical software are based on the second derivatives of the likelihood function, which reflect curvature.

2.10   ORDINARY AND NONLINEAR LEAST SQUARES ESTIMATION

Ordinary least squares (OLS) estimation offers an alternative to MLE for estimation problems that are linear in parameters, whereas nonlinear least squares (NLS) is an alternative for estimation of parameters that are in a nonlinear form. OLS estimates of parameters minimize the sum of the squared residuals in a linear model, whereas NLS pursues a similar objective for nonlinear models. In fact, the estimates obtained through MLE and OLS/NLS will coincide in many problems and are very similar in cases where the number of sample observations is large. Estimated standard errors of parameter estimates will exhibit similarities.

To see the close relationship between least squares estimation and MLE, observe how OLS, applied to estimate the parameters of the consumption function considered in the last section, seeks to solve the following problem by choosing values of parameters a and b:

$$\text{Minimize} \sum (c_i - a - b\, y_i)^2.$$

MLE seeks to solve the following problem by choosing the values of parameters a, b, and σ:

$$\text{Maximize } L = \prod [f_{Ci}(c_i)],$$

$$\text{where } f_{C_i}(c_i) = \frac{1}{\sqrt{2\pi\sigma^2}} \exp\left[-\frac{1}{2\sigma^2}(c_i - a - by_i)^2\right].$$

Using the properties of natural logarithm reviewed in Section 2.4, we see that an equivalent problem can be used to define the MLE:

$$\text{Maximize } \ln L = \sum [\ln f_{C_i}(c_i)]$$

or

$$\text{Maximize } \ln L = \sum \left[\frac{1}{2\pi\sigma^2}\right] - \sum \left[\frac{1}{2\sigma^2}(c_i - a - by_i)^2\right].$$

Hence, the MLE involves making the likelihood function large, which necessitates minimizing the second term in the expression for $\ln L$. As a result, the OLS and MLE estimates of the parameters are identical in the case of the consumption function. Moreover, parameter estimates associated with MLE and minimum distance methods, such as NLS, have the same large sample distribution in the cases where both estimators are feasible. In such cases, parameter estimates and their estimated standard errors may be regarded as equally efficient whether derived via MLE or minimum distance alternatives.

SUMMARY

- Managerial economics relies on quantitative methods because of the precision and rigor such methods introduce to economic analysis. Functions are special mathematical relationships that have found application in managerial economic models and comparative statics analysis. Exponents and logarithms are important functions that are used throughout the subfields of managerial economics, including demand, production, cost, and forecasting. Calculus tools enable analysis of functional relationships as well as optimization and constrained optimization. Inequality constrained optimization is most commonly accomplished in linear programming models. Statistical notions such as random variables, probability, probability density function, and likelihood provide the foundation for estimation and economic forecasting based on the method of maximum likelihood and least squares techniques.

- This chapter provided a review of the mathematical and statistical methods needed to fully understand the topics covered in this book and regularly used by managerial economists. By "review" we mean that the mathematical and statistical topics covered in this chapter have been presented to refresh your memory about quantitative material covered in the prerequisites for an upper division course in managerial economics. The prerequisites we refer to usually include methods that are introduced as part of courses in intermediate microeconomic theory, introductory calculus, statistics and/or econometrics, and quantitative methods featuring decision analysis and constrained optimization. We hope that renewing acquaintance with the quantitative foundations of this past coursework will enable a smooth transition to useful applications that form the field of managerial economics.

- This chapter began with the general notion of a mathematical function. Functional relationships are prevalent throughout economics and statistics. Understanding of functions is essential to every quantitative method covered in this chapter as well as comparative statics analysis in economics. The review then focuses on two specific functions, logarithms and exponents, both of which are used frequently in economic theory and statistical analysis based on the theory.

- Optimization and constrained optimization also lie at the center of both economic theory and statistical analysis. Because differential calculus plays such an important role in applied optimization, this chapter provides a comprehensive review of the techniques you have learned during your previous study of calculus. In particular, ordinary, partial, first, and higher order derivatives were reviewed with examples to remind you of these concepts, which are used repeatedly in the chapters that follow. An immediate application of the calculus techniques reviewed was made in our review of multivariate and constrained optimization methods, including the Lagrangian method, which followed the calculus presentation. The widely used technique for optimization with inequality constraints, known as linear programming, was also reviewed. Linear programming was undoubtedly the centerpiece of your previous coursework in quantitative methods for management.

- Following the review of functions, calculus, and optimization, the focus shifted to statistics and estimation, which, once founded on economic theory, form the basis of empirical analysis that is so common in managerial economics. Critical statistical concepts, including the notions of random variable, probability, probability density function, and likelihood function, detailed in your previous statistics and econometrics coursework, were reviewed with examples to reinforce their meaning. Each of these statistical concepts found immediate use in our review of statistical inference based on the method of maximum likelihood, ordinary least squares, and nonlinear least squares criteria. These estimation techniques, particularly the method of maximum likelihood, have been used repeatedly throughout the remainder of this book and throughout empirical analysis in economics.

KEY TERMS

function

exponents

comparative statics analysis

limit of function

maximization

Lagrange multiplier

value function

linear programming

probability density function

nonlinear least squares
  estimation

mathematician's graph
  of demand and supply

economist's graph of
  demand and supply

differentiation

partial derivative

minimization

objective function

indirect function

maximum likelihood

random variable

number e

logarithms

derivatives

equality constrained
  optimization

Lagrangian method

constraint function

inequality constrained
  optimization

probability

ordinary least squares
  estimation

LIST OF FORMULAS

Exponents:

$$a^n = a\,a\,a\,\ldots\,a\ (n \text{ times}; n \text{ is a nonnegative integer}),$$

$$a^{-n} = \frac{1}{a^n},$$

$$a^n a^m = a^{n+m},$$

$$\frac{a^n}{a^m} = a^{n-m},$$

$$(a^n)^m = a^{n\,m},$$

$$(a\,b)^n = a^n\,b^n,$$

$$\left(\frac{a}{b}\right)^n = \frac{a^n}{b^n},$$

$$a^{m/n} = \text{the } n\text{th root of } a^m.$$

Calculus:

$$\frac{dy}{dx_1} = \text{Lim}_{h \to 0} \left[\frac{f\,(x_1 + h) - f\,(x_1)}{h} \right],$$

$$y = f(x_1) = a(a \text{ is a constant}) \Rightarrow \frac{dy}{dx_1} = 0,$$

$$y = x_1^b \Rightarrow \frac{dy}{dx_1} = b\,x_1^{b-1},$$

$$y = af(x_1) \Rightarrow \frac{dy}{dx_1} = a\,f'(x_1),$$

$$y = f(x_1) + g(x_1) \Rightarrow \frac{dy}{dx_1} = f'(x_1) + g'(x_1),$$

$$y = f(x_1)g(x_1) \Rightarrow \frac{dy}{dx_1} = f(x_1)g'(x_1) + g(x_1)f'(x_1),$$

$$y = \frac{f(x_1)}{g(x_1)} \Rightarrow \frac{dy}{dx_1} = \frac{[g(x_1)f'(x_1) - f(x_1)g'(x_1)]}{(g(x_1))^2},$$

$$y = g(u); \quad u = f(x_1); \quad y = g(f(x_1)) \Rightarrow \frac{dy}{dx_1} = \left(\frac{dy}{du}\right)\left(\frac{du}{dx_1}\right),$$

$$y = \ln x_1 \Rightarrow \frac{dy}{dx_1} = \frac{1}{x_1},$$

$$y = e^{x_1} \Rightarrow \frac{dy}{dx_1} = e^{x_1},$$

$$\frac{d}{dx_1}\left(\frac{dy}{dx_1}\right) = \frac{d^2y}{dx_1^2} = f''(x_1),$$

$$\frac{\partial y}{\partial x_1} = \text{Lim}_{h \to 0}\left(\frac{f(x_1 + h, x_2, \ldots, x_n) - f(x_1, x_2, \ldots, x_n)}{h}\right).$$

Multivariate and constrained optimization:

$$\text{Maximize } f(x_1, x_2),$$

$$\frac{\partial f}{\partial x_1} = 0; \ \frac{\partial y}{\partial x_2} = 0.$$

$$\text{Maximize } f(x_1, x_2), \text{ subject to } g(x_1, x_2) = b,$$

$$L(x_1, x_2, \lambda) = f(x_1, x_2) - \lambda[g(x_1, x_2) - b],$$

$$\frac{\partial L}{\partial x_1} = \frac{\partial f}{\partial x_1} - \lambda\frac{\partial g}{\partial x_1} = 0,$$

$$\frac{\partial L}{\partial x_2} = \frac{\partial f}{\partial x_2} - \lambda\frac{\partial g}{\partial x_2} = 0,$$

$$\frac{\partial L}{\partial \lambda} = b - g(x_1, x_2) = 0,$$

$$f^*(b) = f[x_1^*(b), x_2^*(b)],$$

$$\frac{df^*(b)}{db} = \lambda.$$

Linear programming model:

$$\text{Maximize } c_1 x_1 + c_2 x_2.$$

$$\text{Subject to } a_{11} x_1 + a_{12} x_2 \leq b_1,$$

$$a_{21} x_1 + a_{22} x_2 \leq b_2,$$

$$\text{where } x_1, x_2 = 0.$$

Probability:

$$X \sim N(\mu, \sigma),$$

$$f_X(x) = \frac{1}{\sqrt{2\pi\sigma^2}} \exp\left[-\frac{1}{2\sigma^2}(x-\mu)^2\right].$$

Expectation:

$$E(X) = \text{average value of rv } X,$$

$$SD(X) = \sqrt{E[(X - E(X))^2]} = \text{standard deviation of rv } X,$$

$$E(X) = \mu \Rightarrow E(aX) = aE(X) = a\mu \text{ for any constant } a \text{ and any rv } X,$$

$$E(X + Y) = E(X) + E(Y) \text{ for any rvs } X \text{ and } Y,$$

$$SD(X) = \sigma \Rightarrow SD(aX) = a\,SD(X) \text{ for any constant } a.$$

Estimation:

$$\text{MLE: Maximize } L = \prod f_{X_i}(x_i).$$

EXERCISES

1. What is the difference between the mathematician's and economist's graphs for demand and supply? Take any set of demand and supply functions and graph them according to both perspectives.

2. How are exponents related to logarithms? Provide an example to illustrate your explanation.

3. What is a derivative and how important is it to economics?

4. What is optimization? What are the types of optimization and how significant is this mathematical concept in economic applications?

5. Explain the following statistical concepts and their need in economics and, specifically, their application in managerial economics:

- Random variable
- Probability density function
- Maximum likelihood
- Ordinary squares method

6. Evaluate: $(3.14159^{2.71828})(3.14159^{-2.71828})$.

7. Evaluate: $3.4159^{2.1828}/3.14159^{-2.71828}$.

8. Maximize $x + y$; subject to $x\,y = 100$.

9. Interpret the symbol ln graphically.

10. Maximize x, y; subject to $x + y = 10$.

UNIT II

DECISIONS AT THE CONSUMER LEVEL

3

THEORY OF CONSUMER CHOICE

According to the economic theory of consumer choice, consumers are rational enough to choose the best possible bundle of commodities that they can afford. In other words, this theory explains the notion of choice, at its core, as a continuous interaction between people's preferences and the constraints they face. Therefore, it can be summarized that **consumer choice** is often made on the basis of interaction between two major elements:

1. Consumer's preferences and willingness to trade among the available alternatives of commodities.
2. Consumer's affordability or ability to buy those alternatives.

3.1 CONSUMER PREFERENCES

Economists model consumer preferences by assuming that consumers have a set of preferences that are formed on the basis of personal taste. Since people are substantially different in their tastes, their preferences of commodity alternatives would be highly subjective, given certain circumstances. However, on general and universal bases, consumer preferences are supposed to have specific properties, which confirm the assumption that consumers have the ability to rank their preferences in a logically consistent manner. Such properties can be illustrated by the following axioms.

Axiom 1 Completeness
Preferences are said to be complete if the consumer

(a) prefers x-bundle over y-bundle $(x_1, x_2) \succ (y_1, y_2)$;

Managerial Economics: A Mathematical Approach, First Edition. M. J. Alhabeeb and L. Joe Moffitt.
© 2013 John Wiley & Sons, Inc. Published 2013 by John Wiley & Sons, Inc.

(b) prefers y-bundle over x-bundle $(y_1, y_2) \succ (x_1, x_2)$; or

(c) prefers them equally well (the consumer would be indifferent to have either of the bundles).

$$(x_1, x_2) \sim (y_1, y_2).$$

This axiom rules out the case where the consumer cannot make any choice among these alternatives. In other words, the consumer would certainly have one clear choice from the three possibilities stated above.

Axiom 2   Transitivity

Preferences are transitive when a consumer prefers x-bundle over z-bundle $(x_1, x_2) \succ (z_1, z_2)$, usually as a result of

(a) preferring x-bundle over y-bundle $(x_1, x_2) \succ (y_1, y_2)$ and

(b) preferring y-bundle over z-bundle $(y_1, y_2) \succ (z_1, z_2)$.

Axiom 3   Nonsatiation

This axiom states that given a desirable bundle of commodities, a consumer would prefer more over less. Technically, this would require that all first-order partial derivatives of the **utility** function or the marginal utilities to be positive:

$$U = f(x_1, x_2, \ldots, x_n),$$

$$MU_j = \frac{\partial U}{\partial x_j} > 0 \quad j = 1, \ldots, n.$$

Geometrically, a nonsatiated preference can be illustrated as in Figure 3.1. Compared to the bundle of x and y offered by point Z, all the points in the shaded area such as A, B, and C would offer

(a) either more of x and equal amount of y;

(b) or more of y and equal amount of x;

(c) or more of x and y.

While all points outside the shaded area, such as D, E, and F, would offer at least one commodity less, if not less of both commodities, than in Z. Therefore,

$$A, B, C, \succ Z, \quad \text{but} \quad Z \succ D, E, F.$$

Axiom 4   Convexity

This axiom basically describes the consumer's tendency to prefer an average of the desired bundles of commodities over extreme bundles. For example, if a consumer prefers X and

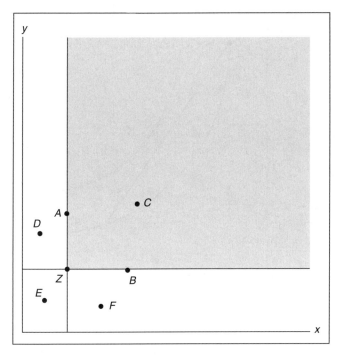

FIGURE 3.1

Y over Z, then this consumer would most likely prefer a combination of X and Y or their weighted average over Z:

$$\beta X + (1 - \beta)Y \succ Z, \quad 0 < \beta < 1.$$

Geometrically, and as a matter related to the shape of the **indifference curve** (IC), a set of points is said to be convex if any two points within the set can be reached by a straight line (DE in Figure 3.2) that is entirely contained within the set. This would imply a diminishing **marginal rate of substitution** (MRS), which will be explained later. However, the notion of preference for the average over the extremes can be explained in Figure 3.2.

Point A offers the bundle of (x_1, y_2), and point B offers the bundle of (x_2, y_1). Both points would yield the same satisfaction. In other words, a consumer would be equally satisfied at both points because if A offers less of x, it certainly offers more of y, and if B offers less of y, it would offer more of x. Now, if we consider points such as x_3 and y_3, which are midpoints between the two amounts of x and y offered earlier, these points would offer the averages of x and y:

$$x_3 = \frac{x_1 + x_2}{2} \quad \text{and} \quad y_3 = \frac{y_1 + y_2}{2}.$$

If we extend a vertical line from x_3 and a horizontal line from y_3, the two lines would meet at C, which is clearly outside IC_1. This indicates that C is on a higher indifference curve

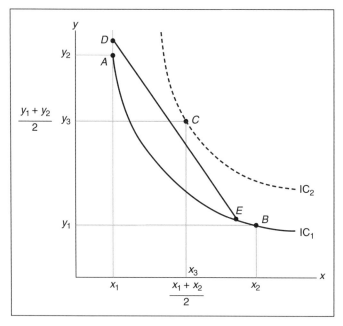

FIGURE 3.2

such as IC$_2$, which offers a higher level of utility, making the consumer better off than on either A or B.

3.1.1 Indifference Curve

Based on the preference axioms, economists modeled the theory of consumer choice on a geometrical tool called an indifference curve. As shown in Figure 3.3, an **indifference curve** is a locus of points representing commodity bundles that a consumer would prefer equally well. These points are supposed to yield the same level of utility, despite the different combination of commodities they stand for. This tool is called an indifference curve to signify that a consumer would be indifferent in terms of satisfaction level obtained if he/she moves to any point on the same curve. This implies that higher or lower levels of satisfaction can be obtained by different bundles depending on higher or lower ICs running parallel, above and below the one with which we started. This would lead to the existence of what is called an **indifference space** or **indifference map**. It contains an infinite number of curves representing all the possibilities of consumer tastes and preferences. The typical shape of an IC, as shown in Figure 3.3, is convex to the origin, and running from northwest to the southeast. However, there are exceptions to this typical shape of the IC. The geometrically different shapes can be obtained depending on the nature of commodities and the extent of consumer preference toward these commodities. Technically, the shape of the ICs would be dictated by the marginal rate of substitution (MRS). However, all ICs have to share the following fundamental properties:

1. **Total utility** remains constant at any point on a single curve. However, it increases as the ICs move away from the origin, and decreases as they move toward the origin.

2. Any single IC is basically one of many in the commodity plane.

3. ICs on a single plane cannot intersect.

Let us consider the following case:

Suppose we make IC_1 intersect with IC_2 at point A, and we consider two other points on the curves, B on IC_1 and C on IC_2, then

$A \sim B$ and $A \sim C$ (based on property #1), then
$B \sim C$ (based on the transitivity axiom), but
$C \succ B$ (based on property #1 again).

Therefore, if we allow the ICs to intersect, we would be violating the transitivity axiom, and for this reason ICs must not intersect.

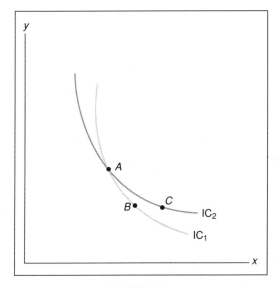

FIGURE 3.3

Typically shaped ICs share the following properties (see Figure 3.4):

1. They slope downward from the northwest to the southeast. Therefore, they have a declining (negative) value of MRS.

2. They are convex to the origin:

$$A \sim B \sim C,$$
$$E \succ (D, A, B, C),$$
$$D \succ (A, B, C).$$

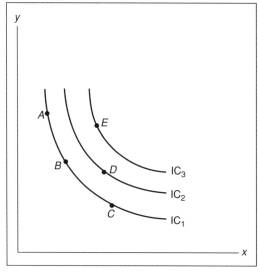

FIGURE 3.4

3.1.2 Marginal Rate of Substitution (MRS)

The IC provides a great technical tool to analyze how consumers can trade off between their available alternatives of bundles to reach their best choice. A central concept in this analysis is the **marginal rate of substitution**. It is defined as the amount of commodity (y) that a consumer is willing to give up in order to have one unit of the other commodity (x). Therefore, it can be measured by the change in commodity y (a loss) with respect to a standardized change in commodity x (a gain by one unit). In this case, the MRS would be equal to the negative slope of the IC at the point of change (see Figure 3.5):

$$\text{MRS} = \text{Slope of IC} = -\frac{\Delta y}{\Delta x}.$$

Since the change in x is standardized by only one unit ($\Delta x = 1$), the MRS would end up equaling to the **marginal value** (MV):

$$\text{MRS} = -\frac{\Delta y}{\Delta x} = \frac{-\Delta y}{1} = -\Delta y = \text{MV}.$$

Let us assume that a consumer's choice is to have the bundle (x_1, y_1) at point A. If this consumer wants to have one more unit of x (moves to x_2), but does not want his overall satisfaction to diminish as a result of this change, then he must give up some amount of y in order to gain a unit of x and still enjoy the same level of satisfaction (being on the same IC). Having this particular slope of IC would dictate that this consumer has to give up an amount of (y) measured by ($y_1 - y_2$) when he/she moves to point B (x_2, y_2), which would offer an additional unit of x ($x_2 - x_1$). Note that if this consumer would want to have one more unit of x, he can still move down along the curve to C and D. However, every time in which one unit of x is gained, the consumer would lose less and less of commodity (y) than he/she did before. This would illustrate the diminishing MRS (losing 3 units, 2 units,

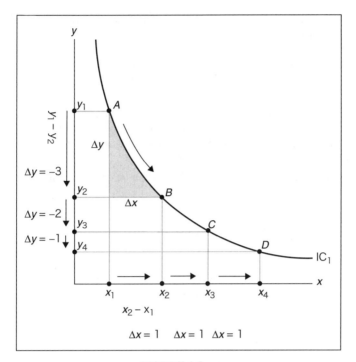

FIGURE 3.5

1 unit) consecutively, as the consumer moves from A to B to C, where one additional unit of x is gained each time.

The essence of the diminishing **marginal utility** is reflected by the fact that when we move from one point to another on an IC, for example from A to B, we are going to give up some of commodity y, and as a result our utility gets reduced. This reduction in utility must be compensated by an alternative gain in utility by getting more of commodity x. This can be mathematically expressed as

$$\left[\Delta y \cdot \frac{\Delta TU}{\Delta y}\right] + \left[\Delta x \cdot \frac{\Delta TU}{\Delta x}\right] = 0,$$

$$\left[\Delta y \cdot \frac{\Delta TU}{\Delta y}\right] = -\left[\Delta x \cdot \frac{\Delta TU}{\Delta x}\right],$$

$$\Delta y = (-\Delta x)\frac{\left[\dfrac{\Delta TU}{\Delta x}\right]}{\left[\dfrac{\Delta TU}{\Delta y}\right]},$$

$$-\frac{\Delta y}{\Delta x} = \frac{\left[\dfrac{\Delta TU}{\Delta x}\right]}{\left[\dfrac{\Delta TU}{\Delta y}\right]},$$

where the left-hand side of the last equation is the MRS, and the right-hand side is the ratio of the marginal utilities of the two commodities x and y:

$$\text{MRS} = -\frac{\Delta y}{\Delta x} = \frac{\text{MU}_x}{\text{MU}_y}.$$

It is important here to note that a common mistake often made by students is to keep x and y in the same order when they write the equation above. The right format, though, is to switch their places between the top and bottom when you equate the ratio of the change in quantities with the ratio of their marginal utilities.

Using the utility function $U = f(x, y)$, the MRS can be expressed in calculus as

$$\text{MRS} = \frac{dy}{dx}$$

$$= -\frac{\dfrac{\partial U}{\partial x}}{\dfrac{\partial U}{\partial y}}$$

$$= -\frac{\text{MU}_x}{\text{MU}_y},$$

which can be read as the negative ratio of the marginal utilities of the two commodities x and y. If we consider, for example, a Cobb–Douglas utility function such as

$$U = x^a y^{1-a}, \quad \text{where} \quad a > 0,$$

we can obtain the MRS between x and y from the marginal utilities of x and y and dividing them by each other. The marginal utilities are the first derivatives of the function with respect to x and y, respectively:

$$U = x^a y^{1-a},$$

$$\text{MU}_x = \frac{\partial U}{\partial x} = a x^{a-1} y^{1-a}$$

$$= a x^{-1} x^a y^{1-a}$$

$$= a \frac{1}{x} x^a y^{1-a}$$

$$= a \frac{x^a y^{1-a}}{x}$$

$$= a \frac{U(x, y)}{x}. \tag{3.1}$$

Similarly,

$$\text{MU}_y = \frac{\partial U}{\partial x} = (1-a)\frac{U(x,y)}{y},$$

$$\text{MRS} = -\frac{\dfrac{\partial U}{\partial x}}{\dfrac{\partial U}{\partial y}}$$

$$= -\frac{a\dfrac{U(x,y)}{x}}{(1-a)\dfrac{U(x,y)}{y}}$$

$$= -\frac{a}{1-a}\cdot\frac{U(x,y)}{x}\cdot\frac{y}{U(x,y)}$$

$$\text{MRS} = -\frac{a}{1-a}\cdot\left[\frac{y}{x}\right]. \tag{3.2}$$

Example 3.1

If x is the amount of white meat and y is the amount of red meat that Jack purchases in a week, what would be his MRS between red and white meats for a weekly amount of 8 lb of hamburger and 4 lb of chicken, given that "a" in the general Cobb–Douglas equation for a typical consumer is 0.75.

Solution:

$$\text{MRS} = -\frac{a}{1-a}\cdot\frac{y}{x}$$

$$= -\frac{0.75}{1-0.75}\cdot\frac{4}{8}$$

$$= -\frac{3}{2} = -1.5.$$

This MRS value means that Jack has to give up $1\frac{1}{2}$ lb of hamburger for every additional pound of chicken he may want to consume.

3.1.3   Nontypical Indifference Curves

For all consumer preferences, where the MRS is not declining, the IC would not be typically convex to the origin. It would take different shapes (see Figures 3.6, 3.7, 3.8, 3.9, 3.10, and 3.11):

1. Straight downward line exhibiting constant MRS in the case of the commodities that are perfect substitutes (Fig. 3.6).
2. L-shaped, exhibiting proportional MRS in the case of the commodities that are perfect complements (Fig. 3.7).
3. Vertical or horizontal line with unidentified MRS in the case of neutral commodities (Figs. 3.8 and 3.9).
4. Straight upward sloping line exhibiting an increasing MRS in the case of undesirable commodities (Fig. 3.10).
5. Concave curve with an increasing MRS in the case of concave preferences (Fig. 3.11).

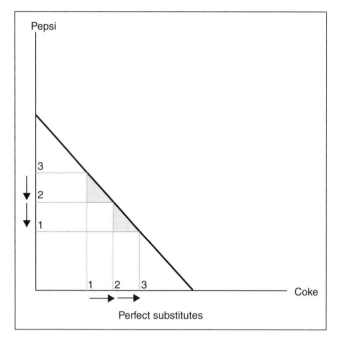

FIGURE 3.6

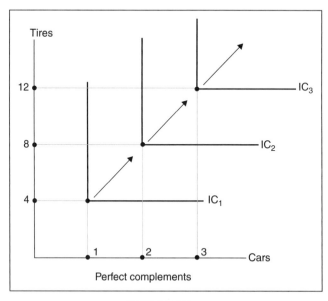

FIGURE 3.7

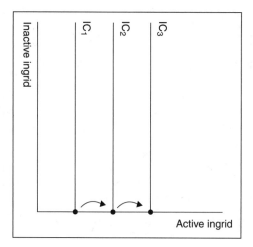

FIGURE 3.8

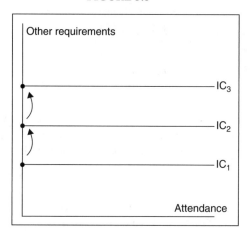

FIGURE 3.9

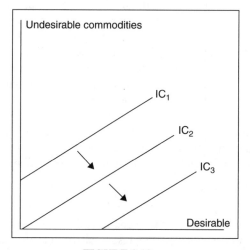

FIGURE 3.10

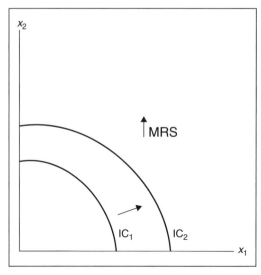

FIGURE 3.11

3.2   CONSUMER'S AFFORDABILITY

Affordability is the second major element of consumer choice. It refers to consumer's ability to buy the alternatives of the commodities he/she prefers. While the consumer's preferences were analyzed by the indifference curve as an appropriate technical tool, his/her affordability would be analyzed by another technical tool called the **budget line**.

3.2.1   Budget Line

The budget line refers to the geometrical boundary between two zones, what a consumer can and cannot afford to buy. In particular, it is a tool to depict the two fundamental constraints: size of income or budget a consumer has, and prices of the commodities to be purchased. A **budget line** is, therefore, defined as the line representing all maximum combinations of commodities that a consumer can buy, given a certain income and specific prices. It implies that the line would be a locus of all points that refer to the bundles which would require spending the entire available budget. In this perspective, the whole area below the line would logically contain an infinite number of points referring to all possible bundles that are affordable but require less than the maximum budget available. This area is called the **opportunity set** or the **affordability zone**. We can, therefore, conclude that the area above the line would be the zone of unaffordability.

Let us imagine a consumer having a certain budget such as (I) and that this consumer is interested in spending that budget on two commodities, x and y, priced at P_x and P_y, respectively. In a two-dimensional scenario, a budget line equation would be

$$xP_x + yP_y = I.$$

In order to draw the budget line, first we need to find out the two intercepts: the vertical and horizontal. Those **intercepts** would represent the extreme affordable bundles. In other words, each one of them would stand for the maximum possible amount of a commodity if the entire budget is spent on that commodity alone. This would require assuming that none would be spent on the other commodity. For such assumption, we set the expenditures on the skipped commodity to zero:

$$x P_x + 0 = I$$

$$x = \frac{I}{P_x}, \text{ the horizontal intercept.}$$

That would stand for the maximum affordable amount of x, which can be obtained if the entire budget is spent only on x. Similarly, we can obtain the maximum affordable amount of y, if the entire budget is spent only on y:

$$0 + y P_y = I$$

$$y = \frac{I}{P_y}, \text{ the vertical intercept.}$$

The budget line can then be drawn as the line extended between the two intercepts.

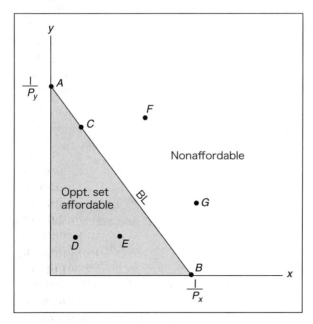

FIGURE 3.12

In Figure 3.12, we can observe that

A, B are the extreme bundles;

A, B, C are affordable bundles that require the entire budget;

D, E are affordable bundles that require less than the entire budget;

F, G are nonaffordable bundles.

The fact that points such as A, B, and C require exhausting the whole budget implies that if a consumer is at any point on the line, the desire to increase any of the commodities requires giving up some of the other commodity, unless there is a change in either income or prices. Therefore, a trade-off must occur to achieve any movement from one point to another on the line.

3.2.2   Slope of the Budget Line

The most important characteristic of the budget line is its slope, especially what it means and how it changes or stays fixed. Obviously, the **slope** visually depicts how flat or steep the line is. The value of the slope is determined by the negative ratio of the prices of the two commodities x and y. It stands for the rate at which commodity y can be substituted for commodity x, while still satisfying the budget constraint:

$$\text{Slope} = \frac{\Delta y}{\Delta x} = -\frac{P_x}{P_y}.$$

This is why the slope of the budget line is called the **marginal rate of transformation (MRT)** in the same fashion as the marginal rate of substitution (MRS) was identified. From a slightly different perspective, the slope of the budget line or MRT expresses how the price of commodity x stands, in the market relative to the price of commodity y. From this perspective, we can understand that the higher the price of x, relative to the price of y, the higher the slope and steeper the budget line. In contrast, the lower the price of x, relative to the price of y, the lesser the slope and flatter the budget line. This will be clearly seen when we discuss how the slope changes in the next section. From yet another perspective on the slope, economists believe that the slope of the budget line can actually measure the opportunity cost of consuming commodity x. This notion logically refers to the fact that in order to increase the consumption of x, you must give up some of the consumption of y, and that can measure the true cost of the gained amount of x.

3.2.3   Shift, Swing, and Kink of the Budget Line

There are three important changes in the budget line: the shift, the swing, and the kink.

The Shift   The shift of the budget line, right and left, occurs due to changes in the size of the consumer budget or when consumer income increases or decreases. The higher the budget, the farther the budget line from the origin, making the affordability zone larger, and vice versa. Technically, this would occur because changes in income would only affect the intercept term in the budget line equation:

$$x P_x + y P_y = I.$$

If we rewrite this budget line equation in the form of the linear function $Y = a + bx$, where "a" is the y-intercept and "b" is the slope:

$$y P_y = I - x P_x,$$

$$y = \frac{I}{P_y} - \frac{P_x}{P_y} x. \tag{3.3}$$

In this form, the intercept would be (I/P_y) and the slope would be $-(P_x/P_y)$.

Now let us assume that consumer income has changed in the following manner:

1. In period 1, income increases from I to I_1.
2. In period 2, income decreases from I to I_2.

Equation (3.3) would be adjusted to these changes as follows:

1. $y = \dfrac{I_1}{P_y} - \dfrac{P_x}{P_y}x$

2. $y = \dfrac{I_2}{P_y} - \dfrac{P_x}{P_y}x$

Since $I_1 > I$ and $I_2 < I$, the y-intercept (I_1/P_y) in the first change would be higher than the original intercept (I/P_y). Also, in the second change, the intercept I_2/P_y would be lower than the original I_2/P_y. Furthermore, since the slope $-(P_x/P_y)$ did not change in both cases, the line would only shift right or left, in a parallel manner, following the new intercepts, respectively.

Example 3.2
Suppose that a consumer budget (I) is equal to \$12, and spent on meat (x) and potatoes (y) where the price of meat is \$3 per pound, and the price of potatoes is \$2 per pound. Draw the budget line and show how it would shift in two cases: (1) when the budget increases to \$18 and (2) when the budget decreases to \$9. Assume that the prices remain unchanged in both cases (see Figure 3.13):

Solution:

$$P_x x + P_y y = I,$$
$$3x + 2y = 12.$$

- The horizontal intercept:

$$P_x x + 0 = I,$$
$$P_x x = I,$$
$$x = \frac{I}{P_x} = \frac{12}{3} = 4.$$

- The vertical intercept:

$$0 + P_y y = I,$$
$$P_y y = I,$$
$$y = \frac{I}{P_y} = \frac{12}{2} = 6.$$

1. When the budget or income increases to 18:

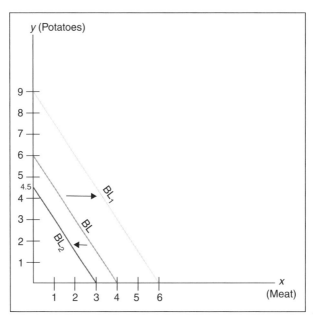

FIGURE 3.13

- The horizontal intercept:

$$x = \frac{I}{P_x} = \frac{18}{3} = 6.$$

- The vertical intercept:

$$y = \frac{I}{P_y} = \frac{18}{2} = 9.$$

2. When the budget or income decreases to 9:

- The horizontal intercept:

$$x = \frac{I}{P_x} = \frac{9}{3} = 3.$$

- The vertical intercept:

$$y = \frac{I}{P_y} = \frac{9}{2} = 4.5.$$

The Swing   The other change of the budget line is the inward and outward swing from the origin point, while pivoting on one intercept. It occurs due to changes in the price of either of the two commodities. Unlike the shift of the line, which is brought about by changes in both intercepts, the swing of the line would be characterized by changes in both, the slope of the line and the intercept of the commodity whose price has changed. Technically, this time, both terms on the right side of the modified budget equation would be affected:

$$y = \frac{I}{P_y} - \frac{P_x}{P_y}x,$$

$$x = \frac{I}{P_x} - \frac{P_y}{P_x}y,$$

we can see that any change in the price of x or y would affect the value of the slope $\left(-\frac{P_x}{P_y}\right)$, as well as the value of the intercepts, $\left(\frac{I}{P_x}\right)$ and $\left(\frac{I}{P_y}\right)$, resulting in a certain swing of the line.

Example 3.3

Follow the changes in the budget line of the last example when (1) the price of meat goes up to $6 one time, and down to $1.50 the other time, while the price of potatoes remains the same; and (2) the price of potatoes goes up to $4 one time and down to $1 the other time, while the price of meat remains the same. Also, income would remain the same at $12 throughout the changes in price:

Solution:

1. Since the change is only in the price of meat (x), y-intercept would not change and the budget line would pivot over y and swing around x-axis:

$$x = \frac{I}{P_x} = \frac{12}{6} = 2 \left(\begin{array}{l} \text{Line pivots at } y = 6 \text{ and} \\ \text{swings inward to BL}_1 \\ \text{slope} = -\frac{6}{2} = -3 \end{array} \right),$$

$$x = \frac{I}{P_x} = \frac{12}{1.50} = 8 \left(\begin{array}{l} \text{Line pivots at } y = 6 \text{ and} \\ \text{swings outward to BL}_2 \\ \text{slope} = -\frac{1.5}{2} = -0.75 \end{array} \right).$$

2. Since the change is only in the price of potatoes (y), x-intercept would be the pivot point and the budget line would swing around y-axis (see Figure 3.14):

$$y = \frac{I}{P_y} = \frac{12}{4} = 3 \left(\begin{array}{l} \text{Line pivots at } x = 4 \text{ and} \\ \text{swings inward to BL}_3 \\ \text{slope} = -\frac{3}{4} = -0.75 \end{array} \right),$$

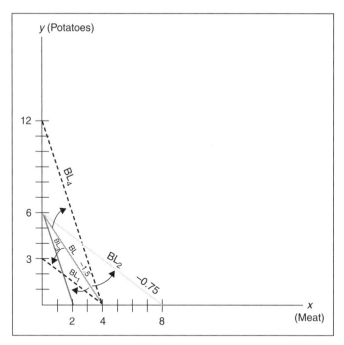

FIGURE 3.14

$$y = \frac{I}{P_y} = \frac{12}{1} = 12 \begin{pmatrix} \text{Line pivots at } x = 4 \text{ and} \\ \text{swings outward to BL}_4 \\ \text{slope} = -\frac{3}{1} = -3 \end{pmatrix}.$$

The Kink   Typically, the budget line is a straight line unless there is a **price change** related to a certain quantity of one of the commodities. In such case, the budget line would be kinked either inward or outward to reflect the nonuniform price of one of the commodities. Let us consider one of the last swing cases, say when the budget line swung from BL to BL$_2$ due to the decrease in the price of meat from \$3 to \$1.50 per pound and the resulting purchase of 8 lb of meat (see Figure 3.15).

Now, let us assume that a grocery store sale coupon states that the low price of \$1.50 per pound is good only for the first 2 lb purchased, and the original price of \$3 would apply on all quantities beyond 2 lb. In this case, 2 lb would be purchased at \$1.50 per pound. That would exhaust \$3 from the budget, leaving \$9 that would buy 3 additional pounds at \$3.00 each.

$$2 \times \$1.50 = \$3.00,$$

$$\$12.00 - \$3.00 = \$9.00,$$

$$\frac{\$9.00}{\$3.00} = 3 \text{ lb.}$$

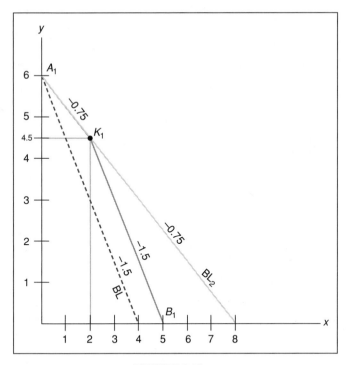

FIGURE 3.15

So, the maximum amount of meat that can be purchased under this two-price system would be 5 lb, and that is the x-intercept:

$$2 \ @\$1.50 + 3@\$3 = 5 \text{ lb.}$$

If the consumer buys 2 lb at \$1.50 spending \$3, the remaining \$9 would buy 4.5 lb of potatoes at \$2 per pound, and if the consumer chooses to spend the rest of the money on potatoes:

$$2 \text{ lb of meat} @\$1.50 = \$3.00,$$

$$\$12.00 - \$3.00 = \$9.00,$$

$$\frac{\$9.00}{\$2.00} = 4.5 \text{ lb of potatoes.}$$

This 4.5 lb of potatoes would be the y-intercept and together with the 2 lb of meat, it would give us point of K_1 on BL_2, which is the kink point. The kinked budget line, then, would be $A_1 \ K_1 \ B_1$, with two segments: $A_1 \ K_1$ with a slope of -0.75 just like BL_2 and segment K_1 B_1 with a slope of -1.5 just like BL.

In addition to this type of kink, the budget line can also be kinked down. Let us assume there is a different type of grocery store sale that benefits consumers who buy in bulk, one such sale states: the low meat price of \$1.50 per pound is applicable only on large purchases, that is more than 2 lb. In this case, the consumer would pay the original price of

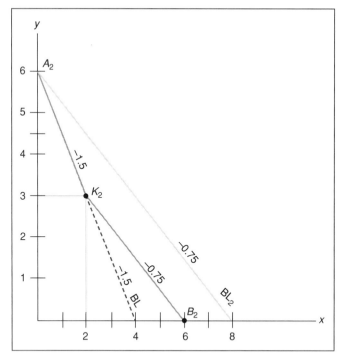

FIGURE 3.16

$3 per pound for the first 2 lb, and pay $1.50 for all that he can buy beyond the first 2 lb. That would be 4 lb in the remaining budget of $6.00:

$$2 \text{ lb } @\$3.00 = \$6.00,$$
$$\$12.00 - \$6.00 = \$6.00,$$
$$\frac{\$6.00}{\$1.50} = 4 \text{ lb.}$$

This would make the total purchases of meat 6 lb (2 + 4), and that is the new x-intercept of the kinked line. Now, after purchasing the initial 2 lb of meat and spending $6.00, the remaining $6.00 would buy 3 lb of potatoes, if that consumer still wants to buy some potatoes after buying 2 lb of meat. This point, together with the 2 lb of meat, would form the kink point K_2 on the original BL. Therefore, a kinked budget line $A_2 K_2 B_2$ is formed with a down kink point of K_2. Segment $A_2 K_2$ would have a slope of -1.5, and segment K_2 B_2 would have a slope of -0.75 (see Figure 3.16).

3.2.4   Three-Dimensional Budget

Suppose the consumer in the last example wants to add green vegetables along with meat and potatoes while his budget is still $12.00, given that the price of green vegetables is $2.40 per pound, we can construct a three-dimensional budget constraint graph by adding a third axis, Z, to represent green vegetables. We can also find the z-intercept for the maximum amount spent on green vegetables, assuming the entire budget of $12.00 would be spent on them:

$$z\text{-intercept: } Z = \frac{I}{P_z} = \frac{12.00}{2.40} = 5.$$

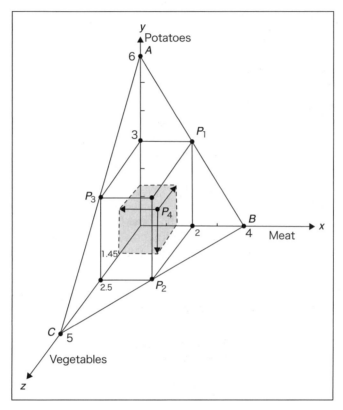

FIGURE 3.17

Here, the consumer would have four choices to split his budget (see Figure 3.17):

1. between potatoes and meat, along AB line;
2. between potatoes and vegetables, along AC line;
3. between vegetables and meat, along CB line;
4. between meat, potatoes, and vegetables, around the triangle.

For example, we can consider the following bundles:

$$P_1 : 2x + 3y,$$
$$2(\$3) + 3(\$2) = \$12,$$

$P_2 : 2x + 2.5Z,$

$2(\$3) + 2.5(\$2.40) = \$12,$

$P_3 : 3y + 2.5Z,$

$2(\$3) + 2.5(\$2.40) = \$12.$

If the budget is split between the three commodities, the fourth bundle, P_4, has to be somewhere inside the cube. Such a bundle would be

$P_4 : 1.5x + 2y + 1.45Z,$

$1.5(\$3) + 2(\$2) + 1.45(\$2.40) = \$12.$

3.3   THE OPTIMAL CHOICE

The consumer's optimal goal is to gain the highest possible satisfaction that is affordable. In other words, it is to maximize utility within the constraints of one's income and market prices. This ultimate goal can be achieved by combining the two aforementioned elements of choice and deriving the optimality produced by their interaction. Figure 3.18 shows that a consumer would like to have his bundles of commodities at the highest possible IC, such as at D on IC_3. But this bundle is not affordable because it is outside the affordability zone. All of A, D, C, and E are within the affordability zone, but they are on lower ICs. A, B, and C exhaust the entire budget, but C is on a higher IC than A and B. In fact, C is absolutely the

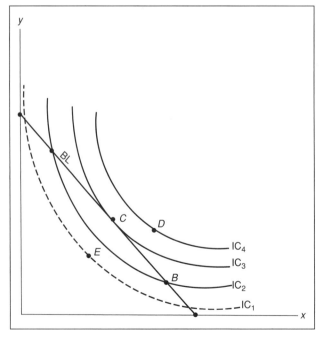

FIGURE 3.18

best bundle for it is the only point that is on the highest affordable IC. This would establish the rule that the consumer's **optimal choice** would be at the point of tangency between the budget line and the highest possible IC. Technically, the **point of tangency** is where the slope of the IC (MRS) is equal to the slope of the budget line (MRT):

$$\text{Slope}^c \text{ IC}_3 = \text{Slope}^c \text{ BL},$$

$$\text{MRS} = \text{MRT},$$

$$\frac{\text{MU}_x}{\text{MU}_y} = \frac{P_x}{P_y} \left(\begin{array}{l} \text{No sign is assigned because} \\ \text{both slopes are negative.} \end{array} \right).$$

This means that the optimal point implies the equality between the **marginal utility** (MU) of x in terms of y marginal value and the relative price of x in terms of y price. If we rearrange this equality, we obtain

$$\frac{\text{MU}_x}{P_x} = \frac{\text{MU}_y}{P_y},$$

which refers to the general condition of **consumer equilibrium**. This condition states that a consumer's optimal choice occurs at a point when he implicitly equates between the marginal value of the commodities as they are related to their prices. Specifically, we can say that a consumer would make an optimal choice of two commodities when the marginal utility of the last dollar spent on one commodity (x) is equal to the marginal utility of the last dollar spent on the other commodity (y). This equality is logical for the following reason:

Let us assume that the marginal utility of x relative to its price MU_x/P_x is larger than the marginal utility of y relative to its price MU_y/P_y. A consumer would then act wisely by pulling out \$1 from the expenditure on y and spending it on x. Such an act would increase the consumption of x by certain additional units, and as a result, it would reduce its marginal utility. On the other hand, decreasing the expenditure on y by \$1 would reduce its consumption by certain units leading to an increase in its marginal utility. If this process continues, MU_x/P_x would decrease while MU_y/P_y increases until there will be no incentive to have either term changed. That would be the point where they experience no changes and become equal, and that explains the logic behind the equality of those terms in the equilibrium condition.

3.3.1   Interior and Corner Solutions

Achieving an optimal choice at the point of tangency (C) between the highest possible IC and the budget line would be called the "interior" solution. It would still be considered an **interior solution** as long as that point of tangency lies anywhere on the budget line between its ends. However, if this point of tangency occurs exactly on either of the budget line ends, then the solution is called the corner solution and the point is called the **boundary optimum**. The **corner solution** case occurs when a consumer is interested in buying only one of the two commodities, and his budget would be entirely spent on that commodity alone while the other commodity remains irrelevant. In other words, his marginal utility obtained from the purchased commodity would be larger than the marginal utility obtained by the skipped commodity. For example, if a consumer is not interested in purchasing a cell phone and he would rather spend his budget on other electronics, his optimum purchase would occur on the other electronics intercept.

Technically, he would have

$$\frac{MU_o}{P_o} > \frac{MU_c}{P_c},$$

where (o) refers to the other electronics measured on the x-axis and (c) refers to a cell phone measured on the y-axis. His optimal choice would be at C in the corner (see Figure 3.19).

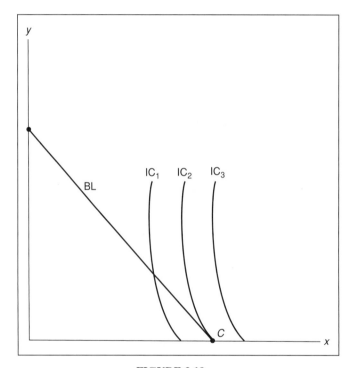

FIGURE 3.19

It is important here to remind that having only the tangency point between the budget line and the IC may not assure optimality of the choice, although it is a necessary requirement. What guarantees optimality is the second necessary condition, and that is the convexity of the IC. In the graph shown in Figure 3.20, points A, B, and C are all tangency points but only A and C achieve optimality of the consumer choice in terms of the **utility maximization**. Point B cannot achieve any maximization since it is on the concave segment of the IC.

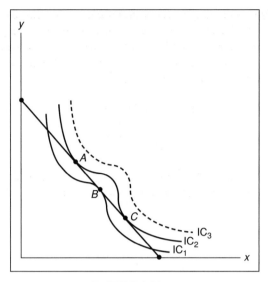

FIGURE 3.20

3.3.2 Utility and Its Measurability

Consumer utility is a term coined by the British philosopher Jeremy Bentham in 1823. In classical economic literature, utility has been a synonym to satisfaction, welfare, and happiness. The most commonly used definition of utility states that it is the satisfaction derived by a consumer through the use or consumption of goods and services. Another definition focuses on the consumed products more than on the consumer response to them. Such a concept would consider utility as the ability or power of a commodity to satisfy consumer's needs and wants. Yet another view would shift focus to the measurability issue. Utility, according to this view, would be the index for the consumer's sense of well-being. The issue of measurability of utility gave two doctrines:

1. **Ordinalism**, which assumes that utility can only be measured by ranking the preferences by unspecified and unquantifiable relationships between certain levels such as higher, lower, or in-between. This ordinal measure and its relative ranking is the cornerstone of the neoclassical theory of consumer choice despite the fact that it would not provide a discrete level of satisfaction, nor would it be able to provide the magnitude of the change in satisfaction. Most economists believe that when it comes to understanding consumer preferences, it is only important to know which bundle of commodities is preferred over what?

2. **Cardinalism**, which assumes that utility can be measured either by (a) units of absolute values such as *a* **util** where a consumer can determine that 6 utils were obtained by consuming two apples and can also determine the magnitude of change in the utility as in determining that the second apple added only 2 utils, while the rest of 4 utils were attributed to the first apple; or (b) quantifying the comparison between interval levels such as in saying the difference between level 1 and level 2 of utility is twice as much the difference between level 3 and level 4 of utility.

Classic economists theorized that consumers' satisfaction or utility gained out of con-suming commodity x can be expressed in proportion to the logarithm of x:

$$U(x) = \ln x,$$

such that as x increases the utility of x would increase in a decreasing rate (Figure 3.21) where the slope is

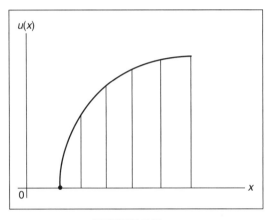

FIGURE 3.21

$$\frac{dU}{dx} = \frac{1}{x} > 0$$

and

$$\frac{d^2U}{dx^2} = \frac{1}{x^2} < 0.$$

This forms the basis of classifying utility into **total utility** (TU) and **marginal utility** (MU) and establishes the law of diminishing marginal utility. TU is the overall satisfaction derived from consuming a particular number of units of a product, while the marginal utility is the change in the total utility that results from consuming the last unit of that product.

Example 3.4
Let us consider that a number of small pieces of chocolate are being offered to a chocolate lover who is able to translate the overall satisfaction he gets out of chocolate consumption as shown in the total utility column of Table 3.1.

TABLE 3.1

Q	TU	MU
1	16	16
2	30	14
3	42	12
4	52	10
5	60	8
6	66	6
7	70	4
8	72	2
9	72	0
10	69	−3

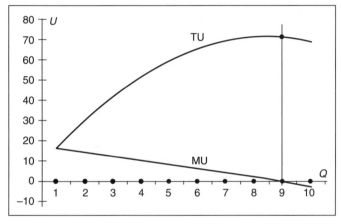

FIGURE 3.22

Considering Table 3.1 and the graph in Figure 3.22, we can make the following observations:

- Total utility is a function that increases all the way but at a decreasing rate. It reaches its maximum of 72 utils on the consumption of the ninth piece of chocolate.
- Marginal utility is a function that is decreasing all the way. It reaches zero on the consumption of the ninth piece of chocolate and it continues to decrease to reach a negative value (−3). This would establish the "law of diminishing marginal utility," which states that "consumption of successive units of a given commodity would eventually cause the marginal utility to decline as shown by adding smaller and smaller contributions to the overall satisfaction."
- Since the marginal utility represents the change in total utility that is brought about by the last unit, it is clear that the zero value indicates that the ninth piece consumed did not do any good because the total utility remains at 72 utils, the same as in the eighth piece. This is where the consumer has to stop eating. The consumption of the

ninth piece gave the signal that the total utility has reached its maximum. Any further consumption would be detrimental. At the consumption of the ninth unit, a consumer would have reached the **point of saturation**.

- If the total utility function is known, the marginal utility function would be $\frac{dU(x)}{dx}$.

Example 3.5

Given below is the total utility (TU_x) and the marginal utility (MU_y) that are derived from consuming a combination of two commodities x and y.

$$TU_x: 7, 13, 18, 22, 25, 27, 27, 26, 25, 23.$$
$$MU_y: 4, 10, 8, 6, 4, 2, 0, -1, -2, -3$$

(a) Derive a column for the marginal utility of x (MU_x), and a column for the total utility of y (TU_y).

(b) On separate graphs, plot the total and marginal utilities of each commodity.

(c) Determine at what unit of each commodity a consumer would reach the point of saturation.

(d) If the consumer buys a combination of the two commodities and if their prices are $2.00 for commodity x and $1.00 for commodity y, where would his equilibrium be?

(e) What would be the consumer budget for his equilibrium combination?

Solution:

TABLE 3.2

1	2	3	4	5	6	7
Q	TU_x	MU_x	TU_y	MU_y	MU_x/P_x	MU_y/P_y
1	7	7	4	4	3.5	4
2	13	6	14	10	3.0	10
3	18	5	22	8	2.5	8
4	22	4	28	6	2	6
5	25	3	32	4	1.5	4
6	27	2	34	2	1.0	2
7	27	0	34	0	0.0	0
8	26	-1	33	-1	$-\frac{1}{2}$	-1
9	25	-1	31	-2	$-\frac{1}{2}$	-2
10	23	-2	28	-3	-1	-3

(a) Each value of the marginal utility of x in Column 3 in Table 3.2 is the corresponding value of total utility minus the one before. So, 7 is $(7 - 0)$, 6 is $(13 - 7)$, and so on. Opposite to that is the creation of total utility of y. Each value in Column 4 is the sum of the corresponding value of marginal utility and all other values before it. So, 14 is $(10 + 4)$, 22 is $(8 + 10 + 4)$, and so on.

(b) See Figure 3.23.

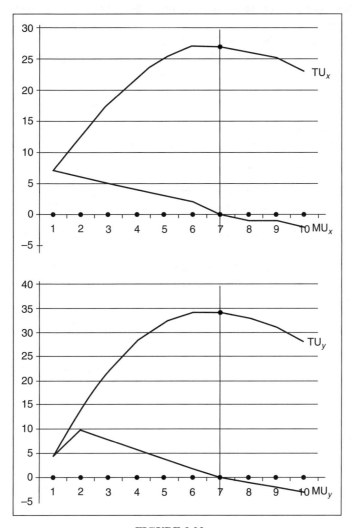

FIGURE 3.23

(c) Point of saturation is reached at the seventh unit for both commodities where the total utility of x reaches the maximum of 27 and the marginal utility of x reaches zero. Also, when the total utility of y reaches the maximum of 34 and the marginal utility of y reaches zero.

(d) Consumer equilibrium is achieved when

$$\frac{MU_x}{P_x} = \frac{MU_y}{P_y}.$$

After creating Columns 6 and 7, we can where the equality occurs: It occurs at 2 and 0. Since the case of zero is negligible, the equality of 2 is the equilibrium. It indicates that the consumer equilibrium is achieved when buying 4 units of x and 6 units of y.

(e) The consumer's budget would be

$$xP_x + yP_y = I.$$

$$4(\$2.00) + 6(\$1.00) = \$14.00.$$

3.3.3 Utility Maximization

The consumer preference that we discussed earlier can be viewed as a utility function that can be mathematically maximized, subject to the consumer budget constraint. In this manner, the utility maximizing bundle of consumer commodities can be determined, if not for estimating the individual optimal consumption per se, it would be more important for the many interesting implications that can be drawn on the aggregate resource allocation and the maximization of the efficiency of such allocation.

So, on the basis of mathematical logic, consumer utility can be viewed as a function of the consumed commodities, the purchase of which is constrained by a certain income or budget available to a consumer, and by the prevailing market prices of the commodities that consumer is interested in. Such a function can be maximized using calculus methods:

$$\max U = f(x, y), \tag{3.4}$$

$$\text{s.t. } xP_x + yP_y = I. \tag{3.5}$$

This constrained function can be converted into an unconstrained function in order to solve the optimum quantities of x and y that would grant the maximum consumer satisfaction. There are two ways to turn the constrained function into an unconstrained one: (1) by substituting the budget constraint equation into the original objective function, and (2) by the **Lagrangian method**.

1. *By substitution*: Rearrange Equation (3.5) to express y-value:

$$xP_x + yP_y = I,$$

$$yP_y = I - xP_x,$$

$$y = \frac{I - xP_x}{P_y},$$

$$y = \frac{I}{P_y} - \frac{P_x}{P_y}x. \tag{3.6}$$

Substitute the value of y from Equation (3.6) into Equation (3.4):

$$\max U = f\left(x, \frac{I}{P_y} - \frac{P_x}{P_y}x\right).$$

Differentiate the function in terms of x, and set it to zero for the first-order condition (FOC):

$$\frac{\partial U(x, y)}{\partial x} + \frac{\partial U(x, y)}{\partial y} \cdot \frac{d_y}{d_x} = 0. \tag{FOC}$$

Now, we differentiate Equation (3.6) in terms of x:

$$y = \frac{I}{P_y} - \frac{P_x}{P_y} x,$$

$$\frac{d_y}{d_x} = -\frac{P_x}{P_y}, \tag{3.7}$$

and substitute the value of $\dfrac{d_y}{d_x}$ from Equation (3.7) into $\dfrac{d_y}{d_x}$ in FOC:

$$\frac{\partial U(x, y)}{\partial x} + \frac{\partial U(x, y)}{\partial y} \cdot -\frac{P_x}{P_y} = 0,$$

$$\frac{\partial U(x, y)}{\partial x} = \frac{\partial U(x, y)}{\partial y} \cdot \frac{P_x}{P_y},$$

$$\frac{\dfrac{\partial U(x^*, y^*)}{\partial_x}}{\dfrac{\partial U(x^*, y^*)}{\partial_y}} = \frac{P_x}{P_y},$$

$$\frac{\mathrm{Mu}_x}{\mathrm{Mu}_y} = \frac{P_x}{P_y},$$

or MRS = MRT,

which states that the optimal quantities (x^*, y^*) would satisfy the condition where the slope of the indifference curve (MRS) would be equal to the slope of the budget line (MRT), and that was the case of consumer equilibrium that we have seen before at point C.

2. *By the Lagrangian Method*: Using the **Lagrangian function** developed by the Italian-French mathematician Joseph Louis Lagrange in 1804, we can maximize our utility function by first setting the L-function as a sum of the objective function, which is to be maximized $U = f(x, n)$, and the budget constraint function:

$$\max U = f(x, y),$$

$$\text{s.t. } x P_x + y P_y = I,$$

$$x P_x + y P_y - I = 0,$$

$$\max L(x, y, \lambda, I) = f(x, y) - \lambda(x P_x + y P_y - I).$$

First, we obtain the FOC for x, y, and λ:

$$\frac{\partial L}{\partial x} = \frac{\partial U(x^*, y^*)}{\partial x} - \lambda P_x = 0, \qquad\qquad \text{FOC} \quad (3.8)$$

$$\frac{\partial L}{\partial y} = \frac{\partial U(x^*, y^*)}{\partial y} - \lambda P_y = 0, \qquad\qquad \text{FOC} \quad (3.9)$$

$$\frac{\partial L}{\partial \lambda} = P_x x^* + P_y y^* - I = 0. \qquad\qquad \text{FOC} \quad (3.10)$$

Dividing FOC (3.8) by FOC (3.9), we get

$$\frac{\dfrac{\partial U(x^*, y^*)}{\partial x}}{\dfrac{\partial U(x^*, y^*)}{\partial y}} = \frac{P_x}{P_y},$$

$$\frac{MU_x}{MU_y} = \frac{P_x}{P_y}.$$

$$MRS = MRT,$$

while FOC (3.10) remains as the budget constraint.

Example 3.6

Maximize the utility function of the Cobb–Douglas form $U = f(x^a\, y^{1-a})$, subject to the usual budget constraint $xP_x + yP_y = I$:

$$\max U = f(x^a, y^{1-a}), \qquad\qquad (3.11)$$

$$\text{s.t. } xP_x + yP_y = I. \qquad\qquad (3.12)$$

Solution:

First, we take the natural logarithm of the objective function (3.11), and then we maximize it:

$$\ln U(x, y) = a \ln x + (1 - a) \ln y,$$

$$\max va \ln x + (1 - a) \ln y, \qquad\qquad (3.13)$$

$$\text{s.t. } xP_x + yP_y = I.$$

- *Substitution Solution*: First, we obtain MRS from Equation (3.13):

$$U(x, y) = a \ln x + (1 - a) \ln y,$$

$$\text{MRS} = \frac{\dfrac{\partial U(x, y)}{\partial x}}{\dfrac{\partial U(x, y)}{\partial y}}$$

$$= \frac{a \cdot \dfrac{1}{x}}{(1 - a) \cdot \dfrac{1}{y}}$$

$$= \frac{\dfrac{a}{x}}{\dfrac{1 - a}{y}}$$

$$= \frac{a}{x} \cdot \frac{y}{1 - a}$$

$$\text{MRS} = \frac{ay}{(1 - a)x}.$$

Obtaining y-value from Equation (3.12),

$$P_x x + P_y y = I,$$

$$P_y y = I - P_x x,$$

$$y = \frac{I - P_x x}{P_y}. \tag{3.14}$$

Since MRS $= \frac{P_x}{P_y}$, we can use the value of MRS for this particular function that was obtained in Equation (3.14), and substitute for y-value obtained in Equation (3.15) to get x-value:

$$\frac{ay}{(1 - a)x} = \frac{P_x}{P_y},$$

$$\frac{a\left(\dfrac{I - P_x x}{P_y}\right)}{(1 - a)x} = \frac{P_x}{P_y},$$

$$a\left(\frac{I - P_x x}{P_y}\right) P_y = (1 - a)P_x x,$$

$$a(I - P_x x) = (1 - a)P_x x,$$

$$aI - aP_x x = P_x x - a \, P_x x,$$

$$aI = P_x x,$$

$$\frac{aI}{P_x} = X. \tag{3.15}$$

Substitute x-value from Equation (3.16) into x in Equation (3.15) to get y-value:

$$y = \frac{I - P_x \left(\frac{aI}{P_x} \right)}{P_y},$$

$$y = \frac{I - aI}{P_y},$$

$$y = \frac{I(1 - a)}{P_y}.$$

- *The Lagrangian Solution*:

$$\max L = a \ln x + (1 - a) \ln y - \lambda(P_x x + P_y y - I),$$

we obtain the FOCs:

$$\frac{\partial L}{\partial x} = \frac{a}{x} - \lambda P_x = 0, \qquad\qquad \text{FOC} \quad (3.16)$$

$$\frac{\partial L}{\partial x} = \frac{(1 - a)}{y} - \lambda P_y = 0, \qquad\qquad \text{FOC} \quad (3.17)$$

$$\frac{\partial L}{\partial y} = P_x x + P_y y - I = 0. \qquad\qquad \text{FOC} \quad (3.18)$$

From FOC (3.17), we get

$$\frac{a}{x} = \lambda P_x,$$

$$a = \lambda P_x x. \tag{3.19}$$

From FOC (3.18), we get

$$\frac{1 - a}{y} = \lambda P_y,$$

$$1 - a = \lambda P_y y. \tag{3.20}$$

Adding Equation (3.20) to Equation (3.21), we get $a + 1 - a = \lambda P_x x + \lambda P_y y$,

$$1 = \lambda(P_x x + P_y y),$$

$$1 = \lambda I,$$

$$\frac{1}{I} = \lambda. \tag{3.21}$$

Substituting the value of λ from Equation (3.22) into λ in Equation (3.20):

$$a = \lambda P_x x,$$

$$a = \frac{1}{I} P_x x,$$

$$\frac{a}{\frac{P_x}{I}} = x,$$

$$\frac{aI}{P_x} = x. \tag{3.22}$$

Substitute the value of λ from Equation (3.22) into λ in Equation (3.21):

$$1 - a = \lambda P_y y,$$

$$1 - a = \frac{1}{I} P_y y,$$

$$\frac{1-a}{\frac{P_y}{I}} = y,$$

$$\frac{(1-a)I}{P_y} = y.$$

3.4 EFFECTS ON THE OPTIMAL CHOICE

There are two major changes that would directly and effectively affect the consumer's optimal choice and for which consumer demand would respond accordingly. They are the change in income and consequently in the consumer's ability to buy, and the change in the market price of commodities, and consequently in the willingness to trade among the alternatives of those commodities.

3.4.1 Change in Income

We have seen earlier how an increase or decrease in consumers' budget or income would only affect the intercepts, resulting in a parallel shift of the budget line to the right or left, which either expands or shrinks the affordability zone. This, of course, would occur under the assumption of holding the prices of commodities constant. The question now is what would happen to the optimum point (C) when the budget line shifts right or left? The answer would be visually clear in the graph shown in Figure 3.24 where we assume that an increase in income would cause the budget line, BL, to shift right to BL_1. The optimum point C can literally move to any spot on the new budget line BL_1, but here are the five general representative possibilities:

- C could move to A, which would offer more x (increase from x_c to x_a) and more y (increase from y_c to y_a).

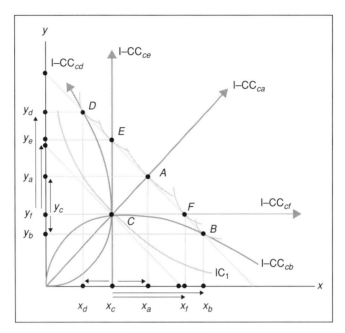

FIGURE 3.24

- C could move to F, which would offer more of x (increase from x_c to x_f), but the same amount of y.
- C could move to E, which would offer more of y (increase from y_c to y_e), but the same amount of x.
- C could move to B, which would offer more of x (increase from x_c to x_b), but less of y (decrease from y_c to y_b).
- C could move to D, which would offer less of x (decrease from x_c to x_d), but more of y (decrease from y_c to y_d).

Another question is: What would determine which of these moves would be most likely to occur? The answer lies in knowing the nature of the commodity, especially whether it is normal or inferior.

Normal and Inferior Commodities   A **normal commodity** is a commodity for which the consumption would increase as consumer income increases and would decrease as income decreases. The movement from C to A indicates that this specific consumer would consider both x and y as normal commodities since the quantities of both increased as income increased. The majority of the commodities we deal with are most likely to be normal commodities. Specifically, we can say that good-quality goods and services are normal commodities. In technical terms, we can say that the demand for normal commodities has a positive relationship with income. If x is a normal good, then

$$\frac{\Delta x}{\Delta I} > 0.$$

An **inferior commodity** is the commodity for which the consumption would decrease as income increases, and would increase as income decreases. The movement from C to B when the consumption of y decreased and x increased, and the movement from C to D, when the consumption of x decreased and y increased indicated that y and x, respectively, were inferior commodities compared with their counterparts x and y in the same movements. Generally, as shown in Figure 3.24, the consumption of whichever commodities decreased were inferior commodities. In other words, income had a negative effect on the consumption of the inferior commodities. If x is an inferior commodity, then

$$\frac{\Delta x}{\Delta I} < 0.$$

Income–Consumption Curve   In the graph shown in Figure 3.24, we saw the possibilities of how the initial optimal point C may move to either A, B, D, E, or F depending on the consumer preference and the type of commodities. If we follow any of these movements by connecting the points with a line, we would get what is called the **income–consumption curve** (I–CC), which is defined as a locus of all the points representing the optimum pattern obtained as income changes while prices of commodities are held constant. In Figure 3.24, we can identify a number of major I–CCs associated with movements of the optimum point. Here are five types of I–CCs:

1. I–CC$_{ca}$, which is an upward sloping curve indicating a pattern of normal commodities.
2. I–CC$_{cf}$, which is a horizontal straight line indicating a pattern of having more of x and keeping y unchanged.
3. I–CC$_{ce}$, which is a vertical straight line indicating a pattern of having more of y and keeping x unchanged.
4. I–CC$_{cd}$, which is a backward sloping curve indicating a pattern of having normal y and inferior x.
5. I–CC$_{cb}$, which is a downward sloping curve indicating a pattern of having normal x and inferior y.

Engel Curve: Nominal and Real   The first scientific survey research on the way families spent their income was conducted by a German statistician Ernest Engel in 1857. It was famous for coining what is now known as the **Engel curve** that describes the relationship between income and quantity demanded for commodities. This curve is defined as a locus of all points representing the quantities of a commodity demanded at various levels of consumer's budget. Such a curve can be geometrically derived from the I–CC. But since we can look at the value of income in two ways, the nominal income and the real income, we can actually produce two curves: an Engel curve based on nominal income and an Engel curve based on real income:

1. *Nominal Income Engel Curve*: Let us assume a certain consumer's nominal in-come of level I_1 which has increased to level I_2, and let us assume that this con-sumer is interested in increasing the consumption of both x and y, which are normal

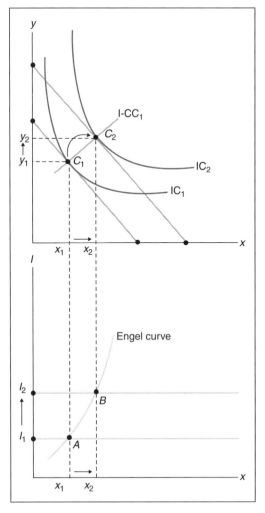

FIGURE 3.25

commodities. The optimum would move from C_1 to C_2 producing an I–CC$_1$. Now, in a panel (see Figure 3.25), let us set the nominal income on the y-axis and keep the x commodity on the x-axis. To draw a nominal income Engel curve on this panel, we take the following steps to mark two points A and B:

(a) Drop two vertical lines from the optimum points C_1 and C_2.

(b) Extend two horizontal lines from the two levels of nominal income I_1 and I_2.

(c) Mark the intersection of the first vertical and first horizontal by A, and the intersection of the second vertical and second horizontal by B.

(d) Connecting A to B would produce a nominal income Engel curve, for commodity x.

2. *Real Income Engel Curve*: **Real income** is basically what nominal or money income can buy. In other words, it is the consumer budget after consideration of the market

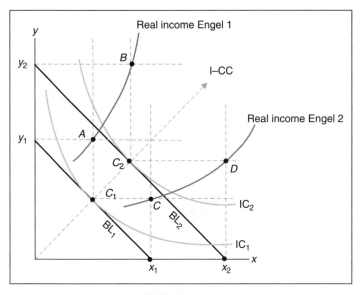

FIGURE 3.26

prices of goods and services. So, if we have nominal income (I), real income would be $\frac{I}{P}$. Specifically, we would have a real income for x and y.

$$\text{RI}_x = \frac{I}{P_x} \quad \text{and} \quad \text{RI}_y = \frac{I}{P_y}.$$

Therefore, we can obtain the following real income Engel curves (see Figure 3.26):

(a) *Engel curve for x in terms of y prices*: Raise verticals from C_1 and C_2 and cross them with horizontals from the y-intercepts y_1 and y_2. Reach the two points of intersections A and B to produce a real income Engel curve AB.

(b) *Engel curve for y in terms of x prices*: Extend horizontals from C_1 and C_2 and cross them with verticals raised from the x-intercepts x_1 and x_2. Reach the two points of intersections C and D to produce a real income Engel curve CD.

Engel Curve and Income–Consumption Curve for Homothetic and Quasi-Linear Preferences A **homothetic preference** means that a consumer would increase or decrease his demand of a commodity by the same proportion of his increase or decrease in income:

$$\frac{x_1}{I_1} = \frac{x_2}{I_2} = \cdots = \frac{x_n}{I_n} = \frac{\partial x}{\partial I},$$

$$\frac{\frac{\partial x_j}{\partial I}}{x_j} = 1 \quad j = 1, 2, \ldots, n.$$

This equality in the way demand is scaled up or down with income results in a straight I–CC through the origin as well as a similar straight line Engel curve. As for a **quasi-linear**

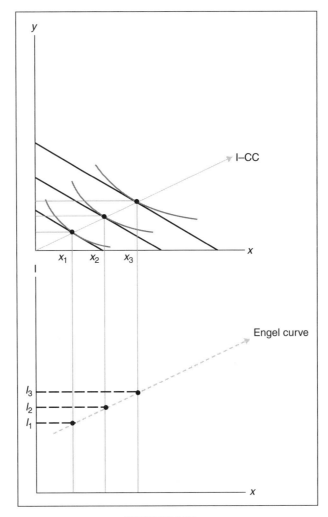

FIGURE 3.27

preference, it is where a consumer would divert any change in income only toward one of the commodities, say y, while the other, x, stays unchanged, the result would be a perfectly vertical I–CC, as well as a vertical Engel curve (see Figures 3.27 and 3.28).

Income Elasticity of Demand   We have seen the effect of income on the demand of commodities but only in general terms. Now, we will be able to see to what extent the demand responds to **income change**. That would be what is called the **income elasticity of demand** that measures the degree of responsiveness of demand to income change. Specifically, the term "income elasticity" is defined as the percentage change in the demand of a commodity as a response to a 1% change in income. So, for example, the demand for commodity

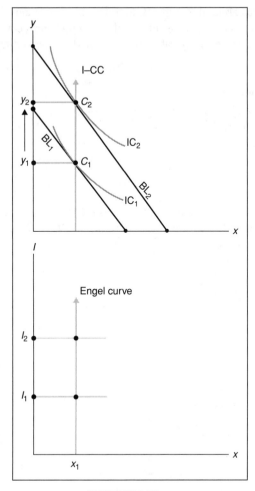

FIGURE 3.28

(x) in response to a change in income (I) can be measured by the income elasticity of demand (ε):

$$\varepsilon_x = \frac{\%\Delta x}{\%\Delta I}$$

$$= \frac{\dfrac{\Delta x}{x} \times 100}{\dfrac{\Delta I}{I} \times 100}$$

$$= \frac{\Delta x}{x} \cdot \frac{I}{\Delta I}$$

$$= \frac{\Delta x}{\Delta I} \cdot \frac{I}{x}$$

$$= \frac{x_2 - x_1}{I_2 - I_1} \cdot \frac{I}{x}.$$

Elasticity can tell us about the shape of the I–CC and Engel curve as well as about the type of commodities for a certain consumer. Although consumers consider commodities in a subjective way, we can generally categorize commodities according to their elasticities in this manner:

- For normal commodities, $\varepsilon \geq 0$.
- For inferior commodities, $\varepsilon < 0$.
- For **necessities**, $0 \leq \varepsilon \leq 1$.
- For **luxuries**, $\varepsilon > 1$.

Example 3.7
Calculate the income elasticity of demand for music CDs when Jack purchased 8 CDs in October, at a time his monthly income was $2000, and 10 CDs in February when his income raised to $3000 (Table 3.3).

TABLE 3.3

	I	$1x$
October	2000	8
February	3000	10

$$\varepsilon_x = \frac{x_2 - x_1}{I_2 - I_1} \cdot \frac{I}{x}$$
$$= \frac{10 - 8}{3000 - 2000} \cdot \frac{2000}{8} = 0.5 \text{ at the lower level.}$$

This is the **elasticity at the lower level**. Note that we can use $I = 3000$ and $x = 10$ to in substituting for (I/A) get the **elasticity at the upper level**, and we can use an average of (I) as well as of (x) to get what is called the **arc elasticity**:

$$\varepsilon_x = \frac{10 - 8}{3000 - 2000} \cdot \frac{3000}{10} = 0.6 \text{ at the upper level,}$$
$$\varepsilon_{\text{arc}} = \frac{10 - 8}{3000 - 2000} \cdot \frac{2000 + 3000}{8 + 10} = 0.55 \text{ Arc elasticity.}$$

3.4.2   Change in Prices

In the budget line discussion, we have seen how the budget line would swing inward or outward when the price of x decreased or increased, or swing downward or upward when the price of y decreased or increased. This, of course, would occur under the assumption that consumer budget or income as well as the price of one of the commodities remain constant. Similar to the income change discussion, we can ask again. "What would happen

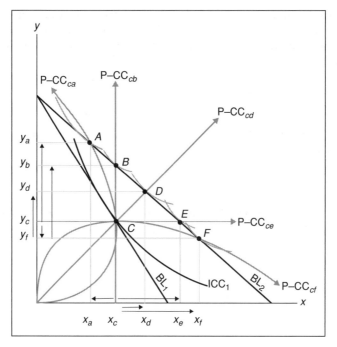

FIGURE 3.29

to the optimum point when such a swing in the budget line occurs?" The answer can be seen in the graph given in Figure 3.29. Let us assume that the price of x has decreased, and let us recall that such a decrease would cause the change of both the slope of the budget line and the x-intercepts. The slope value would be smaller, leading to a flatter budget line, and the intercept would move right, which would mean causing the line to swing outward on the x-axis, away from the origin.

The original optimum point C on BL_1 can move to any spot on the new budget line BL_2. It would depend on consumer's specific preference and the type of commodities. Generally, we can identify the following five typical possibilities, where consumer equilibrium at C could move to:

1. D, which would offer more of x (an increase from x_c to x_d) and more of y (an increase of y_c to y_d);
2. B, which would offer the same amount of x but more of y (an increase from y_c to y_b);
3. E, which would offer the same amount of y but more of x (an increase from x_c to x_e);
4. A, which would offer less of x but much more of y (a big increase from y_c to y_a);
5. F, which would offer less of y but much more of x (a big increase from x_c to x_f).

Because the move from the original optimum point C to any of the alternative points above is induced by a change in price, the nature of commodities in regards to their price change would play a major role in those moves. Commodities, in this respect, can be categorized as Giffen and non-Giffen.

Giffen and Non-Giffen Commodities   A **Giffen commodity** is a concept coined after the nineteenth-century economist Robert Giffen who made a unique observation on the Irish poor who increased their consumption of potatoes when their prices rose during a local hardship. Since then, a Giffen commodity concept became known as any commodity that would defy the common law of demand, which states a rise in price would cause a drop in demand, and that the demand curve would be downward sloping. A Giffen commodity, therefore, would be demanded more as its price rises and demanded less as its price drops. Therefore, its demand curve would have a positive slope:

$$\frac{\partial x}{\partial P_x} > 0.$$

Practically, it is very rare to find such a commodity. Logic dictates that for any commodity to be Giffen, there would be two general conditions that have to be satisfied:

1. This commodity has to be an inferior one in the first place.
2. It has to be in a time and place that makes it requiring a substantial proportion of consumer's budget despite its inferiority.

The Irish potatoes at Giffen's time must have satisfied these conditions, but generally speaking, it is very uncommon to find a Giffen commodity for today's consumers, and therefore, this notion remains only a theoretical concept.

A non-Giffen commodity is the ordinary commodity that would normally obey the law of demand and would exhibit a negative sloping demand curve:

$$\frac{\partial x}{\partial P_x} < 0,$$

which reflects the inverse relationship between the demand for a commodity and its own price. The vast majority of the commodities in our life are non-Giffen commodities.

Price–Consumption Curve   Just like we did in our discussion of income change, we can follow the movement possibilities of the optimum point to create a general pattern curve called **price–consumption curve** (P–CC). We can also define such a curve in the same manner we defined the I–CC. Price–consumption curve is, therefore, a locus of all points representing the optimum pattern obtained as the price of a commodity changes while income and price of the other commodity are held constant. Following the possible movements outlined earlier, we can identify five major P–CCs:

1. P–CC$_{cd}$, which is an upward-sloping curve indicating a pattern of consumer prefer-ence toward having more of both commodities. Here, the decrease in the price of x not only offered the consumer an opportunity to buy more of x, but also allowed the consumer to buy more of y.
2. P–CC$_{ce}$, which is a horizontal line indicating that the consumer entirely dedicated the gain offered by the decrease in the price of x to increase his consumption of x. None was spared to buy more of y.

3. P–CC_{cb}, which is a vertical line. Here is the opposite case to the previous one. The opportunity obtained by the decrease in the price of x was not used to buy more of x but entirely dedicated to buy more of y.

4. P–CC_{cf}, which is a downward sloping curve indicating that this consumer takes the opportunity of the drop in the price of x to significantly increase the consumption of x even on the expense of dropping the consumption of y.

5. P–CC_{ca}, which is a backward bending curve to confirm that x is an inferior commodity and its consumption is reduced despite the drop in its own price. All benefits gained from the price decrease are directed toward increasing the consumption of y.

Price Change and the Demand Curve   Since the demand curve describes the relationship between consumption of a commodity and its own price, this curve can be traced out of the change in the optimum point and the resulting changes in the quantities induced by the price change. Let us create a new panel below the previous graph as shown in Figure 3.30. In this panel, the vertical axis would be the price where we mark the original price (P_1) and the dropped price (P_2). The horizontal axis would measure the quantities of x. A demand curve can then be obtained by

- dropping a vertical line from the first optimum point C, passing through XC_1 in the first graph and down to the x-axis in the second panel to mark x_1;
- dropping a vertical line from the second optimum point, C_z, passing through XC_2 and down to mark x_2 on the second panel.

Mark the intersection between the first vertical and a horizontal line extended from P_1 as point a, and mark the intersection between the second vertical and a horizontal line extended from P_2 as point b. Join a and b to form a demand curve D-curve.

Price Elasticity of Demand   Just like in the case of income change, we can measure to what extent the demand for commodities responds to the change in their own prices. This kind of measure is what we call "**the price elasticity of demand,**" which is defined as the percentage change in the quantity demanded of a commodity in response to a 1% change in its own price, given that consumer budget and the price of the other commodity remain constant:

$$\eta_x = \frac{\%\Delta x}{\%\Delta P_x}$$

$$\eta_x = \frac{\dfrac{\Delta x}{x} \cdot 100}{\dfrac{\Delta P_x}{P_x} \cdot 100},$$

$$\eta_x = \frac{\Delta x}{x} \cdot \frac{P_x}{\Delta P_x},$$

$$\eta_x = \frac{\Delta x}{\Delta x} \cdot \frac{P_x}{x},$$

$$\eta_x = \frac{x_2 - x_1}{P_x^2 - P_x^1} \cdot \frac{P_x}{x}.$$

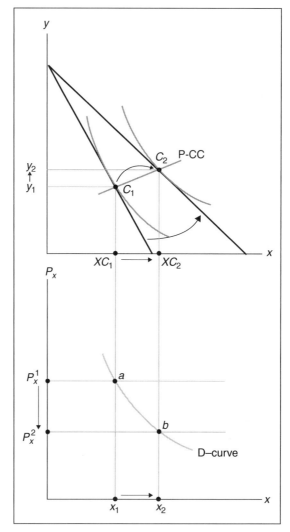

FIGURE 3.30

Just like with the income elasticity of demand, the second term of this formula $\dfrac{P_x}{x}$ can be specified to calculate three types of elasticity: (1) at the lower level, where P_x is the lower price and x is its corresponding quantity of x; (2) at the upper level, where P_x is the upper price and x is its corresponding quantity; and (3) arc elasticity, where P_x is the average of the lower and upper prices and x is the average of the quantities:

$$\eta_{\text{arc}} = \frac{x_2 - x_1}{P_x^2 - P_x^1} \cdot \frac{P_x^1 + P_x^2}{x_1 + x_2} \quad \text{arc elasticity.}$$

Example 3.8

Find the lower, upper, and arc price elasticities of demand for eggs (x) if Jim buys the following dozens a year (Table 3.4).

TABLE 3.4

Eggs (x)	Price (P_x)
22	2.25
30	1.95

Solution:

$$\eta_x = \frac{x_2 - x_1}{P_x^2 - x_x^1} \cdot \frac{P_x}{x},$$

$$\eta_x = \frac{30 - 22}{1.95 - 2.25} \cdot \frac{1.95}{30} = 1.73 \text{ elasticity at the lower level,}$$

$$\eta_x = \frac{30 - 22}{1.95 - 2.25} \cdot \frac{2.25}{22} = 2.72 \text{ elasticity at the upper level,}$$

$$\eta_{\text{arc}} = \frac{30 - 22}{1.95 - 2.25} \cdot \frac{1.95 + 2.25}{30 + 22} = 2.15 \text{ arc elasticity.}$$

Note that since the demand would typically change in the opposite direction of the price change according to the demand law, price elasticity would usually be negative for all ordinary commodities. The resulting number of elasticity would just reflect the rate of change in demand with respect to price change.

Substitutes and Complements   We have seen how the price elasticity of demand measures the response of demand to a change in the commodity's own price. What if the demand for a commodity responds to a change in the price of the other commodity? That would produce the **cross price elasticity of demand**. But before we get into that, we need to define two related types of commodities, the substitutes and the complements.

The **substitutes** are the commodities in pair for which an increase in the price of one would cause an increase in the demand for the other commodity, or a decrease in the price of one would cause a decrease in the demand for the other commodity. Basically, the cross-relationship between the price of one and the demand for the other is positive:

$$\frac{\partial x}{\partial P_y} > 0 \quad \text{or} \quad \frac{\partial y}{\partial P_x} > 0.$$

Typical substitutes are the commodities such as Pepsi and Coke or regular and herbal tea that can easily replace each other. Usually the effect of a change in the price of x would go to the quantity of y through the quantity of x. For example, a person is used to buying Pepsi

(x). But, if the price of Pepsi (P_x) increases, the purchased quantity of Pepsi (Q_x) would decrease because this person would most likely switch to Coke (y) leading to an increase in the purchase quantity of Coke (Q_y) would increase, assuming its price P_y has not changed:

$$P_x \uparrow \rightarrow Q_x \downarrow \rightarrow Q_y \uparrow \underbrace{}_{+} ,$$

also

$$P_x \downarrow \rightarrow Q_x \uparrow \rightarrow Q_y \downarrow \underbrace{}_{+} .$$

The complements are a pair of commodities for which an increase in the price of one would cause a decrease in the quantity of the other, or a decrease in the price of one would cause an increase in the quantity demanded of the other. In other words, there is a negative cross-relationship between the price of one commodity and the demand for the other commodity:

$$\frac{\partial x}{\partial P_y} < 0 \quad \text{or} \quad \frac{\partial y}{\partial P_x} < 0.$$

Typically, the complements are the commodities that are put to use together so that they are needed at the same time and the demand for them is connected for an integrated consumption. A classic example is cameras and films or cars and tires, or pancake and syrup. The connection in use dictates that the effect of a change in price of one (P_x) would be passed on to the purchased quantity of the other (y) through the own quantity (x). Suppose that the price of cameras dropped, people would buy more cameras and as a natural result, they would buy more films:

$$P_x \downarrow \rightarrow Q_x \uparrow \rightarrow Q_y \uparrow \underbrace{}_{-}$$

or

$$P_x \uparrow \rightarrow Q_x \downarrow \rightarrow Q_y \downarrow \underbrace{}_{-} .$$

Cross-Price Elasticity of Demand We can modify the price elasticity formula by introducing the price of one commodity and the quantity of the other commodity:

$$e_{x,y} = \frac{\Delta x}{\Delta P_y} \cdot \frac{P_y}{x},$$

$$e_{x,y} = \frac{x_2 - x_1}{P_y^2 - P_y^1} \cdot \frac{P_y}{x} \quad \text{lower and upper.}$$

$$e_{x,y} = \frac{x_2 - x_1}{P_y^2 - P_y^1} \cdot \frac{P_y^1 + P_y^2}{x_1 + x_2} \text{arc.}$$

Example 3.9

Find the three forms of **cross-price elasticity** for the following data of the prices of cameras (P_y) and the purchased quantities of film (x) (Table 3.5).

TABLE 3.5

P_y	x
$400	2000
$200	5000

Solution:

$$e_{x,y}^{lower} = \frac{X_2 - X_1}{P_y^2 - P_y^1} \times \frac{P_y}{X}$$

$$= \frac{5000 - 2000}{200 - 400} \times \frac{200}{5000} = 0.6,$$

$$e_{x,y}^{upper} = \frac{5000 - 2000}{200 - 400} \times \frac{400}{2000} = 3,$$

$$e_{x,y}^{arc} = \frac{5000 - 2000}{200 - 400} \times \frac{200 + 400}{5000 + 2000} = 1.2.$$

3.5   INCOME AND SUBSTITUTION EFFECTS

The change in price of a commodity usually affects the quantity demanded in two inter-twined effects, the substitution effect and the **income effect**. The **substitution effect** is about the change in the relative price and the marginal value of the commodity. It reflects the change in the balance between the marginal value and the new price because consumers usually would not buy any commodity whose marginal value is less than the price paid. That is why when the price of a commodity increases, a consumer would buy less so as to avoid buying any extra units whose price became above their marginal value. By the same token, if the price of a commodity falls, a consumer would want to buy more of a commodity whose marginal value became more than what is paid for. Such consumer adjustments of the quantity demanded refer to the substitution effect or the Hicksian substitution after the British economist J.R. Hicks.

The **income effect** is about the change in the alternative opportunity offered by the change in the consumer's purchasing power brought about by the change in the price of one of the commodities. So, if the price of a commodity falls, the consumer would be able to buy more for the same money available. In other words, there will be some gain in real income that would be translated into buying more commodities. Let us see how the entire change in price can be decomposed into those two effects, substitution and income effects. In the graph shown in Figure 3.31, suppose a consumer is originally at the optimum point A, buying x_a and y_a. If the price of x falls, BL_1 would swing to BL_2, and the consumer's optimum point would move to another point such as C on a higher IC, offering more of

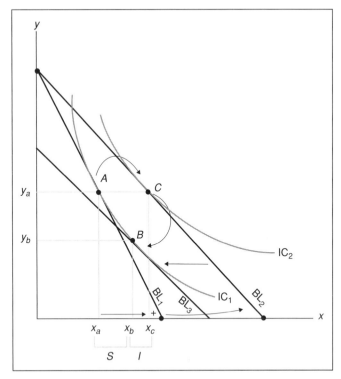

FIGURE 3.31

x. This increase in *x* from x_a to x_c is the full price change that includes two parts by two effects, substitution and income. In order to separate these two parts, we can assume that the decrease in the price of *x* offered the opportunity to have a higher real income or higher purchasing power. It became possible for the consumer to achieve the same satisfaction or level of utility of bundle *A* with less money. We can represent that assumption by creating another budget line such as BL₃ that represents a lower budget than what BL₂ projects. This new budget line would touch IC₁ at *B* as a third optimum point that offers the same previous level of utility of *A* but with lower budget. The bundle offered by *B* is x_b and y_b. Therefore, the movement of the optimum from *C* to *B* refers to the income effect while the movement of the optimum from *A* to *B* refers to the substitution effect. In other words, the entire price effect (x_a to x_c) is divided by the substitution part (x_a to x_b) and the income part (x_b to x_c).

3.6   SLUTSKY EQUATION

Slutsky equation is a mathematical formulation that shows how the full change in price is decomposed into the substitution and income effects. It is named after the nineteenth-century Russian economist Eugene Slutsky. The original budget constraint equation is rewritten after a price change such as fall in the price of x from, say P_x to P'_x:

$$P_x x + P_y y = I,$$

$$P'_x x + P_y y = I, \quad P'_x < P_x.$$

Such a fall in price from P_x to P'_x would cause a total effect on the quantity in a form of increase from x to x'_1, where

$$\text{Total effect} = \frac{\partial x}{\partial P_x} < 0$$

when the optimum point B was introduced on the new budget line BL$_3$, in Figure 3.31 it had to be to the right of the original optimum A because of the strict convexity of the IC, and because of the need to keep the original level of utility at IC$_1$. This implies that the new bundle at B would have more of x and less of y, hence the substitution effect has to be negative:

$$\frac{\partial x^S}{\partial P_x} < 0, \quad \text{where} \quad dU = 0.$$

This would define what is called **the compensated law of demand** where for a constant level of utility, price and quantity would have an inverse relationship.
As for the change in income it would be expressed by:

$$\frac{\partial I}{\partial P_x} = x,$$

a decline in P_x to P'_x leads to an increase in the real income I_r:

$$\frac{\partial I_r}{\partial P_x} = -x,$$

where the minus sign refers to the negative relationship between price and real income. As price decreases, the purchasing power and real income would increase. The income effect can be obtained by multiplying two elements:

$$\frac{\partial I_r}{\partial P_x},$$

which refers to the impact of the change in the price of x over real income, and

$$\frac{\partial x}{\partial I},$$

which refers to the impact of income on the quantity of x:

$$\text{Income effect} = \frac{\partial I_r}{\partial P_x} \times \frac{\partial x}{\partial I}$$

$$\text{Since } \frac{\partial I_r}{\partial P_x} = -x, \text{ then}$$

$$\text{Income effect} = -\frac{\partial x}{\partial I}x.$$

The full effect can, therefore, be formulated by adding both, the substitution and income effects:

$$\underbrace{\frac{\partial x}{\partial P_x}}_{\substack{\text{Full price} \\ \text{effect}}} = \underbrace{\frac{\partial x^s}{\partial P_x}}_{\substack{\text{Substitution} \\ \text{effect}}} - \underbrace{\frac{\partial x}{\partial I}x}_{\substack{\text{Income} \\ \text{effect}}}$$

and this is the Slutsky equation.

SUMMARY

- This chapter establishes that consumer choice is based on the interaction between his preferences and willingness to trade among the available commodities and his affordability.
- Consumer preferences are characterized by four major properties: completeness, transitivity, nonsatiation, and convexity. Preferences and the consumer's willingness to trade among the commodities are represented by a technical tool called the indifference curve, which has a certain shape and characteristics and a capacity to depict all the bundles of commodities for which the consumer would be indifferent to choose.
- The marginal rate of substitution (MRS) is another technical tool to show how much a consumer is willing to give up one commodity in favor of another. MRS is equal to the negative slope of the indifference curve.
- Consumer's affordability to obtain the desired goods and services is represented by his budget line, which, in turn, is determined by consumer's income and the price of commodities. Analogous to the marginal rate of substitution is the marginal rate of transformation (MRT), which is the ratio of the market prices of the commodities, and it is equal to the negative slope of the budget line. The budget line has been shown through its major changes: the shift, swing, and kink that can be brought about by changes in income and the market prices. Also, a three-dimensional budget line has been constructed as an example of dealing with three desired commodities.
- Consumer's optimal choice has been addressed by matching his preferences to his affordability. It is shown technically by combining the two technical tools, the indifference curve and the budget line, such that his optimal choice is located at the point of tangency between the highest possible indifference curve and his available budget line.
- Consumer utility and the way of measuring it have been discussed and the concepts of total utility, marginal utility, and diminishing marginal utility have been addressed. Utility maximization is detailed technically and examples have been given.
- The most common effects on the optimal choice are addressed under the topic of changes in consumer's income and changes in market prices. Changes in income lead to classifying commodities into normal and inferior and result into deriving the income–consumption

curve, Engel curve, and the income elasticity of demand. Price changes lead to the Giffen and non-Giffen goods, price–consumption curve, demand curve, and the price elasticity of demand, as well as substitutes and complements.

- The effect of the change in market price lead to the discussion of income and substitution effect, which is a technical analysis to dissect the effect of price change into two parts: one that is related to the change in the marginal value of the commodity in the eyes of consumers when the commodity price changes, and the other that is related to the change in consumer's real income that would result from the price change. Finally, the Slutsky equation is constructed to echo the income and substitution effects.

KEY TERMS

consumer preference
consumer affordability
transitivity
nonsatiation
convexity
indifference curve
indifference space
indifference map
utility
Cobb-Douglas function
marginal utility
total utility
marginal rate of substitution
marginal rate of
  transformation
diminishing utility

budget line
optimal choice
consumer equilibrium
interior solution
corner solution
utility maximization
Lagrangian method
income change
price change
normal commodity
inferior commodity
Engel curve
income–consumption
  curve
income elasticity
homothetic preference

quasi-linear preference
necessities
luxuries
Giffen commodity
non-Giffen commodity
price elasticity
price–consumption curve
substitute goods
complement goods
cross-price elasticity
income effect
substitution effect
compensated law of demand
Slutsky equation

LIST OF FORMULAS

- Marginal rate of substitution:

$$\text{MRS} = -\frac{\Delta y}{\Delta x} = \frac{\text{MU}_x}{\text{MU}_y}.$$

- Marginal value:

$$\text{MV} = -\Delta y.$$

- Marginal utility of x:

$$\text{MU}_x = \frac{\partial U}{\partial x}.$$

- Budget line for x and y:

$$xp_x + yp_y = I.$$

- Horizontal intercept:

$$x = \frac{I}{p_x}.$$

- Vertical intercept:

$$y = \frac{I}{p_y}.$$

- Marginal rate of transformation:

$$\text{MRT} = \text{Slope}_{\text{BL}} = -\frac{P_x}{P_y}.$$

- Consumer equilibrium condition:

$$\frac{\text{MU}_x}{p_x} = \frac{\text{MU}_y}{P_y}.$$

- Cobb–Douglas Utility function:

$$U = f(x^a y^{1-a}).$$

- Income elasticity of demand:

$$\varepsilon_x = \frac{x_2 - x_1}{I_2 - I_1} \cdot \frac{I}{x}.$$

- Arc income elasticity:

$$\varepsilon_{\text{arc}} = \frac{x_2 - x_1}{I_2 - I_1} \cdot \frac{I_1 + I_2}{x_1 + x_2}.$$

- Price elasticity of demand:

$$\pi_x = \frac{x_2 - x_1}{p_x^2 - p_x^1} \cdot \frac{p_x}{x}$$

- Arc price elasticity:

$$\pi_{\text{arc}} = \frac{x_2 - x_1}{p_x^2 - p_x^1} \cdot \frac{p_x^1 + p_x^2}{x_1 + x_2}$$

- Cross-price elasticity:

$$e_{x,y} = \frac{x_2 - x_1}{p_y^2 - p_y^1} \cdot \frac{p_y}{x}.$$

- Arc cross-price elasticity:

$$e_{x,y}^{arc} = \frac{x_2 - x_1}{p_y^2 - p_y^1} \cdot \frac{p_y^1 + p_y^2}{x_1 + x_2}.$$

- Slutsky equation:

$$\frac{\partial x}{\partial p_x} = \frac{\partial x^s}{\partial p_x} - \frac{\partial x}{\partial I} x.$$

EXERCISES

1. Explain how convexity of the indifference curve indicates that consumers generally prefer average choices over extremes.

2. Compare the marginal rate of substitution (MRS) with the marginal rate of transformation (MRT) and explain what would each one convey about consumer choices.

3. Explain what would logically justify the equality of the following terms in the consumer equilibrium condition:

$$\frac{MU_x}{P_x} = \frac{MU_y}{P_y}.$$

4. Think of two more examples of each of the following and determine the type of MRS and draw the appropriate indifference curve for each:
   - Perfect substitutes
   - Perfect complements
   - Neutral commodities
   - Undesirable commodities

5. Explain why it is rare to find Giffen commodities in real life.

6. Find the optimal choice for Martin who buys ham (H) and potatoes (P) when their prices are: $P_h = \$4.00$ and $P_p = \$1.50$. His utility function is

$$U = 5H + 2\tfrac{1}{4}P.$$

7. Where would the consumer equilibrium be if the utility function is: $U = 3x + 6y$ and the price of x is \$2.00 and the price of y is \$4.00?

8. If a CES utility function is

$$U(x_1, x_2) = x_1^{\alpha} + x_2^{\alpha},$$

where α is a positive constant. Find the MRS.

9. Tina has $40 to spend between chocolate (C) and milk (M) where the price of chocolate is $8.00 and the price of milk is $4.00. Draw her budget line and redraw when (a) the price of chocolate drops by 50% and the price of milk increases by 25%, (b) the price of milk decreases to $2.00 and the price of chocolate remains the same at $8.00, and (c) the price of chocolate decreases by 75% and the price of milk remains the same at $4.00.

10. Using both the substitution and Lagrangian solutions, maximize the following utility function:

$$U = 5x + 3y$$

$$\text{s.t. } 2x + 4y = 100.$$

4

CONSUMER DEMAND: THEORETICAL ANALYSIS

4.1 DEMAND AND SUPPLY: FUNCTIONS AND LAWS

The model of demand and supply is the cornerstone of economics and a striking feature of its theoretical analysis. It is an applicable model in the market that can be tested and utilized as a significant analytical tool in market predictions.

Demand and **quantity demanded** are often used interchangeably, but it might be helpful to distinguish between the two terms, especially at the technical observation and the separation between the individual and the aggregate scales. **Demand** (D) is a set of quantities of a good or service that consumers are willing and able to purchase at certain prices in a specific frame of time and place. **Quantity demanded** (Q_d) is the amount of a good or service that consumers would buy at a certain price among alternative set of prices. An individual **demand function** is often expressed by Q_D and it shows the relationship between the individual demand of a good or service in relation to some major determinants. For example, we can write the demand function for coffee (Q_D^C) as

$$Q_D^C = f(P_c, P_t, P_s, Y),$$

where the amount of coffee a person purchases is determined by related factors such as the price of coffee (P_c), the person's income (Y), as well as the prices of related goods such as tea (P_t) and soft drink (P_s). There are many determinants that can be included in the function as the theory and life experience dictate. Suppose that this function is empirically translated as

$$Q_D^C = 80 - 18P_c + 15P_t + 7P_s + 2Y.$$

Managerial Economics: A Mathematical Approach, First Edition. M. J. Alhabeeb and L. Joe Moffitt.
© 2013 John Wiley & Sons, Inc. Published 2013 by John Wiley & Sons, Inc.

However, the typical demand function in economics textbooks includes only the price of the good. This is because the analysis focuses on the influence of price, holding the other factors constant. We can do this, for instance, by assuming that income and other prices are held at their average values. Suppose that the average price of tea is $5 and of soft drinks $3, and let us assume that the consumer's income is $25,000. We can adjust the function as

$$Q_D^C = 80 - 18P_c + (15 \times 5) + (7 \times 3) + (2 + 25)$$

$$\boxed{Q_D^C = 226 - 18P_c.}$$

This is the typical format of the demand function from which we can draw the demand curve, derive the demand table, and observe all of their characteristics. In the same manner, we can talk about supply, **quantity supplied**, and the supply function. **Supply** (*S*) is a set of quantities of a good or service that producers (sellers) are willing and able to offer at certain prices in a specific frame of time and place. **Quantity supplied** (Q_S) is the amount of a good or service that a producer or seller would produce (sell) at a certain price among alternative set of prices. An individual supply function of a firm is often expressed by Q_S, which is determined based on some factors such as the price of the good or service offered, the cost of producing this commodity, and other production-related factors such as technology of production. As for the last example of coffee, we can express the supply function as

$$Q_S^C = g(P_C, P_B, P_L, T),$$

where the amount of coffee that can be produced and offered in the market by this firm depends on the selling price of the produced coffee P_C, the purchase price of coffee beans (P_B), the price of labor (wages) the firm pays to its employees, and the cost of technology (*T*). As with the demand function, we focus on the selling price of the produced coffee (P_C) after holding the rest of the variables constant. The final typical supply function after such adjustment can be given as

$$\boxed{Q_S^C = 170 + 35P_C.}$$

This equation can be used to draw the supply curve and derive the supply table in a way analogous to the operations on the demand function.

In drawing these two functions, the common way in economics is to put the price on the *y*-axis, and both quantity demanded and supplied on the *x*-axis. This is different from the typical way in mathematics, where the dependent variable (in this case *Q*) is assigned to the vertical *y*-axis and the independent variable (in this case *P*) is assigned to the horizontal *x*-axis. This difference in the axis assignment leads to the fact that the **slope** of both the demand curve and the supply curve is equal to the reciprocal of the derivative of their functions:

$$Q_D = 226 - 18P_C,$$

$$\frac{dQ_D}{dP_C} = -18,$$

$$\text{Slope}_D = \left[\frac{1}{\frac{dQ_D}{dP_C}} \right] = \frac{1}{-18} = -0.055.$$

Similarly for the slope of the supply curve (Slope_S),

$$Q_S = 170 + 35P_C,$$

$$\frac{dQ_S}{dP_C} = 35,$$

$$\text{Slope}_S = \left[\frac{1}{\dfrac{dQ_S}{dP_S}} \right] = \frac{1}{35} = 0.028.$$

The slope can also be found by dividing the change on the vertical axis (the rise) by the change on the horizontal axis (the run):

$$\text{Slope} = \frac{\Delta P}{\Delta Q}.$$

The slope in this direct sense describes how the quantity demanded by consumers and the quantity offered by firms relate to the price change. The slope of the demand curve of −0.055 means that consumers would be willing to buy one more unit for each 5.5 cents reduction in the price. Also, the supply curve slope of 0.028 means that firms would be encouraged to produce one more unit if the product price rises by 2.8 cents.

Assuming that the demand and supply functions are continuous and differentiable, their derivatives express demand and **supply laws**, respectively. The derivative of demand function is negative, indicating that consumers would buy more of a commodity if its price drops, and vice versa:

$$\frac{dQ_D}{dP} < 0,$$

which is a direct expression of the **demand law**.

Also, the derivative of the supply function is positive, indicating that the firms tend to produce and offer more of their products if the selling price goes up:

$$\frac{dQ_S}{dP} > 0.$$

This is a direct expression of the **supply law**. However, demand and supply curves can take shapes other than the typical downward sloping and upward sloping, respectively.

4.2   DERIVING A DEMAND FUNCTION FROM UTILITY MAXIMIZATION

We can derive a demand function directly from the utility maximization process. Suppose that we have a household utility function of two commodities x and y:

$$U = f(x, y),$$

$$U = 9 \ln x + 7 \ln y,$$

$$\max U = 9 \ln x + 7 \ln y,$$

$$\text{s.t. } xP_x + yP_y = I.$$

Forming the Lagrangian function gives us

$$L(x, y, \lambda) = 9 \ln x + 7 \ln y - \lambda [P_x + P_y - I].$$

Taking the first-order conditions (FOCs):

$$\frac{\partial L}{\partial x} = \frac{9}{x^*} - P_x \lambda^* = 0,$$

$$\frac{\partial L}{\partial y} = \frac{7}{y^*} - P_y \lambda^* = 0,$$

$$\frac{\partial L}{\partial \lambda} = P_x X^* + P_y y^* - I = 0.$$

Getting the marginal rate of substitution (MRS) (y for x) from the first two FOCs,

$$\text{MRS} = \frac{9y^*}{7x^*} = \frac{P_x}{P_y},$$

and solving for y^*,

$$9y^* P_y = 7x^* P_x,$$

$$y^* = \frac{7}{9} \left[\frac{P_x}{P_y} \right] x^*.$$

This equation represents the **income consumption line**, which can be substituted into the budget constraint in its FOC format to obtain the demand function:

$$P_x x^* + P_y y^* = I,$$

$$P_x x^* + P_y \left[\frac{7}{9} \left(\frac{P_x}{P_y} \right) x^* \right] = I,$$

$$P_x x^* + \frac{7}{9} P_x x^* = I,$$

$$P_x x^* \left(1 + \frac{7}{9} \right) = I,$$

$$\frac{16}{7} P_x x^* = I,$$

$$x^* = \frac{9I}{16 P_x},$$

which is the demand function for the commodity x. It can be rewritten as

$$Q_x = 9I \left(\frac{1}{16 P_x} \right).$$

$$\text{Or} \quad \boxed{Q_x = \frac{9}{16} - P_x^{-1}}$$

To make sure that the demand curve is negatively sloping, we take the first derivative of the function with respect to the price of x, and see if it has a negative value:

$$Q_x = \frac{9}{16}IP_x^{-1},$$

$$\frac{\partial Q_x}{\partial P_x} = -\frac{9}{16}IP_x^{-2},$$

$$\frac{\partial Q_x}{\partial P_x} < 0.$$

By taking the second derivative, we can test if the demand curve is convex to the original when the second derivative is positive:

$$\frac{\partial^2 Q_x}{\partial P_x^2} = \frac{9}{8}IP_x^{-3},$$

$$\frac{\partial^2 Q_x}{\partial P_x^2} > 0.$$

Now we can obtain the demand function for commodity y by substituting the obtained demand function for x into the budget constraint equations:

$$P_x x^* + P_y y^* = I,$$

$$P_x\left[\frac{9I}{16P_x}\right] + P_y y^* = I,$$

$$P_y y^* = I - \frac{9}{16}I,$$

$$P_y y^* = I\left(1 - \frac{9}{16}\right),$$

$$y^* = \frac{I}{P_y}\frac{7}{16},$$

$$y^* = \frac{7I}{16P_y},$$

$$\text{or} \quad \boxed{Q_y = \frac{7}{16}IP_y^{-1}.}$$

Similar to the demand function of x, the demand function of y has a negative slope with convexity to the origin due to the negative first derivative and positive second derivative:

$$\frac{\partial Q_y}{\partial P_y} = -\frac{7}{16}IP_y^{-2},$$

$$\frac{\partial Q_y}{\partial P_y} < 0,$$

$$\frac{\partial^2 Q_y}{\partial P_y^2} = \frac{7}{8}IP_y^{-3},$$

$$\frac{\partial^2 Q_y}{\partial P_y^2} > 0.$$

For graphing the demand curve from these derived functions for x and y, we can assume certain values for income and prices of x and y (Figure 4.1). Suppose that income is \$100, and the price of x rises from \$5 to \$10,

$$Q_x = 9I\left(\frac{1}{16P_x}\right),$$

$$Q_{x1} = 9(100)\left[\frac{1}{16(5)}\right] = 11.25,$$

$$Q_{x2} = 9(100)\left[\frac{1}{16(10)}\right] = 5.62.$$

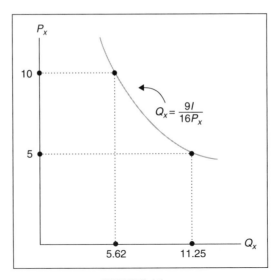

FIGURE 4.1

As for y, let us assume the price rises from \$3 to \$6, and income remains at \$100 (see Figure 4.2):

$$Q_y = 7I\left(\frac{1}{16P_y}\right),$$

$$Q_{y1} = 7(100)\left[\frac{1}{16(3)}\right] = 14.6,$$

$$Q_{y2} = 7(100)\left[\frac{1}{16(6)}\right] = 7.3.$$

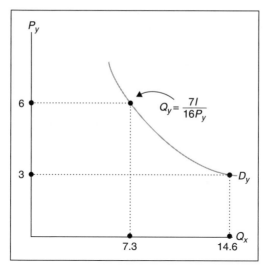

FIGURE 4.2

4.3   HOMOGENEITY AND THE NUMERAIRE

Consumer demand function is said to be "**homogeneous of degree zero.**" This is illustrated by

$$Q_x^* = f(P_x, P_y, \ldots\ldots, I)$$
$$= f(kP_x, kP_y, \ldots\ldots, kI), \quad \text{for } k > 0,$$

which means that if all prices and income are multiplied by any positive constant, the real optimal quantity demanded of a commodity would remain the same. This is basically because the budget constraint

$$P_x x + P_y y = I$$

is essentially the same as

$$5P_x x + 5P_y y = 5I$$

and also as

$$kP_x x + kP_y y = kI.$$

The common implication of this characteristic is that if people's income is raised by the same proportion as inflation, there will be no change in their cost of living, given that it is pure consistent inflation, and people would not have what is called "**money illusion.**"

Homogeneity of the demand function can be shown by the graph below (see Figure 4.3) in which the consumer budget line BL would remain the same as both the slope and intercepts do not change, and therefore the **equilibrium point** would not change either.

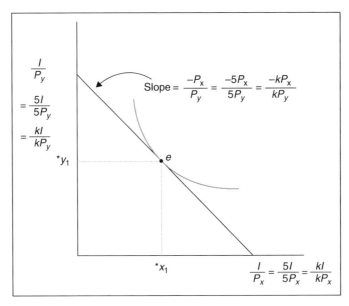

FIGURE 4.3

The **numeraire price** is an extension to the homogeneity in the demand function. It is one of the prices of the commodities that would become the base for relative measurement of other prices and income. If we consider that the k constant equals one of the prices, either x price or y price, and this time we divide all the terms of the budget constraint by it, then we would actually count that price as having the value of 1:

$$P_x x + P_y y = I,$$

$$\frac{P_x}{P_y} x + \frac{P_y}{P_y} y = \frac{I}{P_y},$$

$$P_x x + y = I.$$

This last equation can be understood as if P_y was equal to 1. This would practically mean eliminating the price of y and measuring the price of x relative to the price of y. This is why the ratio of prices is called the **relative price**, and the ratio of income to price is called the **relative or real income**.

We can also divide by income to get

$$P_x x + P_y y = I,$$

$$\frac{P_x}{I} x + \frac{P_y}{I} y = 1,$$

and in both ways setting either one of the prices or income to 1 would not change the essence of the budget constraint.

4.4   INVERSE DEMAND FUNCTION

The typical demand function is a direct function in that the quantity Q_x is a function of price P_x, meaning that the quantity is the dependent variable and the price is the independent variable. In the inverse function, price P_x would be the dependent variable and the quantity would be the independent variable. The common example is the auction where price usually follows the quantity demanded. The more people want an item, the higher the price goes. Another example would be the bulk buying in which higher quantity demand would lower the price per unit.

The implication of having an inverse function on the MRS is to flip the ratio of the change in commodities around between the MRS of a direct function (MRS_d) and the MRS of an inverse function (MRS_i):

$$MRS_d = -\frac{\Delta Q_y}{\Delta Q_x} \rightarrow MRS_i = -\frac{\Delta Q_x}{\Delta Q_y}.$$

This means how much a consumer would be willing to give up of commodity x in order to have more of commodity y.

4.5   DEMAND AND SUPPLY: TABLE AND CURVES

Demand and supply functions of two variables allow us to obtain values for these variables and tabulate them in a demand and supply table in which a set of quantities that would be demanded and supplied are shown corresponding to a set of prices. Let us consider the following set of demand and supply equations for a certain market product:

$$Q_D = 200 - 1.75P,$$

$$Q_S = 12 + 1.5P.$$

We can plug in possible product prices, for example, from \$10 to \$110 and calculate the corresponding quantities demanded and supplied, as shown in Table 4.1.

TABLE 4.1

Q_D	P	Q_S
182.5	10	27
165	20	42
147.5	30	57
130	40	72
112.5	50	87
95	60	102
77.5	70	117
60	80	132
42.5	90	147
25	100	162
7.5	110	177

We can, then, plot both columns of Q_D and Q_S on the horizontal axis against price on the vertical axis. Each curve we obtain would be a locust of all the quantities demanded or supplied at their corresponding prices to form the whole **Demand** or **Supply** into **demand curve** or **supply curve**, respectively, as shown in Figure 4.4.

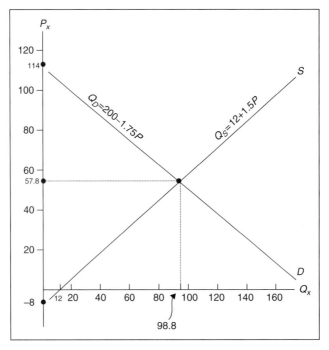

FIGURE 4.4

Observations:

(a) To technically distinguish between quantity demanded (Q_D) and demand (D) on the one hand, and between quantity supplied (Q_S) and supply (S) on the other hand, we go back to the definitions stated earlier. Q_D and Q_S are any single quantities demanded or supplied displayed at any price. D and S are the whole set of quantities demanded or supplied at the corresponding set of prices, namely, that the combined columns of Q_D and P constitute the demand (D), and the combined columns of Q_S and P constitute the supply (S).

(b) As prices go up, the quantities demanded go down and the quantities supplied go up. These types of relationships result in having a downward sloping demand curve and an upward sloping supply curve. It confirms the negative relationship between price and quantity demanded (**demand law**), and the positive relationship between price and the quantity supplied (**supply law**):

$$\left.\begin{array}{l} P \uparrow \rightarrow Q_D \downarrow \\ P \downarrow \rightarrow Q_D \uparrow \end{array}\right\} \ominus \text{Demand law,}$$

$$\left.\begin{array}{l} P \uparrow \rightarrow Q_S \uparrow \\ P \downarrow \rightarrow Q_S \downarrow \end{array}\right\} \oplus \text{Supply law.}$$

(c) As one column goes down and the other goes up, there has to be a point when they meet. That occurs when the price is $57.85, resulting in the equality between the quantity demanded and the quantity supplied at 98.77. This is where the demand curve and supply curve cross each other. The point of intersection is called the **equilibrium point**, the $57.85 is called the **equilibrium price**, and the 98.77 is called the **equilibrium quantity**.

(d) At all prices below the equilibrium price, such as $20 or $40, the quantity to be demanded would exceed the quantity to be supplied, creating an excess quantity demanded called "**shortage**." It would be the difference between quantity demanded and quantity supplied at all the prices below the equilibrium price:

$$\text{Shortage} = Q_D - Q_S$$

$$= 165 - 42 = 123 \text{ at price } \$20$$

$$= 130 - 72 = 58 \text{ at price } \$40.$$

It is illustrated by the lines between the two curves such as AB and CD at the prices $20 and $40, respectively. For all prices below the equilibrium price, there will be shortages, and, therefore, all the area between the two curves below the equilibrium point would represent the market shortage (Table 4.2).

TABLE 4.2

	P	Q_D	Q_S	Shortage	Surplus
	10	182.5	27	155.5	–
	20	165	42	123	–
	30	147.5	57	90.5	–
	40	130	72	58	–
	50	112.5	87	25.5	–
Equilibrium	57.85	98.77	98.77	0	0
	60	95	102	–	7
	70	77.5	117	–	39.5
	80	60	132	–	72
	90	42.5	147	–	104.5
	100	25	162	–	137
	110	7.5	177	–	169.5

Similarly, for all the prices above the equilibrium price, such as $80 or $100, the quantity to be supplied would exceed the quantity to be demanded, creating an excess quantity supplied called "surplus" (Figure 4.5). It would be the difference between quantity supplied and quantity demanded:

$$\text{Surplus} = Q_S - Q_D$$

$$= 132 - 60 = 72 \quad \text{for price } \$80$$

$$= 162 - 25 = 137 \quad \text{for price } \$100.$$

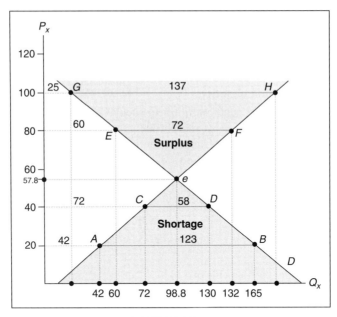

FIGURE 4.5

It is illustrated by the lines between the curves such as *EF* and *GH* at the prices $80 and $100, respectively. Also, for all the prices above the equilibrium price, the whole triangular area between the curves above the equilibrium point would represent the market surplus.

4.6   MARKET EQUILIBRIUM

There is a natural universal conflict in the interests of buyers and sellers. Each would want to deal with a price that serves them best. For the buyer, the price better be the lowest possible, and for the seller, the price better be the highest possible. Any market for any product includes this implicit conflict among traders until they agree with each other in an implicit and aggregate sense. From that agreement, their product price is born, and the product market would be in equilibrium.

   Market equilibrium is a case that reflects the mutual satisfaction for both sides of the market traders so that there "are" no frustrated buyers who will bid prices up, nor any desperate sellers who cut prices down. There will be no incentive for either party to change their mind. Figure 4.6 illustrates that the equilibrium occurs only at point e for the following reason: at a price lower than P_e, for example, P_L, buyers would love to buy the largest amount of the commodity they can afford, for example, Q_L^b, but sellers would not find it in their interest and would offer less quantity, for example, Q_L^s. In this case, buyers will be willing to offer a higher price as an incentive to make sellers offer more and also because their marginal value is higher than the price they pay. So, they would be willing to bid the price up for more commodities. For those reasons, the price will go higher than P_L to anywhere between P_L and P_V on the second panel. Similarly, at a higher price than P_e, for example, P_H, sellers would be glad to sell the largest amount they can, for example, Q_H^s, but buyers may not afford this high price and fewer of them would be willing to buy less amount, for example, Q_H^b. So, automatically all prices lower than the equilibrium price would go up and all prices higher than the equilibrium price would go down until they are on P_e, where $Q_D = Q_S = Q_e$.

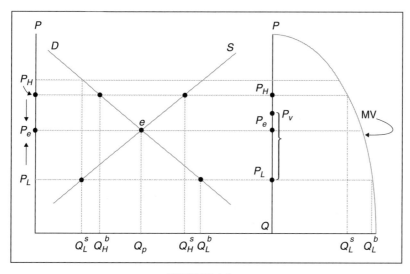

FIGURE 4.6

Mathematically, we can obtain the equilibrium price and equilibrium quantities by setting the demand and supply functions equal to each other and solve for the price, then substitute for it to get the quantities:

$$Q_D = 200 - 1.75P,$$

$$Q_S = 12 + 1.5P,$$

$$Q_D = Q_S,$$

$$200 - 1.75P = 12 + 1.5P,$$

$$200 - 12 = 1.75P + 1.5P,$$

$$188 = 3.25P,$$

$$\frac{188}{3.25} = P,$$

$$57.85 = P.$$

We can plug this equilibrium price in any of the equations to get the equilibrium quantity:

$$Q_D = 200 - 1.75P$$

$$= 200 - 1.75(57.85)$$

$$= 98.77.$$

$$Q_S = 12 + 1.5P$$
$$= 12 + 1.5(57.85)$$
$$= 98.77.$$

Example 4.1

Suppose the individual demand function for a specific contractual project (measured by millions of dollars) is given by

$$Q_D = 12 - 2P,$$

and the individual supply function for the same project is given by

$$Q_S = 20P.$$

Suppose also that there are in the market 1000 contractors willing and able to submit their bids to the 100 offices which want to contract out these projects:

(a) Find the market demand and supply functions for this project.
(b) Mathematically derive the equilibrium price and quantity.
(c) Construct the demand and supply table and mark the equilibrium price and quantity.
(d) Plot the demand and supply curves and show where the market equilibrium occurs.
(e) Add to the table obtained in point (c) above the market potential shortage and surplus quantities and mark their areas on the graph.

Solution:

(a) Market demand:
$$Q_D = 1000 \; Q_D$$
$$= 1000(12 - 2P)$$
$$= 12{,}000 - 2000P,$$

and market supply:

$$Q_S = 100Q_S$$
$$= 100(20P)$$
$$= 2000P.$$
$$Q_D = Q_S$$
$$12{,}000 - 2000P = 2000P$$

(b) $4000P = 12{,}000$
$$P = \frac{12{,}000}{4000} = 3 \text{ million the equilibrium price of the project.}$$

We substitute the equilibrium price into either market demand or supply function to get the equilibrium quantity:

$$Q_D = 12,000 - 2000P$$
$$= 12,000 - 2000(3).$$

(c) $Q_D = 6000$ project (see Table 4.3).

TABLE 4.3

P	Q_d	Q_s	
0	12,000	0	
1	10,000	2,000	
2	8,000	4,000	
3	6,000	6,000	Equilibrium price and quantities
4	4,000	8,000	
5	2,000	10,000	
6	0	12,000	

(d) See Figure 4.7.

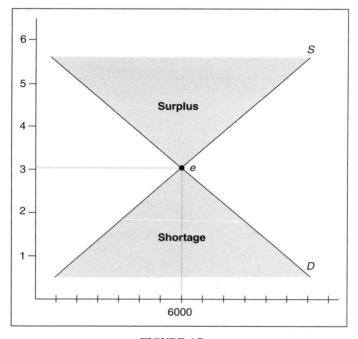

FIGURE 4.7

(e) See Table 4.4.

TABLE 4.4

P	Q_D	Q_S	Shortage	Surplus
0	12,000	0	12,000	–
1	10,000	2000	8000	–
2	8000	4000	4000	–
3	6000	6000	0	0
4	4000	8000	–	4000
5	2000	10,000	–	8000
6	0	12,000	–	12,000

Example 4.2

The following set of simultaneous equations represents the demand and supply functions for beef (B) and chicken (C) fillets in the barbeque market:

$$\text{For beef} \quad Qd_B = 82 - 3P_B + P_C,$$
$$Qs_B = -5 + 15P_B.$$
$$\text{For chicken} \quad Qd_C = 92 - 2P_B + 4P_C,$$
$$Qs_C = -6 + 32P_C.$$

(a) Mathematically, find the equilibrium condition (price and quantity) for beef and chicken.

(b) Show the equilibrium on a graph for each product.

Solution:

(a) First, we set the equilibrium condition for beef:

$$Qd_B = Qs_B,$$
$$82 - 3P_B + P_C = -5 + 15P_B,$$
$$P_C = -87 + 18P_B. \tag{4.1}$$

Second, we set the equilibrium for chicken:

$$Qd_C = Qs_C,$$
$$92 - 2P_B + 4P_C = -6 + 32P_C,$$
$$98 = -2P_B + 36P_C. \tag{4.2}$$

Now, we substitute P_C value from (4.1) in (4.2):

$$98 = -2P_B + 36(-87 + 18P_B),$$
$$98 = -2P_B - 3,132 + 648P_B,$$

$$3230 = 646P_B,$$

$$\frac{3230}{646} = P_B,$$

$$\$5 = P_B \quad \text{equilibrium price of beef.}$$

We substitute the price of beef into (4.1) to get the price of chicken:

$$P_C = -87 + 18P_B$$

$$= -87 + 18(5)$$

$$= \$3 \quad \text{equilibrium price of chicken.}$$

Now we substitute the price of both beef and chicken in either of the functions in the first set to get the equilibrium condition for beef:

$$Qd_B = 82 - 3P_B + P_C$$

$$= 82 - 3(5) + 3$$

$$= 70$$

or

$$Qs_B = -5 + 15P_B$$

$$= -5 + 15(5)$$

$$= 70 \quad \text{equilibrium quantity of beef.}$$

(b) See Figures 4.8 and 4.9.

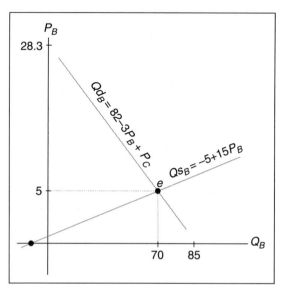

FIGURE 4.8

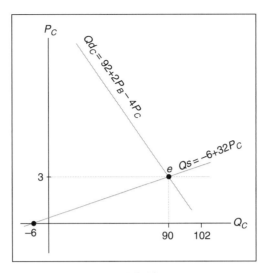

FIGURE 4.9

We also substitute the prices in the second set of functions to get the equilibrium condition for chicken:

$$Qd_C = 92 + 2P_B - 4P_C$$
$$= 92 + 2(5) - 4(3)$$
$$= 90$$

or

$$Qs_C = -6 + 32P_C$$
$$= -6 + 32(3)$$
$$= 90 \quad \text{equilibrium quantity of chicken.}$$

4.7   FROM INDIVIDUAL TO MARKET DEMAND

Market demand is an aggregate concept obtained by adding up all the individual demands for any commodity for any price at any market. Technically, the market demand function is the mathematical sum of all individual demand functions comprising a specific market. Let us take, for example, three hypothetical individuals who are demanding commodity x, facing the same prices (P_x) but having three different incomes (I_1, I_2, I_3). Their individual demand functions are written as

$$Q_x^1 = \alpha_1 + \beta_1 P_x + I_1,$$
$$Q_x^2 = \alpha_2 + \beta_2 P_x + I_2,$$
$$Q_x^3 = \alpha_3 + \beta_3 P_x + I_3.$$

Adding up these three functions would give us the market aggregate demand function for commodity x, Q_x^m:

$$Q_x^m = Q_x^1 + Q_x^2 + Q_x^3$$

$$= \alpha_1 + \beta_1 P_x + I_1 + \alpha_2 + \beta_2 P_x + I_2 + \alpha_3 + \beta_3 P_x + I_3$$

$$= (\alpha_1 + \alpha_2 + \alpha_3) + (\beta_1 + \beta_2 + \beta_3)[P_x] + I_1 + I_2 + I_3)$$

$$= \sum_{i=1}^{n} [\alpha_i + \beta_i P_x + I_i] \, i = 1, 2, 3, \ldots, n.$$

As for the market demand curve of a certain commodity, it is too a horizontal summation of all the individual demand curves for that commodity. Figure 4.10 shows how the market demand curve D^m is derived by adding the three individual curves representing the following demand equations for commodity x:

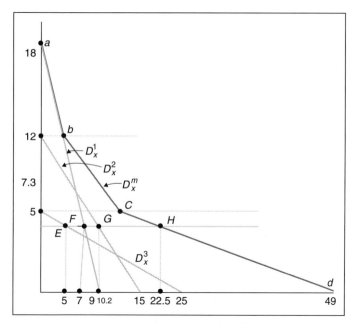

FIGURE 4.10

$$Q_x^1 = 9 - 0.5 P_x,$$

$$Q_x^2 = 15 - 1.2 P_x,$$

$$Q_x^3 = 25 - 5 P_x,$$

$$Q_x^m = 49 - 6.7 P_x.$$

The aggregate demand curve D_x^m is the kinked line abcd. The kink points b and c are on horizontal lines originating from the upper extreme points of D_x^2 and D_x^3. These points indicate that consumer 2 cannot afford to buy x if its price exceeds \$12, whereas consumer

3 can only afford it if its price is less than $5. We can, for example, observe how much of commodity x each of those individuals would buy if its price is $4:

$$Q_x^1 = 9 - 0.5(4) = 7,$$

$$Q_x^2 = 15 - 1.2(4) = 10.2,$$

$$Q_x^3 = 25 - 5(4) = 5,$$

$$Q_x^m = 49 - 6.7(4) = 22.2.$$

Graphically, a horizontal line extended from $4 price would intersect with three individual demand curves as well as with the market demand curve. From the intersection points e, f, g, h, we can drop vertical lines to mark the individual quantities demanded, that is, 7, 10.2, 5, as well as the market quantity demanded, that is, 22.2.

Note also that the market demand of 22.2 units of commodity x is the mathematical sum of the three individual demands of 7, 10.2, and 5, that is, 22.2.

4.8   DEMAND AND NETWORK EXTERNALITIES

When we defined market demand as the horizontal summation of all individual demands, we assumed that consumers in the market made their purchase decisions independently. However, reality shows a different picture in which consumers are increasingly influencing each other, and their tastes and preferences get intertudine as the means of communication increase rapidly and efficiently. This kind of mutual influence forms what is called a **network externality**, which describes the extent to which the demand of individual consumers can be affected by the demand of other consumers in a specific market.

This externality can be either positive, which is also called the "**bandwagon effect**," or negative, which is called the "**snob effect.**"

4.8.1   The Case of the Bandwagon Effect

The bandwagon effect on market demand appears when consumers tend to increase their demand of a particular commodity just because it is demanded more by others. The utility of these consumers is derived from "going with the joneses," or being fashionable, or desiring to own a popular brand, or just to be associated with other. Firms understand this economic externality very well and prefer to spend hundreds of millions of dollars on celebrity endorsements to their products. Such endorsement campaigns have proved time and time again to have significantly increased the demand for the endorsed products. It would still do more of boosting the demand, the more famous and likable the endorsing celebrity is.

When the bandwagon effect is counted for, the derived market demand becomes more price elastic and tends to look flatter than any individual demand for that product. Let us see this in Figure 4.11. Suppose we start with one demand curve such as D_1 representing a certain group of popular consumers buying a particular commodity, the quantity demanded of which is initially 2000 units at a price of $100. Now suppose that the price falls down to $80. This group of consumers will increase their quantity demanded to 2500, moving from a to b on D_1. This drop in price will enable even larger groups of consumers to buy this

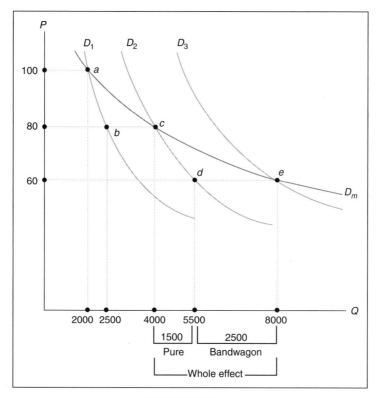

FIGURE 4.11

commodity for its popularity or the popularity of its initial consumers. The second group is represented by the demand curve D_2 and will buy 4000 more units at the reduced price of $80. Let us assume that the price falls again to $60. This will encourage the second group to increase their consumption from 4000 to 5500, moving from c to d on D_2. However, the increasing popularity of the product and the two consecutive drops in its price will again entice another group of consumers such as those who are represented by D_3 to buy 8000 more units. In deriving the market demand curve D_m, we connect points a, c, and e for they are the transfer points based on the bandwagon effect. They are different from points such as b and d, which are the transfer points based on the pure price effect and each lies on its own curve, namely, D_1 and D_2, respectively.

Market demand curve is more price elastic, as we calculate its price elasticity, compared with the individual demand (Table 4.5).

TABLE 4.5

D_1				D_2				D_3			
P		Q		P		Q		P		Q	
P_1	100	2000	Q_1	P_1	80	4000	Q_1	P_1	100	2000	Q_1
P_2	80	2500	Q_2	P_2	60	5500	Q_2	P_2	60	8000	Q_2

$$\eta_Q = \frac{Q_2 - Q_1}{P_2 - P_1} \cdot \frac{P_1 + P_2}{Q_1 + Q_2},$$

$$\eta_Q^1 = \frac{2500 - 2000}{80 - 100} \cdot \frac{100 + 80}{2000 + 2500}$$

$$= -1,$$

$$\eta_Q^2 = \frac{5500 - 4000}{60 - 80} \cdot \frac{80 + 60}{4000 + 5500}$$

$$= -1.10,$$

$$\eta_Q^m = \frac{8000 - 2000}{60 - 100} \cdot \frac{100 + 60}{2000 + 8000}$$

$$= 2.4.$$

If we consider one movement on the market demand curve D_m, for example, moving from c to e, we will observe that the whole price effect on the market demand was to increase the quantity demanded from 4000 to 8000 as the price dropped from \$80 to \$60. But only 1500 units were increased due to the pure price effect and the rest of 2500 units were up due to the bandwagon effect.

4.8.2   The Case of the Snob Effect

The snob effect on market demand is the opposite case of the bandwagon effect. It appears when certain groups of consumers are driven to have an exclusive consumption of a commodity. They derive their utility from seeing fewer and fewer of other people buying the commodity they desire. They would reduce or even stop their purchase if they see more consumers obtaining that commodity. Rare collectible items are typical for the commodity that becomes a subject for the snob effect.

As shown in Figure 4.12, it is assumed that there are three groups of snob consumers who, for some commodities, prefer to be the exclusive buyer. Those groups are represented by the demand curves D_1, D_2, and D_3. They are set in a way that the higher the demand (D_3 is the highest), the fewer the potential snob consumers who would be willing to buy this highly collectible item, and vice versa, the lower the demand (D_1 is the lowest), the more the snob consumers who would be willing to purchase this item. Suppose at a price \$60,000 there would be 10 snob consumers on D_1 willing to buy, and if the price goes up to \$100,000, those consumers would be only 3. This is the movement from point a to point b on D_1. The rise in price and the reduction in the number of people buying the item would entice consumers of D_2 to buy eight items. The third group, who are the most snobbish, are waiting to see even fewer others to buy no matter how much the price will be. Now suppose the price goes further up to \$200,000 where only the group of D_3 is willing and able to buy five items. The market demand curve would be derived by connecting points a, c, d each on an individual curve representing the transfer points due to the snob effect. Point b on D_1 would not be included because it is the transfer point from point a due to the pure price effect. The whole reduction in the quantity is 7 (from 10 to 3), but 5 of which is due to the snob effect. The market demand curve is steeper than any of the individual demand curves for it has the lowest elasticity of all. Compared with D_1, market demand curve (D_m) has -0.62 price elasticity while D_1 has -2.15.

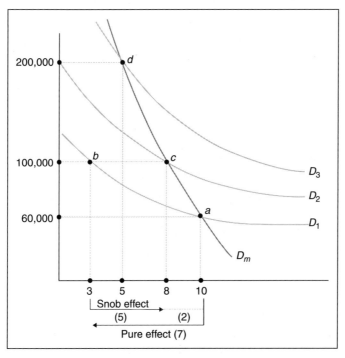

FIGURE 4.12

Individual demand:

	D_1				D_2		
	P	Q			P	Q	
P_1	60,000	10	Q_1	P_1	60,000	10	Q_1
P_2	100,000	3	Q_2	P_2	200,000	5	Q_2

$$\eta_Q^1 = \frac{3-10}{100,000-60,000} \cdot \frac{60,000+100,000}{10+3}$$

$$= -2.15,$$

$$\eta_Q^m = \frac{5-10}{200,000-60,000} \cdot \frac{60,000+200,000}{10+5}$$

$$= -0.62.$$

4.9   DERIVING A MARKET DEMAND FUNCTION UNDER EXTERNALITIES

Mathematically, we can show the effect of the positive and **negative externalities** on market demand. Let us first assume that we have two households, A and B, represented by the following demand functions for commodity X:

$$X_A = \frac{5}{4P_x}[I_A],$$

$$X_B = \frac{5}{4P_x}[I_B],$$

where I_A and I_B are the two households income, respectively, and P_x is the price of X.

First, we find the market demand function without any effect of an externality. It is simply the horizontal summation of the individual demand functions:

$$
\begin{aligned}
X_M &= X_A + X_B \\
&= \frac{5}{4P_x}[I_A] + \frac{5}{4P_x}[I_B] \\
&= \frac{5}{4P_x}[I_A + I_B].
\end{aligned}
$$

(4.3)

Now, let us consider the effect of the **positive externalities** where households positively affect each other. Their demand functions can reflect this mutual effect as

$$X_A = \frac{5}{4P_x}[I_A] + \frac{1}{2}X_B,$$

$$X_B = \frac{5}{4P_x}[I_B] + \frac{1}{2}X_A,$$

where

$$\frac{\partial X_A}{\partial x_B} = \frac{1}{2} \quad \text{and} \quad \frac{\partial X_B}{\partial X_A} = \frac{1}{2}.$$

Substituting X_B into X_A function, we get

$$X_A = \frac{5}{4P_x}[I_A] + \frac{1}{2}\left[\frac{5}{4P_x}[I_B] + \frac{1}{2}X_A\right],$$

$$X_A = \frac{5}{4P_x}I_A + \frac{5}{8P_x}I_B\frac{1}{4}X_A,$$

$$\frac{3}{4}X_A = \frac{5}{4P_x}I_A + \frac{5}{8P_x}I_B,$$

$$X_A = \frac{5I_A}{3P_x} + \frac{5I_B}{6P_x},$$

and substituting X_A into X_B, we get

$$X_B = \frac{5}{4P_x}[I_B] + \frac{1}{2}\left[\frac{5}{4P_x}[I_A] + \frac{1}{2}X_B\right],$$

$$X_B = \frac{5I_B}{4P_x} + \frac{5I_A}{8P_x}\frac{1}{4}X_B,$$

$$\frac{3}{4}X_B = \frac{5I_B}{4P_x} + \frac{5I_A}{8P_x},$$

$$X_B = \frac{5I_B}{3P_x} + \frac{5I_A}{6P_x}.$$

Market demand would be

$$X_M = X_A + X_B$$
$$= \frac{5I_A}{3P_x} + \frac{5I_B}{6P_x} + \frac{5I_B}{3P_x} + \frac{5I_A}{6P_x}$$
$$= \frac{15[I_A + I_B]}{6P_X} \qquad (4.4)$$
$$= \frac{5}{2P_x}[I_A + I_B].$$

Finally, let us consider the effect of the negative externalities where households affect each other negatively. Their demand function can reflect this mutual negative effect as

$$X_A = \frac{5}{4P_x}[I_A] - \frac{1}{2}X_B,$$

$$X_B = \frac{5}{4P_x}[I_B] - \frac{1}{2}X_A.$$

Substituting X_B into X_A, we get

$$X_A = \frac{5I_A}{4P_x} - \frac{1}{2}\left[\frac{5I_B}{4P_x} - \frac{1}{2}X_A\right],$$

$$X_A = \frac{5I_A}{4P_x} - \frac{5I_B}{8P_x} + \frac{1}{4}X_A,$$

$$\frac{3}{4}X_A = \frac{5I_A}{4P_x} - \frac{5I_B}{8P_x},$$

$$X_A = \frac{5I_A}{3P_x} - \frac{5I_B}{6P_x}.$$

Substituting X_A into X_B, we get

$$X_B = \frac{5}{4P_x} I_B - \frac{1}{2}\left[\frac{5I_A}{4P_x} - \frac{1}{2}X_B\right],$$

$$X_B = \frac{5I_B}{4P_x} - \frac{5I_A}{8P_x} + \frac{1}{4}X_B,$$

$$\frac{3}{4}X_B = \frac{5I_B}{4P_x} - \frac{5I_A}{8P_x},$$

$$X_B = \frac{5I_B}{3P_x} - \frac{5I_A}{6P_x}.$$

Market demand would be

$$
\begin{aligned}
X_M &= X_A + X_B \\
&= \frac{5I_A}{3P_x} - \frac{5I_B}{6P_x} + \frac{5I_B}{3P_x} - \frac{5I_A}{6P_x} \\
&= \frac{10I_A - 5I_B + 10I_B - 5I_A}{6P_X} \\
&= \frac{5[I_A + I_B]}{6P_x} \\
&= \frac{5}{6P_x}[I_A + I_B].
\end{aligned}
\tag{4.5}
$$

If we assume that household A income is \$20,000, household B income is \$40,000, and the market price for X is \$5.00, then market demand for X before any externality effect and as determined by Equation (4.3) would be

$$
\begin{aligned}
X_M &= \frac{5}{4P_x}[I_A + I_B] \\
&= \frac{5}{4(5.00)}[20,000 + 40,000] \\
&= 15,000 \text{ units of } X.
\end{aligned}
$$

Market demand for X under the positive externalities effect as determined by Equation (4.4) would be

$$
\begin{aligned}
X_M &= \frac{5}{2P_x}[I_A + I_B] \\
&= \frac{5}{2(5.00)}[20,000 + 40,000] \\
&= 30,000 \text{ units of } X.
\end{aligned}
$$

Market demand for X under the negative externalities effect as determined by Equation (4.5) would be

$$X_M = \frac{5}{6P_x}[I_A + I_B]$$

$$= \frac{5}{6(5.00)}[20,000 + 40,000]$$

$$= 10,000 \text{ units of } X.$$

As shown in Figure 4.13, the market demand curve would shift right under the positive externalities and shift left under the negative externalities.

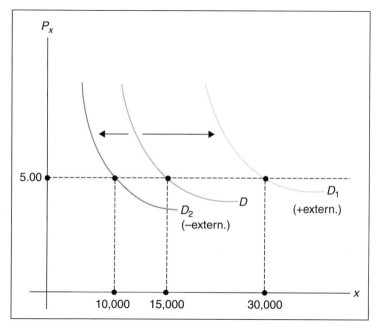

FIGURE 4.13

4.10 CHANGES IN Q_D AND Q_S VERSUS CHANGES IN D AND S

We have already distinguished between the terms quantity demanded/supplied and demand/supply. The changes in them ought to be distinguished too, for they occur due to different reasons. Those reasons are related to the affecting factors (independent variables) and their changes as mentioned below:

1. Changes in the commodity's price would result in changes in the quantities demanded or supplied, causing movements along the same curve (demand or supply).

2. Changes in any of the affecting factors other than the commodity's price would result in shifting the entire curve right or left. Those affecting factors in case of the shift in demand curve are, for example, consumer income, price of related commodities, government interventions such as taxes and subsidies, consumer expectations, tastes, and preferences, and alike. In the case of the shift in supply curve, those factors could be cost of production, level of production technology, market expectations, and alike.

The vertical axis of the graph below shows that as the price of x increases from P_1 to P_2, the quantity demanded would decrease from Q_{D1} to Q_{D2}, and if the price drops from P_2 to P_1, the quantity demanded would increase from Q_{D2} to Q_{D1}. This type of change in the commodity's price can be traced down as a movement along the demand curve D_x from a to b or the other way around, from b to a (Figure 4.14).

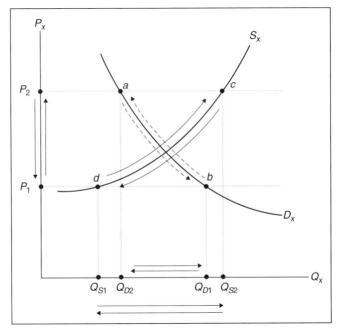

FIGURE 4.14

Also, along the supply curve we can observe a similar type of movement. If the price of x goes up from P_1 to P_2, the quantity supplied would go up from Q_{S1} to Q_{S2} and point d would move up to point c. If the price drops from P_2 to P_1, the quantity supplied would follow, dropping from Q_{S2} to Q_{S1} and point c moves down to point d along the supply curve. If any affecting factor other than the commodity's price changes, the effect on the demand or supply curves would be shifting the whole curve right (for more) or left (for less). If, for example, consumer income increases and as a result consumer demand of commodity x increases too, this demand change would be represented by a shift in the demand curve to the right such as from D_{x1} to D_{x2} in graph 4.15. The curve would shift to the left from D_{x1} to D_{x3} if income decreases, causing a decrease in demand. Similarly, supply curve can shift right to indicate higher supply due, for example, to a decrease in the cost of production or it could shift left to indicate a lower supply for facing an increase in the production cost (Figure 4.15).

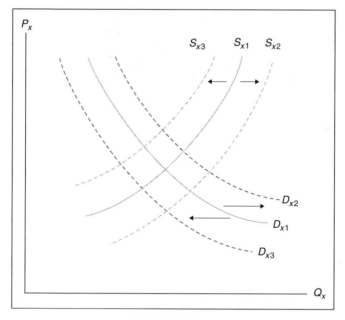

FIGURE 4.15

It is the shift in either demand or supply curves or both that would lead to a change in equilibrium, as it is illustrated in the following case of taxes.

4.11   CHANGES IN EQUILIBRIUM

Changes in equilibrium point, price, and quantities occur only when there are shifts in demand or supply. Normally in the free market system, any shift in either of the curves or in both would automatically trigger the price mechanism that would control the situation and bring back equilibrium. It is usually the price that follows any change in either demand or supply, and then the quantities follow the price into a new equilibrium. Figure 4.16 illustrates the possibilities of shift in both demand and supply and in both directions, rise and fall. In the upper panel we see four possible cases, increase and decrease in demand, and increase and decrease in supply. In the first case, only demand increases and its curve shifts right causing the price to rise from P_{e1} to P_{e2} and the quantity from Q_{e1} to Q_{e2}, establishing a new equilibrium point at $e2$. In the second case, demand would fall shifting left and causing the price to drop from P_{e1} to P_{e2} and the quantity to drop too, from Q_{e1} to Q_{e2}. In the third case, supply would increase and demand remains the same as before. This would cause the price to drop from P_{e1} to P_{e2} but for an equilibrium quantity that is higher than before. In the fourth case, supply would decrease and shift left. The price would increase but for an equilibrium quantity that is lower than before.

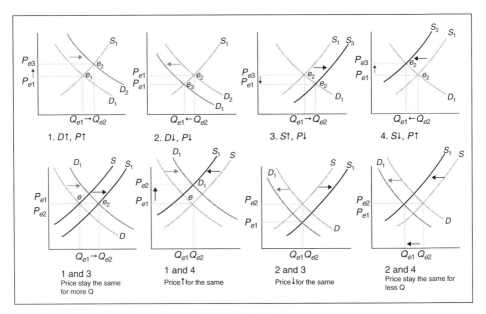

FIGURE 4.16

What happens when both demand and supply change in the same time? We can see this possibility in the lower panel of the graph, assuming the changes occur in the same proportion for simplicity. The first case combines cases 1 and 3 discussed above, that is, a rise in demand and supply that causes the price to stay at the same level of last equilibrium but for new equilibrium quantity that is higher than before. The second case combines cases 1 and 4 discussed above, that is, an increase in demand but a decrease in supply. That would be a double reason to increase the price probably to a double of the previous level but for the same equilibrium quantity as before. The third case combines cases 2 and 3 discussed above, that is, a decrease in demand but an increase in supply. This would be a double reason to lower the price, probably to half as it was before but for the same equilibrium quantity as it was before. The last case combines cases 2 and 4 discussed above, that is, a decrease in both demand and supply that would keep the price at the same equilibrium level as before but for lower quantity than before.

The chances of both demand and supply to change in exactly the same percentage are only a hypothetical situation that is good for the illustration of theory. In reality, the magnitude of the changes in the equilibrium price and quantity depends not only on the differential in demand and supply change but also on the shape and slopes of the curves, as it is shown in the following cases.

4.11.1   The Case of Thanksgiving Turkey

In this case, we show that the changes in equilibrium price and equilibrium quantity also depend on the nature and slope of the curves. The largest ever surge in sales of turkey (fresh and frozen) usually occurs in the week before Thanksgiving. Figures 4.17 and 4.18 show how the difference in the slope of supply curves between the fresh and frozen birds affect the equilibrium price and quantity for an assumed same surge in demand. The right shift in demand from D_1 and D_2 represents the surge in demand for the turkey in the days before Thanksgiving and it is kept the same in both panels. The supply of the fresh birds is relatively price inelastic and its curve is steeper than the supply for frozen birds. The reason is that producer's and retailer's capacity to prepare frozen birds and build up large stocks of them during the year is much higher than their capacities to raise birds and prepare their fresh meat for that week before Thanksgiving. That is why the supply of the fresh birds is somehow limited even when the price rises substantially, such as from P_{e1} to P_{e2} in the upper panel, resulting in increasing the equilibrium quantity only from Q_{e1} to Q_{e2}. On the other hand, the large supply of frozen birds stocked ahead of time would naturally allow the price to perhaps rise just a little or stay unchanged. In some cases, it can even go down a little bit.

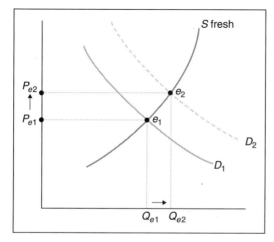

FIGURE 4.17

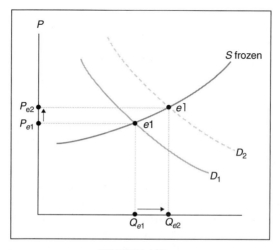

FIGURE 4.18

4.11.2   The Case of Sales and Excise Taxes

Let us take the case of imposing a sales tax on a certain commodity, say 50¢ per pound of lamb sold. In Figure 4.19, suppose that P_{e1} is the equilibrium price and Q_{e1} is the equilibrium quantity in the lamb market before imposing the tax. Now the tax will be an additional burden carried by consumers and will cause a drop in their demand of lamb represented by shifting the D_1 curve left to D_2, where the vertical distance $ae2$ is equal to the amount of tax per pound (50¢). Now with the new demand curve D_2, we would have a new equilibrium point ($e2$), and a new equilibrium quantity Q_{e2}, which is less than the previous equilibrium quantity Q_{e1}. As for the equilibrium price, it would be P_{e2}, which is the price received by producers, and P_{e3} (which is equal to $P_{e2} + 50¢$) would be the price paid by consumers, and the difference between them is the amount of tax, 50¢ ($P_{e3} - P_{e2}$).

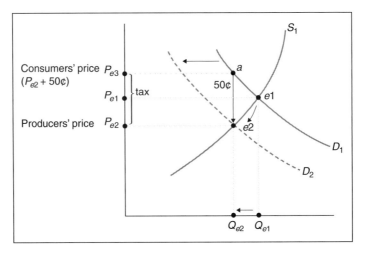

FIGURE 4.19

Similarly, Figure 4.20 shows the case of the excise tax. If a 50¢ excise tax is imposed on the producers of lamb, it will be considered an increase in the production cost, and it would, therefore, cause the supply of lamb to fall and its curve to shift left to S_2 where the vertical distance between S_1 and S_2 represents the 50¢ excise tax. Assuming the original demand stays the same, the equilibrium point will move from $e1$ to $e2$. The equilibrium quantity will decrease from Q_{e1} to Q_{e2}, and the equilibrium price will be P_{e2} that would be the price that consumers pay, now that their demand is faced with less supply. However, producers would not keep this whole price since they have to pay 50¢ to the tax collector. So, the producer's price would be P_{e3} (which is equal to $P_{e2} - 50¢$) and the difference between the two prices would be the 50¢ excise tax ($P_{e2} - P_{e3}$).

Although **the legal incidence of taxes** places the burden of paying the sales taxes on consumers and excise taxes on producers, in reality both parties share paying both types of taxes. In other words, the **economic incidence of taxes** is shared between consumers and producers. Their shares are determined by the slopes of the curves. The following is an example to calculate the shares of a sales tax between consumers and producers.

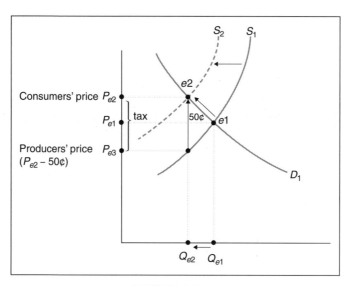

FIGURE 4.20

Example 4.3
The following are the market demand and supply functions for salmon steak:

$$Q_D = 8000 - 1000P,$$

$$Q_S = 2000P - 4000.$$

Suppose that the local government imposes a sales tax of $0.75 per pound of salmon steak, find the following:

(a) The original equilibrium price and quantity.
(b) The after-tax equilibrium price and quantity.
(c) The absolute and percentage share for consumers and producers of the tax burden.
(d) Graphically show the tax burden and how it is divided between consumers and producers.

Solution:
(a) Let us start with equating the functions to solve for the equilibrium price and equilibrium quantity:

$$Q_D = Q_S,$$

$$8000 - 1000P = 2000P - 4000,$$

$$12,000 = 3000P,$$

$$\frac{12,000}{3000} = P = \$4.00 \quad \text{the original equilibrium price.}$$

We substitute the equilibrium price in either of the functions to get the equilibrium quantity:

$$Q_D = 8000 - 1000(4)$$
$$= 4000 \text{ pounds of quantity demanded of salmon steak,}$$
$$Q_S = 2000(4) - 4000$$
$$= 4000 \text{ pounds of quantity supplied.}$$

(b) Since it is a tax problem, it would be better to modify the demand and supply function in terms of price instead of in terms of quantity:

$$Q_D = 8000 - 1000P,$$
$$P = \frac{8000}{1000} - \frac{Q_D}{1000},$$
$$P = 8 - \frac{1}{1000}Q_D,$$
$$Q_S = 2000P - 4000,$$
$$P = \frac{4000}{2000} - \frac{Q_S}{2000},$$
$$P = 2 - \frac{1}{2000}Q_S.$$

Since introducing the sales tax causes a drop in demand equal to the amount of tax, the demand function above would be modified as

$$P = 8 - \frac{1}{1000}Q_D - \$0.75.$$

Now we get the new equilibrium after imposing the tax by equating the above after-tax demand function with the supply function:

$$8 - \frac{Q}{1000} - 0.75 = 2 + \frac{Q}{2000},$$
$$8 - 0.75 - 2 = \frac{Q}{1000} + \frac{Q}{2000},$$
$$5.25 = \frac{3Q}{2000},$$
$$3Q = 10,500,$$
$$Q = \frac{10,500}{3} = 3500 \text{ the new equilibrium quantity.}$$

We substitute the new equilibrium quantity into either function to get the new equilibrium price:

$$P = 8 - \frac{3500}{1000} = -\$0.75,$$

$$P = \$3.75,$$

$$\text{or } P = 2 + \frac{3500}{2000},$$

$$P = \$3.75 \quad \text{the new equilibrium price.}$$

Since consumers bear the legal burden to pay the sales tax, they would pay

$$\$3.75 + \$.75 = \$4.50 \quad \text{consumer's price.}$$

Though the producers collect \$4.50, they keep only \$3.75 and they forward \$0.75 to the government (see Figure 4.21).

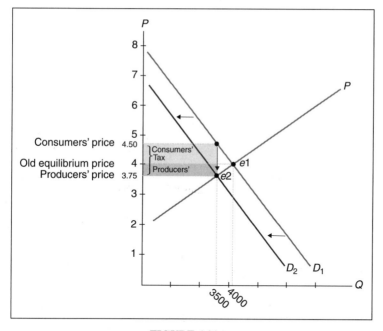

FIGURE 4.21

Another way to look into this solution is to equate the before-tax functions but modifying the demand function by replacing its price (P) with the price plus tax ($P + \$0.75$):

$$Q_D = 8000 - 1000P,$$

$$Q_S = 2000P - 4000,$$

$$Q_D = Q_S,$$

$$8000 - 1000(P + 0.75) = 2000P - 4000,$$

$$3000P = 11{,}250,$$

$$P = \frac{11{,}250}{3000} = \$3.75 \quad \text{the new equilibrium price.}$$

We substitute this new equilibrium price into either of the functions to get the equilibrium quantity:

$$Q_D = 8000 - 1000(3.75 + 0.75),$$

$$Q_D = 3500,$$

$$Q_S = 2000(3.75) - 4000,$$

$$Q_S = 3500 \quad \text{the new equilibrium quantity.}$$

(c) The sales tax made consumers pay \$4.50, which is 50¢ more than what they used to pay before taxes. The 50¢ is their absolute share of the tax burden, which is equal to two-thirds of the tax (0.50/0.75) or 66.6%.

As for producers, they now collect \$3.75. That is 25¢ less than what they used to get before the imposition of the sales tax. So, their absolute share is 25¢, which is one-third of the tax (0.25/0.75) or 33.4%.

(d) Figure 4.21 shows the consumer's share of the tax as the large rectangular area constituting 2/3, as compared to 1/3 for the producer's share shown in the smaller rectangular area.

4.12   MARKET DISEQUILIBRIUM

In what is known as "**the rationing function of prices**," market price plays a crucial role in controlling the market forces and brings back the state of market equilibrium any time the interplay between demand and supply and their influencing factors pushes the market away from the stable state of equilibrium. So, it is the nature of the free market system that market prices have the ability to converge toward equilibrium when some external factors disturb it. However, under certain circumstances, powerful external factors such as the government can interfere and short-circuit the mechanism of the price rationing function and bring about a state of market disequilibrium. It should be noted here that many government policies may lead to shifts in demand or supply here and there, but the effect of such policies can naturally be mitigated by the price self-adjusting mechanism. It is only those policies that tamper with market price that would lead to disequilibrium; this is because once the price is set by the conscious choice of anybody other than the market natural forces, the self-rationing function would not work anymore. Needless to say that in most cases, government interventions often come with the best intentions. But despite the fact that those intervention policies may be morally justified for fairness and protecting the public interest, they often end up backfiring and defeating their own purpose, and sometimes even causing many negative consequences, the aggregate cost of which may exceed any benefit. The typical examples of such policies are the price control in its two faces, the price ceiling and **price floor**.

4.12.1 The Case of a Price Ceiling

A **price ceiling** refers to the maximum level of price that can be mandated by law under certain circumstances. When such a price is imposed on a particular good or service that is subject to government control, it would mean that this commodity must not be sold for a price above the legislated level. A price ceiling is usually either equal or below the previous equilibrium price for that commodity. There have been many real-life price ceilings imposed by the government for a certain period of time. The most popular examples are rent control, a cap for gas prices, upper limit for insurance premium, and alike. Figure 4.22 shows an example of a price ceiling application on gasoline. Suppose that due to war in the Middle East, the supply of gasoline in the United States dropped from S_1 to S_2, which caused the price to rise from P_1 to P_2, given that the demand for gasoline stayed at the same level D_1. Suppose that this hike in the gasoline price is high enough that most people cannot afford it; it would eventually constitute a compelling reason for the government to act and impose a price level and declare it as a maximum that gasoline prices must not go beyond.

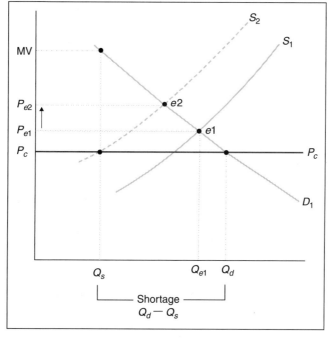

FIGURE 4.22

Suppose that the imposed price ceiling is P_c. At this price, consumers would love to buy Q_D, but producers would be willing to only offer Q_S. This is a classic case of market disequilibrium where quantity demanded Q_D exceeds quantity supplied Q_S, creating a market shortage equal to $(Q_D - Q_S)$. At the offered quantity supplied of Q_S, some able consumers may become willing to pay a higher price than P_c in order to get the amount of gasoline they used to get. The offered price may reach up to the marginal value at MV. It is also seen that the added cost of time and energy the rest of consumers indirectly incur trying to get the gasoline they need would be considered and may push the real price for them up to MV too. People may spend many hours standing in lines or offer whatever they can afford as bribes, or pay more in the black market to get some gasoline. All of these possibilities would be example of the additional cost that would raise the real price to MV. Eventually and collectively the gasoline price may practically settle somewhere definitely above P_c but below MV. Most likely, the price may get stabilized between the two equilibrium prices P_{e1} and P_{e2}.

Let us consider the following numerical example (see Figure 4.23).

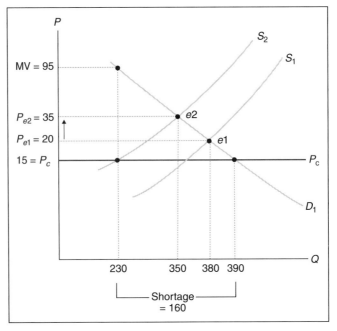

FIGURE 4.23

Example 4.4
The following are the market demand and supply functions for a product:

$$Q_D = 420 - 2P,$$

$$Q_S = 260 + 6P.$$

Suppose that some unexpected circumstances caused a rise in the cost of production that led the supply to fall to

$$Q_S = 140 + 6P,$$

which caused the price to rise beyond the affordability of most consumers. What would happen in the market of this product if the government imposes a ceiling price equal to 25% less than the equilibrium price?

Solution:

First, we find the market equilibrium before the imposition of the legislated ceiling price:

$$Q_D = Q_S,$$

$$420 - 2P = 260 + 6P,$$

$$160 = 8P,$$

$$\frac{160}{8} = P_{e1} = \$20, \quad \text{the market equilibrium price}$$

$$Q_{e1} = 420 - 2(20) = 260 + 6(20),$$

$$Q_{e1} = 380.$$

Second, we find the market equilibrium when supply fell:

$$Q_D = Q_S,$$

$$420 - 2P = 140 + 6P,$$

$$280 = 8P,$$

$$\frac{280}{8} = P_{e2} = \$35,$$

$$Q_{e2} = 420 - 2(35) = 0.140 + 6(35),$$

$$Q_{e2} = 350.$$

Price ceiling $= 20 - (20 \times 0.25) = 15$.

At this price, consumers will demand

$$Q_D = 420 - 2(15)$$

$$= 390.$$

But producers will only offer

$$Q_S = 140 - 6(15),$$

$$Q_D = 230.$$

The market shortage will be

$$Sh = 390 - 320 = 160.$$

The price equalling the consumer's marginal value will be

$$Q_D = 420 - 2P,$$

$$230 = 420 - 2P,$$

$$2P = 190,$$

$$P = \frac{190}{2} = 95.$$

4.12.2   The Case of a Price Floor

Similar to the price ceiling, a **price floor** is a legislated price too, but it refers to the minimum level, below which prices of goods and services subject to control must not fall. It is usually either at or above the previous equilibrium price. The typical example for the actual price floor is the price of some agricultural commodities that the government wants to protect in support of their farmers. Another typical example is the labor price in terms of a minimum wage that the government imposes to protect workers and assure decent living conditions for them. Once again, although such policies may seem normally sound, they most likely create negative economic consequences. The big problem with the price floor is that it eventually leads to a market surplus, as shown in Figure 4.24.

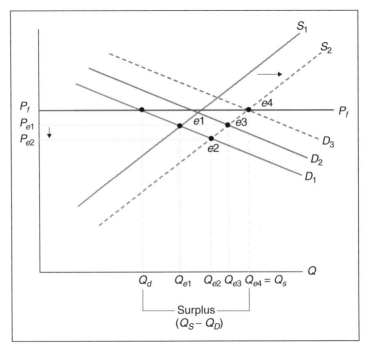

FIGURE 4.24

If, for any reason, the supply of a good increases to the point way beyond the current demand (S_1 shifting to S_2), the price would automatically decrease (from P_{e1} to P_{e2}) to bring about a new equilibrium at $e2$. But a decrease like this may sometimes go below the level necessary to sustain production, which may collectively hurt the majority of producers. In this case, the government may interfere and impose a better price to save producers. This is the price floor P_f, which could be above the first equilibrium price. Producers would be thrilled to sell Q_S at this price, but consumers would not be willing to buy at this price but a maximum amount of Q_D, and that is what sets the market for big surplus equal to ($Q_S -$ Q_D). It happened in reality many times where the government found itself eventually either subsidizing producers for what they cannot sell or buy out the excess amount of production that cannot be sold in the market normally. In this latter case, the government would act as if it is creating a shadow extra demand represented by D_2 to partially absorb the excess supply and bring about a new market equilibrium at $e3$, or go all the way to D_3 in order to accommodate all the surplus in the market and achieve a new equilibrium at $e4$ at the price floor. The bigger problem is that the cost of any of these corrective actions would be carried by the taxpayers. In some cases of mandating a price floor in the form of a minimum wage for the unskilled workers, the eventual detrimental economic consequences may be as dire as to increase a wide-scale unemployment, although it would help employ a certain group of workers.

Example 4.5

The following are demand and supply functions for lettuce:

$$Q_D = 12 - 3\frac{1}{2}P,$$
$$Q_S = 3 - 2\frac{1}{2}P.$$

Suppose that at some point the price of lettuce fell to a level below what keeps the lettuce farmers coping and maintaining their living. Also, suppose that the local government found it necessary to intervene to protect the farmers and their community by imposing a price floor of $2.50 per head of lettuce sold (see Figure 4.25). What would be the consequences on the lettuce market?

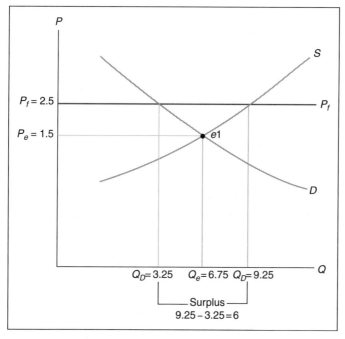

FIGURE 4.25

Solution:

First, let us obtain the original equilibrium condition in the lettuce market:

$$Q_D = Q_S,$$
$$12 - 3^1/_2 P = 3 + 2^1/_2 P,$$
$$9 = 6P,$$
$$\frac{9}{6} = P = \$1.50 \quad \text{the original equilibrium price,}$$
$$Q_D = 12 - 3^1/_2/(1^1/_2) = 3 + 2^1/_2(1^1/_2) = 6.75 \quad \text{equilibrium quantity.}$$

When the price floor of $2.50 is imposed, the quantity demanded will be

$$Q_D = 12 - 3^1/_2(2^1/_2)$$
$$= 3.25,$$

and the quantity supplied would be

$$Q_S = 3 + 2^1/_2(2^1/_2),$$
$$Q_S = 9.25,$$
$$Q_S > Q_D.$$

That would create a surplus of

$$Q_S - Q_D = 9.25 - 3.25 = 6.$$

4.13   MARSHALLIAN VERSUS HICKSIAN DEMAND CURVES

Let us recall the income and substitution effect that we discussed in the previous chapter. It showed that the price effect on the quantity demanded was dissected into income effect and substitution effect. Let us also recall from the previous chapter how demand curve was derived from subsequent changes in price and the responses of the quantity demanded to them. The demand curve we obtained was the regular demand curve that is commonly used everywhere in microeconomics. It is called the **Marshallian demand** curve after Alfred Marshall (1842–1924). It reflects both of the changes in price effects on the quantity demanded, that is, income and substitution effects combined. However, because the income effect was shown by hypothetically assuming different income (another budget line) to keep the consumer on the same utility level, the segment becomes compensatory and would allow to create another demand curve called the **compensated demand** curve that would reflect only the substitution effect of the price change and quantity demanded holding the utility level constant. Given the fact that only the substitution effect is reflected, and that it is negative since increasing the price of a commodity with holding utility constant would result in cutting the consumption of that commodity, the compensated law of demand would act exactly like the regular law of demand in that the price and the quantity of a non-Giffen commodity would always move in opposite direction to each other when consumer utility is maintained at a certain level. The compensated demand curve is also called the

Hicksian demand curve after John Hicks. It reflects a compensated demand function of the price of commodities and the consumer utility level:

$$Q_D^{comp} = f(P_x, P_y, U).$$

The compensated demand function can be derived according to **Shephard lemma**.

4.13.1   Shephard Lemma and the Expenditure Function

We have seen in the previous chapter that for consumer equilibrium we maximize consumer utility subject to a budget constraint. Analogous to this is the approach of minimizing consumer expenditures subject to a certain level of utility. This would lead to

$$\text{Min } E = P_x x + P_y y,$$

$$\text{s.t. } U = u(x, y).$$

Solving this by the same Lagrangian method we had before would express what is called the **expenditure function**:

$$E = e(P_x, P_y, u),$$

which is to say that the consumer expenditures for the optimal utility is a function of the prices of the commodities and the utility level that is to be maintained.

It is this expenditure function that, according to Shephard lemma, would give us the compensated demand function when it is differentiated with respect to the price of one of the commodities.

Example 4.6

1. Obtain the expenditure function from the utility function

$$u = x^a y^{1-a}.$$

2. Derive the compensated demand function from the expenditure function.
3. How the compensated demand function would look like if $a = 0.45$.

Solution:

1. We start with the Lagrangian expression[1]

$$L = P_x x + P_y y + \lambda[u - x^a y^{1-a}],$$
$$\frac{\partial L}{\partial x} = P_x - \lambda_a x^{a-1} y^{1-a},$$
$$\text{substitute for } y^{1-a} = \frac{u}{x^a} = u_x^{-a}, \tag{4.6}$$
$$\frac{\partial L}{\partial x} = P_x - \lambda_a x^{a-1} u_x^{-a},$$
$$= P_x - \lambda_a \frac{u}{x} = 0,$$

---

[1]The form of the Langrangian in this minimization problem is consistent with the Language multiplier being interpreted as improvement in the optimal value of the objective function. Improvement in this case of minimization means becoming smaller. However, the Lagrangian form used in Chapter was for maximization problems.

$$\frac{\partial L}{\partial y} = P_y - \lambda(1-a)x^a y^{1-a-1},$$

substituting for $x^a = \dfrac{u}{y^{1-a}} = u\, y^{-(1-a)} = u_y^{a-1},$

$$\frac{\partial L}{\partial y} = P_y - \lambda(1-a)u\, y^{a-1}y^{-a},$$

$$\frac{\partial L}{\partial y} = P_y - \lambda(1-a)\tfrac{u}{y} = 0,$$

(4.7)

$$\frac{\partial L}{\partial y} = u - x^a y^{1-a} = 0. \tag{4.8}$$

Dividing (4.6) by (4.7) we obtain

$$(1-a)P_x x = a\, P_y y. \tag{4.9}$$

From (4.9), we get the value of $P_y y$ as

$$P_y y = \frac{(1-a)P_x x}{a}. \tag{4.10}$$

If we substitute (4.10) into the expenditure equation E, we get

$$\begin{aligned}
E &= P_x x + P_y y \\
&= P_x x + \frac{(1-a)P_x x}{a} \\
&= \frac{aP_x x + (1-a)P_x x}{a} \\
&= \frac{P_x x(a + 1 - a)}{a} \\
&= \frac{P_x x}{a}.
\end{aligned}$$

From this, we obtain the value of x:

$$x = a\frac{E}{P_x}. \tag{4.11}$$

Similarly, we can obtain the value of y from getting $P_x x$ from (4.9) and substituting it in E. It would be equal to

$$y = (1-a)\frac{E}{P_y}. \tag{4.12}$$

Now we substitute x and y values above into the utility function:

$$U = x^a y^{1-a}$$

$$= \left[a \frac{E}{P_x} \right]^a \left[(1-a) \frac{E}{P_y} \right]^{1-a}$$

$$= E \left[\frac{a}{P_x} \right]^a \left[\frac{(1-a)}{P_y} \right]^{1-a},$$

and the expenditure function E would be

$$E = \frac{U}{\left[\dfrac{a}{P_x} \right]^a \left[\dfrac{(1-a)}{P_y} \right]^{1-a}}$$

or

$$E = U \left[\frac{P_x}{a} \right]^a \left[\frac{P_y}{1-a} \right]^{1-a}.$$

2. Now that we have the expenditure function E, we can differentiate it with respect to the price of x (P_x) in order to get the compensated demand function for x:

$$\frac{\partial E}{\partial P_x} = U \left[\frac{a}{1-a} \left(\frac{P_y}{P_x} \right) \right]^{1-a},$$

and if the demand function is often expressed by the quantity of the commodity, this one would be

$$Q_D^x = U \left[\frac{a}{1-a} \right]^a \left(\frac{P_y}{P_x} \right)^{1-a}.$$

3. If $a = 0.45$, then $1 - a = 1 - 0.45 = 0.55$, and the function would be

$$Q_D^x = U \left[\frac{0.45}{0.55} \left(\frac{P_y}{P_x} \right) \right]^{0.55}$$

$$= 0.9U \left[\frac{P_y}{P_x} \right]^{0.55}.$$

4.14   DERIVING THE HICKSIAN (COMPENSATED) DEMAND CURVE

The next two figures show that the Hicksian or compensated demand curve can be derived from an equilibrium change due to price change scenario. Figure 4.26 shows an initial equilibrium $e1$ for the original budget line BL_1 and the indifference curve IC. When the price of x goes up and down, budget lines BL_2 and BL_3 represent the adjusted income so as to keep the utility level the same as before the change in price. This is why all budget lines stay in tangency with the same IC, forming the equilibrium points $e2$ and $e3$. This is where the compensation term comes to make more sense. The consumer's income is compensated, positively or negatively, where the price of x increases and decreases, respectively, so that the equilibrium can stay on the same indifference curve. In this case, the corresponding quantities of x projected in Figure 4.27 from the three equilibrium points in the upper panel would represent only the substitution effect of the price change. Along with their corresponding prices, they form points A, B, and C to create the compensated demand curve (Figure 4.27).

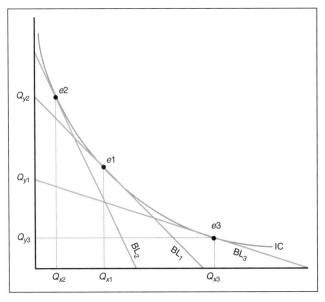

FIGURE 4.26

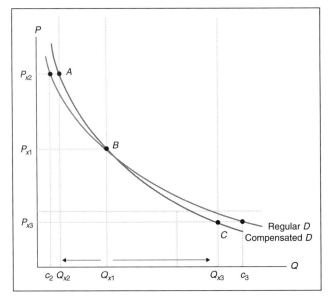

FIGURE 4.27

Compared with the regular demand curve, the only common point between the two curves is the original equilibrium $e1$ since the consumer was able to get Q_{x1} at P_{x1} without any compensation. This is exactly why the two curves would intersect at B. At higher prices than P_{x1}, such as P_{x2}, there would be an increase in the consumer income (positive compensation) and more of x is demanded on the compensated than on the regular curve ($Q_{x2} > C_2$). At prices lower than P_{x1}, such as P_{x3}, the consumer income is decreased (negative compensation) and as a result less x is demanded on the compensated than on the regular curve ($Q_{x3} < C_3$).

Another point of comparison between the two curves is that the compensated curve is steeper than the regular because it reflects only the substitution effect compared with the regular curve that reflects both substitution and income effects.

4.15   REVEALED PREFERENCES

The notion of the revealed preferences goes back to the economic literature of the 1940s, specifically to the book published in 1947, *Foundation of Economic Analysis*, by Paul Samuelson who proposed that consumer preference could be inferred from consumer behavior. That notion was opposite to what had been known in the traditional economic theory that built a model of consumer behavior based on his preferences. Such a proposal depended on the fact that we can observe people's actual choices of goods and services, given a certain combination of income and prices. Knowing more and better information about consumer preferences would lead to better estimation of consumer demand and the substitution effect.

The basic idea of the revealed preferences is illustrated in Figure 4.28. Suppose that a consumer is to choose between A and B bundles of commodities. Point A with the coordinates (x_1, y_1) is on budget line 1 (BL$_1$) and point B with the coordinates (x_2, y_2) is on budget line 2 (BL$_2$). Whereas both points are affordable to this consumer, let us suppose that he chooses A over B. In such a choice, A would be considered revealed preferred. This scenario is qualitatively different from saying that the consumer just prefers A over

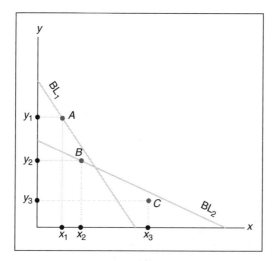

FIGURE 4.28

B, although he would in the final analysis. **Revealed preferred** is a term to indicate that the consumer chose A while he could have chosen B at a time where both A and B were affordable. In other words, it might be more succinct to say that this consumer has chosen A over B, or B has been passed on in favor of A. This implies that the major condition for the revealed preference is the affordability of both commodities but the choice of one. If consumer income is I and price of commodities is P, then choosing A bundle means spending all income, and therefore,

$$x_1 P_x + y_1 P_y = I,$$

and for B being affordable means that

$$x_2 P_x + y_2 P_y \leq I.$$

Taking the left-hand side of both equations gives us

$$x_1 P_x + y_1 P_y \geq x_2 P_x + y_2 P_y. \tag{4.13}$$

This describes the relationship between the bundle of commodities that could have been demanded and those that have actually been demanded. This relation can be stated as that the bundle (x_1, y_1) is directly revealed preferred to the bundle (x_2, y_2). If that means that the consumer is choosing the most preferred bundle that he could afford (x_1, y_1) over the less preferred that he could afford too, then it can be stated unequivocally that bundle A is preferred over bundle B:

$$(x_1, y_1) \succ (x_2, y_2).$$

If we repeat the same scenario of A and B but between B and another point, for example, C, where B and C are affordable for B being on BL_2 and C being inside of it, then we would reach to a similar relation as the one in (4.13):

$$x_2 P_x + y_2 P_y \geq x_3 P_x + y_3 P_y. \tag{4.14}$$

Combining with (4.13), we get

$$x_1 P_x + y_1 P_y \geq x_2 P_x + y_2 P_y \geq x_3 P_x + y_3 P_y, \tag{4.15}$$

which ends up as

$$(x_1, y_1) \succ (x_2, y_2) \succ (x_3, y_3),$$

and by transitivity

$$(x_1, y_1) \succ (x_3, y_3)$$

or

$$A \succ C.$$

This is to say that bundle A is indirectly revealed preferred to bundle C.

This discussion leads to what is called the weak and **strong axioms of revealed preference**. The **weak axiom of revealed preference** states that if A is directly revealed preferred to B, given that they are different, then B can never be directly preferred to A. A stronger axiom includes the indirect revealed preference too. The **strong axiom of revealed preference** states that if A is directly or indirectly revealed preferred over B, then it must not happen that B is directly or indirectly revealed preferred over A. The distinction of the strong axiom here is its inclusion of the indirect revealed preference.

Knowing more on the consumer-revealed preferences allows us to derive where his indifference curve would lie. Let us assume that we add three more budget lines to the earlier BL_1 and BL_2. In Figure 4.29, we introduce five budget lines. Let us take three points, for example, D, E, F on the added three budget lines BL_3, BL_4, BL_5, and let us assume that all are revealed preferred to A. If we assume that consumer preference is convex and monotone, then we can state that the weighted average values of D, E, and F are preferred to x. Also, we can say that any bundle which can offer more of the two commodities than any of the points D, E, and F would be preferred to x. This, in other words, says that the whole shaded area to the northeast of these points would offer more than A can offer. Contrary to that, the whole area to the southwest of the BL_1 and BL_2 would offer less than A can offer. From that we can conclude that the indifference curve where A is at must lie in the remaining area between the upper and lower shaded areas.

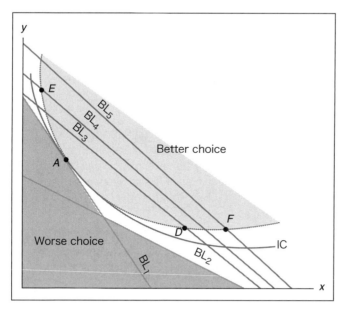

FIGURE 4.29

In addition to deducing consumer preferences from consumer's behavior and the actual choices he makes in the marketplace, the theory of revealed preference can also help estimate the substitution effect and prove its negativity.

Let us assume that a consumer is indifferent between two bundles of goods, $A(x_a, y_a)$ and $B(x_b, y_b)$, and let us assume that these bundles are purchased for the prices P_x^a, P_y^a and P_x^b, P_y^b. If this consumer finds himself indifferent between A and B but he still chooses A, the logical conclusion would be that A must cost less than B:

$$P_x^a x_a + P_y^a y_a < P_x^a x_b + P_y^a y_b, \tag{4.16}$$

and if he chooses B, it must be that B cost less:

$$P_x^b x_b + P_y^b y_b < P_x^b x_a + P_y^b y_a. \tag{4.17}$$

If we rearrange (4.16) into (4.17),

$$\begin{aligned} P_x^a x_a + P_y^a y_a - P_x^a x_b - P_y^a y_b &< 0, \\ P_x^a(x_a - x_b) - P_y^a(y_a - y_b) &< 0, \end{aligned} \tag{4.18}$$

and rearrange (4.17) into (4.18):

$$\begin{aligned} P_x^b x_b + P_y^b y_b - P_x^b x_a - P_y^b y_a &< 0, \\ P_x^b(x_b - x_a) - P_y^b(y_b - y_a). \end{aligned} \tag{4.19}$$

Now, if we assume that only the price of x changes and the price of y remains the same $\left(P_y^a = P_y^b\right)$, and if we add (4.18) to (4.19), we get

$$P_x^a(x_a - x_b) + P_x^b(y_b - y_a) < 0$$

or

$$P_x^a(x_a - x_b) - P_x^b(x_a - x_b) < 0$$

and we rearrange it to

$$\left(P_x^a - P_x^b\right)[x_a - x_b] < 0. \tag{4.20}$$

Expression 5 says that the product of the difference in prices and the difference in quantities is less than zero. It means that prices and quantities go in opposite directions to each other, which is to confirm the negativity of the substitution effect when the utility is held constant. This is traditionally expressed as

$$\left. \frac{\partial Q_x}{\partial P_x} \right|_{U:\,\text{constant}} < 0 \, .$$

4.16   INTERDEPENDENT DEMAND

Some firms produce multiple products or multiline products. Sometimes, there is a competitive relationship between these products or lines of products, and at other times, there is a complementarity between them. How does such a firm draw a collective strategy in production, pricing, and marketing in order to maximize profits for the firm as a whole and allow that maximization to occur in the individual subsection of the firm? Let us take, for example, a giant automaker such as Ford or General Motors, which produce many models and many lines within, where it is possible that a marketing or price policy in one plant may inadvertently end up hurting the other. The parent firm has always to consider all potential effects of business policies in one of its companies on the other affiliated companies, taking into consideration whether the products are compliments or substitutes. Suppose that Sears compa produces the lines of appli Sears ad Kent and consider for example, what a reduction in pricing of Kenmore washing machines would do to Sears washing machines and to Kenmore and Sears dryers when all of these items are produced by companies belonging to Sears. The typical strategy for maximizing profits for the entire firm is to go by the equimarginal principle that stipulates equating the marginal revenue with the marginal cost to get the optimal quantities and prices that would maximize profits.

Let us consider two products, x and y, produced by the same company C. The profit of the company would be reached by subtracting the total cost (TC) of both products from the total revenue (TR) of both items:

$$\pi_C = TR_C - TC_C$$
$$= [TR_x + TR_y] - [TC_x + TC_y].$$

The marginal revenue for product x would be

$$MR_x = \frac{\partial TR_x}{\partial Q_x} + \frac{\partial TR_y}{\partial Q_x}, \tag{4.21}$$

and the marginal revenue for product y would be

$$MR_y = \frac{\partial TR_y}{\partial Q_y} + \frac{\partial TR_x}{\partial Q_y}. \tag{4.22}$$

The last term in the equation, which is $\partial TR_y/\partial Q_x$ in Equation (4.21) and $\partial TR_x/\partial Q_y$ in Equation (4.22), is the **cross-marginal revenue (CMR)**. It is the sign of this term that indicates whether the products are complements, substitutes, or just not connected by any relation (independent from each other):

$$CMR < 0 \quad \text{for substitutes,}$$
$$CMR > 0 \quad \text{for compliments,}$$
$$CMR = 0 \quad \text{for independents.}$$

Compared with the case of independent products, having CMR negative would lead to cutting on the optimal quantities and increasing the optimal price. Inversely, having a positive CMR would lead to increasing the optimal quantities and reducing their optimal prices. This type of knowledge would alert the company to adopt a strategy of neither lowering the price nor increasing the supply of its substitute products, and may do the opposite for its complement products.

Example 4.7

Consider the following demand functions for two substitute products, (x and y), which are produced by the same company. Their marginal costs are 160 and 80, respectively:

$$P_x = 560 - 4Q_x,$$
$$P_y = 360 - 2Q_y - 4Q_x.$$
$$\begin{aligned} \mathrm{TR}_x &= Q_x P_x \\ &= Q_x[650 - 4Q_x] \\ &= 560Q_x - 4Q_x^2. \end{aligned} \quad (4.23)$$

$$\begin{aligned} \mathrm{TR}_y &= Q_y P_y \\ &= Q_y[360 - 2Q_y - 4Q_x] \\ &= 360Q_y - 2Q_y^2 - 4Q_x Q_y. \end{aligned} \quad (4.24)$$

We combine the total revenues of the two products, (4.23) and (4.24), into the company's total revenue TR_C:

$$\begin{aligned} \mathrm{TR}_C &= \mathrm{TR}_x + \mathrm{TR}_y \\ &= 560Q_x - 4Q_x^2 + 360Q_y - 2Q_y^2 - 4Q_x Q_y. \end{aligned} \quad (4.25)$$

For marginal revenue of the two products, we take the partial derivative with respect to Q_x and Q_y, respectively:

$$\mathrm{MR}_x = \frac{\partial \mathrm{TR}_C}{\partial Q_x} = 560 - 8Q_x - 4Q_y. \quad (4.26)$$

$$\mathrm{MR}_y = \frac{\partial \mathrm{TR}_C}{\partial Q_y} = 360 - 4Q_y - 4Q_x. \quad (4.27)$$

Applying the equimarginal principle $\mathrm{MR} = \mathrm{MC}$, we get

$$560 - 8Q_x - 4Q_y = 160, \quad (4.28)$$

$$360 - 4Q_x - 4Q_y = 80. \quad (4.29)$$

Subtracting (4.28) from (4.29), we get

$$200 - 4Q_x = 80,$$
$$120 = 4Q_x,$$
$$30 = Q_x.$$

We substitute Q_x into the original demand function for x to get the price of x:

$$\begin{aligned} P_x &= 560 - 4Q_x \\ &= 560 - 4(30) \\ &= 440. \end{aligned}$$

We substitute this Q_x value into (4.29) to get the value of Q_y:

$$260 - 4(30) - 4Q_y = 80,$$
$$160 = 4Q_y,$$
$$40 = Q_y.$$

We substitute Q_x into the original demand function for y to get the price of y:

$$P_y = 360 - 2Q_y - 4Q_x$$
$$= 360 - 2(40) - 4(30)$$
$$= 160.$$

These are the equilibrium quantities $Q_x = 30$ and $Q_y = 40$ and the equilibrium prices $P_x = 440$ and $P_y = 160$ that would maximize profit. Had the company let these product managers maximize profits individually and without any consideration for the other product, the result would have been different. The equilibrium quantities will not be able to maximize the entire company's profit. Let us see what would be those optimal quantities and prices if the maximization is done independently:

$$\mathrm{TR}_x = 560Q_x - 4Q_x^2,$$
$$\mathrm{MR}_x = \frac{\partial \mathrm{TR}_x}{\partial Q_x},$$
$$\mathrm{MR}_x = 560 - 8Q_x,$$
$$\mathrm{MR}_x = \mathrm{MC}_x,$$
$$560 - 8Q_x = 160,$$
$$400 = 8Q_x,$$
$$50 = Q_x,$$
$$P_x = 560 - 4(50),$$
$$P_x = 360.$$

We have seen previously that to maximize profit in the case of having substitute products, the firm should avoid increasing output or lowering the price. Acting as an independent manager of product x resulted in higher quantity (50 instead of 30) and lower price (360 instead of 440), an equilibrium set that will not lead to maximizing profit for the firm as a whole.

SUMMARY

- This chapter discusses the fundamental topics of demand and supply. It starts by making a distinction between the two basic terms that are very frequently confused: quantity demanded/supplied and demand/supply. Quantities refer to one case in which a certain quantity would be purchased or sold at a certain price. That is one point on the demand or supply curve. Demand or supply refers to an entire set of those quantities that a consumer or producer is willing and able to purchase or sell at a set of corresponding prices. Demand and supply laws were explained, their curves were illustrated, and the demand function was derived from the utility function. Homogeneity and the numeraire of the demand function was explained as a property that let the optimal quantity demanded remain the same when income and prices were multiplied by a positive constant. Related to the format in which the demand function is expressed, the inverse demand function has also been explained.

- Market demand was addressed as the horizontal summation of the individual demands, and the effects of the network externalities were detailed in both the positive and negative impacts on the market demand. The bandwagon and snob effects represented both sides of the externalities and the market demand function was derived from both of these influences.

- Market equilibrium was explained in detail and two types of changes were addressed. Changes in the quantities demanded and supplied are due to price change, and changes in the entire demand or supply are due to several factors other than the price. Changes in the quantities demanded or supplied were depicted as movements along the same curves; and changes in the entire demand or supply were depicted as shifts of the whole demand or supply curves, either to the right, in the case of an increase, or to the left, in the case of a decrease. This shift type of change is what usually leads to changes in equilibrium. Two popular cases illustrated the change in equilibrium, the case of Thanksgiving turkey and the case of sales and excise taxes.

- Along the market equilibrium, market disequilibrium cases were addressed too. Under certain circumstances, the natural market equilibrium, which occurs because of the rationing function of prices in the free market system, may not exist. Powerful external forces such as the government may sometimes impose policies that tamper with market price and may lead to the state of disequilibrium. Two typical examples of government intervention were addressed, the case of price ceiling and the case of price floor.

- Related to the discussion of the income and substitution effect in Chapter 3, the compensated or Hicksian demand curve was addressed as the curve that could be created to reflect the compensatory effect of the income effect segment in the state of the income and substitution effect on consumer choice after a price change. Shephard lemma was also explained in relation to the expenditure function that would lead to the derivative of the compensated demand function when differentiated with respect to the price of one of the commodities.

- Revealed preferences were discussed as the notion that consumer preferences, and their indifference curve could be inferred from observing consumer behavior as in the case of knowing consumer choices of commodities at various income levels and different prices. Two states of the revealed preferences were defined, the strong axiom and the weak axiom of the revealed preferences.

- The last topic in this chapter was the interdependent demand where firms produced multiple products, and the demand of one would be affected by the other whether the commodities were substitutes or complements. Examples were given to illustrate the best strategy from these firms to maximize their profits under the conditions of the interdependent demand on their various products.

KEY TERMS

quantity demanded	demand	quantity supplied
supply	demand law	supply law
money illusion	relative price	relative income
demand function	equilibrium point	equilibrium quantity
equilibrium price	market equilibrium	network externalities
positive externalities	negative externalities	bandwagon effect
snob effect	market disequilibrium	price ceiling
price floor	compensated demand	Hicksian demand
Marshallian demand	Shephard lemma	expenditure function
weak axiom of revealed preference	interdependent demand	revealed preference
strong axiom of revealed preference	cross-marginal revenue (CMR)	

LIST OF FORMULAS

- Marshallian demand function:

$$Q_x^M = f(P_x, P_y, I).$$

- Hicksian (compensated) demand function:

$$Q_x^H = g(P_x, P_y, U).$$

- Expenditure function:

$$E = e(P_x, P_y, u).$$

EXERCISES

1. While the change in quantity demanded or supplied is only caused by price change, list as many factors as you can that would cause shift in demand and supply separately.

2. If there is a new sales tax of $100 on wide-screen TVs and an excise tax of $1.00 on tobacco farmers, how would the demand of wide-screen TVs and the supply of tobacco be affected?

3. Explain the difference between the legal incidence of taxes and the economic incidence of taxes.

4. What does it mean to say a demand function is homogeneous of degree zero and what is the significance of that?

5. Compare the weak axiom of revealed preference with the strong axiom of revealed preference.

6. Suppose that the demand and supply functions of pineapples are given by

$$Q_d = 2000 - 400P,$$
$$Q_s = 1600P.$$

(a) Find the equilibrium price and quantity.

(b) Find the equilibrium price and quantity after the local government imposes a 20¢ sales tax on pineapples.

(c) Find the equilibrium price and quantity if there is a 20¢ excise tax on growers instead of the sales tax.

7. The following are the total utilities of commodities x and y:

Q	TU_x	TU_y
1	30	20
2	55	38
3	75	54
4	90	68
5	100	80

(a) Find the marginal utilities of both commodities.

(b) Draw the total utility and marginal utility curves for both commodities separately.

(c) Find the consumer's optimal combination choice if $P_x = \$5.00$ and $P_y = \$4.00$.

(d) Find the necessary consumer budget required to purchase the optimal choice.

8. The following are the demand and supply functions of milk:

$$Q_D = 100 - 20P,$$
$$Q_S = 40 + 5P.$$

(a) Find the equilibrium price and quantity.

(b) If a price ceiling of $6.00 is imposed and the demand rises to $Q_D = 150 - 20P$, what would be the consequences in the market?

9. The following are the demand and supply functions of all-purpose flour:

$$Q_D = 6000 - 3000P,$$
$$Q_S = 2400 + 3000P.$$

(a) Find the equilibrium price and quantity.

(b) If the government imposes a price floor of $1.20 on this commodity, what would happen to the quantities demanded and supplied?

10. Consider a consumer's demand function for a small window air conditioner:

$$P = 100 - 2Q.$$

(a) If this consumer is willing to pay $96.00 a piece, how many units would he or she buy?

(b) If at the store the consumer finds this item on sale for $82.00, how many units would he or she buy?

(c) How would these scenarios be depicted on a graph?

(d) Calculate the arc price elasticity of demand for this item.

5

CONSUMER DEMAND: EMPIRICAL ESTIMATION

The theory of consumer demand that was explained in the previous chapters would not be valid unless it is tested and verified in the real world. However, demand estimation not only is necessary to merely validate the theory but also can serve as a powerful tool for managers to explore and test the nature of market, behavior of consumers, appropriateness of strategies, and effects of policies, all in order to make the best managerial decisions in production, pricing, promotion, and expansion of the business.

Technically, demand estimation means identifying the demand function, recognizing its determinants, and quantifying the impact of the significant determinants. This can be done in many ways ranging from the simple common-sense **market experimentation** to the most prominent statistical method of **regression analysis**.

5.1 SIMPLE MARKET EXPERIMENTATION

Suppose that a manager of a small pizza restaurant wants to estimate the demand of his pizza in a simple way of trial and error by changing the price and watching the response of the sale. In this case, he would implicitly assume that his pizza demand function is linear, where the amount of sale or demand depends only on the price of the product. Suppose that he took a look at his records and saw that his pizza had been sold for a while for $14.00 and averaging 15,000 pizzas in annual sales. He decided to test the response of demand if he cut the price to $10.00. Suppose that after a year he watched the sale climbed to 20,000 pizzas. Right here, the manager can draw the simplest demand curve by identifying two points *A* and *B* for two pairs of price–quantity readings (Table 5.1; Figure 5.1).

Managerial Economics: A Mathematical Approach, First Edition. M. J. Alhabeeb and L. Joe Moffitt.
© 2013 John Wiley & Sons, Inc. Published 2013 by John Wiley & Sons, Inc.

TABLE 5.1

	P	Q
A	$14	15,000
B	$10	20,000

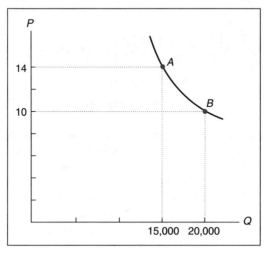

FIGURE 5.1

Due to the assumption that the demand function is linear, it can be written as

$$Q = a + \beta P,$$

and it can be switched in terms of price as

$$P = \alpha + \beta Q.$$

Now, values can be plugged in from the table as

$$14 = \alpha + \beta(15{,}000), \tag{5.1}$$

$$10 = \alpha + \beta(20{,}000). \tag{5.2}$$

α and β can be solved by subtracting Equation (5.2) from (5.1):

$$14 = \alpha + 15{,}000\,\beta,$$
$$-10 = -\alpha - 20{,}000\,\beta,$$
$$4 = -5000\,\beta,$$
$$\frac{4}{-5000} = \beta = -0.0008.$$

Plugging in β in either of the functions (5.1) or (5.2), one can get α:

$$14 = \alpha + (-0.0008)(15,000),$$

$$14 + 12 = \alpha = 26,$$

or

$$10 = \alpha + (-0.0008)(20,000),$$

$$10 + 16 = \alpha = 26.$$

The manager can now construct the general demand function for pizza as

$$P = \alpha + \beta(Q),$$

$$P = 26 - 0.0008Q.$$

He can now use this general demand function to predict what would happen to the sales of pizza if he increases or decreases the price to any level he wants. However, he should realize that the prediction would be reasonable only to prices close to the range of $10–$14 and may not be applicable to any extreme change in the price. He can also know the appropriate price he must charge if his production increases or decreases for any reason.

Inspecting the impact of price change on the restaurant revenue reveals that dropping the price of pizza to $10 results in reducing the annual revenue by $10,000:

$$TR = Q \cdot P$$

$$= 15,000(\$14.00) = \$210,000$$

$$= 20,000(\$10.00) = \$200,000$$

$$= \$200,000 - \$210,000$$

$$= -\$10,000.$$

Therefore, it is obvious that the drop of $4 per pizza boosted the sales but was not enough to increase the revenue or even to keep it close. In this case, the experimenting manager would realize that he went too far cutting the price by $4 (from $14 to $10). He may try to cut it by a lesser amount, such as $2, so the price would become $12. With the help of the demand function he has constructed, he can see what kind of revenue this new price of $12 would bring. First, see how much would be the sales:

$$P = 26 - 0.0008Q,$$

$$12 = 26 - 0.0008Q,$$

$$0.0008Q = 26 - 12,$$

$$Q = \frac{14}{0.0008} = 17,500.$$

The size of sales would bring a revenue of

$$TR = Q \cdot P,$$

$$= 17,500(\$12.00) = \$210,000.$$

It is exactly the same as the revenue when the price was $14.00. In this case, it would not make any sense to drop the price. Therefore, there has to be a price that would give the maximum possible revenue. So, what would that price be? If the manager knows a little bit of economics, he would remember that the total revenue is maximized when the marginal revenue reaches zero. This would lead him to get the marginal revenue function by taking the first derivative of the total revenue function, and set the marginal revenue function to zero and solve for P, which would be the optimal price that would maximize revenue:

$$\text{TR} = Q \cdot P$$
$$= Q(26 - 0.0008Q)$$
$$= 26Q - 0.0008Q^2.$$
$$\text{MR} = \frac{\partial \text{TR}}{\partial Q},$$
$$\text{MR} = 26 - 0.0016Q = 0,$$
$$26 = 0.0016Q,$$
$$\frac{26}{0.0016} = Q = 16,250.$$

He can plug the quantity of 16,250 into the original demand equation to find the price:

$$P = 26 - 0.008(16,250),$$
$$P = 13.$$

So, $13.00 would be the optimal price for the pizza that would result in selling 16,250 pizzas a year, which would maximize the revenue to $211,250:

$$\text{TR} = Q \cdot P$$
$$= 16,250(\$13.00) = \$211,250.$$

This revenue is more by $1250 than the revenue that would be obtained when the price is $14.00 or $12.00, and more by 11,250 than when the price is $10.00.

The conclusion is that a manager can experiment with affecting factors, such as price, advertising expenditures, packaging expenditures, and see what happens. This method, of course, is risky as it may result in a drop in revenue or profits. It is also limited to its range of flexibility.

5.2 LINEARITY OF THE DEMAND FUNCTION: FROM VISUAL TO REGRESSION

As seen before, demand function is primarily a relationship between the quantity demanded and the price of a product. We further know from the demand law that this relation is typically negative especially for the non-Giffen commodities, which constitute the vast majority of the goods and services we deal with. We may further know from experience that this relationship is often linear. These two important characteristics of the function, linearity and negative correlation, can actually be observed visually before the utilization of more involved mathematical or statistical methods. Plotting data where each point would represent a pair of readings, the quantity purchased for a price, would be the way to visually and roughly observe those characteristics of the relation. This plotting of data would form what is known as the "scatter diagram." The major advantage of this two-dimensional graph is to enable us to visually recognize the general relationship between the two variables.

Let us consider the following data on the number of TV sets sold at various prices and locate 10 points for 10 pairs of data where the price would be on the vertical axis and the quantity on the horizontal axis (Table 5.2; Figures 5.2 and 5.3).

TABLE 5.2

Price	1,000	1,100	1,200	1,300	1,400	1,500	1,600	1,600	17,000	2,000
Quantity	17	20	15	10	12	12	10	5	5	6

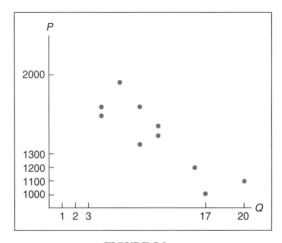

FIGURE 5.2

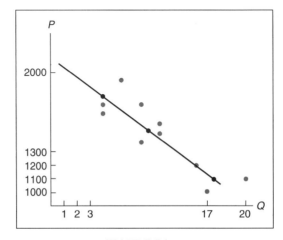

FIGURE 5.3

From a general look at the diagram we can note that the scattered points visually reveal three clusters of points (1, 2, 3), (4, 5, 6, 7), and (8, 9, 10). These clusters are placed as if on a line running from southeast to northwest. This would hint that the relationship of quantity and price is linear. We can also visually recognize that the higher the price, the lesser the quantity. This would hint that the linear relation is negative. Now, we can take a step further and attempt to visually place a line that would be as close as possible to each and every one of the 10 observations. One approximation method to locate this line is to take an average of each of the three clusters to produce three points (A, B, and C). The line connecting these three points would be the best fit possible, determined visually. However, since visual fitting is an arbitrary and subjective process and can result in certain differences in the subsequent estimation, the statistical technique of regression would present the best alternative and the most objective fitting process to date. The regression analysis is based on what is called the ordinary least squares (OLS) method . The major premise of this method is to minimize the vertical distances between the observations and the regression line.

The regression line is assumed to be a straight line with the typical equation of

$$Y = \alpha + \beta x,$$

where the value of x is given as the independent or explanatory variable that would have an impact on the value of the dependent variable Y. The purpose of the regression method is to estimate the value of Y and quantify the effect of x on Y. Throughout this process, x (Y-intercept), and β (slope of the line) are also estimated, in addition to adding the **error term** (e) that would sum up all other factors that may contribute to the reasons why, and to what extent, the estimated value of Y is different from the actual observation. The estimated values of Y, α, and β would be marked by ($^$):

$$\hat{Y} = \hat{\alpha} + \hat{\beta}x.$$

The value of the error term (e) would be obtained by the difference between the actual observation (Y) and the estimated value of it ($\hat{Y}$) for each observation:

$$e = Y - \hat{Y},$$

and if we substitute $\hat{Y}$ from the previous equation, we get

$$e = Y - \hat{\alpha} - \hat{\beta}x.$$

This would stand for the deviation in value for each observation as it is estimated. Those deviations would be squared and summed up as

$$\Sigma e^2 = \Sigma[Y - \hat{\alpha} - \hat{\beta}x]^2.$$

It is this sum of all deviations that would be minimized to get the best fit of the line, where the values β and α are determined:

$$\hat{\beta} = \frac{\Sigma[x - \bar{x}][Y - \bar{Y}]}{\Sigma[x - \bar{x}]^2},$$

$$\hat{\alpha} = \bar{Y} - \hat{\beta}\bar{x},$$

where $\bar{x}$ and $\bar{Y}$ are the mean values of the x and Y observations. In addition to the estimation of the **parameters**, the regression process should also examine how significant these estimators are, and to what extent (i.e., the confidence level in these values), as well as how effective the explanatory role of the model is as a whole.

Now, let us use the OLS method on the following example, performing the manual calculations first and then the usual computer analysis so that we can clearly comprehend the connection:

Example 5.1
Table 5.3 shows the monthly revenues and the advertising expenditures from an appliance store records.

TABLE 5.3

Monthly Revenue	13,000	12,000	8,500	18,000	16,000	18,000	8,000	16,800	17,000	22,000
Monthly Adv. Exps.	1,000	750	580	1,400	1,500	1,250	550	1,100	1,600	2,000

Assess how spending on advertisement can affect the sales revenue by estimating and testing the regression equation (Table 5.4).

TABLE 5.4

Obs.	Y Revenue	X Adv.	$[Y - \bar{Y}]$	$[x - \bar{x}]$	$[Y - \bar{Y}][x - \bar{x}]$	$[x - \bar{x}]^2$
1	13,000	1,000	−1,930	−173	333,890	29,929
2	12,000	750	−2,930	−423	1,239,390	178,929
3	8,500	580	−6,430	−593	3,812,990	351,649
4	18,000	1,400	3,070	227	696,890	51,529
5	16,000	1,500	1,070	327	349,890	106,929
6	18,000	1,250	3,070	77	236,390	5,929
7	8,000	550	−6,930	−623	4,317,390	388,129
8	16,800	1,100	1,870	−73	136,510	5,329
9	17,000	1,600	2,070	427	883,890	182,329
10	22,000	2,000	7,070	827	5,846,890	683,929
	$\Sigma Y = 149{,}300$	$\Sigma x = 11{,}730$	$\Sigma[Y - \bar{Y}]$	$\Sigma[x - \bar{x}]$	$\Sigma[Y - \bar{Y}][x - \bar{x}]$	$\Sigma[x - \bar{x}]^2$
	$\bar{Y} = 14{,}930$	$\bar{x} = 1173$	$= 0$	$= 0$	$= 17{,}854{,}120$	$= 1{,}984{,}610$

Solution:
First, we need to construct a calculation table so that we can obtain $\hat{\beta}$:

$$\hat{\beta} = \frac{\sum_{i=1}^{10} [Y - \bar{Y}][x - \bar{x}]}{\sum_{i=1}^{10} [x - \bar{x}]^2},$$

$$\hat{\beta} = \frac{17,854,120}{1,984,610},$$

$$\hat{\beta} = 8.86.$$

Now, we can obtain $\hat{\alpha}$ by

$$\hat{\alpha} = \bar{Y} - \hat{\beta}\bar{x},$$
$$= 14{,}930 - (8.86)(1173)$$
$$= 4538.$$

We can also obtain $\hat{\alpha}$ by using the original equation but substituting for Y and x by their mean values $\bar{Y}$ and $\bar{x}$:

$$Y = \alpha + \beta x,$$
$$\bar{Y} = \hat{\alpha} + \hat{\beta}\bar{x},$$
$$14{,}930 = \hat{\alpha} + (8.86)(1173),$$
$$\hat{\alpha} = 14{,}930 - 10{,}392,$$
$$\hat{\alpha} = 4538.$$

Now, we can write the equation of the estimated regression line:

$$\hat{Y} = \hat{\alpha} + \hat{\beta}x,$$
$$\hat{Y} = 4538 + 8.86x.$$

We can simply draw the regression line by substituting the two extreme values of x in the observed data. The lowest advertising expenditure is at observation 7, which is equal to $550, and the highest expenditure on advertisement in these data is at observation 10, which is equal to $2000. Plugging these values into the equation would give us the corresponding revenues and enable us to locate two points of the two pairs of values:

$$\hat{Y} = 4538 + 8.86x$$
$$= 4538 + 8.86(550) = 9{,}411.$$

This is point B (550, 9411) on the graph.

$$\hat{Y} = 4538 + 8.86(2000) = 22{,}258.$$

This is point C (2000, 22,258) on the graph.

Connecting B to C would give us the regression line. Furthermore, we can extend the line until it crosses the vertical axis. The intersection point would be the Y-intercept. We can see that it occurs at 4538, which is exactly the value of x.

The estimated α of $4538 means that when the firm does not spend any dollars on advertisement, it can still sell some appliances and collect revenue equal to $5438 per month:

$$\text{If } x = 0, \quad \text{then}$$
$$\hat{Y} = 5538 + 8.86(0),$$
$$\hat{Y} = 4538.$$

It is shown on the graph that at $x = 0$, Y is represented by the vertical distance A0, which is equal to 4538.

Plugging in any value of x from these data will produce a value of Y based on the relationship between x and Y that is explained by β. This β is the slope of the line. It indicates how the firm's revenue changes according to how much is spent on advertisement $\left(\frac{\Delta Y}{\Delta x}\right)$. On the graph, we marked an arbitrary change in advertisement expenditures equal to $400, say from $100 to $500. This change is shown as a movement along the line from point i to ii, which can be translated on the vertical axis as an increase from $5400 to $8944. That is the change in $Y(\Delta Y)$ due to the change in $x(\Delta x)$, which is the slope of the line:

$$\text{Slope} = \frac{\Delta Y}{\Delta x}$$
$$= \frac{8944 - 5400}{400}$$
$$= 8.86,$$

and this is exactly the value of β.

β means that for each $100 increase in advertisement, the revenue will increase by $886. It can be generalized in these data that any expenditure on advertisement would bring more than eight times its value in more revenue. However, it is not wise to generalize this beta power for much more than the range of data in this specific example. In other words, we can predict the size of revenue the firm would collect if it spends $3,000 on advertisement, but we should not rely on the prediction if we move further than that.

5.3   RELIABILITY OF THE ESTIMATION

We have established that the regression equation explained how x can affect Y, namely, how spending on advertisement would increase sales and revenue. We have also established the quantitative impact of x in obtaining the value of β. However, the question is, how reliable is the role of β that we calculated and how confident can we be in this estimated value? For the answer, we need to run a t-statistic test or a t-ratio test. It is a ratio of the estimated β to the standard deviation of β. So, having calculated β already, we now need to calculate the standard deviation s_β, which is obtained by

$$s_\beta = \sqrt{\frac{\Sigma \varepsilon^2}{(n-k)\Sigma[x-\bar{x}]^2}}$$

$$= \sqrt{\frac{\Sigma[Y-\hat{Y}]^2}{(n-k)\Sigma[x-\bar{x}]^2}}$$

where $\Sigma \varepsilon^2$ is the sum of the squared errors, which is the sum of the squared differences between the actual and estimated values of Y (revenues) $[Y - \hat{Y}]^2$, $n - k$ is the **degree of freedom** (DF) or the difference between the number of observations and the number of coefficients in the regression equation including the constant term (α), and $\Sigma[x - \bar{x}]^2$ is the sum of the squared deviations of the advertising expenditures from its mean. Table 5.5

allows us to obtain the standard deviations of β by calculating the terms needed, including creating the column of the estimated quantitative $\hat{Y}$. Each value in this column is calculated by substituting the corresponding x in the regression equation. For example, the first value of $\hat{Y}$ is that obtained by substituting the first value of x in the equation:

$$\hat{Y} = \alpha + \beta x,$$

$$= 4538 + (8.86)(1000) = 13{,}398.$$

TABLE 5.5

Obs.	X	Y	$\hat{Y}$	$\varepsilon = [Y - \hat{Y}]$	$\varepsilon^2 = [Y - \hat{Y}]^2$	$[x - \bar{x}]^2$
1	1,000	13,000	13,398	−398	158,404	193,600
2	750	12,000	11,183	817	667,489	115,600
3	580	8,500	9,677	−1,177	1,385,329	57,600
4	1,400	18,000	16,942	1,058	1,119,364	19,600
5	1,500	16,000	17,828	−1,828	3,341,584	1,600
6	1,250	18,000	15,613	2,387	5,697,769	3,600
7	550	8,000	9,411	−1,411	1,990,921	25,600
8	1,100	16,800	14,284	2,516	6,330,256	25,600
9	1,600	17,000	18,714	−1,714	2,937,796	67,600
10	2,000	22,000	22,258	−258	66,564	313,600
					$\Sigma \varepsilon^2 =$	$\Sigma(x - \bar{x})^2 =$
					23,695,476	1,984,610

DF is $n - k = 10 - 2 = 8$:

$$s_\beta = \sqrt{\frac{\Sigma[Q - \hat{Q}]^2}{n - k[P - \hat{P}]^2}}$$

$$s_\beta = \sqrt{\frac{23{,}695{,}476}{8(19{,}846(0)}}$$

$$s_\beta = 1.22.$$

Now we get t-statistics by dividing β by its standard error (s_β):

$$t = \frac{\beta}{s_\beta},$$

$$t = \frac{8.86}{1.22} = 7.26.$$

We compare this calculated value of t with the critical value of the t-distribution given in Table A.2 in the appendix. We choose the two-tailed test because it is also important to test for the sign of the coefficient ($+$ or $-$). The calculated value of 7.26 is larger than the critical values at both 95% confidence (value $= 2.306$) and 99% confidence (value $= 2.355$). The reading of the table value is across both the DF ($n - k = 10 - 2 = 8$) and the chosen confidence level. Typically, 95% is the level of choice, which is listed at the 5% column of the table. The 99% confidence level is listed in the 1% column. Choosing this level of confidence means that there would only be a chance of 1% of being wrong. Therefore, having a t-ratio value larger than the critical value under 5% and 1% means that there is indeed a positive and significant relationship between spending on advertisement and revenue growth.

Furthermore, the critical value of the t-test can be used to establish the confidence interval of the true value of the estimated coefficient. For example, at 95% confidence, the true value of the coefficient would be in the range specified as

$$+\hat{\beta} \pm [(\text{table value})(s_\beta)],$$

that is, between

$$8.86 - [(2.306)(1.22)] = 6.05,$$

and

$$8.86 + [(2.306)(1.22)] = 11.67.$$

That is, there is a 95% chance that the true value of our coefficient estimate is between 6.05 and 11.67 and if we choose the 99% chance, then we replace the 2.306 by 3.355.

Naturally, if we increase our confidence from 95% to 99%, the range of the true value would increase so as to say that there is a 99% chance that the true value of the coefficient is between

$$8.86 - [(3.333)(1.22)] = 4.77$$

and

$$8.86 + [(3.355)(1.22)] = 12.95.$$

That is, β is between 4.77 and 12.95, and there is only 1% chance to be wrong about that.

5.4 QUALITY OF FITTING

To test how well the explanatory variable(s) can explain the variation in the dependent variable, we utilize the **coefficient of determination (R^2)**. It is calculated as the proportion of the explained variation in the dependent variable $\Sigma[\hat{Y} - \bar{Y}]^2$ to the total variation in the dependent variable $\Sigma[Y - \bar{Y}]^2$:

$$R^2 = \frac{\Sigma[\hat{Y} - \bar{Y}]^2}{\Sigma[Y - \bar{Y}]^2}.$$

Note that while the total variation in the dependent variable is $\Sigma[Y - \bar{Y}]^2$ and the explained variation is $\Sigma[\hat{Y} - \bar{Y}]^2$, the unexplained variation would be $\Sigma[Y - \hat{Y}]^2$. Let us note these differences on one observation on the graph, say observation 4 in the table where Y is $18,000 and x is $1400. The total variation is the difference between the observation at point D, which is $18,000, and the mean value, which is $14,930; that is, the vertical distance between D and F. The explained part of the variation is the difference between the estimated value, which is $16,942, and the mean value, which is the vertical distance between E and F. So the remaining is the unexplained portion of the variation, which is the difference between the observation value of $18,000, and the estimated value of $16,942. This portion is what constitutes the error term (e). Similarly, the whole error term of the model would be the sum of all the vertical distances between the observations and the regression line. Note that the error terms are squared mathematically to treat both the negative and positive values of the errors, as they tend to cancel each other out and defeat the purpose (Table 5.6).

$$R^2 = \frac{\Sigma[\hat{Y} - \bar{Y}]^2}{\Sigma[Y - \bar{Y}]^2},$$

$$R^2 = \frac{102,144,404}{179,441,000} = 0.57,$$

$$r = \sqrt{R^2} = \sqrt{0.57} = 0.76.$$

TABLE 5.6

Obs.	X	$\hat{Y}$	$[\hat{Y} - \bar{Y}]$	$[\hat{Y} - \bar{Y}]^2$	$[Y - \bar{Y}]$	$[Y - \bar{Y}]^2$
1	13,000	13,398	−1,532	2,347,024	−1,930	3,724,900
2	12,000	11,183	−3,747	14,040,009	−2,930	8,584,900
3	8,500	9,677	−5,253	27,594,009	−6,430	41,344,900
4	18,000	16,942	2,012	4,048,144	3,070	9,424,900
5	16,000	17,828	2,898	8,398,404	1,070	1,144,900
6	18,000	15,613	683	466,489	3,070	9,424,900
7	8,000	9,411	−5,519	30,459,361	−6,930	48,024,900
8	16,800	14,284	−647	418,609	1,870	3,496,900
9	17,000	18,714	3,784	14,318,656	2,070	4,284,900
10	22,000	22,258	7,328	53,699,584	7,070	49,984,900
$n = 10$	$\bar{Y} =$ 14,930			$\Sigma(\hat{Y} - \bar{Y})^2 =$ 102,144,404		$\Sigma(Y - \bar{Y})^2 =$ 179,441,000

Since R^2 is suited for multiple regression in testing how effective the **independent variables** is in explaining the variation in the dependent variable, here we would rely on the correlation coefficient (r), which is the square root of R^2. This measure is suited for simple regression in that it would test how a single independent variable is able to explain the variation in the dependent variable by simply referring to how correlated the two variables are and in which direction. A result of 0.75 for the correlation coefficient indicates that spending on advertisement is positively related to the growth of revenue and that the two variables are associated with each other by 75%. However, in multiple regression, when there are more than one independent variable, the R^2 would tend to have a higher value simply because more variables can explain more than one variable (see Figure 5.4).

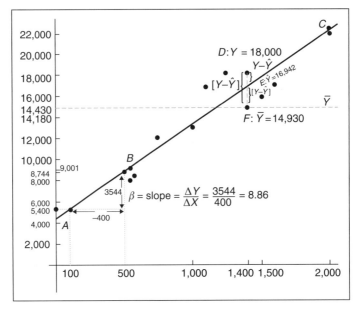

FIGURE 5.4

5.5 FITTING BY COMPUTERIZED REGRESSION

There is no need to perform tedious calculations of any mathematical or statistical technique such as regression since they can be done in a few minutes by computers and calculators. However, it is very important to know the manual operation in order to understand what the computer does. Running the previous example by computer would give us the following information in a printout complete with a graph of the scatter diagram and the regression line (Tables 5.7, 5.8, 5.9, 5.10, 5.11, 5.12, 5.13, and 5.14):

x: Exogenous variable = monthly advertisement expenditures $.

Y: Exogenous variable = monthly revenue $.

TABLE 5.7

Data Y	Data x
13,000	1,000
12,000	750
8,500	580
18,000	1,400
16,000	1,500
18,000	1,250
8,000	550
16,800	1,100
17,000	1,600
22,000	2,000

TABLE 5.8

	Simple Linear Regression—Ungrouped Data			
Parameter	Value	SE	*T*-Stat	Notes
Constant	4538.723981			
Beta	8.858718	1.221647	7.251455	H0: beta = 0
Elasticity	0.696000	0.095981	−3.167306	H0: elast. = 1

TABLE 5.9

	Simple Linear Regression—Analysis of Variance		
ANOVA	DF	Sum of Squares	Mean Square
Regression	1.000000	1.557460 E + 8	1.557460 E + 8
Residual	8.000000	2.369500 E + 7	2.961874 E + 6
Total	9.000000	1.794410 E + 8	1.993789 E + 7
F-Test		52.583594	

TABLE 5.10

	Simple Linear Regression—Autocorrelation
Statistic	Value
Durbin–Watson	3.646751
Von Neumann ratio	4.051946
Rho-least squares	−0.830393
Rho-serial correlation	−0.920104
Rho-Goldberger	−0.832020

TABLE 5.11

	Simple Linear Regression—Descriptive Statistics
Statistic	Value
Mean x	1173.000000
Biased variance X	198461.000000
Biased SE X	445.489618
Mean Y	14930.000000
Biased variance Y	1.194410 E + 7
Biased SE Y	4236.047686
Mean F	14930.000000
Biased variance F	1.557460 E + 7
Biased SE F	3946.466826
Mean e	0.000000
Biased variance e	2.369500 E + 6
Biased SE e	544.231062

TABLE 5.12

Student Distribution Probability (Mathematical Equation Plotter)

T-Test	7.2514545805782
DF	8
Tails (1 or 2)	2
Student Probability	

TABLE 5.13

Student Distribution Probability (Mathematical Equation Plotter)

T-Test	$-$ 3.1673059922745
DF	8
Tails (1 or 2)	2
Student Probability	

TABLE 5.14

Fisher Distribution Probability (Mathematical Equation Plotter)

T-Test	52.5835
DF numerator	1
DF denominator	2
Fisher Probability	

Note that the manual calculations gave very close results, and the slight differences were due to the rounding up of values. The printout contains more information that would make more sense to explain in the following case of multiple regression.

5.6   DEMAND ESTIMATION BY THE MULTIPLE REGRESSION METHOD

The multiple regression method uses the same technique as in simple regression except that there is more than one independent variable to explain the variation in the independent variable. With more variables in the regression equation, the manual calculations become more complex and tedious to the point they warrant the use of computers or calculators equipped with a regression program. But all the calculations are based on the same techniques except that they are performed with much more accuracy and speed when done electronically.

The simple regression equation of

$$Y = \alpha + \beta x + e$$

would be expanded to more than one x to represent all the major variables that would be hypothesized to influence the dependent variable by theory, experience, or most likely both.

Our typical demand function is

$$Q_x = \alpha + \beta P_x + e,$$

where demand (Q) of a commodity (x) would depend on the price of that commodity (P_x). This function can be expanded to include other variables such as consumer income (I), the price of an alternative commodity P_y, advertising expenditures in order to sell more of that commodity (Adv_x), the size of the market in which the commodity is sold $(MSize_x)$ and any other variables that we may think have the potential to be influential in changing the amount of demand on that commodity.

The regression equation would then be adjusted in the following way to include all of the aforementioned variables:

$$Q_x = \alpha + \beta^1 P_x + \beta^2 I + \beta^3 P_y + \beta^4 Adv_x + \beta^5 MSize_x + \beta^6 T + e.$$

Here, we have six independent variables in addition to the constant term and the error term. T is the time sequence of the data.

Table 5.15 shows the demand data on frozen pizza with the influential variables as they are specified in the equation above. The regression analysis was run by computer and the following were obtained: the estimated regression equation, the results of the analysis as they appear on the computer printout, and their interpretation.

The estimated demand equation is

$$Q_x = 2,047,850 - 75,554 P_x - 52 I + 34,039 P_y + 5.43 Adv_x$$
$$+ 0.06 MSize + 8,927 T + e,$$

where

Q_x is the demand for frozen pizza;

P_x is the unit price of frozen pizza;

I is the consumer's disposable income;

P_y is the price of an alternative good such as a frozen pocket pizza;

Adv_x is expenditures on advertising for this pizza;

MSize is the market size (population) where the pizza is sold;

T is the time sequence;

e is the error term.

TABLE 5.15

Obs.	Quantity (Sales, Q_x)	Price (P_x)	Income (I)	Alternative (P_y)	Advertising Expenditure (Adv_x)	Market Size (MSize)	Time (T)
1	247,709	5.75	33,599	5.28	14,062	4,218,965	1
2	183,259	6.75	33,797	6.17	16,973	4,226,070	2
3	282,118	6.36	33,879	6.36	18,815	4,278,912	3
4	203,396	5.98	34,186	4.88	14,176	4,359,442	4
5	167,447	6.64	35,691	5.22	17,030	4,363,494	5
6	361,677	5.30	35,950	5.80	14,456	4,380,084	6
7	321,972	7.24	35,898	5.82	34,367	9,254,182	7
8	445,236	6.08	36,113	6.05	26,895	9,272,758	8
9	479,713	6.40	36,252	5.37	30,539	9,300,401	9
10	459,379	6.00	36,449	4.86	26,679	9,322,168	10
11	444,040	5.96	37,327	5.29	26,607	9,323,331	11
12	376,046	7.21	37,841	4.89	32,760	9,348,725	12
13	330,271	5.62	35,972	6.03	15,743	5,386,134	13
14	313,485	6.06	36,843	5.08	17,512	5,409,350	14
15	311,500	5.83	37,573	5.29	16,984	5,409,358	15
16	370,780	5.38	37,781	6.19	15,698	5,425,001	16
17	152,338	7.41	37,854	6.94	22,057	5,429,300	17
18	320,804	6.19	39,231	6.38	17,460	5,442,595	18
19	699,051	5.03	28,633	5.04	37,364	4,657,425	19
20	628,838	6.76	28,833	4.61	50,602	4,655,395	20
21	631,934	7.04	29,242	5.85	53,562	4,658,743	21
22	651,162	6.70	29,876	5.63	48,911	4,668,078	22
23	765,124	6.54	30,327	6.94	49,422	4,671,693	23
24	741,364	5.73	30,411	6.37	44,061	4,671,793	24
25	574,486	5.94	30,598	6.70	31,631	2,989,720	25
26	375,396	7.00	30,718	4.58	39,176	3,020,244	26
27	590,190	5.19	30,922	5.17	33,538	3,021,618	27
28	288,112	7.02	31,199	5.15	53,643	3,025,298	28
29	276,619	7.02	31,354	5.46	60,284	3,042,834	29
30	522,446	5.23	31,422	6.06	53,595	3,063,011	30
31	451,321	5.95	39,552	6.31	25,734	7,710,368	31
32	352,181	6.01	39,776	6.24	23,777	7,713,007	32
33	317,322	7.02	41,068	4.86	27,544	7,752,393	33
34	422,455	5.71	41,471	4.86	23,852	7,754,204	34
35	290,963	7.36	41,989	5.32	30,487	7,782,654	35
36	395,314	5.80	39,992	6.56	24,626	7,611,304	36
		$\bar{P} = 5.56$	$\bar{I} = 25,027$		$\bar{Adv} = 19,036$	$\bar{MSize} = 4,538,692$	

Economic Regression Equation (Tables 5.16, 5.17, 5.18, 5.19, 5.20, 5.21, 5.22, 5.23, and 5.24)

TABLE 5.16

Multiple Linear Regression—Estimated Regression Equation

Quant[t] = -75554.380995695 Price[t] $- 52.093823650183$ Income[t] $+ 34039.145543355$
Altprice[t] $+ 5.4264602658647$ Advs[t] $+ 0.062648748988615$ Msize[t] $+ 8927.0959264093$
Time[t] $+ 2047850.9667688 + e[t]$

TABLE 5.17

	Multiple Linear Regression—Ordinary Least Squares				
Variable	Parameter	SE	T-Stat H0: Parameter = 0	Two-Tail p-Value	One-Tail p-Value
Price[t]	−75554.380996	24092.234634	−3.136047	0.003905	0.001953
Income[t]	−52.093824	9.92233	−5.25016	1.3 E − 5	6.0E − 6
Altprice[t]	34039.145543	18958.255227	1.795479	0.083006	0.041503
Advs[t]	5.42646	1.262363	4.298654	0.000177	8.8 E − 5
Msize[t]	0.062649	0.010421	6.012041	2.0 E − 6	1.0 E − 6
Time[t]	8927.095926	2359.896594	3.782834	0.000719	0.00036
Constant	2047850.966769	305081.19038	6.712479	0	0

TABLE 5.18

Variable	Elasticity	SE[a]	T-Stat H0: [Elast] = 1	Two-Tail p-Value	One-Tail p-Value
%Price[t]	−1.153956	0.367965	0.418399	0.678738	0.339369
%Income[t]	−4.450076	0.847608	4.070369	0.00033	0.000165
%Altprice[t]	0.470024	0.261782	−2.024496	0.052215	0.026108
%Advs[t]	0.403103	0.093774	−6.36525	1.0 E − 6	0
%Msize[t]	0.877863	0.146018	−0.836452	0.40974	0.20487
%Time[t]	0.403206	0.106588	−5.599066	5.0 E − 6	2.0 E − 6
%Constant	4.999688	0.744835	5.369899	9.0 E − 6	5.0 E − 6

[a]*Note*: Computed against deterministic endogenous series.

TABLE 5.19

Variable	Stand. Coeff.	SE[a]	T-Stat H0: Coeff. = 0	Two-Tail p-Value	One-Tail p-Value
S-Price[t]	−0.312537	0.09966	−3.136047	0.003905	0.001953
S-Income[t]	−1.260259	0.240042	−5.25016	1.3 E − 5	6.0 E − 6
S-Altprice[t]	0.141319	0.078708	1.795479	0.083006	0.041503
S-Advs[t]	0.451487	0.10503	4.298654	0.000177	8.8 E − 5
S-Msize[t]	0.8331	0.138572	6.012041	2.0 E − 6	1.0 E − 6
S-Time[t]	0.577989	0.152793	3.782834	0.000719	0.00036
S-Constant	0	0	0	1	0.5

[a]*Note*: Computed against deterministic endogenous series.

TABLE 5.20

Variable	Partial Correlation
Price[t]	−0.503236
Income[t]	−0.698075
Altprice[t]	0.316295
Adv[t]	0.623856
Msize[t]	0.744874
Time[t]	0.57481
Constant	0.780007

Critical Values (Alpha = 5%)

One-tail CV at 5%	1.7
Two-tail CV at 5%	2.05

TABLE 5.21

Multiple Linear Regression—Regression Statistics

Multiple R	0.908842
R-squared	0.825994
Adjusted R-squared	0.789993
F-Test	22.943549
Observations	36
Degrees of freedom	29

Multiple Linear Regression—Residual Statistics

Standard error	74570.802224
Sum squared errors	161263331785.2
Log likelihood	−451.091927
Durbin–Watson	1.493541
Von Neumann ratio	1.536214
$e[t] > 0$	18
$e[t] < 0$	18
Number of runs	19
Stand. normal runs statistic	0

TABLE 5.22

Multiple Linear Regression—Analysis of Variance

ANOVA	DF	Sum of Squares	Mean Square
Regression	6	765507562071.02	127584593678.5
Residual	29	161263331785.2	5560804544.3173
Total	35	926770893856.22	26479168395.892
F-Test		22.943549	
p-Value		0	

TABLE 5.23

Student Distribution Probability (Mathematical Equation Plotter)

T-Test	$\boxed{-3.1360470352051}$
DF	$\boxed{29}$
Tails (1 or 2)	$\boxed{1}$
$\boxed{\text{Student Probability}}$	

TABLE 5.24

Fisher Distribution Probability (Mathematical Equation Plotter)

T-Test	$\boxed{22.9435}$
DF numerator	$\boxed{6}$
DF denominator	$\boxed{29}$
$\boxed{\text{Fisher Probability}}$	

5.6.1   Results and Interpretation

All the variables in the equation except the price of the alternative good were significant. Therefore, it would be wise to drop the alternative price from the estimated equation:

$$Q_x = 2,047,850 - 75,554P_x - 52I + 5.43\text{Adv}_x + 0.6\text{MSize} + 8,927T + e.$$

Significance of the variables was determined due to having *t*-values larger than the critical values in Table A.2 in the appendix). The coefficient *t*-statistics values were as follows (Table 5.25):

TABLE 5.25

−3.136047	For the price of pizza (P_x)
−5.25016	For consumer's income (I)
1.795479	For the alternative good price (P_y)
4.298654	For advertising expenditures (Adv_x)
6.012041	For market size (MSize)
3.782834	For time (T)
6.712479	For constant term (α)

All of the *t*-values except the alternative price value (1.795479) are larger than the critical value (in the table) at both 95% and 99% levels of confidence. This critical value is determined by looking across the confidence level and the DF:

$$\text{DF} = n - k$$
$$= 36 - 7 = 29.$$

The third column of the table gives the 95% confidence level at one- and two-tail probabilities. The last column gives the 99% level. The critical values are 2.045 and 2.756, respectively.

The computer calculated these values by dividing each value of the coefficient by its standard error:

$$t\text{-Statistics} = \frac{\text{Coeff. value}}{\text{SE}}.$$

For example,

$$\frac{-75554.380996}{24092.234634} = -3.136047.$$

If we look at the 2-tail p-value column in the printout and across the alternative price coefficient, we will read 0.083006. This number indicates that the alternative price estimate came at 91.6994% confidence and this was rejected because we wanted the confidence to be at least 95%.

All coefficients reflect the potential changes in revenue due to changes in the independent variables individually, and the signs reflect the direction of the relationship between the affecting factor (the independent variable) and the affected factor (the dependent variable). The price has a negative sign as it is consistent with the inverse relationship between price and demand. It is interesting enough that consumer income came with a negative relationship with demand contrary to the typical positive relationship for normal commodities. Here, it indicates that the frozen pizza has been considered by these consumers as an inferior good. It is most likely that the majority of those consumers would switch to fresh pizza or any other better-quality good as their income increases; hence, they divert from frozen pizza consumption the more they earn.

Advertising expenditures, market size, and time came with positive signs, indicating that demand or revenue would increase as the firm spends more on advertising as the size of the market increases, and as time moves forward. All of these results are consistent with the expected outcome.

As far as how the coefficients are explained in terms of quantifying the impact of the independent variable on the variation of the dependent variable, we can state the following:

- A drop in the price of frozen pizza by $1 per unit would result in increasing the demand and eventually the sales by $75,554.
- For each dollar the company spends on advertising, the sales of frozen pizza would increase by more than $5 ($5.43).
- As for the negative impact of income, we can state that for each dollar increase in the consumer's disposable income, the makers of this frozen pizza would experience a decrease in their sales by $52.09.
- Since market size is proxied by the population size in those specific areas where the frozen pizza is sold, we can state that for each additional consumer in the market, the sales of frozen pizza would increase by 6¢.
- The data in this example were collected quarterly. Therefore, we can state that moving forward from one quarter to the next has increased the sales by $8,927.

- The demand for frozen pizza was found elastic in terms of both price and income. Both price elasticity of demand and income elasticity of demand had values larger than 1, specifically 1.15 and 4.45, respectively.

In practice, we can calculate an estimated value of sales (Q_x) based on the average value of the independent variables:

$$Q_x = 2,047,850 - 75,554P_x - 52I + 5.43\text{Adv}_x + 0.06\text{MSize},$$

$$Q_x = 2,047,850 - 75,554(5.56) - 52(25,027) + 5.43(19,036) + 0.06(4,538,692),$$

$$Q_x = \$702,052.$$

Now, let us suppose the manager wants to see how much revenue he may expect if he raises the price of pizza by 44¢, that is, to make it $6.00.

The predicted sales, according to the equation above, would be

$$Q_x = 2,047,850 - 75,554(6.00) - 52(25,027) + 5.43(19,036) + 0.06(4,538,692),$$

$$Q_x = \$668,808.$$

So, raising the price by 44¢ would result in reducing the sales revenue to $668,808, that is, by $33,244.

5.6.2   Goodness of Fit

In order to test how good the choice of that group of independent variables is as they impact the dependent variable, and to what extent they work as explanatory factors in the variation of the dependent variable, we need to look at the coefficient of determination (R^2). It is a measure of how much all the independent variables together can explain the variation in the dependent variable. In other words, it is a measure of how well the regression equation fits the data or how fit the estimation model is to reality:

$$R^2 = \frac{\text{Explained variation by all indepednent variables}}{\text{Total variation in the dependent variable}}.$$

Between the two extreme values of R^2, giving a 100 for all the observations lined up perfectly on the regression line and zero for no relationship between the observations and the line, we should be able to understand any figure for R^2. In our printout, the R^2 is 82.6%, which is considered a very good fit. However, it is statistically advisable to rely on the adjusted R^2 when the number of observations gets larger.

While R^2 is obtained by subtracting the ratio of **sum of squared errors (SSE)** to sum of squared total (SST) from 1:

$$R^2 = 1 - \frac{\text{SSE}}{\text{SST}}.$$

The adjusted R^2 considers the sample size or the number of observations (N) and the DF ($N - k$) in that ratio:

$$\text{adj } R^2 = 1 - \frac{\left(\dfrac{\text{SSE}}{N - k}\right)}{\left(\dfrac{\text{SST}}{N - 1}\right)},$$

where k is the number of coefficients including the constant term (α). Our printout shows an adjusted R^2 of 79%, which is still a very good indication of a good fit. It means that all the independent variables together are able to explain 79% of the variation in the dependent variable.

5.6.3   The Overall Explanatory Power of the Model

How significant is the explanatory capacity of all the independent variables in their impact on the dependent variable can be tested by the **analysis of variance (ANOVA)** or F-statistics.

F-ratio uses R^2 and its complement in consideration of the number of observations and the DF:

$$F = \frac{\left(\dfrac{R^2}{k - 1}\right)}{\left(\dfrac{1 - R^2}{N - k}\right)},$$

where R^2 represents the explained portion of the variation in the dependent variable, $1 - R^2$ stands for the unexplained portion, k is the number of coefficients, and N is the number of observations.

The model would be significant if the calculated value of F-statistics is larger than the critical value in the table. The calculated value is

$$F = \frac{\dfrac{0.825994}{7 - 1}}{\dfrac{1 - 0.825994}{36 - 7}}$$

$$= \frac{0.137665666}{0.006000206897} = 22.9435.$$

The critical value is to be seen in the table across $k - 1$ and $N - k$, and depending on a level of significance (Tables A.3 and A.4 in the appendix):

$$k - 1 = 7 - 1 = 6,$$

$$N - k = 36 - 7 = 29.$$

Moving 6 rows vertically and 29 columns horizontally, we read the critical value of 2.43 at 5% significance and 3.50 at 1% significance. Our printout shows an F-ratio of 22.94. So the regression equation is significant at 95% and 99% confidence.

5.6.4   Major Problems to Check On

Multicollinearity   The regression model requires that there be no or at most weak correlations among the set of independent variables so that the model can accurately show the individual impact of those independent variables on the dependent variable. If it happens that there is some strong correlation among the independent variables, we would know that we have a problem of "**multicollinearity**." Most of the regression programs have the capacity to prompt an error message when the system detects strong correlations, and probably cease to perform the analysis. However, most systems would probably continue to perform with some degrees of correlation. This is why it would be up to the researcher to check the correlation matrix that would calculate and list all the correlations between all possible pairs of the independent variables. Strongly correlated variables should be dropped off the analysis. If, for example, there are five independent variables in the regression equation (x_1 to x_5), the correlation matrix may look similar to Table 5.26.

TABLE 5.26

	x_1	x_2	x_3	x_4	x_5
x_1	100				
x_2	0.32	100			
x_3	0.25	0.87	100		
x_4	0.41	0.38	0.43	100	
x_5	0.37	0.91	0.19	0.36	100

The diagonal line always shows perfect correlation of 1 or 100 since variables are perfectly correlated with themselves. The triangle above the diagonal line is usually left blank because it contains complete symmetrical values to the lower triangle since, for example, there is no difference between the correlation of x_1 and x_4, and x_4 and x_1. A correlation matrix like this clearly shows that there is a strong correlation between x_2 and x_5 (0.87) and between x_2 and x_3 (0.91). This suggests that x_2 should be dropped off the model. All the rest are tolerable correlations. There is another way to detect multicollinearity in the regression model. It is related to the major problem caused by multicollinearity shown by inflating the variance of the regression coefficient. Let us assume that we take the variable that showed a high correlation such as x_2 in the last correlation matrix, and run a new regression with it as a dependent variable for all the other independent variables. Then we can use the R^2 obtained in this regression $R^2_{x_2}$ as a measure for the variance inflation factor (VIF):

$$\text{VIF} = \frac{1}{1 - R^2_{x_2}}.$$

Most of the computer programs for running regression can report the VIF data. Having a list of VIF for all coefficients in the equation can tell a great deal. For example, a VIF of 5.5 across from the coefficient of x_3 means that the variance of the regression coefficient is 5.5 times what it would be had the multicollinearity problem not existed. The following graph depicts the relationship between $R^2_{x_2}$ and VIF, which shows that at a perfect coefficient of determination ($R^2_{x_2} = 1$), the VIF would reach infinity. The point is that higher $R^2_{x_2}$ are associated with higher VIFs (see Figure 5.5).

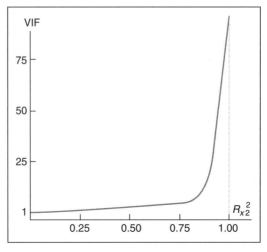

FIGURE 5.5

The conclusion is that multicollinearity can be a serious problem in producing less than reliable coefficient estimates. It can affect the regression model by inflating the variance of coefficient, altering their magnitude, and changing their signs. Remedies for multicollinearity include dropping off the culprit variable, creating a new variable by combining the highly correlated ones, running different regressions such as ridge regression and other statistical methods to remove or minimize the effects of multicollinearity.

Autocorrelation   Another problem that regression estimation may face could stem from violating one of the basic assumptions of the regression model, that is, the independence of the error terms through observations. So, if it happens that the error terms are found to be correlated through the lagged terms, we would have another problem at hand called "**autocorrelation**." It is defined as the correlation among the values of a variable throughout time, between the current time (t) and the previous periods ($t - 1, t - 2, \ldots t - n$).

The Durbin–Watson statistical test was developed in 1951 to detect any evidence of a first-order autocorrelation in the regression model. Its value (d) is calculated as

$$d = \frac{\sum_{t=2}^{n} [e_t - e_{t-1}]^2}{\sum_{t=1}^{n} e_t^2}.$$

Most statistical programs for running regression analysis would produce the Durbin–Watson value, which should be compared against the critical values of the lower and upper d (Tables A.5 and A.6 in the appendix). The critical value is read based on either 95% or 99% level of significance (5% and 1% tables) where n is the number of observations and k is the number of independent variables in the regression equation. This test is good only for regression equations estimated for at least 15 observations. The test of the estimated

Durbin–Watson statistic (d) against the critical value can be done for both positive and negative autocorrelations:

If $d > d_u$: There is **no** evidence of positive autocorrelation.

If $d < d_L$: There is evidence of positive autocorrelation.

If d between d_L and d_u: The test is inconclusive.

As for the negative autocorrelation, we use four as the maximum value of d according to its range (0–4):

If $d > (4 - d_L)$: There is evidence of negative autocorrelation.

If $d < (4 - d_u)$: There is **no** evidence of negative autocorrelation.

If d between $(4 - d_L)$ and $(4 - d_u)$: The test is inconclusive.

Generally, we can say that if the estimated d turns out to be equal to two or more, it would be a sure confirmation that there is no evidence of any autocorrelation.

In our printout, the Durbin–Watson statistic is 1.49. Looking at the 5% table, across $n = 36$ and $k = 5$ (the maximum value in the table), we find that $d_L = 1.18$ and $d_u = 1.80$, which says that the test for positive autocorrelation is inconclusive since the estimated value of 1.49 is in between the lower and upper critical values. The estimated d is also in between the critical values in the 1% table where $d_L = 0.99$ and $d_u = 1.59$.

As for the negative autocorrelation, the estimated d of 1.49 is less than $4 - d_u$ ($4 - 1.80 = 2.20$) at the 5% table, and less than ($4 - 1.59 = 2.41$) at the 1% table, which indicates that there is no evidence of any negative autocorrelation.

If the **Durbin–Watson test** confirms the existence of autocorrelation, it would be a reason to doubt the accuracy of the estimates. In such cases, there are several remedies to remove or reduce the harmful effects of autocorrelation. These remedies include adding time as an independent variable to give the trend dimension to data, adding other important but missed independent variables, rerunning the regression in a nonlinear format, and changing the OLS method to an alternative technique such as the generalized least squares (GLS) method.

Heteroscedasticity   Another problem that may distort the regression estimation is **heteroscedasticity**. One of the basic assumptions in the regression model is that the error term would have a normal distribution with zero mean and constant variance. Therefore, if it happens that the variance of the error term is nonconstant, whether decreasing or increasing, the model would suffer heteroscedasticity. Look at the following scatter graph to make sense of both decreasing and increasing variances of the error term around the regression line, and the increase in the value of the independent variable.

One of the ways to test for the existence of heteroscedasticity is to divide the errors (the difference between actual and predicted data) into two groups based on low and high values of the independent variable and test whether the two groups differ from each other significantly. If they do, then that would be a sign for heteroscedasticity. To overcome the effects of heteroscedasticity on the accuracy and reliability of the estimates, many options may be tried such as running the logarithmic form of the regression equation, using weighted data such as dividing all variables including the dependent variable by the value of the variable that is the source of heteroscedasticity, and last but not least, using the GLS (see Figures 5.6 and 5.7).

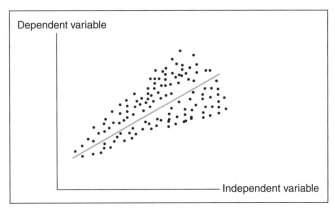

FIGURE 5.6

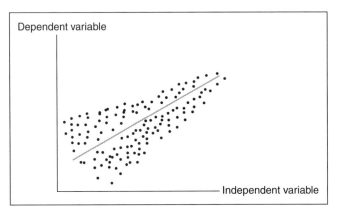

FIGURE 5.7

5.7   NONREGRESSION APPROACHES TO ESTIMATION

There are many ways other than regression, and its highly involved statistical procedures, to estimate market demand and assess its parameters. Many managers have handled market information and understood consumer behavior and preferences and in many respects succeeded to capture a good picture of the market demand. We can briefly group these nonregression methods into three categories.

5.7.1   Market Experimentation

This method takes place in the real market and in real time. It basically involves changing one major factor such as price, packaging, taste, and flavor and recording the consumer response to that change. It can be done either across different markets, different group-ing of consumers, or in the same market against a competitor. Fast-food franchises and soft-drink and food companies are typical examples of firms practicing this method. Mc-Donalds may come up with a new menu or modified recipe to test the response of its customers as well as to test against the products of its competitors such as Burger King or Wendy's. Pepsi Cola may come up with a new flavor or introduce a new sweetener in its diet Pepsi and gauge the response against its own products and the competitor's products. Price can always be the factor to change in such experiments to see how the demand would respond. One of the disadvantages of this method is that only one factor is being changed in each experiment and in conditions that may not be fully controlled. Also, these experiments are expensive, short run, small scale, and there are many questions about their generalizability.

5.7.2 Observational Studies

Watching what consumers buy and do not buy is one of the most basic and oldest ways to directly know about market demand without any complications. However, the expansion of the market and of the variety of products, and the change in consumers' tastes and preferences made this simple way harder to be efficient. Asking consumers directly about what they prefer and how they feel about these changes opens the way for a wide variety of market research. The research methodology includes questioning a sample of consumers and obtaining their direct answers by email or phone surveys, market interviews, focus groups, panel or case studies, consumer seminars or clinics, and laboratory and experimental economies. All these methods can provide a wealth of valuable information on consumers and their demand, but they all remain, by their nature, subject to serious shortcomings such as the extent to which the studied sample is highly representative of all consumers, and to what extent consumer answers are reliable. It is very well known that most consumers cannot or would not provide accurate answers to some questions, either because they are hypothetical, involves memory, or because consumers usually give the answers that they may think are more acceptable than the true answers. This is why it becomes much wiser for firms to supplement data obtained by these methods by more accurate data obtained by observations. Nowadays, store scanners can provide very accurate information on demand on everything that is sold. This information is truly valuable in the whole scheme of estimating consumer demand.

5.7.3 Micromarketing and Virtual Shopping

Micromarketing is the latest trend that narrows down the scale of targets and focuses on smaller units such as individual stores or specific groups of consumers or even individual consumers. Information from secondary data such as the census or primary data such as shop scanners and marketing research are used to identify specific targets for specific marketing schemes. For example, the demographics of consumers such as income, age, sex, family size, hobbies and interests, number of children, and number of pets are the pieces of information needed to tailor the marketing strategies to such a population of consumers. Banking industries, financial services, and insurance companies were among the first to try one-on-one marketing in which products are fitted to individual consumers. Dell is considered among the first to individually customize orders. Also, the auto industries have done that but on a very limited scale that got expanded later. Nowadays, online firms of many products can target and individually customize orders.

With the remarkable advancement in computers and their applications, along with expansion in their acceptance and use by people, many new marketing strategies have been played out in the market. One of these innovative ways is virtual shopping. It is an entire shopping experience done visually through a computer screen. A simulation program can create an entire store that a consumer can go through visually and inspect and compare products, read labels, and know other information, then choose and pay for them, all in visual effects. After overcoming the initial cost of this technology, this method can be economical in conducting consumer and marketing research without the real work of tracking down consumer purchases in the real market.

5.8   ADVANCED DEMAND ESTIMATION: THE PAD MODEL

Economists have frequently modeled consumer demand in the presence of consumer habit persistence using the **partial adjustment demand (PAD)** model. The use of the model has also sometimes been motivated by consumer capital goods rigidities. Because of the apparent pervasiveness of habit persistence in the consumption of basic goods, this model of demand has achieved widespread use in modeling demand for consumer goods.

There are two standard forms of the PAD model—linear and constant elasticity. A critical feature of the linear PAD is its distinction between "desired" and "actual" demand for a good at a point of time. The change in actual quantity demanded is specified as a linear function of the difference between the desired quantity demanded and lagged consumption. The lag period used in the PAD is very often 1 year. (This means that the lag period is 1 when annual data are being used, 4 when quarterly data are being used, 12 when monthly data are being used, etc.) Hence, the PAD comprises two equations—an equation that expresses **desired demand** and an equation that expresses the adjustment in actual demand. However, as shown below, only one equation (the "estimating equation" or more formally the "reduced form of the PAD") need be estimated statistically in order to have estimates of all the unknown parameters in the linear PAD.

5.8.1   Model Specification

The complete specification of the PAD in its linear form is as follows.

Desired Demand   Desired demand during period t, Q_t^*, is expressed as a linear function of the demand variables such as price, income, other prices, and so on. Hence, desired demand is the demand derived from consumer utility maximization subject to an income constraint. It would arise in the same manner as the demand for any product would and in a manner that we have already seen. The linear form of desired demand is given by

$$Q_t^* = a + bP_t + cI_t.$$

Note that for brevity in the exposition of the PAD here, desired demand is expressed as a function of only price and income, with the understanding that other variables can also be included when it is important to do so.

Adjustment Equation   Due to habit persistence, desired demand is not assumed to be observed in the PAD during period t, but rather, only the actual quantity demanded during period t is observed. The change in the actual quantity demanded between periods t and $t-1$ is assumed to be proportional to the difference between the desired quantity demanded during period t and the lagged (by 1 year, typically) actual quantity demanded. Algebraically,

$$Q_t - Q_{t-1} = \rho \left(Q_t^* - Q_{t-1} \right).$$

This latter equation is referred to as the adjustment equation since it shows how actual quantity demanded adjusts over time. The adjustment parameter is traditionally represented by the Greek letter ρ (pronounced "row").

To find the estimating equation that follows from the equations for desired demand and the adjustment equation shown above, first substitute the desired demand into the adjustment equation to obtain

$$Q_t - Q_{t-1} = \rho(a + bP_t + cI_t - Q_{t-1}).$$

Estimating Equation Solving the expression immediately above for the actual quantity demanded at time t, Q_t, would give us

$$Q_t = \rho a + \rho b P_t + \rho c I_t + (1 - \rho)Q_{t-1},$$

which is the **estimating equation**. Given observations on the actual quantity demanded, price, and income, all of the unknown parameters can be estimated using a method such as maximum likelihood estimate (MLE).

5.8.2 Graph of the Linear PAD Model

To get a better understanding of the PAD model of consumer demand, consider Figure 5.7, which shows how it works. For simplicity, the income variable is omitted from the exposition.

Initially, the market is in equilibrium (P_0, $Q_0 = Q_0^*$) with the same actual and desired demand:

$$Q_0 = \rho a - \rho b P_0 + (1 - \rho)Q_0^*,$$
$$= \rho a - \rho b P_0 + (1 - \rho)Q_0 \left(\text{since } Q_0 = Q_0^*\right),$$

so

$$Q_0 - (1 - \rho)Q_0 = \rho a - \rho b P_0.$$

Simplifying the left-hand side gives

$$\rho Q_0 = \rho a - \rho b P_0,$$

or

$$Q_0 = a - b P_0.$$

Now, suppose that price increases to $P_1 > P_0$:

Period 1

$$\text{Desired demand: } Q_1^* = a - bP_1.$$

$$\text{Actual demand: } Q_1 = \rho a - \rho b P_1 + (1 - \rho)Q_0^*.$$

Note that Q_1 is found by moving along the actual demand curve. This is the short-run demand curve labeled Q_1 on the diagram.

Period 2

$$\text{Desired demand: } Q_2^* = a - bP_1,$$

which is the same as during period 1.

$$\text{Actual demand: } Q_2 = \rho a - \rho b P_1 + (1 - \rho)Q_1.$$

Note that the actual demand curve shifts down (the downward shift occurs because $Q_1 < Q_0^*$) and that Q_2 is shown as the new (shifted) actual demand curve on the diagram. $Q_2 < Q_1$, as some further adjustment toward desired demand at the higher price has occurred.

Beyond period 2

The actual demand curve continues to shift down each period until it passes through P_1, Q_1^*. This is the new long-run equilibrium (desired) demand. In practice, the number of periods until at least 90% of the shifting to Q_1^* is regarded as the long run (later we will see how to find out how long the long run is).

Short- and long-run price and income elasticities and the length of the long run

Short- and long-run prices and income elasticities are found as

$$\text{SRPrice} = \rho b_1 \left[\frac{\text{Mean of } \dfrac{P_t}{\text{CPI}_t}}{\text{Mean of } \dfrac{Q_t}{\text{Pop}_t}} \right],$$

$$\text{SRInc} = \rho b_2 \left[\frac{\text{Mean of } \dfrac{I_t}{\text{CPI}_t \text{Pop}_t}}{\text{Mean of } \dfrac{Q_t}{\text{Pop}_t}} \right],$$

$$\text{LRPrice} = b_1 \left[\frac{\text{Mean of } \dfrac{P_t}{\text{CPI}_t}}{\text{Mean of } \dfrac{Q_t}{\text{Pop}_t}} \right],$$

$$\text{LRInc} = b_2 \left[\frac{\text{Mean of } \dfrac{I_t}{\text{CPI}_t \text{Pop}_t}}{\text{Mean of } \dfrac{Q_t}{\text{Pop}_t}} \right].$$

The number of periods (usually years) until at least 90% of the effect of a change in price or income is realized is taken to be the long run.

With this definition, it can be shown that for the PAD, the long run is the smallest value of n that solves

$$\rho(1 - \rho)^0 + \rho(1 - \rho)^1 + \rho(1 - \rho)^2 + \cdots + \rho(1 - \rho)^n \geq 0.90.$$

The complete specification of the PAD in its constant elasticity form is as follows:

Desired demand

$$Q_t^* = aP_t^b I_t^c.$$

Adjustment equation

$$\frac{Q_t}{Q_{t-1}} = \left[\frac{Q_t^*}{Q_{t-1}}\right]^\rho.$$

Estimating equation

$$Q_t = \rho a P_t^{\rho b} I_t^{\rho c} Q_{t-1}^{1-\rho}.$$

Short- and long-run price and income elasticities are found as

$$\text{SRPrice} = \rho b_1,$$

$$\text{SRInc} = \rho b_2,$$

$$\text{LRPrice} = b_1,$$

$$\text{LRInc} = b_2.$$

The number of periods (usually years) until at least 90% of the effect of a change in price or income is realized is taken to be the long run.

With this definition, it can be shown that, as for the linear case, for the constant elasticity PAD, the long run is the smallest value of n that solves

$$\rho(1 - \rho)^0 + \rho(1 - \rho)^1 + \rho(1 - \rho)^2 + \cdots + \rho(1 - \rho)^n \geq 0.90.$$

Example 5.2
Estimates of US Gasoline Demand with the PAD Model
We estimate the linear and constant elasticity PAD models with parameter vectors, θ_j by MLE as discussed in Chapter 2. First, a monthly linear demand relationship in the gasoline market is estimated assuming a partial adjustment framework consisting of desired demand,

an adjustment equation, and an estimating equation with an additive normal error where Q_t is the gasoline quantity demanded, I_t is the personal income divided by the consumer price index, and P_t is the gasoline price divided by the consumer price index, all at time t. The disturbance term, u_t, is assumed to be independent and identically normally distributed with mean zero and constant variance:

Desired demand: $Q_t^* = a + bP_t + cI_t; t = 1, 2, \ldots, T$,

Adjustment equation: $Q_t - Q_{t-12} = \rho(Q_t^* - Q_{t-12})$,

Estimating equation: $Q_t = \rho a + \rho b P_t + \rho c I_t + (1 - \rho)Q_{t-12} + u_t$,

or $\qquad Q_t = \theta_{01} + \theta_{11} P_t + \theta_{21} I_t + \theta_{31} Q_{t-12} + u_t$,

where $u_t \sim N(0, \sigma_1^2)$ and $\theta_1 = \left(\theta_{01}, \theta_{11}, \theta_{21}, \theta_{31}, \sigma_1^2\right)$.

The log-likelihood function is

$$\ln L(\theta_1) = -(T - 12) \ln \left[\sqrt{2\pi\sigma_1^2}\right] - \frac{1}{2\sigma_1^2} \Sigma_{t=13}^{T} [Q_t - \theta_{01} + \theta_{11} P_t + \theta_{21} I_t \theta_{31} \theta_{t-12}]^2.$$

With the same notation, a constant elasticity demand relationship in the gasoline market is estimated assuming a partial adjustment framework consisting of desired demand, an adjustment equation, and an estimating equation with an additive normal error:

Desired demand: $Q_t^* = aP_t^b I_t^c; t = 1, 2, \ldots, T$,

Adjustment equation: $\dfrac{Q_t}{Q_{t-1}} = \left(\dfrac{Q_t^*}{Q_{t-12}}\right)^\rho$,

Estimating equation: $Q_t = a^\rho P_t^{\rho b} I_t^{\rho c} Q_{t-12}^{1-\rho} + u_t$,

or $\qquad Q_t = \theta_{02} P_t^{\theta_{12}} I_t^{\theta_{22}} Q_{t-12}^{\theta_{32}} + u_t$,

where $u_t \sim N(0, \sigma_2^2)$ and $\theta_2 = \left(\theta_{02}, \theta_{12}, \theta_{22}, \theta_{32}, \sigma_2^2\right)$.

The log-likelihood function is

$$\ln L(\theta_2) = -(T - 12) \ln \left[\sqrt{2\pi\sigma_2^2}\right] - \frac{1}{2\sigma_2^2} \sum_{t=13}^{T} \left[Q_t - \theta_{02} P_t^{\theta_{12}} I_t^{\theta_{22}} Q_{t-12}^{\theta_{32}}\right]^2.$$

Data used to estimate the linear and constant elasticity PAD models are shown in Table 5.27. MLEs of the parameters in the linear and constant elasticity PAD models of US gasoline demand are shown in Table 5.28, while estimates of short-run and long-run price and income elasticities and the length of the long run are shown in Table 5.29 (see Figure 5.8).

TABLE 5.27   Gasoline Quantity, Gasoline Price, Personal Income, and Consumer Price Index, January 2000–December 2005

Date	Gasoline Quantity (1000 barrels)	Gasoline Price (< per gallon)	Personal Income (billion $)	Consumer Price Index (1967 = 100)
2000				
January	237,243	135.6	8056.4	505.8
February	232,148	142.2	8099.6	508.7
March	257,455	159.4	8161.6	512.8
April	251,250	156.1	8209.3	513.2
May	268,491	155.2	8237.6	513.6
June	264,720	166.6	8279.5	516.5
July	267,902	164.2	8300.0	517.5
August	276,551	155.9	8326.5	517.6
September	255,540	163.5	8420.6	520.3
October	260,927	161.3	8405.7	521.2
November	251,520	160.8	8420.1	521.5
December	268,770	154.4	8455.5	521.1
2001				
January	244,528	152.5	8504.3	524.5
February	219,016	153.8	8640.2	526.7
March	248,341	150.3	8676.2	528.0
April	253,500	161.7	8697.0	529.9
May	268,181	181.2	8709.3	532.2
June	259,110	173.1	8737.6	533.3
July	262,911	156.5	8768.5	531.6
August	256,587	150.9	8775.9	531.8
September	251,430	160.9	8771.0	534.0
October	261,826	144.2	8761.4	532.2
November	250,980	132.4	8760.0	531.3
December	257,331	120.0	8794.6	529.2
2002				
January	252,061	120.9	8766.8	530.6
February	227,836	121.0	8807.2	532.7
March	250,263	132.4	8836.3	535.5
April	258,180	149.3	8865.5	538.6
May	271,188	150.8	8904.9	538.5
June	259,830	148.9	8971.7	538.9
July	268,987	149.6	8965.0	539.5
August	268,088	150.8	8992.2	541.2
September	251,370	150.7	9022.2	542.1
October	253,146	153.5	9048.7	543.2
November	253,530	153.4	9078.3	543.1
December	271,777	147.7	8994.1	541.9

(Continued)

TABLE 5.27 (*Continued*)

Date	Gasoline Quantity (1000 barrels)	Gasoline Price (< per gallon)	Personal Income (billion $)	Consumer Price Index (1967 = 100)
2003				
January	243,970	155.7	9012.5	544.2
February	218,400	168.6	9046.9	548.5
March	239,444	179.1	9086.6	551.8
April	244,830	170.4	9100.8	550.5
May	257,641	158.7	9151.0	549.7
June	248,790	155.8	9186.0	550.4
July	257,920	156.7	9219.6	550.9
August	259,005	167.1	9239.6	553.0
September	246,840	177.1	9268.4	554.7
October	255,843	164.6	9285.1	554.3
November	253,500	157.8	9317.0	552.7
December	264,740	153.8	9335.8	552.1
2004				
January	246,636	163.5	9404.1	554.9
February	223,412	171.5	9445.9	557.9
March	251,162	180.9	9484.9	561.5
April	246,990	187.5	9550.0	563.2
May	261,857	205.0	9603.8	566.4
June	250,080	208.3	9624.2	568.2
July	259,470	198.2	9668.5	567.5
August	259,067	194.1	9706.3	567.6
September	239,790	193.4	9726.4	568.7
October	259,904	207.2	9800.0	571.9
November	250,380	205.3	9924.9	572.2
December	268,429	192.6	10204.9	570.1
2005				
January	250,914	186.6	10025.2	571.2
February	229,712	196.0	10072.9	574.5
March	249,240	210.7	10122.0	579.0
April	254,640	232.5	10145.1	582.9
May	260,741	225.7	10180.6	582.4
June	256,110	221.8	10231.5	582.6
July	256,959	235.7	10274.7	585.2
August	255,595	254.1	10058.7	588.2
September	238,260	296.9	10359.6	595.4
October	245,018	278.5	10413.1	596.7
November	251,160	234.3	10442.9	592.0
December	259,532	218.6	10504.9	589.4

TABLE 5.28   Estimated Linear and Constant Elasticity PAD Models of US Gasoline Demand, January 2000–December 2005

Model	Parameter	Maximum Likelihood Estimate	Estimated Asymptotic Standard Error	Estimated Asymptotic t-Statistic
Linear	θ_{01}	−20228.2	46968.7	−0.43067
lnL	θ_{11}	−37409.2	21996.8	−1.70067
−611.864	θ_{21}	5103.11	2834.4	1.80042
	θ_{31}	0.761989	0.067879	11.2257
	σ_1	6495.1	592.919	10.9544
Constant Elasticity	θ_{02}	7.0888	7.2768	0.974164
lnL	θ_{12}	−0.047263	0.029151	−1.62131
−611.828	θ_{22}	0.348746	0.189944	1.83605
	θ_{32}	0.758617	0.068130	11.1348
	σ_2	6491.13	592.556	10.9544

TABLE 5.29   Estimated Linear and Constant Elasticity PAD Model of US Gasoline Demand, January 2000–December 2005

	Linear	Constant Elasticity
Price elasticity		
Short run	−0.047155	−0.047263
Long run	−0.198121	−0.195801
Income elasticity		
Short run	0.361091	0.348746
Long run	1.51712	1.44478
Length of long run	8.5	8.3

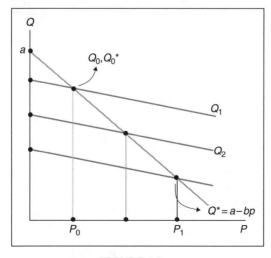

FIGURE 5.8

SUMMARY

- In this chapter, we moved from the theoretical analysis of demand, discussed in the previous chapter, to the empirical estimation of demand in order to validate the theory that we learned throughout Chapters 3 and 4. We started with the most simple market experimentations that were commonly tried by many managers to estimate the demand for their products and to adjust to what they experienced and expected.

- The central part of the chapter was the method of estimation by regression, which is the most common and dependable way to provide reasonable and reliable results. The discussion included the fitting process, reliability of the estimated results, and the interpretation of the results, along with examining the estimated parameters and checking their ability to explain. The discussion also included an overview of the potential estimation problems and the appropriate ways to deal with them. Among these problems are multicollinearity, autocorrelation, and heteroscedasticity. Practical and comprehensive examples were worked out to show the process of estimation by regression analysis.

- Other nonregression methods of estimation were discussed, such as market experimentation, observational studies, micromarketing, and virtual shopping. The chapter was concluded by a section on advanced demand estimation where the partial adjustment demand (PAD) model was explained.

KEY TERMS

market experimentation
regression analysis
reliability of estimation
goodness of fit
coefficient of
   determination (R^2)
parameters
independent variable
dependent variable
   intercept

error term
explanatory power
analysis of variance
   (ANOVA)
F-ratio
sum of squared errors
   (SSE)
degree of freedom
multicollinearity
autocorrelation

Durbin–Watson test
heteroscedasticity
observational studies
micromarketing
virtual shopping
partial adjustment demand
   (PAD) model
desired demand
adjustment equation

LIST OF FORMULAS

- The estimated value of Y:

$$\hat{Y} = \hat{\alpha} + \hat{\beta}x.$$

- The error term:

$$e = Y - \hat{Y}$$

$$e = Y - \hat{\alpha} - \hat{\beta}x.$$

- Sum of squared errors:

$$\sum e^2 = \sum [Y - \hat{\alpha} - \hat{\beta}x]^2.$$

- Estimated β:

$$\hat{\beta} = \frac{\sum [x - \bar{x}][y - \bar{y}]}{\sum [x - \bar{x}]^2}.$$

- Estimated α:

$$\hat{\alpha} = \bar{Y} - \hat{\beta}\bar{x}.$$

- Standard deviation:

$$S_\beta = \sqrt{\frac{\sum [Y - \hat{Y}]^2}{(n - k) \sum [x - \bar{x}]^2}}.$$

- t-Statistic:

$$t = \frac{\beta}{S_\beta}.$$

- Coefficient of determination:

$$R^2 = \frac{\sum [\hat{Y} - \bar{Y}]^2}{\sum [Y - \bar{Y}]^2},$$

$$\text{also}: \quad R^2 = 1 - \frac{\text{SSE}}{\text{SST}}.$$

- Adjusted R^2:

$$\text{Adj } R^2 = 1 - \frac{\left[\dfrac{\text{SSE}}{N - K}\right]}{\left[\dfrac{\text{SST}}{N - 1}\right]}.$$

- Correlation coefficient:

$$r = \sqrt{R^2}.$$

- Estimated demand function:

$$Q_x = \alpha + \beta P_x + e.$$

- Degree of freedom:

$$df = n - k.$$

- *F*-statistic:

$$F = \frac{\left[\dfrac{R^2}{K-1}\right]}{\left[\dfrac{1-R^2}{N-K}\right]}.$$

- Variance inflation factor:

$$\text{VIF} = \frac{1}{1 - R^2_{x_2}}.$$

- Durbin–Watson statistic:

$$d = \frac{\displaystyle\sum_{t=2}^{n}[e_t - e_{t-1}]^2}{\displaystyle\sum_{t=1}^{n} e_t^2}.$$

- Desired demand:

$$Q_t^* = a P_t^b I_t^c.$$

- Adjustment equation:

$$\frac{Q_t}{Q_{t-1}} = \left[\frac{Q_t^*}{Q_{t-1}}\right]^{\rho}.$$

- Estimating equation:

$$Q_t = \rho a P_t^{\rho b} I_t^{\rho c} Q_{t-1}^{(1-\rho)}.$$

EXERCISES

1. What is the significance of demand estimation? Discuss how it is important to the theory and to managers and their business strategies.

2. Review and compare the advantages and disadvantages of the different methods available for demand empirical estimation.

3. Describe the process of demand estimation by the regression method from the beginning to the end and specify what it needs to be a reliable method of estimation.

4. What are the major problems that may arise in the execution of the regression method? Explain how they are checked, their effects on the results and their interpretation, and how they are corrected.

5. What is PAD? How does it work? How important is it to empirically estimate market demand?

6. The following data are for a small firm:

Revenue	Advertising Expenditures
88,000	20,000
80,000	18,000
84,000	22,000
92,000	24,000
96,000	22,000
104,000	24,000
108,000	26,000
116,000	26,000
118,000	28,000
120,000	30,000

(a) Use the regression method to show how spending on advertisement affects the firm's revenue.

(b) Draw the estimated regression line to illustrate the errors, the slope, and the intercept.

(c) Estimate the firm's revenue if the expenditure on advertisement becomes $45,000.

7. Estimate the regression equation (Q) for the following demand data where the independent variables are price (P) and consumer income (I). Also, test the statistical significance of the estimated parameters at the 5% level and show to what extent the independent variables can explain the variation in the quantities demanded.

Q_x	P_x	I
2880	12.00	32,000
3600	8.00	31,500
3241	10.00	34,600
3420	8.00	33,160
3042	10.00	33,980
3600	8.00	35,610
3423	10.00	36,720
3600	8.00	38,000
3965	8.00	37,190
3786	8.00	39,890

6

CONSUMER DEMAND: ECONOMIC FORECASTING

Demand forecasting is closely related to the process of estimation explained in Chapter 5. Both processes are mostly related on the common ground of regression analysis, which involves setting the real data into dependent–independent variables and quantifying their impact by obtaining the estimated values of parameters.

Forecasting is the process of predicting the future state and value of economic variables and their change using current knowledge and present and past data. It is all about projecting the past and present into the future. Some might say that it is very difficult to be accurate to the point of certainty because forecasting is an adventure into the practically unknown and what has not happened yet. Ironically, though, the major justification of forecasting is the very need to reduce life's uncertainties and minimize risks. All decisions taken today are connected to past experience as given facts and are to be connected to potential future development. This is the reason why decision makers in public and private enterprises, as well as at an individual level, need to predict the future events.

Most business managers know that forecasting can be a difficult and daunting process, but they also recognize it as one of the most important tasks to facilitate decision making. Managerial choice to predict sales, for example, would have a significant impact on planning for material and equipment capacities for production, employment size, inventories and storage requirements, and maintenance services. It would impact the financial manager's plans for the firm's cash flow, investment and capital budgeting, and projected profits and losses. In marketing, the sales forecast would be essential to plan for a sensible distribution program, promotional strategy, and marketing budget. Forecasts of future sales would also be used in personnel plans for hiring, promotion, staff structure, reward and retirement programs, and so on. The major point to emphasize here is that any decision would not be sound if it is isolated from the future development of the contributing and related factors.

Managerial Economics: A Mathematical Approach, First Edition. M. J. Alhabeeb and L. Joe Moffitt.
© 2013 John Wiley & Sons, Inc. Published 2013 by John Wiley & Sons, Inc.

6.1 FORECASTING MODELS

Forecasting is both an art and science. Its major objective is to help make the best possible judgment about the future circumstances and conditions as they are predicted by a variety of methods. The most sensible approach is to combine the hard statistical fact with thoughtful, unbiased, and fair subjective judgment that utilizes solid experience and practical wisdom. There are many types of forecasting models. Each can be more appropriate than the others depending on a host of determinants such as

- what is being predicted and whether the purpose is to examine the trend continuation or certain turning points;
- the time factor, which includes
  - projection time, whether it is for a short or long term;
  - time frame available to conduct the forecasting;
  - lead time, during which the firm can make decisions using the estimations of the forecasting model;
- cost of the process;
- the accuracy level needed for the forecasts;
- availability of the data needed;
- complexity of the forecasting model.

In terms of the scale of the process and its variables, forecasting can be either **macro-forecasting**, where the subjects are at the aggregate level such as the gross domestic product, national employment, national inflation rate, interest rate fluctuation, and national money supply, or **micro-forecasting**, which involves variables at the level of an industry, a firm, or specific market such as predicting the demand of a certain product or a product line. Forecasting can also be conducted at a subset micro-level or an individual level of consumers, markets, and products.

Types of forecasting depend on the use of analytical methods, which can be broadly categorized into quantitative and qualitative models.

6.1.1 Quantitative Models

Quantitative models involve utilizing historical data and relying on numerical representation of the observations for the purpose of describing and explaining the trend and changes that the observations reflect. There are two kinds of the quantitative models:

(a) **Structural models**, which focus on the dependent–independent relationships between variables for the purpose of quantifying the impact of the independent variables on the variations in the dependent variable. Econometric models of forecasting are representative of the structural type.

(b) **Nonstructural models**, which are concerned with observing patterns of change in the variables over time. The time series models and barometric models are representative of this type.

6.1.2 Qualitative Models

These models use nonnumerical examination and interpretation of observations for the purpose of discovering the underlying patterns of relationships and inferring their meaning and significance. Value judgment is the major tool in the qualitative analysis in contrast to relying on the objective technical facts as in the case of quantitative models. Models that depend on expert opinion, polls and market research, and consumer surveys are representative of qualitative forecasting models.

In this chapter, first we focus on quantitative models and then briefly describe qualitative models. We start here with the most common model of time series, which constitutes more than two-thirds of the forecasting techniques used by businesses in the United States, according to a recent survey by the Institute of Business Forecasting.

6.2 TIME SERIES ANALYSIS

The time series method of forecasting uses historical data and applies the ordinary least squares statistical techniques to obtain predictions of future values. It basically extrapolates data from the past and present into the future period for the purpose of identifying general patterns in the development of a single variable throughout the time. This method allows us to make forward projections from the data that have long-term trends through the utilization of a simple bivariate regression model, where the time trend (t) serves as the explanatory variable for the changes in the dependent variable.

The long-term development of a variable can be plain and smooth if it follows a straightforward **secular trend**, but often, it contains several sorts of variations that would affect the real value of the variable if it is predicted from the general unadjusted progress. This is why an essential part of this analysis is to recognize and count for these possible fluctuations within the general flow of data. Calculating the impact of these variations allows the adjustment of the forecasts made on the basis of the estimates that the regression equation yields for more realistic values. Most of the variations in the time series data are due to the following common patterns.

6.2.1 Secular Trends

A secular trend is a long-term consistent development in a variable value that is often characterized by a general steadily increasing or decreasing pattern and most likely represented by a solid smooth line going upward or downward. Population growth and per capita income are typical examples of the increasing secular trend, whereas goods that go out of date over time such as typewriters, cable phones, and personal train transportation are typical decreasing secular trends.

6.2.2 Seasonal Variations

These are recurring rhythmic fluctuations that usually reflect certain seasons, weather conditions, or specific periodic occasions such as school time or holidays like Christmas or Thanksgiving. The sales of many products can reflect typical seasonality such as air conditioners, fans, swimsuits, shorts, and tourism services in summer; snow blowers, snow tires, heavy coats in winter; garden products in spring; turkey on Thanksgiving; and gifts during Christmas times.

6.2.3   Cyclical Fluctuations

These are long-term patterns of expansion and contraction in the economic activityin general that reflect the recurring conditions of the economic business cycle that characterizes the free-market economy. The construction and housing sector, for example, exhibits a typical long-term cycle in its activity that could last 10 years or more, whereas other sectors may experience shorter cycles.

6.2.4   Random Changes

These changes are reflection of the irregular, unpredictable fluctuations that are due to events such as war, political instability, natural disasters, and strikes. This type of variation is very difficult to count for in any modeling due to the random nature of its occurrence and the degree of its impact.

Mathematically, the actual value of a variable in the time series data (Y_t) can be expressed as a function of all of the above variations:

$$Y_t = f[\text{Sec}_t, \text{Sea}_t, \text{Cyc}_t, \text{Ran}_t],$$

where

$\quad$ Sec_t is the secular effect for t period;

$\quad$ Sea_t is the seasonal effect for t period;

$\quad$ Cyc_t is the cyclical effect for t period;

$\quad$ Ran_t is the random effect for t period.

Geometrically, Figure 6.1 shows each of the patterns.

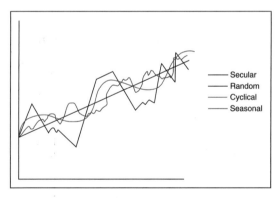

FIGURE 6.1

6.3   FROM SYMBOLIC TO NUMERIC FITTING

Time series data are different in terms of their appropriateness to fit into a certain function for the purpose of regression estimation. Fortunately, most of the economic data can easily fit into the linear function

$$Y_t = \alpha + \beta t.$$

However, some may fit better into the quadratic function

$$Y_t = \alpha + \beta t + \gamma t^2,$$

where the coefficient of t^2 reflects the type of growth. A positive coefficient ($\gamma > 0$) refers to an increasing rate of growth and a negative coefficient ($\gamma < 0$) refers to a decreasing rate of growth. Figure 6.2 shows both quadratic functions against the linear trend.

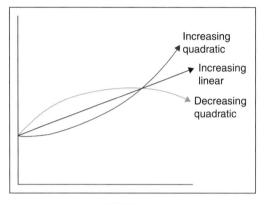

FIGURE 6.2

Some data may need to be fitted into an exponential function of the form

$$Y_t = \alpha \beta^t,$$

which has to be transformed into a linear function by the logarithmic function in order to be estimated by the ordinary least squares method,

$$\text{Log } Y_t = \text{Log } \alpha + t \text{ Log } \beta,$$

and with a slight rearrangement, we can better identify the parameters:

$$\text{Log } Y_t = \text{Log } \alpha + t \text{ Log } \beta \, t,$$

where Log α is the constant term and Log β is the time coefficient. The antilog function would return the parameters to their original state after estimation:

$$Y_t = \text{Antilog } \alpha \text{ and Antilog } \beta(t).$$

The following example shows how supportive information about a product can be used in the fitting of a certain function.

Example 6.1
This example uses the linear function. It is about forecasting the size of membership in an athletic gym of a club. Suppose that the firm that owns the club has conducted a survey and

collected a list of related information:

- During any time period (t), the number of members of the club who resume their membership from a previous period is a certain percentage (x) of the total number of members in the previous period [M_{t-1}]. Therefore, we can say that the number of members of the club during any time period t [M_t] would include those who were carried over from the previous period (xM_{t-1}).

- Also, during any time period (t), there would be a number of new members joining the club for the first time. Suppose that this number is a certain percentage (y) of the estimated total market demand on this particular service (D). Therefore, this number can be expressed as a y-percentage of D after excluding those who already joined before:

$$y[D - M_{t-1}].$$

- Total number of members during period (t) can then be obtained by adding the two previous parts:

$$M_t = x[M_{t-1}] + y[D_{t-1}].$$

Combining the similar terms, we get

$$M_t = x[M_{t-1}] + yD - y[M_{t-1}],$$
$$M_t = yD + (x - y)[M_{t-1}].$$

- Now, let us go back to the firm's survey. Suppose that the survey has revealed that the total demand on this service in the market is estimated at 1200 members and that those who carry their membership over to the next period average 76% of those who already have membership from the last period, and that those who join the club for the first time are usually an average of 18% of the market demand. Plugging these real figures in the equation will give us the numeric form of the function:

$$M_t = 0.18[1200] + [0.76 - 0.18]M_{t-1}$$

or

$$M_t = 216 + 0.58M_{t-1}.$$

This is the linear function format that is to be used to forecast for the next period using the previous period. So, if, for example, we look at the record of membership for the last year and find it to be 450 members, we can immediately extrapolate an estimation of the next year membership and probably for a few more years into the future:

$$M_{\text{next}} = 216 + 0.58(450),$$
$$M_{\text{next}} = 477.$$

However, this kind of function is usually obtained by running a simple bivariate regression analysis on two columns of data. The first is the membership size for a number of previous periods, say years, and second, the trend of time from 1 to n.

The number 216 above would be the y-intercept of the equation or the constant term, and 0.58 would be the β-value or the slope of the regression line. If the last year membership was 450, we can project the membership status for the next 7 years to see that it is a secular trend that is increasing but at a decreasing rate. Table 6.1 shows the membership forecasts for the next 7 years.

TABLE 6.1

T	M_{t-1}	M_t	ΔM_t
0	450	477	
1	477	493	16
2	493	502	9
3	502	507	5
4	507	510	3
5	510	512	2
6	512	513	1
7	514	514	0

It is essential for the manager to know that the growth of membership is decreasing and that 7 years from now there will be not be a single person joining the club when the number of members in the current year would equal the number in the previous year. It is a wakeup call to change strategies and try to turn the tide around into an increasing rate of growth.

The function to estimate the data at hand could be nonlinear, had the conditions and information been different. Let us assume that the data would fit an exponential function such as

$$M_t = \beta[N]^t,$$

where the coefficients to be estimated are β and N. The value of M_t or the membership size during any period (t) would grow proportionally with time if N is larger than 1 ($N > 1$). However, it would decline proportionally with time if N is less than 1 ($N < 1$).

For example, if running the regression yields that N is 1.23, it would mean that M_t or annual membership would increase by ($N-1$) or by 23% annually. However, if the estimate of N is 0.89, it would mean that membership would decline annually by 11%.

As we have seen before, an exponential function should be transformed into a linear function by applying the logarithms in order to be estimated by the ordinary least squares method:

$$\log[M_t] = \log[\beta N^t],$$

$$\log[M_t] = \log[\beta] + \log N[t].$$

To estimate M_t, we need to take the antilog of both coefficients,

$$M_t = \text{Antilog } \beta + \text{Antilog } N(t),$$

and the figures of antilog will be the values of the parameters.

6.4 ADJUSTING FOR SEASONALITY

Since time series data are inherently characterized by the sorts of variations mentioned above, it is essential to adjust the estimation of the regression equation for those variations so that we can get forecasts that reflect the realities of data. We focus on seasonal variation as it is the most common variation in the time series data, and we calculate its impact using more than one method. It is worth noting here that isolating these variations and adjusting the value of data according to their impacts is called the "decomposition process."

Let us first consider some quarterly data on a product's sales for 20 quarters and let us use the following fitted regression equation to calculate quarterly forecasts from the actual data:

$$S_t = S_0 + \beta t,$$
$$S_t = 479.1 + 3.01 t,$$

where S_0 (value 479.1) is the constant coefficient that stands for the average of initial sales and β (value 3.01) is the coefficient of t. Table 6.2 shows the actual and forecasted sales from the first quarter in 2006 to the fourth quarter in 2010 and Table 6.3 illustrates simple average errors.

TABLE 6.2 Sales Forecasts for 20 Quarters

1	2	3	4
Year.Quarter	t	Actual Sale (A)	Forecasted Sale (F)
2006.1	1	529.8	482.11
2006.2	2	487.6	485.12
2006.3	3	505.7	488.13
2006.4	4	512.2	491.14
2007.1	5	507.0	494.15
2007.2	6	486.5	497.16
2007.3	7	466.2	500.17
2007.4	8	474.7	503.18
2008.1	9	492.7	506.19
2008.2	10	496.0	509.20
2008.3	11	490.6	512.21
2008.4	12	483.1	515.22
2009.1	13	519.0	518.23
2009.2	14	510.6	521.24
2009.3	15	515.4	524.25
2009.4	16	525.6	527.26
2010.1	17	526.7	530.27
2010.2	18	526.2	533.28
2010.3	19	560.7	536.29
2010.4	20	598.6	539.30

TABLE 6.3   Simple Average Errors

1	2	3	4
Year.Quarter	Actual Sales (A)	Forecasted Sales (F)	Errors ($F - A$)
2006.1	529.80	482.11	−47.69
2007.1	507.00	494.15	−12.85
2008.1	492.70	506.19	13.49
2009.1	519.00	518.23	−0.77
2010.1	526.70	530.27	3.57
Average error for the first quarter			−8.85
2006.2	487.60	485.12	−2.48
2007.2	486.50	497.16	10.66
2008.2	496.00	509.20	13.2
2009.2	510.60	521.24	10.64
2010.2	526.20	533.28	7.08
Average error for the second quarter			7.82
2006.3	505.70	488.13	−17.57
2007.3	466.20	500.17	33.97
2008.3	490.60	512.21	21.61
2009.3	515.40	524.25	8.85
2010.3	560.70	536.29	−24.41
Average error for the third quarter			4.49
2006.4	512.20	491.14	−21.06
2007.4	474.70	503.18	28.48
2008.4	483.10	515.22	32.12
2009.4	525.60	527.26	1.66
2010.4	598.60	539.30	−59.3
Average error for the fourth quarter			−4.28

The following subsections discuss three methods to capture the impact of seasonality.

6.4.1   The Simple Average of Errors Method

According to this method, we calculate the simple average of errors for each quarter and adjust the next prediction by its value. So, let us rearrange Table 6.3 first by grouping the similar quarters together. The next step is to create Column 5 for the errors that show difference between the forecasted and the actual values. Then we calculate the simple average for each similar quarter individually.

If we want to predict the four quarters of 2011, their t-values would be 21, 22, 23, and 24. Plugging these t-values into the regression equation gives us the forecast for 2011 (see Tables 6.4, 6.5, 6.6, 6.7 and Figure 6.3).

TABLE 6.4

Year.Quarter	t	$S_t = 479.1 + 3.01t$	Forecasted Sale (F)
2011.1	21	479.1 + 3.01(21)	542.31
2011.2	22	479.1 + 3.01(22)	545.32
2011.3	23	479.1 + 3.01(23)	548.33
2011.4	24	479.1 + 3.01(24)	551.34

TABLE 6.5

Multiple Linear Regression—Estimated Regression Equation
Sales [t] = + 479.097368421053 + 3.01406015037595 Time[t] + $e[t]$

TABLE 6.6

Multiple Linear Regression—Ordinary Least Squares					
Variable	Parameter	SD	T-Stat ($H0$: Parameter = 0)	Two-Tail p-Value	One-Tail p-Value
Intercept	479.097368421053	11.742379	40.8007	0	0
Time	3.01406015037595	0.980235	3.0748	0.006529	0.003264

TABLE 6.7

Multiple Linear Regression—Regression Statistics	
Multiple R	0.586832495103272
R-Squared	0.344372377309132
Adjusted R-Squared	0.307948620492972
F-Test (value)	9.45460895336176
F-Test (DF numerator)	1
F-Test (DF denominator)	18
p-Value	0.00652875667517216
Multiple Linear Regression—Residual Statistics	
Residual standard deviation	25.2778977211252
Sum squared residuals	11501.498037594

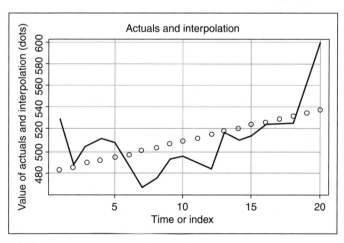

FIGURE 6.3

However, these forecasts are not adjusted for any seasonal variation as reflected by the simple average errors. This is why we should perform the adjustment (Table 6.8). Looking at the average of errors, we get that the forecast for the first quarter was, in general, less than the actual by an average of 8.85. So, we can add back this difference to the forecast of the first quarter in 2011:

$$S_{21} = 542.31 + 8.85 = 551.16.$$

For the second quarter of 2011, the forecasted value was more than the actual by an average of 7.82. So, this difference should be discounted:

$$S_{22} = 545.32 - 7.82 = 537.50.$$

For the third quarter, the average error is 4.49. So, the third quarter of 2011 would be adjusted by discounting 4.49:

$$S_{23} = 548.33 - 4.49 = 543.84.$$

The fourth quarter has a -4.28 average error, which means it is underestimated by 4.28. So, adjusting the fourth quarter of 2011 requires adding this amount:

$$S_{24} = 551.34 + 4.28 = 555.62.$$

TABLE 6.8

Year.Quarter	$F_{sa} = F \pm SAE$	F_{sa}
2011.1	542.31 + 8.85	551.16
2011.2	545.32 − 7.82	537.50
2011.3	548.33 − 4.49	543.84
2011.4	551.34 + 4.28	555.62

6.4.2   The Actual-to-Forecast (A/F) Ratio Method

We arrange our data as in Table 6.8, where similar quarters of all years are grouped together. This time we calculate the A/F ratio by dividing the actual data by the forecasted data. Then, we obtain a 5-year average of the ratio for the similar quarters individually. It is the A/F ratio for a specific quarter that would serve as a multiplier of the predicted values to adjust them for seasonality:

$$F_{sa} = F(A/F)_q, \quad q = 1, 2, 3, 4.$$

Here F_{sa} is the seasonally adjusted forecast, F is the unadjusted forecast, and $(A/F)_q$ is the quarterly average ratio (see Tables 6.9 and 6.10):

$$(A/F)_1 = 1.02,$$
$$(A/F)_2 = 0.98,$$
$$(A/F)_3 = 0.99,$$
$$(A/F)_4 = 1.00.$$

TABLE 6.9   Five-Year Quarterly Average Ratio

Year	Quarter	Actual Sale (A)	Forecasted Sale (F)	A/F Ratio	
2006	1	529.80	482.11	1.10	
2007	1	507.00	494.15	1.03	
2008	1	492.70	506.19	0.97	
2009	1	519.00	518.23	1.00	
2010	1	526.70	530.27	0.99	
5-year average ratio for the first quarter				1.02	$(A/F)_{q1}$
2006	2	487.60	485.12	1.01	
2007	2	486.50	497.16	0.98	
2008	2	496.00	509.20	0.97	
2009	2	510.60	521.24	0.98	
2010	2	526.20	533.28	0.97	
5-year average ratio for the second quarter				0.98	$(A/F)_{q2}$
2006	3	505.70	488.13	1.04	
2007	3	466.20	500.17	0.93	
2008	3	490.60	512.21	0.96	
2009	3	515.40	524.25	0.98	
2010	3	560.70	536.29	1.04	
5-year average ratio for the third quarter				0.99	$(A/F)_{q3}$
2006	4	512.20	491.14	1.04	
2007	4	474.70	503.18	0.94	
2008	4	483.10	515.22	0.94	
2009	4	525.60	527.26	0.99	
2010	4	598.60	539.30	1.11	
5-year average ratio for the fourth quarter				1.00	$(A/F)_{q4}$

TABLE 6.10

Year.Quarter	$F_{sa} = F(A/F)_q$	F_{sa}
2011.1	542.31(1.02)	553.16
2011.2	545.32 (0.98)	534.41
2011.3	548.33 (0.99)	542.85
2011.4	551.34 (1.00)	551.34

6.4.3 The Dummy Variables Method

We can adjust for seasonality by using the regression equation obtained from the run that includes dummy variables for the quarters:

$$S_t^d = 482.1 + 3.06t + Q_i,$$

where Q_i is the estimated coefficient for each quarter (Q_1, Q_2, Q_3), whereas the fourth quarter (Q_4) is represented by the intercept only. So, the estimation of the forecasted value of sales for the first quarter of 2011 would use the intercept t (21) and the Q_1 coefficient (5.39). The forecasted value for the second quarter would use the intercept t (22) and the Q_2 coefficient (-11.33). The forecasted value for the third quarter would use the intercept t (23) and the Q_3 coefficient (-8.06). The fourth quarter would not have any Q_4 coefficient since it is considered the base period.

Table 6.11 shows the calculations of the forecasted sales for the four quarters of 2011 as they are adjusted for the seasonal variation according to the regression with the dummy variables method (also see Tables 6.12, 6.13, 6.14 and Figures 6.4 and 6.5).

The results of the adjusted forecasts by the three methods would have been much closer if it were not for rounding.

TABLE 6.11

Year.Quarter	t	Regression with Dummy Variables Equation ($S_t^d = \alpha + \beta t + Q_i$)	Adjusted Forecast (F_{sa}^d)
2011.1	21	S21 = 482.1 + 3.06(21) + 5.39	551.75
2011.2	22	S22 = 482.1 + 3.06(22) − 11.33	538.09
2011.3	23	S23 = 482.1 + 3.06(23) − 8.06	544.42
2011.4	24	S24 = 482.1 + 3.06(24)	555.54

TABLE 6.12

Multiple Linear Regression—Estimated Regression Equation
Sales [t] = + 482.09 + 3.06250000000001 Time [t] + 5.38749999999994 Q_1 [t] − 11.335 Q_2[t] − 8.05750000000001 Q_3[t] + e[t]

TABLE 6.13

		Multiple Linear Regression—Ordinary Least Squares			
Variable	Parameter	SD	T-Stat ($H0$: Parameter = 0)	Two-Tail p-Value	One-Tail p-Value
(Intercept)	482.09	17.359597	27.7708	0	0
Time	3.06250000000001	1.05258	2.9095	0.010784	0.005392
Q_1	5.38749999999994	17.134764	0.3144	0.757533	0.378767
Q_2	−11.335	16.972345	−0.6679	0.514374	0.257187
Q_3	−8.05750000000001	16.874144	−0.4775	0.639885	0.319943

TABLE 6.14

Multiple Linear Regression—Regression Statistics	
Multiple R	0.627458670627651
R-Squared	0.393704383345819
Adjusted R-Squared	0.232025552238038
F-Test (value)	2.43510161873548
F-Test (DF numerator)	4
F-Test (DF denominator)	15
p-Value	0.0926907022517692
Multiple Linear Regression—Residual Statistics	
Residual standard deviation	26.6284058854449
Sum squared residuals	10636.08

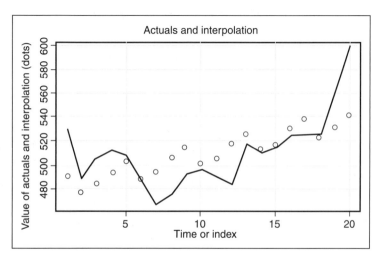

FIGURE 6.4

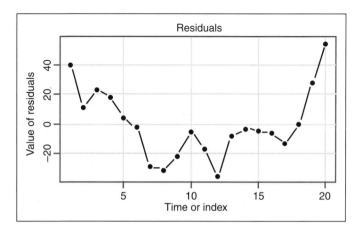

FIGURE 6.5

6.5   SMOOTHED FORECASTS

Smoothing techniques are other ways to produce forecasted values based on past observations. It is more suited for the time series data that have a slow and infrequent change in the underlying pattern and the data that exhibit a noticeable degree of randomness or irregularity. The objective of these techniques is to smooth out such irregularities and reduce or eliminate the distortions arising from the random variations. The forecasted value of a variable according to these techniques is basically an average of some previous data. The most common of these techniques are the moving average smoothing and the exponential smoothing.

6.5.1   Simple Moving Average Method

This method calculates the predicted value of a variable as a simple average of a number of observations (p) that would overlap throughout the prediction list by adding the latest observation while dropping off the earliest. For example, if we are at the end of July and want to predict the sales for August, we can use the data we have for the previous months to get an average to represent a predicted value for August. A 3-month average would include the sales of July, June, and May divided by 3. If at the end of August and after recording the actual sales of August, we want to predict for September, the 3-month moving average requires that we add August (being the latest) and drop off May (being the earliest) so that the September value becomes an average of August, July, and June. The predicted sales for October would be an average of September, August, and July, while June is dropped off, and so on—the average would move forward throughout the series, hence the name "moving" average.

   We can obtain the general formula for the moving average this way. Let us call the actual data of sales A_t, where t is the current time and can reflect the number of observations, such that if we are in July, A_t would be A_7; the previous month is June and can be denoted by A_6, which is also $A_{t-1} = A_{7-1} = A_6$; the month after July is August, which can be denoted by A_8 or $A_{t+1} = A_{7+1} = A_8$. So, the forecast for August is an average of July, June, and May:

$$A_8 = \frac{A_7 + A_6 + A_5}{3}$$

or

$$A_{t+1} = \frac{A_t + A_{t-1} + A_{t-2}}{3}.$$

The denominator, 3, is the number of periods (P) that would constitute the elements of the average according to the forecaster, and it could be any number the forecaster chooses. This would make the formula more general as

$$A_{t+1} = \frac{A_t + A_{t-1} + A_{t-2} + \cdots + A_{t-p+1}}{P}.$$

So, if we are in November [11] and want to calculate a 5-month forecast for December [12], the forecasted value for December sales would be

$$A_{t+1} = \frac{A_t + A_{t-1} + A_{t-2} + A_{t-3} + A_{t-4}}{P},$$

$$A_{11+1} = \frac{A_{11} + A_{11-1} + A_{11-2} + A_{11-3} + A_{11-4}}{5},$$

$$A_{12} = \frac{A_{11} + A_{10} + A_9 + A_8 + A_7}{5}.$$

The last observation is A_7 and it is equal to the last term in the general formula:

$$A_{t-p+1} = A_{11-5+1} = A_7.$$

Column 3 of Table 6.15 shows the actual sales of customized computers at a local store during the 16 quarters of 2008–2011. The three-quarter forecasts are shown in Column 4 starting at the fourth observation, 184.3, as the first average of observations 1, 2, and 3.

$$184.3 = \frac{170 + 187 + 196}{3}.$$

TABLE 6.15   Three-Quarter and Five-Quarter Moving Average

1	2	3	4	5	6	7	8	9
Observation	Year. Quarter	Actual Sale (A)	Three-Quarter MA (F_1)	$A - F_1$	$[A - F_1]^2$	Five Quarter MA (F_2)	$A - F_2$	$[A - F_2]^2$
1	2008.1	170						
2	2008.2	187						
3	2008.3	196						
4	2008.4	204	184.5	19.7	388.09			
5	2009.1	153	195.6	−42.6	1814.76			
6	2009.2	195	184.3	10.7	114.49	182	13	169
7	2009.3	162	184	−22	484	187	−25	625
8	2009.4	144	170	−26	676	182	−38	1444
9	2010.1	188	167	21	441	171.6	16.4	268.96
10	2010.2	196	164.6	31.4	985.96	168.4	27.6	761.76
11	2010.3	150	176	−26	676	177	−27	729
12	2010.4	194	178	16	256	168	26	676
13	2011.1	154	180	−26	676	174.4	−20.4	416.16
14	2011.2	190	166	24	576	176.4	13.6	184.96
15	2011.3	159	179.3	−20.3	412.09	176.8	−17.8	316.84
16	2011.4	140	167.6	−27.6	261.76	169.4	−29.4	864.36
17	2012.1		163		7762.15	167.4		6456.04

MA, moving average.

Next on the column is 195.6 as the forecast value for sales in the first quarter of 2009. It is obtained by averaging only the previous three observations and dropping off the earliest:

$$195.6 = \frac{204 + 196 + 187}{3}.$$

Column 7 of Table 6.15 shows the forecasts using a five-quarter moving average. For example, the predicted value of sales for the third quarter in 2011 (176.8) is obtained by averaging out the previous five actual values:

$$176.8 = \frac{190 + 154 + 194 + 150 + 196}{5}.$$

As to why and when the forecast uses a specific value of p, it depends on the forecaster's design, objectives, and justifications of the forecast. Generally speaking, the larger the p or the number of observations constituting the average, the smoother the forecasts and the more effective the impact on dealing with randomness that would be spread out over more observations, each of which would get less weight ($1/P$) as P increases. If we graph this time series in its three columns of estimates as they are Table 6.16, it would be clearer that the forecast values obtained by using five-quarter moving average produced a smoother curve (C) as compared to the other curves [the actual data curve (A) and the three-quarter moving average forecasts curve (B)]. It is a visual confirmation to the notion that a greater value of p would result in ironing out most of the randomness in the time series data (Figure 6.6).

TABLE 6.16   Time Series Data of Sales: Actual Versus Two Forecasts

Observation	Year.Quarter	A	Three-Quarter MA (F_1)	Five-Quarter MA (F_2)
1	2008.1	120		
2	2008.2	187		
3	2008.3	196		
4	2008.4	204	184.3	
5	2009.1	153	195.6	
6	2009.2	195	184.3	182
7	2009.3	162	184	187
8	2009.4	144	170	182
9	2010.1	188	167	171.6
10	2010.2	196	164.6	168.4
11	2010.3	150	176	177
12	2010.4	194	178	168
13	2011.1	154	180	174.4
14	2011.2	190	166	176.4
15	2011.3	159	179.3	176.8
16	2011.4	140	167.6	169.4

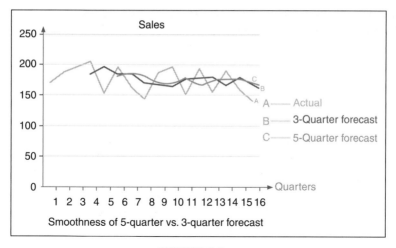

FIGURE 6.6

The RMSE Check   We can run a simple test to check which of the two procedures, the three-quarter forecast or the five-quarter forecast, is better in the sense of being closer to the actual data. This test uses the squared forecast errors and calculates and compares what is called the **root-mean-square error (RMSE)**. The smaller the RMSE, the better it is:

$$\text{Min RMSE} = \sqrt{\frac{\Sigma[A_t - F_t]^2}{n - p}}.$$

Here n is the total number of observations, and p is the number of terms constituting the average.

Columns 6 and 9 of Table 6.15 calculate the summation of the squared errors for both procedures. Plugging the values in the formula above reveals the following.

For the three-quarter forecast, the RMSE is

$$\text{RMSE}_3 = \sqrt{\frac{7762.15}{16 - 3}} = 24.44,$$

and for the five-quarter forecast, the RMSE is

$$\text{RMSE}_5 = \sqrt{\frac{6456.04}{16 - 5}} = 24.22.$$

Since the five-quarter procedure has a relatively smaller RMSE, it would be a little better than the three-quarter procedure. So, if we want to predict for the first quarter of 2012, we will use the five-quarter procedure that produces 167.4 instead of using the three-quarter procedure that produces 163:

$$F_{17} = \frac{140 + 159 + 190 + 154 + 194}{5} = 167.4,$$

$$F_{17} = \frac{140 + 159 + 190}{3} = 163.$$

6.5.2   The Weighted Moving Average

The simple moving average method assumes uniformity among the observations of time series data in terms of their impact on forming the predicted value. It is, in fact, one of the shortcomings that counteracts the simplicity of the model. As a response to such a major pitfall, forecasters came up with the idea of weighing the importance of the observations constituting the average. The weighted moving average, therefore, allows the forecasters to assign certain weights to each observation in the average based on their discretion, and consistent with the external influences they may consider in giving more or less importance to a specific observation or term of the observation. All assigned weights may or may not total to 1. The forecast value for the next period (F_{t+1}) will be calculated as

$$F_{t+1} = \frac{w_1(A_t) + w_2(A_{t-1}) + w_3(A_{t-3}) + \cdots + w_p(A_{t-p+1})}{\Sigma w_i}.$$

Here $w_i = w_1, w_2, \ldots, w_p$: the number of weights assigned to as many observations as available in the average. That is, the 3-month moving average, has a $p = 3$ and, therefore, has three weights (w_1, w_2, w_3) assigned to each of the three observations forming the average.

Example 6.2
Suppose that the forecaster assigned the following weights to the four quarters of 2011: 0.15, 0.25, 0.37, and 0.23. What would be the four-quarter predicted sales for the first quarter of 2012? Use the actual sales as mentioned in Table 6.16:

$$F_{2012.1} = \frac{w_1 A_{2011.1} + w_2 A_{2011.2} + w_3 A_{2011.3} + w_4 A_{2011.4}}{\sum w_i}.$$

Solution:
Since the summation of weights is 1, we can skip dividing by $\sum w_i$ and simply calculate the numerator part of the equation:

$$F_{2012.1} = 0.15(140) + 0.25(159) + 0.37(190) + 0.23(154),$$
$$F_{2012.1} = 166.5.$$

Example 6.3
What if the weights are 0.18, 0.24, 0.33, and 0.20?

Solution:

$$F_{2012.1} = \frac{0.18(140) + 0.24(159) + 0.33(190) + 0.20(154)}{0.95},$$

$$F_{2012.1} = 165.12.$$

Example 6.4

Suppose that at the end of the first quarter of 2012 the sales turn out to be 164. Use the four-quarter weighted moving average to predict the sales in the second quarter of 2012 assuming the same weights as in the last example.

Solution:

Since we use the four-quarter moving average and we have new actual sales of the first quarter of 2012, we should drop off the earliest quarter in the group, which is the first quarter of 2011 (154). So, the four quarters forming the average now are 2012.1, 2011.4, 2011.3, and 2012.2:

$$F_{2010.2} = \frac{0.18(164) + 0.24(140) + 0.33(159) + 0.20(190)}{0.95},$$

$$F_{2012.2} = 161.7.$$

6.5.3 Exponential Smoothing

The exponential smoothing model is another way to respond to the uniformity assumption of the moving average method as it treats all time periods in the series equally. This method assumes that the most recent past is more predictive of the future value of the forecast than the distant past. This assumption has prompted the introduction of a constant (α) to signify the weight of the immediate past, while the earlier data take a ($1 - \alpha$) weight. In this case, α is assigned by forecasters based on their discretion and the extent of their belief in how strong the impact of the most recent data is on the prediction. The value of α is between 0 and 1, but traditionally has been assigned values between 0.10 and 0.35.

So, the exponential model calculates the value of the forecast for the next period (F_{t+1}) as a weighted average of the actual observation in the current period (A_t) and the forecast value for the same period (F_t), where α is assigned to the current actual and ($1 - \alpha$) is assigned to the smoothed forecast (F_t):

$$F_{t+1} = \alpha A_t + (1 - \alpha)F_t. \tag{6.1}$$

Logically, if we write this equation for the current period (t), we get

$$F_t = \alpha A_{t-1} + (1 - \alpha)F_{t-1}, \tag{6.2}$$

and if we substitute (6.2) into (6.1), we get

$$F_{t+1} = \alpha A_t + (1 - \alpha)[\alpha A_{t-1} + (1 - \alpha)F_{t-1}],$$
$$F_{t+1} = \alpha A_t + (1 - \alpha)\alpha A_{t-1} + (1 - \alpha)^2 F_{t-1},$$

and if we substitute for F_{t-1} as

$$F_{t-1} = \alpha A_{t-2} + (1 - \alpha)F_{t-2},$$

we get

$$F_{t+1} = \alpha A_t + \alpha(1 - \alpha)A_{t-1} + (1 - \alpha)^2[\alpha A_{t-2} + (1 - \alpha)F_{t-2}].$$
$$F_{t+1} = \alpha A_t + \alpha(1 - \alpha)A_{t-1} + \alpha(1 - \alpha)^2 A_{t-2} + (1 - \alpha)^3 F_{t-2}.$$

If we keep substituting for the forecast of the past periods F_{t-2}, F_{t-3}, and earlier, we will realize that we have an equation of an exponentially weighted moving average with its weights forming a geometric progression:

$$\alpha, \alpha(1-\alpha), \alpha(1-\alpha)^2, \alpha(1-\alpha)^3, \ldots, \alpha(1-\alpha)^n.$$

It illustrates that any value of α would produce a decreasing value of weights. For example, if α is 0.40, the rest of the weights would be calculated as shown in Table 6.17.

TABLE 6.17

Term	Weight	Value
1	α	0.40
2	$\alpha(1-\alpha)1$	0.24
3	$\alpha(1-\alpha)2$	0.144
4	$\alpha(1-\alpha)3$	0.0864
5	$\alpha(1-\alpha)4$	0.0518
6	$\alpha(1-\alpha)5$	0.0311
7	$\alpha(1-\alpha)6$	0.0186
8	$\alpha(1-\alpha)7$	0.0111

This shows that the weights get smaller and smaller as we go back in the past. It dropped here to 1% at the eighth term back. It is a confirmation that assigning a higher α would place greater importance on the most recent past as a predictor of the future, and logically place less importance on the earlier observations. However, a greater value of α produces less smoothing, so for a smoother line a smaller α would help. If we slightly rearrange the original format of the exponential smoothing model,

$$F_{t+1} = \alpha(A_t) + (1-\alpha)F_t,$$

$$F_{t+1} = \alpha(A_t) + F_t - \alpha F_t,$$

we can get the most practical format for calculations:

$$F_{t+1} = F_t + \alpha[A_t - F_t].$$

We use this equation to produce forecasts in the F_1 and F_2 columns of Table 6.18 using two values of α, 0.20 and 0.45. For the first forecast of the first quarter of 2008, we use the actual observation (170) for A_t and the general average of the actual (173.9) for F_t, but for the rest of the forecasts, F_t would be the previous F. For example, to predict the sales for the second quarter of 2010, using an α of 0.20, we use 188 for A_t and 170.9 for F_t as they are the current data at the time to predict for the following quarter:

$$F_{t+1} = F_t + \alpha[A_t - F_2],$$

$$F_{2010.2} = F_{2010.1} + .20[A_{2010.1} - F_{2010.1}],$$

$$F_{2010.2} = 170.9 + .20[188 - 170.9],$$

$$F_{2010.2} = 174.3.$$

TABLE 6.18   Exponential Smoothing with Two Values of α

Observation	Year.Quarter	Actual Sale (A)	$\alpha = 0.20$			$\alpha = 0.45$		
			F_1	$A - F$	$[A - F_1]^2$	F_2	$A - F_2$	$[A - F_2]^2$
1	2008.1	170	173.9	−3.9	15.2	173.9	−3.9	15.2
2	2008.2	187	173.1	13.9	193.2	172.1	14.9	222
3	2008.3	196	175.9	20.1	404	178.8	17.2	295.8
4	2008.4	204	179.9	24.1	580.8	186.5	17.5	306
5	2009.1	153	184.7	−31.7	1004.9	194.4	−41.4	1714
6	2009.2	195	178.4	16.6	275.5	175.8	19.2	368.6
7	2009.3	162	181.7	−19.7	388	184.4	−22.4	501.8
8	2009.4	144	177.7	−33.7	1135.7	174.3	−30.3	918.1
9	2010.1	188	170.9	17.1	292.4	160.7	27.3	745.3
10	2010.2	196	174.3	21.7	470.9	173.0	23	529
11	2010.3	150	178.6	−28.6	817.9	183.3	−33.3	1108.9
12	2010.4	194	172.9	21.1	445.2	168.3	25.7	660.5
13	2011.1	154	177.1	−23.1	533.6	179.8	−25.8	665.6
14	2011.2	190	172.5	17.5	306.2	168.2	21.8	475.2
15	2011.3	159	176.0	−17	289	178.0	−19	361
16	2011.4	140	172.6	−32.6	1062.7	169.4	−29.4	864.4
Average = 173.9					8215			9737

As for the moving average method, we can use the RMSE test to see which α-value produces a better forecast. For the forecasts produced with $\alpha = 0.20$, we get

$$\text{RMSE} = \sqrt{\frac{\Sigma [A_t - F_t]^2}{n}},$$

$$\text{RMSE} = \sqrt{\frac{8215}{16}},$$

$$\text{RMSE} = 22.6,$$

and for the forecasts produced with $\alpha = 0.45$, we get

$$\text{RMSE} = \sqrt{\frac{9737}{16}},$$

$$\text{RMSE} = 24.7.$$

Since using α of 0.20 produced a smaller RMSE, it means that this α-value is more appropriate to bring the forecasts closer to their actual values.

This concludes that if we want to predict the sales of the first quarter of 2012, we should rely on the estimate of 166.08 instead of the estimate of 157.9 as the first one uses an α of

0.20 and the second uses an α of 0.45:

$$F_{2012.1} = F_{2011.4} + \alpha[A_{2011.4} - F_{2011.4}]$$
$$= 172.6 + 0.20[140 - 172.6]$$
$$= 166.08$$

or

$$F_{2012.1} = 172.6 + 0.45[140 - 172.6]$$
$$= 157.9.$$

Graphing the time series in its three forms, the actual, the forecasts using an α of 0.20, and the forecasts using an α of 0.45, as they are in Table 6.19, shows that a smaller α (0.20) produces a smoother line (see Figure 6.7).

TABLE 6.19

Observation	Year.Quarter	A	F_1 ($\alpha = 0.20$)	F_2 ($\alpha = 0.45$)
1	2008.1	170	173.9	173.9
2	2008.2	187	173.1	172.1
3	2008.3	196	175.9	178.8
4	2008.4	204	179.9	186.5
5	2009.1	153	184.7	194.4
6	2009.2	195	178.4	175.8
7	2009.3	162	181.7	184.4
8	2009.4	144	177.7	174.3
9	2010.1	188	170.9	160.7
10	2010.2	196	174.3	173.0
11	2010.3	150	178.6	183.3
12	2010.4	194	172.9	168.3
13	2011.1	154	177.1	179.8
14	2011.2	190	172.5	168.2
15	2011.3	159	176.0	178.0
16	2011.4	140	172.6	169.4

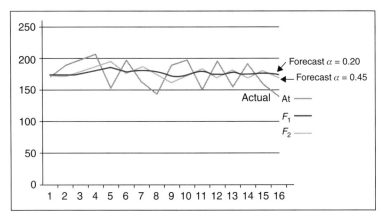

FIGURE 6.7

Mean Absolute Deviation (MAD)   This is similar to RMSE to test for the appropriateness of the forecasting technique in terms of how close the estimates are to the actual data, especially when conducting short-range forecasts such as those performed by the moving average and the exponential smoothing. MAD is a simple measure of the overall forecast error. It depends on the absolute value of the error terms, as opposed to squaring them (as in the RMSE calculations). The absolute value is obtained by ignoring the signs of the deviation between the actual and predicted values, or deeming all of them positive as they are squeezed in between the two vertical lines:

$$\text{MAD} = \frac{\Sigma |A - F|}{n}.$$

Table 6.20 shows the absolute values of the deviations between the actual sales and four different forecasts as we calculated them earlier. In the last row of Table 6.20, MAD is calculated for every forecast method. The results are very similar to what we got earlier by the RMSE tests. The results confirm again that the least forecast error is found in the exponential smoothing technique using an α-value of 0.20, a reason to consider this method the best among the four methods followed for this specific time series. The results also confirm that using the four-quarter moving average is better than the three-quarter moving average, and using an α of 0.20 is better than an α of 0.45.

TABLE 6.20

Observation	Year.Quarter	$|A - F_1|$ (Three-Quarter MA)	$|A - F_2|$ (Four-Quarter MA)	$|A - F|$ ($\alpha = 0.20$)	$|A - F|$ ($\alpha = 0.45$)
1	2008.1			3.9	3.9
2	2008.2			13.9	14.9
3	2008.3			20.1	17.2
4	2008.4	19.7		24.1	17.5
5	2009.1	42.6		31.7	41.4
6	2009.2	10.7	13	16.6	19.2
7	2009.3	22	25	19.7	22.4
8	2009.4	26	38	33.7	30.3
9	2010.1	21	16.4	17.1	27.3
10	2010.2	31.4	27.6	21.7	23
11	2010.3	26	27	28.6	33.3
12	2010.4	16	26	21.1	25.7
13	2011.1	26	20.4	23.1	25.8
14	2011.2	24	13.6	17.5	21.8
15	2011.3	20.3	17.8	17	19
16	2011.4	27.6	29.4	32.6	29.4
$\Sigma |A - F|$		313.3	254.2	342.4	372.1
n		13	11	16	16
MAD		24.1	23.1	21.4	23.2

MA, moving average.

6.6 BAROMETRIC FORECASTING

Because of the continuous and significant overlap between micro- and macro-levels of economic activities, firm managers have traditionally realized the need to be aware of the directions of the major macroeconomic variables when they forecast for their own variables at the micro-level. For example, predicting the sales or profits for a specific product is inextricably connected to consumer demand, income and employment levels, inflation, and many aggregate economic variables. Generally, any business activity at the firm's level can be connected to the general conditions of the economy. Economists have noticed the significant impact that some economic variables can have on the rest of the economy, and the acquired importance in the prediction of many other variables at both macro- and micro-levels. Researchers at the National Bureau of Economic Research have considered some major economic variables as "indicators," and have classified them into three groups:

1. *The leading indicators*: Those variables that change first, prompting other variables to follow the change.
2. *The lagging indicators*: Those variables whose changes tend to follow the changes of others.
3. *The coincident indicators*: Those variables whose changes simply coincide with the changes of other variables.

This categorization and the fact that in practice certain variables tend to move ahead of others implies that the changes in the leading economic indicators (LEIs) can be used to predict the changes in others that follow. Figure 6.8 shows a typical set of time series for these three groups. We can see that the turning points of peak and trough occur first in the leading indicators followed after a period of time by the lagged indicators, while the coincidental indicators move almost in tandem with the leading group.

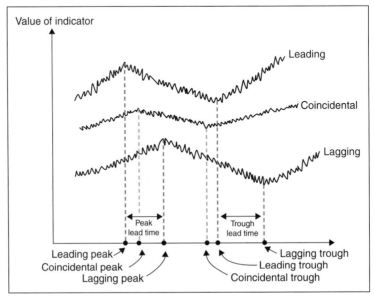

FIGURE 6.8

The time during which the leading change precedes the following change is called the lead time. It varies from cycle to cycle and it is different in the peak and trough cases. In the graph, we can see that the lagging indicator takes shorter time to follow the peak of the leading as compared to the time it takes to follow the trough. This variability is a classic characteristic of the business cycle. Recorded data on reference dates of all peaks and troughs of the United States business cycle since 1854 show a great deal of variability, especially in the lead time and how long each phase lasts. For example, in 1990–1991 the trough lead time was 2 months and the peak lead time was 6 months. In 2001, the trough lead time was 8 months and the peak lead time was 14 months.

Once again, the main idea of the barometric forecasting is to utilize the LEIs as a predictor or barometer for short-term changes in a set of time series data that exhibits a good correlation of their changes over time. A typical example to illustrate the plausibility of this idea is the causal relationship among some variables: the changes in the number of building permits issued in the entire economy can serve as a predictor of the activity in the construction sector. An increase in the new consumer orders can indicate an increase ahead in the production, employment, income, and so on. The other typical example is the fluctuation of the stock market indices such as the Down Jones and Nasdaq and how they are used as predictors of the state of the economy.

Economic indicators data are published monthly in Business Cycle Indicators that is issued by The Conference Board. There are more than 300 major indictors, but the short list of the most common ones include 21:10 in the leading category, 7 in the lagging, and 4 in the coincidental, as shown in Table 6.21.

TABLE 6.21   Major Economic Indicators

Leading Indicators
1	Average weekly hours in manufacturing
2	Initial claims for unemployment insurance
3	Manufacturer's new orders, consumer goods and material
4	Vendor performance, slower deliveries diffusion index
5	Manufacturer's new orders, nondefense capital goods
6	Building permits, new private housing units
7	Stock prices, 500 common stocks
8	Money supply
9	Interest rate spread, 10-year treasury bonds less federal funds
10	Index of consumer expectations

Lagging Indicators
1	Average duration of unemployment
2	Ratio, manufacturing and trade inventories to sales
3	Change in labor cost per unit of output, manufacturing
4	Average prime rate charged by banks
5	Commercial and industrial loans outstanding
6	Ratio, consumer installment credit to personal income
7	Change in consumer price index for services

Coincidental Indicators
1	Employees on nonagricultural payrolls
2	Personal income less transfer payments
3	Industrial production
4	Manufacturing trade sales

Barometric forecasting depends on the composite indices that are developed from each group of these indicators. Each composite index is, in fact, a weighted average of the components of the group to signify the direction of movement in the whole group. Since some of the components move up and some move down, a so-called diffusion index has been developed to represent the collective movement in the group. A diffusion index value of 100 means that all of the components in the group are increasing, a value of zero means all of them are decreasing, and any other percentage would refer to the increasing aspect. For example, a value of 60% means 6 out of 10 components are going up.

One of the most popular composite measures is the LEI. It has been developed by the US Bureau of Economic Analysis. Typically, the LEI can signal the march toward recession or the way to recovery. One of the known criteria is that three consecutive months of decline is a strong signal for a recession, and three consecutive quarters of decline is a confirmation to be in a recession. As for the diffusion index, history has shown that a value of about 50 reflects growth in the economic activity and a value under 50 reflects a downturn. Despite the fact that the leading indicators have correctly predicted all recessions that occurred since 1948, it has also predicted some recessions that did not occur. This is a matter of the extent of its accuracy that may have become part of its shortcomings in forecasting in addition to its inability to measure the magnitude of the change and being restricted to identifying only the direction of the change. Despite all the shortcomings of the economic and business indicators, they remain an important tool in the prediction of short-term changes in the general economic activity and the turning points in business cycles. Their prediction can be highly useful, especially in conjunction with other types of forecasting techniques.

6.7 ECONOMETRIC MODELS

Econometric models utilize a perfect combination of economic theory and mathematical and statistical methods to identify and quantify relationships between variables and examine their relative importance and elasticities toward each other. They are characterized by being explanatory and rely on causal reasoning as opposed to other models of forecasting that depend on extrapolating past data and projecting their extensions. This very feature of distinction among other forecasting techniques sets econometric models on a higher ground of advantages, which are as follows:

- They allow making explicit assumptions on how variables of the model are linked to each other.
- They have the capability not only to identify the direction of the changes but also to quantify the magnitude of changes in the related variables.
- They enable the forecaster to have more consistency and reliability in capturing the interdependence of the components, not only at the firm's level but also for the entire economy, and make it possible to explain the whole economic picture in certain conditions.
- They allow a flexible degree of adaptability, especially when managers can experiment with changing the values of explanatory variables under their control after knowing their measured impact.

Econometricians usually approach the task of forecasting by following the typical procedures that may include the following:

- Identify a set of variables that are related to the variable being predicted. The choice of these variables is often governed by economic theory, other theories, and past experience. However, the choice of variables must be, in the first place, closely related to the purpose of prediction. All variables have to operationalize in a sense that their measurements have to be clear.
- Develop a set of hypotheses on the directional links of the variables. These too have to be drawn based on the logic of the theory and in light of past experience and other empirical work.
- Determine the mathematical link among variables by choosing the most suitable functional equation to be estimated, especially whether the function is linear or nonlinear, additive or otherwise.
- Identify a reliable source and select the appropriate breadth and depth of the data to be used in the application of the model.
- Select the appropriate statistical technique to run the data through and achieve the task of estimating the equation parameters.
- Run all the possible tests on the results to assure their specification, accuracy, reliability, significance, and the extent of their relevance to the hypotheses set earlier.
- Explain the results and perform the forecast by plugging in new values of the exogenous variables that affect the next value of the endogenous variable being subject to forecast.

Forecasts performed by econometric models are successful if they are able to produce the following:

- Correct signs of the parameters that are consistent with the theoretical model and the set of hypotheses that was put forward.
- Significant t-test of all or most of the major parameters.
- Good adjusted R^2, which shows that the model explains a great deal of variation in the value of the variable to be predicted.
- Successful test of multicollinearity, autocorrelation, and heteroscedasticity.
- Ability to adapt the model into the forecast of the next period by changing the values of the exogenous variables into the values that influence the next readings of the forecasted variable.

Econometric models vary tremendously in terms of being simple or complex, plain or sophisticated, macro or micro, as well as single-equation or **multiple-equation models**.

6.7.1 Single-Equation Model

This is the basic and most common econometric model in use. It is represented by a single-equation containing one dependent variable, the subject of forecast, and a set of independent variables. For example, a simple single-equation model for the sales of a manual SLR camera can be formulated as

$$S = \alpha + \beta_1 P_c + \beta_2 Y + \beta_3 P_f + \beta_4 P_d + \beta_5 A + \varepsilon,$$

where the quantity of manual SLR cameras sold is a linear function of

P_c = price of camera;
Y = consumer's disposable income;
P_f = price of film as a complement commodity;
P_d = price of compact digital camera as a substitute commodity;
A = expenditures on advertising for the SLR camera;
ε = the error term that sums all of the other influencing (but not included) variables, the measurement errors, and all other irregularities in data and their collections.

Suppose that after collecting the appropriate data and running the model into the ordinary least squares method, we obtain the following estimated equation:

$$S = 225 - 3.84P_c + 0.002Y + 0.0015P_f + 0.129A.$$

Suppose that both income and price of films turn out to be insignificant. They should be dropped off the equation to be used for forecasting. This equation will predict the next period sales of SLR cameras S_{t+1} and will use only two variables, price of camera and advertising expenditures that have to have their values in the next period. The manager has to decide here what will be the price of the camera next year and what is allocated for advertisement spending. So, the variables that have to be plugged in are P^c_{t+1} and A_{t+1}:

$$S_{t+1} = 225 - 3.84P^c_{t+1} + .129A_{t+1}.$$

This will give the forecasted sales of the SLR camera for next year, assuming that the estimated model passed all the necessary tests of specification and reliability.

Another example of the single-equation econometric model is one that would express the dependent variable in a different format from the usual time series of amount of sales. Suppose that a forecaster is targeting the percentage change in the stock of the product between the current and the past period. In this case, it is expressed as

$$\Delta S = \frac{S_t}{S_{t-1}} = \alpha + \beta_1 P_p + \beta_2 V + \beta_3 P_a + \beta_4 M = \varepsilon,$$

$$\log \left[\frac{S_t}{S_{t-1}} \right] = \alpha + \beta_1 \log P_p + \beta_2 \log V + \beta_3 \log P_a + \beta_4 \log M,$$

where the percentage change of the stock of this product between the current time and the previous time is a fraction of

P_p = price of the product;
V = inventory capacity;
P_a = price of the competitive product;
M = is the market size.

The function is transformed into a logarithmic function to be estimated by the ordinary least squares and is turned back to the antilog function to perform the appropriate forecasting.

6.7.2   Multiple-Equation Model

Most of the firm's predictions can be performed using a single-equation econometric model that involves one dependent variable whose value is determined by a set of independent variables. The major assumption is that the values of these independent variables are determined by the factors and circumstances outside the model system. Sometimes a forecaster faces a situation when values of some of those independent variables are determined within the model system. In this case, a single-equation model can no longer be helpful. A system of multiple equations would be the appropriate model. Such a model has endogenous variables whose values are determined from within the system and exogenous variables whose values are determined outside the system. Macroeconometric models dealing with national-scale data can include a huge number of equations that may reach 1000 equations and require a very sophisticated statistical method of analysis.

The multi-equation econometric model usually contains two kinds of equations: (1) structural or behavioral equations, where the relationship among its variables comes in the exogenous–endogenous format that is usually set up according to the researcher's hypotheses and in light of the theoretical model; (2) definitional or identity equations, which state a fact or make a statement that is true by definition. It is the structural (behavioral) equation that is to be estimated using the facts given by the identity equations. Since there would be more than one endogenous variable, each need to have its own equation such that the number of equations would match the number of endogenous variables in the system. Having many equations simultaneously would warrant solving the system in order to reach what is called the "reduced form" that is appropriate to perform the prediction. The reduced form of an equation expresses the value of the endogenous variable in an estimatable format in that it has the determinant variables and their coefficients.

Let us consider a macroeconomic multiple-equation system to show the structural and identity components and how to reach the reduced form. It is about the value of the gross national product (GNP), which is equal to the aggregate consumption (AC) and the gross capital investment (V), where the AC is expressed as a function of GNP for the previous period and the percentage change in GNP between the last and the current period (ΔGNP). The gross capital investment is determined by the interest rate (r):

$$\text{GNP}_t = \text{AC}_t + V_t, \tag{6.3}$$

$$\text{AC}_t = \alpha + \beta_1 \text{GNP}_{t-1} + \beta_2 \Delta \text{GNP} + \varepsilon, \tag{6.4}$$

$$\Delta \text{GNP} = [\text{GNP}_t - \text{GNP}_{t-1}], \tag{6.5}$$

$$\text{AC}_t = \alpha + \beta_1 \text{GNP}_{t-1} + \beta_2 \text{GNP}_t - \beta_3 \text{GNP}_{t-1} + \varepsilon, \tag{6.6}$$

$$V_t = \beta_3 r. \tag{6.7}$$

Substituting (6.6) and (6.7) into (6.3),

$$\text{GNP}_t = \alpha + \beta_1 \text{GNP}_{t-1} + \beta_2 \text{GNP}_t - \beta_2 \text{GNP}_{t-1} + \beta_3 r + \varepsilon.$$

Subtracting $\beta_2 \text{GNP}_t$ from both sides and factoring out GNP_t,

$$\text{GNP}_t - \beta_2 \text{GNP}_t = \alpha + \beta_1 \text{GNP}_{t-1} - \beta_2 \text{GNP}_{t-1} + \beta_3 r + \varepsilon,$$

$$\text{GNP}_t[1 - \beta_2] = \alpha + \beta_1 \text{GNP}_{t-1} - \beta_2 \text{GNP}_{t-1} + \beta_3 r + \varepsilon,$$

$$\text{GNP}_t = \frac{\alpha + \beta_1 \text{GNP}_{t-1} - \beta_2 \text{GNP}_{t-1} + \beta_3 r + \varepsilon}{(1 - \beta_2)},$$

$$\text{GNP}_t = \left[\frac{\alpha}{1 - \beta_2}\right] + \left[\frac{\beta_1 - \beta_2}{1 - \beta_2}\right] \text{GNP}_{t-1} + \left[\frac{\beta_3}{1 - \beta_2}\right] r + \left[\frac{1}{1 - \beta_2}\right] \varepsilon. \quad (6.8)$$

This is the reduced form of GNP for the current period expressed as a function of GNP of the last period and the interest rate, where the parameters are as follows:

$$\left[\frac{\alpha}{1 - \beta_2}\right] : \text{the constant term,}$$

$$\left[\frac{\beta_1 - \beta_2}{1 - \beta_2}\right] : \text{the coefficient for the GNP of the last period,}$$

$$\left[\frac{\beta_3}{1 - \beta_2}\right] : \text{the coefficient for the interest rate.}$$

As for the reduced form of AC, we substitute the value of the current GNP from the reduced form (6.8) into Equation (6.6):

$$\text{AC}_t = \alpha + \beta_1 \text{GNP}_t + \beta_2 \left[\frac{\alpha}{1 - \beta_2} + \frac{\beta_1 - \beta_2}{1 - \beta_2} \text{GNP}_{t-1} + \frac{\beta_3}{1 - \beta_2} r + \frac{1}{1 - \beta_2} \varepsilon\right]$$

$$- \beta_2 \text{GNP}_{t-1} + \varepsilon,$$

$$\text{AC}_t = \alpha + \beta_1 \text{GNP}_{t-1}$$

$$+ \beta_2 \left[\left(\frac{\alpha}{1 - \beta_2}\right) + \left(\frac{\beta_1 - \beta_2}{1 - \beta_2} - 1\right) \text{GNP}_{t-1} + \left(\frac{\beta_3}{1 - \beta_2}\right) r + \left(\frac{1}{1 - \beta_2}\right) \varepsilon\right] + \varepsilon,$$

$$\text{AC}_t = \alpha + \left[\frac{\beta_2 \alpha}{1 - \beta_2}\right] + \left[\frac{\beta_2(\beta_1 - \beta_2)}{1 - \beta_2} - \beta_2 + \beta_1\right] \text{GNP}_{t-1} + \left[\frac{\beta_2 \beta_3}{1 - \beta_2}\right] r$$

$$+ \left[\frac{\beta_2}{1 - \beta_2}\right] \varepsilon + \varepsilon,$$

$$\text{AC}_t = \left[\frac{\alpha}{1 - \beta_2}\right] + \left[\frac{\beta_1 - \beta_2}{1 - \beta_2}\right] \text{GNP}_{t-1} + \left[\frac{\beta_2 \beta_3}{1 - \beta_2}\right] r + \left[\frac{1}{1 - \beta_2}\right] \varepsilon. \quad (6.9)$$

This is the reduced form of the current AC expressed as a function of GNP in the last period and the interest rate. The reduced forms in Equations (6.8) and (6.9) are the suited forms to be used in the prediction after estimating the parameters. A statistical method more advanced than the ordinary least squares is required to estimate the parameters of this system.

Once the parameters are estimated, the value of the next GNP (GNP$_{t+1}$) and next AC (AC$_{t+1}$) can be forecasted using the reduced form equations and plugging in the current values of the determinants.

6.8   INPUT–OUTPUT MATRIX

The idea of forecasting using the input–output relations in the economy is related to the famous analysis of the input–output matrix introduced by Wassily Leontief and his colleagues in their book *Studies in the Structure of the American Economy*, published in 1953. An input–output matrix shows the interconnection among the economy's industries and sectors as they produce their goods and services and use other goods and services as inputs to their output. It traces down all the inter-industry and intra-industry transactions and record them in dollar values. For example, an increase in the production of furniture as an output will lead to an increase in the production of many inputs such as wood, fabric, leather, plastic, nails, glue, and the equipment and machinery required to produce them. Then, an increase in each of these inputs may lead to increases in what is producing it. Producing more wood would require cutting more trees and having the equipment and services necessary for that and so on. It is a domino effect that would run through the entire economy to illustrate the interdependence among its components. Tracking down this flow of input–output in the entire economy requires constructing a comprehensive and intricate set of tables of interconnection among the various components of the economy. It has been done by the federal government under the responsibility of the US Department of Commerce. Table 6.22 is a basic sample to show how the input–output flow is arranged. Sectors of the economy are listed both horizontally and vertically; the final markets are shown in their individual, institutional, and governmental consuming units; and the value added is listed at the bottom in its three components: employees, employers, and government. The table culminates into producing the GNP at the lower right corner as a summation of both directions.

There are many tables in the matrix set; some involve more details and specifications. Three of these types of tables are worth mentioning for their relevance to forecasting:

1. *The output-distribution table*: The values in this table are obtained by dividing the rows of the input–output flow table by the row totals. It shows the patterns of industry in comparison to the patterns of individual firms.

2. *The direct-requirement table*: The values in this table are obtained by dividing each entry in the columns of producers by the column table. It shows the interdependencies in the economy by relating each of the inputs to the total output in the industry. In this table, the values stand for the amount of money each input requires for each dollar of output in each industry.

3. *The total-requirement table*: It shows the direct and indirect requirements of each industry to produce one dollar of output. This table is called the Leontief inverse matrix. It takes into consideration all of the interrelations among the input and output of all industries.

Despite the high significance of the input–output analysis, it may not be as important nowadays for the purpose of forecasting. Among the shortcomings is the tedious,

TABLE 6.22 Input–Output Flow

	Producers								Final Markets			
	Agriculture	Mining	Construction	Manufacturing	Trade	Transportation	Services	Other	Persons	Investors	Foreigners	Government
Agriculture												
Mining												
Construction												
Manufacturing												
Trade												
Transportation												
Services												
Other												
Employee compensation												
Owners of businesses and capital	Profit-type income and capital consumption allowances								GNP			
Government	Indirect business taxes and current surplus of government enterprises, etc.											

Source: US Department of Commerce, Bureau of the Census, Historical Statistics of the United States.

232

time-consuming, and complex process of following all matrix details even if the tables are constructed by the Department of Commerce. Also, the matrix is usually constructed later in time. The lag may last 2 or 3 years during which many factors may change in this rapidly moving world. Another shortcoming is that all changes between input and output are assumed to be constant in addition to the lack of any explicit consideration of prices.

6.9   JUDGMENTAL MODELS

Judgmental models are qualitative in nature. These models depend on people's intuitiveness and experience in determining what product sells, what consumers want or do not want, and what conditions and circumstances the market will experience. On these bases, they would decide the size of production needed and the sales or profits expected. A bright example is the late Steve Jobs of Apple Inc., who exhibited this ability as well as it has ever been exhibited.

6.9.1   Opinions and Polls

Firms often seek the opinions and views of others who are in touch with the market and are knowledgeable about the product and its customers. It can take the form of polling several groups, such as executives, the sales staff, the customers, and the market experts. Firms can also use the Delphi method, which uses a panel of corporate executives and experts but questioning them separately, which makes it different from the jury of executives mentioned above that meet together and form a collective view. If the firm has an international connection through its product, it can also form a council of distinguished foreign dignitaries and business people to get their global perspectives on the events and issues related to its market share and international consumer behavior.

6.9.2   Surveys and Market Research

The idea of utilizing surveys in forecasting stems from the fact that most major decisions of individuals and firms are usually preconceived and mostly predetermined. The required expenditures are planned and allocated before the actual spending. This constitutes a good rationale for surveying people on their plans and intentions, which is most likely to reveal valuable information for forecasting. This is why it is justified for US firms to spend billions of dollars on surveys that enlist millions of people who are asked variety of questions that ultimately have strong economic relevance. Among the famous surveys are the surveys of consumer's expenditures that are conducted by the Bureau of the Census; surveys of business executives, which are conducted by a consortium of institutions such as the US Department of Commerce, the Securities and Exchange Commission, the National Industrial Conference Board, and McGraw-Hill Publishing Company. The third famous set of surveys is the surveys of inventory changes and sales expectations that are conducted by the US Department of Commerce, the Institute for Supply Management, and Dun & Bradstreet Company. Another important survey related to consumers in the national context is the Survey of Consumer Confidence, which produces three monthly indexes: the Consumer Confidence Index, the Present Situation Index, and the Expectations Index.

When it comes to the short-term projections, surveying people proves most significant, as people are assumed to provide insights into their intended actions on financial and economic matters. This technique is perhaps the only available way to predict consumer's responses on a new product. Over time, surveys have proved their great capacity to reveal the nature and direction of changes in consumer tastes and preferences.

As for market research, it is a general area that may include questionnaires, observations, "clinical tests," field interviews, and focus groups. The primary purpose is to know the consumer well, demographically, economically, socially, and psychologically. Knowing the consumer means knowing what to produce and how to market the product. Market research is often used to introduce a new product, a new improvement on an existing product, or even to introduce a new business or new market. Data obtained through the various research techniques are often extrapolated qualitatively and quantitatively to form certain predictions.

6.10   FORECASTING ACCURACY AND RELIABILITY

Forecasting accuracy and reliability refer to the predictive consistency and effectiveness of the forecasting process and to its capacity to come up with forecast values that are as close as possible to the actual values that would be realized later. Such closeness and consistency between the forecast value and the actual value mean that the difference between them has to be kept as minimum as to make it totally insignificant. The difference or the error term is typically due to many reasons related to the design of the model, its specifications, the type of data and the way of collecting them, and the process of data analysis. The major reasons of errors are as follows:

- The omitted variables.
- The equation misspecification.
- The random fluctuations.
- The economic misinterpretations.
- The explanatory variables identification and reliance.

As we have seen, there are typical tests of the forecast goodness that target the value of error and see if it is at its minimum. Among these are the following:

- The average absolute error (AAE) or MAD:

$$\text{AAE or MAD} = \frac{\Sigma \, |A - F|}{n}.$$

- The RMSE or the sample mean forecast error (SMFE):

$$\text{RMSE} = \text{SMFE} = \sqrt{\frac{\Sigma_1 [A - F]^2}{n - p}}.$$

- Correlation coefficient (r):

$$r = \frac{\sigma_{AF}}{\sigma_A \cdot \sigma_F}.$$

Accuracy of any forecast has an inverse relationship with the time horizon of the forecast. The shorter the past period of time the forecaster uses and the shorter the future period he would predict for, the more accurate the forecast. In other words, the recent past is much more predictive for the near future. Accuracy is often related to more careful and sophisticated procedures that cost a lot, which should make managers aware that the more the desire and enthusiasm to get accurate forecast, the more willingness is required to bear the necessary cost. Despite the fact that the very idea of forecasting is invented basically to help managers make educated and confident judgment in their decision process for the future, sound subjective judgment about forecasting is required of them, so much as to make this a circle of interdependent subjectivity in decision making.

SUMMARY

- Following both the theoretical analysis and empirical estimation of demand in Chapters 4 and 5, this chapter completes the trend of thought into forecasting demand. Forecasting is the process of predicting the future state and value of economic variables and probing into their potential changes. It is about projecting the past and present data into the future using the current knowledge and skills. The major justification of forecasting is to learn from past experience, reduce life's uncertainties, and minimize risks. As for the managerial purposes, economic forecasting helps in both the short-term operational decisions as well as in the planning for the long-term growth and stability.

- There are many forecasting methods. Each can be used for the most appropriate condition. Choosing the right method depends on several factors such as the nature of what is being predicted and the purpose of the forecast, time frame for the projection, time available and lead time, cost of the process, the accuracy level, data availability and appropriateness, and the complexity of the forecasting model.

- Models of forecasting are categorized into quantitative and qualitative models based on the analytical methods used. Quantitative models are those that utilized numerical historical data. They have two subcategories: (1) structural models, such as econometrical models, depend on assessing the relationship between the related variables as dependent and independent; (2) nonstructural models are concerned with observing the patterns of change in variables over time. Barometric and time series models are representative of the nonstructural types of models. The qualitative models depend on descriptive ways to examine and interpret the observation in order to discuss the underlying patterns of relationships and to infer their meaning and significance. These models utilize value judgment, but by experts and collective measures such as polls, surveys, and market research.

- This chapter focuses on the time series model as one of the most common and practical models of forecasting. It uses historical data and utilizes a simple bivariate regression analysis, where time trend serves as the explanatory variable for the changes in the dependent variables. Several common possibilities of variation in the time series data were addressed such as the secular trend, seasonal variations, cyclical fluctuations, and random changes. Recognizing these variations requires that the regression estimates be adjusted according to these variations in order to more closely and fairly reflect the reality. Three methods to capture the impact of seasonality were addressed: the simple average of errors method, the actual-to-forecast ratio method, and the dummy variables method.

- Smoothed forecast is another way to treat the time series data that are characterized by slow and infrequent changes or certain degree of randomness and irregularity. Three smoothing techniques were explained: the simple moving average, the weighted moving average, and the exponential smoothing. Two more methods were addressed to check for the appropriateness of the forecasting techniques in terms of how close the estimates were to the actual data. These methods are the root-mean-square error (RMSE) and the mean absolute deviation (MAD).

- Barometric forecasting is another way that depends on the composite indices of the economy as they are assumed to smooth out random variations and provide more reliable predictions and less confusing signals. One of the most popular composite indices is the leading economic indicator (LEI), which can typically signal the march toward economic recession or the way to recovery.

- The most common and reliable techniques used in forecasting are the econometric models, whether they use the single-equation model or multiple-equation model. They are distinct from other forecasting models in that they rely on causal reasoning as opposed to mere extrapolating of past data. The process of forecasting in the econometric models involves substituting the predicted values of the explanatory variables into the estimated regression equation to obtain the predicted value of the dependent variable during the period of forecast.

- Another way of forecasting involves using an input–output table that would show the extent and degree of interdependence among the various variables, sectors, and industries. Other judgmental ways of forecasting can also include consumer surveys, market research, people's poles, and expert views and opinions. The last topic in this chapter addresses forecasting accuracy and reliability, which refers to the predictive consistency and effectiveness of the forecasting process and its capacity to deliver forecasted values that are as close as possible to the actual values that will be realized later.

KEY TERMS

forecasting	smoothing technique	coincidental indicators
structural models	simple moving average	single-equation model
nonstructural models	root-mean-square error (RMSE)	multiple-equation model
time series analysis	weighted moving average	input–output matrix
secular trend	exponential smoothing	direct-requirement table
seasonal variation	mean absolute deviation (MAD)	output-distribution table
cyclical fluctuations	barometric forecasting	total-requirement table
random changes	leading indicators	judgmental models
dummy variable	lagging indicators	forecasting accuracy

LIST OF FORMULAS

- The linear function:

$$Y_t = \alpha + \beta t.$$

- The quadratic function:

$$Y_t = \alpha + \beta t + \gamma t^2.$$

- The exponential function:

$$Y_t = \alpha \beta^t.$$

- The logarithmic function:

$$\log Y_t = \log \alpha + t \, \log \beta.$$

- Seasonally adjusted forecast:

$$F_{\text{sa}} = F[A/F]_q.$$

- Sample moving average:

$$A_{t+1} = \frac{A_t + A_{t-1} + A_{t-2} + \ldots A_{t-p+1}}{p}.$$

- Root-mean-square error (RMSE):

$$\min \text{RMSE} = \sqrt{\frac{\sum [A_t - F_t]^2}{n - p}}.$$

- Weighted moving average:

$$F_{t+1} = \sqrt{\frac{w_1(A_t) + w_2(A_{t-1}) + w_3(A_{t-2}) + \ldots .w_p(A_{t-p+1})}{\sum wi}}.$$

- Smoothed forecast:

$$F_{t+1} = F_t + \alpha[A_t - F_t].$$

- Mean absolute deviation (MAD):

$$\text{MAD} = \frac{\sum |A - F|}{n}.$$

- Econometric equation:

$$Y = \alpha + \beta_1 x_1 + \beta_2 x_2 + \ldots \beta_n x_n + \varepsilon.$$

- Reduced form for the current AC:

$$AC_t = \left[\frac{\alpha}{1 - \beta_2}\right] + \left[\frac{\beta_1 + \beta_2}{1 - \beta_2}\right] GNP_{t-1} + \left[\frac{\beta_2 + \beta_3}{1 - \beta_2}\right] r + \left[\frac{1}{1 - \beta_2}\right] \varepsilon.$$

EXERCISES

1. Explain the nature and purpose of economic forecasting and how significant it is in the context of managerial economics.

2. List and compare the various models of forecasting in terms of their advantages, disadvantages, and how they fit into specific needs of the business firms.

3. List and explain the possible variations in the time series data. How are they different from each other? How would they affect the data and how would they be counted for?

4. Explain the concept of smoothing in forecasting. List and compare the various types of smoothing techniques and when they would be needed and how would they work.

5. Explain the econometric method of forecasting and describe the process from specifying the econometric equation to having the final results of forecasted variables. How would you rank the econometric models among the rest of the forecasting models and why?

6. Consider the following actual data for sales during the 12 months of 2012.

Month	Actual Sales	Three-Month Moving Average	MAD$_1$	MAD$_2$
January	71,290			
February	70,912			
March	62,540			
April	64,258			
May	68,912			
June	70,512			
July	72,436			
August	70,887			
September	68,500			
October	64,312			
November	61,850			
December	66,275			

   (a) Fill in the third column of 3-month moving average.
   (b) Calculate the forecast value of sales in January of 2013.
   (c) Calculate the forecast value of sales in February 2013 if January sales turn out to be 70,937.

7. Use the data in question 6 to calculate 5-month weighted moving average to obtain the forecast value of sales in January 2013 if the last 5 months of 2012 are weighted by 0.12, 0.17, 0.15, 0.21, 0.19, respectively.

8. Use the exponential smoothing technique to predict the sales value of January 2013 given that the actual sales for December 2012 is 66,275 and the forecast sale is what you got in Column 3. Consider an α-value of 0.31.

9. Use Columns 2 and 3 of the table in question 6 as the actual and forecasted values to calculate the mean absolute deviation (MAD) for the period April to December. Record the results in Column 4 of the table.

10. Repeat the process in question 9 to obtain the mean absolute deviation (MAD) after dropping April values and adding January 2013 values as calculated and given in questions 6(b) and 6(c). Record your results in Column 5.

UNIT III

MANAGERIAL DECISIONS
AT THE FIRM LEVEL

7

PRODUCTION THEORY

As is clear from the previous chapters, the focus of managerial economics is on the parts of microeconomics that are useful in practical application. The unique contribution of managerial economics is its formulation and the use of analytical models to facilitate application of microeconomic principles. Managerial economics connects theory with quantitative methods using analytical models. For example, microeconomics provides a general model of consumer behavior that leads to the notion of consumer demand for a product and related concepts such as elasticity. Quantitative methods provide tools for estimating unknown parameters. Demand models bring the theory and methods together to enable applied demand analysis. Similarly, microeconomics provides a general model of production and related concepts such as the **marginal rate of technical substitution** (MRTS) and **returns to scale**. Again, quantitative methods provide tools for estimating any unknown parameters. This chapter provides a review of the economic theory of production, but more importantly, it provides analytical models that tie the theory and quantitative methods together. This leads to methods for measuring concepts such as factor substitution and returns to scale.

Neither theory nor quantitative methods can have much practical use without the critical link between them. Due to epistemic (systems) and aleatory (random) uncertainty, the analytical model should ideally be robust; that is, it should enable acceptable performance in both kinds of uncertainty. As we continue, the managerial economics approach will be applied to facilitate analysis of production.

7.1 VARIABILITY OF INPUTS THROUGHOUT TIME

In terms of how inputs of production are related to the time span, a simplified (but practical) model of production considers three periods through which production takes place: (1) **market period**, when all inputs are considered fixed; (2) **short-run period**, when at least

Managerial Economics: A Mathematical Approach, First Edition. M. J. Alhabeeb and L. Joe Moffitt.
© 2013 John Wiley & Sons, Inc. Published 2013 by John Wiley & Sons, Inc.

one input is fixed; and (3) **long-run period**, when all inputs become variable. The span of these periods progresses from shorter to longer. For example, for a young entrepreneur who has just started his own landscape job, everything would seem fixed in the morning after the storm. He might manage to clear a couple of driveways of the falling branches using a handsaw and wheelbarrow. In the short run, he might buy a chainsaw and a larger cart, but in the long run, every factor in his production setup would be subject to change. He will have more employees, some of whom will be skillful and experienced; more equipment, some of which will be sophisticated; a fleet of trucks; and a host of other services. This period is extended into the future, and that is why it is called the long run.

In a more advanced analysis, dynamic models go beyond the assumptions of these three discrete stages to a continuous and more flexible concept of variability of production inputs throughout the time span.

7.2 PRODUCTION FUNCTION

The economic theory of production provides a framework for quantitative analysis of production and cost. In addition, though not obvious, this theory provides a qualitative guide to production decisions; this is illustrated in the following example.

The Wall Street Journal reports the case of a manufacturing firm in Connecticut, which moved its operations from Bristol, CT, to Juarez, Mexico, and then moved back to Connecticut 4 years later, for economic reasons. Why do you think the firm may have moved in the first place? Although there is usually a standard explanation for this type of move, can you guess why it moved back; that is, what were the economic reasons for the return to Connecticut? Is it possible that a production economics principle could have been considered "on the back of an envelope" rather than being ignored in making the move to Juarez? Let us begin with an overview of some basic concepts such as the production function.

The **production function** is usually the starting point for describing the theory of production economics. It describes the relationship between inputs and output of production. In particular, it refers to the various ways to transform inputs into output. The production function specifies the maximum level of output obtainable from any given inputs. In other words, the production function implies (and targets) efficiency, specifically what is called **technological efficiency**, the process that yields the highest possible level of output when employing a particular set of inputs.

Using a very general algebraic form, the production function for a single product is expressed as

$$y = f(x_1, x_2, \ldots, x_n),$$

where both sides of production, y the output and x_i the input vector, are usually measured in physical units. Table 7.1 gives numerical examples of how we can obtain various levels of output by choosing different combinations of labor units (the first row) and capital units (the first column). For example, employing 20 workers and 10 pieces of equipment gives 60 units of output. However, if we want to increase production tenfold, that is, to obtain 600 units of output, we would need to increase the number of workers to 50 and pieces of equipment to 20. The 600 units of output can also be produced by other combinations such as 80 workers and 10 pieces of equipment, or 60 workers and 15 pieces of equipment, and so on. The choice of a specific combination of inputs to produce a certain level of output is a managerial decision that takes several economic factors into consideration. Figure 7.1 discreetly depicts the production

TABLE 7.1   Production Function

Labor → ↓Capital	10	20	30	40	50	60	70	80	90	100
5	10	20	40	60	160	290	440	500	550	520
10	30	60	160	290	430	550	580	600	590	560
15	60	160	290	440	550	600	620	620	610	590
20	100	240	440	550	600	620	630	630	630	620
25	160	290	550	580	610	630	640	640	640	640
30	160	320	550	600	620	630	640	650	650	650
35	160	440	550	600	620	630	640	650	660	660
40	130	440	500	550	600	620	640	650	660	670

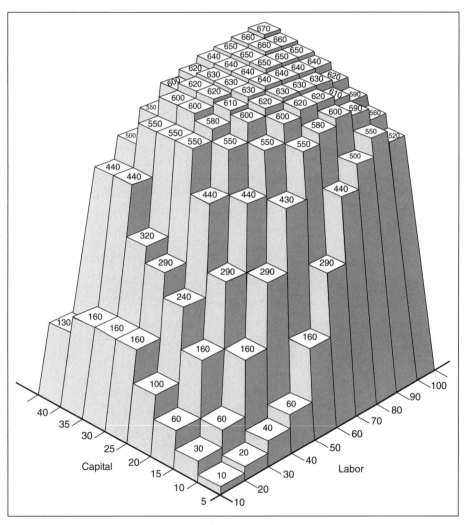

FIGURE 7.1

surface as it forms out of the top surfaces of the vertical bars, which represent the possible levels of output that can be produced by various sets of inputs. The height of the bars stands for the levels of output, while the right dimension on the ground displays the labor units and the left dimension shows the capital units.

7.3   GRAPHICAL REPRESENTATION OF THE PRODUCTION FUNCTION

Let us consider a more specific model of the production function with a single variable input using algebra. Assume an output of a synthesized hormone, y, and input of a microbe used in its manufacture, x_1. With this notation, we can characterize the manufacturing process algebraically by the following production function with parameters, a and b, which could, of course, be estimated by the maximum likelihood method using experimental data:

$$y = ax^b.$$

Let us take a look at the curve of this production function as it changes for different values of parameter a, to see how it behaves. Note that as the value of parameter a increases, the **total product** (TP) curve shifts upward (Figure 7.2a). Now, let us look at this production function for different values of parameter b, as shown in Figure 7.2b. Note how the TP curve pivots upward with increasing values of parameter b. If we focus on a particular

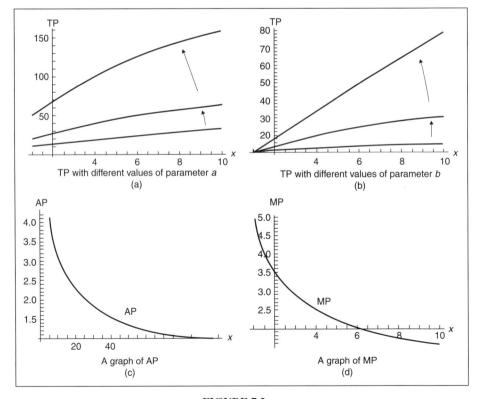

FIGURE 7.2

production function such as $y = 10x_1^{0.5}$, we can see how the **average product** (AP) and the **marginal product** (MP) get their shapes. Although we will discuss AP and MP later in detail, it is sufficient to say here that AP is the output per unit of input at a certain level of that input; that is, $AP = y/x_1$. In this case, it is expressed as $AP = 10x_1^{-0.5}$. AP can be interpreted as a measure of the productivity of an input, where its value can be very small but does not go below zero. MP of an input is the first derivative of output with respect to that input, or (dy/dx_1). In this case, it is expressed as $MP = 5x_1^{-0.5}$. MP is interpreted as the change in output per unit increase in input at a particular input level. Figures 7.2c and 7.2d show AP and MP, respectively.

The three popular analytical production functions involving two or more variable inputs are (1) the linear function, given as $y = ax_1 + bx_2$; (2) Cobb–Douglas type, given as $y = ax_1^b x_2^c$; and (3) the **Leontief production function**, expressed as $y = \min(ax_1, bx_2)$.

These functions are analytical models of production that can accommodate any number of inputs. Each has implications for the ability to substitute one input for another and for returns to scale.

If the number of inputs is 2 or if employment of all but two of the inputs is fixed, then the production function is graphed as a surface in three dimensions. If output is on the vertical axis, then the points of intersection between the production surface and a plane parallel to either the y–x_1 or y–x_2 planes show TP. The points of intersection between the production surface and a plane parallel to the x_1–x_2 plane reveal the input combinations on the x_1–x_2 plane, which correspond to a given level of output.

Let us look at the three-dimensional graphs (Figures 7.3, 7.4, and 7.5) for these production functions. In this example, parameters for the linear function are $a = 2$ and $b = 3$, the Cobb–Douglas function are $a = 10$, $b = 0.2$, and $c = 0.5$, and for the Leontief function, $a = 3$ and $b = 3$.

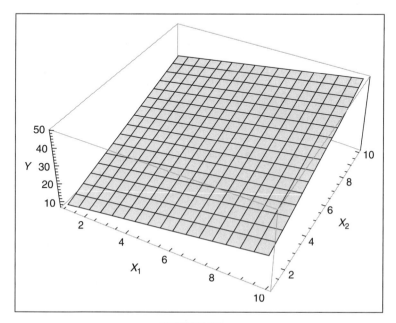

FIGURE 7.3

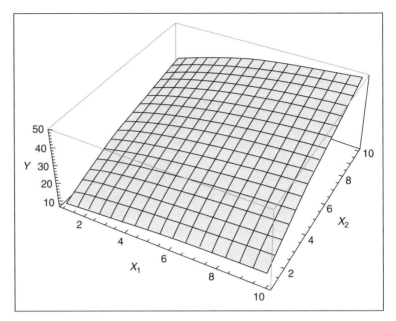

FIGURE 7.4

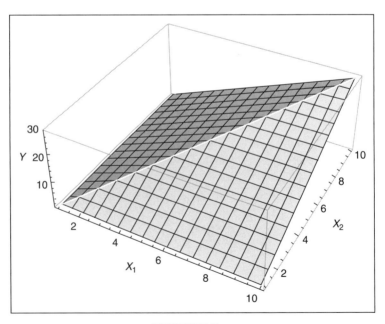

FIGURE 7.5

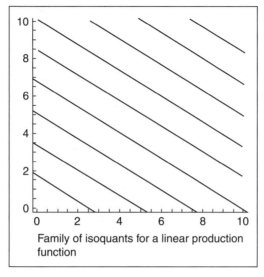

Family of isoquants for a linear production function

FIGURE 7.6

Any input combinations corresponding to a certain level of output form a contour line called an **isoquant**, the slope of which is called the MRTS. This slope indicates how well the inputs substitute for one another.

Factor substitution is an important characteristic of production with two or more variable inputs. It can be investigated by a statistical analysis of production and, therefore, can be studied to provide information of interest for management decisions. Substitution possibilities are indicated by the shape of isoquants. Linear isoquants show that

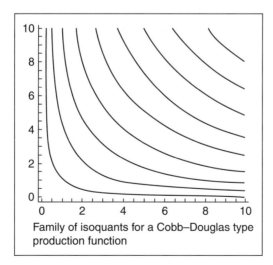

Family of isoquants for a Cobb–Douglas type production function

FIGURE 7.7

substituting one input for another can be easily accomplished to maintain production levels. They appear like parallel straight lines between the axes. Traditionally looking iso-quants that are bowed toward the origin are exhibited by a production function such as the Cobb–Douglas. They show that substitution is possible but becomes increasingly difficult. Isoquants that are bowed to be L-shaped indicate that input substitution is not possible. These types of isoquants are exhibited by the Leontief production function. Isoquant maps associated with the three production functions are shown in Figures 7.6, 7.7, and 7.8.

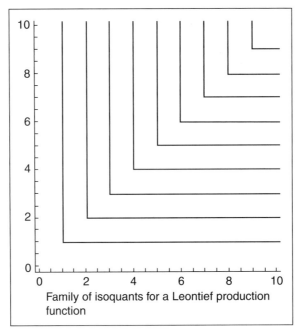

FIGURE 7.8

7.4   SHORT-RUN, ONE VARIABLE INPUT FUNCTION

Let us specify the production function (Y) as a short-run function for a certain product that is produced by using two inputs, capital (K) and labor (L). Let us also assume that we hold capital constant at a certain level and allow labor (L) to vary while we observe how the output (Q) changes according to the change in labor:

$$Q_L = f(K_0, L). \tag{7.1}$$

Table 7.2 shows a similar scenario in numbers. The units of labor (L) used in production are listed in Column 1, and the TP produced by the utilization of those labor units is listed in Column 2 and shown in the upper panel of Figure 7.9.

TABLE 7.2

L	TP	MP_L	AP_L	ε_L	Stages
0	0	0	0	0	I
1	8	8	8	1	
2	20	12	10	1.2	Stage I
3	33	13	11	1.18	$\varepsilon_L > 1$
4	47	14	11.75	1.19	Stage II
5	60	13	12	1.08	$0 < \varepsilon_L < 1$
6	69	9	11.5	0.78	
7	75	6	10.7	0.56	
8	77	2	9.6	0.21	Stage III
9	76	−1	8.4	−0.12	$\varepsilon_L < 0$
10	73	−3	7.3	−0.41	

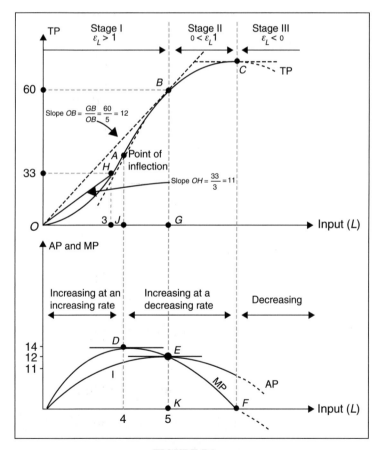

FIGURE 7.9

Equation (7.1) can also be written as equal to the TP related to the variable input, which in this case is labor (L):

$$Q_L = f(K_0, L) = \text{TP}_L,$$

where TP_L is the TP of labor, defined as the maximum amount of product that can be produced using a certain set of capital and labor inputs, K is constant, and L is variable. The marginal product of labor (MP_L) is the change in the total product of labor (TP_L) as a result of the change in units of labor. It is the change in TP_L brought about by the last unit of labor entering production. This change can be expressed as the partial derivative of the production function with respect to labor:

$$\text{MP}_L = \frac{\Delta \text{TP}_L}{\Delta L},$$

$$\text{MP}_L = \frac{\partial f(K_0, L)}{\partial L},$$

$$\text{MP}_L = \frac{\partial \text{TP}_L}{\partial L}.$$

Column 3 of Table 7.2 and the lower panel of Figure 7.9 shows how the MP_L changes according to the change in TP.

Similarly, we can express the marginal product of capital (MP_K) if we hold labor constant and allow capital to vary:

$$\text{MP}_K = \frac{\Delta \text{TP}_K}{\Delta K},$$

$$\text{MP}_K = \frac{\partial f(K_0, L_0)}{\partial K},$$

$$\text{MP}_K = \frac{\partial \text{TP}_K}{\partial K}.$$

Average product of labor (AP_L) is obtained by dividing TP_L by the input units (L):

$$\text{AP}_L = \frac{\text{TP}_L}{L}.$$

Note how AP_L changes with the addition of more units of labor, as shown in Table 7.2 and Figure 7.9.

7.5 DYNAMIC RELATIONS AMONG PRODUCTION CURVES

Looking closely at Table 7.2 and Figure 7.9, we can make the following observations, which point out how the total, marginal, and average products are related to each other:

1. As labor input increases, such as hiring additional workers, while equipment stays the same, the total output or TP_L would change in three different ways:

(a) It would increase at an increasing rate between points O and A on the upper panel of the graph. This is represented by the number of workers up to 4 in Table 7.2. Point A is called the point of inflection. It is the point at which the rate of growth in TP changes from increasing to decreasing.

(b) It would continue to increase between points A and C but at a decreasing rate at C, and TP reaches its maximum. Table 7.2 shows that this phase of growth occurs between adding the fifth and the eighth worker. To be precise, it is a little beyond the eighth unit, but we approximate it at the eighth unit since we are using workers as non-divisible units.

(c) It would decrease right after point C, as shown by the dashed segment of the TP_L curve. Table 7.2 shows the decrease beyond the eighth worker as TP drops from 77 to 76 and 73 units when the ninth and tenth workers are added.

2. Since MP_L is equal to the partial derivative of the TP_L function, it is equal to the slope of TP_L at any point. The slope gets to its maximum at point A, corresponding to point D in the lower panel of the graph, where MP_L reaches its maximum. The slope of TP_L decreases to zero as it becomes a horizontal line at point C where TP_L reaches its maximum. This corresponds to point F in the lower panel where MP_L reaches zero.

3. Since AP_L is obtained by dividing TP by the number of units of labor $\left(AP_L = \frac{TP_L}{L}\right)$, it can also be obtained as the slope of any line (cord) extended from the origin (O) to any point on the TP curve. For example, the slope of OB can be obtained by

$$\text{Slope OB} = \frac{\text{Rise}}{\text{Run}}$$
$$= \frac{GB}{OB} = \frac{60}{5} = 12.$$

It is the same as

$$AP_L = \frac{TP_L}{L} = \frac{60}{5} = 12.$$

This corresponds to point E on the lower panel of the graph, which happens to be the highest point on the AP_L curve. Similarly, we can consider another cord such as OH:

$$\text{Slope } OH = \frac{\text{Rise}}{\text{Run}}$$
$$= \frac{HJ}{OJ} = \frac{33}{3} = 11.$$

It is the same as

$$AP_L = \frac{TP_L}{L} = \frac{33}{3} = 11.$$

It corresponds to point I on the AP_L curve.

4. MP_L intersects with AP_L at the point when AP_L reaches its maximum. This is point E in the lower panel of the graph. Mathematically, this case can be derived by differentiating the AP function and setting the first derivative with respect to labor to zero:

$$AP_L = \frac{TP_L}{L} = \frac{f(K_0, L)}{L} = \frac{Q_L}{L},$$

$$\frac{\partial AP_L}{\partial L} = \frac{L\left[\frac{\partial Q}{\partial L}\right] - Q}{L^2},$$

$$\frac{\partial AP_L}{\partial L} = \frac{L[MP_L] - Q}{L^2} = 0,$$

$$L[MP_L] - Q = 0,$$

$$L[MP_L] = Q,$$

$$MP_L = \frac{Q}{L},$$

$$MP_L = AP_L.$$

The level of input (the number of workers in this case) at which this equality occurs is called the extensive margin of production, because any added input beyond this point (point K in the lower panel of the graph) would cause AP to fall.

5. At any level of input before the extensive margin of production (point K), MP is higher than AP, but AP is rising to the top:

$$MP_L > AP_L,$$

$$\frac{\partial AP_L}{\partial L} > 0.$$

At any level of input beyond the extensive margin of production (point K), MP is lower than AP, which is falling from the top throughout this phase:

$$MP_L < AP_L,$$

$$\frac{\partial AP_L}{\partial L} = 0.$$

This implies that only at the point of equality (E) does AP_L remain stationary, neither rising nor falling:

$$MP_L = AP_L,$$

$$\frac{\partial AP_L}{\partial L} > 0.$$

6. Relating MP_L to AP_L would also produce what is called the **production elasticity** of labor (ε_L). It is defined as the responsiveness of output to changes in input. In this case, it would reflect how TP responds if we hire five additional workers.

Like any elasticity, this is measured by the proportionate rate of change in Q with respect to L:

$$\varepsilon_L = \frac{\partial Q}{\partial L}\left[\frac{L}{Q}\right],$$

$$\varepsilon_L = \frac{\frac{\partial Q_L}{\partial L}}{Q_L},$$

$$\varepsilon_L = \frac{MP_L}{AP_L}.$$

So, the production elasticity is obtained by the ratio of MP to AP. It is calculated in Column 5 of Table 7.2. We can observe that when

$$\varepsilon_L > 1 = MP_L > AP_L,$$

$$0 < \varepsilon_L < 1 = 0 < MP_L < AP_L,$$

$$\varepsilon_L < 1 = MP_L < 0.$$

7. The above-mentioned ranges of production elasticity are distinctively related to what is known as the three stages of production:

   (a) *Stage I*: This stage of production extends from the start to the point of equality between MP and AP at E. It is characterized by a steadily rising AP_L until it reaches its maximum. The firm can continue to add additional workers during this stage. MP_L is above AP_L throughout this stage, although it has both rising and declining segments. Production elasticity during this stage is larger than 1. The number of labor units (K) that corresponds to the maximum AP_L is called the extensive margin.

   (b) *Stage II*: This stage extends between the extensive margin and the intensive margin (F), which is the level of labor at which MP reaches zero. During this stage, both AP_L and MP_L decline, but AP_L is higher than MP_L throughout this stage. The production elasticity is larger than zero but less than 1.

   (c) *Stage III*: This stage is beyond the intensive margin of labor at F, where MP_L becomes negative beyond that point. Both TP_L and AP_L decline during this stage, and production elasticity is negative. An effective management would not recommend operating at this stage. In fact, even during Stage I, operation is not recommended. Only Stage II would be recommended for the firm to operate; that is to specify the maximizing profit operation between the extensive and intensive margins of labor.

Example 7.1
Consider the following **Cobb–Douglas production function**:

$$TP = 70(K)^{0.6}(L)^{0.4}.$$

(a) Find AP_K and AP_L.

(b) Find MP_K and MP_L.

Consider (a) and (b) if $K = 20$ and $L = 100$ units.

Solution:

(a) $\text{TP} = 70(K)^{0.6}(L)^{0.4}$:

$$\text{AP}_K = \frac{\text{TP}}{K}$$

$$= \frac{70\,(K)^{0.6}\,(L)^{0.4}}{K}$$

$$= 70(K)^{-0.4}(L)^{0.4}$$

$$= 70\left[\frac{L}{K}\right]^{0.4}$$

$$= 70\left[\frac{100}{20}\right]^{0.4}$$

$$= 133.26.$$

$$\text{AP}_L = \frac{\text{TP}}{L}$$

$$= \frac{70\,(K)^{0.6}\,(L)^{0.4}}{L}$$

$$= 70(K)^{0.6}(L)^{-0.6}$$

$$= 70\left[\frac{K}{L}\right]^{0.6}$$

$$= 70\left[\frac{20}{100}\right]^{0.6}$$

$$= 26.65.$$

(b) $\text{TP} = 70(K)^{0.6}(L)^{0.4}$:

$$\text{MP}_K = \frac{\partial \text{TP}}{\partial K} = \frac{\partial[70\,(K)^{0.6}\,(L)^{0.4}]}{\partial K}$$

$$= (0.6)(70)(K)^{-0.4}(L)^{0.4}$$

$$= 42\left[\frac{L}{K}\right]^{0.4}$$

$$= 42\left[\frac{100}{20}\right]^{0.4}$$

$$= 79.95.$$

$$\text{MP}_L = \frac{\partial \text{TP}}{\partial L} = \frac{\partial[70\,(K)^{0.6}\,(L)^{0.4}]}{\partial L}$$

$$= (0.6)(70)(L)^{-0.6}(K)^{0.6}$$

$$= 42 \left[\frac{K}{L} \right]^{0.6}$$

$$= 42 \left[\frac{20}{100} \right]^{0.6}$$

$$= 15.99.$$

Example 7.2

Q is a Cobb–Douglas production function using two inputs, capital (K) and labor (L), and expressed as

$$Q = 90(K)^{1/3}(L)^{2/3}. \tag{7.2}$$

Derive the reduced formulas for (a) MP_K, (b) MP_L, (c) AP_K, and (d) AP_L.

Solution:

(a)

$$MP_K = \frac{\partial Q}{\partial K} = \frac{\partial [90\,(K)^{1/3}\,(L)^{2/3}]}{\partial K},$$

$$MP_K = \frac{90}{3}\,(K)^{-2/3}\,(L)^{2/3}.$$

Substituting the value of $(L)^{2/3}$ from Equation (7.2), $(L)^{2/3} = \dfrac{Q}{90(K)^{1/3}}$:

$$MP_K = 30(K)^{-2/3} \left[\frac{Q}{90(K)^{1/3}} \right],$$

$$MP_K = \frac{Q}{3}(K)^{-1}$$

or

$$MP_K = \frac{Q}{3K}.$$

(b)

$$MP_L = \frac{\partial Q}{\partial L} = \frac{\partial [90\,(K)^{1/3}\,(L)^{2/3}]}{\partial L},$$

$$MP_L = 60\,(L)^{-1/3}\,(K)^{1/3}.$$

Substituting the value of $(K)^{1/3}$ from Equation (7.2), $(K)^{1/3} = \dfrac{Q}{90(L)^{1/3}}$:

$$MP_L = 60(L)^{-1/3}\left[\frac{Q}{90(L)^{2/3}}\right],$$

$$MP_L = \frac{2Q}{3}(L)^{-1}$$

or

$$MP_L = \frac{2Q}{3L}.$$

(c)

$$AP_K = \frac{90\,(K)^{1/3}\,(L)^{2/3}}{K}$$

$$AP_K = 90\,(K)^{-2/3}\,(L)^{2/3},$$

$$AP_K = 90\left[\frac{(L)^{2/3}}{(K)^{2/3}}\right].$$

Substituting the value of $(L)^{2/3}$ from Equation (7.2), $(L)^{2/3} = \dfrac{Q}{90(K)^{1/3}}$:

$$AP_K = 90\left[\frac{\dfrac{Q}{90(K)^{1/3}}}{(K)^{2/3}}\right],$$

$$AP_K = QK^{-1},$$

$$AP_K = \frac{Q}{K}.$$

(d)

$$AP_L = \frac{90\,(K)^{1/3}\,(L)^{2/3}}{L}$$

$$AP_L = 90\,(K)^{1/3}\,(L)^{-1/3},$$

$$AP_L = 90\left[\frac{(K)^{1/3}}{(L)^{1/3}}\right].$$

Substituting $(K)^{1/3} = \dfrac{Q}{90(L)^{2/3}}$:

$$AP_L = 90 \left[\frac{\dfrac{Q}{90(L)^{2/3}}}{(L)^{1/3}} \right],$$

$$AP_L = QL^{-1},$$

$$AP_L = \frac{Q}{L}.$$

Example 7.3

Find the values of TP, AP_K, AP_L, MP_K, and MP_L, if $K = 15$ and $L = 65$.

Solution:

$$TP = Q = 90(15)^{1/3}(65)^{2/3} = 3588,$$

$$AP_K = \frac{Q}{K} = \frac{3588}{15} = 239.2,$$

$$AP_L = \frac{Q}{L} = \frac{3588}{65} = 55.2,$$

$$MP_K = \frac{Q}{3K} = \frac{3588}{3 \times 15} = 79.7,$$

$$MP_L = \frac{2Q}{3L} = \frac{2(3588)}{3 \times 65} = 36.8.$$

Example 7.4

Find the production elasticity of capital (ε_K) and labor (ε_L), given the production function $Q = 20(K)^{1/5}(L)^{4/5}$.

Solution:

$$MP_K = \frac{Q}{5K},$$

$$AP_K = \frac{Q}{K},$$

$$\varepsilon_K = \frac{MP_K}{AP_K}$$

$$= \frac{\dfrac{Q}{5K}}{\dfrac{Q}{K}}$$

$$= \frac{Q}{5K} \times \frac{K}{Q}$$

$$= \frac{1}{5}.$$

$$\text{MP}_L = \frac{4Q}{5L},$$

$$\text{AP}_L = \frac{Q}{L},$$

$$\varepsilon_L = \frac{\text{MP}_L}{\text{AP}_L}$$

$$= \frac{\dfrac{4Q}{5L}}{\dfrac{Q}{L}}$$

$$= \frac{4Q}{5L} \times \frac{L}{Q}$$

$$= \frac{4}{5}.$$

7.6   LAW OF DIMINISHING MARGINAL RETURNS

The law of diminishing returns refers to the declining MP after a certain point in production. It is a short-run concept and considered one of the major technical relationships in economics that has crucial implications. It states that adding successive units of a specific input to production, while holding other inputs constant, would eventually cause productivity to decline. It is associated with the classic notion by Malthus who observed that continuous addition of labor into a particular piece of land would eventually cause land production to decline. Graphically, this decline starts to occur beyond the point of inflection (point A) on the upper panel and the peak of MP at point D on the lower panel. The TP will continue to increase but at a decreasing rate and the MP would still be positive but decline all the way to zero and negative levels. Table 7.2 shows how the increments in TP go from the top 14 to 13, 9, 6, 2, -1, -3 as reflected by the MP figures beyond point D. Mathematically, the case of diminishing marginal returns requires the first partial derivative of TP to be positive and the second partial derivative be negative for any input that is variable:

$$\frac{\partial \text{TP}}{\partial L} = \text{MP}_L > 0,$$

$$\frac{\partial^2 \text{TP}}{\partial L^2} = \frac{\partial \text{MP}_L}{\partial L} < 0,$$

or

$$\frac{\partial \text{TP}}{\partial K} = \text{MP}_K > 0,$$

$$\frac{\partial^2 \text{TP}}{\partial K^2} = \frac{\partial \text{MP}_K}{\partial K} < 0.$$

7.7   LONG-RUN, TWO VARIABLE INPUT FUNCTION

The short-run analysis was about the production function with only one variable input, holding the rest constant. In the long run, all inputs have the potential to become variable. Here, we focus on a production function with two inputs, both of them variable. We can assume that managerial decisions would allow the use of any appropriate combination of the two inputs to produce a certain level of output. This should remind us of the theory of consumer choice, when we discussed the utilization of two commodities, in different combinations, to obtain a certain level of consumer utility. The technical tool for that was the indifference curve (IC). Here, we use a parallel concept of isoquants and its related concepts such as MRTS, which is an analogous tool to the marginal rate of substitution (MRS) in consumer choice.

Isoquants   An isoquant (IQU) is a locus of points representing various combinations of two inputs to produce a certain level of output. The combination is assumed to be the most technologically efficient way of combining the inputs. This refers to the combination that is least costly to obtain the target level of output. As with the IC, a movement along the isoquant changes the ratio of the inputs but does not change the level of output. The utility level remains the same on the IC, so does the level of output on any given isoquant. Figure 7.10 shows a typical map of isoquants on a plane.

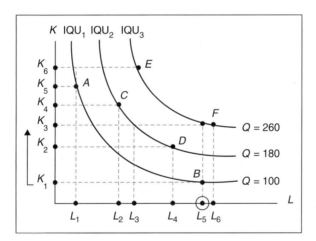

FIGURE 7.10

The three isoquants represent three levels of output: 100, 180, and 260. Each can be produced by a combination of labor and capital determined by the location of a point on the curve. Both points A and B on IQU_1 can produce 100 units of product but A uses an amount of labor represented by L_1 and an amount of capital represented by K_5, while B also produces 100 units but with L_5 and K_1. The same conclusion can be drawn from the other two isoquants and the points on them. Suppose that the firm wants to increase its output from 100 to 260 but wants to keep the same number of workers at L_5. Moving to the isoquant of 260 holding L_5 the same means that capital has to be increased from K_1 to K_3.

We can visualize a map of isoquants in a three-dimensional graph as shown in Figure 7.11. As isoquants represent increasing output, if they are placed progressively away from the origin in a two-dimensional graph, they would be projected up and toward the northeast in a three-dimensional image. Collectively, their outer surface would form the production surface that would resemble a half tent. Each projected contour would reflect the level of production on the vertical axis. This is a more continuous visualization of production surface compared with the discreet visualization shown previously in Figure 7.1.

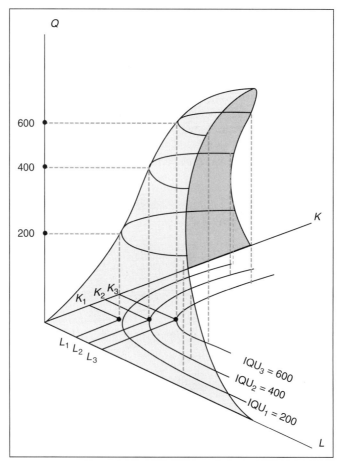

FIGURE 7.11

Isoquants hold the same major characteristics of the ICs:

- They run parallel and do not cross each other.
- The farther they are from the origin toward the northeast, the higher the level of output they represent.

- They slope downward from northwest to southeast. This characteristic reveals the nature of substitution between the two inputs if output is held constant. It leads to the next topic of MRTS. As with the IC, the shape of an isoquant is typical unless the production has a special case, such as the case of inputs as perfect substitutes or the case of fixed-proportion production, in which the shape of isoquants would be, respectively, a straight line going across the axis and a right-angle isoquant.

7.8 MARGINAL RATE OF TECHNICAL SUBSTITUTION (MRTS)

The concept of MRTS is parallel to the concept of MRS, which is related to the IC for consumer choice. The negatively sloped, convex to the origin isoquant curve implies that employing more labor units would require reducing capital units if output is to be held at the same level. The MRTS shows how many units of capital have to be given up for each additional unit of labor added to production, keeping the output level constant. It can be expressed as the ratio of change in capital and change in labor, which in itself is equal to the ratio of the partial derivatives related to the inputs, capital and labor, and ultimately equal to the negative reverse ratio of MP of the two inputs:

$$\text{MRTS} = \frac{\Delta K}{\Delta L} = \frac{dK}{dL} = -\frac{\text{MP}_L}{\text{MP}_K}.$$

Mathematically, this can be obtained by taking the total derivative of the standard production function $Q = f(K, L)$:

$$dQ = \left[\frac{\partial Q}{\partial L}\right] dL + \left[\frac{\partial Q}{\partial K}\right] dK,$$
$$= (\text{MP}_L)dL + (\text{MP}_K)dK.$$

Since the output level is held constant along the isoquant, we can say that dQ is equal to zero ($dQ = 0$):

$$0 = (\text{MP}_L)dL + (\text{MP}_K)dK,$$
$$-(\text{MP}_K)dK = (\text{MP}_L)dL.$$

Rearranging the terms, we get

$$\frac{dK}{dL} = -\frac{\text{MP}_L}{\text{MP}_K},$$

where Q is constant and $dQ = 0$,

$$\left.\frac{dK}{dL}\right|_{dQ=0} = -\frac{\text{MP}_L}{\text{MP}_K} = \text{MRTS}_{K/L},$$

and this is the MRTS of capital for labor.

The strict convexity of the isoquant dictates that the MRTS is a diminishing value along the curve if we descend from northwest to southeast. This can be observed in the graph shown in Figure 7.12. As we move from A to B, we gain 1 unit of labor for giving up 3 units of capital, which makes the MRTS equal to (-3). However, if we move further down from B to C, we still gain 1 unit of labor but lose only $1/2$ unit of capital, which makes the MRTS equal to $\left(-\frac{1}{2}\right)$. So, the amount of input we give up declines for the same amount of input we gain.

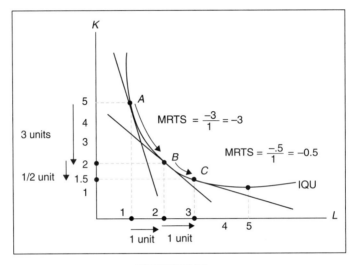

FIGURE 7.12

In essence, as we gain L, its MP_L decreases, and as we lose K, its MP_K increases. Consequently, their ratio (which is the MRTS) decreases because of the division of a smaller value by a larger value: $(MRTS_{K/L} = \frac{MP_L}{MP_K})$.

Consider a Cobb–Douglas production function such as

$$Q = C(K)^{\alpha}(L)^{\beta}.$$

The MRTS between labor and capital is obtained as the ratio of MP_L and MP_K:

$$MP_L = \frac{\partial Q}{\partial L} = \alpha C(L)^{\alpha-1}(K)^{\beta}$$

$$= \frac{\alpha Q}{L},$$

$$MP_K = \frac{\partial Q}{\partial K} = \beta C(L)^{\alpha}(K)^{\beta-1}$$

$$= \frac{\beta Q}{K},$$

$$\text{MRTS} = -\frac{\text{MP}_L}{\text{MP}_K} = -\frac{\dfrac{\alpha Q}{L}}{\dfrac{\beta Q}{K}}$$

$$= \frac{\alpha Q}{L} \times \frac{K}{\beta Q}$$

$$= -\frac{\alpha}{\beta}\left[\frac{K}{L}\right].$$

Example 7.5

Suppose that, for an isoquant of 150 units, the production function is $Q = 15(K)^{1/2}(L)^{1/2}$. Find

(a) the isoquant equation in terms of labor; and

(b) prove that this isoquant is descending from northwest to southeast and convex at the origin.

Solution:

(a) $150 = 15(K)^{1/2}(L)^{1/2}$

$$(K)^{1/2} = \frac{150}{15L^{1/2}} = 10,$$

$$(K)^{1/2} = 10L^{-1/2},$$

$$\sqrt{K} = \frac{10}{L^{1/2}},$$

$$K = \left[\frac{10}{L^{1/2}}\right]^2,$$

$$K = \frac{100}{L}.$$

(b) The down-sloping isoquant must have a negative derivative:

$$\frac{\partial K}{\partial L} = -\left[\frac{100}{L^2}\right] = -100L^{-2} < 0.$$

The convexity to the origin requires a positive second derivative:

$$\frac{\partial^2 K}{\partial L^2} = 200L^{-3} = \frac{200}{L^3} > 0.$$

7.9   THE ECONOMICALLY EFFICIENT REGION OF PRODUCTION

The economically efficient region of production is where the firm restricts its production. Technically, it is where the MPs of inputs is positive, which leads to a negatively sloped isoquant. When the MP turns negative and the production reaches its third stage, it would not be wise to produce because isoquants would have positive slopes and the total production would go down. We can see in Figure 7.13 where that economically efficient point of production lies. It is where the isoquants take the typical shape; that is, the negatively sloped segments between the two ridgelines, *OAE* and *OBE*. The dashed segments on both sides of each isoquant are not suitable for production since the slope (MRTS) is either zero, where the tangent line is perfectly horizontal such as at point *B* of the second isoquant, or is equal to ∞, where the tangent line is perfectly vertical such as at point *A*. In between *A* and *B*, the isoquant would have its normal negative slope, which would make that region the best time of production and which corresponds to Stage II. So, collectively all good segments of the entire isoquant map would be stretched between the two ridgelines, *OAE* and *OBE*, shown as the shaded area in the graph.

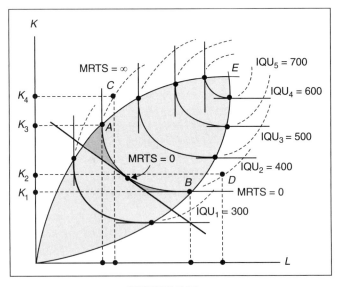

FIGURE 7.13

Generally, the firm would prefer to produce at a negatively sloped segment of the isoquant because it can minimize the cost of production. We can clearly see that on the graph. Let u's consider IQU_2, where production is 400 units. The firm would prefer achieving this level production at *B*, employing L_3 of labor and K_1 of capital, over achieving it at *D* by employing more of both inputs (L_4 and K_2). It would also prefer achieving the same level of production (400 units) at *A*, by employing L_1 and K_3, over achieving it at *C*, which must employ more of both inputs (L_2 and K_4). Any point between A and B on the isoquant would be more cost effective than any other point on the dashed segments on both sides of the isoquant.

7.10   RETURNS TO SCALE

Returns to scale refers to how output responds to proportionate changes (increase and decrease) in all inputs. Three major types of responses can be observed:

(a) **Constant returns to scale** are obtained when output changes by the same percentage as the change in inputs. For example, if both inputs, labor and capital, are doubled and, consequently, the output is also doubled, we say that the production function has exhibited constant returns to scale. We can express this mathematically. Suppose that both inputs, labor and capital, are increased by a constant (C), then the output would also increase by a factor equal to (C):

$$f(CL, CK) = Cf(L, K)   C > 0$$
$$Cf(L, K) = hQ   h = C.$$

  Constant returns to scale is a condition that results from the production function being homogeneous of degree 1.

(b) **Increasing returns to scale** are obtained when output changes by a higher percentage than the percentage of change in inputs. For example, if the inputs are doubled, then the output would be more than double:

$$f(CL, CK) = Cf(L, K)   C > 0$$
$$Cf(L, K) = hQ   h > C.$$

  Increasing returns to scale is a condition that results from the production function being homogeneous of degree greater than 1.

(c) **Decreasing returns to scale** are obtained when output changes by a lower percentage than the percentage of change in inputs. If the inputs are doubled, then the resulting output would be less than double:

$$f(CL, CK) = Cf(L, K)   C > 0.$$
$$Cf(L, K) = hQ   h < C.$$

  Decreasing returns to scale is a condition that results from the production function being homogeneous of degree less than 1.

  In Figure 7.14, the inputs of labor and capital are doubled, from $(L = 4$ units; $K = 2$ units) to $(L = 8$ units, $K = 4$ units), in all of the three panels. On the top panel, the output increases from 400 units to 800 units illustrating the constant returns to scale, with a 100% increase in output. On the middle panel, the output increases from 400 to 1000 units, which is a 150% increase. On the bottom panel, the output increases from 400 units to 600 units, which is a 50% increase.

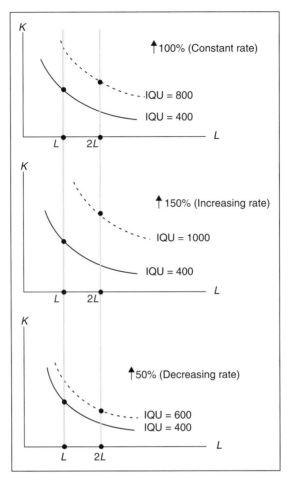

FIGURE 7.14

Example 7.6

What would happen to the total output, Q, of the Cobb–Douglas production function, $Q = C(L)^\alpha(K)^\beta$, if we triple the amount of both inputs, labor and capital?

Solution:

$$Q^* = C(3L)^\alpha(3K)^\beta$$
$$= (3)^{\alpha+\beta}C(L)^\alpha(K)^\beta$$
$$= (3)^{\alpha+\beta} Q$$

The amount of new output Q^* would depend on the value of $(\alpha + \beta)$:

- If $(\alpha + \beta) = 1$, $Q^* = 3Q$ and the function would exhibit constant returns to scale.
- If $(\alpha + \beta) > 1$, $Q^* > 3Q$ and the function would exhibit increasing returns to scale.
- If $(\alpha + \beta) < 1$, $Q^* < 3Q$ and the function would exhibit decreasing returns to scale.

7.11 ELASTICITY OF SUBSTITUTION

The elasticity of substitution in the production function refers to the extent to which one input can substitute for another. More practically, it describes how easy or difficult it is for a firm to substitute one input for another, such as the typical case of substituting capital for labor. We know that the MRTS changes as we move along the typical isoquant. In fact, it has been assumed that the MRTS decreases as the capital–labor ratio (K/L) decreases. Substitution of input may be considered easy if MRTS does not change when there is a change in K/L, and may otherwise be considered difficult if MRTS changes in response to any change in K/L. The elasticity of substitution offers a measure of the proportionate change in K/L relative to the proportionate change in MRTS. Since these changes occur along one isoquant, they would determine the shape of the isoquant, as they reflect the degree of its curvature. Mathematically, the elasticity of substitution (ε_S) can be expressed as

$$\varepsilon_S = \frac{\%\Delta \dfrac{K}{L}}{\%\Delta(\text{MRTS})}$$

$$= \frac{\dfrac{d(K/L)}{K/L}}{\dfrac{d\text{MRTS}}{\text{MRTS}}}$$

$$= \frac{d(K/L)}{K/L} \times \frac{\text{MRTS}}{d\text{MRTS}}.$$

Rearranging:

$$\varepsilon_S = \frac{d(K/L)}{d\text{MRTS}} \times \frac{\text{MRTS}}{K/L}.$$

Since both MRTS and K/L are positive along the same direction, elasticity can be expressed as a logarithmic derivative:

$$\varepsilon_S = \frac{d\ln(K/L)}{d\ln(\text{MRTS})}.$$

Figure 7.15 shows how moving from one point (A) to another (B) along an isoquant changes both the slope (MRTS) and the capital–labor ratio K/L, as in from $\frac{AC}{OC}$ to $\frac{BD}{OD}$, and how elasticity ε_S is simply an expression of that relative change:

$$\%\Delta(K/L) = \frac{(K/L)_B - (K/L)_A}{(K/L)_A},$$

$$\%\Delta(\text{MRTS}) = \frac{(\text{MRTS})_B - (\text{MRTS})_A}{(\text{MRTS})_A},$$

$$\varepsilon_S = \frac{\%\Delta(K/L)_{A-B}}{\%\Delta(\text{MRTS})_{A-B}}.$$

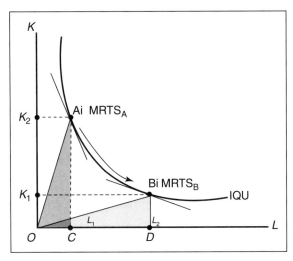

FIGURE 7.15

The elasticity of substitution can also be expressed in terms of the production function derivatives:

$$\varepsilon_S = \frac{\left[\dfrac{\partial Q}{\partial L}\right]\left[\dfrac{\partial Q}{\partial K}\right]}{Q\left[\dfrac{\partial^2 Q}{\partial K\,\partial L}\right]}.$$

The elasticity of substitution (ε_S) is commonly assumed to be constant. There are four values of elasticity according to the type of production function, as explained in Sections 7.11.1, 7.11.2, 7.11.3, and 7.11.4.

7.11.1 Elasticity of the Cobb–Douglas Production Function

This function has an elasticity of substitution equal to 1. It is characterized by the typical convexity of the isoquant, which implies the diminishing MRTS:

$$Q = f(K, L) = C(K)^{\alpha}(L)^{\beta},$$

$$F(aK, aL) = C(aK)^{\alpha}(aL)^{\beta}$$

$$= Ca^{\alpha+\beta}(K)^{\alpha}(L)^{\beta}.$$

The function would exhibit constant returns to scale when $\alpha + \beta = 1$. However, when the constant $\alpha + \beta$ exceeds 1, the function would exhibit increasing returns to scale, and when $\alpha + \beta < 1$, it would show decreasing returns to scale.

It is linear in its logarithmic form:

$$\ln Q = \ln C + \alpha \ln K + \beta \ln L.$$

To find that the elasticity of substitution in this case is equal to 1, let us take MPs of the two inputs:

$$Q = C(K)^{\alpha}(L)^{\beta},$$

$$\mathrm{MP}_K = \alpha C(K)^{-1}Q,$$

$$\mathrm{MP}_L = \beta C(L)^{-1}Q,$$

$$\mathrm{MRTS} = \frac{\mathrm{MP}_L}{\mathrm{MP}_K} = \frac{\beta C(L)^{-1}Q}{\alpha C(K)^{-1}Q},$$

$$\mathrm{MRTS} = \frac{\beta}{\alpha}\left(\frac{K}{L}\right),$$

$$\frac{K}{L} = \frac{\mathrm{MRTS}}{\frac{\beta}{\alpha}} = \frac{\alpha}{\beta}\,\mathrm{MRTS}.$$

Taking the natural log of both sides,

$$\ln\left(\frac{K}{L}\right) = \ln\left(\frac{\alpha}{\beta} + \ln \mathrm{MRTS}\right),$$

$$\varepsilon_S = \left[\frac{\partial\left(\frac{K}{L}\right)}{\partial \mathrm{MRTS}}\right] \times \left[\frac{\mathrm{MRTS}}{\left(\frac{K}{L}\right)}\right]$$

$$= \frac{\partial \ln\left(\frac{K}{L}\right)}{\partial \ln(\mathrm{MRTS})} = 1.$$

7.11.2   Elasticity of the Leontief Production Function

This function is also called the fixed-proportion production function. It has an elasticity of substitution equal to zero. It is characterized by a single-point isoquant taking a right-angle or L-shaped curve. There are only single points along a ray from the origin in which the firm can operate, since the ratio K/L is fixed. It is similar to the case of perfect complements for consumer commodities. The output in this function is given by the smaller of the two inputs:

$$Q = \min\left[\frac{K}{a}, \frac{L}{b}\right] a, b > 0,$$

$$\mathrm{MRTS} = -\left[\frac{L}{K}\right]^{-\infty},$$

where MRTS approaches zero if $L > K$, and reaches infinity if $L < K$:

$$\varepsilon_s = \frac{1}{-\infty} = 0.$$

This function also exhibits constant returns to scale:

$$f(\alpha K, \alpha L) = \left[\frac{\alpha K}{a}, \frac{\alpha L}{b}\right]$$

$$= \alpha \min\left[\frac{K}{a}, \frac{L}{b}\right]$$

$$= \alpha f(K, L).$$

7.11.3 Leontief Technology and Linear Programming

The Leontief production function does not permit the flexibility in factor substitution or variety in returns to scale that often dominate the nature of production models in microeconomic theory. Even so, the Leontief model has special importance as a model of production in the short run; that is, a period of time during which at least one input is fixed (as discussed earlier). If substitution possibilities and returns to scale are actually associated with a choice of production process or technology, then the flexibility and variety envisioned by microeconomic theory will be possible only in the long run, when investments permit changes in technology. Under this circumstance, short-run factor substitution and returns to scale may be very limited or nonexistent, and the Leontief production function will characterize the nature of the production function faced by managers. The Leontief production function is especially useful in multioutput situations with resource limits, as the following example reveals. Suppose that two products that employ some of the same types of inputs are denoted by y_1 and y_2 and that the amount of the inputs, x_1 and x_2, available is fixed during the short run at x_1^0 and x_2^0. Due to past investments in production processes, the production of each can be characterized by the Leontief model: $y_1 = \min(a_1 x_{11}, b_1 x_{21})$:

$$y_2 = \min(a_2 x_{12}, b_2 x_{22}),$$

where x_{ij} is the amount of input i used to make output j. The production function for y_1 indicates that $(1/a_1)$ units of input x_1 and $(1/b_1)$ units of input x_2 are required to produce a single unit of y_1. The production function for y_2 indicates that $(1/a_2)$ units of x_1 and $(1/b_2)$ units of x_2 are needed to produce a single unit of output y_2. If the price of output y_1 is p_1 and the price of output y_2 is p_2, then the optimal allocation of the resources between the outputs can be found from the solution of an inequality constrained optimization problem, which features maximization of TVP (total value product) from both products subject to resource limits:

Maximize $p_1 \min(a_1 x_{11}, b_1 x_{21}) + p_2 \min(a_2 x_{12}, b_2 x_{22})$,

Subject to $x_{11} + x_{12} = x_1^0$,

$x_{21} + x_{22} = x_2^0$,

where $x_{11}, x_{12}, x_{21}, x_{22} = 0$.

While in this description the optimization problem faced by a multioutput firm yields an optimal production plan, a reformulation of the problem focused on the choice of output levels results in the linear programming model described in Section 2.7, which is more easily solved using the widely available computer programs. As an added bonus, the following formulation also reduces the number of decision variables by half:

$$\text{Maximize } p_1 \, y_1 + p_2 \, y_2,$$

$$\text{Subject to } a_1 \, y_1 + a_2 y_2 = x_1^0,$$

$$p_1 \, y_1 + p_2 \, y_2 = x_2^0,$$

$$\text{where } y_1, y_2 = 0.$$

This linear programming formulation is known as a product-mix model. We are able to leverage solution methods due to linear programming, courtesy of the Leontief production function.

7.11.4 Elasticity of the Linear Production Function

This production function is also called the perfect-substitute production function. It exhibits an infinite elasticity, and it is analogous to the case of perfect substitutes for consumer commodities. It is characterized by a straight-line isoquant parallel to the slope $(-\frac{b}{a})$, where MRTS is constant ($\%\Delta\text{MRTS} = 0$):

$$Q = aK + bL,$$

$$E_S = \frac{\%\Delta \left(\dfrac{K}{L} \right)}{\%\Delta\text{MRTS}},$$

where K/L is constant,

$$\text{MRTS} = -\frac{dK}{dL} = 0$$

$$= \frac{1}{0} = \infty.$$

It can also be shown how this function exhibits constant returns to scale:

$$F(\alpha K, \alpha L) = a\alpha K + b\alpha L$$

$$= \alpha(aK + bL)$$

$$= \alpha f(K, L) = \alpha Q.$$

7.11.5   Elasticity of the CES Production Function

This function is well known as the constant elasticity of substitution (CES) production function. It is characterized by an elasticity value that is equal to any positive value. Mathematically, it is specified by

$$Q = \gamma[\delta K^{-\rho} + (1 - \delta)L^{-\rho}]^{-\frac{1}{\rho}}.$$

Here

γ is an efficiency parameter with a positive value: $\gamma > 0$.

δ is a distribution parameter with a value between zero and one: $0 \leq \delta \leq 1$.

ρ is a substitution parameter with a value equal to or above -1: $\rho \geq -1$.

Parameter ρ determines the value of elasticity as follows:

$$\text{when} \quad \rho = 0, \, \varepsilon_S = 1,$$
$$\rho = \infty, \, \varepsilon_S = 0,$$
$$\rho = -1, \, \varepsilon_S = \infty.$$

Generally, the elasticity of substitution for this function is

$$\varepsilon_S = \frac{1}{1 + \rho}.$$

It also exhibits constant returns to scale:
For $a > 0$:

$$f(aK, aL) = \gamma[\delta(aK)^{-\rho} + (1 - \delta)(aL)^{-\rho}]^{-\frac{1}{\rho}}$$
$$= \gamma(a^{-\rho})^{-\frac{1}{\rho}}[\delta K^{-\rho} + (1 - \delta)L^{-\rho}]^{-\frac{1}{\rho}}$$
$$= af(K, L).$$

Example 7.7
What would be the elasticity of substitution for the following CES production function?

$$Q = 10[0.75K^{-11} + 0.25L^{-11}]^{-\frac{1}{11}},$$
$$\varepsilon_S = \frac{1}{1 = \rho} = \frac{1}{1 + 11}$$
$$= 0.083.$$

7.11.6   Graphical Representation of CES

Let us consider a more general form of the CES production function with output y and inputs x_1, x_2:

$$y = a(a_1 x_1^\rho + (1 - \alpha_1) x_2^\rho)^{\varepsilon/\rho},$$

where $x_1, x_2 > 0$; $a > 0$; $0 \le a_1 \le 1$; $\rho \le 1$; $\varepsilon \ge 0$.

This takes on the linear, Cobb–Douglas-type, and Leontief forms as special cases; hence, the CES model may be regarded as relatively robust with respect to the shape of the isoquants it can accommodate and the returns to scale it can exhibit. This means that there are values of the parameters $(a, a_1, \rho, \varepsilon)$ that enable this form to be essentially linear, Cobb–Douglas type, or Leontief. Hence, statistical analysis of production based on this form enables the data to inform about both input substitution and returns to scale. In fact, the CES model is the workhorse of applied production analysis.

Because of the importance of the CES model in production analysis, we provide an expression for it that can involve an arbitrary number of inputs. The CES production function with output y and inputs $x_1, x_2, \ldots, x_n$ has the form:

$$y = a \left(a_1 x_1^\rho + a_2 x_2^\rho + \cdots + (1 - \Sigma a_i) x_n^\rho \right)^{e/\varepsilon},$$

$x_1 > 0, x_2 > 0, \ldots, x_n > 0$; $a > 0$; $0 \le a_1 \le 1$; $\rho \le 1$; $\varepsilon \ge 0$ for $i = 1, 2, \ldots, n - 1$.

As already mentioned, the shape of the CES production function surface depends on the values of its parameters. The shape of its isoquants is determined by the value of parameter ρ. Figure 7.16 shows the production surface of a CES when $\rho = 1$. The isoquants associated with this function resemble the family of isoquants for the linear function, as shown in

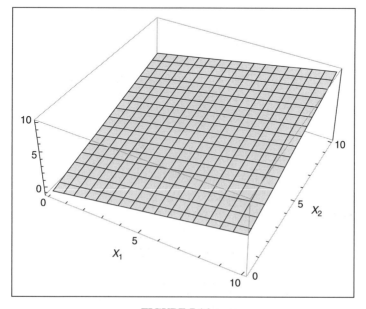

FIGURE 7.16

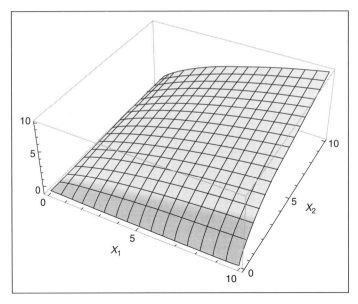

FIGURE 7.17

Figure 7.6 earlier. When $\rho = 0$, the production surface would seem to be bowed downward, as shown in Figure 7.17. The isoquants for this function are similar to the isoquants of the Cobb–Douglas function in their standard convexity to the origin, as shown in Figure 7.7. If parameter ρ is a large (in an absolute value) negative number approaching $-\infty$, then the production surface would look like a corner of a pyramid with a ridge at the diagonal line and two triangles sloping downward (Figure 7.18). The isoquants look like those of the Leontief of the L-shaped isoquant, as shown in Figure 7.8.

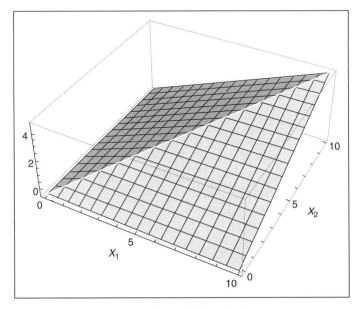

FIGURE 7.18

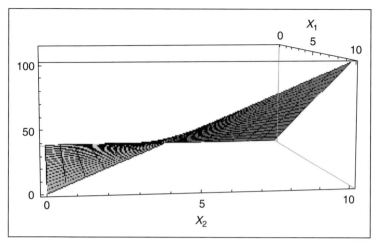

FIGURE 7.19

Note that the value of parameter ρ has no effect on returns to scale. It only affects the shape of isoquants. The returns to scale exhibited by the CES production function are determined by the value of parameter ε. If $\varepsilon < 1$, then decreasing returns to scale are evident. If $\varepsilon = 1$, there are constant returns to scale, and if $\varepsilon > 1$, there are increasing returns to scale. Figure 7.19 shows a CES function with ρ value near 0 and $\varepsilon > 1$.

The statistical estimates of parameters ρ and ε inform about factor substitution and returns to scale, respectively. The linear, Cobb–Douglas-type, and Leontief production functions are special cases of the CES function when these parameters have particular values. Table 7.3 summarizes the conclusions that can be drawn on the basis of statistical analysis of production data with the CES model.

TABLE 7.3   Factor Substitution and Returns to Scale of the CES Production Function Depending on Parameter Values

Parameter $\rho \rightarrow \varepsilon \downarrow$	<0	0	1
<1	No substitution, decreasing RTS	Some substitution, decreasing RTS	Good substitution, decreasing RTS
1	No substitution, constant RTS	Some substitution, constant RTS	Good substitution, constant RTS
>1	No substitution, increasing RTS	Some substitution, increasing RTS	Good substitution, increasing RTS

7.12   OPTIMAL EMPLOYMENT OF AN INPUT

A major question that many managers might ask is: "What would be the optimal amount of a certain input to be employed in order to maximize profit?" The answer lies in one of the most fundamental tools in economics: the **"Equimarginal Principle,"** which generally

TABLE 7.4

Units of Input (Q)	TB	MB (ΔTB)	TC (QP)	MC (ΔTC)	NG (TB − TC)
1	12	12	6	6	6
2	22	10	12	6	10
3	30	8	18	6	12
{4	36	6	24	6	12}
5	40	4	30	6	10
6	42	2	36	6	6

states that an activity ought to be pursued until the marginal benefit (MB) equals the marginal cost (MC). Let us take a look at Table 7.4.

Suppose that we are given the overall benefit that is obtained by adding successive units of an input into a production process, such as what 1–6 units of that input generate and what is in Column 2 of Table 7.4. On the basis of this column, we can track down the change that each unit of input would cause; that is, the MB, calculated as the change in total benefit: MB = ΔTB (Column 3). Suppose that each unit of input used costs the company \$6. The total cost can be obtained by multiplying the units used by per unit cost: TC = Q × P (Column 4). As we could track down the change in benefits as a result of adding any additional unit of input, we can track down the change in cost that is caused by any additional unit of input used; that is, the MC, which is the change in the total cost for successive units of input. There should be no surprise that every number in Column 5 is 6, because it is \$6 cost per unit the firm may decide to use. Now, in order to decide the optimal number of units of input to use for maximizing the benefit, we apply the equimarginal principle and note where MB equals MC. It would be at 4 units of input, where MB = MC = 6. To prove that it maximizes the benefit, we can generate Column 6 to record the net gain, which is simply the difference between the total benefit and the total cost. At the fourth unit of input, the net benefit reaches its maximum of 12. One might ask the reason for not choosing the third unit, where also the net gain is 12! The answer is that, at the third unit, the MB is still larger than the cost (8 > 6), which keeps on the motivation to use more input until the MB becomes equal to the MC, signaling the point to stop. After that point, the MB would be smaller than the MC (4 < 6), which would cause the net gain to decline from 12 to 10, incurring a loss of 2. Graphically, we can see the optimal size of input of 4 where the MB curve crosses the MC curve on the upper panel of Figure 7.20. On the lower panel, we can see that, at the fourth unit of input, the total benefit curve rises above the total cost, producing the longest vertical distance between the two curves. This distance is the maximum net benefit of 12.

7.13 TECHNOLOGICAL PROGRESS, INVENTION, AND INNOVATION

Technological progress refers to how much our knowledge has expanded and how the advances are applied in the production of goods and services. It is a systematic process and endogenous to the economic system. It has an incremental nature that spreads over the long

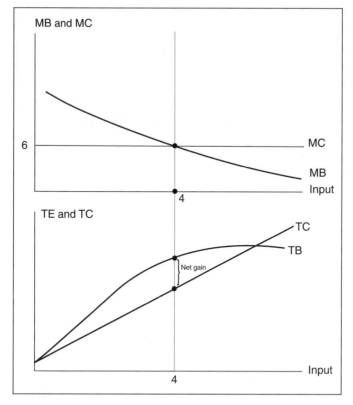

FIGURE 7.20

run. Invention is a form of technological progress. It refers to coming up with new products or new ways of using a product or rendering a service. Those new ways are most likely to increase efficiency, especially in terms of increasing output, improving its quality, reducing cost, or any combination of these objectives. Innovation has to do with the applications of the new discoveries and inventions, especially in their first commercial use. This too is a long-run concept that is tied to the way the economic system is structured and run. Successful innovation pivots around two major economic requirements: (1) supportive and sustained demand, and (2) willingness and capacity to reduce cost. It is highly affected by competition among firms and can easily become the "make it or break it" factor in the market. Staying ahead of competition has become a major survival tool for firms in the business market. Firms would compete not only for quantity and quality of innovative techniques but also for the speed with which innovation spreads. Generally, the dissemination of innovation passes through three stages by which a forward S-shaped curve emerges (Figure 7.21). The first is the initial adaptation stage, which is characterized by an increasing growth rate. The second stage is characterized by a decreasing growth rate. The third is the settling stage, where the curve becomes flat toward the end of that innovation and the emergence of others. Firms, industries, and economies can have various S-shaped curves for their own innovation spread status. Figure 7.21 shows three random examples in which the innovation spread curves are distinguished by their own three stages.

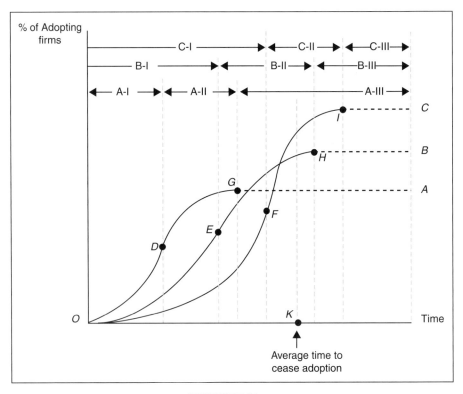

FIGURE 7.21

For example, the first stage has different lengths of time for the three firms and probably different rates of growth (compare *OD*, *OE*, and *OF*). The same observation can be made by comparing the other stages, such as the second stage where we can see how the growth of dissemination starts and ends (compare *DG*, *EH*, and *FI*). Points *G*, *H*, and *I* show where the growth of innovation spread ceases and signals that the attention is shifting to a newer and better innovation. We can observe that this stage starts and extends differently for the three firms, but we can also see that an average time among the three firms, or say in an industry or country, can be estimated by the length of line segment *OK*.

7.14 TECHNOLOGICAL PROGRESS AND PRODUCTION FUNCTION

The collective advances in production technology that we witnessed, especially in the last two centuries, have profoundly changed the production process and its reflections on the dynamics of the production function. Of specific interest is the change in substitution among inputs and the change in their quality. Naturally, any change in the production function would mirror the status of the innovative activities and nature and structure of the economic system. It has been observed that total output has increased beyond the effects of the changes in inputs. This has prompted economists to theorize on the impact of other factors over time and express it in the following form of the production function:

$$Q = O(t)f[L, K],$$

where $O(t)$ reflects the impact of all other determining factors than the typical inputs. Including (t) stresses that the changes in other factors over time are the right form of representation where $dO(t)/dt > 0$. It was further hypothesized that the impact of other factors can be brought about in three different forms:

1. When $O(t)$ affects inputs in equal proportions; it would be the typical format of the function, $Q = O(t) f[L, K]$.
2. When $O(t)$ specifically focuses its impact on labor, $Q = f[O(t)L, K]$.
3. When $O(t)$ specifically focuses its impact on capital, $Q = f[L, O(t)K]$.

The structure of the economic system, the fundamental needs of a society, and the philosophy on the orientation of the progress are the determinants of what form of production function is followed. For example, it would not be wise to adopt a production format that would cut back on labor as an input in a country like China, where labor is abundantly available and need to be employed. Empirically, the impact of other factors over time versus the impact of the two typical inputs, labor and capital, has been estimated using the following formula:

$$G_Q = G_O + G_{in},$$

where G_Q is the rate of growth in output, G_O is the rate of growth in other factors over time, and G_{in} is the rate of growth in inputs, which can be broken down into two different rates of growth in labor and capital in consideration of their own elasticities. The growth in **technical progress** has been taken to represent G_O. It is denoted by G_{tp}:

$$G_Q = G_{tp} + [\varepsilon_{QL}(GL) + \varepsilon_{QK}(GK)],$$

where ε_{QL} is the output elasticity of capital, and ε_{QK} is the output elasticity of labor.

Example 7.8
What would be the rate of growth in technological progress for a country's output that has been growing by 3.6% under the following growth conditions for labor and capital?

$$GL = 1.6, GK = 1.2, \quad \varepsilon_{QL} = 0.75, \quad \varepsilon_{QK} = 0.25,$$
$$G_Q = G_{tp} + [\varepsilon_{QL}(GL) + \varepsilon_{QK}(GK)],$$
$$3.6 = G_{tp} + [(0.75)(1.6) + (0.25)(1.2)],$$
$$G_{tp} = 3.6 - 1.5,$$
$$G_{tp} = 2.1.$$

SUMMARY

- This first chapter of the unit discussed the managerial decisions at the firm level. It addressed the basic topics in the production theory. As the production process basically meant the transformation of various resources (as inputs) into certain identified outputs, called products, the discussion started with an explanation of the variability of inputs throughout time. It clarified the frequently used terms in this field, such as short run and long run. In the short run, at least one input is fixed, while in the long run, all inputs are variable.

- The production function was the central topic in this chapter. It referred to the relationship between the inputs into the production process and the resulting output. It was explained and illustrated graphically with examples. A discussion on short-run, one variable input flowed in where the typical inputs, capital and labor, were used and capital was held constant. It was to illustrate the essential concepts related to changing labor units and observing the resulting change in output. These concepts were total product (TP), marginal productivity of labor (MP_L), and average productivity of labor (AP_L). They were all explained mathematically and graphically to show the dynamic relationships that hold them together. Output elasticity was obtained to depict the percentage change in output relative to the percentage change in input. This elasticity value characterizes the three stages of production: (1) larger than 1 in the first stage, (2) between 0 and 1 in the second stage, and (3) less than 0 in the third stage.

- The three stages of production show the law of diminishing marginal returns, which states that, after a certain point in production, the marginal productivity starts to decline. So, as to the stages of production, during the first stage the average productivity usually increases. During the second stage, the average productivity starts decreasing from its maximum to the point when the marginal productivity becomes zero. During the third stage, the marginal productivity decreases from zero to negative.

- The long-run, two variable input function was discussed asto continue the discussion of the short-run, one variable input function. Here, the analytical tools were the isoquant, **isocost**, and the marginal rate of technical substitution (MRTS), which are all analogous to the consumer choice analytical tools of the indifference curve (IC), budget line, and the marginal rate of substitution (MRS). The isoquant shows the possible combination of two inputs to produce a certain level of output, while the isocost depicts a certain cost required to produce a certain level of output. The MRTS represents the slope of the isoquant, which, like the consumer's MRS, declines as we move down the isoquant. The optimal choice of production for the firm is achieved at the point of frequency between the highest possible isoquant and the lowest possible isocost.

- Given the visualization of the isoquant map, the economically efficient region is where the isoquants take their typical shape of the negatively sloped curves, for that is where the MP of input is positive. In other words, a look at a group of isoquants reveals the two areas that are not recommended for production: (1) where the tangents to the isoquants have zero slope (horizontal lines) and (2) where the tangents are vertical lines. Anywhere between these two areas are the segments of the negatively sloped isoquants, which should be the target area for production.

- The term returns to scale refers to three cases in which output responds to changes in inputs. Increasing returns to scale is where output changes by a larger proportion than the changes in input. Decreasing returns to scale is the case of having an output changed by a proportion less than the change in inputs, and finally constant returns to scale is where output and inputs change by an equal proportion.

- Elasticity of substitution refers to the extent to which one input can substitute for another. Aside from the assumption that this elasticity is normally constant, there are four types of production functions, which exhibit different values of elasticity of substitution. The Cobb-Douglas function is where elasticity equals 1, the Leontief function is where elasticity equals zero, the linear function is where elasticity equals ∞, and finally there is the constant elasticity of substitution function (CES).

- The last topic discussed in this chapter covered technological progress, invention, and innovation, which refers to the impact of knowledge and skills development over time on the production process and products. Invention is concerned with producing new and improved products, whereas innovation has to do with the applications of new discoveries and methods that would impact the production process. They are vital for a firm in the competitive system, not only to survive but also to go along with the trends, be able to satisfy ever-changing consumer demand, and to carve its own place in the industry.

KEY TERMS

short-run production
long-run production
production function
total product
marginal product
average product
law of diminishing
    marginal returns
isoquant
isocost

marginal rate of technical
    substitution
returns to scale
economically efficient
    region of production
increasing returns to scale
decreasing returns to scale
constant returns to scale
production elasticity
elasticity of substitution

Cobb–Douglas production
    function
Leontief production
    function
linear production function
CES production function
equimarginal principle
technical progress
invention
innovation

LIST OF FORMULAS

- Short-run, one variable production function:

$$Q = f(K_0, L).$$

- Marginal product of labor:

$$MP_L = \frac{\Delta TP_L}{\Delta_L} = \frac{\partial f(K_0, L)}{\partial L}.$$

- Marginal product of capital:

$$MP_K = \frac{\Delta TP_K}{\Delta_K} = \frac{\partial f(K, L_0)}{\partial K}.$$

- Average product of labor:

$$\text{AP}_L = \frac{\text{TP}_L}{L}.$$

- Production elasticity of labor:

$$\varepsilon_L = \frac{\partial Q}{\partial L}\left[\frac{L}{Q}\right] = \frac{\text{MP}_L}{\text{AP}_L}.$$

- Marginal rate of technical substitution:

$$\text{MRTS} = \frac{\Delta K}{\Delta L} = \frac{dK}{dL} = -\frac{\text{MP}_L}{\text{MP}_K}.$$

- Elasticity of substitution:

$$\varepsilon_S = \frac{d(K/L)}{d\,\text{MRTS}} - \frac{\text{MRTS}}{K/L}.$$

$$\text{also}\quad \varepsilon_S = \frac{d\ln(K/L)}{d\ln(\text{MRTS})}$$

and

$$\varepsilon_S = \frac{\left[\dfrac{\partial Q}{\partial L}\right]\left[\dfrac{\partial Q}{\partial K}\right]}{Q\left[\dfrac{\partial^2 Q}{\partial K\,\partial L}\right]}.$$

- CES function:

$$Q = \gamma[\delta K^{-\rho} + (1-\delta)L^{-\rho}]^{-\frac{1}{\rho}}.$$

- CES elasticity of substitution:

$$\varepsilon_S = \frac{1}{1+\rho}.$$

- Growth in technical progress:

$$G_Q = G_{t\rho} + \left[\varepsilon_{QL}(GL) + \varepsilon_{QK}(GK)\right].$$

EXERCISES

1. Explain the concepts of short run and long run in production. Are they defined by certain periods of time? What is the significance of this type of term variability in production?

2. List as many aspects as you can of the dynamic relationships between total product, marginal product of a variable of your choice, and the average product. Support your explanation with graphs.

3. What is the production function? List and explain its various types. Also, explain its significance in the managerial decision making context.

4. How would you tie the discussion on the three stages of production: production elasticity, the law of diminishing returns, and the returns to scale?

5. Provide a comparative explanation of the analytical tools for the optimal decision-making process between an individual consumer and a firm's manager.

6. The following table shows the number of units produced (Q), total revenue (TR), and the total cost (TC) of a product in a small firm. What would be the optimal size of production? How would you determine it and what would be the firm's profit at the level of production? Is it the maximum profit that can be obtained?

   Note: You need to fill in the blank columns to get your answer.

Q	TR	TC
100	1000	900
200	1800	1100
300	2400	1400
400	2800	1800
500	3000	2300
600	3000	2900
700	2800	3600
800	2400	4400

7. On a two-panel figure, plot the following curves:
   - Total revenue (TR) and total cost (TC).
   - Marginal revenue (MR) and marginal cost (MC).
   - Show the maximum profit and the optimal production.

8. In the first and second columns of the following table, you find the units of labor (L) used in a production process, and the total output (TP_L) obtained. Calculate the average production of labor (AP_L), the marginal product of labor (MP_L), and the production elasticity (ε_S). Fill in the columns with the results of your calculations.

L	TP_L	AP_L	MP_L	ε_L	Stages
10	700				
20	2,600				
30	5,400				
40	8,800				
50	12,500				
60	16,200				
70	19,600				
80	22,400				
90	24,300				
100	25,000				
110	24,200				
120	21,600				

9. (a) Mark the three stages of production in the previous table based on the elasticity values.

   (b) Draw the three curves of TP_L, AP_L, and MP_L, and show the following:
   - The three stages of production
   - The inflection point
   - The maximum production

10. The following is the production function of a small firm:

$$Q = 3K^{0.45}L^{0.55}.$$

   (a) Obtain the MP_L and the AP_L functions.
   (b) Obtain the MP_K and the AP_L functions.
   (c) Calculate the values of MP_L, AP_L, and MP_K, AP_K if $K = 35$ and $L = 15$.
   (d) What would be the total product?

8

COST THEORY

8.1 COST CONCEPTS AND CATEGORIES

Fundamental understanding of the nature of cost, its types, conceptualization, measurement, and use is a major requirement to be a successful manager. This is particularly true for managers who pursue efficiency in their managerial decisions to offer better, more affordable products of higher quality and faster services. Cost has never been evaluated in isolation from other variables. Its judgment is inextricably bound with assessing, first and foremost, the associated benefits. There are many concepts and categories of cost. The most obvious distinction is between explicit and implicit costs. **Explicit cost** is the direct monetary expenditure or out-of-pocket expenses paid for the firm's obligations, such as material, wages, interest on loans, rent, and other similar types of expenditures. **Implicit cost** is the indirect nonmonetary cost that can only be estimated by the **opportunity cost**. Here, we can refer to the economic versus accounting perspectives to recognizing and measuring cost. From the efficiency standpoint, economists consider the **foregone cost** as opportunity cost. It is the cost of the best alternative use of a resource. For example, energy can be used to produce many different products. The accounting cost of a therm of heat is simply the expenditure involved for the energy. The opportunity cost of a therm of heat energy to produce one product is the value of the alternative product that could be produced using that energy.

The efficient choice of a resource dictates that its value must be at least equal to its opportunity cost. In other words, opportunity cost represents the payment necessary to keep a resource in its present employment. Accounting perspective does not take opportunity cost into consideration. It focuses mainly on what is called the historical cost that is explicit. This signifies that implicit cost does not enter the accountant's calculation. A typical example of the implicit cost is the salary of an entrepreneur or self-employed manager, which is not

Managerial Economics: A Mathematical Approach, First Edition. M. J. Alhabeeb and L. Joe Moffitt.
© 2013 John Wiley & Sons, Inc. Published 2013 by John Wiley & Sons, Inc.

really paid but can be estimated by what the person would get, had he been employed in the market. So, the implicit cost can be estimated by the opportunity cost.

The accounting perspective relies on **historical cost**, which is the actual cash outlay or what is paid for the production operations regardless of any market influences on the value of what the payment was for. This is why the historical cost is the suitable measure for formal purposes such as tax calculations, report to stockholders, and financial statements for governmental purposes. The opposite of the historical cost is the **current cost**, which takes into consideration the current market conditions that change the value of an asset, such as inflation, supply and demand, consumer taste, alternative products, technology, and appreciation and depreciation of the asset. For example, a piece of equipment that was purchased 10 years ago for $20,000 has depreciated now to $8000. The original cost, $20,000, is the historical cost and $8000 is the current cost. Another concept of the cost that is related to the current cost is the **replacement cost**, which refers to the expenditures in the real (adjusted) dollar value that is required to procure the asset. It means that the replacement cost is similar to the current cost in terms of accounting for the current market conditions. Not only inflation but also the state of technology can play a role here. For example, computers are cheaper to replace now than 10 years ago, due to the advancement of technology. This is why replacement cost is sometimes defined as the cost of duplicating productive capacities under the utilization of an updated technology. A concept of cost that is closely related to the direction of managerial decisions is the **incremental cost**, which refers to the changes in cost due to implementation of certain courses of action by management. An example of incremental cost is the extra cost incurred for a new product line, establishing an extra labor shift, or renting some of the firm's equipment. In this sense, we can connect incremental cost to the concept of **marginal cost** (MC), which could be considered a special case of incremental cost, as long as it means the cost incurred for producing another unit of output. Managerial decisions on the incremental cost can be related to considering another cost, namely, the sunk cost. **Sunk cost** is the cost that has to be paid due to certain obligations that are unrelated to the efficiency of a current decision. So, it is the cost that does not vary across alternative courses of action, and which cannot play a role in the optimality of outcome. Suppose that for a reason related to the schedule of operations, some equipment of the firm remains unemployed for a period of time. If the manager decides to rent these pieces of equipment to another firm, he would bring about a negative incremental cost that would reduce the original cost of paying for the maintenance and storage of the equipment, which, in this case, is considered sunk cost since it will be paid whether the equipment is used or not.

In terms of how it is related to output, cost can either be fixed, variable, or sometimes cross-listed between the two types. **Fixed costs** (FC) are those that are not connected to the size of production. Typical examples include rent, interest paid on loans, taxes, and insurance. The firm would pay these costs whether it is producing or not, or whether it is producing more or less. **Variable costs** (VC) are those that are tied directly and positively to the size of production. The more the production, the higher the VC. Typical examples include labor, material, and energy. During a production period, FC often refers to the cost of assets that will be useful during multiple production periods. It may be measured by the change in the market value of assets during the production period. Practically, it is often evaluated as the sum of interest, taxes, insurance, depreciation, and other typical FC that are not tied to the size of output.

The cost function or cost–output relation brings about one more major categorization of cost, that is, short-run and **long-run costs**. **Short-run cost** refers to a period of time during which one or more factors of production cannot be changed. It reflects a phase of production characterized by input inflexibility and where operating decisions are constrained by previous capital expenditures. This is why the curves of short-run cost are called operating curves, as opposed to planning curves, which depict the long-run costs. **Long-run cost** refers to costs over a sufficiently long period of time, which permits all factors of production to be changed. Long-term cost reflects much more flexible use of inputs. We focus on the accounting perspective of cost for it is the relevant measure for the majority of managerial decisions. Also, as far as the cost function is concerned, we focus on short-run and long-run analyses of cost.

8.2 SHORT-RUN COSTS

Short-run costs are basic indicators for managerial operating decisions. They stand for the minimum possible cost of production for a certain output level at a particular operating condition. The basic component is the **total cost** (TC), which includes two parts: FC and VC. To mark these costs for a short-run analysis, they can be preceded by S or SR such as in the short-run total cost (STC or SRTC) though that is not often done:

$$STC = SFC + SVC.$$

As for the **average cost** (AC), it is a cost per unit of production. Since we have three measures of cost—total, fixed, and variable—each can be expressed as per unit of production. Therefore, dividing each by the size of output Q produces the AC of any particular measure of the three concepts:

- Average cost (AC) $= \dfrac{TC}{Q}$.
- **Average fixed cost** (AFC) $= \dfrac{FC}{Q}$.
- **Average variable cost** (AVC) $= \dfrac{VC}{Q}$.

Therefore, the AC is the sum of the two averages:

$$AC = AFC + AVC.$$

The MC is the cost of the last unit of output. So, it is the change in TC (or VC) due to producing one more unit of production:

$$MC = \frac{\Delta TC}{\Delta Q} = \frac{\partial TC}{\partial Q}$$
$$= \frac{\Delta VC}{\Delta Q} = \frac{\partial VC}{\partial Q} \text{ since } \frac{\partial FC}{\partial Q} = 0.$$

Let us assume, for the purpose of illustration, that we follow the cost of production of a certain product for the first 10 units of production. Suppose that the FC for this production is 50, which remains the same throughout all units of production. Also, suppose that the VC changes throughout production in the following manner: 10, 19, 26, 31, 38, 45, 55, 67, 82, 100. We can construct a table (Table 8.1) and calculate all the cost measures.

TABLE 8.1

Q	FC	VC	TC	AC	AFC	AVC	MC
1	50	10	60	60	50	10	
2	50	19	69	34.5	25	9.5	9
3	50	26	76	25.3	16.66	8.66	7
4	50	31	81	20.25	12.5	7.75	5
5	50	38	88	17.6	10	7.6	7
6	50	45	95	15.83	8.33	7.5	7
7	50	55	105	15	7.14	7.86	10
8	50	67	117	14.62	6.25	8.37	12
9	50	82	132	14.67	5.55	9.11	15
10	50	100	150	15	5	10	18

Plotting the data obtained in this table would produce the short-run cost curves as shown in Figure 8.1. Looking carefully at the graph, we can observe most of the characteristics of the cost curves.

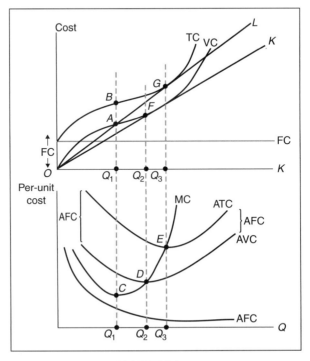

FIGURE 8.1

Observations:

- The TC and VC curves in the upper panel are vertically parallel to each other. They both are increasing all the way, but at a decreasing rate up to the inflection points *A* and *B*, and at an increasing rate beyond those points. The TC mimics the changes of the VC since the difference between them is the FC, which is a constant. Graphically, the vertical distance between them (*AB*) represents the FC, which is also shown as a horizontal line along increasing levels of output. The reason for the change in the increasing rate of both TC and VC is that only after the inflection points the law of diminishing marginal returns starts to work.
- The lowest point on the MC curve (point *C*) corresponds to the points of inflection. The MC would pick up after *C*, and both VC and TC soar.
- The AFC curve descends all the way as output level increases. This is because it is a constant value divided by an increasing value. It is also shown as a gradually shrinking vertical distance between ATC and AVC curves.
- All other cost curves in the lower panel (MC, ATC, AVC) take roughly a U-shape in a sense that they have two phases, decreasing and increasing, and they reach their lowest points in between the two phases. For example, in the case of the marginal cost curve this happens because the marginal product of an input, say labor (MP_L), would naturally rise up to its maximum then start to fall. The MC of such an input would behave in the opposite direction. That is to say, it would gradually fall, reach a minimum, then rise, and that is what the MC curve depicts:

$$MC = \frac{\Delta TVC}{\Delta Q}.$$

The relationship between marginal and average products and costs can be rigorously developed in the context of optimizing behavior by a firm, we can being to see the relationship now. Since the total variable cost (TVC), say labor, is obtained by multiplying the wage rate (w) by the amount of labor (L),

$$TVC = wL,$$

then

$$MC = \frac{\Delta wL}{\Delta Q},$$

$$MC = \frac{w\Delta L}{\Delta Q},$$

$$MC = \frac{w}{\frac{\Delta Q}{\Delta L}},$$

and since the marginal product of labor (MP_L) is the change in output due to the change in labor, that is, $\frac{\Delta Q}{\Delta L}$,

$$MC = \frac{w}{MP_L},$$

which confirms that the MC value would fluctuate in the opposite direction to the MP_L value, given a certain wage rate.

We can use a similar argument to justify the U-shape for AVC:

$$AVC = \frac{TVC}{Q},$$

$$AVC = \frac{wL}{Q},$$

$$AVC = \frac{w}{\frac{Q}{L}}.$$

Since $\frac{Q}{L}$ is the average product of labor AP_L, then

$$AVC = \frac{w}{AP_L},$$

and this again means that the AVC would fluctuate in the opposite direction to AP_L. So, when AP_L is high, AVC would be low, and when the average product starts to fall, AVC would rise. As for the AC curve, it would follow the changes of AVC where only AFC is between them.

- The MC curve intersects with both the AVC curve and the AC curve at their lowest points of D and E. These points correspond to output levels Q_2 and Q_3, respectively. They also correspond to the points of tangency on VC and TC in the upper panel. This is where the AVC curve and the AC curve would equal the slope of the cords OK and OL at the tangency points F and G, respectively.
- The AVC curve and the AC curve would never intersect, although they get closer as the output level increases. The shorter distance between them represents the minimum value of the AFC, which cannot be zero.

Example 8.1

The TC function for a small business firm is given by

$$TC = 3000 + 10Q - 20Q^2 + Q^3,$$

where this firm produces 50 units.

1. Calculate the FC, VC, AC, AFC, AVC, and MC.
2. Verify the answers.

Solution:
Since TC = FC + VC, we conclude that

$$FC = 3000,$$

$$VC = 10Q - 20Q^2 + Q^3$$

$$= 10(50) - 20(50)^2 + (50)^3$$

$$= 75,500.$$

$$AC = \frac{TC}{Q}$$

$$= \frac{3000}{Q} + 10 - 20Q + Q^2$$

$$= \frac{3000}{50} + 10 - 20(50) + (50)^2$$

$$= 1570.$$

$$AFC = \frac{FC}{Q}$$

$$= \frac{3000}{50} = 60.$$

$$AVC = \frac{VC}{Q}$$

$$= 10 - 20Q + Q^2$$

$$= 10 - 20(50) + (50)^2$$

$$= 1510.$$

$$MC = \frac{\partial TC}{\partial Q}$$

$$= 10 - 40Q + 3Q^2$$

$$= 10 - 40(50) + 3(50)^2$$

$$= 5510.$$

$$TC = 3000 + 10(50) - 20(50)^2 + (50)^3$$

$$= 78,500.$$

$$TC = FC + VC$$

$$= 3000 + 75.500 = 78,500.$$

$$AC = AFC + AVC$$

$$1570 = 60 + 1510 = 1570.$$

$$\text{MC} = \frac{\partial \text{TC}}{\partial Q} = \frac{\partial \text{VC}}{\partial Q},$$

$$5510 = 10 + 40Q + 3Q^2,$$

$$5510 = 10 + 40(50) + 3(50)^2,$$

$$5510 = 5510.$$

Example 8.2

Consider the TC function that is expressed as

$$\text{TC} = 9375 + 15Q^2.$$

1. What would be the size of production that minimizes the AC?
2. Calculate the actual AC, TC, and MC at that level of output.

Solution:

$$\text{AC} = \frac{\text{TC}}{Q},$$

$$\text{AC} = \frac{9375 + 15Q^2}{Q},$$

$$\text{AC} = 9375Q^{-1} + 15Q.$$

The level of output that would make the AC at its minimum can be obtained when the first derivative of this function is set to zero:

$$\frac{\partial \text{AC}}{\partial Q} = -9375Q^{-2} + 15 = 0$$

$$= \frac{9375}{Q^2} = 15.$$

$$Q^2 = \frac{9375}{15} = 625$$

$$Q = \sqrt{625} = 25.$$

So, at 25 units of production, the average cost would be at its minimum, which is

$$\text{AC} = \frac{9375}{Q} + 15Q$$

$$= \frac{9375}{25} = 15(25)$$

$$= 375 + 375 = 750.$$

The AC curve would have its lower point when AC is $750 at output level of 25 as shown in the graph (Figure 8.2).

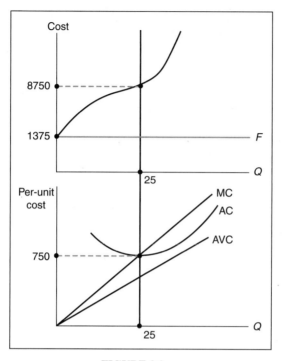

FIGURE 8.2

The TC would be

$$TC = 9375 + 15Q^2,$$
$$= 9375 + 15(25)^2,$$
$$= 18,750.$$

The TC can also be obtained by multiplying the AC by production size:

$$TC = AC(Q)$$
$$= 750(25)$$
$$= 18,750.$$

The MC can be obtained as the first derivative of the TC with respect to the calculated output level:

$$MC = \frac{\partial TC}{\partial Q} = 30Q,$$
$$= 30(25) = 750.$$

Example 8.3

Follow the previous example and show the following:

1. The MC curve intersects with the AC curve at its lower point.
2. How many units of output would be produced to minimize the AVC?
3. Calculate the AVC, TC, and MC at that level of output.

Solution:

The fact that the MC turned out to be equal to $750—the same as the AC at the same level of output (25 units)—means that the two curves intersect corresponding to point 25 on the output axis. In order to prove that the point of intersection is the minimum, or that it is at the dip of the curve, the first derivative of the MC has to be positive:

$$MC = 30Q,$$

$$\frac{\partial MC}{\partial Q} = 30 > 0.$$

Since the TC function is $TC = 9375 + 15Q^2$, the FC would be $9375 and the VC would be $15Q^2$:

$$AVC = \frac{VC}{Q},$$

$$AVC = \frac{15Q^2}{Q} = 15Q.$$

Unlike the AC function, this AVC function is linear and can be minimized at the origin when $Q = 0$:

$$AVC = 15(0) = 0.$$

The TC would then be

$$TC = 9375 + 15(0)^2,$$

$$TC = 9375.$$

This means that even when there is no production, the firm would incur $9375, which is the FC. The MC would be zero when there is no production:

$$MC = 30Q$$

$$= 30(0) = 0.$$

This means that both curves of AVC and MC emerge from the origin.

8.3   THE OPTIMAL COMBINATION OF INPUTS

Before we understand the long-run costs, we need to know the analysis of optimal combination of inputs, which would offer helpful tools to derive the long-run costs. Let us recall the analysis of optimal choice in the consumer decision making, where equilibrium is reached at the point where the highest possible indifference curve touches the lowest possible budget line. Here, in the managerial decision making, we follow a similar analysis to reach the optimal combination of inputs in order to maximize the firm's profits. We shall employ the previously explained isoquant with a new tool called isocost.

8.3.1   Isocost

Just as the budget line shows the combination of commodities that a consumer can afford, given a certain budget, an isocost shows the combination of inputs that a firm can employ, given a certain cost. Analogous to the budget-line equation, an isocost equation can be expressed as a sum of the firm's expenditures on the employed inputs, such as labor and capital:

$$TC = wL + vK,$$

where TC is the total cost to employ two inputs: labor (L) at a wage rate (w) and capital (K) at a unit price (v). This is often referred to as **total factor cost**; we use TC without fear of confusion with total cost discussed earlier. Solving this equation for K would provide us with what we need to draw the isocost, analogous to the way we drew the budget line:

$$TC = wL + vK,$$

$$TC - wL = vK,$$

$$\frac{TC - wL}{v} = K,$$

or

$$K = \frac{TC}{v} - \frac{w}{v}L,$$

where $\frac{TC}{v}$ is the vertical intercept obtained by dividing the firm's assigned cost by the rental price of capital, and $-\frac{w}{v}$ is the slope of the isocost. Suppose that the price of capital is $10 and the wage rate is $5. For a given cost such as $100, the firm can allocate its budget among various combinations of labor and capital where all of the possible combinations lie on the following isocost with $\max(K) = 10$; $\max(L) = 20$; slope $= -\frac{1}{2}$:

$$K = \frac{100}{10} - \frac{5}{10}L.$$

The isocost represents all the possible combinations of capital and labor that can be employed, keeping the TC at $100 (Figure 8.3). Two examples are points A and B:

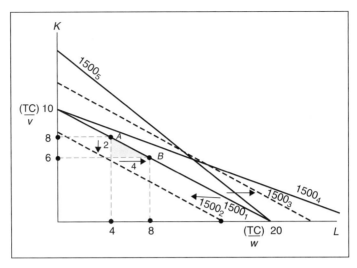

FIGURE 8.3

$$A = 8 \text{ units of } K \ \& \ 4 \text{ units of } L,$$

$$\text{TC} = wL + vK,$$

$$100 = (5)(4) + (10)(8),$$

$$B = 6 \text{ units of } K \ \& \ 8 \text{ units of } L,$$

$$100 = (5)(8) + (10)(6).$$

If we move from A to B, we would have to exchange some units of capital for some units of labor. The slope of the isocost $(-\frac{1}{2})$ dictates that two units of capital would have to be given up in order to gain four units of labor. The slope, being a negative ratio of wage to capital price, refers to the market rate at which capital is traded for labor. It is also called the **economic rate of substitution (ERS)**.

If the prices of inputs or their ratio stays the same and the given cost goes down, say to $80, the isocost1 (isoc1) would shift left to isocost2 (isoc2), in a parallel way, and would shift right to isocost3 (isoc3), also in a parallel way, in case the cost goes up, say to $120. However, the isocost would swing to either isocost4 (isoc4) or isocost5 (isoc5), depending on how the ratio of input prices changes.

8.4   MINIMIZING INPUT COST AND MAXIMIZING OUTPUT

The fundamental managerial objective is to either minimize the cost of inputs for a given level of output or maximize output for a given TC of inputs. Recall that an isoquant is to show all the combinations possible of inputs required to produce a certain level of output. If this level of output is given, a firm can achieve it with the least possible cost. Also, if the firm wants to adhere to a certain cost, it can maximize the output as much as possible within that cost limitation. Technically, this goal can be achieved at the point of tangency between the highest possible isoquant (maximum output) and the lowest possible isocost (minimum cost). This point is the firm's equilibrium, which is the counterpart to the equilibrium point for consumer choice. Let us imagine a full map of isoquants representing various levels of output, and also a group of isocosts representing various costs of inputs. Let us focus on a few of them in the following graph, and assume that a firm wants to produce a level of output represented by the second isoquant (Iqu2) (Figure 8.4).

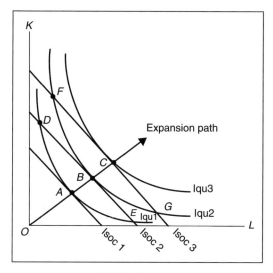

FIGURE 8.4

Any point on this isoquant would yield the same level of output. So points F, B, and G are all producing the level of output the firm seeks. However, B has to be preferred over both F and G for being on a lower isocost. By the same logic, we can conclude that if the firm seeks a higher level of output such as the one represented by Iqu3, it has to expect to pay higher cost such as the cost represented by isoc3. If the firm wants to reduce the cost of isoc2, say to isoc1, it must realize that it cannot keep output at Iqu2 because the highest output that the cost of isoc1 can afford is Iqu1.

Point B assures the minimum cost to produce the output level of Iqu2, and therefore, it is the cost-minimizing equilibrium point. The reason for it to be the absolute best is that if we move either up toward F or down toward G, we can face a higher cost at a higher isocost. So, this is where the **long-run total cost (LTC)** would be minimized. Since it is a point of tangency, it would be where the slope of isoquant equals the slope of the isocost, and the ERS equals the marginal rate of technical substitution (MRTS):

$$\text{ERS} = \frac{w}{v} = \text{MRTS} = \frac{MP_L}{MP_K},$$

and by rearranging we obtain

$$\frac{w}{MP_L} = \frac{v}{MP_K},$$

which states that the ratios of input prices to their marginal products must be equal at the equilibrium state in order to minimize the TC for a certain level of output. In contrast to this balance are all the possible cases at any other point along the isoquant Iqu2, such that

$$\text{at point } F: \quad \frac{w}{MP_L} < \frac{v}{MP_K},$$

$$\text{and at point } G: \quad \frac{w}{MP_L} > \frac{v}{MP_K}.$$

We can arrive to the equilibrium condition (8.1) by mathematically minimizing the LTC function, subject to the production function:

$$\min \ LTC = \min(wL + vK),$$

$$\text{s.t. } Q = f(L, K).$$

By forming the Lagrangian equation, we get

$$\mathbf{L}(L, K, \lambda) = wL + vK + \lambda[Q - f(L, K)].$$

Taking the first-order conditions,

$$\frac{\partial \mathbf{L}}{\partial L} = w - \lambda^* \left[\frac{\partial f}{\partial L} \right] = 0, \tag{8.1}$$

$$\frac{\partial \mathbf{L}}{\partial K} = v - \lambda^* \left[\frac{\partial f}{\partial K} \right] = 0, \tag{8.2}$$

$$\frac{\partial \mathbf{L}}{\partial \lambda} = Q - f(L, K) = 0. \tag{8.3}$$

Rearranging (8.1) and (8.2) into (8.4) and (8.5),

$$w = \lambda^* \left[\frac{\partial f}{\partial L} \right], \tag{8.4}$$

$$v = \lambda^* \left[\frac{\partial f}{\partial K} \right]. \tag{8.5}$$

Dividing (8.4) by (8.5),

$$\frac{w}{v} = \frac{\left[\dfrac{\partial f}{\partial L} \right]}{\left[\dfrac{\partial f}{\partial K} \right]},$$

which is

$$\frac{w}{v} = \frac{MP_L}{MP_K} = MRTS.$$

If we connect the tangency points *A*, *B*, and *C* by a line and we extend it to the origin, we will obtain what is called the "**expansion path**," which is generally a positive sloping curve. It can either be a straight line, like 0*ABC*, or a crooked or smooth curve.

8.5   LONG-RUN COSTS

Since the expansion path is a locus of all the points of tangency that stand for the cost-minimizing combination of inputs, we can use the expansion path to directly derive the LTC curve. This curve stands for the least possible cost in the long run to produce a certain level of output, using the optimal combination of inputs.

Figure 8.5 shows that if we transfer the information related to the equilibrium points on the expansion path *ABCDEF* from the upper panel to the lower, we can create an LTC curve that measures TC for various levels of output.

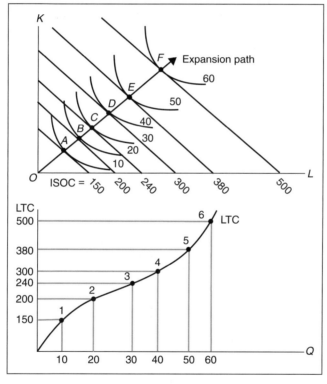

FIGURE 8.5

Points 1–6 on the curve in the lower panel correspond to the equilibrium points on the expansion path. For example, point 1 is obtained by recording the level of output (10) from the first isoquant and the least cost to produce it ($150) from the first isocost. Point 2 is associated with output size 20 units (second isoquant) at a cost of $200 (second isocost), and so on for the rest of the points on the lower panel. If we reach these points 1–6, we will get an LTC.

Just as we did in the short-run costs, we can obtain other long-run costs from the LTC. The **long-run average cost (LAC)** is still derived by dividing the LTC by the size of the output:

$$LAC = \frac{LTC}{Q}.$$

In the lower panel of Figure 8.6, we can derive the LAC by dividing all the TC figures by their corresponding output size and recording the results on the vertical axis. For example, point *a* refers to an output level of 10 and AC of 15$\left(\frac{150}{10}\right)$. Point *b* refers to output level of 20 and an AC of 10 $\left(\frac{200}{20}\right)$, and likewise for all other remaining points *c*, *d*, *e*, *f*. Reaching these points gives us the LAC. Note that the LAC declines to its lowest point *d* then picks up. This manner is associated with changes in the slopes of the cords that run from the origin to the LTC curve in the upper panel. The slopes continue to decline up to point 4, which corresponds to point *d* in the lower panel. Beyond point 4, the slopes bounce back again.

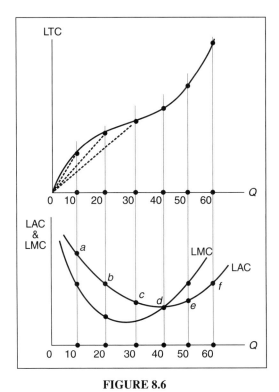

FIGURE 8.6

As for the **long-run marginal cost (LMC)**, it is the change in the LTC for each unit of output. It is also equal to the slope of the LTC:

$$LMC = \frac{\partial LTC}{\partial Q}.$$

It is noteworthy to mention here that the LMC does not represent the cost of the last unit of production as much as it represents the increase in production cost when there is an extra increment in output. As Figure 8.6 shows, the LMC curve descends as long as the LAC exceeds it. Once they are equal at d, they will both rise, but this time the LMC will exceed the LAC. The point of their intersection continues to be the lowest point of the LAC.

8.6   SHORT-RUN AND LONG-RUN AVERAGE COSTS: ECONOMIES OF SCALE

Let us assume that a firm has five plants progressing in scales of operation from the smallest to the largest. The upper panel of Figure 8.7 shows the short-run average cost (SAC) of each scale of operation. On the smallest scale, the first plant (SAC_1), the firm can produce output level Q_1 at an AC of C_1 (point A). On point B, the firm would be indifferent to producing Q_2 at either plant 1 (SAC_1) or plant 2 (SAC_2) because both require the same AC of C_2. However, if the firm wants to produce Q_3, plant 1 could offer its minimum AC of C_3 (point C) but plant 2 can beat the best of plant 1 by offering to produce the same level of output Q_3 at the much lower cost of C_4 (point D). Plant 2 can go further to offer even the larger output of Q_4 at the even lower cost of C_5 (point E). The larger plant 3 can beat them all and offer the highest possible output Q_5 at the least possible cost of C_6. This illustrates that in the long run and with larger scale plants, the firm would have higher flexibility and better choices. Considering these five plants all together and in the long run, the firm's general LAC curve would look like the solid part of the bottom curves in the upper panel. However, with more plants in a more extended future, this curve stretches and becomes smoother like

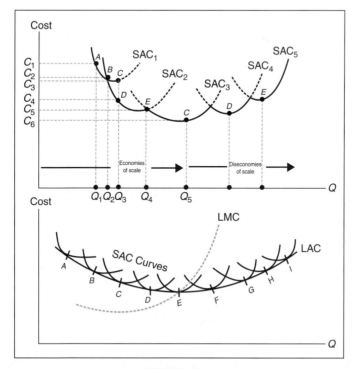

FIGURE 8.7

the large curve in the lower panel. This is why the LAC for a large and multifaceted firm is described as the envelope for the firm's many SAC curves.

This observation of the decline of average or per unit cost of production with larger scale production refers to what is known in economics as "**economies of scale.**" It is due to the fact that the firm would operate on the declining section of the LAC curve, where $\partial \text{LAC}/\partial Q < 0$. This occurs up to output level Q_5. In other words, the firm would face increasing returns to scale up to Q_5. Beyond Q_5, the firm would operate on the rising section of the LAC ($\partial \text{LAC}/\partial Q > 0$), and would face decreasing returns to scale. The firm would, then, face the opposite phase called "**diseconomies of scale.**" A good question is: what happens right at point Q_5? Well, the answer is that, if the firm does not face either increasing or decreasing returns to scale, then it must be facing constant returns to scale where $\partial \text{LAC}/\partial Q = 0$. This very level of output (Q_5) is called the "**minimum efficient scale**" (**MES**). The existence of either economies or diseconomies of scale can be detected by checking the cost elasticity (ε_c), which measures the percentage change in the LTC due to a 1% change in output:

$$\varepsilon_c = \left[\frac{\partial \text{LTC}}{\partial Q} \right] \left[\frac{Q}{\text{LTC}} \right],$$

where ε_c is just a point elasticity. But for an arc elasticity, the formula would be

$$\varepsilon_c = \left[\frac{\text{LTC}_2 - \text{LTC}_1}{Q_2 - Q_1} \right] \left[\frac{Q_1 + Q_2}{\text{LTC}_1 + \text{LTC}_2} \right],$$

where

$\varepsilon_c < 1$ = economies of scale occur;
$\varepsilon_c > 1$ = diseconomies of scale occur.

One might wonder, what in reality causes the changes of returns to scale. The answer would typically be that as the firm grows larger and gets more established, its specialization increases, which would bring higher productivity that may exceed the increase in operating cost. This may happen along with an increase in sales and more favorable consumer response and higher demand and ultimately more opportunities for better marketing, higher research and development, and more expansion. All of these events may result in higher efficiency, that is, increasing the benefits and reducing the cost. These are the practical reasons for the increasing returns to scale and the economies of scale. The opposite conditions might throw the firm in diseconomies of scale, when expansion in operation increases the burden and liabilities, and results in a loss of coordination and control, especially over curbing the skyrocketing AC.

Example 8.4
Consider the LTC function that is given by

$$\text{LTC} = 1125Q - 8Q^2 + 0.016Q^3.$$

Find the following:

1. The LAC function.

2. The MES output level.

3. The minimum per unit cost at the MES output level.

Solution:

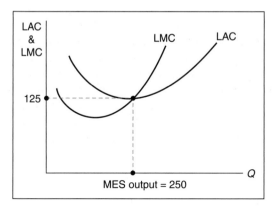

FIGURE 8.8

1.

$$LAC = \frac{LTC}{Q},$$

$$LAC = \frac{1125Q - 8Q^2 + 0.016Q^3}{Q},$$

$$LAC = 1125 - 8Q + 0.016Q^2.$$

2. The MES occurs at the output level corresponding to the minimum point at the bottom of the LAC curve. It can be found by taking the first derivative of the LAC function with respect to Q, setting it to zero and solving for Q:

$$LAC = 1125 - 8Q + 0.016Q^2,$$

$$\frac{\partial LAC}{\partial Q} = -8 + 0.032Q = 0,$$

$$0.032Q = 8,$$

$$Q = \frac{8}{0.032} = 250.$$

This output level can also be found by equating the LAC function with the LMC function and solving for Q (see Figure 8.8):

$$LMC = \frac{\partial LTC}{\partial Q} = 1125 - 16Q + 0.048Q^2,$$

$$LMC = LAC,$$

$$1125 - 16Q + 0.048Q^2 = 1125 - 8Q + 0.016Q^2,$$

$$1125 - 1125 - 16Q + 8Q = 0.048Q^2 + 0.016Q^2 = 0,$$

$$-8Q = -0.032,$$

$$Q = \frac{8}{0.032},$$

$$Q = 250.$$

To prove that this output level can be realized when the AC is at its minimum, the second derivative of the LAC with respect to Q has to be positive:

$$\frac{\partial^2 \text{LAC}}{\partial Q^2} = 0.032 > 0.$$

3.

$$\text{LAC} = 1125 - 8Q + 0.016Q^2,$$

$$= 1125 - 8(250) + 0.016(250)^2,$$

$$= 125.$$

This can be confirmed by obtaining the TC and dividing it by MES:

$$\text{LTC} = 1125Q - 8Q^2 + 0.016Q^3,$$

$$= 1125(250) - 8(250)^2 + 0.016(250)^3,$$

$$= 31{,}250.$$

$$\frac{\text{LTC}}{\text{MES}} = \frac{31{,}250}{250} = 125.$$

8.7   DERIVATION OF THE COST FUNCTION

On the surface, analyzing "cost" appears to involve only simple arithmetic and, under certain circumstances, this is correct. This section reviews economic cost concepts and provides the epistemic framework that underlies statistical analysis of cost. The focus of a statistical analysis of cost is to learn about scale economies and cost control. Let us consider this definition of total cost: total cost (TC) is the minimum expenditure associated with a level of output. Let us use this definition to derive TC for the case where there are only two inputs. Note that this may mean that the production process involves only two distinct inputs or that inputs other than these two are fixed inputs, meaning their employment cannot be readily changed. In the former case, we derive the LTC function. In the latter case, we derive the STC function. As alternative interpretations, the production process may involve only a single input that is applied during two stages of a production process or only a single variable input (other inputs fixed) applied during two stages of a production process. Again, the former results in the derivation of LTC while the latter results in the derivation of STC.

Let us focus on the case of a single variable input (other inputs fixed) that is used during two stages of a production process. Call the amount of the input used during the first stage, x_1, and the amount of the input used during the second stage, x_2. Call the prices paid per unit of x during the first and second stages, c_1 and c_2, respectively. Total factor cost (TFC) is simply the amount of money spent on the two inputs; namely, $\text{TFC}(x_1, x_2)$ is $c_1 x_1 + c_2 x_2$. To find $\text{TC}(y)$ for a level of output, y, we need to find the smallest TFC such that output is the amount y. So, we need to solve the following problem:

$$\text{Minimize } c_1 x_1 + c_2 x_2,$$

$$\text{Subject to } f(x_1, x_2) = y,$$

where $f(x_1, x_2)$ is the production function. Assuming that the solution to this problem involves the use of both inputs, this algebraic statement reveals that finding a point on TC amounts to solving an equality constrained optimization problem. The Lagrangian method is a suitable solution method for problems of this type, and, as an added bonus, the value of the Lagrange multiplier at the solution reveals how TFC increases with an expansion of output by one unit. Recall that the Lagrangian has the general form:

$$L(x_1, x_2, \lambda) = \text{Objective function} - \lambda(\text{Constraint function} - \text{Constraint constant}),$$

where λ is a new variable (known as the Lagrange multiplier) that has been introduced to help solve the problem.

In this particular case, the Lagrangian is

$$L(x_1, x_2, \lambda) = c_1 x_1 + c_2 x_2 - \lambda[f(x_1, x_2) - y].$$

Also, recall that a saddle point of the Lagrangian is sufficient for a solution to the equality constrained optimization problem. Assuming that the production function is smooth, a saddle point is necessarily found as a point where the derivatives of the Lagrangian with respect to x and the Lagrange multiplier, λ, are simultaneously zero. For the Lagrangian above (letting MP_i denote the marginal product of input i), the saddle point conditions are

$$c_1 - \lambda\, MP_1 = 0,$$

$$c_2 - \lambda\, MP_2 = 0,$$

$$y - f(x_1, x_2) = 0.$$

Among other things, these conditions require that

$$\frac{MP_1}{c_1} = \frac{MP_2}{c_2}.$$

First, let us take a look at these conditions and see what they might mean in a qualitative sense. Note what these conditions say about cost minimization. Cost minimization requires that the ratio of marginal product to marginal factor cost be the same for all inputs. This amounts to the tangency condition between an isoquant and an isocost line, where

$$MRS = \frac{MP_1}{MP_2} = \frac{c_1}{c_2}.$$

Second, and at a more general level, these conditions from the Lagrangian only seem to take on practical importance when the constraint in the problem actually binds; that is, when the same solution would have resulted from an inequality constraint in the problem rather than the strict equality constraint. This is the case for which resources are not adequate to accomplish all one wants to accomplish and allocation of scarce resources must actually take place to achieve the best (though perhaps not good) outcome available, which leads to the third point. At a much more general level, note that these conditions associated with cost minimization seem to be capable of extension to more general management efforts. Moreover, it is not clear that the extension needs to be quantitative to have an impact on the quality of management decisions. In cases where resources are actually scarce as indicated above, the conditions from the Lagrangian suggest to the (perhaps overworked) manager to balance the ratio of the marginal fruit of effort to the marginal sacrifice of effort for all efforts. This condition, at the very least, provides a manager with a target. It is a rule of thumb that may be more or less applicable without quantification or, at least, may provide a useful mindset from time to time in guiding management decisions. Contrast this condition to related advice such as "make a list of the ten things you want to accomplish and hope to accomplish five or six of them." Or contrast it to the stochastic analog to this latter advice: "figure out what you want to happen and then take action to maximize the probability that the preferred event occurs." This advice for an uncertain environment may be contrasted in a similar manner to related efficiency conditions derived from the economics of risk and uncertainty. The critical point here is that economic efficiency, as depicted by the saddle point of the Lagrangian, requires balanced efforts across all endeavors. This balancing of efforts seems to run throughout microeconomic theory probably because the nature of the economizing problems being considered is so similar across different fields.

Now let us consider finding a specific TC. This will be accomplished by dispensing with interpretation and actually solving the efficiency conditions derived from the Lagrangian above. Suppose that we know the production function is a Cobb–Douglas type, that is, we know the values of a, b, and c in

$$y = a\, x_1^b x_2^c,$$

and we know the input prices, c_1 and c_2, as well.

Then the Lagrangian is

$$L(x_1, x_2, \lambda) = c_1\, x_1 + c_2\, x_2 - \lambda \left(a\, x_1^b x_2^c - y \right).$$

Solving the saddle point conditions,

$$c_1 - ba\, x_1^{b-1} x_2^c \lambda = 0,$$
$$c_2 - ca\, x_1^b x_2^{c-1} \lambda = 0,$$
$$y - a\, x_1^b x_2^c = 0,$$

and inserting the solution values for x_1 and x_2 gives the expression for TC as

$$\text{TC}(y) = \left[\frac{(b+c)c_2}{c} \right] \left[\left(\frac{bc_2}{cc_1} \right)^{-b} \left(\frac{y}{a} \right) \right]^{\frac{1}{b+c}}.$$

Note that this expression gives the minimum possible expenditure on x_1 and x_2, which results in y units of output. TC depends on the input prices, c_1 and c_2, and the technical coefficients from the production function, a, b, and c, as well as on the level of output, y. Note that in the case above, TC has the form

$$TC(Q) = A\, y^B,$$

where $B = 1/(b+c)$. You should be able to determine the shape of TC as a function of returns to scale, which, in the case of the Cobb–Douglas type production function, is indicated by the value of $b + c$. In particular, what does TC look like if the production function exhibits constant returns to scale? (Answer: Constant slope).

Note that $0 \leq B \leq 1$ suggests economies of scale (i.e., decreasing AC); $B = 1$ suggests constant AC; $B > 1$ suggests diseconomies of scale (i.e., increasing AC). As demonstrated later, this TC function could also have been derived using a more robust specification of the epistemic production model such as the CES.

Average cost (AC) is $TC(y)/y$. Note the form of AC is determined entirely by the form of TC and is a function of y. VC is $TC(y) - FC$. Note that the form of VC is identical to the form of TC and VC is also a function of y. AVC is $VC(y)/Q$. Its form is similar to that of AC. AVC is a function of y. AFC is FC/y. AFC has the form of a rectangular hyperbola regardless of the technology. AFC is a decreasing function of y. The MC is $dTC(y)/dy$. It is a function of y and approximates the change in TC due to a one-unit expansion in output. You should be able to show that MC $>$ AVC implies that AVC is increasing. Suppose that the production function is $y = 100\, x_1{}^{0.2}\, x_2{}^{0.5}$. The prices of x_1 and x_2 are \$4 and \$5 per unit, respectively. Fixed cost is \$250. You should be able to derive, plot, and interpret TC, VC, FC, AC, AVC, AFC, and MC. Ignoring FC, a robust epistemic model of cost is given by

$$TC(y) = A\, y^B,$$
$$A \geq 0 \quad \text{and} \quad B \geq 0.$$

This form for TC will follow from the linear, Cobb–Douglas type, Leontief, and more importantly, the CES production models. Hence, it is robust with respect to uncertainty about factor substitution and returns to scale. This means there are values of its parameters, A and B, which enable the data to inform about economies of scale. Hence, the statistical analysis of cost based on this form will enable the data to inform, without artificial restriction, about returns to scale. Of course, at all times, remain mindful that statistical analysis is but a single piece of information to assist decision –making among multiple pieces of information that may be available to a manager.

We know from the discussion in Chapter 7 that the CES production function can admit linear, Leontief, and Cobb–Douglas type factor substitution and returns to scale characteristics depending on the values of its parameters. Hence, it will be reassuring to find that a cost function derived from CES technology leads to the epistemic model that we have already arrived at. While somewhat tedious to show, this turns out to be the case. Let us first consider the problem that needs to be solved to yield a cost function based on CES technology:

$$\text{Minimize } c_1 x_1 + c_2 x_2,$$
$$\text{Subject to: } a \left[a_1 x_1^\rho + (1 - a_1) x_2^\rho \right]^{\varepsilon/\rho} = y.$$

After simplifying the constraint function, the Lagrangian is

$$L(x_1, x_2, \lambda) = c_1 x_1 + c_2 x_2 - \lambda \left[a^{\rho/\varepsilon} \left(a_1 x_1^\rho + (1-a_1) x_2^\rho \right) - y^{\rho/\varepsilon} \right].$$

The conditions based on the Lagrangian are

$$c_1 - a^{\rho/\varepsilon} a_1 x_1^{\rho-1} \lambda \rho = 0,$$

$$c_2 - a^{\rho/\varepsilon}(1-a_1) x_2^{\rho-1} \lambda \rho = 0,$$

$$y^{\rho/\varepsilon} - a^{\rho/\varepsilon} \left[a_1 x_1^\rho + (1-a_1) x_2^\rho \right] = 0.$$

Solving the first equation for x_1 gives

$$x_1 = a^{\frac{\rho}{\varepsilon}} \left(\frac{y^{\frac{\rho}{\varepsilon}} - a^{\frac{\rho}{\varepsilon}} x_2^\rho + a^{\frac{\rho}{\varepsilon}} a_1 x_2^\rho}{a_1} \right)^{\frac{1}{\rho}}.$$

Observing that the first two conditions imply that

$$x_1 = \left[\frac{(1-a_1) c_1 x_2^{\rho-1}}{a_1 c_2} \right]^{\frac{1}{\rho-1}},$$

and the solving for x_1 gives

$$x_1 \left(\left((1-a_1) c_1 x_2^{\rho-1} \right) / (a_1 c_2) \right)^{1/(\rho-1)},$$

or equivalently that

$$x_1 = (1-a_1)^{\frac{1}{\rho-1}} a_1^{-\frac{1}{\rho-1}} c_1^{-\frac{1}{\rho-1}} c_2^{-\frac{1}{\rho-1}} x_2.$$

The two expressions for x_1 can be simplified by first raising both sides of each expression to the power ρ and then simplifying the right-hand side of each expression to give

$$a^{\frac{\rho}{\varepsilon}} \left(\frac{y^{\frac{\rho}{\varepsilon}} - a^{\frac{\rho}{\varepsilon}} x_2^\rho + a^{\frac{\rho}{\varepsilon}} a_1 x_2^\rho}{a_1} \right) (1-a_1)^{\frac{\rho}{\rho-1}} a_1^{-\frac{\rho}{\rho-1}} c_1^{\frac{\rho}{\rho-1}} c_2^{\frac{\rho}{\rho-1}} x_2^\rho.$$

Solving this equation for x_2 gives

$$x_2 = \left[-a^{\frac{\rho}{\varepsilon}} a_1 y^{\frac{\rho}{\varepsilon}} \left(1 - \frac{1}{a_1} - (1-a_1)^{\frac{\rho}{\rho-1}} a_1^{\frac{\rho}{\rho-1}} c_1^{\frac{\rho}{\rho-1}} c_2^{\frac{\rho}{\rho-1}} \right) \right]^{-\frac{1}{\rho}}.$$

This expression for x_2 can be simplified to yield

$$x_2 = \left[a^{\frac{\rho}{\varepsilon}} y^{\frac{\rho}{\varepsilon}} \left(1 - a_1 + (1-a_1)^{\frac{\rho}{\rho-1}} a_1^{\frac{1}{\rho-1}} c_1^{\frac{\rho}{\rho-1}} c_2^{\frac{\rho}{\rho-1}} \right) \right]^{-\frac{1}{\rho}}.$$

Substituting this expression for x_2 into $x_1 = (1 - a_1)^{\frac{1}{\rho-1}} a_1^{-\frac{1}{\rho-1}} c_1^{\frac{1}{\rho-1}} c_2^{-\frac{1}{\rho-1}} x_2$ obtained earlier gives

$$x_1 = (1 - a_1)^{\frac{1}{\rho-1}} a_1^{-\frac{1}{\rho-1}} c_1^{\frac{1}{\rho-1}} c_2^{-\frac{1}{\rho-1}} \left[a^{\frac{\rho}{\varepsilon}} y^{-\rho}_{\varepsilon} \left(1 - a_1 + (1 - a_1)^{\frac{\rho}{\rho-1}} a_1^{\frac{1}{\rho-1}} c_1^{-\frac{\rho}{\rho-1}} c_2^{-\frac{\rho}{\rho-1}} \right) \right]^{-\frac{1}{\rho-1}}.$$

Substituting the expressions obtained for x_1 and x_2 into $c_1 x_1 + c_2 x_2$ and simplifying the outcome gives an expression for TC:

$$\text{TC}(y) = a^{-\frac{1}{\varepsilon}} \left[c_2 + (1 - a_1)^{\frac{1}{\rho-1}} a_1^{\frac{1}{1-\rho}} c_1^{\frac{\rho}{\rho-1}} c_2^{\frac{1}{1-\rho}} \right] \left[1 - a_1 + (1 - a_1)^{\frac{\rho}{\rho-1}} a_1^{\frac{1}{1-\rho}} c_1^{\frac{\rho}{\rho-1}} c_2^{\frac{-\rho}{\rho-1}} \right]^{-\frac{1}{\rho}} y^{\frac{1}{\varepsilon}},$$

or

$$\text{TC}(y) = A\, y^B,$$

where $B = 1/\varepsilon$.

Note that if $B < 1$, then $\varepsilon > 1$ (economies of scale; increasing returns to scale); if $B = 1$, then $\varepsilon = 1$ (no economies of scale; constant returns to scale); if $B > 1$, then $\varepsilon < 1$ (diseconomies of scale; decreasing returns to scale). In view of the results in this section, this form of epistemic model can be based on the CES production function and so will be robust with respect to the underlying technology/factor substitution (linear, Cobb–Douglas type, Leontief).

8.8 ECONOMIES OF SCOPE: BASIC CONCEPT AND COST COMPLEMENTARITIES

Economies of scope refer to the cost reduction resulting from producing two or more products together compared with producing them separately. It can be expressed as

$$\text{TC}(Q_1, Q_2) < [\text{TC}(Q_1, 0) + \text{TC}(0, Q_2)],$$

and the cost savings (CS) can be expressed as

$$\text{CS} = \frac{[\text{TC}(Q_1) + \text{TC}(Q_2)] - \text{TC}(Q_1, Q_2)}{[\text{TC}(Q_1) + \text{TC}(Q_2)]}.$$

Typical examples are the companies that produce beef and can easily produce leather. These firms would enjoy favorable economies of scope compared with firms that have two separate plants. Soft drink companies can easily produce other types of drinks, such as iced tea or energy drinks. Companies producing butter and cream can market the milk by-product as skim milk and create a market for it that may prove to be even more lucrative than the market for the original products. There is no secret to how the cost is reduced by the collective scope. Companies capitalize on their comparative advantages and exploit all the experience gained with the original products. They can make an excellent use of their facilities, equipment, labor, and management skills. Also, they can utilize the same distribution and supply networks they dealt with over the years, as well as tap into the same market base and consumer loyalty that they have developed over a long time.

Example 8.5

Suppose that a company estimates that producing its two products jointly would cost $7.56 million while currently it costs $5.2 million to produce product 1 and $3.8 million to produce product 2. How can the economies of scope be expressed?

Solution:

$$CS = \frac{[5.2 + 3.8] - 7.56}{[5.2 + 3.8]} = 0.16$$

TC would be reduced by 16% and that is due to the economies of scope.

Not only the TC of production is involved in measuring the economies of scope but the MC also plays a role in the existence of the economies of scope through what is called **cost complementarity**. When the MC of producing one product (MCQ_1) is reduced by the increase in production of another product (Q_2), a cost complementarity is said to exist. This can be proven when the cross second partial derivative of the joint product cost is negative:

$$\left[\frac{\partial MC_1(Q_1, Q_2)}{\partial Q_2} \right] < 0.$$

Since the MC is the first derivative of the TC, this condition can also be written as

$$\left[\frac{\partial^2 TC}{\partial Q_1 \partial Q_2} \right] < 0,$$

and for the other product, this condition would be

$$\left[\frac{\partial MC_2(Q_1, Q_2)}{\partial Q_1} \right] < 0,$$

or

$$\left[\frac{\partial^2 TC}{\partial Q_2 \partial Q_1} \right] < 0.$$

So, by this, the MC of Q_1 can be reduced if the production of Q_2 is increased or the other way around.

Example 8.6

Consider the following TC function:

$$TC = 500 - 2Q_1 Q_2 + Q_1^2 + Q_2^2$$

1. Would there be any cost complementarity?
2. If $Q1 = 10$ and $Q^2 = 15$, would there be any economies of scope?

Solution:

1.

$$\frac{\partial TC}{\partial Q_1} = -2Q_2 + 2Q_1,$$

$$\frac{\partial^2 TC}{\partial Q_1 \partial Q_2} = -2 < 0,$$

Also,

$$\frac{\partial TC}{\partial Q_2} = -2Q_1 + 2Q_2,$$

$$\frac{\partial^2 TC}{\partial Q_2 \partial Q_1} = -2 < 0.$$

Yes, the cost complementarity exists.

2.

$$TC(Q_1, Q_2) < [TC(Q_1, 0) + TC(0, Q_2)],$$

$$TC(Q_1, Q_2) = 500 - 2(10)(15) + (10)^2 + (15)^2 = 525,$$

$$TC(Q_1, 0) = 500 - 2(10)(0) + (10)^2 + (0)^2 = 600,$$

$$TC(0, Q_2) = 500 - 2(0)(15) + (0)^2 + (15)^2 = 725,$$

$$525 < (600 + 725),$$

$$525 < 1325.$$

Economies of scope exist.

8.9   ECONOMIES OF SCOPE: SYNERGY AND INPUT INDIVISIBILITY

Economies of scope may result from (1) a synergistic relationship between production processes and/or (2) input indivisibility. For example, suppose that there are two potential outputs, y_1 and y_2, with production functions:

$$y_1 = f(x_1, x_2, y_2),$$

$$y_2 = g(x_1, x_2).$$

Note the interrelatedness of the production of good y_1 with good y_2 indicated by the presence of the output level of the second good in the first good's production function. If y_1 is presently being produced, then synergism would be present if making y_2 increased the output of y_1. Such synergism could occur if an activity associated with the production of y_2 also served in the production of y_1.

The question "What can be added to an existing product line to increase profit?" is a very common management consideration in both production and retailing. This question can often be viewed as an inquiry into the existence and identity of economies of scope. Musing or simple logic and engineering may be useful in identifying synergistic effects in production. Analysis of production and factor usages may be helpful in identifying economies of scope due to input indivisibility. The following discussion provides a detailed description of a quantitative procedure that may be used to identify a new product to add in the case when economies of scope can be pursued owing to the existence of input indivisibility. This is a common situation, though sometimes synergistic effects are realized as a by-product of taking on another output, even if the motive for adding the output was input indivisibility.

First of all, what is meant by input indivisibility (sometimes referred to as lumpiness in factor supply)? This term refers to the fact that many inputs cannot be varied continuously but rather must usually be purchased in particular, discrete quantities. For example, the 40-h workweek is fairly common in the United States. Machines come with various discrete capacities. Additional workspace may come in round numbers, and so on. It is highly likely that some inputs in a production process will be fully employed at some times and unemployed (or employed at less than full capacity) at other times. This is likely to occur because the discrete amount of an input that can be acquired will not always correspond in a timely manner to the precise needs of a production process. Economies of scope may be achieved by fitting a new product into the "seams" of the production processes of the existing products. Note that the existence of economies of scope here does not depend on any synergistic relationship between the products. The different production processes can be completely unrelated except for the fact that there are common types of inputs used in some or all of them.

For example, a restaurant that sells meals and ice-cream desserts may analyze its production processes and determine that an ice-cream bar and/or a walk-up window can be staffed by existing management and other personnel. The new product ("carry-out" ice cream) can be added to the existing product line with minimal fixed cost and essentially no additional variable factor cost. The new product may significantly improve the firm's profitability owing entirely to economies of scope and input indivisibility. Moreover, additional synergistic economies of scope may be realized if it turns out that some synergistic effects occur as a result of adding the new product.

A quantitative procedure to identify economies of scope due to input indivisibility is described by an abstract example. The fact that this description is an example should not be taken as a reason to devalue its importance. In an actual situation, successful identification of economies of scope may be the critical difference for businesses such as the restaurant mentioned above. An abstract example is used to illustrate the main elements of the procedure in a comprehensive manner; that is, a manner that avoids the nonessential complexities of a real situation. The main technique used in the analysis is from a quantitative-methods course you have probably already taken and leverages the review of linear programming.

Suppose that the firm in this example produces two products. The first product, y_1, uses two inputs, x_1 and x_2. The second product, y_2, uses the same inputs plus an additional input, x_3. Production takes place over two time periods with finished products available after the second period. The firm must first determine the amount of each input required for each period to make a unit of each product. From the firm's first task, can you identify the type of production functions that are assumed for the outputs in this very obviously multioutput example? (Answer: Leontief).

Measurements are undertaken to characterize minimum input requirements for each product and for each input. Actually, averages of the measured requirements may be used rather than the minimum observed, though the minimum would be ideal. It is determined that producing a unit of y_1 requires 4 units of x_1 and 6 units of x_2 during period 1 and 5 units of x_1 and 10 units of x_2 during period 2 (Figures 8.9 and 8.10). Producing a unit of y_2 requires 20 units of x_1, 10 units of x_2, and 5 units of x_3 during period 1 and 10 units of x_1 and 5 units of x_3 during period 2 (Figures 8.11 and 8.12).

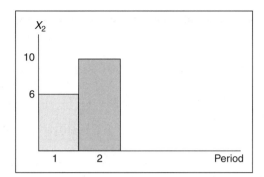

FIGURE 8.9

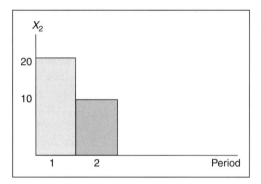

FIGURE 8.10

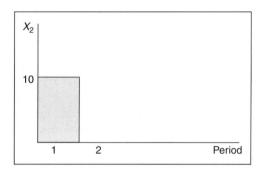

FIGURE 8.11

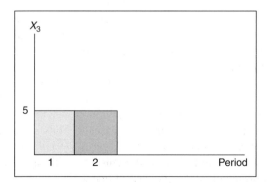

FIGURE 8.12

Let x_{jt} denote an amount of input j during period t. In view of the input requirements, the production function for y_1 is

$$y_1 = \min(1/4x_{11},\, 1/6x_{21},\, 1/5x_{12},\, 1/10x_{22}),$$

while the production function for y_2 is

$$y_2 = \min(1/20x_{11},\, 1/10x_{21},\, 1/5x_{31},\, 1/10x_{12},\, 1/5x_{32}).$$

The firm's estimates of the demand for its products suggest that it can sell 4 units of y_1 and 5 units of y_2. Due to input indivisibility, the firm must procure none or 200 units of x_1, none or 200 units of x_2, and none or 100 units of x_3 for use during the production cycle. Assume that each of the products is equally profitable with a profit per unit of \$50, and that the firm plans to acquire the maximum amount of input prior to the beginning of the production cycle. From section 7.6, the form of the multioutput model reflecting product demand, production, and resource constraints during the production cycle is

Maximize $50\,y_1 + 50\,y_2$.

Subject to $4\,y_1 + 20\,y_2 \le 200$,

$6y_1 + 10y_2 \le 200$,

$5y_2 \le 100$,

$4y_1 + 20y_2 + 5y_1 + 10y_2 \le 200$,

$6y_1 + 10y_2 + 10y_1 \le 200$,

$5y_2 + 5y_2 \le 100$,

$y_1 \le 4$,

$y_2 \le 5$,

where $y_1, y_2 \ge 0$.

The firm's multioutput decision problem can be solved by computer or graphical techniques. The optimal solution is $y_1 = 4$ and $y_2 = 5$, which yields a profit of 450 at the end of the production cycle. With these levels of output, the firm's optimal production plan uses 116 units of x_1, 74 units of x_2, and 25 units of x_3 during period 1 and 70 units of x_1, 40 units of x_2, and 25 units of x_3 during period 2. At the end of the production cycle, the firm will possess 14 units of x_1, 86 units of x_2, and 50 units of x_3. The firm can achieve economies of scope due to input indivisibility, by identifying a product or products that can make use of these unused inputs during the periods of the production cycle. Hence, the firm would need to evaluate promising new products that involve these inputs with unit requirements over the periods of the production cycle that fall within these ranges.

8.10   THE LEARNING CURVE

It is common sense to expect that if you do something long enough, it would not only become easier over time but also take less energy, time, and whatever other inputs it needs.

To put it formally, it is the experience that gets more intensive, highly flexible, and more applicable. This has been formalized as the learning curve effect. It refers to the reduction in inputs and input cost that can be observed as the cumulative size of output increases. In other words, accumulating learning and experience in the production process leads to a decline in the average cost of inputs for a given output level at a certain time. This phenomenon is specifically evident in labor as input and was observed initially during the 1930s in the aircraft industry. The observation was that the number of work hours required to produce one unit of output kept declining as production increased. However, it is not exclusively related to labor. It can be applied to many inputs, including the raw material, which can also be reduced as a longer and better experience is gained. For example, as the amount of scraps and wastes can be cut down with improvements in the method, design, and tools. However, not all production inputs can be subject to the learning curve effect.

Mathematically, the relationship between the reduction in input or its cost and the increased output can be expressed as

$$C = \alpha Q^{\beta}, \tag{8.6}$$

where C is the average cost of input, Q is any output level, α is the average cost of the first unit of production, and β is a measure of the learning effect. It is a negative value that makes the learning curve downward sloping (the upper panel of Figure 8.13). The greater the absolute value of β, the faster the decline in the per-unit cost (C).

Equation (8.6) can be expressed logarithmically as

$$\log C = \log \alpha + \beta \log Q.$$

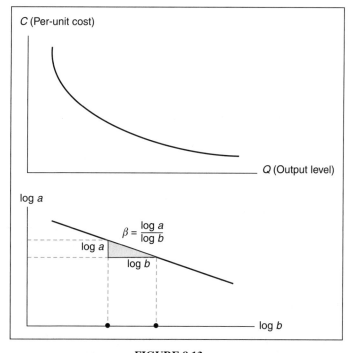

FIGURE 8.13

This form is linear resulting in a learning curve that is a downward-sloping straight line (lower panel of Figure 8.13). The slope of the line is β, which is typically obtained by

$$\beta = \frac{\log a}{\log b}.$$

As a measure of the learning effect, β is a ratio of the logarithms of two factors: the first is the learning factor a that refers to the rate at which the learning process occurs and the experience accumulates. Its value is between zero and one ($0 \leq a \leq 1$). As the value of this factor approaches zero, β would become very large, and the learning effect gets more significant.

The second factor is the factor of output proportionality that has been standardized as doubling the production so that β measures how much the average cost would decline every time the output is doubled. This factor is represented by the denominator ($\log b$) and, in this case, it would become log 2, which is equal to 0.30103. Table 8.2 shows three selected values of the learning factor, a, and their effects on the reduction of the cost of the initial unit of production at \$100,000.

TABLE 8.2

Q	$a = 0.9$	$a = 0.6$	$a = 0.3$
1	100,000	100,000	100,000
2	90,000	60,000	30,000
4	81,000	36,000	9,000
8	72,900	21,600	2,700
16	65,610	12,960	810
32	59,049	7,776	243
64	53,144	4,666	72.9
128	47,830	2,799	21.87
256	43,047	1,680	6.56
512	38,742	1,008	1.97
	$\beta = -0.152$	$\beta = -0.737$	$\beta = -1.736$

We can look up the value of the reduced cost at any of the production size in the Q column. Each Q is a double of the one before. For example, if the output level doubles from 16 to 32, the average cost of the first unit of production would be cut to \$59,049 if the learning factor is 0.9, and to \$7776 if the learning factor is 0.6, and to \$243 if the learning factor is 0.3, given that the average cost of the initial unit is \$100,000.

When $a = 0.9$,

$$\beta = \frac{\log a}{\log b}$$

$$= \frac{\log 0.9}{\log 2}$$

$$= -0.152,$$

$$C = \alpha Q^\beta$$

$$= (100,000)[32]^{-0.152}$$

$$= 59,049.$$

When $a = 0.6$,

$$\beta = \frac{\log 0.6}{\log 2}$$

$$= -0.737,$$

$$C = (100{,}000)[32]^{-0.737}$$

$$= 7776.$$

When $a = 0.3$,

$$\beta = \frac{\log 0.3}{\log 2}$$

$$= -1.74,$$

$$C = (100{,}000)[32]^{-1.736}$$

$$= 243.$$

Note that the higher the absolute value of β, the more dramatic the reduction in the average cost would be.

The learning curve effect has been applied in a wide range of fields in manufacturing and assembly lines of many industries. It has also been utilized in forecasting the requirements of equipment, material, and personnel, also in planning production schedules and pricing the products and services. The following graph (Figure 8.14) shows how the learning curve can be compared with a current price and how the saving in the LAC can be tracked down as the production grows from Q_1 to Q_2 to Q_3. For up to production size of Q_2, the average cost is above price, bringing about a disadvantage area of A. At Q_2, the cost is equal to the price, but after Q_2, the cost would be cut dramatically allowing a huge area of gain (B).

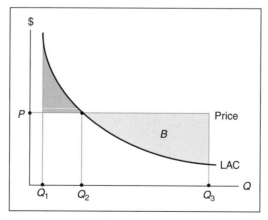

FIGURE 8.14

Example 8.7
If the average cost of producing the first piece of equipment in an assembly plant is $3500, the learning factor is 0.68, and the output proportionality factor is 3. Find the following:

1. The percentage of reduction in the average cost of producing 500 pieces of equipment.
2. The number of work hours required to produce the first piece of equipment given that the wage rate is $25 per hour of work.
3. The number of work hours required to produce each of the 500 pieces of equipment.

Solution:

1.
$$\beta = \frac{\log a}{\log b},$$
$$= \frac{\log 0.68}{\log 3},$$
$$= -0.35,$$
$$C = \alpha Q^{\beta}$$
$$= (3500)[500]^{-0.35}$$
$$= 395, \text{ the reduced cost}$$
$$\frac{3500 - 395}{3500} \times 100 = 88.7\%.$$

The 500th unit is reduced by 88.7% or the cost of the 500th unit became only 11.3% of the cost of the first unit:

$$\frac{395}{3500} \times 100 = 11.3.$$

2. If the average cost of the first unit is $3500 and the wage rate is $25, then the number of work hours would be

$$\frac{3500}{25} = 140 \text{ work hours.}$$

3. Since the cost of 500 units is $395 and the wage rate is $25 per hour, then the number of work hours required to produce 500 units is

$$\frac{395}{25} = 15.8 \text{ h.}$$

The last word about the learning curve is to distinguish its effect from the effect of economies of scale, since both are involved in the cost reduction owing to production increase. Figure 8.15 shows the difference clearly: the economies of scale effect on the cost reduction is measured by the vertical distance $C_2 C_1$ as we move down the curve from point A to point B

and as production size increases from Q_1 to Q_2. In the case of the learning curve, the same cost reduction would be due to shifting the entire curve down from LAC_1 to LAC_2.

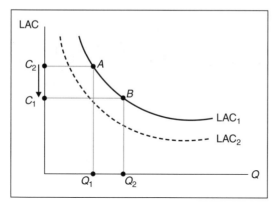

FIGURE 8.15

8.11   COST–VOLUME–PROFIT ANALYSIS AND OPERATING LEVERAGE

The major objective of the cost–volume–profit analysis is to identify the smallest output level necessary to secure a nonnegative level of profit. That specific output level would first and foremost be able to cover the fixed cost. This analysis is also called **break-even analysis** where it is considered an important tool for business performance and profit planning that utilizes the restructuring of the fundamental relationship between cost and revenue. This analytical tool offers the manager or business planner a plausible approximation of the point when profits begin to be collected according to the realization of the stage during which TC of production has been recovered by revenues from the production sales.

The **cost–volume–profit** can be defined as the process determining the level of output that must be produced and sold before any profit can be earned. It can also be the determination of the amount of revenue that can be collected before earning any profit. The reliance on finding the revenue instead of the production size can be more practical and convenient if the firm produces or sells multiproducts. For example, General Motors can easily determine how many Chevy Malibu cars should be sold before that plant starts to earn profits, but this method cannot be easily used for Walmart, because Walmart stores sell tens of thousands of products. It is, therefore, more appropriate to determine how much sales revenue should be collected before a certain Walmart store starts to earn profits.

Technically, the break-even analysis is to find the point that refers to both the break-even quantity of product and the break-even revenue of sales. This point is called the **break-even point**, at which profit would be zero and TC would equal the total revenue. Geometrically, it is the point of intersection between TC and total revenue curves. Once we locate this point, we would know that all production before that point incurs some loss and any product produced and sold after that point would yield some profits.

8.11.1   Break-Even Quantity and Break-Even Revenue

If total cost (C) includes both FC and VC, then

$$C = \text{FC} + \text{VC}.$$

Since VC changes with the size of production, let us consider v the variable cost per unit of production. If production is Q, then

$$\text{VC} = vQ, \text{ and}$$
$$C = \text{FC} + vQ. \tag{8.7}$$

Also, revenue (R) will depend on how many units of product are sold. If we consider p as the price per unit of product, then

$$R = pQ. \tag{8.8}$$

Profit (Pr), sometimes called **operating profit** or **EBIT** (earnings before interests and taxes) is the difference between total revenue and total cost, then

$$\text{Pr} = R - C, \tag{8.9}$$
$$\text{Pr} = pQ - (\text{FC} + vQ),$$
$$\text{Pr} = pQ - \text{FC} - vQ,$$
$$\text{Pr} = Q(p - v) - \text{FC},$$

and since profit is zero at the break-even point,

$$0 = Q(p - v) - \text{FC},$$
$$Q(p - v) = \text{FC},$$
$$Q = \frac{\text{FC}}{p - v}.$$

This Q is the quantity of products at the break-even point, and it is called the **break-even quantity (BEQ)**:

$$\text{BEQ} = \frac{\text{FC}}{p - v},$$

where again, FC is the fixed operating cost, p is the price per unit of product, and v is the variable operating cost per unit of a product.

Similarly, we can find the revenue at the break-even point; we start with Equation (8.9):

$$\text{Pr} = R - C,$$
$$\text{Pr} = R - (\text{FC} + vQ),$$
$$\text{Pr} = R - \text{FC} - vQ.$$

We substitute for the Q value that is obtained from Equation (8.8):

$$R = pQ,$$

$$\frac{R}{p} = Q,$$

$$\text{Pr} = R - \text{FC} - v\left(\frac{R}{p}\right).$$

At the break-even point $\text{Pr} = 0$,

$$0 = R - \text{FC} - v\left(\frac{R}{p}\right),$$

$$\text{FC} = R\left(1 - \frac{v}{p}\right),$$

$$R = \frac{\text{FC}}{1 - \dfrac{v}{p}}.$$

This is the revenue at the break-even point, and it is called the **break-even revenue** (BER):

$$\text{BER} = \frac{\text{FC}}{1 - \dfrac{v}{p}}.$$

By knowing the BEQ or BER, a firm can

1. determine and control its operations in order to sustain the proper level of output to cover all operating costs;
2. assess and control its ability and timing to earn profits at different levels of production and volumes of sale.

Before we apply the break-even technique, we should be able to know the operational definitions of the variables involved, especially to distinguish between the FC and VC, which is the first task to perform before solving any BEQ or BER problems.

Fixed Cost   Fixed costs are the costs that are not associated with the size of production or sale of products. They are a function of time, not sales or production, and therefore, they are incurred whether or not the firm produces anything or sells any product. Typical examples of FC are rent, lease payments, insurance premiums, regular utilities, executive and clerical salaries, and debt services. All these are expenses that have to be paid regardless of how much the firm produces or sells. Geometrically, they are represented by a horizontal line.

Variable Cost   Variable costs are any costs that are associated with the size of production or sale. They fluctuate up and down with the volume of production in a positive relationship.

Typical examples of VC are production material, production labor and production utilities such as the cost of electricity and gas consumed by the productive machines and equipment, merchandise insurance, transportation, and storage. The more the firm produces, the more the VC it incurs. In this sense, VC would be a product of the size of production (Q) and the VC per unit of a product (v).

Contribution Margin   The CM is the amount of profit earned on each unit sold above and beyond the break-even quantity, and similarly, it would be the amount of loss the firm would incur on each unit produced below the break-even point. Technically, it is equal to the unit price of the product discounted for the unit variable cost. Mathematically, CM would be

$$CM = p - v$$

and that is, in fact, the denominator of the BEQ formula.

Example 8.8

A small home business incurs \$3860 FC and \$0.75 variable cost per unit. If it sells its product for \$2.75, how many units of the product have to be produced and how much revenue has to be collected before this business starts earning a profit?

Solution:

$$BEQ = \frac{FC}{p - v},$$

$$BEQ = \frac{3860}{2.75 - 0.75},$$

$$BEQ = 1930 \text{ units},$$

$$BER = \frac{FC}{1 - \dfrac{v}{p}},$$

$$BER = \frac{3860}{1 - \dfrac{0.75}{2.75}},$$

$$BER = 5307.50,$$

Also,

$$BER = BEQ \cdot p,$$

$$BER = (1930)(2.75),$$

$$BER = 5307.50.$$

Example 8.9

Table 8.3 shows the cost data as in the records of Modern Books, a company that specializes in custom book-binding and sells its service for \$30 per book. Calculate the break-even quantity and the break-even revenue.

TABLE 8.3

Item	Frequency	Cost ($)
Rent	Monthly	2800
Property taxes	Semiannually	1665
Insurance	Quarterly	1112
Administrative salaries	Monthly	6580
Employees benefits	Annually	5312
Wages	Per book	3.00
Paper	Per book	2.15
Cardboard	Per book	1.35
Glue, take, thread	Per book	0.55
Leather	Per book	1.95
Ink and paint	Per book	0.95
Shipping and handling service	Per book	2.00

Solution:

- The first task is to separate FC and VC on the basis of our understanding of the concepts:
  - Fixed costs are rent, property taxes, insurance administrative salaries, and employee benefits.
  - Variable costs are wages, paper, cardboard, glue, tape, and thread, leather, ink and paint, and shipping and handling.
- The second task is to unify the frequencies of the cost items. The standard is to convert every fixed cost item into annual and energy variable cost item per unit.

Fixed costs:

$$\text{Rent} = \$2800 \times 12 = \$33,600,$$

$$\text{Property taxes} = \$1665 \times 2 = \$3300,$$

$$\text{Insurance} = \$1112 \times 4 = \$4448,$$

$$\text{Admin.salaries} = \$6580 \times 12 = \$78,960,$$

$$\text{Employee benefits} = \$5312 \times 1 = \$5312,$$

$$\text{Total} = \$125,620.$$

Variable costs:

$$\text{Wages} = \$3.00,$$

$$\text{Paper} = \$2.15,$$

$$\text{Cardboard} = \$1.35,$$

$$\text{Glue, tape, thread} = \$.55,$$

$$\text{Leather} = \$1.95,$$

$$\text{Ink and paint} = \$4.95,$$

$$\text{Shipping \& handling} = \$2.00,$$

$$\text{Total} = \$11.95,$$

$$\text{BEQ} = \frac{\text{FC}}{p - v},$$

$$\text{BEQ} = \frac{125{,}620}{30 - 11.95} = 6959 \text{ books},$$

$$\text{BER} = \frac{\text{FC}}{1 - \dfrac{v}{p}},$$

$$\text{BER} = \frac{125{,}620}{1 - \dfrac{11.95}{30}} = \$208{,}786.$$

Also,

$$\text{BER} = \text{BEQ} \cdot p,$$

$$\text{BER} = (6959.56)(30.00) = 208.786.$$

8.11.2   Cash Break-Even Technique

Sometimes, there are a lot of noncash charges that a company has to deal with as a significant part of its operating FC. Often, these noncash charges are the depreciation charges, which have to be deducted from the operating FC in order to prevent the overestimation of the break-even point. In such a case, the formula to calculate the break-even point would be adjusted to "cash break-even quantity" (CBEQ), which is equal to

$$\text{CBEQ} = \frac{\text{FC} - \text{NC}}{p - v},$$

where NC is any noncash charges constituting a sizeable portion of the FC.

Example 8.10

The records of the Riverbent Company indicate a \$5700 FC, depreciation charges of \$1767, which is a little more than one-third of the FC. Suppose also that the VC per unit is \$2.30 and the product sells for \$7.00. What would be the company's CBEQ and how would it compare to the regular break-even quantity (BEQ)?

Solution:

$$\text{CBEQ} = \frac{\text{FC} - \text{NC}}{p - v},$$

$$\text{CBEQ} = \frac{5700 - 1767}{7.00 - 2.30},$$

$$\text{CBEQ} = 837,$$

$$\text{CBER} = (\text{CBEQ})(p) = (837)(7.00) = \$5859.$$

If we calculate the regular BEQ, we would not discount the depreciation out of the FC. In this case, BEQ would be

$$BEQ = \frac{FC}{p - v},$$

$$BEQ = \frac{5700}{7.00 - 2.30},$$

$$BEQ = 1213,$$

$$BER = (BEQ)(p) = (1213)(7.00) = \$8491,$$

which is a case of overstating the break-even point (Figure 8.16).

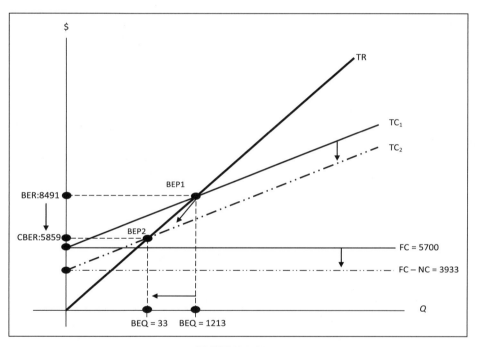

FIGURE 8.16

Excluding the noncash charges reduces the FC and TC, resulting in lowering the break-even point from BEP1 to BEP2. This would lead to a lower CBEQ, and lower CBER.

8.11.3   The Break-Even Point and Target Profit

If a business owner has a specific objective to achieve a certain profit specified in advance as a certain amount of money, then that specific profit figure would be called a "**target profit.**" It can be preset by making it part of the FC in order to determine the size of the BEQ and **break-even revenue (BER)**. The BEQ and BER formulas would then have to be adjusted by adding that target profit (TP) to their FC in the numerator and the new BEQ_{tp} and BER_{tp} would be

$$BEQ_{tp} = \frac{FC + TP}{p - v},$$

and

$$BER_{tp} = \frac{FC + TP}{1 - \frac{v}{p}}.$$

Example 8.11

Let us assume that the Riverbent Company in the last example decided to collect at least $6000 profit as a first step. What would the BEQ and the BER be?

Solution:

$$TP = \$6000,$$

$$BEQ_{tp} = \frac{FC + TP}{p - v},$$

$$BEQ_{tp} = \frac{5700 + 6000}{7.00 - 2.30},$$

$$BEQ_{tp} = 2490,$$

$$BER_{tp} = \frac{FC + TP}{1 - \frac{v}{p}},$$

$$BER_{tp} = \frac{5700 + 6000}{1 - \frac{2.30}{7.00}},$$

$$BER_{tp} = 17,425,$$

or

$$BER_{tp} = (2489.36)(7.00),$$

$$BER_{tp} = 17,425.$$

This is an opposite case to the cash break-even (Figure 8.17). Here a TP is added to the FC pushing the TC up from TC_1 to TC_2 and as a result, moving up both the BEQ and BER. The second break-even point would have a different meaning this time. It is no longer the point at which the profit is equal to zero as was the first point, but it is the point beyond which profits would move higher than the achieved target.

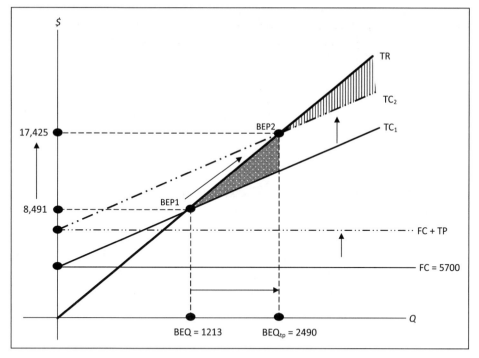

FIGURE 8.17

8.11.4   An Algebraic Approach to the Break-Even Point

Corenza's home business produces dolls at a VC of $20 per doll and a FC of $300. If it sells the doll for $50 apiece, we can write the cost (C) and revenue (R) equations in the following way:

$$C = \text{FC} + vQ,$$
$$C = 300 + 20X,$$
$$R = pQ,$$
$$R = 50Q.$$

At the break-even point, cost would equal revenue, then

$$C = R,$$
$$300 + 20Q = 50Q,$$
$$300 = 50Q - 20Q,$$
$$300 = 30Q,$$

$$Q = \frac{300}{30},$$

$Q = 10,$ this is the BEQ,

$R = 50Q,$

$R = 50(10),$

$R = 500,$ this is the BER.

8.11.5 Break-Even Time

Since the break-even point has been expressed in terms of production size and revenue amount, it can also be expressed in terms of time, especially if a firm knows its production capacity, which is stable and consistent and can be measured in time units. In the light of the time value of money, it becomes significant to identify the break-even point in terms of time (Figure 8.18). Suppose that a firm knows its production rate (e.g., q). If the time required to produce a certain size of production is t, and if Q refers to the break-even quantity, then we can write

$$Q = qt. \tag{8.10}$$

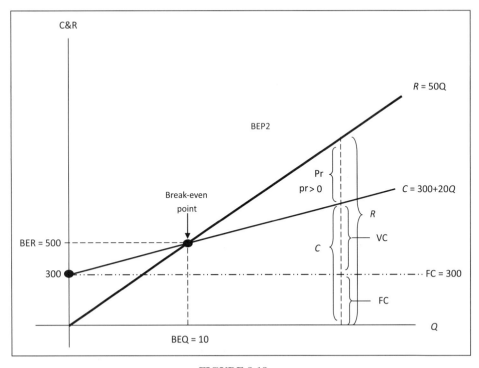

FIGURE 8.18

Suppose that the family business in the last example can only produce two dolls a day. Their break-even time would be 5 days:

$$Q = qt,$$
$$10 = 2t,$$
$$t = \frac{10}{2},$$
$$t = 5 \text{ days.}$$

In reality, products take some time to be sold, which means there is a time lag between manufacturing a product and selling it, and actually collecting revenue from its sale. So, let us denote this time lag by t_L and go back to the original cost and revenue equations and substitute for the Q value from Equation (8.10):

$$C = FC + vQ,$$

$$C = FC + vqt, \tag{8.11}$$

$$R = pQ,$$

$$R = pqt.$$

We can factor in the time lag in the revenue equation:

$$R = pq(t - t_L). \tag{8.12}$$

Now, let us equate C and R Equations (8.11) and (8.12) under the break-even condition and solve for t as the break-even time:

$$C = R,$$
$$FC + vqt = pq(t - t_L),$$
$$FC + vqt = pqt - pqt_L,$$
$$FC + pqt_L = pqt - vqt,$$
$$FC + pqt_L = pt(p - v),$$
$$t = \frac{FC + pqt_L}{q(p - v)}.$$

This t is the break-even time (BET), which is expressed in terms of the FC, unit price of the product (p), production rate (q), time lag (t_L), and variable cost per unit (v):

$$\text{BET} = \frac{\text{FC} + pqt_L}{q(p - v)}.$$

Example 8.12

Suppose Corenza's family business in the last example decided to produce beach-craft souvenirs at the rate of four pieces a day at a \$28 variable cost per piece. Assume its FC stays the same at \$300. Each souvenir would sell for \$60, but it will take 3 days for the revenue to start coming in. When would this business break even and at what BEQ, and with what BER?

Solution:

$$\text{BET} = \frac{\text{FC} + pqt_L}{q(p - v)},$$

$$= \frac{300 + (60)(4)(3)}{4(60 - 28)},$$

$$= 7.97 \text{ or } 8 \text{ days to break even.}$$

$$R = pq(t - t_L),$$

$$= (60)(4)(8 - 3),$$

$$\text{BER} = \$1200.$$

$$\text{BEQ} = \frac{\text{BER}}{P},$$

$$= \frac{1200}{60},$$

$$= 20 \text{ dolls.}$$

Example 8.13

Find BET, BER, and BEQ for Goodtract, a tire manufacturing firm that has the following data (Figure 8.19):

$$\text{Fixed cost} = \$80,000,$$

$$\text{Variable cost per tire} = \$20,$$

$$\text{Daily production rate} = 100 \text{ tires,}$$

$$\text{Selling price per tire} = \$80,$$

$$\text{Time lag for revenue} = 20 \text{ days.}$$

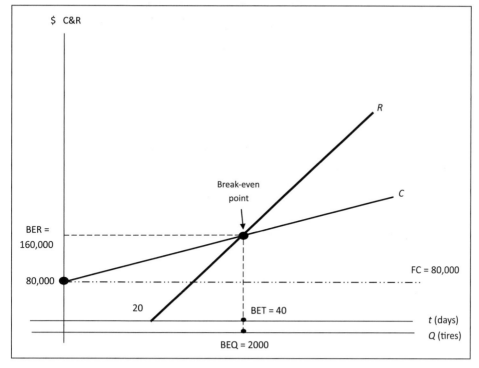

FIGURE 8.19

Solution:
First, we construct the cost and revenue equations in which a time element is involved:

$$C = \text{FC} + vqt,$$
$$C = 80,000 + (20(100)t,$$
$$C = 80,000 + 2000\,t,$$
$$R = pq(t - t_L),$$
$$R = (80)(100)(t - 20),$$
$$R = 8000\,t - 160,000.$$

At the break-even point, $C = R$

$$80,000 + 2000\,t = 8000\,t - 160,000,$$
$$240,000 = 6000\,t,$$
$$t = \frac{240,000}{6000}.$$
$$\text{BET} = t = 40 \text{ days to break even.}$$

$$\text{BER} = R = 8000\,t - 160{,}000$$
$$= 8000(40) = 160{,}000$$
$$= \$160{,}000.$$
$$\text{BEQ} = \frac{\text{BER}}{P},$$
$$= \frac{160{,}000}{80},$$
$$= 2000 \text{ tires.}$$

8.11.6   The Dual Break-Even Points

As we have seen so far, the revenue and cost functions have been either linear or approximated as linear, and the graphs of the two functions have been straight lines intersecting one time at one point, forming a single break-even point. Usually to the left of the break-even point, the TC line is above the total revenue to indicate the loss area, and to the right of the point, the TC line runs below the total revenue line indicating the profit area. In other cases, either both or one of the functions would be nonlinear, a case that might result in having the two curves intersect each other at more than one point, often at two points resulting in the creation of two break-even points. The area formed between the two curves up and down, and between the two break-even points left and right is the area of gain. Profit usually starts low right after the first break-even point, which is called "**the lower break-even point**" and it would increase until it reaches the maximum at some point of production. Then it starts to decrease until it gets to zero again at the second break-even point, which is called "**the upper break-even point**." After that point, losses would incur again. Let us consider the following revenue and cost functions:

$$R = -2Q^2 + 86Q,$$
$$C = 16Q + 140,$$

and let us

1. locate the two break-even points;
2. find out at what size of production the profit reaches its maximum;
3. calculate how much the maximum profit (Pr^m) would be

$$\text{Pr} = R - C,$$
$$\text{Pr} = -2Q^2 + 86Q - 16Q - 140,$$
$$\text{Pr} = -2Q^2 + 70Q - 140.$$

At the break-even point(s), profit would be zero, so we set the equation to zero:

$$\text{Pr} = -2Q^2 + 70Q - 140 = 0,$$

and solve for Q as the break-even point. The function is quadratic and Q will have two values. The function is of the following form:

$$Y = ax^2 + bx + c.$$

We can solve for Q by following the quadratic formula:

$$x = \frac{-b \pm \sqrt{b^2 - 4ac}}{2a}.$$

In the case of our function above, those values are

$$a = 2, \; b = 70 \quad \text{and} \quad c = -140.$$

$$Q = \frac{-b \pm \sqrt{b^2 - 4ac}}{2a},$$

$$Q = \frac{-70 \pm \sqrt{(70)^2 - 4(-2)(-140)}}{2(-2)},$$

$$Q = \frac{-70 \pm \sqrt{3,780}}{-4},$$

$$Q_1 = \frac{-70 + 61.48}{-4} = 2.13, \text{ the lower break-even point,}$$

$$\text{and} \quad Q_2 = \frac{-70 + 61.48}{-4} = 32.87, \text{ the upper break-even point.}$$

Maximum profit would occur at a production size of Q_v that would be obtained as the vertex of the quadratic function. The vertex point can be found by

$$Q_v = \frac{-b}{2a},$$

$$Q_v = \frac{-70}{2(-2)} = 17.5.$$

Substituting for this amount of production in the profit function would give us the maximum profit (Pr^m):

$$\text{Pr}^m = -2Q_v^2 + 70Qv - 140,$$

$$\text{Pr}^m = -2(17.5)^2 + 70(17.5) - 140,$$

$$\text{Pr}^m = 472.50.$$

To prove this value of the function is the maximum, two checks have to be verified:

1. The first derivative of the function has to have a value of zero when the Q_v is plugged in $\frac{d\,Pr}{dQ} = 0$. The first derivative of the profit function refers to the marginal profit and the zero indicates that the tangent at the maximum point is a horizontal line (Figure 8.20):

$$Pr^m = -2Q_v^2 + 70Qv - 140,$$

$$\frac{d\,Pr^m}{dQ_v} = -4Qv + 70,$$

$$= -4(17.5) + 70,$$

$$= 0.$$

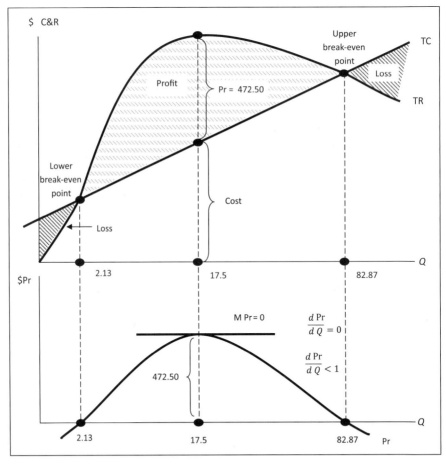

FIGURE 8.20

2. Since both points, the maximum point at the top of the down-opened parabola and the minimum point at the bottom of the up-opened parabola have horizontal line

tangents, we need a second check to refer to the maximum condition. That is the second derivative of the profit function that has to have a negative value when the Q_v is plugged in $\frac{d^2 \text{Pr}}{dQ^2} < 0$, the negativity refers to the fact that the function is going down. If it were a minimum, it would go up:

$$\frac{d\,\text{Pr}}{dQ} = -4Qv + 70,$$

$$\frac{d^2\,\text{Pr}}{dQ^2} = -4.$$

This condition can simply be expressed as the fact that the coefficient of x^2, which is a in the quadratic function, has to be negative.

8.12   LEVERAGE

The break-even analysis provides the tool to calculate the break-even point after which the firm would start to collect profits as it produces and sells more products. Then, the crucial question is to what extent the production and sales would have to increase in order to achieve a certain level of profits. This is a question of the profit sensitivity to the variability of the product sales, and that is what the "**leverage**" is all about. From another perspective, leverage refers to the relationship between FC and VC. If FC is larger than VC for a firm, then the firm is said to be highly leveraged. An important implication of being highly leveraged is that profit variation due to variation in output will be more significant than for a firm that is not highly leveraged. To understand this, note that high leverage means that cost (VC plus FC) will not change much if output declines. Revenue will be sensitive to output; however, cost will not be. If output declines, profit will decline by a relatively large percentage when compared with a firm that is not highly leveraged and whose costs are also closely tied to output.

Profit elasticity is a measure of profit variability with respect to output and can illustrate the profit variability that is associated with leverage. Profit elasticity is interpreted as the percent change in profit due to a 1% change in output. An applicable formula for profit elasticity is

$$\left[\frac{\%\Delta\,\text{Pr}}{\%\Delta Q}\right]\left[\frac{Q}{\text{Pr}}\right].$$

This can be reduced to

$$\frac{Q(P - v)}{Q(P - v) - \text{FC}}.$$

Later, this will be called the **degree of operating leverage** (DOL), in which a relatively large value for FC implies a relatively large value for profit elasticity, which suggests a larger vulnerability to output reductions.

8.12.1 Operating Leverage

Operating leverage is one of three kinds of leverage. The other two are the **financial leverage**, and **total leverage**. We focus on operating leverage here for it is more relevant to sales and profits of the business. It refers to the responsiveness of the change in profits due to the change in sales. Specifically, it is the potential use of fixed operating costs to magnify the effects of changes in sales on operating income or earnings before interests and taxes (EBIT). The fixed operating cost includes those items at the top of the balance sheet such as leases, executive salaries, property taxes, and alike.

The DOL measures that responsiveness of profit as a percentage change in operating income (OY) relative to the percentage change in sales (S):

$$DOL = \frac{\%\Delta OY}{\%\Delta S},$$

$$DOL = \frac{\dfrac{OY_2 - OY_1}{OY_1} \times 100}{\dfrac{S_2 - S_1}{S_1} \times 100},$$

$$DOL = \frac{\left[\dfrac{(OY_2 - OY_1)}{OY_1}\right]}{\left[\dfrac{S_2 - S_1}{S_1}\right]}.$$

Example 8.14

If the operating income of a small business increased from \$884 to \$1680 as it expanded the sales of its product from \$4200 to \$5880, what would be the DOL (Table 8.4)?

TABLE 8.4

	S	OY	
S_1	4200	884	OY_1
S_2	5880	1680	OY_2

Solution:

$$DOL = \frac{\left[\dfrac{(OY_2 - OY_1)}{OY_1}\right]}{\left[\dfrac{(S_2 - S_1)}{S_1}\right]},$$

$$= \frac{\left[\dfrac{(1680 - 884)}{884}\right]}{\left[\dfrac{(5880 - 4200)}{4200}\right]},$$

$$DOL = \frac{0.90}{0.40} = 2.25.$$

This means that for every 1% change in sales, there would be a 2.25% change in operating income (profit or EBIT). In other words, as sales increased by 40%, profits rose by 90% as it is shown in the denominator and nominator of the DOL, respectively. It is also shown in Figure 8.21. The move from Q_1 to Q_2 on the units of sale (or R_1 to R_2 on the dollars of revenue) would result in the move from Pr_1 to Pr_2. This effect would hold the same in the other direction, meaning that a reduction in sales (units of product or dollars of revenue) by 40% would result in a drop in the profit by 90%. We can calculate a move in sales on the opposite direction from Q_1 to Q_0 or in revenue from R_1 to R_0, which is about 40% less (420 to 252 units or \$4200 to \$2520) and see the profit drop 90% from $Pr_1 = 884$ to $Pr_0 = 88.4$:

$$\text{DOL} = \dfrac{\left[\dfrac{884 - 88.4}{884}\right]}{\left[\dfrac{4200 - 2520}{4200}\right]},$$

$$\text{DOL} = \dfrac{0.90}{0.4} = 2.25.$$

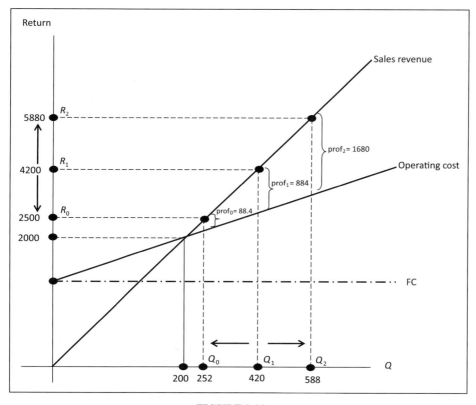

FIGURE 8.21

So, the DOL can actually be considered a multiplier of the effect that a change in sales would have on profit. In other words, DOL is a concept of elasticity. It is the elasticity of profit with respect to sales. In such a sense, we can express it as the partial change in profit (π) relative to the partial change in output (Q):

$$\text{DOL} = \frac{\dfrac{\partial \pi}{\pi}}{\dfrac{\partial Q}{Q}}.$$

This DOL can be obtained at any level of output. If FC is constant, the change in profit ($\partial \pi$) would be

$$\partial \pi = \partial Q(p - v). \tag{8.13}$$

Also profit π is

$$\pi = R - C,$$
$$\pi = PQ - (FC + vQ),$$
$$\pi = PQ - FC - vQ,$$
$$\pi = Q(P - v) - FC. \tag{8.14}$$

Substituting (8.13) and (8.14) in the DOL equation above,

$$\text{DOL} = \frac{\partial Q(P - v)}{Q(P - v) - FC} \cdot \frac{Q}{\partial Q}.$$

Cancelling out ∂Q, we get

$$\text{DOL} = \frac{Q(P - v)}{Q(P - v) - FC},$$

which is the DOL at any level of output, also called "profit elasticity."

Example 8.15
Find and interpret the DOL for a firm that has the following data:

$$FC = \$2500,$$
$$\text{Variable cost per unit} = \$5,$$
$$\text{Unit price} = \$10,$$
$$\text{Units of product sold} = 1000.$$

Solution:

$$DOL = \frac{Q(P - v)}{Q(P - v) - FC},$$

$$DOL = \frac{1000(10 - 5)}{1000(10 - 5) - 2500},$$

$$DOL = 2.$$

The DOL of 2 means that for every 1% change in sales, operating income would change by 2%.

8.12.2 Operating Leverage, Fixed Cost, and Business Risk

A major observation can be made on the above DOL formula. This observation is related to the fixed operating cost and its effect on DOL. Mathematically, since the term $Q(p - v)$ is present in both the numerator and the denominator, the role of FC becomes crucial. Any increase in FC would make the denominator smaller and the DOL larger, and any decrease in FC would make the denominator larger and the DOL smaller. We can then conclude that the higher the firm's fixed operating cost, relative to its variable cost, the greater the degree of operating leverage and ultimately higher the profit. Let us try this by observing the change in DOL if the FC in the last example increases from 2500 to 4000:

$$DOL = \frac{1000(10 - 5)}{1000(10 - 5) - 4000},$$

$$DOL = 5.$$

A DOL of 5 means that the profit would increase by 5% instead of 2% when the sales increase by 1%. Table 8.5 shows how the DOL and the profit(Pr) would change, as the FC increases, notably across three firms selling the same product for the same price. However, as we have seen before, operating leverage works in the opposite direction too. This means that if we take the figures of the previous example, a decrease in sale by 1% would be more damaging by lowering profits by 5%. So, the increase in the FC would really make the situation more sensitive in both ways, which can translate into presenting a source of business risk. Such a potential risk can come from two sides:

1. In the case of seeking more profits through the increase in the FC, the firm would take the risk of not being able to cover all of the high cost and additional risk of not being able to maintain the increase in sales.
2. In the case of a slight drop in the sales, the firm would take a risk of facing its profit dropping significantly. It may drop to the point to threaten any reasonable recovery.

So, the ever-increasing temptation to benefit from new technology, modernize production and replace labor-intensive by capital-intensive technology would most likely increase

TABLE 8.5

		Q	R	$FV + vQ$	Pr	Apr	$DOL = \dfrac{Q(p-v)}{Q(P-v-FC)}$
	B-even	1,000	3,000	3,000	0	0	FC = $1000;
F		1,500	3,500	4,000	500	500	VC = $2.00; P = $3.00
i		2,000	6,000	5,000	1,000	500	
r		2,500	7,500	6,000	1,500	500	$DOL = \dfrac{3500(3-2)}{3500(3-2)-1000}$
m		3,000	9,000	7,000	2,000	500	
		3,500	10,500	8,000	2,500	500	$DOL = 1.4$
1	→	4,000	12,000	9,000	3,000	500	
		1,000	3,000	4,000	−1,000	/	FC = $2250;
F	B-even	1,800	5,400	5,400	0	−1,000	VC = $1.75; P = $3.00
i		2,500	7,500	6,625	875	625	
r		3,000	9,000	7,500	1,500	625	$DOL = \dfrac{3500(3-1.75)}{3500(3-1.75)-2250}$
m		3,500	10,500	8,375	2,125	625	
	→	4,000	12,000	9,250	2,750	625	$DOL = 2.06$
2		4,500	13,500	10,125	3,375	625	
F		1,000	3,000	5,000	−2,000	/	FC = $3750;
i	B-even	2,143	6,429	6,429	0	−2,000	VC = $1.25; P = $3.00
r		2,500	7,500	6,875	625	625	
m		3,000	9,000	7,500	1,500	875	$DOL = \dfrac{3500(3-1.25)}{3500(3-1.25)-3700}$
3		3,500	10,500	8,125	2,375	875	
	→	4,000	12,000	8,750	3,250	875	$DOL = 2.58$
		4,500	13,500	9,375	4,125	875	

efficiency but require incurring a lot more FC, which, if done, has to be with much more caution and consideration by financial managers who have to carefully and rationally weigh the benefits of increasing the profits with all of the risks associated with them.

Table 8.5 shows three firms selling the same product at the same price but facing three different cost functions. It confirms that the higher their FC, the higher their DOL, and ultimately the higher the profits (see Figure 8.22).

SUMMARY

- It is obvious for a chapter on cost theory to start with the various concepts of costs. The first section of the chapter described many common concepts that we would frequently read in business and economic literature. They included explicit and implicit costs, opportunity or foregone cost, historical and current costs, replacement cost, incremental cost, total and marginal and average costs, sunk cost, fixed and variable costs, and short-run and long-run costs.

- In the short-run production, cost of production would be at its minimum possible for a certain level of output under particular operating conditions. The major player is the total cost, which includes both fixed and variable costs. The shape of the variable cost curve is determined by the law of diminishing returns. The total cost curve imitates the shape

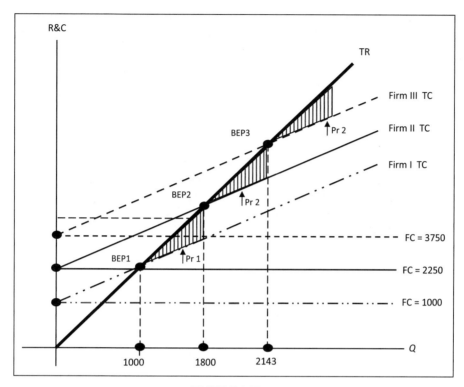

FIGURE 8.22

of the variable cost curve, but both curves are separated by a vertical distance equal to the fixed cost. Marginal cost is the change in total cost, and the average cost is the total cost per unit of production. The average variable cost is the variable cost per unit of production. Marginal cost, average cost, and average variable cost all take a U-shape. Average fixed cost is a descending curve. Marginal cost crosses both average cost and average variable cost at their minimum points.

- Employing the combination of isoquant and isocost to reach the optimal choice for production produces the expansion path, which, in turn, becomes the basis for the long-run cost analysis. It offers firms the capability to build several plants for several scales of operations to produce various levels of output at the minimum cost possible. The basic relationships remain the same, as the long-run marginal cost represents the change in the long-run total cost (LTC), and the long-run average cost (LAC) is the per unit total cost over the long run or the LTC divided by the output size. The LAC curve takes a wide U-shape to envelope all short-run average cost curves. Still, at the minimum point of this wide LAC, the long-run marginal cost makes the intersection. Economies of scale refer to the decline of average cost as the scale of production rises. However, the opposite case of diseconomies of scale occurs at the rising section of the LAC when the firm faces decreasing returns to scale.

- Different from economies of scale, economies of scope refer to the cost reduction that results from producing two or more products together compared with producing them separately. Cost complementarity refers to the situation where the marginal cost of producing one product is being reduced by the increase in production of another product. Generally, economies of scope may result from either some synergistic relationship in the production process or from the state of input indivisibility.

- The notion of economies of scope is closely associated with the idea of learning curve. This curve is convex to the origin and has a negative slope to confirm that the average cost declines as the size of production increases. There have been many uses of the learning curve in the field of marginal economics such as forecasting the requirements of production, scheduling operations, and pricing both inputs and output.

- Cost–volume–profit analysis was covered for its managerial significance in identifying the minimum output level necessary to secure a nonnegative level of profit. It can also be applied to secure a certain desired level of profit, if that is the target. Break-even quantity and revenue and break-even time were calculated and several examples were given. We also covered an algebraic treatment to find the break-even point and the case of dual break-even points. Leverage was detailed in its operating and financial types and three degrees of leverage were calculated.

KEY TERMS

explicit cost
opportunity (foregone) cost
current cost
incremental cost
average cost
average fixed cost
sunk cost
long-run cost
variable cost
expansion path
long-run average cost (LAC)
economies of scale
minimum efficient scale
   (MES)
cost complementarity
learning curve
break-even analysis

financial leverage
break-even quantity (BEQ)
EBIT (operating profit)
cash break-even
target profit
upper break-even point
implicit cost
historical cost
replacement cost
marginal cost
average variable cost
total cost
short-run cost
fixed cost
economic rate of
   substitution (ERS)
long-run total cost (LTC)

long-run marginal cost
   (LMC)
diseconomies of scale
economies of scope
input indivisibility
cost-volume-profit analysis
operating leverage
total leverage
break-even revenue (BER)
contribution margin (CM)
break-even time
lower break-even point
degree of operating leverage

LIST OF FORMULAS

- Total cost:

$$TC = FC + VC.$$

- Average cost:

$$AC = \frac{TC}{Q} = AFC + AVC.$$

- Average fixed cost:

$$AFC = \frac{FC}{Q}.$$

- Average variable cost:

$$AVC = \frac{VC}{Q}.$$

Also, for labor:

$$AVC = \frac{w}{AP_L}.$$

- Marginal cost:

$$MC = \frac{\Delta TC}{\Delta Q} = \frac{\partial TC}{\partial Q}.$$

Also, for labor:

$$MC = \frac{w}{MP_L}.$$

- Economic rate of substitution:

$$ERS = \frac{w}{v} = MRTS = \frac{MP_L}{MP_K}.$$

- Equilibrium condition:

$$\frac{w}{MP_L} = \frac{v}{MP_K}.$$

- Long-run average cost:

$$LAC = \frac{LTC}{Q}.$$

- Long-run marginal cost:

$$LMC = \frac{\partial LTC}{\partial Q}.$$

- Cost elasticity:

$$\varepsilon_c = \left[\frac{\partial LTC}{\partial Q}\right]\left[\frac{Q}{LTC}\right].$$

- Arc cost elasticity:

$$\varepsilon_{care} = \left[\frac{LTC_2 - LTC_1}{Q_2 - Q_1} \right] \left[\frac{Q_1 + Q_2}{LTC_1 + LTC_2} \right].$$

- Cost function based on Cobb–Douglas type technology:

$$TC_{(y)} = \left[\frac{(b+c)c_2}{c} \left(\frac{bc_2}{cc_1} \right)^{-b} \left(\frac{y}{a} \right) \right]^{\frac{1}{b+c}}.$$

- Cost function based on CES technology:

$$TC_{(y)} = a^{-\frac{1}{\varepsilon}} \left[c_2 + (1-a_1)^{\frac{1}{\rho-1}} a_1^{\frac{1}{1-\rho}} c^{\frac{\rho}{\rho-1}} \right] \left[1 - a_1 + (1-a_1)^{\frac{\rho}{1-\rho}} a_1^{\frac{1}{1-\rho}} c_2^{\frac{-\rho}{\rho-2}} \right]^{-\frac{1}{\rho}} Y^{\frac{1}{\varepsilon}}.$$

- Learning curve effects:

$$C = \alpha Q^{\beta},$$

$$\log C = \log \alpha + \beta \log Q,$$

$$\beta = \frac{\log a}{\log b}.$$

- Break-even quantity:

$$BEQ = \frac{FC}{p - v}.$$

- Break-even revenue:

$$BER = \frac{FC}{1 - \dfrac{v}{p}},$$

$$BER = BEQ \cdot P.$$

- Cash break-even quantity:

$$CBEQ = \frac{FC - NC}{p - v}.$$

- Break-even quantity with target profit:

$$BEQ_{tp} = \frac{FC + TP}{p - v}.$$

- Break-even revenue with target profit:

$$\text{BER}_{tp} = \frac{\text{FC} + \text{TP}}{1 - \frac{v}{p}}.$$

- Break-even time:

$$\text{BET} = \frac{\text{FC} + pqt_L}{q(p - v)}.$$

- Quadratic formula:

$$x = \frac{-b \pm \sqrt{b^2 - 4ac}}{2a}.$$

- Degree of operating leverage:

$$\text{DOL} = \frac{\left[\dfrac{0y_2 - 0y_1}{0y_1} \right]}{\left[\dfrac{s_2 - s_1}{s_1} \right]}.$$

EXERCISES

1. List as many cost concepts as you recall and explain each one and the purpose and justification for it.

2. What would distinguish the short-run cost from the long-run cost? Compare their major concepts.

3. What would determine the shape of the average cost curve in both the short-run and long-run? List the similarities and differences and draw both curves.

4. Explain and compare the following concepts:
   - Economies of scale
   - Diseconomies of scale
   - Economies of scope
   - The learning curve

5. Explain the concept of break-even point in at least four types of that point. Compare and give the formula for each one.

6. The following table shows the units of labor used to produce a certain product, the fixed cost, and the variable cost in the first three columns. Fill in the rest of the columns after calculating all the required values.

L	FC	VC	TC	AC	AFC	AVC	MC
0	40	0					
1	40	16					
2	40	32					
3	40	48					
4	40	64					
5	40	80					
6	40	96					
7	40	112					
8	40	128					
9	40	144					
10	40	160					

7. Draw all the seven cost curves based on the calculations you made in the previous table.

8. If the long-run total cost function of a product is expressed as

$$\text{LTC} - 10{,}000Q - 25Q^2 + 0.025Q^3,$$

   (a) find the long-run average function;
   (b) find the long-run marginal function;
   (c) find the minimum efficient scale (MES);
   (d) check if MES is really at its minimum.

9. The following table shows the cost data for a product that would be sold at $15.00.

Cost $	Item	Frequency
2500	Rent	Monthly
5600	Salaries	Monthly
2000	Employee benefits	Annually
1700	Insurance	Quarterly
3250	Property taxes	Annually
2.25	Material 1	Per unit
6.00	Material 2	Per unit
4.75	Shipping	Per unit
15.00	Labor	Per unit

   (a) Find the break-even quantity and the break-even revenue.
   (b) What would be the break-even quantity and revenue if the firm wants to secure 5000 in profit?

10. If the company above produces and sells 6000 units, what would be the degree of operating leverage (DOL) and what would it mean for the company?

9

PRODUCTION AND COST: ESTIMATION AND FORECASTING

The statistical methods reviewed in Chapter 2 can be applied when data are available to estimate the **epistemic models** of production and cost that have been discussed in Chapters 7 and 8. This chapter focuses on estimating the constant elasticity of substitution (CES) production model and the form of cost function that is derived from it. The primary objective of these estimations is to reveal statistical evidence related to factor substitution, returns to scale, and economies of scale when data permit. Additionally, this chapter brings a relatively robust approach to dealing with aleatory uncertainty in terms of both modeling and **estimation**. Of course, at all times, it is important to remain mindful that statistical analysis is but a single piece of information to assist decision making among multiple pieces of information that may be available to a manager.

In the second part of this chapter, we introduce the use of **computer simulation** for the purpose of forecasting decision-driven production and cost at the firm's level. The outcome of alternative input and output decisions is described using graphical tools developed from the simulation, which can help shed light on the implications of different decisions. It should be noted that the time series forecasting techniques presented in Chapter 6 are also valid approaches to forecasting that may be applied to production and cost; however, these techniques are not discussed further or applied in this chapter. The reason is that the extension of the techniques in Chapter 6 to production and cost time series data is relatively straightforward and can be left to the reader. However, time series forecasting techniques are perhaps less easily adapted to forecasting decision-driven outcomes than is computer simulation, which seems to have an advantage of accommodating a future that is influenced by today's choices. In addition, we will revisit simulation briefly in Chapter 12 when we consider analysis of risky alternative decisions.

Managerial Economics: A Mathematical Approach, First Edition. M. J. Alhabeeb and L. Joe Moffitt.
© 2013 John Wiley & Sons, Inc. Published 2013 by John Wiley & Sons, Inc.

9.1 ESTIMATION OF THE PRODUCTION FUNCTION

Recall that the CES production function with output y and inputs x_1 and x_2 has the form

$$y = a\left[a_1 x_1^\rho + (1 - a_1)x_2^\rho\right]^{\varepsilon/\rho},$$

where $x_i > 0$; $a > 0$; $0 \le a_1 \le 1$; $\rho \le 1$; $\varepsilon \ge 0$.

As demonstrated in Chapter 7, the CES takes on the linear, the Cobb–Douglas type, and the Leontief forms as special cases; hence, the CES model is relatively robust with respect to uncertainty about factor substitution and returns to scale. This means that there are values of its parameters $(a, a_1, \rho, \varepsilon)$ that enable this form to be linear, Cobb–Douglas type, or Leontief. Hence, statistical analysis of production based on this form enables the data to inform, without undue artificial restriction, about both factor substitution and returns to scale.

The use of sample data to make inferences about uncertain circumstances is an important component of managerial decision making today. Marketing (demand) and production decisions are no exceptions to this. This practice may become more sophisticated and important in the future. Data related to production of goods and services are available for analysis. For example, Table 9.1 shows a sample of data. The specific issue pursued in this section is how best we can analyze the data to learn about factor substitution and returns to scale that were reviewed conceptually in Chapter 7.

TABLE 9.1   Data Sample for Production Analysis

Observation (i)→ ↓ Variable	1	2	3	4	5	6	7	8	9	10	11	12
y_i	10	15	17	26	12	11	20	9	19	23	14	21
x_{1i}	2	3	3	5	2	3	4	1	3	4	3	5
x_{2i}	1	3	6	9	8	1	5	1	7	8	2	5

Due to its robustness with respect to factor substitution and returns to scale, we choose the CES production function as our epistemic model. Note that we have not said or done anything about aleatory uncertainty or robustness to it yet; however, we will focus on this shortly. Estimation of the CES model can be based on the method of **maximum likelihood** estimation/estimate (MLE) detailed in Chapter 2 once a stochastic structure has been specified to the epistemic model. The process, as indicated in Chapter 2, is to form the likelihood function (joint probability of the observations) and then choose as the estimate of the parameters the value that makes the observations most likely.

We begin with a very simple statistical model comprising an additive, normally distributed disturbance denoted by u. Specifically, we begin with the following statistical model:

$$y = a\left[a_1 x_1^\rho + (1 - a_1)x_2^\rho\right]^{\varepsilon/\rho} + u,$$

where it is assumed that $u \sim N(0, \sigma)$.

Note that

$$E[u] = a[a_1 x_1^\rho + (1 - a_1)x_2^\rho]^{\varepsilon/\rho} \quad \text{and} \quad SD[u] = \sigma.$$

The parameters to be estimated are a, α_1, ρ, ε, and σ.

The probability density function (pdf) associated with each y_i is

$$f_{yi}(y_i) = \left[\frac{1}{\sqrt{2\pi\sigma^2}}\right] \exp\left[\frac{1}{2\sigma^2}(y_i - a)[a_1 x_1^\rho + (1 - a_1)x_2^\rho]^{\frac{\varepsilon}{\rho}}\right]^2.$$

Assuming independent sampling, the likelihood of the sample data $y_1, y_2, \ldots, y_{12}$ is

$$L = \prod f_{yi}(y_i).$$

The MLEs of a, a_1, ρ, ε, and σ are the values of a, α_1, ρ, ε, and σ that solve

$$\text{Maximize } L = \prod f_{yi}(y_i).$$

We know that $a \geq 0$, $0 \leq a_1 \leq 1$, $\rho \leq 1$, $\varepsilon \geq 0$, and $\sigma \geq 0$. Nearly always, it is best to maximize $\ln L = \sum \ln f_{yi}(y_i)$ rather than $\prod f_{yi}(y_i)$.

Maximization of $\ln L$ by computer reveals the MLEs of the parameters a, a_1, ρ, ε, and σ. The estimates are $a = 7.35$, $a_1 = 0.66$, $\rho = -1.38$, $\varepsilon = 0.69$, and $\sigma = 1.11$. Some factor substitution is indicated since ρ is negative but not all that far from 0. Decreasing returns to scale are suggested by the value of ε below 1.

The **stochastic specification** that we have used is not robust. By simply adding u, our specification requires that the standard deviation of output be a constant, σ, regardless of the level of input use. Although this might be true, the variability of output may change with the level of input use. A more robust stochastic specification would permit the data to inform about variability of output rather than imposing a rigid condition.

Instead of the production model,

$$y = a[a_1 x_1^\rho + (1 - a_1)x_2^\rho]^{\varepsilon/\rho} + u,$$

where it is assumed that $u \sim N(0, \sigma)$, we can use this stochastic specification:

$$y = a[a_1 x_1^\rho + (1 - a_1)x_2^\rho]^{\varepsilon/\rho} + \beta \, x_1^{\beta 1} x_2^{\beta 2} \varepsilon,$$

where it is assumed that $\varepsilon \sim N(0, 1)$.

Now, it is the case that

$$E[y] = a[a_1 x_1^\rho + (1 - a_1)x_2^\rho]^{\varepsilon/\rho} \quad \text{and} \quad SD[y] = \beta x_1^{\beta 1} x_2^{\beta 2}.$$

Both the mean and standard deviation of y can now vary with input use. Note that the impact of the inputs on SD[y] depends on the parameter, β_i. If $\beta_i = 0$ for all i, then the simple stochastic specification we have used previously will apply since output variability will be constant regardless of input use. If $\beta_i < 0$, then output variability will decrease with use of input x_i. If $\beta_i > 0$, then output variability will increase with use of input x_i. This stochastic specification is relatively robust with respect to aleatory uncertainty because it allows the data to inform about the relationship between input use and output variability rather than requiring that output variability be constant regardless of the level of input. The MLE of the parameters β_i suggests the degree of production control that can be exerted if input use is ramped up. Hence, this model is relatively robust with respect to both epistemic and aleatory uncertainties.

The pdf associated with each y_i is

$$\left[f_{yi}(y_i) = \left[\frac{1}{\sqrt{2\pi} \left(\beta x_1^{\beta_2} \beta x_2^{\beta_2} \right)^2} \right] \exp\left[\frac{1}{2 \left(\beta x_1^{\beta_1} \beta x_2^{\beta_2} \right)^2} \right] (y_i - a) \left[a_i x_1^\rho + (1 - a_1) x_2^\rho \right]^{\frac{\varepsilon}{\rho}} \right]^2 .$$

Assuming independent sampling, the likelihood of the sample data $y_1, y_2, \ldots, y_{12}$ is

$$L = \prod f_{yi}(y_i).$$

The MLEs of a, a_1, ρ, ε, β, β_1, and β_2 are the values of these parameters that solve

$$\text{Maximize } L = \prod f_{yi}(y_i).$$

We know that $a \geq 0$, $0 \leq a_1 \leq 1$, $\rho \leq 1$, $\varepsilon \geq 0$, and $\beta \geq 0$. Again, nearly always, it is best to maximize the log-likelihood, that is, to solve

$$\text{Maximize } \ln L = \sum \ln f_{yi}(y_i).$$

The MLEs of the parameters are $a = 4.28$, $a_1 = 0.78$, $\rho = 0.94$, $\varepsilon = 1.03$, $\beta = 3.63$, $\beta_1 = -0.61$, and $\beta_2 = -0.16$. From Table 7.1, factor substitution is indicated since ρ is near 1. Constant returns to scale are suggested by the value of ε near 1. Both inputs serve to reduce the variability of output, that is, increase control of the production process since both β_1 and β_2 are negative.

9.2 ESTIMATION OF THE COST FUNCTION

It almost goes without saying that most important management decisions are made without knowing for sure what the outcome will be. There seems to be no way to completely avoid sources of uncertainty, and so, most managers try their best to cope with them instead. Understandably, decisions that seem likely to work out are popular. Managerial economics helps by integrating the conceptual framework, analytical models, and quantitative methods for identifying these decisions. In short, managerial economics brings economic models a step closer to the real world by recognizing and incorporating uncertainty (uncontrolled elements) into them. As already emphasized, the model and the estimation method illustrated in this chapter are applicable to analysis of cost.

With regard to recognizing and incorporating uncertainty in analytical models, attention must be paid to **stochastic specification** (i.e., how the error term and decision variables interact) in a statistical model of cost. Without a robust stochastic specification, measurements and decisions based on economic models may be misleading—almost surely will be misleading if the purpose of the effort is to measure and understand the magnitude of the risk associated with a decision. For example, if the usual additive error (say u) is used in a statistical model (say $y = f(x) + u$), then the decision (independent) variable can only affect the mean of the outcome (it can have no effect on the standard deviation of the outcome). If a multiplicative error term is used (say $y = f(x)e^u$), then the decision (independent) variable's effect on the variability of the outcome can only be the same as its effect on the mean of the outcome. Neither of these possibilities seems very attractive. The following describes a relatively robust alternative and illustrates its estimation.

Cost analysis for the purpose of estimating economies of scale involves the following specific problem. We have some data related to the cost of production of a good or service (see Table 9.2).

TABLE 9.2   Cost and Output Data

Month	Cost	Output
January	5.46	25
February	5.64	27
March	6.30	35
April	5.90	30
May	5.46	25
June	5.81	29
July	5.08	21
August	6.14	33
September	5.64	27
October	6.22	34
November	4.99	20
December	5.98	31

How best can we analyze the data to learn about economies of scale and cost control? Due to its robustness, we choose $\text{TC}(Q) = A\, y^B$ as our epistemic model. (Note that we have not said or done anything about aleatory uncertainty or robustness to it yet; we will do that subsequently to estimate cost control.) We will allow the data to inform about economies of scale through estimation of this relatively robust epistemic model. The relatively robust stochastic specification developed subsequently will deal with aleatory uncertainty and enable the data to inform about cost control. Estimation of the model can be based on the method of MLE. As we continue, we will apply MLE to estimate the TC model.

To do MLE, recall the problem. Suppose that you have a sample of independent observations on a random variable and you believe that the observations occur with relative frequencies given by a pdf that has unknown parameters. In other words, you have some data and you assume that those were drawn from a pdf with a known form, such as the normal, bell-shaped curve, but with an unknown parameter. The MLE approach is to form the likelihood function (joint probability of the observations) and then choose as the estimates of the parameters the values that make the observations most likely. We will apply this procedure to cost analysis by first considering estimation of the robust epistemic model using a simple model of aleatory uncertainty:

$$\text{TC} = A\, y^B + u,$$

where it is assumed that $u \sim N(0, \sigma)$.

Note that

$$E[\text{TC}] = A\,y^B \text{ and SD}[\text{TC}] = \sigma.$$

The parameters to be estimated are A, B, and σ. The pdf associated with TC_i is given by

$$f_{\text{TC}_i}(\text{TC}_i) = \left[\frac{1}{\sqrt{2\pi\sigma^2}}\right]\exp\left[\frac{1}{2\sigma^2}\left(\text{TC}_i - A\,y_i^B\right)^2\right].$$

Assuming independent sampling and the likelihood of the sample data, TC_1, TC_2, ..., TC_{12}, the MLEs of A, B, and σ are the values of A, B, and σ that solve

$$\text{Maximize } \ln L = \sum \ln f_{\text{TC}_i}(\text{TC}_i).$$

We know that $A \geq 0$, $B \geq 0$, and $\sigma \geq 0$. We maximize $\ln L$ to find the MLEs of the parameters A, B, and σ and find $A = 1.41812$, $B = 0.419102$, and $\sigma = 0.00541058$.

In this case, the MLE of B (<1) suggests the existence of scale economies.

The stochastic specification that we have used is not robust. By simply adding u, our specification requires that the standard deviation of TC be a constant, σ, regardless of the level of output. Although this might be true, the variability of cost or, equivalently, our ability to manage and control cost, may change with the level of output. A relatively robust stochastic specification should permit the data to inform about variability of TC rather than imposing a rigid condition.

An alternative stochastic specification can provide a relatively robust approach to aleatory uncertainty:

$$\text{TC} = A\,y^B + C\,y^D\varepsilon,$$

where it is assumed that $\varepsilon \sim N(0, 1)$.

With this specification, we have

$$E[\text{TC}] = A\,y^B \quad \text{and} \quad \text{SD}[\text{TC}] = C\,y^D.$$

Both the mean and the standard deviation of TC can now vary with y. Note that the impact of y on SD[TC] depends on parameter D. If $D = 0$, then the simpler stochastic specification that we have already used will apply since cost variability will be constant regardless of output. If $D < 0$, then cost variability will decrease with output. If $D > 0$, then cost variability will increase with output. The stochastic specification above is relatively robust with respect to aleatory uncertainty because it allows the data to inform about the relationship between output and cost variability rather than requiring that cost variability be constant regardless of the level of output. The MLE of parameter D suggests the degree of cost control that can be exerted if production is ramped up. Hence, this model is relatively robust with respect to both epistemic and aleatory uncertainties.

The pdf associated with TC_i is

$$f_{\text{TC}_i}(\text{TC}_i) = \left[\frac{1}{\sqrt{2\pi\left(C\,y_i^D\right)^2}}\right]\exp\left[\frac{1}{2\left(C\,y_i^D\right)^2}\left(\text{TC}_i - A\,y_i^B\right)^2\right].$$

Assuming independent sampling and the likelihood of the sample data $TC_1, TC_2, \ldots,$ TC_{12}, the MLEs of $A, B, C,$ and D are the values that solve

$$\text{Maximize } \ln L = \sum \ln f_{TCi}(TC_i).$$

We know that $A \geq 0, B \geq 0,$ and $C \geq 0$. We maximize $\ln L$ to find the MLEs of parameters $A, B, C,$ and D and find $A = 1.38769, B = 0.425441, C = 12938.5,$ and $D = -4.55413$.

The MLE of B (<1) again suggests the existence of scale economies. The MLE of D (<0) suggests that cost variability is decreasing with output, suggesting that cost control can be exerted as output expands. Note that the analytical model used for estimation is based on robustness considerations with respect to both epistemic and aleatory uncertainties.

9.3   FORECASTING OUTPUT

We consider characterizing future output by basing the forecast on the relatively robust production model we estimated via the method of MLE explained above. Our goal is to use the estimated production function to gain a sense of the frequency distribution of output corresponding to different input combinations. Recall that production data were used to estimate a production function that was relatively robust with respect to both epistemic and aleatory uncertainties. The CES production function with output y and inputs x_1 and x_2 has the following epistemic model:

$$y = a\big[a_1 x_1^\rho + (1 - \alpha_1)x_2^\rho\big]^{\varepsilon/\rho},$$

where $x_1, x_2 > 0; a > 0; 0 \leq a_1 \leq 1; \rho \leq 1; \varepsilon \geq 0$.

Also recall that this CES takes on the linear, Cobb–Douglas type, and Leontief forms as special cases; hence, the CES model may be regarded as a relatively robust epistemic model with respect to the shape of the isoquants it can accommodate and the returns to scale that it can exhibit. In addition to this relatively robust epistemic model of production, we also employed a relatively **robust model** of aleatory uncertainty which permitted, but did not require, the employment of inputs to impact the standard deviation of output:

$$y = a\big[(a_1 x_1^\rho + (1 - a_1)x_2^\rho\big]^{\varepsilon/\rho} + \beta x_1^{\beta_1} x_2^{\beta_2}\varepsilon,$$

where $\beta > 0$ and $\varepsilon \sim N(0, 1)$.

The pdf of output conditional on input use is

$$f_{yi}(y_i) = \left[\frac{1}{\sqrt{2\pi}\left(\beta x_1^{\beta_1} x_2^{\beta_2}\right)^2}\right] \exp\left[\frac{-1}{2\left(\beta x_1^{\beta_1} x_2^{\beta_2}\right)^2}\left(y_i - a\big[a_1 x_1^\rho + (1 - a_1)x_2\big]^{\frac{\varepsilon}{\rho}}\right)^2\right].$$

MLEs of the parameters were found to be $a = 4.28, a_1 = 0.78, \rho = 0.94, \varepsilon = 1.03, \beta = 3.63, \beta_1 = -0.61,$ and $\beta_2 = -0.16$. Using these parameter estimates in conjunction with the form of the pdf provides a specific pdf from which random numbers can be generated to simulate output. The histogram of output conditional on input use $x_1 = 10$ and $x_2 = 10$ based on 1000 simulated outputs is shown in Figure 9.1. Note that the vertical scale of the histogram is probability. The histogram of output using the same 1000 random elements

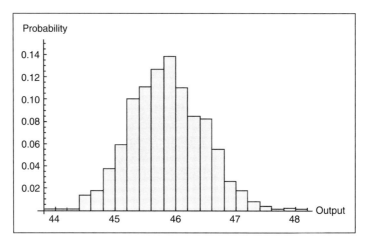

FIGURE 9.1

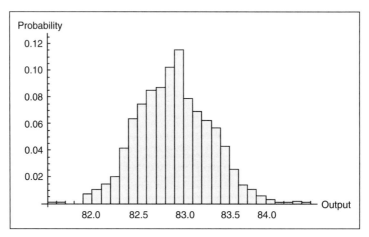

FIGURE 9.2

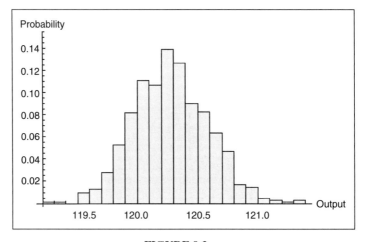

FIGURE 9.3

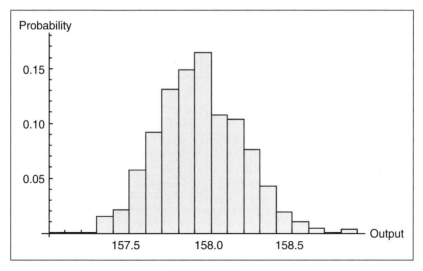

FIGURE 9.4

is shown in Figures 9.2, 9.3, 9.4, and 9.5 for $x_1 = 20$, $x_1 = 30$, and $x_1 = 40$ in conjunction with $x_2 = 10$, respectively. The figures highlight the role of x_1 as a productive input in moving the distribution of output that will be experienced to the right and reducing the dispersion associated with the distribution as well. The figures provide an idea of the range of outputs that are likely as employment of the factor is increased.

Findings of a similar nature are shown diagrammatically in Figures 9.1, 9.6, 9.7, and 9.8, respectively, where input x_1 is held at 10 units and input x_2 is increased by 10 units increments. Note that increasing x_2 also moves the anticipated output distribution to the right and reduces its dispersion; however, the effects are not nearly as pronounced as those that will be associated with the other factor.

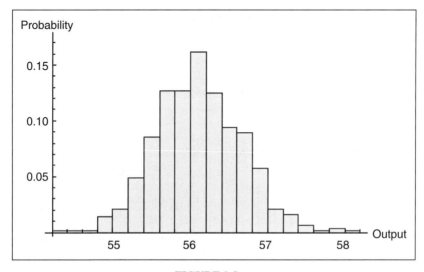

FIGURE 9.5

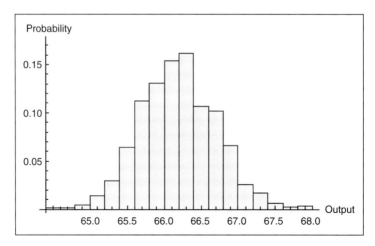

FIGURE 9.6

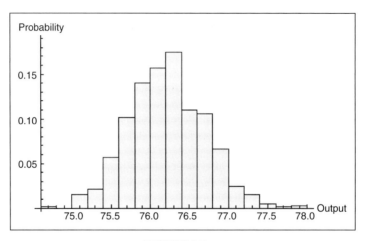

FIGURE 9.7

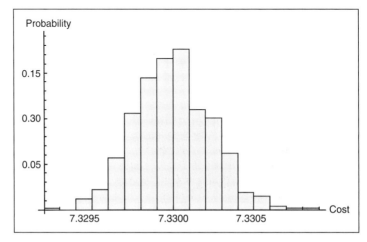

FIGURE 9.8

9.4   FORECASTING COST

We can simulate histograms for the cost of production conditional on the output level using the relatively robust epistemic and aleatory models that were estimated from cost data as we have seen earlier. Probability will again be the vertical scale of the histograms. It is presumed that relative factor prices will remain the same for the relevant forecast period. Of course, if that is not the case, then the time series methods described in Chapter 6 can be used to forecast factor prices that appear in the cost function developed here and can then be updated with the price forecasts prior to engaging in the simulations reported here.

Our goal is to use the estimated cost function to gain a sense of the probability of costs corresponding to different levels of output. Recall that cost data were used to estimate a cost function that was relatively robust with respect to both epistemic and aleatory uncertainties. The cost function was derived from the CES production function with output y, which led to the following epistemic model:

$$TC = A\,y^B,$$

where $A > 0$.

Also recall that this form, based on the CES production model, is relatively unrestrictive with respect to the substitution of inputs in production and returns to scale. In addition to this relatively robust epistemic model of cost, we also employed a relatively robust model of aleatory uncertainty that permitted alternative scenarios regarding cost control as output increases:

$$TC = A\,y^B + C\,y^D\,\varepsilon,$$

where $C > 0$ and $\varepsilon \sim N(0, 1)$.

The pdf of cost conditional on level of output is

$$f_{TC_i}(TC_i) = \left[\frac{1}{\sqrt{2\pi}\,(Cy_i^D)^2}\right]\exp\left[\frac{-1}{2\,(Cy_i^D)^2}\left(TC_i - Ay_i^B\right)^2\right].$$

MLEs of the parameters were found to be $A = 1.38769$, $B = 0.425441$, $C = 12938.5$, and $D = -4.55413$. Using these parameter estimates in conjunction with the form of the pdf provides a specific pdf from which random numbers can be generated to simulate cost of production. For example, the histogram of cost conditional on an output of 50 based on 1000 simulated outputs is shown in Figure 9.8. The histogram of cost using the same 1000 random elements is shown in Figures 9.9 and 9.10 for output of 100 and 500, respectively. The figures highlight the role of the output level in moving and shaping the distribution of production cost that will be experienced. The figures provide an idea of the range of costs that are likely as output is raised.

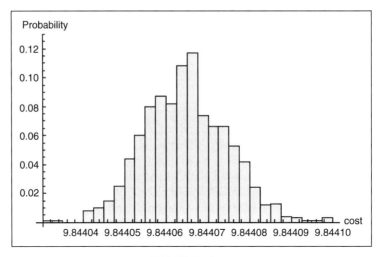

FIGURE 9.9

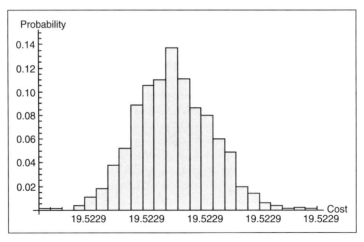

FIGURE 9.10

9.5   MEETING OBLIGATIONS THROUGH DECISIONS WITH PROBABILISTIC RESULTS

This section focuses on the choice of inputs and output when the outcome of the decision is uncertain. A more general consideration of managerial choice under uncertainty is pursued in Chapter 12. For now, the conditional distributions of output and cost shown in this chapter can provide guidance for decisions when, for example, contractual requirements mandate that a particular level of output be delivered or that cost overruns be avoided.

Consider again Figure 9.3 in which the first input takes on the value $x_1 = 30$, whereas the second input is employed at $x_2 = 10$. Suppose that a contractual arrangement mandates that 120 units of output be delivered. In this case, the probability that at least 120 units of output will result from production with this combination of factors is approximately $1 - (0.01 + 0.015 + 0.03 + 0.05 + 0.08) = 1 - 0.185 = 0.815$; that is, 1 minus the sum of the probabilities as measured by the height of each of the first five bars of the histogram in Figure 9.3. This arithmetic is determined by noting that the probability of output being at least 120 units when $x_1 = 30$ and $x_2 = 10$ is the probability that output exceeds 120. The latter is found by subtracting the probability that output is less than 120 from 1. Note that the contractual obligation can be met with probability .815 when $x_1 = 30$ and $x_2 = 10$. Other input combinations can make the chance of meeting the obligation much higher. For example, if x_1 is raised to 40 while x_2 remains at 10, the chance that the obligation will not be met is negligible.

Histograms developed through simulation of cost can be used to identify the probability of a cost overrun. Suppose that $7.3295 has been budgeted for production. The probability of exceeding the budget is the height of the left-most bar in the histogram and is only .01 when output is 50 units. Other scenarios to help with decisions under uncertainty can also be investigated via simulation of histograms for output and cost.

SUMMARY

- This chapter focused on the use of the method of maximum likelihood to estimate the unknown parameters in production and cost functions. Relatively robust epistemic models of production and cost were estimated drawing on the functional forms reviewed in Chapters 7 and 8. Attention was paid to specifying relatively robust models of aleatory uncertainty, and estimation of these specifications by the method of maximum likelihood was also pursued. Interpretation of MLE of parameters in both the relatively robust epistemic model and the aleatory model was given for both production and cost.

- Estimated production and cost functions that are relatively robust with respect to epistemic and aleatory uncertainties can be used to simulate output and cost of production. Creation of histograms of output and cost with the vertical component equal to probability enables a convenient and an easily interpreted range of likely output and costs to be identified and associated with input and output choices, respectively. Such histograms facilitate simple analysis of a number of management decisions. For example, the histograms permit analysis of the probability that a particular combination of inputs will enable a contractual obligation to supply an amount of a product to be evaluated. Similarly, the probability of a cost overrun can be very conveniently determined. The last section of Chapter 13 focuses deeply on management decision making under uncertainty.

KEY TERMS

estimation	forecasting cost	maximum likelihood
stochastic specification	epistemic model	robust model
computer simulation	forecasting output	simulated histogram

LIST OF FORMULAS

- The CES epistemic model of production:

$$y = a\left[a_1 x_1^\rho + (1 - a_1)x_2\rho\right]^{\varepsilon/\rho},$$

where $x_i > 0$; $a > 0$; $0 \le a_1 \le 1$; $\rho \le 1$; $\varepsilon \ge 0$.

- The statistical model of CES technology:

$$y = a\big[a_1 x_1^\rho + (1 - a_1)x_2^\rho\big]^{\varepsilon/\rho} + u,$$

where it is assumed that $u \sim N(0, \sigma)$.
- Mean and standard deviation of CES technology:

$$E[u] = a\big[a_1 x_1^\rho + (1 - a_1)x_2^\rho\big]^{\varepsilon/\rho} \quad \text{and} \quad SD[u] = \sigma.$$

- The pdf of the CES epistemic model:

$$f_{yi}(y_i) = \left[\frac{1}{\sqrt{2\pi\sigma^2}}\right] \exp\left[\frac{1}{2\sigma^2}(y_i - a)\big[a_1 x_1^\rho + (1 - a_1)x_2^\rho\big]^{\frac{\varepsilon}{2}}\right]^2.$$

- The relatively robust statistical model of CES technology:

$$y = a\big[a_1 x_1^\rho + (1 - a_1)x_2^\rho\big]^{\varepsilon/\rho} + \beta\, x_1^{\beta 1} x_2^{\beta 2}\varepsilon,$$

where it is assumed that $\varepsilon \sim N(0, 1)$.
- Mean and standard deviation of the relatively robust model of CES technology:

$$E[y] = a\big[a_1 x_1^\rho + (1 - a_1)x_2^\rho\big]^{\varepsilon/\rho} \quad \text{and} \quad SD[y] = \beta x_1^{\beta 1} x_2^{\beta 2}.$$

- The pdf of the relatively robust statistical model of CES technology:

$$f_{yi}(y_i) = \left[\frac{1}{\sqrt{2\pi}\left(\beta x_1^{\beta_2}\beta x_2^{\beta_2}\right)^2}\right] \exp\left[\frac{1}{2\left(\beta x_1^{\beta_1}\beta x_2^{\beta_2}\right)^2}(y_i - a)\big[a_i x_1^\rho + (1 - a_1)x_2^\rho\big]^{\frac{\varepsilon}{\rho}}\right]^2.$$

- Maximum likelihood estimation for production analysis:

$$\text{Maximize } \ln L = \sum \ln f_{yi}(y_i).$$

- The statistical model of cost:

$$TC = A\, y^B + u,$$

where it is assumed that $u \sim N(0, \sigma)$.
- Mean and standard deviation of cost:

$$E[TC] = A\, y^B \quad \text{and} \quad SD[TC] = \sigma.$$

- The pdf of the cost function:

$$f_{TC_i}(TC_i) = \left[\frac{1}{\sqrt{2\pi\sigma^2}}\right] \exp\left[\frac{1}{2\sigma^2}\left(TC_i - A\, y_i^B\right)^2\right].$$

- The relatively robust model of cost:

$$TC = A\, y^B + C\, y^D \varepsilon,$$

where it is assumed that $\varepsilon \sim N(0, 1)$.

- Mean and standard deviation of the relatively robust model of cost:

$$TC = A\, y^B + C\, y^D \varepsilon,$$

where it is assumed that $\varepsilon \sim N(0, 1)$.

- The pdf of the relatively robust statistical model of cost:

$$f_{TC_i}(TC_i) = \left[\frac{1}{\sqrt{2\pi}\,(C y_i^D)^2}\right] \exp\left[\frac{1}{2\left(C y_i^D\right)^2}\left(TC_i - A y_i^B\right)^2\right].$$

- Maximum likelihood estimation for cost analysis:

$$\text{Maximize } \ln L = \sum \ln f_{TC_i}(TC_i).$$

- The CES epistemic model of production:

$$y = a\left[\left(a_1\, x_1^\rho + (1 - \alpha_1)\, x_2^\rho\right]^{\varepsilon/\rho}\right.,$$

where $x_1, x_2 > 0$; $a > 0$; $0 \le a_1 \le 1$; $\rho \le 1$; $\varepsilon \ge 0$.

- The relatively robust model of production under epistemic and aleatory uncertainties:

$$y = a\left[\left(a_1\, x_1^\rho + (1 - a_1)x_2^\rho\right]^{\varepsilon/\rho} + \beta x_1^{\beta_1} x_2^{\beta_2} \varepsilon,\right.$$

where $\beta > 0$ and $\varepsilon \sim N(0, 1)$.

- The pdf of output with a particular input combination:

$$f_{yi}(y_i) = \left[\frac{1}{\sqrt{2\pi}\left(\beta x_1^{\beta_1} x_2^{\beta_2}\right)^2}\right] \exp\left[\frac{-1}{2\left(\beta x_1^{\beta_1} x_2^{\beta_2}\right)^2}\left(y_i - a\left[a_1 x_1^\rho + (1 - a_1)x_2^\rho\right]^{\frac{\varepsilon}{\rho}}\right)^2\right].$$

EXERCISES

1. What is the estimation process? What is the rationale behind it and how would it be different in estimating the cost in estimating the output?

2. What is the epistemic model and how appropriate is it for a CES production function to represent such a model in a matter of the empirical estimation?

3. Why would forecasting cost and output be important and how would it serve managers in their decision making?

4. Are there any noticeable differences between the methods of forecasting consumer demand and forecasting a firm's cost or output?

5. Are there any differences between estimating and forecasting the short-run variables and the long-run variables? What would be the difficulties associated with any or both?

6. Assume that the pdf of total cost (million dollars) for a particular output level has been estimated and is depicted by the histogram shown immediately below. Using the histogram, estimate the probability that the total cost experienced in a future production run for this same level of output lies within the range $7.3298 m–$7.3302 m.

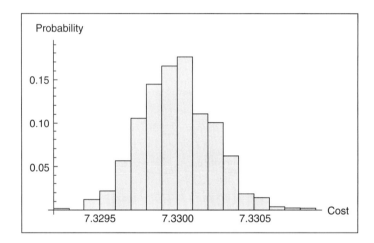

7. Find the mean and standard deviation of total cost, TC, when $TC = A Q^B + FC + C Q^D \varepsilon$, where it is assumed that $\varepsilon \sim N(0, 1)$.

8. Assume that independent sampling has provided data on total cost, $TC_1, TC_2, \ldots, TC_n$, and corresponding observations on output, $q_1, q_2, \ldots, q_n$. Find the pdf of the random variable, TC_i, and log-likelihood function associated with the sample given the following statistical model of total cost:

$$TC = AQ^B + FC + CQ^D \varepsilon \text{ with } \varepsilon \sim N(0, 1).$$

9. Find the mean and standard deviation of output, Q, as a function of inputs, X_1 and X_2, when $Q = f(X_1, X2) = a (a_1 x_1^\rho + (1 - a_1) x_2^\rho)^{\varepsilon/\rho} + u$, where it is assumed that $u \sim N(0, \sigma)$.

10. Find the pdf of output, Q, in Exercise 9.

UNIT IV

MANAGERIAL DECISIONS
AT THE MARKET LEVEL

10

MARKET STRUCTURE AND BUSINESS ORGANIZATION

In the previous units, we dealt with managerial decisions made at consumer and firm levels. In this unit, we shall put together what we have learned into a model of price and output determination at the market level. For profit-maximizing firms, the nature and direction of the managerial decisions to determine output and prices are significantly influenced and guided by the market structure and organization. A market refers to any interaction between those who produce or sell and those who consume or buy. It includes the potential sellers and buyers of resources and products. Market structure is the economic atmosphere in which sellers and buyers behave and operate, especially in consideration of competition and organization. There are generally four criteria by which market structure is categorized. They are as follows:

1. *Type of product*: Whether the product is (a) homogeneous or identical for all producers, which would lead to the prevalence of a single price across all firms, or (b) differentiated, where producers compete to make different products, which would justify the imposition of different prices.

2. *Scope of supply and demand for the product*: It can be translated to how large the size and influence of the firms producing and selling the product, and how wide the circle of consumers buying the product.

3. *Mobility of inputs into the product*: It defines how flexible the firm is in the matter of getting in and out of the business market or its own industry.

4. *Player's information status*: It refers to how informed the economic agents are about the market on both sides, producers and consumers, and how familiar they are on production cost, input supplies, competition, product prices, rules and regulations, and similar vital information about the market.

Managerial Economics: A Mathematical Approach, First Edition. M. J. Alhabeeb and L. Joe Moffitt.
© 2013 John Wiley & Sons, Inc. Published 2013 by John Wiley & Sons, Inc.

On the basis of these criteria, market structure is classified into four types: **perfect competition, monopoly, monopolistic competition**, and **oligopoly**.

10.1 PERFECT COMPETITION

10.1.1 Characteristics of Perfect Competition

A perfectly competitive market is distinguished by the following characteristics:

1. A large number of economic players of producers and consumers. They are small enough to influence the price of product. The price is considered "given" and they are all considered "price takers."
2. The product is homogeneous across all the producing firms so that consumers would be indifferent to products of all firms.
3. The resources are perfectly mobile, implying that no input of production is monopolized by its supplier and all firms are free to enter and exit their industry with ease and at no extra cost.
4. Economic players are assumed to have perfect knowledge of prices and costs, and market conditions.
5. Economic players incur no extra cost for market transactions or exchanges.

Although these economic conditions are more of theoretical assumptions than reality, they play an important role in providing the knowledge to comprehend reality, predict changes, and be able to exert positive influence and improve it. All the five conditions stated above would lead to the establishment of one price and justify what is called the "law of a single price" of a competitive market. This price for a competitive firm would be equal to its marginal revenue (MR) and its demand (**D**). Since no firm alone can affect the price and all firms would just follow one price, the demand curve for a competitive firm would be just a horizontal line while the demand curve for the industry or all markets would remain as downward sloping. Both demand and supply for the market would be the horizontal summation of individual demand and supply.

The graph in Figure 10.1 shows the demand curve for a competitive firm as a horizontal line, set at one-price level and equal to the marginal revenue, while the demand curve for the entire industry or market remains a typical down sloping curve. In the figure, p is market price and Q is quantity of the good.

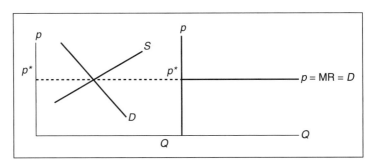

FIGURE 10.1

The following example shows that the market supply curve is the horizontal summation of the individual supply curves of the competitive firms in that industry.

Example 10.1

If the following three functions represent the supply of three competitive firms, then the industry supply curve can be obtained by adding all three functions (Figure 10.2):

$$\text{Firm 1: } Q_1^s = -14 + 2p.$$

$$\text{Firm 2: } Q_2^s = -4 + p.$$

$$\text{Firm 3: } Q_3^s = -6 + 3p.$$

$$\text{Industry: } Q^s = -24 + 6p.$$

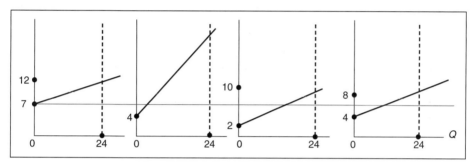

FIGURE 10.2

10.1.2   Profit Maximization for Competitive Firms

Let us begin with the universal notion of profit maximization for any business regardless of the type of market structure. Making as much profit as possible is the basic objective for business survival and improvement. Let us take a look at the following graph (Figure 10.3) while realizing that profit (Pr) is defined by the difference between total revenue (TR) and total cost (TC):

$$\text{Pr} = \text{TR} - \text{TC}.$$

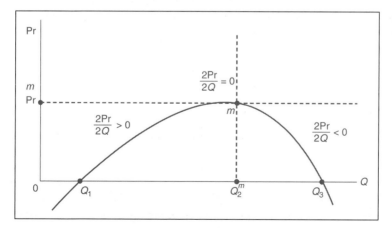

FIGURE 10.3

Up to the output level Q_1 and beyond the output level Q_3, the firm would incur losses, but between Q_1 and Q_3, the firm would make a profit. The profit earned is not consistent throughout between Q_1 and Q_3. It would go through two distinct phases: first when it would increase at an increasing rate between Q_1 and Q_2, and the second when it would increase at a decreasing rate between Q_2 and Q_3. These phases are expressed by looking at the change in profit as the output level changes from Q_1 to Q_3, namely, the derivative of profit with respect to output:

$$\text{Pr} = \text{TR} - \text{TC},$$

$$\frac{\partial \text{Pr}}{\partial Q} = \frac{\partial \text{TR}}{\partial Q} - \frac{\partial \text{TC}}{\partial Q}.$$

Since $\frac{\partial \text{TR}}{\partial Q}$ and $\frac{\partial \text{TC}}{\partial Q}$ are the marginal revenue and the marginal cost (MC), respectively,

$$\frac{\partial \text{Pr}}{\partial Q} = \text{MR} - \text{MC}.$$

This change in profit would be positive between Q_1 and Q_2 for the marginal revenue and exceeds the marginal cost, and it would be negative between Q_2 and Q_3 since the marginal cost would increase above the marginal revenue. In the stage between these phases, the change in profit would neither be positive nor negative. It would be equal to zero. This is where the profit is maximized at P_r^m when the output level is optimum at Q_2:

$$\frac{\partial \text{Pr}}{\partial Q} = 0 = \text{MR} - \text{MC},$$

$$\text{MR} = \text{MC},$$

and this is where the golden rule of the **equimarginal principle** came from. It states that the output would be optimal and the profit would reach its maximum when the marginal revenue is equal to the marginal cost.

To prove that point (m) on the profit curve represents the maximum profit point, we check the second derivative of the profit. If it is found to be negative, point (m) would be the maximum, because then it means that the slope of the marginal revenue curve is less than the slope of the marginal cost curve:

$$\frac{\partial^2 \text{Pr}}{\partial Q^2} = \frac{\partial^2 \text{TR}}{\partial Q^2} - \frac{\partial^2 \text{TC}}{\partial Q^2},$$

$$\frac{\partial^2 \text{Pr}}{\partial Q^2} = \frac{\partial \text{MR}}{\partial Q} - \frac{\partial \text{MC}}{\partial Q} < 0.$$

Specifically, for a competitive firm, profit maximization in the short run occurs when the market price of a product is equal to the marginal cost of producing it. This is simply because the competitive firm's demand curve is a horizontal line determined at the price level and it is equal to the marginal revenue. We can observe this on the lower panel of Figure 10.4 at point E, corresponding to output level Q_2. This point is the point of equilibrium for the competitive firm where profit is maximized at point C in the upper panel. Maximum profit Pr^m is represented by the longest vertical distance between TR and TC curves (line *AB*), which is exactly equal to line *CD*. The shaded area between points *F* and *G* is the cumulative profit earned when producing output level Q_1 through Q_3. In the lower panel, we can see the total profit earned by producing the optimum level of output Q_2.

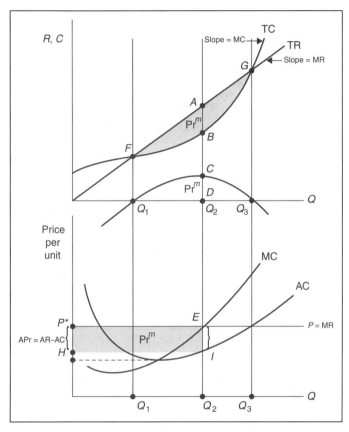

FIGURE 10.4

Total profit is represented by the shaded rectangular area where the length is Q_2 and the height is the average profit (APr), which is the difference between the product's average revenue (AR) and the product's average cost (AC):

$$APr = AR - AC,$$

where the average revenue is essentially the product's market price:

$$APr = P - AC.$$

This is because

$$APr = \frac{Pr}{Q} = \frac{TR}{Q} - \frac{TC}{Q}.$$

Because

$$TR = PQ \quad \text{and} \quad \frac{TC}{Q} = AC,$$

$$APr = \frac{PQ}{Q} - \frac{TC}{Q}$$

$$= P - AC.$$

Example 10.2

A competitive firm has the following cost function:

$$TC = 20 + 4Q + 0.003Q^2.$$

Given that the market price for the firm's product is $16.00, find the following:

1. The equilibrium output level that would maximize its profit.
2. How much would be the maximum profit?

Solution:
The firm would maximize its profit when its marginal cost is equal to its marginal revenue. Being a competitive firm dictates that its marginal revenue is equal to its product market price ($16.00), we shall find its marginal cost:

$$MC = \frac{\partial TC}{\partial Q} = 4 + 0.006Q,$$

$$MC = MR,$$

$$4 + 0.006Q = 16 - 4,$$

$$0.006Q = 12,$$

$$Q = \frac{12}{0.006} = 2000, \quad \text{the equilibrium output level,}$$

$$Pr = TR - TC$$

$$= PQ - [20 + 4Q + 0.003Q^2]$$

$$= (16)(2000) - 20 - 4(2000) - 0.003(2000)^2$$

$$= 11,980.$$

Example 10.3

An industry is consisted of 5000 perfectly competitive firms with market demand and supply function described by

$$Q_d = 35,000 - 20P,$$

$$Q_s = 5000 + 10P.$$

1. What would be the profit-maximizing output level for the industry and what would be the uniform market price for the product?

2. What would be the market share of output for each firm?

3. What would be the marginal cost for each firm?

Solution:

$$Q_d = Q_s,$$

$$35{,}000 - 20P = 5000 + 10P,$$

$$30P = 30{,}000,$$

$$P = 1000.$$

Substituting the market price ($1000) in either the demand or supply equation would yield the equilibrium quantity of the industry:

$$Q_d = 35{,}000 - 20(1000) = 15{,}000,$$

$$Q_s = 5000 + 10(1000) = 15{,}000.$$

Since the industry contains 5000 competitive firms, each firm would produce

$$\frac{15{,}000}{5000} = 3000 \text{ units.}$$

Since the profit-maximizing condition is achieved when

$$P = \text{MR} = \text{MC},$$

the marginal cost should be the same as the price. That is $1000.

10.1.3   The Decision to Shut Down

At the equilibrium price P^*, as shown in Figure 10.4, the firm was producing output level Q_2 and earning a total profit equal to the area P^*EIH. If the market price falls to a level that would not cover the average cost such as P_1 in the following graph (Figure 10.5), which is below the bottom of the average cost curve (AC), then the equilibrium point would shift to E_1 and the company would suffer a loss equal to the area ABE_1P_1, and the output would be reduced to Q_1. The company would continue to operate and try to minimize its loss as much as possible. However, if the product market price continued to fall further to a level equal to or below the company's average variable cost (AVC) such as P, the firm would rather shut down at this point because the revenue can no longer cover the fixed cost (FC). So, the decision to shut down is tied to the fact that the revenue falls below the firm's short-run variable cost:

$$\text{TR} < \text{VC},$$

$$PQ < \text{VC}.$$

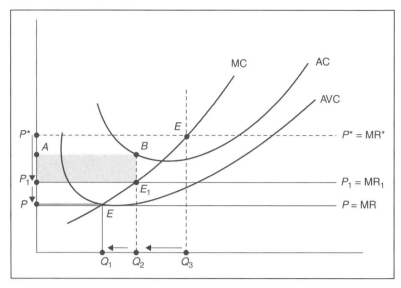

FIGURE 10.5

Dividing by Q,

$$\frac{PQ}{Q} < \frac{VC}{Q},$$

$$P < AVC.$$

Given that $\frac{VC}{Q}$ is the average variable cost, hence the **shut-down rule**, which states that a competitive firm would shut down its production when the product market price becomes equal to the average variable cost of the product:

$$P = AVC.$$

Output level Q becomes the last output the company produces at the shut-down point.

Example 10.4
Consider a competitive firm with a fixed cost of $800 and a variable cost function of

$$VC = 75Q - 12Q^2 + 2Q^3.$$

1. When would this firm prefer to shut down?
2. Draw a graph to show the price and quantity of the **shut-down decision**.

Solution:
The firm would shut down when the price of its product falls to a point where the price is equal to its average variable cost (i.e., $P = AVC$). So, we have to find the average variable cost (Figure 10.6):

$$AVC = \frac{VC}{Q} = \frac{75Q - 12Q^2 + 2Q^3}{Q},$$

$$AVC = 75 - 12Q + 2Q^2.$$

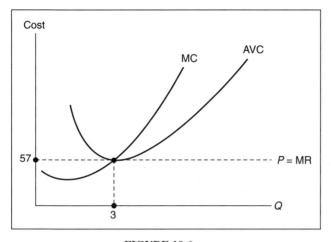

FIGURE 10.6

Taking the first derivative of the AVC, setting it to zero, and solving for Q would give us the output level at which the firm would shut down:

$$\frac{\partial\,\text{AVC}}{\partial Q} = -12 + 4Q = 0,$$

$$4Q = 12,$$

$$Q = 3.$$

To find the price, we know that a competitive firm has a price equal to its marginal revenue which is equal to marginal cost. Marginal cost is the first derivative of the total cost, which is

$$\text{TC} = \text{FC} + \text{VC},$$

$$\text{TC} = 800 + 75Q - 12Q^2 + 2Q^3,$$

$$\text{MC} = \frac{\partial\text{TC}}{\partial Q} = 75 - 24Q + 6Q^2.$$

This is the marginal cost that would be equal to the price

$$P = \text{MC} = 75 - 24Q + 6Q^2$$

$$= 75 - 4(3) + 6(3)^2$$

$$= 57.$$

So, the firm would prefer to shut down once the price falls to $57 or below.

Example 10.5

Suppose that a competitive firm's total cost function is

$$TC = 250 + 5Q + 0.025Q^2.$$

If the product market price is $15, find the following:

1. What would be the firm's maximum profit, and at which size of production?
2. What would be the level of output at which the firm would break even? Plot it on a graph.

Solution:

1. Let us take the first derivative of the profit function, set it to zero, and solve it for Q:

$$Pr = TR - TC$$
$$= PQ - (250 + 5Q + 0.025Q^2)$$
$$= 15Q - 250 - 5Q - 0.025Q^2$$
$$= 10Q - 250 - 0.025Q^2.$$

$$\frac{\partial Pr}{\partial Q} = 10 - 0.05Q = 0,$$

$$10 = 0.05Q,$$

$$Q = 200,$$

$$Pr = 10Q - 250 - 0.025Q^2$$
$$= 10(200) - 250 - 0.025(200)^2$$
$$= 750.$$

To prove that this is the maximum profit, the second derivative has to be negative:

$$\frac{\partial^2 Pr}{\partial Q^2} = -0.05 < 0.$$

2. The break-even level of output occurs when the total cost is equal to the total revenue:

$$TC = TR,$$
$$250 + 5Q + 0.025Q^2 = 15Q,$$
$$0.025Q^2 - 10Q + 250 = 0.$$

We use the quadratic formula to solve for Q where

$$a = 0.025,$$
$$b = -10,$$

$$c = 250,$$

$$Q = \frac{-b \pm \sqrt{(b^2 - 4ac)}}{2a}$$

$$= \frac{-(-10) \pm \sqrt{[(-10)^2 - 4(0.025)(250)]}}{2(0.025)}$$

$$= \frac{10 \pm 8.66}{0.05}$$

$$Q = 373$$

or

$$Q = 27.$$

When Q has two values, it means that the firm's break even is at two different levels of output, as shown in Figure 10.7.

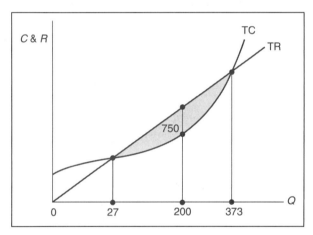

FIGURE 10.7

10.1.4   The Competitive Firm in the Long Run

The long run is characterized by the variability of all inputs, their cost, and the wide-ranging possibilities for any firm to set its scale of operations. As stated before, a competitive firm enjoys full freedom of entering and exiting the industry market at any time. These two prerequisites, among others, imply that if the competitive firm succeeds to earn a decent profit in the short run, as we have seen before, many other firms in the industry would be willing and able to employ their resources in order to earn the same amount of profit. In the long run, more and more firms would decide to enter the market. This would increase the market supply and shift its curve to the right, as seen in Figure 10.8, causing the market price to drop from P_1 to P_2. The right panel of the figure shows, the competitive firm making a profit equal to area A ($abc\,E_1$) in the short run when the market price is P_1. Now that the price drops to P_2, the competitive firm would have a new lower point of equilibrium E_2 resulting in reducing the profit to area B ($def\,E_2$).

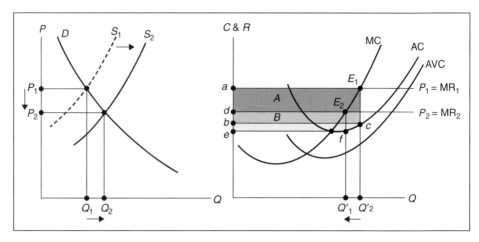

FIGURE 10.8

As more and more competitive firms enter the market pursuing good profits, the market supply curve would shift further to the right causing further drop in the price and reducing the profits even further. In the long run, this cycle would continue and its effects widen until all the possible profits are squeezed out. It is theoretically safe to see that in the long run competitive firms would not be able to make any profit. This happens when the market price drops to the level of break even, when total revenue would equal total cost. There will be no incentive for any firm to enter the market at and after that point. The long-run equilibrium for the entire competitive industry is defined where all competitive firms produce at the lowest point on their long-run average cost (LAC). Figure 10.9 shows

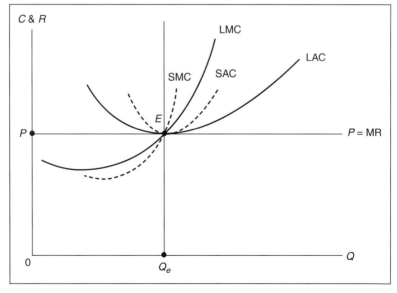

FIGURE 10.9

that the long-run equilibrium point E exists not only when long-run marginal cost is equal to the long-run marginal revenue (LMR) or price (P), but also when the point at which the short-run average cost (SAC) and the long-run average cost are tangential to each other.

The long-run competitive equilibrium may be considered more theoretical than real, but it remains a useful analytical tool for managers and economists to examine the effects of market changes.

Example 10.6

Consider an industry that consists of 500 competitive firms. The uniform total cost function in the industry is

$$\text{TC} = Q^3 - 8Q^2 + 20Q$$

and the market demand function is

$$Q_d = 2016 - 4P.$$

1. What would be the long-run equilibrium output for each competitive firm and at what market price would it occur?
2. Confirm the break-even point, if it occurs.

Solution:

The long-run equilibrium for the competitive term occurs at the lowest point of its average cost function. Therefore, we have to obtain the average cost function and take the first derivative of it, set it to zero, and solve for Q. We would also make sure it is the lowest point by checking the minimum condition:

$$\text{TC} = Q^3 - 8Q^2 + 20Q,$$

$$\text{AC} = \frac{\text{TC}}{Q} = Q^2 - 8Q + 20,$$

$$\frac{\partial \text{AC}}{\partial Q} = 2Q - 8,$$

$$\frac{\partial^2 \text{AC}}{\partial Q^2} = 2 > 0 \text{ (minimum)},$$

$$2Q - 8 = 0,$$

$$2Q = 8,$$

$$Q = 4.$$

Each competitive firm would produce 4 units, which is its equilibrium output level. Now, we obtain the value of the average cost:

$$\text{AC} = Q^2 - 8Q + 20$$
$$= (4)^2 - 8(4) + 20 = \$4.$$

Since the average cost would be equal to the price in the long run ($P = AC = MC$), these firms would produce 4 units and sell them at $4 each. The total revenue would be

$$TR = PQ$$
$$= (4)(4) = 16,$$

and the total cost would be

$$TC = Q^3 - 8Q^2 + 20Q$$
$$= (4)^3 - 8(4)^2 + 20(4)$$
$$= 16.$$

Therefore, at the output level of 4 units, each of the 500 firms would break even, since the total revenue is equal to the total cost. It is the zero-profit point:

$$Pr = TR - TC$$
$$= 16 - 16 = 0.$$

Since the market demand function is

$$Q_d = 2016 - 4Q$$
$$= 2016 - 4(4) = 2000.$$

The total industry would produce 2000 units distributed among 500 firms, making the market share of production 4 units for each competitive firm (Figure 10.10):

$$\frac{D_m}{500} = \frac{2000}{500} = 4 \text{ units.}$$

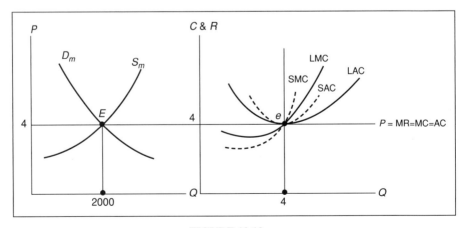

FIGURE 10.10

10.2 MONOPOLY

At the opposite extreme of perfect competition is the imperfect competition of the market structure. At the very end of the spectrum of the imperfect competition is monopoly. It is a market organization that is reverse in terms of perfect competition. Characteristics of monopoly include the following:

1. A single producer who dominates the production of a unique product, which has no close substitute.
2. The characteristic mentioned above leads to the natural result that the monopolistic firm representing the entire industry single handedly has total control on the market. Although its market power is not unlimited, it is extremely significant.
3. Based on points 1 and 2 above, the entry of new firms into the industry is totally blocked, implying that a monopolistic firm can enjoy earning profits in the long run, unlike its counterparts in the fully competitive industry.
4. Information for the economic agents on production, cost, price, and quality is not perfect as it is assumed in the perfect competition scenario.

There are several plausible reasons for monopoly to exist. Here are the most important of them:

1. A monopolistic firm may have total control over a natural resource that may be the only source of supply of its raw material requirements. This is the case for firms that own gold mines, petrol fields, and so on.
2. A monopolistic firm may own a certain patent or exclusively hold a copyright to its sources and products. In the United States, a patent can be exclusively held by law for 17 years, as a reward for inventors and incentive for them to progress with protection.
3. A monopolistic firm may obtain a legal right to be the sole producer for a certain commodity. Federal government usually grants such rights for certain advantages of a particular producer. This could be the case of companies that provide electric power or public transportation or water. Another example is a post office, which holds an exclusive right to provide postal services. These are called regulated monopolies for the right of the government to exercise some control in order to protect the public from the unlimited market power that may be exercised by those monopolies, if left unchecked.

10.2.1 Monopoly's Equilibrium in the Short Run

Like any other type of firm, a monopoly would reach its equilibrium level of output that maximizes its profits when its marginal revenue is equal to its marginal cost. But because in a monopoly, the average revenue curve is the product's market demand curve, we need to first set the relationship between the market demand curve and the firm's marginal revenue curve before obtaining the equilibrium point.

Let us show that a marginal revenue curve is

1. down sloping just like the demand curve;
2. lower than the demand curve, as shown in Figure 10.11.

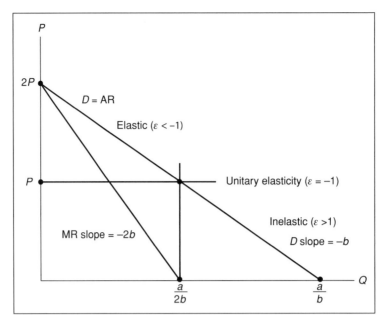

FIGURE 10.11

Marginal revenue is defined as the change in total revenue with respect to output change:

$$MR = \frac{\partial TR}{\partial Q}$$

$$= \frac{\partial PQ}{\partial Q}$$

$$= P\frac{\partial Q}{\partial P} + Q\frac{\partial P}{\partial Q}$$

$$= P + \frac{\partial P}{\partial Q}Q,$$

where $\frac{\partial P}{\partial Q}$ is the slope, and since the change in price with respect to quantity is related to a down sloping demand curve, it must be negative:

$$MR = P - \frac{\partial P}{\partial Q}Q.$$

This would mean that the marginal revenue is less than the price for any given positive level of output Q.

For any linear demand curve, the marginal revenue curve would be linear too, but with a slope that is twice as the slope for the demand curve. This would make the marginal revenue curve steeper than the demand curve (located closer to the origin) and have an x-intercept equal to half of the x-intercept of the demand curve.

Let us take an inverse linear demand function, such as

$$P = a - bQ.$$

Given that total revenue is

$$TR = PQ$$
$$= (a - bQ)Q$$
$$= aQ - bQ^2,$$

and the marginal revenue is

$$MR = \frac{\partial TR}{\partial Q}$$
$$= a - 2bQ,$$

where $-2b$ is the slope of the marginal revenue curve, which is twice as the slope of the demand curve $(-b)$.

Now that we established both the demand curve and the marginal revenue curve, let us take a look at the graph in Figure 10.12 to see how monopoly determines equilibrium output level and maximizes profit.

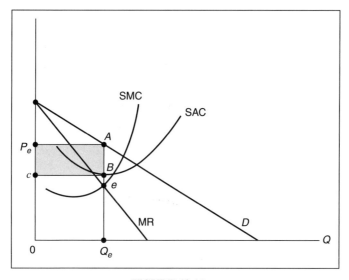

FIGURE 10.12

A monopolistic firm would produce its optimum level of output Q_e, where its marginal revenue is equal to its marginal cost at point e. This level of output would be sold at price P_e, as determined by the market demand curve D at point A. The price P_e is determined indirectly by the firm because of the firm's influence on the quantity, given the state of the market demand. This is why a monopoly is considered **price maker**, not a **price taker**, unlike the case with perfect competition. Selling Q_e at a price P_e would mean that the firm's total revenue would be the area $Q_e A P_e 0$, but the cost incurred is equal to the area $Q_e B C 0$, which means that the maximum profit that can be obtained would be the shaded area of $B A P_e C$. The firm can still earn some profit as long as the market price would not fall below C where it would be less than the average cost. Also, the profit would still be earned as long as the average cost would not go higher than P_e. If it does for any reason, the firm would suffer a loss as shown in Figure 10.13.

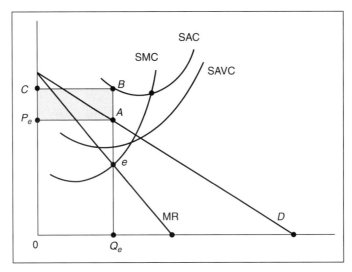

FIGURE 10.13

The equilibrium level of output is Q_e and the price is P_e, making the total revenue equal to the area $Q_e A P_e 0$. However, since the average cost would exceed the price level P_e, the firm's total cost would be equal to the average cost, that is, $Q_e B$ times the quantity Q_e:

$$AC = (Q_e B)(Q_e) = \text{Area } Q_e B C 0,$$

which is larger than the total revenue, that is, $Q_e A P_e 0$, and the difference would be a loss represented by the shaded area of $ABCP_e$:

$$\text{Area } Q_e B C 0 - \text{Area } Q_e A P_e 0 = \text{Area } ABCP_e.$$

Example 10.7
A monopoly has the following total cost function:

$$TC = 80 - 8Q + Q^2.$$

Find its equilibrium output and price and calculate its maximum profits, given that the market demand function is

$$Q = 32 - \frac{1}{3}P.$$

First we have to find the total revenue function, for which we need the price. We get the price function by taking the inverse demand function:

$$Q = 32 - \tfrac{1}{3}P.$$
$$P = 96 - 3Q,$$
$$TR = PQ,$$
$$TR = [96 - 3Q]Q,$$
$$TR = 96Q - 3Q^2,$$
$$Pr = TR - TC,$$
$$Pr = 96Q - 3Q^3 - 80 + 8Q - Q^2,$$
$$Pr = 104Q - 4Q^2 - 80,$$
$$\frac{\partial Pr}{\partial Q} = 104 - 8Q = 0,$$
$$8Q = 104,$$
$$Q = \tfrac{104}{8} = 13.$$

This is the equilibrium quantity at which the profit is maximized. The second derivative is negative to confirm the maximum profit:

$$\frac{\partial^2 Pr}{\partial Q^2} = -8 < 0.$$

This equilibrium quantity is sold at market price, which is

$$P = 96 - 3Q$$
$$= 96 - 3(13)$$
$$= 57.$$

The maximum profit earned would be

$$Pr = 104Q - 4Q^2 - 80$$
$$= 104(13) - 4(13)^2 - 80 = 596.$$

10.2.2 Monopoly's Equilibrium in the Long Run

In the long run, a monopolist will earn profit, as entry to the industry remains exclusive. The equilibrium point occurs when the firm marginal revenue is equal to its long run marginal cost. That would be at point E in Figure 10.14. This point would determine the optimum level of output at Q_e. This output can be sold at price P_e according to what is determined by the market demand curve at point A. Total revenue for the firm would be $0Q_e$ times $0P_e$. That is the entire area of $0Q_eAP_e$. The best scale of plant would be established in the long run when the short-run average cost curve (SAC) curve touches the long-run average cost

(LAC curve at the optimum level of input. That is at point B. It should be noted here that while the marginal cost curves both in the short run (SMC) and in the long run (LMC) still cross the related average cost curves at their lowest point, it is not necessary this time that the SAC curve touches the LAC curve at their lowest points. Figure 10.14 shows that point B is not the lowest of the two curves. However, this tangency must still occur at the equilibrium level of output Q_e. In the long run, the firm would incur cost equal to the area $Q_e BC0$, which would leave a pure profit equal to the shaded area of $BAP_e C$.

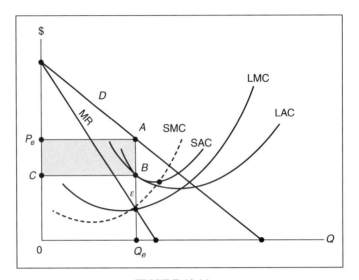

FIGURE 10.14

Example 10.8

Consider a monopoly with a cost function of

$$\text{TC} = 120 + 6Q + \frac{Q_2}{270}.$$

1. Find the equilibrium quantity and price.
2. Calculate the firm's maximum profit in the long run.

Solution:

If the market demand is expressed by

$$Q_d = 4500 - 90P.$$

First, let us express the demand function in terms of the price:

$$Q_d = 4500 - 90P,$$

$$90P = 4500 - Q,$$

$$P = 50 - \frac{Q}{90}.$$

Second, we obtain the firm's total revenue function as $P \cdot Q$:

$$TR = PQ,$$

$$TR = \left[50 - \frac{Q}{90}\right]Q,$$

$$TR = 50Q - \frac{Q^2}{90}.$$

Third, we obtain the marginal revenue function as the first derivative of the total revenue function:

$$MR = \frac{\partial TR}{\partial Q} = 50 - \frac{Q}{45}.$$

Similarly, the marginal cost function is the first derivative of the total cost function:

$$MC = \frac{\partial TR}{\partial Q} = 6 + \frac{Q}{135}.$$

The equilibrium occurs when $MR = MC$:

$$50 - \frac{Q}{45} = 6 + \frac{Q}{135},$$

$$50 - \frac{Q}{45} - 6 - \frac{Q}{135} = 0,$$

$$44 = \frac{4Q}{135},$$

$$4Q = 5940,$$

$$Q = 1485 \text{ the optimum level of output.}$$

We substitute Q into the demand function to obtain the price:

$$P = 50 - \frac{Q}{90},$$

$$P = 50 - \frac{1485}{90}$$

$$= 33.50, \text{ the equilibrium price.}$$

Now, we can calculate the firm's profit:

$$Pr = TR - TC$$

$$= PQ - \left[120 + 6Q + \frac{Q^2}{270}\right]$$

$$= (33.50)(1485) - 120 - 6(1485) - \frac{(1485)^2}{270}$$

$$= 32{,}550.$$

10.2.3   Monopoly Power and the Lerner Index

We stated earlier that a monopoly is a price maker, unlike a firm in perfect competition, which is considered a price taker. Monopolies set their prices on the basis of a down sloping market demand curve. It is, therefore, a matter of the monopoly's ability to set its product price above its marginal cost so that it can make the highest possible profit. It is this ability for a monopoly to have what is called market power. The **Lerner index** is a measure of monopoly power for it shows the effect of price elasticity of demand on monopoly price, relative to the product marginal cost. It is named after Abba Lerner and defined as the ratio of the difference between price and marginal cost relative to the price. It can also be considered the negative inverse of the price elasticity of demand. Let us derive the Lerner index, starting with the first derivative of the profit:

$$\text{Pr} = \text{TR} - \text{TC},$$

$$\frac{\partial \text{Pr}}{\partial Q} = \frac{\partial \text{TR}}{\partial Q} - \frac{\partial \text{TC}}{\partial Q}$$

$$= \frac{\partial [PQ]}{\partial Q} - \text{MC}$$

$$= P \frac{\partial Q}{\partial P} + P \frac{\partial P}{\partial Q} - \text{MC}$$

$$= P + Q \frac{\partial P}{\partial Q} - \text{MC}.$$

Setting $\frac{\partial \text{Pr}}{\partial Q}$ to zero and rearranging, we get

$$P - \text{MC} + Q \frac{\partial P}{\partial Q} = 0,$$

$$P - \text{MC} = -Q \frac{\partial P}{\partial Q}.$$

Dividing both sides by P, we get

$$\frac{P - \text{MC}}{P} = -\frac{Q}{P} \frac{\partial P}{\partial Q}. \tag{10.1}$$

Recall that the price elasticity of demand is

$$\varepsilon = \frac{\partial Q}{\partial P} \times \frac{P}{Q},$$

and if we reverse it, it would be

$$\frac{1}{\varepsilon} = \frac{\partial P}{\partial Q} \times \frac{Q}{P},$$

which is the right-hand side of Equation (10.1). So, the difference between price and marginal cost would be equal to negative inverse of the price elasticity of demand:

$$\frac{P - MC}{P} = -\frac{1}{\varepsilon},$$

which is the Lerner index or as sometimes called the "price markup." Given that the marginal cost has a positive value, the Lerner index would mean that the elasticity value ranges are

$$-1 \leq \varepsilon \leq -\infty,$$

so that a monopoly would only produce on the upper elastic portion of the demand curve as it was seen in Figure 10.11. The price elasticity of demand would indicate whether the marginal revenue would be positive or negative:

$$MR > 0 \quad \text{if } \varepsilon < -1 \text{ (elastic)},$$
$$MR < 0 \quad \text{if } \varepsilon > -1 \text{ (inelastic)},$$
$$MR = 0 \quad \text{if } \varepsilon = -1 \text{ (unit elasticity)}.$$

The Lerner index takes a value between 0 and 1, but greater the index, greater the difference between price and marginal cost in favor of the price, which would mean a greater monopoly power. This is naturally confirmed in the case of the perfect competition where the difference between price and marginal cost is zero ($P = MR = MC$), which explains that in a perfect competition there is no monopoly power at all.

10.3   MONOPOLISTIC COMPETITION

This is the third type of market structure, which is a combination of perfect competition and monopoly. The major characteristics of monopolistic competition firms can be identified as follows:

1. A large number of producers or sellers, each of whom produces a small portion of the industry's output, and have no significant influence to affect the market in general.
2. A large number of consumers or buyers, each of whom buys a small portion of the market output.
3. A heterogeneous and differentiated product. Firms in such an industry would strive to offer close substitutes but not identical products. They compete and spend resources on development and advertisement to reinforce the differences of their products and distinguish them from each other in order to secure a higher market share. Typical examples of the monopolistic competition products are soft drink, pizza, fast food, gas, and gas station services.
4. Free and easy entry to and exit from the industry.
5. Perfect information for all economic agents.

6. While the demand curve is perfectly elastic (horizontal line) in perfect competition, it is less elastic in the monopolistic competition, but more elastic (flatter) than the demand curve of a monopoly.

10.3.1 Monopolistic Competition Equilibrium in the Short Run

Since the major product for a monopolistically competitive firm is a heterogeneous product with distinguished characteristics among many close substitutes, the demand curve is highly elastic and negatively sloped and linear. This would make the marginal revenue linear and negatively sloped. It is still below the demand curve just like in the case of monopoly. It also pivots from the same point on y-axis and the slope of demand curve is half of the marginal revenue slope. Looking at Figure 10.15, we can observe that a monopolistic competition like any other market organization would have its equilibrium output at the point where the marginal revenue is equal to the marginal cost. That is at point E, where the optimum output would be determined as Q_e. This optimum level of output would be sold in the market at a price determined by the market demand curve. That is P_e, shown by a horizontal line from point A on the elastic section of the demand curve. Total revenue would be obtained by multiplying Q_e by P_e, which is the entire area of Q_eAP_e0. This firm, like any other, seeks profit and for that it would not sell its product unless market price is higher than its average cost. It can be seen how P_e is higher than P that is equal to point B on the average cost curve. This margin of the price above the average cost is the profit per unit. The total maximum profit would be obtained by multiplying this margin (BA) by the entire output sold, which would be represented by PB that corresponds to $0Q_e$. The result is that the firm's profit is maximized as the shaded area BAP_eP. It is the same area obtained as the difference between total revenue (Q_eAP_e0) and total cost (Q_eBP0).

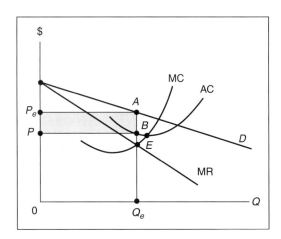

FIGURE 10.15

Similar to other market structures, this monopolistic firm can incur a loss if its average cost rises above market price (AC curve above D curve), and it can minimize the loss if the price falls close to the average variable cost. However, it would be preferable to shut down if the price falls to the same level as the AVC or below it.

10.3.2 Monopolistic Competition Equilibrium in the Long Run

We saw that a monopolistically competitive firm would strive to make its own product differentiated from the products of similar firms in the industry in order to secure a market share that would bring some profits. However, the free and easy entry to the industry coupled with the evidence of earning good profits would encourage more firms to get into the industry and produce closer and better substitutes. In the long run, the rush of more firms into the industry would eventually squeeze the profits for everybody and increase the price elasticity of demand, as the demand curve would shift to the left and become price elastic (flatter).

If the demand curve of individual firms continues to shift left and becomes flatter as the market share shrinks and more close substitute products flood the market, it may finally touch the LAC curve , but in the down sloping portion instead of the lowest point B. This is where the average cost would be equal to the price and the firm breaks even. This point A corresponds to the point of equilibrium E where both the LMC and SMCs are equal to marginal revenue (Figure 10.16):

$$MR = LMC = SMC.$$

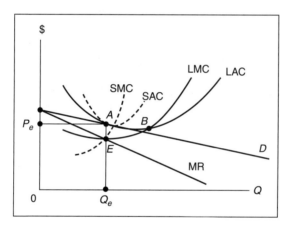

FIGURE 10.16

This is where the optimal level of output is determined at Q_e, and the equilibrium price becomes P_e based on point A on the demand curve. Since the firm faces equal revenue and cost, it will not be able to make any profit. Area $Q_e A P_e 0$ represents both total revenue and total cost. Recording zero profit in the long run is associated with the fact that the fall of demand allowed the price to fall to the level of average cost. This can be expressed by

$$P = AC,$$

$$P - AC = 0.$$

Multiplying by Q, $PQ - ACQ = 0(Q)$.

PQ is total revenue, and ACQ is total cost:

$$TR - TC = 0,$$

and the difference between the total revenue and total cost is profit:

$$Pr = 0.$$

Example 10.9

A monopolistically competitive firm has a total cost function and demand function, respectively, as

$$TC = 200 - 10Q + 2Q^2,$$
$$P = 120 - 2Q.$$

1. What are the equilibrium quantity and price?
2. How much profit would the firm make?
3. If the demand function changes over time to: $Q = \frac{70}{6} - \frac{1}{6}P$, would the firm still earn profit?
4. What can be said about short run and long run?

Solution:

First, we should express the demand function in terms of price in order to obtain the total revenue function:

$$P = 120 - 2Q,$$
$$TR = QP$$
$$= Q(120 - 2Q)$$
$$= 120P - 2Q^2,$$
$$Pr = TR - TC,$$
$$Pr = 120Q - 2Q^2 - 200 + 10Q - 2Q^2,$$
$$Pr = 130Q - 4Q^2 - 200,$$
$$\frac{\partial Pr}{\partial Q} = 130 - 8Q = 0,$$
$$130 = 8Q.$$

1. $Q = \frac{130}{8} = 16.25$ equilibrium output.
   $P = 120 - 2Q$
   $= 120 - 2(16.25) = \$87.5$ equilibrium price.
2. $Pr = 130Q - 4Q^2 - 200$
   $= 130(16.25) - 4(16.25)^2 - 200$
   $= \$856.25.$

3. New demand function is $P = 70 - 6Q$:

$$\mathrm{TR} = QP = Q(70 - 6Q)$$
$$= 70Q - 6Q^2,$$
$$\mathrm{Pr} = \mathrm{TR} - \mathrm{TC},$$
$$\mathrm{Pr} = 70Q - 6Q^2 - 200 + 10Q - 2Q^2,$$
$$\mathrm{Pr} = 80Q - 8Q^2 - 200,$$
$$\frac{\partial \mathrm{Pr}}{\partial Q} = 80 - 16Q = 0,$$
$$16Q = 80,$$
$$Q = \tfrac{80}{16} = 5,$$
$$\mathrm{Pr} = 80Q - 8Q^2 - 200$$
$$= 80(5) - 8(5)^2 - 200$$
$$= 0.$$

4. Since the firm earned a profit of \$856.25 as shown in step 2 above, it was a short-run operation and since it earned zero profit later, it was a long-run operation when the demand function was $P = 70 - 6Q$.

10.4   OLIGOPOLY

Oligopoly is the fourth type of market structure, which is characterized by two or more large firms that dominate a particular industry in the market. They would produce homogeneous or slightly distinctive products such as the case of aluminum and electrical products where the structure is called **pure oligopoly**. They can also produce differentiated products such as automobiles or computers where the structure is called **differentiated oligopoly**.

Entry to the industry is possible but usually hard to achieve for it requires significant capital investment, highly specialized input and products, and possibly exclusive patent. Oligopoly is also characterized by a high degree of interdependence among the firms in the industry. This means that any action by any individual firm in the industry would directly affect the rest of the firms, although they individually set their own production and price strategies, and make profits in the short and long terms. Oligopoly market is also characterized by imperfect information among the economic players in the market. Consumers usually do not have full information on costs, price, product quality, resources, and production strategies.

Oligopolistic firms can sometimes enter into formal mutual agreements to fix production targets and prices, and share profits. If they can operate under such overt collaboration, they would form what is known as a **cartel** or **trust**. However, sometimes a covert agreement between these firms can take place. In this case, they would form what is called a **collusion**. It is illegal to form and operate any of the oligopolistic collaborations in the United States, although it is legal in other countries. These collaborations were prohibited by the Sherman Antitrust Act (SAA) of 1890, and later by the Federal Trade Commission Act of 1914, exclusively to keep competition alive and well in the economic activities of the nation. As a result of prohibiting cartels and collusions in the United States, oligopolistic firms tried to merge together and the law still restricts the ability of firms to form mergers. The reason is to protect competition and prevent the industries from becoming pure monopolies. In some cases, mergers bring higher efficiency because of appropriate scale of operations, integration of technologies, and complementary research and development efforts. In order for mergers to take place, the proposing firms have to win the higher court decision against the challenges of the Federal Trade Commission.

10.4.1   The Concentration Ratio and the Herfindahl Index

The **concentration ratio** refers to the extent to which specific oligopolistic firms have been dominating the industry. It is measured by the volume of sales or revenue for a specific firm or firms as compared with the whole industry. One measure is to gauge the sales of the 4, 8, 12, 20, or 50 largest firms in the industry. It is based on the percentage of market share of a specific company (i) in a particular cluster (n):

$$CR_n = \frac{\sum_{i=1}^{n} s_i}{s_n} \times 100,$$

where n can be any of those clusters of 4, 8, 12, 20, or 50 companies.

The highest ratio of concentration is 100 for the first four firms, which means that the whole market is shared by only four firms. The top four oligopolistic companies in the United States have a typical concentration ratio (CR_4) ranging between 20% and 80%. Another method to measure the concentration ratio is the one developed by Herfindahl and Hirschmann, which is called the **Herfindahl index** (HI) or the **Herfindahl–Hirschmann index** (HHI). It is the sum of the squared market shares for all oligopolistic companies that compete in a particular industry:

$$HHI = \sum_{i=1}^{n} s_i^2,$$

where s_i is the ith company's market share expressed in percentage points:

$$HHI = \sum_{i=1}^{n} \left[\frac{ms_i}{ms_n} \times 100 \right]^2,$$

where ms_i is the market share (sales) for company i, and ms_n is the total sales for the whole industry. For example, if there are only three companies, A, B, and C, dominating the industry so that their sales are as follows:

A: 50% of sales

B: 30% of sales

C: 20% of sales

Then the HHI for this industry would be

$$HHI = (50)^2 + (30)^2 + (20)^2 = 3800.$$

The HHI has been gaining increasing popularity since the 1980s and has been utilized by the US Justice Department for evaluating mergers.

10.4.2   Models of Oligopoly

Unlike competitive and monopolistic markets, oligopolistic markets operate depending on either setting the output level or setting the product price. The following are the most common models of oligopoly divided into two groups: the output-setting group that includes the Cournot and **Stackelberg models**, and the price-setting group that includes the Bertrand and **Sweezy models**.

Cournot Model   Named after the French economist Augustin Cournot, this model of oligopoly dates back to 1838. It illustrates the interdependence in the way a **duopoly** operates. In addition to the general assumption that the production by the two firms of the duopoly would be equal to the production by the entire industry, Cournot assumed that the firms were producing a **homogeneous product** where each decides its own level of output assuming that the other firm would not change its output accordingly. This is to say that the model assumed that the **conjectural variation** between the two firms in the industry was zero:

$$\frac{dQ_1}{dQ_2} = \frac{dQ_2}{dQ_1} = 0.$$

The original Cournot model was about two companies producing spring water at no cost. Figure 10.17 shows that the first firm started as a sole producer in the market. Its demand curve is linear and represented by D_1 where Q_m is the market demand on spring water. The marginal revenue is represented by MR_1 and since the marginal cost is zero, the

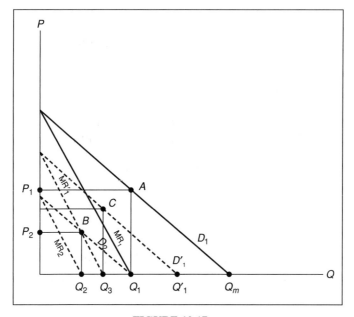

FIGURE 10.17

equilibrium point is at the intersection of MR_1 with the horizontal axis. This is where the first firm produces Q_1 and sells it at P_1 based on point A on the demand curve D_1.

As for the second firm, it gets into the market believing that the first firm would not change its production of Q_1. So the demand curve for the second firm (D_2) starts from Q_1 and extends parallel to D_1. The marginal revenue for this firm (MR_2) will also equate its marginal cost of zero at Q_2. The equilibrium level of output (Q_2) for the second firm would be sold at P_2 based on point B on D_2. Now, the first firm would, in turn, assume that the second firm would continue to produce Q_2 and sell it for P_2 with no change. Firm 1 would react to the amount that the second firm produced by starting at Q_1' on a new demand curve D_1' that is now shifted to the left. The whole process would be repeated when a new equilibrium point (Q_3) is established where the new marginal revenue curve MR_1' crosses the horizontal axis. This new output level for the first firm in the second round would be sold at a price P_3, which is determined by the midpoint C on the demand curve D_1'. The second firm would react and behave just like it did before. Over time, and through the action and reaction between the two firms, each firm will eventually end up taking its share of production that would be equal to one-third of the whole market demand Q_m. Both would produce two-thirds Q_m.

Cournot equilibrium can be illustrated better if we consider the following example: suppose that the following linear demand function is for a duopoly producing a certain product at a marginal cost of $50:

$$P = 400 - Q,$$

where Q is the market output level, that is the sum of the two companies' output (Figure 10.18):

$$Q = Q_1 + Q_2.$$

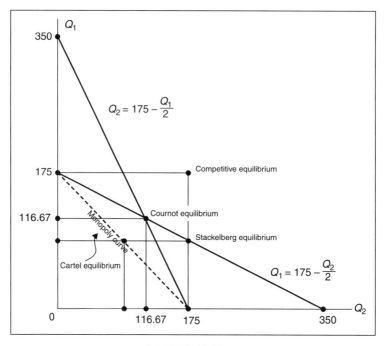

FIGURE 10.18

Since the equilibrium is determined at the equality between the marginal revenue and marginal cost, we need to derive the marginal revenue and equate it to the marginal cost as $MC = 25$, and solve for Q. Let us start with the total revenue for firm 1:

$$TR_1 = Q_1 P$$
$$= Q_1[400 - (Q_1 + Q_2)]$$
$$= 400Q_1 - Q_1^2 - Q_1 Q_2,$$
$$MR_1 = \frac{\partial TR_1}{\partial Q_1} = 400 - 2Q_1 - Q_2,$$
$$MR_1 = MC_1,$$
$$400 - 2Q_1 - Q_2 = 50,$$
$$2Q_1 = 350 - Q_2,$$
$$Q_1 = 175 - \frac{Q_2}{2}, \tag{10.2}$$

$$TR_2 = Q_2 P$$
$$= Q_2[400 - (Q_1 + Q_2)]$$
$$= 400Q_2 - Q_2^2 - Q_2 Q_1,$$
$$MR_2 = \frac{\partial TR_2}{\partial Q_2} = 400 - 2Q_2 - Q_1,$$
$$MR_2 = MC_2,$$
$$400 - 2Q_2 - Q_1 = 50,$$
$$2Q_2 = 350 - Q_1,$$
$$Q_2 = 175 - \frac{Q_1}{2}. \tag{10.3}$$

We can solve Equations (10.1) and (10.2) simultaneously:

$$Q_1 = 175 - 0.5Q_2,$$
$$Q_2 = 175 - 0.5Q_1,$$
$$Q_1 = 175 - 0.5(175 - 0.5Q_1),$$
$$Q_1 = 175 - 87.5 + 0.25Q_1,$$
$$0.75Q_1 = 87.5,$$
$$Q_1 = \frac{87.5}{0.75} = 116.67,$$
$$Q_2 = 175 - 0.5(116.67) = 116.67,$$
$$Q = Q_1 + Q_2,$$
$$Q = 116.67 + 116.67 = 233.33, \tag{10.4}$$

$$P = 40 - Q,$$

$$P = 400 - 233.33 = 166.67, \quad \text{market price.}$$

Since both firms produce an equal output of 116.67 units and face the same market price of $166.67, their total revenue would be

$$(116.67)(166.67) = 19{,}445.39.$$

Given that there is no fixed cost, and the marginal cost is $50, which is equal to the average cost, the total cost for each firm would be

$$(50)(116.67) = 5833.50,$$

which makes the profit for each firm equal to

$$\text{Pr} = 19{,}445.39 - 5833.50 = 13{,}611.89.$$

Example 10.10
What would be the equilibrium output and price if the above case is a monopoly?

Solution:
Under monopoly there would be one output (Q) and the total revenue would be

$$\text{TR} = \text{PQ}$$
$$= (400 - Q)Q$$
$$= 400Q - Q^2,$$
$$\text{MR} = \frac{\partial \text{TR}}{\partial Q} = 400 - 2Q,$$
$$\text{MC} = 50,$$
$$\text{MR} = \text{MC},$$
$$400 - 2Q = 50,$$
$$350 = 2Q,$$
$$175 = Q.$$

The equilibrium price would be

$$P = 400 - Q$$
$$= 400 - 175 = 225,$$
$$\text{TR} = (225)(175) = 39{,}375,$$
$$\text{TC} = (50)(175) = 8750,$$
$$\text{Pr} = 39{,}375 - 8750 = 30{,}625.$$

This shows that the size of market production under duopoly (233.33) turned out to be larger than the market production under monopoly (175), but the monopoly price is higher than the price under duopoly. Finally, the monopoly would earn more profit (30,625) than the duopoly (27,233.78).

Stackelberg Model The Stackelberg model of oligopoly is about the strategic interaction among oligopolistic companies in terms of their production and price decisions. It is an extension of the Cournot model developed and named after the German economist and mathematician Heinrich Von Stackelberg in 1934. We can recognize three essential points that show how the Stackelberg model is different from the Cournot model:

(a) Decision making of the parties is sequential instead of simultaneous.
(b) Parties are interdependent instead of independent.
(c) Parties are classified into leader and follower(s) where the dominant leader company takes the advantage of the first move. It would operate based on the likely reaction of the other competitive company, while the company, being the follower, would behave just like it did in the Cournot model. Generally speaking, the Stackelberg leader company would depend on a stimulus or signal from the Stackelberg follower in drawing its strategy of production, price, and profit maximization.

Let us reconsider the Cournot model and adjust it on the basis of the Stackelberg modification. Let us assume that the first firm is going to be the Stackelberg leader and the second firm is the Stackelberg follower. Assume further that firm 1 would be able to correctly anticipate the output reaction of firm 2 ($Q_2 = 175 - \frac{1}{2} Q_1$) and take it into consideration when deciding the profit-maximizing level of output.

So, the total revenue function of firm 1 would be

$$\begin{aligned} TR_1 &= Q_1 P \\ &= Q_1[400 - (Q_1 + Q_2)] \\ &= 400Q_1 - Q_1^2 - Q_1 Q_2 \\ &= 400Q_1 - Q_1^2 - Q_1(175 - 0.5Q_1) \\ &= 400Q_1 - Q_1^2 - 175Q_1 + 0.5Q_1^2 \\ &= 225Q_1 - 0.5Q_1^2, \end{aligned}$$

the marginal revenue for firm 1 would be

$$MR_1 = \frac{\partial TR_1}{\partial Q_1} = 225 - Q_1,$$

and the equilibrium condition, given that the marginal cost is 50, would be

$$\begin{aligned} MR_1 &= MC_1, \\ 225 - Q_1 &= 50, \\ Q_1 &= 175. \end{aligned} \tag{10.5}$$

So, that would be the output level of the first firm. The output level of the second firm would be

$$Q_2 = 175 - \tfrac{1}{2}Q_1,$$

$$Q_2 = 175 - \tfrac{1}{2}(175),$$

$$Q_2 = 87.5, \tag{10.6}$$

and the industry output (Q) would be

$$Q = Q_1 + Q_2,$$

$$Q = 175 + 87.5 = 262.6, \tag{10.7}$$

which is the market equilibrium quantity that would be sold at the price of

$$P = 400 - Q,$$

$$P = 400 - 262.5 = 137.50. \tag{10.8}$$

We can conclude that the Stackelberg equilibrium brought a market output level (262.5) higher than the Cournot (233.33), but under the Stackelberg strategy market price (\$137.50) was lower than it was under Cournot (\$166.67).

Example 10.11

Consider a duopoly facing a demand function $P = 500 - 5Q$ and an identical cost function $TC_1 = 10Q_1$ and $TC_2 = 10Q_2$:

(a) Find the Cournot equilibrium.
(b) Find the Stackelberg equilibrium if firm 1 follows firm 2.
(c) Compare the equilibrium quantities and prices as well as profits between the two models.

Solution:

(a) We start by forming the total revenue function for firm 1:

$$TR_1 = Q_1 P,$$

$$TR_1 = Q_1[500 - 5Q].$$

Since Q is the output for the entire industry and consists of the outputs of both firms Q_1 and Q_2:

$$TR_1 = Q_1[500 - 5(Q_1 + Q_2)],$$

$$TR_1 = 500Q_1 - 5Q_1^2 - 5Q_1 Q_2.$$

Now we can form the profit function (Pr_1), set its first derivative to zero, and solve for Q_1:

$$\text{Pr}_1 = \text{TR}_1 - \text{TC}_1,$$
$$\text{Pr}_1 = 500Q_1 - 5Q_1^2 - 5Q_1Q_2 - 10Q_1,$$
$$\text{Pr}_1 = 100Q_1 - Q_1^2 - Q_1Q_2 - 2Q_1,$$
$$\text{Pr}_1 = 98Q_1 - Q_1^2 - Q_1Q_2,$$
$$\frac{\partial \text{Pr}_1}{\partial Q_1} = 98 - 2Q_1 - Q_2 = 0,$$
$$2Q_1 = 98 - Q_2,$$
$$Q_1 = 49 - \tfrac{1}{2}Q_2. \tag{10.9}$$

Similarly, Q_2 would be equal to a similar value

$$Q_2 = 49 - \tfrac{1}{2}Q_1. \tag{10.10}$$

Solving (10.9) and (10.10) simultaneously, we obtain the value of Q_1:

$$Q_1 = 49 - 0.5(49 - 0.5Q_1),$$
$$Q_1 = 49 - 24.5 - 0.25Q_1,$$
$$Q_1 - 0.25Q_1 = 24.5,$$
$$0.75Q_1 = 24.5,$$
$$Q_1 = 32.67,$$
$$Q_2 = 49 - 0.5(32.67) = 32.67.$$

Industry output:

$$Q = Q_1 + Q_2,$$
$$Q = 32.67 + 32.67 = 65.33.$$

Market price:

$$P = 500 - 5Q$$
$$= 500 - 5(65.33) = \$173.33,$$
$$\text{Pr}_1 = 500Q_1 - 5Q_1^2 - 5Q_1Q_2 - 10Q_1,$$
$$\text{Pr}_1 = 500(32.67) - 5(32.67)^2 - 5(32.67)(32.67) - 10(32.67),$$
$$\text{Pr}_1 = 5335.$$

Pr_2, the profit for the second firm, would be exactly the same as the profit for the first firm:

(b) Since firm 2 is the Stackelberg leader, we form its profit function and factor in the reaction function of the follower $Q_1 = 49 - 0.5Q_2$:

$$Pr_2 = 500Q_2 - 5Q_2^2 - 5Q_2Q_1 - 10Q_2,$$

$$Pr_2 = 500Q_2 - 5Q_2^2 - 5Q_2(49 - 0.5Q_2) - 10Q_2,$$

$$Pr_2 = 500Q_2 - 5Q_2^2 - 245Q_2 + 2.5Q_2^2 - 10Q_2,$$

$$Pr_2 = 245Q_2 - 2.5Q_2^2,$$

$$\frac{\partial Pr_2}{\partial Q_2} = 245 - 5Q_2 = 0,$$

$$5Q_2 = 245,$$

$$Q_2 = 49, \tag{10.11}$$

$$Q_1 = 49 - 0.5(49) = 24.5, \tag{10.12}$$

$$Q = Q_1 + Q_2,$$

$$Q = 49 + 24.5 = 73.5, \tag{10.13}$$

$$P = 500 - 5Q,$$

$$P = 500 - 5(73.5) = \$132.5, \tag{10.14}$$

$$Pr_1 = 500Q_1 - 5Q_1^2 - 5Q_1Q_2 - 10Q_1,$$

$$Pr_1 = 500(24.5) - 5(24.5)^2 - 5(24.5)(49) - 10(24.5),$$

$$Pr_1 = 3001.25,$$

$$Pr_2 = 500Q_2 - 5Q_2^2 - 5Q_2Q_1 - 10Q_2,$$

$$Pr_2 = 500(49) - 5(49)^2 - 5(49)(24.5) - 10(49),$$

$$Pr_2 = 6002.5.$$

(c) By comparison, this example shows that Stackelberg's market output (73.5) is higher than Cournot's market output (65.33), but market price under the Stackelberg model (132.50) is lower than market price under the Cournot model (\$173.33). Also, while the two firms under the Cournot model earn an identical profit of \$5335, the two firms under the Stackelberg model earned different profits. The leading firm (firm 2) earned more (\$6002.50) than the following firm 1, which earned a total of \$3001.25. Market profit (the combined profit of the duopoly) was higher under the Cournot model (\$10,670) than the market profit under the Stackelberg model (\$9003.75).

Bertrand Model   This model was developed and named after the French economist and mathematician Joseph Louis Bertrand in 1883. It is one of the price-setting models of oligopoly as opposed to the output-setting models such as Cournot and Stackelberg models. Bertrand posited that oligopolistic firms make their production decisions independently and simultaneously. Each firm sets its own price and assumes that the prices of rival firms remain unchanged. The market would set the quantity based on consumer demand, and the given prices. Bertrand further assumed that if firms have identical marginal costs and if they produce homogeneous or identical products, any slight cut in the price of any firm may very well lead to a price war. Consumers may significantly shift to the firm that offers a lower price and indirectly forces the rivals to cut their prices to get their customers back. The first firm to cut price may continue price-cutting to maintain the increased demand for its product. The cycle of price-cutting may not stop until prices offered by all firms go down to the level of marginal cost, squeezing profits to zero.

In order to illustrate how an oligopolistic firm relates to rivals when it comes to its profit-maximizing price level, we consider two firms producing differentiated products and having the following demand equations:

$$Q_1 = 20 - 0.4P_1 + 0.2P_2$$

and

$$Q_2 = 20 - 0.4P_2 + 0.2P_1,$$

where P_1 and P_2 are the price levels set by the two firms to maximize profits. Let us further assume, for simplicity, that both firms produce at no cost:

$$TR_1 = P_1 Q_1,$$
$$TR_1 = P_1[20 - 0.4P_1 + 0.2P_2],$$
$$TR_1 = 20P_1 - 0.4P_1^2 + 0.2P_1 P_2.$$

Since TC is zero, profit would be equal to TR:

$$Pr_1 = TR_1 - TC_1,$$
$$Pr_1 = 20P_1 - 0.4P_1^2 + 0.2P_1 P_2.$$

Since the Bertrand model specifies the firm's price as the determinant of the profit-maximizing strategy, we take the first derivative to Pr_1 with respect to price:

$$\frac{\partial Pr_1}{\partial P_1} = 20 - 0.8P_1 + 0.2P_2 = 0,$$
$$20 + 0.2P_2 = 0.8P_1,$$

$$P_1 = 25 + 0.25P_2. \tag{10.15}$$

Similarly, we can obtain P_2 of the other firm as

$$P_2 = 25 + 0.25P_1, \tag{10.16}$$

and we obtain P_1 value by solving Equations (10.15) and (10.16) simultaneously:

$$P_1 = 25 + 0.25(25 + 0.25P_1),$$
$$P_1 = 25 + 6.25 + 0.0625P_1,$$
$$P_1 = 0.0625P_1 = 31.25,$$
$$0.9375P_1 = 31.25,$$
$$P_1 = \frac{31.25}{93.75},$$
$$P_1 = 33.34,$$
$$P_2 = 25 + 0.25(33.34),$$
$$P_2 = 33.34,$$
$$Q_1 = 20 - 0.4(33.34) + 0.2(33.34),$$
$$Q_1 = 13.33,$$
$$Q_2 = 20 - 0.4(33.34) + 0.2(33.34),$$
$$Q_2 = 13.33.$$

The market output (Q) would be

$$Q = Q_1 + Q_2$$
$$= 13.33 + 13.33 = 26.66.$$

Assuming that the output is measured by thousands of units, market production would be 26,664 units shared equally by the two firms that produce 13,332 units each. When sold at the market price of $33.34, this level of output would generate a profit of

$$\mathrm{Pr}_1 = 20P_1 - 0.4P_1^2 + 0.2P_1P_2$$
$$= 20(33.34) - 0.4(33.34)2 + 0.2(33.34)(33.34)$$
$$= 2445.$$

Also,

$$\mathrm{Pr}_2 = 20P_2 - 0.4P_2^2 + 0.2P_2P_1$$
$$= 20(33.34) - 0.4(33.34)2 + 0.2(33.34)(33.34)$$
$$= 2445.$$

Each of the firms would earn $2,445,000 and the market profit would be $4,890,000.

Figure 10.19 shows how the Bertrand equilibrium point is obtained as the intersection point between the price reaction curves of both firms.

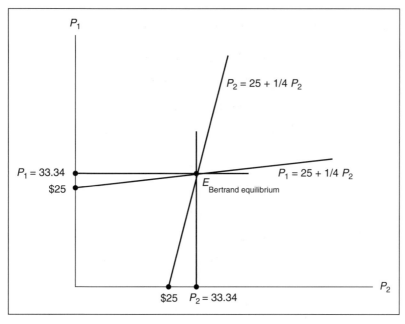

FIGURE 10.19

Example 10.12
Consider a duopoly producing a homogeneous product and facing identical demand and cost functions:

$$Q_1 = 400 - 4P_1 + 2P_2,$$
$$TC_1 = 32Q_1,$$
$$Q_2 = 400 - 4P_2 + 2P_1,$$
$$TC_2 = 32Q_2.$$

Find the Bertrand equilibrium price, output, and profit for each firm.

Solution:

$$TR_1 = P_1Q_1,$$
$$TR_1 = P_1[400 - 4P_1 + 2P_2],$$
$$TR_1 = 400P_1 - 4P_1^2 + 2P_1P_2,$$
$$TC_1 = 32Q_1,$$
$$TC_1 = 32[400 - 4P_1 + 2P_2],$$
$$TC_1 = 12,800 - 128P_1 + 64P_2.$$

Similarly, we can obtain TR$_2$ and TC$_2$ as

$$\text{TR}_2 = 400P_2 - 4P_2^2 + 2P_2P_1,$$
$$\text{TC}_2 = 12,800 - 128P_2 + 64P_1.$$

The profit function for both firms would be

$$\text{Pr}_1 = \text{TR}_1 - \text{TC}_1,$$
$$\text{Pr}_1 = 400P_1 - 4P_1^2 + 2P_1P_2 - 12,800 + 128P_1 - 64P_2,$$
$$\text{Pr}_1 = 528P_1 - 4P_1^2 + 2P_1P_2 - 12,800 - 64P_2,$$
$$\text{Pr}_2 = \text{TR}_2 - \text{TC}_2,$$
$$\text{Pr}_2 = 400P_2 - 4P_2^2 + 2P_2P_1 - 12,800 + 128P_2 + 64P_1,$$
$$\text{Pr}_2 = 528P_2 - 4P_2^2 + 2P_2P_1 - 12,800 - 64P_1,$$
$$\frac{\partial \text{Pr}_1}{\partial P_1} = 528 - 8P_1 + 2P_2 = 0,$$
$$\frac{\partial \text{Pr}_2}{\partial P_2} = 528 - 8P_2 + 2P_1 = 0,$$
$$528 + 2P_2 = 8P_1,$$
$$P_1 = 66 + 0.25P_2, \tag{10.17}$$

$$528 + 2P_1 = 8P_2,$$
$$P_2 = 66 + 0.25P_1. \tag{10.18}$$

Solving Equations (10.17) and (10.18) simultaneously, we get

$$P_1 = 66 + 0.25(66 + 0.25P_1),$$
$$P_1 = 66 + 16.5 + 0.0625P_1,$$
$$P_1 - 0.0625P_1 = 82.5,$$
$$P_1 = 88,$$
$$P_2 = 66 + 0.25(88) = 88,$$
$$Q_1 = 400 - 4P_1 + 2P_2,$$
$$Q_1 = 400 - 4(88) + 2(88),$$
$$Q_1 = 224,$$
$$Q_2 = 400 - 4P_2 + 2P_1,$$
$$Q_2 = 400 - 4(88) + 2(88),$$
$$Q_2 = 224,$$
$$\text{Pr}_1 = 528P_1 - 4P_1^2 + 2P_1P_2 - 12,800 - 64P_2$$

$$= 528(88) - 4(88)^2 + 2(88)(88) - 12,800 - 64(88)$$

$$= 12,544,$$

$$\text{Pr}_2 = 528P_2 - 4P_2^2 + 2P_2P_1 - 12,800 - 64P_1$$

$$= 528(88) - 4(88)^2 + 2(88)(88) - 12,800 - 64(88)$$

$$= 12,544.$$

Sweezy Model   This model of oligopoly behavior was developed by, and named after, Harvard University professor of economics Paul Sweezy in 1939. The purpose was to explain price rigidity in the oligopoly market, where it was observed that prices stayed unchanged for a relatively long time. Sweezy posited that oligopolistic firms get into a race with each other only when a price decrease is initiated by one firm, but would not engage in a similar race when a price increase is initiated. The interpretation is rather simple. When one firm cuts its price, demand shifts significantly towards the product of that firm, causing the other firms to lose their market share. This is enough to make other firms follow the price cut to maintain their customer base. On the other hand, when one firm increases its price, customers shift away from it and there will be no incentive for other firms to follow. However, the decrease in price would not result in a significant increase in demand for the firm that initiates the price cut, simply because other firms quickly match the cut and mitigate the effect. However, in the case of price increase, almost all customers would shift away making the decrease in demand seem very significant for the firm that initiated the increase. This firm would alone carry the burden of the consequences. Because of the little positive effect of the decrease in price, and the large negative effect of the increase in price, oligopolistic firms tend to prefer to keep the prevailing price that results in price rigidity over a relatively long time. Technically, and as is shown in Figure 10.20, this case would be translated into having a kinked demand curve such as *ABC* where the demand is highly elastic for price increase along the segment *AB* (above the kink point *B*, and highly inelastic for price decrease along the segment *BC* (below *B*). This is why the Sweezy model is sometimes called the "Kinked Demand Model."

Following the kinked demand curve, the marginal revenue curve (*ADEFG*) is not a straight line. Reflecting Sweezy's notion that oligopolistic firms would match any price cut but not price increase, the marginal revenue curve would include three segments: (1) *AD*, which corresponds to *AB* segment of the demand curve; (2) *FG*, which corresponds to *BC* segment of the demand curve; and (3) the dashed segment of *DEF*, which represents a region of discontinuity. It is here in this region that Sweezy's equilibrium would occur when the firm's marginal cost is equal to its marginal revenue. In Figure 10.20, MC intersects MR at *E* but it can actually intersect at any point along the discontinuity region and the vertical segment of the marginal revenue. The striped area shows the range in which equilibrium can occur, between MC′ and MC″. If the equilibrium point *E* occurs anywhere on *DF*, there would be no change in the equilibrium quantity and no significant change in the price. Therefore, point *E* would determine the equilibrium output Q_1 that would be sold at the prevailing price (P_1). It is this price that would stay unchanged and rigid for a relatively long period. Only in two cases, the market price (P_1) may change: (1) when the marginal cost MC″ drops below point *F*, the firm would produce more and bring the price below P_1, or (2) when the marginal cost (MC′) rises above point *D*, the firm would cut the output

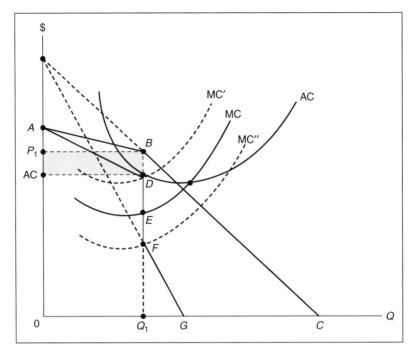

FIGURE 10.20

and be forced to fix the price above (P_1). Since the price stays rigid, the oligopolistic firms would have to find other nonprice ways of competition in order to carve out a good market share. This is why they practically compete on the product quality, services, advertising and other ways to gain consumer loyalty. The oligopolistic firms can gain profits as long as their average cost remains below the price. In Figure 10.20, the average cost is determined when the AC curve crosses the vertical BQ_1 at point D. Since AC is below P_1, the firm would make a profit equal to the shaded area (HBP_1AC), which is the difference between the total revenue (QBP_10) and the total cost (Q_1HAC0).

Example 10.13
Consider the following kinked demand function for a product produced by an oligopolistic firm:

$$Q_1 = 600 - 6P,$$

$$Q_2 = 180 - 1.2P.$$

Given that the firm faces a constant marginal cost of $60.00,

(a) find Sweezy's prevailing price, the firm's output, and how much profit it would make;

(b) find the range of discontinuity in the marginal revenue or the values that marginal cost can take without affecting Sweezy's equilibrium.

Solution:
To get a prevailing price, we equate the two demand functions and solve P:

(a) $600 - 6P = 180 - 1.2P,$
$$4.8P = 420,$$
$$P = \$87.50.$$

The quantity can be obtained from either of the demand functions:

$$Q_1 = 600 - 6P$$
$$= 600 - 6(87.50) = 75 \text{ units},$$
$$Q_2 = 180 - 1.2(87.50) = 75 \text{ units}.$$

To get the profit (Pr), we need to calculate both the total revenue and total cost:

$$\text{TR} = P \cdot Q$$
$$= (87.50)(75) = \$6562.50.$$

Since marginal cost is constant at $60.00, it would be equal to the average cost. Total cost is the average cost times the quantity of output (Q):

$$\text{TC} = AC \cdot Q,$$
$$\text{TC} = (60)(75) = \$4500,$$
$$\text{Pr} = \text{TR} - \text{TC}$$
$$= 6562.50 - 4500 = \$22{,}062.50.$$

(b) Evaluating the marginal revenue of the two demand functions would give us the upper and lower values of the marginal cost, indicating the range in which the marginal cost curve can fluctuate without significantly changing output and price. However, first we have to express the demand functions in terms of price (P):

$$Q_1 = 600 - 6P,$$
$$6P = 600 - Q,$$
$$P = 100 - \tfrac{1}{6}Q,$$
$$\text{TR}_1 = Q \cdot P,$$
$$\text{TR}_1 = Q\left[100 - \tfrac{1}{6}Q\right],$$
$$\text{TR}_1 = 100Q - \tfrac{1}{6}Q^2,$$
$$\text{MR}_1 = \frac{\partial \text{TR}_1}{\partial Q} = 100 - \frac{1}{3}Q, \qquad (10.19)$$

$$Q_2 = 180 - 1.2P,$$

$$1.2P = 180 - Q,$$

$$P = 150 - \tfrac{5}{6}Q,$$

$$TR_2 = Q \cdot P,$$

$$TR_2 = Q \left[150 - \tfrac{5}{6}Q\right],$$

$$TR_2 = 150Q - \tfrac{5}{6}Q^2,$$

$$MR_2 = \frac{\partial TR_2}{\partial Q} = 150 - \frac{5}{3}Q. \qquad (10.20)$$

By evaluating Equations (10.19) and (10.20), we get

$$MR_1 = 100 - \tfrac{1}{3}Q$$

$$= 100 - \tfrac{1}{3}(75) = 75,$$

$$MR_2 = 150 - \tfrac{5}{3}Q,$$

$$= 150 - \tfrac{5}{3}(75) = 25.$$

So, the range of the marginal cost is between $25 and $75 and the current marginal cost is $60 which is somewhere within this range.

SUMMARY

- This is the first chapter in the fourth unit on managerial decisions at the market level. It addresses market structure at the economic atmosphere in which producers and consumers behave, interact, and act to serve their own interests in consideration of free competition and business organization. The categorization of market structure is determined using four criteria: (1) type of product, whether it is homogeneous or differentiated; (2) scope of supply and demand for the product; (3) mobility of inputs; and (4) the information status for producers and consumers. Based on these criteria, market structure is classified into four common markets: (1) perfect competition, (2) monopoly, (3) monopolistic competition, and (4) oligopoly.

- Perfect competition is characterized by a perfectly elastic demand where the demand curve becomes a horizontal line at the price level. Price is determined by the market and the short-run equilibrium is determined where $P = MR = MC$ as long as the price is above the average variable cost. The short-run supply curve for a perfectly competitive firm is the segment of the marginal cost curve above the point of intersection with the average variable cost curve. In the long run, many competitive firms enter the industry as they are completely free to do so, which may eventually squeeze out all the possible profit to be made by any firm. In case some firms incur losses, it would eventually make them leave the industry, and the rest would just manage to break even.

- In a monopoly, one firm in the entire industry dominates the production of a product for which there is usually no close substitute. The demand curve for this product is a normal downward curve with a negative slope. Equilibrium is achieved by the equimarginal principle where MR = MC as long as the market price for the product is higher than the average variable cost. Unlike perfectly competitive firms, a monopoly would earn profit in the long run because it has a hold over the industry and would not allow any entrants into the market.

- In a market of monopolistic competition, the product is differentiated and has many close substitutes. Many firms can enter the industry with no difficulties. The demand for the product is highly elastic and the equimarginal principle is still the name of the game for the best level of output in the short run. In the long run, more and more firms will enter the industry and compete for profits. Eventually, the demand curve for each of these firms would shift left as its market share gets smaller and smaller and they ultimately break even.

- Oligopoly is the market where the product is either homogeneous or differentiated, but there are a few producers in the industry and the entry is possible but usually very difficult for its strict requirements to be satisfied. The extent of domination and concentration of these few firms in the industry has been indexed by the concentration ratio and the Herfindahl–Hirschmann index. Four different models of oligopoly were explained and numerical examples and graphs were provided. The Cournot model assumes that in a duopoly each firm would not change the level of output regardless of what the other one is doing. Each firm would eventually end up producing one-third of the market demand. The Stackelberg model assumes that the oligopolistic firms are interdependent when it comes to the production decisions and that they act as leaders and followers. The Bertrand model is concerned about price decisions among the oligopolistic firms, instead of output size decisions. It assumes that the firms decide on their output independently and simultaneously and that they set their own prices assuming that the other firms in the industry would not change their prices. The last model of oligopoly is the Sweezy model. It explains price rigidity in the oligopolistic market where it has been observed that prices stay unchanged for a relatively long time. The model assumes that firms in the oligopolistic industry compete with each other only when one of them initiates a reduction in price. They compete to reduce their own prices in order to secure their market share. However, such a competition would be pursued when a price increase is initiated.

KEY TERMS

market	market structure	homogeneous product
differential product	perfect competition	price taker
shut-down decision	monopoly	price maker
Lerner index	monopolistic competition	oligopoly
Duopoly	Herfindahl index	concentration ratio
Cournot model	Stackelberg model	Bertrand model
Sweezy model	natural monopoly	monopoly power

LIST OF FORMULAS

- Lerner index:

$$LI = \frac{P - MC}{P} = -\frac{1}{\varepsilon}.$$

- Concentration ratio:

$$CR_n = \frac{\sum\limits_{i=1}^{n} s_i}{s_n} \times 100.$$

- Herfindahl–Hirschmann index:

$$HHI = \sum_{i=1}^{n} \left[\frac{ms_i}{ms_n} \times 100 \right]^2.$$

EXERCISES

1. Construct a table to compare the major characteristics of all four types of market structures: perfect competition, monopoly, monopolistic competition, and oligopoly.

2. Explain the circumstances under which a competitive firm would rather shut down. Support your explanation with a graph.

3. Compare the four types of markets–perfect competition, monopoly, monopolistic competition, and oligopoly—in relation to their profit-earning status in the long run.

4.
   (a) What is the Lerner index? What is it meant for and how significant is it to understand the business market?
   (b) What is the Hefindahl index? What is it meant for and how significant is it to understand the business market?

5. Make a table to compare the major assumptions and ideas of the four models of oligopoly: Cournot, Stackelberg, Bertrand, and Sweezy.

6. A competitive firm sells its product for $50.00. If it has the following cost function, what would be its equilibrium output and how much profit can it make?

$$TC = 5000 + 10Q + 0.05Q^2.$$

7. The following are the demand and supply functions for a product produced by an industry of perfect competition that includes 100 firms:

$$Q_d = 6600 - 12P,$$
$$Q_s = 1600 + 13P_1.$$

   (a) What would be the market price for the product and the equilibrium output for the industry?
   (b) Calculate the marginal cost for each firm in the industry.
   (c) What would be the market share for each firm in the industry?

8. A competitive firm has the following total cost (TC) function:

$$TC = 2400 + 225Q - 36Q^2 + 6Q^3.$$

Calculate at what point will this firm make a decision to shut down?

9. If a monopolistic firm has the following variable cost function:

$$VC = 300 + 15Q + \frac{Q^2}{108}.$$

   (a) What would be its optimum output level if the fixed cost is _____.
   (b) What would be its maximum profit?

10. If there is a duopoly with a demand function for their product such as

$$Q = 100 - \frac{P}{15},$$

and a cost function such as TC $= 30Q$, calculate both the Cournot and the Stackelberg equilibriums and find out how much profits the firms can make according to each model.

11

PRICING DECISIONS AND PRACTICES

11.1 BASICS OF PRICE SETTING

There are some simple and straightforward rules for businesses to set their product prices in order to achieve their major goal of profit maximization. In a perfectly competitive market, all businesses are price takers, economic information is open and free, and the demand curve is a horizontal line reflecting the total revenue. This implies that the demand is set initially at the price level and that the price (P) is the same as the marginal revenue (MR): $P = \text{MR}$. Going by the equimarginal rule to reach the equilibrium that assures the maximum profit, this relation leads to the fact that price is to be equal to the marginal revenue, and marginal cost (MC) as well:

$$P = \text{MR} = \text{MC}.$$

In other imperfectly competitive markets such as monopoly, monopolistic competition, and oligopoly, price is a function of quantity of product, and demand is characterized by a down-sloping curve as opposed to the horizontal line under perfect competition. The marginal revenue and marginal cost still have to be equal as a condition for the equilibrium level of price and output for the maximization of profit. However, their relationship to price would not remain a simple equality as it is in the perfect competition. We can follow this relation in the following way:

$$P = f(Q),$$

$$P \cdot Q = \text{TR},$$

Managerial Economics: A Mathematical Approach, First Edition. M. J. Alhabeeb and L. Joe Moffitt.
© 2013 John Wiley & Sons, Inc. Published 2013 by John Wiley & Sons, Inc.

$$\text{MR} = \frac{\partial \text{TR}}{\partial Q} = \frac{\partial [P \cdot Q]}{\partial Q},$$

$$\text{MR} = P + Q \left[\frac{\partial P}{\partial Q} \right].$$

Multiplying the right-hand side of $1 = P/P$, we get

$$\text{MR} = P \left[\frac{P}{P} \right] + \left[\frac{P}{P} \right] \left[\frac{Q \partial P}{\partial P} \right],$$

$$\text{MR} = P + P \left[\frac{Q}{P} \cdot \frac{\partial P}{\partial Q} \right].$$

Recalling that the term within the brackets is the inverse of the price elasticity of demand ($\varepsilon = \partial Q / \partial P \times P/Q$), we can rewrite the MR equation as

$$\text{MR} = P + P \left[\frac{1}{\varepsilon} \right]$$

or

$$\text{MR} = P \left[1 + \frac{1}{\varepsilon} \right].$$

Equating marginal revenue to marginal cost for equilibrium yields

$$\text{MC} = P \left[1 + \frac{1}{\varepsilon} \right],$$

which means that, for a firm to maximize its profit, it must set the price of its product equal to its marginal cost divided by $(1 + 1/\varepsilon)$, where ε is the point elasticity of demand for that product:

$$P = \frac{\text{MC}}{1 + \dfrac{1}{\varepsilon}}.$$

Firms can set up their market price by considering a **markup** over either marginal cost or purchase price. Both ways of marking up aim at maximizing profit, which is the ultimate objective.

11.2 THE MARKUP RULE

When a firm can estimate the price elasticity of demand for its product, it can simply calculate a markup percentage over its marginal cost. This is called the **optimal markup** on cost and is determined as explained below.

If we calculate the profit margin, which is the difference between price and marginal cost $(P - MC)$ and express it in relation to the marginal cost itself, we obtain what is called the markup on cost (MupC):

$$\text{MupC} = \frac{P - MC}{MC},$$

$$P - MC = (\text{MupC})(MC),$$

$$P = (\text{MupC})(MC) + MC,$$

$$P = MC[\text{MupC} + 1]. \tag{11.1}$$

Recall that price can be expressed in terms of marginal cost and ε $(P = MC/(1 + 1/\varepsilon))$:

$$\frac{MC}{1 + \dfrac{1}{\varepsilon}} = MC[\text{MupC} + 1].$$

Dividing by MC, we get

$$\frac{MC}{1 + \dfrac{1}{\varepsilon}} - 1 = \text{MupC},$$

$$\text{MupC} = -\frac{1}{\varepsilon + 1}, \tag{11.2}$$

which is the optimal markup on cost.

Note that the firm's marginal cost is assumed to be constant at the standard level of output (70–80% of capacity). It implies that the marginal cost is equal to what is called the fully allocated average cost (FAAC):

$$\text{FAAC} = AVC + AOC,$$

where the FAAC is the summation of the firm's estimated average variable cost (AVC) and the average overhead cost (AOC). In reality, firms do not have accurate information on the marginal cost when they have to price their product. So, practically, they find the easiest way to set the profit-maximizing price. They can estimate the variable and fixed costs per unit and combine them to represent the FAAC. They can then replace MC in Equation (11.1) with

$$P = \text{FAAC}[\text{MupC} + 1]. \tag{11.3}$$

Example 11.1
The total variable cost (TVC) for a product is estimated at $3000 and the total overhead cost is $1500. Given that the firm's standard output is 300 units, what would be the price of the product if the firm follows the 32% markup policy?

Solution:

$$AVC = \frac{TVC}{Q} = \frac{3000}{300} = 10,$$

$$AOC = \frac{TOC}{Q} = \frac{1500}{300} = 5,$$

$$FAAC = AVC + AOC$$

$$= 10 + 5 = 15,$$

$$P = FAAC \, [MupC + 1]$$

$$= 15[0.32 + 1] = \$19.80.$$

So, the product that costs \$15 would be priced at \$19.80. This is a markup of 32% as it is confirmed by dividing the profit margin by the cost:

$$\frac{P - FAAC}{FAAC} = \frac{19.80 - 15}{15} = 0.32.$$

However, the markup can also be based on price instead of marginal cost. In this case, the profit margin $(P - MC)$ would be expressed based on how it is related to the price so that the markup would be considered the markup on price (MupP):

$$MupP = \frac{P - MC}{P}.$$

As for expressing the markup in terms of price elasticity of demand, let us recall the marginal cost formula in terms of price and elasticity:

$$MC = P\left[1 + \frac{1}{\varepsilon}\right]$$

$$= P + \frac{P}{\varepsilon}.$$

$$-\frac{P}{\varepsilon} = P - MC.$$

Dividing by P, we get

$$\frac{P - MC}{P} = -\frac{1}{\varepsilon},$$

$$MupP = -\frac{1}{\varepsilon}, \tag{11.4}$$

which is called the optimal markup on price. It should be noted that both markup on cost and markup on price have negative relationships with the elasticity of demand. The higher the elasticity, the lower the markup percentage; and the lower the elasticity, the higher the markup percentage.

Example 11.2
Suppose that a firm has estimated the FAAC of its product as $65, how much would the
market price be if the firm depends on its estimated elasticity of –3.59 of a similar product?

Solution:
We use the markup-on-cost formula:

$$\text{MupC} = -\frac{1}{\varepsilon + 1}$$

$$= -\frac{1}{-3.59 + 1} = 38.6\%,$$

$$P = \text{FAAC}[\text{MupC} + 1]$$

$$= 65[0.386 + 1] = \$90.$$

11.3 MULTIPRODUCT PRICING STRATEGIES

Most firms do not produce only a single product. They usually produce multiple products
that would naturally be related as either substitutes, in the case of producing different models
of the same products, or complements, in the case of producing the necessary accessories of
the main produce. Let us take, for example, the production of personal computers nowadays.
We all know that computers are produced in many models, styles, and sizes. They can also
be produced separately, for example, the screens, keyboards, modems, speakers, extra hard
drives, and more components that serve as complements to the main unit. There are also
other important complements such as the software and the technical service. This requires
the producing company to pay special attention to its pricing strategies for all these units,
simply because their demand is inextricably interrelated. For example, if the firm decides
to reduce the price of computer model A, then the demand will increase not only for model
A but also for all other parts related to this model. In addition, consumers are expected
to shift away from the similar model C produced by the same company. The decrease
in demand for model C may cause some loss, and the increase in demand for model A
may cause increase in the prices of inputs to model A. This is why all actions have to be
coordinated to ensure a healthy balance that would eventually culminate in a positive net
profit for the firm. This would imply that in the first-order condition for profit maximization,
the total revenue for each product appears along with the total revenue for the other
produce:

$$\frac{\partial \text{Pr}}{\partial Q_A} = \frac{\partial \text{TR}_A}{\partial Q_A} + \frac{\partial \text{TR}_C}{\partial Q_A} - \frac{\partial \text{TC}_A}{\partial Q_A} = 0,$$

$$\frac{\partial \text{Pr}}{\partial Q_C} = \frac{\partial \text{TR}_C}{\partial Q_C} + \frac{\partial \text{TR}_A}{\partial Q_C} - \frac{\partial \text{TC}_C}{\partial Q_C} = 0,$$

or

$$\text{MR}_A = \frac{\partial \text{TR}_A}{\partial Q_A} + \frac{\partial \text{TC}_C}{\partial Q_A} = \text{MC}_A, \tag{11.5}$$

$$\text{MR}_C = \frac{\partial \text{TR}_C}{\partial Q_C} + \frac{\partial \text{TR}_A}{\partial Q_C} = \text{MC}_C. \tag{11.6}$$

This means that the profit-maximizing production requires the firm to have its marginal cost equal to not only the change in total revenue of one product but also the change combined with the change in total revenue of the other product. The type of relationship between the two products is determined by the sign of the second term of the combined units in Equations (11.5) and (11.6), namely, if $\partial TR_C/\partial Q_A$ or $\partial TR_A/\partial Q_C$ is positive, the two products are complements, and if the signs are negative, the two products are substitutes. This is because these terms stand for

- the impact on product C's revenue caused by selling an additional unit of product A, in the case of $\partial TR_C/\partial Q_A$;
- the impact on product A's revenue caused by selling an additional unit of product C, in the case of $\partial TR_A/\partial Q_C$.

11.4 JOINT PRODUCTS WITH INDEPENDENT DEMANDS

11.4.1 Product Set of Fixed Proportions

Often firms produce products that are related to each other and share the same set of inputs. In many cases, these products are defined as the pair of a main product and a by-product. Although each has its own demand in the market, they share the same cost function. The classic example of that is the production of beef and hide, where each cow has one carcass and one skin. This is the case of joint products with fixed proportions. As shown in Figure 11.1, products like beef and hide have their independent demand curves, such as D_1 and

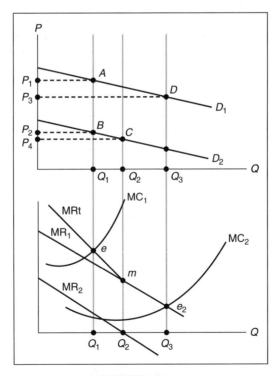

FIGURE 11.1

D_2, respectively, in the upper panel. Since these products are produced in sets of two with fixed proportions, they have their marginal revenue curves MR_1 and MR_2 in the lower panel where combined marginal revenues of the two products form the total marginal revenue (MR_t) as the vertical summation of the two. Note that MR_t merges with MR_1 at point m because MR_2 has reached zero in Q_2 and would be negative beyond that. The optimal output and price are determined when the joint marginal cost (MC_1) crosses the MR_t at point e. The equilibrium output level of the packages of beef and hide is determined at Q_1, which would lead to the prices of the two products as determined by point A on the beef demand curve D_1 and point B on the hide demand curve D_2 in the upper panel. This optimal output level would be sold at P_1 for beef and P_2 for hide (Figure 11.1).

Note that the MR_t would equal the beef marginal revenue (MR_1) to the right of point m because the hide marginal revenue MR_2 becomes irrelevant beyond Q_2. So, if the marginal cost curve crosses the MR_t curve beyond point m, like in the case of MC_2, the equilibrium point would be e_2 and the optimal output level would be Q_3 leading to selling the beef at P_3 as determined from point D on D_1. However, since the marginal revenue for hide is negative at this stage, the firm would have no choice but to offer only Q_2 of hide at P_4 as determined from point C on D_2, and would have to destroy the excess amount of hide, which is equal to $(Q_3 - Q_2)$.

Example 11.3

Two products, x and y, are produced jointly. Find the profit-maximizing price of each and the total profit if their demand functions and the cost function are

$$Q_x = 60 - 3P_x,$$

$$Q_y = 100 - 4P_y,$$

$$TC = 250 + 8Q + 0.25Q^2.$$

Solution:

First, we express the demand functions in terms of prices and obtain the total and marginal revenue for each:

$$P_x = 20 - \frac{1}{3}Q_x,$$

$$P_y = 25 - \frac{1}{4}Q_y,$$

$$TR_x = Q_x\left[20 - \frac{1}{3}Q_x\right],$$

$$TR_x = 20Q_x - \frac{1}{3}Q_x^2,$$

$$MR_x = \frac{\partial TR_x}{\partial Q_x} = 20 - \frac{2}{3}Q_x,$$

$$TR_y = Q_y \left[25 - \frac{1}{4}Q_y \right],$$

$$TR_y = 25Q_y - \frac{1}{4}Q_y^2,$$

$$MR_y = \frac{\partial TR_y}{\partial Q_y} = 25 - \frac{1}{2}Q_y,$$

$$MR_t = MR_x \ z = MR_y,$$

$$MR_t = 20 - \frac{2}{3}Q_x + 25 - \frac{1}{2}Q_y,$$

$$MR_t = 45 - \frac{7}{6}Q,$$

$$MC = \frac{\partial TC}{\partial Q} = 8 + \frac{1}{2}Q,$$

$$MR_t = MC,$$

$$45 - \frac{7}{6}Q = 8 + \frac{1}{2}Q,$$

$$37 = \frac{9}{6}Q,$$

$$24.67 = Q, \text{ the equilibrium output of the two-product package,}$$

$$P_x = 20 - \frac{1}{3}(24.67) = 11.78, \ m \text{ price of product } x,$$

$$P_y = 25 - \frac{1}{4}(24.67) = 18.83, \text{ price of product } y,$$

$$TR_t = TR_x + TR_y,$$

$$TR_t = 20Q_x - \frac{1}{3}Q_x^2 + 25Q_y - \frac{1}{4}Q_y^2,$$

$$TR_t = P_x Q_x + P_y Q_y$$

$$= (11.78)(24.67) + (18.83)(24.67) = 755,$$

$$TC = 250 + 8(24.67) + 25(24.67)^2 = 599,$$

$$Pr = TR_t - TC$$

$$= 755 - 599 = 156.$$

11.4.2 Product Set of Variable Proportions

This is a more common case than the joint products with fixed proportions. The majority of firms produce products that share the same sources of inputs and they are most likely to be substitutes than complements. This leads to the variability in proportions for they compete to employ the largest share of the firm's available resources. A tradeoff must occur where producing more of product x would necessitate producing less of product y. This tradeoff is reflected in the firm's concave isocosts such as $ISCOS_1$, $ISCOS_2$, and $ISCOS_3$ in Figure 11.2. Each of these isocosts would represent a level of total cost, which stays fixed at any point on the curve.

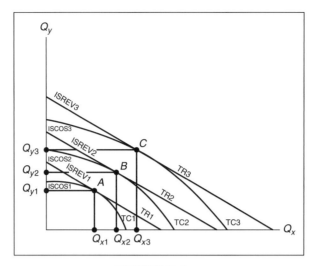

FIGURE 11.2

As for the total revenue from the two products, x and y, the isorevenue lines such as ISREV_1, ISREV_2, and ISREV_3 represent the revenues that stay fixed along the lines. A firm would optimize at points A, B, and C when it can produce the optimal combination of outputs of the two products, reaping the highest possible revenue from both at the lowest possible cost. For example, at a given cost of TC_2, the firm would produce Q_{x2} and Q_{y2} and collect a total revenue of TR_2. The equilibrium point would be the point of tangency (B) between ISCOS_2 and ISREV_2.

Example 11.4

A company produces two joint products using the same production facility. Find the equilibrium quantities and prices of both products if the demand functions and total cost functions are expressed as

$$P_x = 500 - 25Q_x,$$
$$P_y = 100 - 10Q_y,$$
$$\text{TC} = Q_x^2 + Q_x Q_y + 2Q_y^2 + 5,$$
$$\text{TR}_x = Q_x[500 - 25Q_x],$$
$$\text{TR}_x = 500Qx - 25Q_x^2,$$
$$\text{TR}_y = Q_y[100 - 10Q_y],$$
$$\text{TR}_y = 100Q_y - 10Q_y^2,$$
$$\text{Pr} = \text{TR}_x + \text{TR}_y - \text{TC},$$
$$\text{Pr} = 500Q_x - 25Q_x^2 + 100Q_y - 10Q_y^2 - Q_x^2 - Q_x Q_y - 2Q_y^2 - 5,$$
$$\text{Pr} = 500Q_x - 26Q_x^2 + 100Q_y - 12Q_y^2 - Q_x Q_y,$$

$$\frac{\partial \text{Pr}}{\partial Q_x} = 500 - 52Q_x - Q_y = 0,$$

$$\frac{\partial \text{Pr}}{\partial Q_y} = 100 - 24Q_y - Q_x = 0.$$

Solution:

Solving the first-order condition (FOC) simultaneously, we get

$$500 = 52Q_x + Q_y, \tag{11.7}$$

$$100 = 24Q_y + Q_x. \tag{11.8}$$

From (11.8),

$$Q_x = 100 - 24Q_y.$$

Substitute in (11.7):

$$Q_y = 500 - 52(100 - 24Q_y),$$
$$Q_y = 500 - 5200 + 1248Q_y,$$
$$1247Q_y = 4700,$$
$$Q_y = 3.77,$$
$$Q_x = 100 - 24(3.77) = 9.52,$$
$$P_x = 500 - 25(9.52) = 262,$$
$$P_y = 100 - 10(3.77) = 62.30,$$
$$\text{Pr} = 500(9.52) - 26(9.52)^2 + 100(3.77) - 12(3.77)^2 - (9.52)(3.77) - 5$$
$$= 165.55.$$

11.5   TRANSFER PRICING

The expansion of the industry and the rise of giant multidivision firms that structured its operations on the vertical production basis created a considerable conflict in the pricing system among the subsidiaries and the parent company. If we take, for example, the auto industry, we would find that any auto maker has many divisions and subdivisions not only to produce lines of products but also to produce components of the **final product** that would be transferred to other plants for assembly. The industrial system where the output of one plant becomes an input in another plant until the final product is assembled is called the vertical integration system. If each plant and each division operates under the profit-maximizing principle, the final product and the parent company may not end up having an optimal output and price and may not be collecting any profit for the real potential of increasing the cost toward the end in a way that cannot be exceeded by the revenues from the final product. **Transfer pricing** refers to the way of pricing the intermediate products that would be moved to other plants as inputs and would ultimately lead to the final product. The optimal transfer pricing would face one of the three possibilities: (1) when the **intermediate product** cannot be sold in another external market; (2) when it can be sold in a competitive market; and (3) when it can be sold in a noncompetitive market. Figure 11.3 shows that MC is the vertical summation of two marginal costs: MC_i, which is the marginal cost of the intermediate product, and MC_f, which is the marginal cost of the final product. It is the intersection between this collective MC and the marginal revenue of the final product MR_f at e, which would determine the profit-maximizing output level Q_e. This level of production is sold by P_e as it is determined by point A on the market demand for the final product (D_f). Consistent with output level Q_e, point B is the equilibrium point for the intermediate product that sets the price of the intermediate product as input at P_t, allowing a room as wide as ($P_e - P_t$) for the final product to reap the revenue that maximizes the profits. The conclusion is that point B would set the rule that in the case of no external market for the intermediate product, the marginal cost of that intermediate product (MC_i) would become the optimal transfer price (P_t). However, we can contemplate the output level of the intermediate product that is determined at B. If it is more than Q_e, the final product plant will take what it needs and let the rest be sold to other plants in an external market. If, on the other hand, the output of the intermediate product turns out less than Q_e, the final product plant will seek the shortage in an external market. The possibility of involving an external market for the intermediate product can be of two kinds: a perfectly competitive market and an imperfectly competitive market.

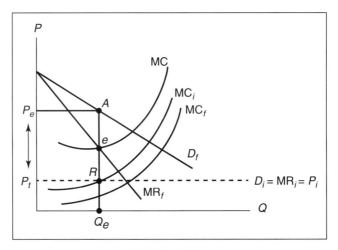

FIGURE 11.3

11.5.1   The Intermediate Product in a Perfectly Competitive Market

Figure 11.4 shows the case in which an excess output of the intermediate product is sold in the external market after the final product firm absorbed the amount it needs.

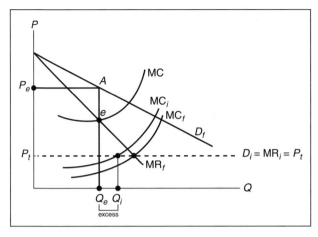

FIGURE 11.4

It is shown in this figure that the intermediate product firm faces lower marginal cost (MC_i) than it faced before, which was the reason to increase output from Q_e to Q_i. Since the final product firm still needs only Q_e, the difference ($Q_i - Q_e$) would be sold at the competitive market where the price (P_t) is determined by the horizontal demand curve D_i which is equal to the marginal revenue (MR_i) and marginal cost (MC_i). Considering its need of the intermediate product (Q_e), the final product firm would still sell its final product output, which is equal to Q_e at the same price P_e, which is determined by the market demand curve D_f, according to point A. The equilibrium point (e) that determined Q_e remains unchanged.

Example 11.5

Consider a vertical integration firm with the following demand function and total cost function:

$$Q = 100,000 - 2000P,$$

$$TC = 156,250 + 12.5Q + 0.00075Q^2.$$

1. Find the equilibrium output, price, and profit.
2. Assuming that there is no external market for the intermediate product, find the transfer price of the intermediate product if the total cost functions of the intermediate and final products were given by

$$TC_i = 125,000 + 10Q + 0.0005Q^2,$$

$$TC_f = 31,250 + 2.5Q + 0.00025Q^2.$$

3. Suppose that there is a perfectly competitive market for a very close substitute to the intermediate product, and suppose further that venders can provide the final product plant with unlimited supply of that product substitute at a competitive price of $17.50. What would happen to the transfer price and the company's profits?

4. Suppose that the intermediate product company found an unlimited demand of its product abroad and that it can sell for $40.00 per unit. What would be the effects on the final product company in terms of its optimal output, price, and profits?

Solution:

1. First, we express the demand function in terms of price:

$$Q = 100{,}000 - 2000P,$$

$$2000P = 100{,}000 - Q,$$

$$P = 50 - 0.0005Q,$$

$$\text{TR} = Q \cdot P,$$

$$\text{TR} = Q[50 - 0.0005Q],$$

$$\text{TR} = 50Q - 0.0005Q^2,$$

$$\text{MR} = \frac{\partial \text{TR}}{\partial Q} = 50 - 0.001Q,$$

$$\text{TC} = 156{,}250 + 12.5Q + 0.00075Q^2.$$

$$\text{MC} = \frac{\partial \text{TC}}{\partial Q} = 12.5 - 0.0015Q,$$

$$\text{MR} = \text{MC},$$

$$50 - 0.001Q = 12.5 + 0.0015Q,$$

$$0.0025Q = 37.5,$$

$$Q = \frac{37.5}{0.0025} = 15{,}000 \text{ equilibrium output,}$$

$$P = 50 - 0.0005(15{,}000) = \$42.50 \text{ equilibrium price,}$$

$$\text{Pr} = \text{TR} - \text{TC}$$

$$= 50Q - 0.0005Q^2 - 156{,}250 - 12.5Q - 0.00075Q^2$$

$$= 37.5Q - 0.00125Q^2 - 156{,}250$$

$$= 37.5(15{,}000) - 0.00125(15{,}000)^2 - 156{,}250$$

$$= 125{,}000.$$

2. The marginal cost MC is the vertical summation of the marginal cost of the intermediate product (MC_i) and the marginal cost of the final product (MC_f):

$$\text{MC}_i = \frac{\partial \text{TC}_i}{\partial Q} = 10 + 0.001Q,$$

$$\text{MC}_f = \frac{\partial \text{TC}_f}{\partial Q} = 2.5 + 0.0005Q,$$

$$MR = MC = MC_i + MC_f,$$

$$50 - 0.001Q = 10 + 0.001Q + 2.5 + 0.0005Q,$$

$$37.5 = 0.0025Q,$$

$$Q = 15,000.$$

This means that the optimal level of output remains the same. The transfer price (P_t) under the assumption of no external market would be equal to the marginal cost (MC_i) at the optimal level of output:

$$P_t = MC_i$$

$$= 10 + 0.001Q$$

$$= 10 + 0.001(15,000) = \$25.$$

3. The transfer price in this case will no longer be $25. It will be the market price of $17.50. In this case, we can find the profit-maximizing output for the final product company:

$$MR = MC_f + P_t,$$

$$50 - 0.001Q = 2.5 + 0.0005Q + 17.50,$$

$$30 = 0.0015Q,$$

$$Q = 20,000.$$

However, the intermediate product plant can only offer a certain amount of the product at this market price:

$$MC_i = P_t,$$

$$10 + 0.001Q = 17.50,$$

$$0.001Q = 7.50,$$

$$Q = 7500.$$

Here, the final product company can take 7500 units from the intermediate product plant and buy the rest $(20,000 - 7500 = 12,500)$ from other venders. The price of the final product will be

$$P = 50 - 0.0005Q$$

$$= 50 - 0.0005(20,000)$$

$$= 40.$$

The total cost to the final product company will be

$$TC = TC_i + TC_f + TC_m,$$

where TC_m is the cost of supply from the external market, which is equal to $P_t Q_m$:

$$TC_i = 125{,}000 + 10Q + 0.0005Q^2$$
$$= 125{,}000 + 10(7500) + 0.0005(7500)^2$$
$$= 228{,}125,$$
$$TC_f = 31{,}250 + 2.5Q + 0.00025Q^2$$
$$= 31{,}250 + 2.5(20{,}000) + 0.00025(20{,}000)^2$$
$$= 181{,}250,$$
$$TC_m = P_t Q_m$$
$$= (17.50)(12{,}500) = 218{,}750,$$
$$TC = 228{,}125 + 181{,}250 + 218{,}750 = 628{,}125,$$
$$TR = 50Q - 0.0005Q^2$$
$$= 50(20{,}000) - 0.0005(20{,}000)^2 = 800{,}000,$$
$$Pr = TR - TC$$
$$= 800{,}000 - 628{,}125 = 171{,}875.$$

The impact of the existence of the competitive external market is positively felt for both—the company, which earned \$46,875 more profits (171,875 – 125,000) or 37.5% more profits, and the general consumers who enjoyed a lower price of the final product (\$40 instead of \$42.50).

4. The output for the final product company would be obtained based on the new price for the intermediate product:

$$MR = MC_f + P_t,$$
$$50 - 0.001Q = 2.5 + 0.0005Q + 40,$$
$$75 = 0.0015Q,$$
$$Q = 5000 \text{ units},$$
$$P = 50 - 0.005Q,$$
$$P = 50 - 0.0005(5000) = \$47.50.$$

The intermediate product company will be able to produce

$$MC_i = Pt,$$
$$10 + 0.001Q = 40,$$
$$0.001Q = 30,$$
$$Q = 30{,}000 \text{ units}.$$

So, an output of 30,000 units will be split between 5000 units for the domestic need to the final product plant and 25,000 units to be sold abroad.

The profit for the final product company will be determined by the difference between its combined revenue and combined cost:

$$Pr = TR - TC,$$

$$TR = Local\ TR + Abroad\ TR,$$

$$Local\ TR = 50Q - 0.005Q^2$$

$$= 50(5000) - 0.0005(5000)^2$$

$$= 237,500,$$

$$Abroad\ TR = P \cdot Q$$

$$= (40)(25,000)$$

$$= 1,000,000,$$

$$TC = TC_i + TC_f,$$

$$TC_i = 125,000 + 10Q + 0.0005Q^2$$

$$= 125,000 + 10(30,000) + 0.0005(30,000)^2 = 875,000,$$

$$TC_f = 31,250 + 2.5Q + 0.00025Q^2$$

$$= 31,250 + 2.5(5,000) + 0.00025(5,000)^2 = 50,000,$$

$$Pr = TR - TC$$

$$= (237,500 + 1,000,000) - (875,000 + 50,000)$$

$$= 312,500.$$

11.5.2   The Intermediate Product in an Imperfectly Competitive Market

The second possibility is that the intermediate product would be sold at an imperfectly competitive market after satisfying the need of the final product plant. Figure 11.5 shows both the negatively sloped demand and marginal revenue curves D_i and MR_i of the intermediate product in such a market. The effective marginal revenue (EMR) is the horizontal sum of the marginal revenue of the intermediate production in both the final product plant and the external market. It is this marginal revenue (EMR) that has to be equal to the marginal cost (MC) in order for the company to maximize its profit at e, producing an optimal level of output Q_e. This total optimal output would include the amount needed for the final product plant (Q_f) and the amount that would be sold in the external market (Q_m). Q_f would be sold at the transfer price P_t as determined by point A on MR_f, and Q_m would be sold at price P_m as determined by point B on D_i. The transfer price P_t would be equal to the marginal cost of producing the intermediate product ($P_t = MC_i$).

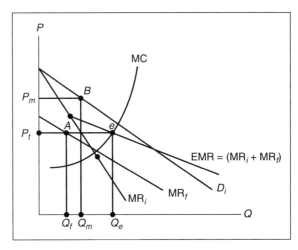

FIGURE 11.5

11.6   PRICING STRATEGIES AND PRACTICES

In addition to what has been addressed about the main concepts and practices of pricing, such as the markup and transfer prices, there are many other concepts and practices adopted by many firms, which are as follows:

- *Peak and off-peak pricing*: This refers to the pricing policies that impose different seasonal or intertemporal prices of products and services that are based on time-related cost differences such as air fares, lodging, and electricity, which have different prices in peak time and in off-peak time. It signifies charging higher prices when the demand of the product or services is high and the production capacity is near-fully or fully used, and charging lower prices when the demand goes down and production capacity has a breather. This is the case of traveling around holidays and electricity prices in core seasons of hot and cold weather.

- *Tying and bundling pricing*: This method of pricing is related to the business practice of requiring consumers to buy a product or service as an attachment to another product or service, in other words, pushing a consumer to buy two products instead of one. Examples are the case of buying specific batteries with a device, bags with vacuum machines, software with computers, and alike. Sometimes businesses justify that for abiding by the technical specifications or insuring proper function and better performance of what they sell. However, in a free market system these practices are illegal if they are done purely for profits for they seriously impede consumer's free choice. **Bundling** is slightly different from tying as pricing practice. The difference is that in bundling, two or more products or services are packaged together, which requires one price instead of separate prices for separate products. The classic example for commodity bundling is a full vacation package that includes transportation, lodging, food, and entertainment, all lumped in one price for all.

- *Two-part tariff pricing*: This is where consumers pay two different prices for the same product or service. Businesses make an artificial breakup in the sold commodity to justify charging two prices. An example of that is the fitness club that requires you to pay a membership fee first just to get into the facility and then pay separately for any activity you choose. A better example is the amusement park that would require you to pay for a ticket first and then pay separately for any ride or activity you choose inside the park. A cell phone service could also be broken into fees to have the service, or maybe to have limited allowances, and separate fees beyond that for any calling or texting or Internet service you use.

- *Skimming pricing*: This pricing practice refers to charging an initial high price for a product or service for a while, after which the price tapers down gradually. It often occurs when a product or service is introduced for the first time, or their demand is unstable or cannot be estimated. Another reason for firms to practice this pricing policy is when their production capacity is limited. If any or all of these reasons loses its justification, prices would be lowered. That happens when other competitors enter the industry and offer more substitutes to the product, when the firm's capacity is expanded and improved, and when the demand for the product picks up and becomes predictable. All of these reasons would push for lowering the initial high price.

- *Prestige pricing*: This refers to consumer-induced significantly high price for a product or service mainly because its brand or other nonquality aspects. It is to answer to some consumer's snob appeal more than any other rational reason. This is when wealthy consumers would love to pay $100,000 for a car for which they can easily find a better substitute for one-third of the price, or when they pay 20 times more to stay in a hotel for which a better substitute can be found for one-fifth of the charge. Prestige price is a very high price in a very special market for very specific consumers who derive their satisfaction not from the quality characteristics of the product but from being unique in buying it such as in the case of buying historical antiques or jewelry items.

- *Competitor's matching pricing*: This is a policy that allows a firm to claim that it would match any price by any competitor that is lower than its own, already low, price. It is a smart and proven to be a successful strategy to attract consumers and give them the confidence to trust the claim. Experience has shown that on most parts, the vast majority of consumers would not take the time to investigate and search for a lower price, although a small negligible percentage of consumers do and win a lower price. This strategy also discourages competitors from going below the advertised price of that firm announcing the match, which helps eliminate the possibilities of undercutting an already low price.

- *Higher value pricing*: This strategy seeks to spread a good intention and better consumer serving in order to gain consumer trust and loyalty and carve out larger market share. It is still within the free and fair competition. Some products are redesigned, repackaged, and improved over the usual version, but all those positive results do not come with any higher price for consumers. Previous prices may stay for much improved product or they can go even lower. A classic example of that is the fast-food restaurants race over the value meals that would really offer a much higher value to consumers as compared to the price paid.

- *Target pricing*: This is also called price lining. It refers to setting a price target first and then having the product that would be priced. It is reversing the usual order where normally the product would determine the price, not the other way around. The best example is the traditional strategy of the automakers to classify their cars to fit the socioeconomic classes of consumers. There is the high class, the middle class, and the lower class. A certain price may be set first before a certain line of Chrysler, for example, is tailored to fit into that price.

- **Penetration and dumping pricing**: This refers to charging a product or service price that is noticeably below the normal prevailing market price of that product or service. It particularly happens when a new corner is just entering an industry and seeking to an immediate foothold. Some severe cases of this strategy is known as predatory dumping where a foreign firm lowers its prices way below the domestic industry in an attempt to beat the existing firms by pulling in most of the market share.

- **Psychological pricing**: This is the most common method of marketing. It is to play on the psychology of consumers by creating the illusion that a product price is being significantly lower while in reality it might not. Sometimes even the knowledgeable consumers are lured by some of these practices. The most common and old practice is to use the 99 cent or the fraction of a cent such as the $9.99 instead of $10, or in the case of gas prices, writing the fractions of a cent as in $3.59^9/_{10}$. Some forms of buy-one-get-one-free offers may be included in this ploy too, when the original price is marked up before applying the sale. Suppose that the normal price of a medium pizza is $12.00. It would be nominally raised to $16.00 and then the buy one get one free sale is applied. The consumer gets two pizzas for $16.00 or $8.00 per pizza. The actual sale would be 33% off instead of what the consumer is led to believe as 50% off. This strategy would also include other illusive pricing methods such as 10 items for $10.00 instead of $1 each.

- **Core charge pricing**: This also is one of the common ways of illusive marketing. It is getting a lot of popularity in the online sale for it fits better in the way the price is told to the consumers. It is basically focusing on the core charge or the main product price and playing down the other extra charges that may raise the total price to more than double. Again, even the knowledgeable consumers may fall into this. Consider a dozen of roses advertised for $19.99. That is what any consumer is attracted to. After going through many steps to complete the order, the consumer will realize that there is $14.99 for standard delivery, $9.99 for guaranteed Valentine Day delivery, $7.99 for handling and care, $9.99 for vase, and $4.95 taxes. The total would come to $67.90. That is a far cry from the $19.99 that attracted the consumer in the first place. Firms understand that consumers have the full choice to approve the final order or not. Still, they can depend only on the percentage of consumers who do finalize the transaction even after realizing it is too much. This percentage is significant and can make the selling firm maximize its profits easily.

- **Leadership pricing**: This is a case specific to oligopoly. As we have seen before, there is usually one dominant oligopolistic firm that has the ability and power to set the product price in the market. Other firms in the industry would follow.

- **Limit pricing**: This is also common in the oligopoly market but can be in other market structures as well. It is the case of setting a limit price for the existing firms in the industry that would still let them make profits but seriously discourage other firms to enter the market, for it would not be economical for the newcomers. Figure 11.6 shows the demand curve and the marginal revenue curve for each firm in the industry that are assumed to share the market in equal proportions. LRAC is the industry's long-run average cost curve, SRAC and SRMC are the short-run average cost and short-run marginal cost, respectively, for the existing firms, which maximize their profit at e, yielding an optimal output Qe and optimal market price Pe. The existing firms in the industry would eventually realize that they could lower P_e to P_L and can still earn positive profits as long as P_L is still above their SRAC and the associated output level Q_L can still be produced at the average cost that is below the new price. This price is the limit price that would serve as a deterrent for any potential newcomers, which may have a SRAC, such as $SRAC_n$, that is above the P_L level.

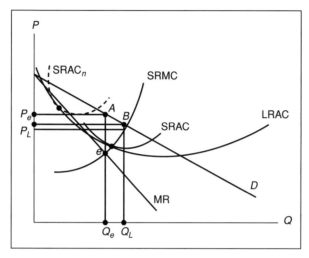

FIGURE 11.6

11.7   PRICE DISCRIMINATION

Price discrimination refers to charging different prices for a product or service from different customers, different markets, different quantities, and different time. The price difference has to be noncost based. The major objective of this practice is to take the opportunities to increase revenue and ultimately maximize profits. Technically, it is a managerial decision to efficiently capture the highest of the consumer surplus by extracting the maximum amount each customer is willing to pay. Typical examples of price discrimination practice that we commonly encounter are as follows: the phone services that charge different rates based on the time of the day or week and also charge higher rates from businesses than from individuals; the quantity discounts that are offered to buyers of large amounts; the medical and legal services that are offered on the basis of customer's income scale; restaurants, transportation, and entertainment services that are offered favorably to elderly and children; power services that are sold at lower rates to local businesses; hotels and resorts with lower rates for conventions and conferences; and so on. The practice of price discrimination requires that the producing firm be imperfectly competitive, for it has to have a control over the price. Also, the basis of differences such as time, quantity, customer, and market must be separable and the market must be segmentable. The other important requirement is that the price elasticity of demand be different according to all these bases of differences, such as being different for different quantities of product, different customers, and different time.

There are three types of price discrimination: the perfect or first degree, the second degree, and the third degree.

11.7.1   First-Degree Price Discrimination

This type is based on the assumption that if a producer (a monopolist) can sell each unit of a product separately and charge the price that a consumer is willing to pay for it, the producer can capture all of the consumer surplus, and the revenue would be the highest and profit would be the absolute maximum, given a certain average cost of the product.

Let us look at Figure 11.7 and recall that if the equilibrium price is P_e, there would have been some consumers who were willing to pay higher prices such as P_4, P_5 but for lower quantities, and there were some willing to pay lower prices (P_2, P_1) for more quantities. The notion of the consumer surplus focuses on the value of benefits that a consumer would receive in excess of what he pays for and can be seen as equal to the triangle (A e Pe) because what the consumer was willing to pay was equal to the entire area of (A e Qe 0) to get a quantity equal to Q_e, but he ended up paying what was equal to the area (Pe e Qe 0).

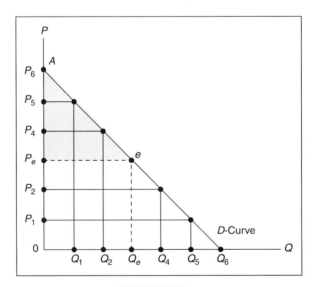

FIGURE 11.7

According to the first degree of price discrimination, a monopolist can take back all of the consumer surplus if he is able to sell each unit of the product separately and change the prices that specific consumers are willing to pay. This type of price discrimination is rare to find in the practical world, but its analysis is still important for it illustrates the essence of price differentials.

Technically, the would-be-obtained consumer surplus (CS) can be explained by

$$\text{CS} = \sum_{i=1}^{n} (P_i \Delta Q_i) = P_n Q_n,$$

where P_n is the market price and Q_n is the quantity demanded by consumer i. P_i and Q_i are the price and quantity, respectively, in the following individual demand function, which is assumed to be linear:

$$P_i = \alpha + \beta Q_i.$$

Substituting for the function, we get

$$CS = \sum_{i=1}^{n} [(\alpha + \beta Q_i)\Delta Q_i] - P_n Q_n.$$

Consumer surplus such as the triangle $A \, e \, Pe$ in Figure 11.7 can be better estimated as Q_i, which becomes smaller and smaller. Considering the linear demand function and as ΔQ approaches zero, consumer surplus (CS) would be calculated as

$$CS = \tfrac{1}{2}[\alpha - P_n]Q_n.$$

Example 11.6
If a demand function is expressed as

$$P_i = 60 - 6Q_i,$$

find the consumer surplus if market price (P_n) is \$18.00 and the change in quantity (ΔQ) is 1 as it approaches zero,

$$CS = \sum_{i=1}^{n} (P_i \Delta Q_i) - P_n Q_n.$$

Solution:
Given that $\Delta Q = 1$, $P_n = 18$, and Q_n is Q_i and can be obtained from the demand function:

$$Q_i = \frac{60}{6} - \frac{18}{6},$$

$$Q_i = 10 - 3 = 7,$$

$$CS = \sum_{i=1}^{n} [60 - 6Q_i](1) - (18)(7),$$

$$CS = \sum_{i=1}^{7} [(60 - 6(1)) + (60 - 6(2)) + (60 - 6(3)) + (60 - 6(4) + (60 - 6(5))$$

$$+ (60 - 6(6) + (60 - 6(7))] - 126$$

$$= [54 + 48 + 42 + 36 + 30 + 24 + 18] - 126$$

$$= 126,$$

and for ΔQ approaching

$$\text{CS} = \tfrac{1}{2}[\alpha - P_n]Q_n$$

$$= \tfrac{1}{2}[60 - 18]7$$

$$= [30 - 9]7 = 147.$$

This means that the more accurate value of consumer surplus is 147 since the change in Q was close to zero, and 126 is an approximate value for the consumer surplus as the change in Q was assumed as equal to 1.

11.7.2   Second-Degree Price Discrimination

This type is relatively more common than the first-degree price discrimination. It is about setting prices on the basis of the quantity purchased. Differential prices are charged by blocks, such as charging the highest price per unit for the block at the top of the demand curve, and progressively lowering the price for the blocks after the first one and toward the bottom of the demand curve. According to this pricing practice, the producer would only extract part of the consumer surplus, but still it is a practice aiming at maximizing revenues and profits. Power, gas, and water companies are known to practice this second-degree price discrimination by offering a higher block rate for certain size of consumption, but it gets lower per unit as the size of consumption increases. This practice is still generally limited, although it is more common than the first-degree price discrimination. It requires that the firms know details about the demand curves of their consumers. Also, it requires that the product consumption can be metered such as in the case of public utilities.

The second-degree price discrimination is also expressed in the block pricing of fixed quantities such as the six-pack soft drink or beer cans or eight- or sixteen-bun package and alike. This practice works easily for the producer as a profit maximizer. Let us take, for example, the six-pack soda cans. Suppose that the demand function is

$$P = 0.9 - 0.0375Q,$$

and the marginal cost per can is fixed at 30 cents (see Figure 11.8). The retailer's block price (BP) would be to add the consumer surplus to the total revenue of the six cans:

$$\text{TR} = P \cdot Q$$

$$= (0.3)(6) = 1.80,$$

$$\text{CS} = \tfrac{1}{2}[\alpha - P_r]Q_n$$

$$= \tfrac{1}{2}[0.9 - 0.3]6$$

$$= 1.80,$$

$$\text{BP} = \text{TR} + \text{CS}$$

$$= 1.80 + 1.80 = 3.60.$$

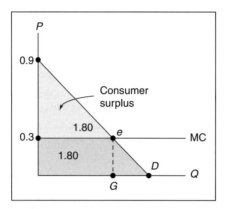

FIGURE 11.8

Given that the total cost is

$$TC = MC \cdot Q$$

$$= (0.30)(6) = 1.80,$$

the retailer would make the following profit:

$$Pr = BP - TC$$

$$= 3.60 - 1.80 = 1.80.$$

11.7.3   Third-Degree Price Discrimination

This type of price discrimination occurs when an imperfectly competitive firm distinctively segments the market into different segments and charges them different prices for the same product. Classic examples of this price discrimination are the seemingly goodwill-driven and community-spirited discounts that are offered to seniors, kids, students, veterans, or any other market segment that is distinguished by a certain characteristic such as age, profession, marital status, and alike. This can also be clear in the market segments distinguished by time of consumption, especially in the case of movie tickets or vacation packages. It is assumed that charging different prices for different markets is practiced until the marginal revenue in each market equals the marginal cost of producing the product. This is to say that the profit-maximizing condition would be

$$MC = MR_1 = MR_2 = \cdots = MR_n,$$

where n refers to the number of markets for different segments. For this type of discrimination to be valid, it is required that the firm be able to control prices; it cannot be a price taker. It also has the following requirements:

1. The firm is able to know and identify demand functions for all the market segments subject to this type of discrimination.

2. Those segments have a different price elasticity of demand, which forms the basis of variation in the price such that the segment exhibiting a higher price elasticity of demand is charged a lower price, and the segment exhibiting a lower price elasticity of demand is charged a higher price. This provides an explanation for granting a lower electricity rates to the business sector and a higher rate to the residential sector; lower hotel rates for members of a big convention than for ordinary customers; and so on.

3. The consumers in each market segment are distinguished on the basis of certain characteristics such as age, profession, marital status, etc.

4. There is no potential trade among the segments in the market so that the group enjoying a lower price cannot sell products to those paying a higher price; if this happens, the whole purpose of price discrimination would be defeated.

Technically, we can see how different price elasticities of demand lead to justifying prices in inverse relationships to the elasticities.

Assuming that there are two market segments, the firm output (Q) would be distributed to both segments (Q_1) and (Q_2):

$$Q = Q_1 + Q_2,$$

and the total and marginal revenues for the firm would be

$$\text{TR} = P \cdot Q,$$

$$\text{MR} = \frac{d\text{TR}}{dQ},$$

$$\text{MR} = \frac{d\text{PQ}}{dQ},$$

$$\text{MR} = P + Q\left[\frac{dP}{dQ}\right].$$

Factoring P out, we get

$$\text{MR} = P\left[1 + \frac{Q}{P}\left(\frac{dP}{dQ}\right)\right].$$

Given that the price elasticity of demand is defined as

$$\varepsilon = \frac{dP}{dP} \cdot \frac{P}{Q},$$

the term inside the bracket would be the reverse of elasticity:

$$\text{MR} = P\left[1 + \frac{1}{\varepsilon}\right].$$

Since we have assumed that there are two market segments with their own marginal revenues MR_1 and MR_2, their own prices P_1 and P_2, and their own elasticities ε_1 and ε_2, and that we equate the marginal revenues, we obtain

$$MR_1 = MR_2,$$

$$P_1\left[1 + \frac{1}{\varepsilon_1}\right] = P_2\left[1 + \frac{1}{\varepsilon_2}\right],$$

$$\frac{P_1}{P_2} = \frac{\left[1 + \dfrac{1}{\varepsilon_2}\right]}{\left[1 + \dfrac{1}{\varepsilon_1}\right]}.$$

(11.9)

This means that if $P_1 > P_2$, then $1 + 1/\varepsilon_1$, and therefore ε_1 has to be smaller than $1 + 1/\varepsilon_2$, and therefore *smaller than* ε_2. Also, if $P_1 < P_2$, then $1 + 1/\varepsilon_1$, and therefore ε_1 has to be larger than $1 + 1/\varepsilon_2$, and therefore *larger than* ε_2. To put it simply, prices and price elasticities of demand have the opposite relationship. This is why higher prices are charged on the product whose price elasticity of demand is low, and lower prices are charged on the product whose price elasticity of demand is high. To confirm, let us give any random numerical values to elasticities and see if they result in the inverse relationship to prices. Let us suppose that product x has a price elasticity of demand equal to –2 and product y has a price elasticity of demand equal to –4. Substituting these values into Equation (11.9), we get

$$\frac{P_x}{P_y} = \frac{\left[1 + \dfrac{1}{\varepsilon_y}\right]}{\left[1 + \dfrac{1}{\varepsilon_x}\right]},$$

$$\frac{P_x}{P_y} = \frac{\left[1 + \dfrac{1}{-4}\right]}{\left[1 + \dfrac{1}{-2}\right]},$$

$$\frac{P_x}{P_y} = \frac{\frac{3}{4}}{\frac{1}{2}},$$

$$\tfrac{1}{2}P_x = \tfrac{3}{4}P_y,$$

$$P_x = \frac{\frac{3}{4}}{\frac{1}{2}}P_y,$$

$$P_x = 1.5P_y.$$

So, $P_x > P_y$ while $\varepsilon_x < \varepsilon_y$ or $|2| < |4|$. We can also illustrate that graphically as it is shown in Figure 11.9. There are three graphs, one each for markets 1 and 2 and the

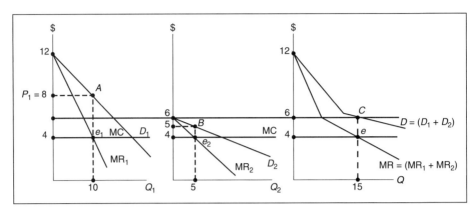

FIGURE 11.9

third one is for the total market. Both the demand curve and the marginal revenue curve show through their slopes that market 1 is more price inelastic (less elastic) with steeper D_1 and MR_1. Market 2 is less price inelastic (more elastic) and therefore has flatter D_2 and MR_2.

The whole market in the far-right third panel shows the market demand D and market marginal revenue MR as horizontal summations of the demand curve and marginal revenue in both markets. As we have seen algebraically that when the marginal revenue equals the marginal cost, we get the equilibrium quantities and prices. In the first market, the equilibrium output turned out to be 10 and the equilibrium price was $8.00 as it was determined from points A on D_1. Also, in the second market, the equality between MR_2 and MC produced the optimal output level 5, which is sold at $5.00 per unit as it was determined by points B on D_2. The marginal cost remained fixed at $4.00 in all markets. As for the whole market, point e is the equality point between market marginal revenue and marginal cost. The optimal market output is 15, which is the combination of outputs in both markets. Market price would be determined from point C on D_3 as $6.00.

It is also confirmed graphically that the less price elastic market 1 charges the higher price, $8.00, and the more price elastic market 2 charges the lower price, $5.00. Once again, the highest profit is achieved through the two price-discriminated markets rather than one unfixed market.

Example 11.7
The following are two demand functions and a total cost function for a product sold in two different market segments. If the marginal cost remains fixed at $4.00 throughout the markets, will the third-degree price discrimination yield higher or lower profit levels?

$$Q_1 = 30 - \tfrac{5}{2}P_1,$$
$$Q_2 = 30 - 5P_2,$$
$$TC = 22.50 + 2(Q_1 + Q_2).$$

Solution:

Before we write the total revenue functions in both markets, we need to express the demand functions in terms of the prices:

$$P_1 = 12 - \tfrac{2}{5}Q_1,$$

$$P_2 = 6 - \tfrac{1}{5}Q_2,$$

$$\text{TR}_1 = Q_1 P_1,$$

$$\text{TR}_1 = Q_1 \left[12 - \tfrac{2}{5}Q_1 \right],$$

$$\text{TR}_1 = 12Q_1 - \tfrac{2}{5}Q_1^2,$$

$$\text{MR}_1 = \frac{\partial \text{TR}_1}{\partial Q_1} = 12 - \frac{4}{5}Q_1,$$

$$\text{TR}_2 = Q_2 P_2,$$

$$\text{TR}_2 = Q_2 \left[6 - \tfrac{1}{5}Q_2 \right],$$

$$\text{TR}_2 = 6Q_2 - \tfrac{1}{5}Q_2^2,$$

$$\text{MR}_2 = \frac{\partial \text{TR}_2}{\partial Q_2} = 6 - \frac{2}{5}Q_2.$$

The profit-maximizing conditions in both markets are achieved by equating both revenues to the same marginal cost of the product:

$$\text{MR}_1 = \text{MC},$$

$$12 - \tfrac{4}{5}Q_1 = 4,$$

$$8 = \tfrac{4}{5}Q_1,$$

$$Q_1 = 10,$$

$$P_1 = 12 - \tfrac{2}{5}Q_1,$$

$$P_1 = 12 - \tfrac{2}{5}(10) = 8,$$

$$\text{MR}_2 = \text{MC},$$

$$6 - \tfrac{2}{5}Q_2 = 4,$$

$$2 = \tfrac{2}{5}Q_2,$$

$$Q_2 = 5,$$

$$P_2 = 6 - \tfrac{1}{5}Q_2,$$

$$P_2 = 6 - \tfrac{1}{5}(5) = 5,$$

$$\text{TR}_1 = 12Q_1 - \tfrac{2}{5}Q_1^2,$$

$$\text{TR}_1 = 12(10) - \tfrac{2}{5}(10)^2,$$

$$\text{TR}_1 = 80,$$

$$\text{TR}_2 = 6Q_2 - \tfrac{1}{5}Q_2^2,$$

$$\text{TR}_2 = 6(5) - \tfrac{1}{5}(5)^2,$$

$$\text{TR}_2 = 25,$$

$$\text{TR} = \text{TR}_1 + \text{TR}_2,$$

$$\text{TR} = 80 + 25 = 105,$$

$$\text{TC} = 22.50 + 2(Q_1 + Q_2)$$

$$= 22.50 + 2(10 + 5) = 52.50,$$

$$\text{Pr} = \text{TR} - \text{TC},$$

$$\text{Pr} = 105 - 52.50 = 52.50.$$

So, the profit under the price discrimination practice is \$52.50. What would it be if this practice is not followed, that is, if there is only one market?

$$Q = Q_1 + Q_2,$$

$$Q = 30 - \tfrac{5}{2}P_1 + 30 - 5P_2.$$

Since there would be only one price, we substitute both P_1 and P_2 with P:

$$Q = 60 - \tfrac{15}{2}P,$$

$$P = 8 - \tfrac{2}{15}Q,$$

$$\text{TR} = Q \cdot P,$$

$$\text{TR} = Q\left[8 - \tfrac{2}{15}Q\right],$$

$$\text{TR} = 8Q - \tfrac{2}{15}Q^2,$$

$$MR = \frac{\partial TR}{\partial Q} = 8 - \frac{4}{15}Q,$$

$$MR = MC,$$

$$8 - \tfrac{4}{15}Q = 4,$$

$$\tfrac{4}{15}Q = 4,$$

$$Q = 15,$$

$$P = 8 - \tfrac{2}{15}Q,$$

$$P = 8 - \tfrac{2}{15}(15) = 6,$$

$$TR = 8(15) - \tfrac{2}{15}(15)^2,$$

$$TR = 90,$$

$$TC = 22.50 + 2(Q_1 + Q_2)$$

$$= 22.50 + 2Q$$

$$= 22.50 + 2(15) = 52.50,$$

$$Pr = TR - TC,$$

$$Pr = 90 - 52.50 = 37.50.$$

The profit in the absence of price discrimination ($37.50) is less than when the practice is applied ($52.50).

Example 11.8
A firm is selling its product in two separate markets as a third-degree price discrimination practice. The demand functions and the total cost function are

$$Q_1 = 120 - 2.4P_1,$$

$$Q_2 = 180 - 6P_2,$$

$$TC = 40 + 10Q.$$

1. Find the firm's profit-maximizing output and price, and calculate the total profits under the third-degree price discrimination.
2. Show that the higher price is charged in the lower price elasticity market and the lower price is charged in the higher price elasticity market.

Solution:

1. First we express the demand functions in terms of price, so we can calculate the total revenues:

$$P_1 = 50 - 0.4167Q_1,$$

$$\text{TR}_1 = Q_1 P_1,$$

$$\text{TR}_1 = Q_1[50 - 0.4167Q_1],$$

$$\text{TR}_1 = 50Q_1 - 0.4167Q_1^2,$$

$$P_2 = 30 - 0.167Q_2,$$

$$\text{TR}_2 = Q_2 P_2,$$

$$\text{TR}_2 = Q_2[30 - 0.167Q_2],$$

$$\text{TR}_2 = 30Q_2 - 0.167Q_2^2,$$

$$\text{TR} = \text{TR}_1 + \text{TR}_2,$$

$$\text{TR}_2 = 50Q_1 - 0.4167Q_1^2 + 30Q_2 - 0.167Q_2^2,$$

$$\text{TC} = 40 + 10Q,$$

$$\text{TC} = 40 + 10(Q_1 + Q_2),$$

$$\text{TC} = 40 + 10Q_1 + 10Q_2,$$

$$\text{Pr} = \text{TR} - \text{TC},$$

$$\text{Pr} = 50Q_1 - 0.4167Q_1^2 + 30Q_2 - 0.167Q_2^2 - 40 - 10Q_1 - 10Q_2,$$

$$\frac{\partial \text{Pr}}{\partial Q_1} = 50 - 0.8334Q_1 - 10 = 0,$$

$$40 = 0.8334Q_1,$$

$$Q_1 = 48,$$

$$P_1 = 50 - 0.4167Q,$$

$$P_1 = 50 - 0.4167(48) = \$30,$$

$$\frac{\partial \text{Pr}}{\partial Q_2} = 30 - 0.334Q_2 - 10 = 0,$$

$$0.334Q_2 = 20,$$

$$Q_2 = 60,$$

$$P_2 = 30 - 0.167Q_2,$$

$$P_2 = 30 - 0.167(60) = \$20,$$

$$\text{Pr} = 50(48) - 0.4167(48)^2 + 30(60) - 0.167(60)^2 - 40 - 10(48) - 10(60),$$

$$\text{Pr} = 1519.$$

2. $Q_1 = 120 - 2.4P_1,$

$$\frac{dQ_1}{dP_1} = -2.4,$$

$$\varepsilon_1 = \left[\frac{dQ_1}{dP_1}\right]\left[\frac{P_1}{Q_1}\right]$$

$$= (-2.4)\left[\frac{30}{48}\right] = -1.5,$$

$$Q_2 = 180 - 6P_2,$$

$$\frac{dQ_2}{dP_2} = -6,$$

$$\varepsilon_2 = \left[\frac{dQ_2}{dP_2}\right]\left[\frac{P_2}{Q_2}\right]$$

$$= -6\left[\frac{20}{60}\right] = -2.$$

In absolute value, $\varepsilon_2 > \varepsilon_1$, or market 2 has more price elasticity of demand than market 1. Also, market 2 has a lower price, $20.00, than that in market 1, $30.00. This verifies that a higher price is charged in the market with lower price elasticity of demand, and a lower price is charged in the market with higher price elasticity of demand.

SUMMARY

- This is the second chapter in the unit on decisions at the market level for an obvious reason that prices and pricing practices and policies stand as one of the central strategies for managers. The chapter starts with the fundamentals of price setting in the business world and makes the distinction between the perfect competitive firms, which are price takers, and the other types of market structures, which set the price of their products based on the market forces of supply and demand, mostly following a down-sloping demand curve and going by the equimarginal principle to maximize their profits. The discussion moves, then, to the markup rule, which adds a certain percentage over the marginal cost of the product and considers the elasticity of demand for that product.
- Joint products with independent demand in the market require a firm policy that would consider the interdependence among the products based on their complementarity and substitutability. Applying the equimarginal principle, the optimal output size for the joint product firm is achieved at the point where the total marginal revenue for the firm equals the marginal cost of the joint products. Prices of the joint products are determined according to their demand curves.
- Some firms produce not only their primary and final product but also some intermediate products that may become components into other products for other plants or firms. Transfer pricing refers to the way of pricing the intermediate products in the case of three possibilities: (1) when the intermediate product cannot be sold in another external

market; (2) when it can be sold in a competitive market; and (3) when it can be sold in noncompetitive markets. In the first case, the transfer price of the intermediate product would be equal to the marginal cost of production. In the second case, the transfer price would be determined as an external competitive price. In the third case, the transfer price of the intermediate product would be determined by the external demand curve.

- There are many other concepts and practices of pricing that are common in the market and followed by many companies for different products under different conditions. These include the tying and bundling prices, peak and off-peak pricing, two-point tariff pricing, skimming pricing, prestige pricing, competitor's matching pricing, higher value pricing, target pricing penetration and dumping pricing, psychological pricing, core charge pricing, leadership pricing, limit pricing, and so on.

- When firms set the prices of their products not based on cost of production and not in the usual way of markup, the prices become the core of an area of pricing policy called price discrimination. It refers to charging prices based on one or more of the following aspects: quantity sold, time of purchase, marketing product, special event, or special group of consumers that could be defined by age, occupation, or some kind of association. Price discrimination requires some conditions under which it can be effectively applied. These conditions include the following: the firm has to be a monopoly or has some monopoly power; the market has to be suitable for segmentation; the product has to have different price elasticity of demand in different markets. There are three degrees of price discrimination. The first degree is defined by selling the product in separate units where the price can be the highest for each unit sold. The second degree of price discrimination is defined by setting a specific price for a specific quantity of product and each additional quantity sold has a lower price. The third degree of price discrimination refers to distinguishing between markets where the same product is sold for a different price in each of these markets. The different prices would continue to be valid in each market until the marginal revenue of the last unit sold in a market equals the marginal cost of the product for that market.

KEY TERMS

markup	joint product	transfer pricing
intermediate product	final product	tying
bundling	off-peak pricing	two-part tariff
skimming	competitor's matching	prestige pricing
higher value pricing	penetration and dumping	target pricing
psychological pricing	core charge pricing	leadership pricing
first-degree price discrimination	price discrimination	limit pricing
second-degree price discrimination	third-degree price discrimination	

LIST OF FORMULAS

- Profit-maximizing price:

$$P = \frac{MC}{1 + \dfrac{1}{\varepsilon}},$$

$$P = FAAC[MupC + 1].$$

- Markup on cost:

$$\text{MupC} = \frac{P - \text{MC}}{\text{MC}},$$

$$\text{MupC} = \frac{1}{\varepsilon + 1}.$$

- Markup price:

$$\text{MupP} = -\frac{1}{\varepsilon}.$$

- Consumer surplus:

$$\text{Approximate value: CS} = \sum_{i=1}^{n} (P_i \Delta Q_i) - P_n Q_n.$$

$$\text{Accurate value: CS} = \frac{1}{2}[\alpha + P_n]Q_n.$$

- Block price:

$$\text{BP} = \text{TR} + \text{CS}.$$

EXERCISES

1. What is the markup? How is it determined and what is the difference between markup on cost and markup on price, and how the price elasticity of demand is relevant?

2. What is the major strategy for firms on multiproduct pricing? How would a firm producing many products ensure its ultimate goal of maximizing profits?

3. List and explain, as many as you remember, the common pricing practices in the market and recall if you have recently dealt with any of them.

4. Explain the pricing strategy for firms producing joint products and give examples of both the case of fixed proportions and the case of variable proportions.

5. Explain and compare with examples the three degrees of price discrimination.

6. Consider the following information for the production of cookies, produced and packaged in boxes by a small firm:

Total overhead cost: $ 1400,

Total variable cost: $ 5600,

Production size: 1000 units,

Price elasticity of demand: -2.57.

What would be the markup percentage and how much would each box of cookies be sold for?

7. The following are the demand functions for two products, A and B, which are jointly produced:

$$P_A = 20 - \frac{Q_A}{5},$$

$$P_B = 24 - \frac{2Q_B}{5}.$$

Given that the firm's costs are as follows:

$$\text{Variable cost: VC} = \frac{15Q}{2} + 0.025Q_2,$$

$$\text{Fixed cost: FC} = 250.$$

(a) Find the profit-maximizing price for each product.
(b) Calculate the firm's maximum profit from the two products.

8. A firm has two divisions, one to produce a major component (intermediate product) and the other to assemble and sell the final product. Suppose that the immediate product cannot be sold in any other market. What would be the equilibrium price and output for the final product and what would be the transfer price for the intermediate product given that the demand function and the marginal revenue function for the final product are as follows?

$$P_f = 32 - 0.20\,Q_f,$$

$$\text{MR}_f = 32 - 0.40\,Q_f.$$

The marginal cost functions of the two products are

$$\text{MC}_f = 2 + 0.20\,Q_f,$$

$$\text{MC}_i = 6 + 0.20\,Q_i.$$

9. Draw a graph for the previous question in which you show
   (a) the equilibrium quantity and price for the final product;
   (b) the transfer price and the output level for the intermediate product.

10. Consider a product, the market price of which is $5, and the individual consumer's demand function is

$$Q = 10 - \tfrac{1}{8}P.$$

Calculate (1) the approximate value of the consumer surplus and (2) the accurate value of consumer surplus.

UNIT V

MANAGERIAL DECISIONS IN THE LONG RUN

12

CAPITAL BUDGETING AND INVESTMENT PROJECT EVALUATION

12.1 WHAT IS CAPITAL BUDGETING?

Most of the topics discussed in the previous chapters were related to managerial decisions on current operational matters leading to short-term profit maximization. In this chapter, we shall discuss capital budgeting that focusses on long-term and strategic plans to sustain a stable and more productive future for the firm. The long-term outlook involves decision making to replace, improve, and expand the firm's major existing resource base compared to only seeking the efficiency of that resource base. The emphasis would primarily be placed on assessing the firm's investment opportunities in order to choose the most viable opportunity. Given that alternative, investment opportunities differ in many aspects, for example in the level of risk associated with them and their capacities to yield returns, the senior management can employ objective, quantitative, and credible methods to evaluate the proposed alternatives and select the best, most feasible in terms of gaining higher profitability, and lower risk option.

Capital expenditure is an outlay of funds that the firm would rely on to generate returns enough to cover and exceed the initial investment. Therefore, capital budgeting is the process of reviewing, assessing, and selecting the business projects that promise the best possible rewards in the medium and long runs. In other words, it is the long-term planning and evaluating capital allocations that are expected to generate cash inflows over a period of time. Figure 12.1 illustrates the major elements of the process of capital budgeting on a timeline.

This is the typical dual cash flow scenario. The first of these flows is the cash outflow, which consists mainly of the initial capital fund allocated for an investment project in the current time, as well as the capital expenditures made throughout the productive life of the assets. The second flow is the cash inflow that includes the annual returns of the project

Managerial Economics: A Mathematical Approach, First Edition. M. J. Alhabeeb and L. Joe Moffitt.
© 2013 John Wiley & Sons, Inc. Published 2013 by John Wiley & Sons, Inc.

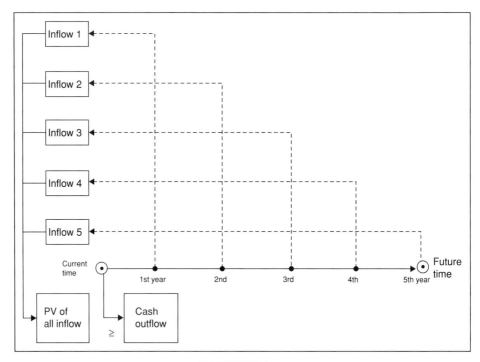

FIGURE 12.1

during its first 5 years. While the cash outflow is normally measured at its current value, the value of cash inflows have to be brought back from their maturity time to the current time. They are discounted at the firm's **cost of capital** rate and added up to form the present value of all returns that has to be either equal or larger than the cash outflow.

Typical examples of capital outlay for a firm's investment projects are funds to finance the purchase of land, buildings, equipment, to expand business, to enhance the working capital for inventories and accounts receivable, to finance research and development, and to pay for promotion and advertisement. Generally, capital budgeting is often associated with the following investment projects:

1. *Expansion*: It includes investment projects involving development and production of either a new product or a new line of product or venturing into a new market. It also includes the extension of service outlets and the distribution and storage facilities.

2. *Replacement*: It includes projects involving replacement of worn-out and damaged machines and equipment as well as renewing structures and technology for efficient production and services.

3. *Cost reduction*: It includes all projects aiming at reducing the cost of production through lower labor cost, raw material, energy, and by employing latest technology to increase production. Projects aimed at moving production to less expensive locations and training personnel could lower the total cost of production.

4. *Conforming*: It includes projects that must comply with federal or state regulations and standards on issues, for example health, safety, pollution, reservation, and so on.

12.2   BASIC MODEL OF CAPITAL BUDGETING

The theoretical framework underlying capital budgeting is based on the equimarginal principle. It states that a firm would continue to engage in an activity until its marginal cost (MC) is equal to its marginal benefit. As for the firm's decisions on investment projects, this principle is applied in such a way that capital would be allocated for investment projects to the point where marginal return on investment as represented by incremental cash flows would be equal to the marginal cost as represented by the added expenditures of new investment capital. Applying this principle would assure maximum return for the firm. The graph in Figure 12.2 shows an example of what firm X has to decide regarding the worthiness of eight proposed investment options, projects I through VIII, which require a total distribution of $25 million on different capital funds of the project that yield different rates of returns (Table 12.1).

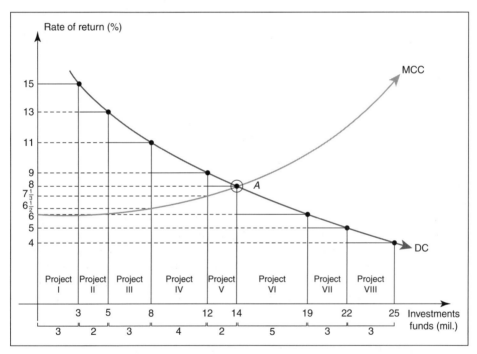

FIGURE 12.2

TABLE 12.1

Project I	$3 million, with 15% return
Project II	$2 million, with 13% return
Project III	$3 million, with 11% return
Project IV	$4 million, with 9% return
Project V	$2 million, with 8% return
Project VI	$5 million, with 6% return
Project VII	$3 million, with 5% return
Project VIII	$3 million, with 4% return
Total capital demanded: $25 million.	

The curve DC is the firm's demand for capital and the curve MCC is the firm's marginal cost of capital. The intersection between the two curves at point A would determine that at maximum the firm could only allocate capitals for the first five projects, I through V, at a total of $14 million. The firm's initial cost of capital rate is 6% that would continue to rise after allocating the first $3 million. Therefore, the first project costs 6% and yields a 15% rate of return ; the second project costs about $6\frac{1}{4}$% and yields 13%; the third project costs $6\frac{1}{2}$% and returns 11%; the fourth project costs $7\frac{1}{3}$% and returns 9%; and the fifth costs 8% and barely returns the same rate. All the remaining projects, VI, VII, and VIII, would cost more than the firm's cost of capital and all of their returns are below the MCC, and this is the reason for rejecting them. Project VI returns 6% but it costs $10\frac{1}{2}$%, Project VII returns 5% but it costs $12\frac{1}{2}$%; and project VIII returns 4% but it costs 15%. The optimal capital allocation for the firm is $14 million.

12.3   SELECTION PROCESS AND PROJECT EVALUATION

Capital budgeting involves a standard, logical, and consistent decision-making process that may consist of the following steps:

1. Exploring a pool of proposed investment projects and generating a list of the most qualified proposals to form the alternative projects under consideration. By focusing on the initially strong and promising projects, this step would also be a screening the projects step to eliminate all unfeasible or unworthy proposals.

2. Estimating the project cash flow, which is a stream of returns that would occur in a future time. It should, therefore, be considered with the appropriate level of uncertainty, risk, and bias. A major bias is the natural tendency to be over-optimistic which may lead to underestimation of costs and overestimation of benefits with a desire to adopt a specific project. It is essential to rely on professionals without bias who use objective measures to minimize any over- or underestimation. This step usually emphasizes three important criteria:

   (a) Cash flow measurement should be done on an incremental basis. It means that a project's cash flow takes a marginal sense as the difference between the firm's cash flow before and after the initiation of that project.

   (b) Cash flow estimation should be considered on after tax basis using the firm's marginal tax rate and should include the effect of depreciation and all other noncash expenses that would be considered for income tax purposes

   (c) Cash flow estimation should include all indirect effects of the project throughout its lifetime, for example, the possible interference and overlap with other products, services, or functions of the firm.

3. Determining the firm's cost of capital that would serve as the discount rate for converting the value of cash flow from the future to the present time. It is equivalent to the required rate of return by the firm's investors.

4. Evaluating the alternative investment projects in order to choose and accept the best alternative project that would yield the maximum value for the firm. The fundamental criterion for establishing the measure of desirability and preference for a specific project is the comparison of the present value of the expected cash inflows with the initial cash outflow. The project that wins the allocation of capital has to have the present value of its expected returns higher than the initial capital outlay.

There are two groups of methods to evaluate the worthiness and desirability of any investment project under consideration.

12.4   METHODS OF EVALUATION FOR PROPOSED INVESTMENT PROJECTS

As decision-making tools for the firm's capital budgeting, there are two groups of methods of evaluation. The first group, which is the most common, is called the value-adjusted method for its utilization of the time value of money in establishing reliable criteria of project worthiness. This group includes the **net present value (NPV)**, the **internal rate of return (IRR)**, and the **profitability index (PI)**. The second group is called the value-unadjusted method because it does not use any time value of money adjustment. This group is represented by the **payback** technique.

12.4.1   Net Present Value

An investment project's net present value is the present value of all future returns or cash inflows minus the initial capital invested in the project. The stream of future cash inflows must be discounted back to the current time using the firm's cost of capital as the discount rate. This rate is determined by the firm based on its assessment of the risk involved in each investment project. High-risk projects are assigned higher discount rate; low risk projects are assigned lower discount rates. NPV is probably the most common technique used to assess how worthy a project is and whether it would be accepted or not. If the present value of all future returns (the cash inflows) is larger than the initial cost of the project (the cash outflows), the NPV would be positive and the project is acceptable. Otherwise, if the present value of the cash inflows is smaller than the cash outflows, the NPV would be negative and the project cannot be accepted.

Let us recall that the current or discounted value (CV) of any future return (FV) can be obtained by

$$CV = \frac{FV}{(1+r)^n},$$

where r is the interest rate used for discounting or bringing the value of return from future back to the present and n is the number of time terms, for example years. If we refer to an annual cash inflow of a project by CF, and to the project cash outflow by I, then the NPV would be the difference between the discounted streams of both flows throughout the life of the project (t):

$$NPV = \sum_{i=1}^{t} \left[\frac{CF_i}{(1+r)^n} \right] - \sum_{i=1}^{t} \left[\frac{I_i}{(1+r)^n} \right].$$

If the project takes into account only the initial capital outlay, then it would already be in its current value, I_0, and does not need to be discounted:

$$NPV = \sum_{i=1}^{t} \left[\frac{CF_i}{(1+r)^n} \right] - I_0.$$

The criteria for project acceptability is for the NPV to be nonnegative:

$$\text{NPV} \geq 0.$$

Example 12.1

A proposal to expand a fast food restaurant calls for the investment of an initial capital of \$42,000 and promises to deliver a return of at least \$14,000 per year during the next 5 years. Would the franchise company approve such an expansion project if its cost of capital is $11\frac{1}{2}\%$?

Solution:

$$\text{NPV} = \sum_{i=1}^{t} \left[\frac{\text{CF}_i}{(1+r)^n} \right] - I_0$$

$$= \frac{\text{CF}_1}{(1+r)^1} + \frac{\text{CF}_2}{(1+r)^2} + \frac{\text{CF}_3}{(1+r)^3} + \frac{\text{CF}_4}{(1+r)^5} - I_0$$

$$= \frac{14,000}{(1+0.115)^1} + \frac{14,000}{(1+0.115)^2} + \frac{14,000}{(1+0.115)^3} + \frac{14,000}{(1+0.115)^4} \frac{14,000}{(1+0.115)^5}$$

$$- 42,000$$

$$= 12{,}556.05 + 11{,}261.03 + 10{,}099.58 + 9057.92 + 8123.69 - 42{,}000$$

$$= 51{,}098.27 - 42{,}000$$

$$= 9098.27.$$

Since the NPV is positive, the expansion project would be accepted (see Figure 12.3).

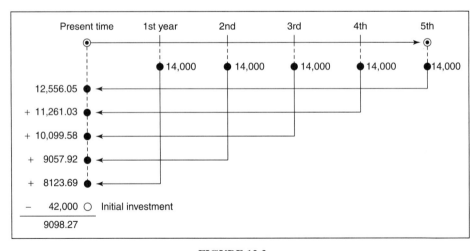

FIGURE 12.3

Example 12.2

The development committee in a construction company is studying two investment proposals whose cash inflows for the next 4 years are as projected in Table 12.2. Both projects require a capital allocation of \$200,000 given that the cost of capital for the first project is 8% and for the second is $7\frac{1}{2}\%$. Which of the two proposals would get an approval?

Solution:

TABLE 12.2

	Project I		Project II	
	Cash Inflows ($)		Cash Inflows ($)	
Year	$r = 8\%$	Cash Outflows ($)	$r = 7.5\%$	Cash Outflow ($)
1	35,000	200,000	40,000	200,000
2	40,000		40,000	
3	50,000		95,000	
4	120,000		100,000	

Project I

$$\text{NPV} = \sum_{i=1}^{4} \left[\frac{\text{CF}_i}{(1+r)^n} \right] - I_0$$

$$= \frac{35,000}{(1+0.08)^1} + \frac{40,000}{(1+0.08)^2} + \frac{50,000}{(1+0.08)^3} + \frac{120,000}{(1+0.08)^4} - 200,000$$

$$= 32,407.40 + 34,293.55 + 39,691.61 + 88,203.58 - 200,000$$

$$= 194,596 - 200,000$$

$$= -5404.26.$$

Project II

$$\text{NPV} = \frac{40,000}{(1+0.075)^1} + \frac{40,000}{(1+0.075)^2} + \frac{95,000}{(1+0.075)^3} + \frac{100,000}{(1+0.075)^4} - 200,000$$

$$= 37,209.30 + 34,613.30 + 76,471.25 + 74,880.05 - 200,000$$

$$= 223,173.90 - 200,000$$

$$= 23,173.90.$$

Project I has a negative NPV and project II has a positive NPV. The committee would accept the second project and reject the first (Figure 12.4).

The cash inflow in the NPV formula could be replaced by the firm's profit for any period (π_i), and adjusted for depreciation and taxes:

$$\text{Since} \quad \pi_i = \text{TR}_i - \text{TC}_i,$$

$$\text{NPV} = \sum_{i=1}^{t} \left\{ \frac{[\text{TR}_i - \text{TC}_i](1-T) + D_i}{(1+r)^n} \right\} - I_0,$$

where TR_i and TC_i are the firm's total revenue and total cost for the ith period; T is the firm's marginal tax rate; D_i is the firm's capital depreciation; and I_0 is the initial investment capital allocated for the project.

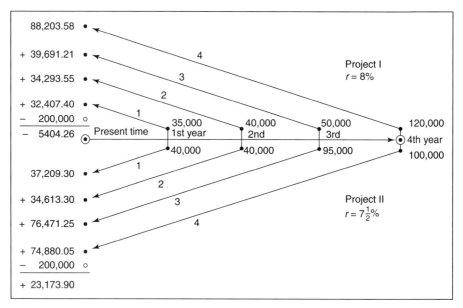

FIGURE 12.4

Example 12.3

A firm received a proposal for an investment project showing estimated projections of the gross profit based on the total cost, total revenue, and depreciation allowances for the first 5 years as shown in Table 12.3. How would the firm decide on accepting or rejecting the request for an initial capital of $650,000, given that the cost of capital is $8\frac{1}{4}\%$ and the firm's marginal income tax is 32%?

Solution:

TABLE 12.3

1	2	3	4	5	6	7
				$(1-T) =$		$\pi_i (1-t) + D_i$
Year	TR_i ($)	TC_i ($)	$\pi_i (3-2)$	$1-0.32$	D_i ($)	$(4 \times 5 + 6)$ ($)
1	600,000	460,000	140,000	0.68	29,400	124,600
2	660,000	475,000	185,000	0.68	31,500	157,300
3	625,000	420,000	205,000	0.68	33,000	172,400
4	620,000	400,000	220,000	0.68	34,100	183,700
5	668,000	418,000	250,000	0.68	35,000	205,000

$$NPV = \frac{124,600}{(1+0.0825)^1} + \frac{157,300}{(1+0.0825)^2} + \frac{172,400}{(1+0.0825)^3}$$

$$+ \frac{183,700}{(1+0.0825)^4} + \frac{205,000}{(1+0.0825)^5}$$

$$= 115{,}103.93 + 134{,}237.21 + 135{,}910.67 + 133{,}781.95 + 137{,}915.90 - 650{,}000$$

$$= 656{,}949.66 - 650{,}000$$

$$= 6949.66.$$

The proposal would be approved for yielding a nonnegative NPV (Figure 12.5).

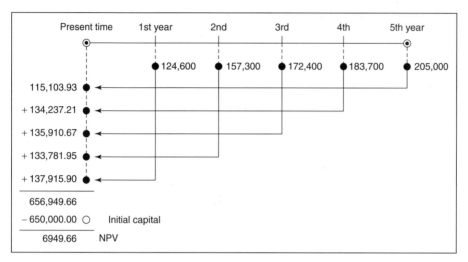

FIGURE 12.5

12.4.2 Internal Rate of Return

Another method used to determine the acceptability of a proposed investment is to compare the internal rate of return with the firm's cost of capital. The criterion for the project to be accepted is that it must yield an internal rate of return larger than or at least equal to the firm's cost of capital:

$$\text{IRR} \geq r,$$

The IRR is sometimes called "the profit rate" or "the marginal efficiency of investment." It is defined as the rate that equates the present value of cash inflows and the cash outflows. In the NPV formula, such a rate that makes the two cash flows equal must make the NPV equal to zero. This would mean that the project is not capable of delivering an earning rate higher than the cost of capital.

Using the NPV formula, we can now replace the firm's cost of capital (r) with the IRR and set the NPV to zero:

$$\text{NPV} = \sum_{i=1}^{n} \left[\frac{\text{CF}_i}{(1 + \text{IRR})^n} \right] - I_0 = 0.$$

To find the right IRR that makes the NPV equal to zero, we have to solve the above equation. IRR can be found by many ways, for example using the table values, trial and error, interpolation, and so on. Computers and sophisticated business calculators can easily find IRR. However, an equation is developed to get the estimate IRR. Once we get such an estimate, we can keep iterating until we get the exact rate that makes the value of NPV zero:

$$\text{IRR} \simeq \left[\frac{\sum_{i=1}^{n} \text{CF}_i - I_0}{\sum i \, \text{CF}_i} \right],$$

where CF is cash inflow for the period I, and i is the number of any year of the discounted term:

$$i = 1, 2, 3, \ldots, n,$$

and I_0 is the initial investment.

Example 12.4

A firm is studying an investment proposal that requires $15,000 as initial capital. The projections for cash inflows during the first 5 years are shown in Table 12.4.

TABLE 12.4

1	2	3
	Cash Inflows	
i	CF_i	$i \, \text{CF}_i \, (1 \times 2)$
1	3,600	3,600
2	4,200	8,400
3	5,500	16,500
4	6,300	25,200
5	7,500	37,500
	27,100	91,200
	$\sum_{i=1}^{5} \text{CF}_i$	$\sum_{i=1}^{5} i \, \text{CF}_i$

$$\text{IRR} \simeq \left[\frac{\sum_{i=1}^{5} \text{CF}_i - I_0}{\sum i \, \text{CF}_i} \right],$$

$$\text{IRR} \simeq \left[\frac{27,100 - 15,000}{91,200} \right],$$

$$\text{IRR} \simeq 13.3\%.$$

But, this is only a rough estimate. However, we can reach the exact rate after some trial and error attempts, by calculating NPV until it reaches zero. That would be possible when the present values of all cash inflows are exactly equal to the initial investment, in this case $15,000.

The first step is to calculate the present value of cash inflows at the discount rate of 13.3% to see how close it would bring the present value to the initial investment of $15,000:

$$PV = \frac{3600}{(1+0.133)^1} + \frac{4200}{(1+0.133)^2} + \frac{5500}{(1+0.133)^3} + \frac{6300}{(1+0.133)^4} + \frac{7500}{(1+0.133)^5}$$

$$= 3177 + 3272 + 3782 + 3823 + 4017$$

$$= 18,071.$$

Therefore, a rate of 13.3 produces a present value of the cash inflows larger than the initial investment of $15,000. Since the rate of discount has an inverse relationship with the present value, we have to increase the rate in the next try to reduce the present value hoping to let it reach $15,000.

At a rate of 18%, the present value of cash inflows would be

$$PV = \frac{3600}{(1+0.18)^1} + \frac{4200}{(1+0.18)^2} + \frac{5500}{(1+0.18)^3} + \frac{6300}{(1+0.18)^4} + \frac{7500}{(1+0.18)^5}$$

$$= 3051 + 3016 + 3347 + 3249 + 3278$$

$$= 15,942.$$

Therefore, we are getting much closer to the $15,000. We need to raise the rate to bring the present value to exactly $15,000. We can also use the $PVIF_{r,n}$ table value (v^n) to ease the tedious calculations. Table A.7 in the appendix shows the discount factor of a dollar for many combinations of r and n:

$$PVIF = v^n = \frac{1}{(1+r)^n}.$$

For example, to get the discounted cash inflow in the third year , we can either divide 5500 by $(1 + 0.18)^3$ or get the discount factor from Table A.7 for $r = 18\%$ and $n = 3$, and multiply it by 5500:

$$PV = FV[PVIF_{r,n}]$$

$$= 5500[PVIF_{0.18,3}]$$

$$= 5500[0.6086]$$

$$= 3347.$$

Other few tries to get the exact rate revealed that

- at 20%, PV = 15,151;
- and at exactly 20.4%, PV = 15,000.

Here, 15,000 is the IRR that brings about the equality between the present value of cash inflows and the initial investment, making the NPV equal to zero (Figure 12.6):

$$NPV = \left[\frac{3600}{(1+0.204)^1} + \frac{4200}{(1+0.204)^2} + \frac{5500}{(1+0.204)^3} + \frac{6300}{(1+0.204)^4} + \frac{7500}{(1+0.204)^5} \right]$$

$$- 15,000$$

$$= [2990 + 2897 + 3151 + 2998 + 2964] - 15,000$$

$$= 15,000 - 15,000 = 0.$$

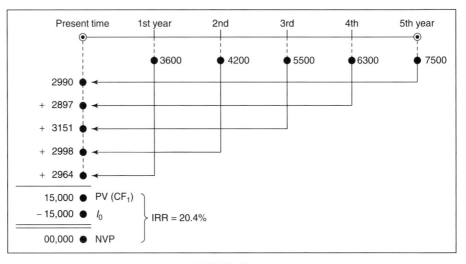

FIGURE 12.6

12.4.3   NPV versus IRR for Mutually Exclusive Projects

The criterion for accepting or rejecting an investment project can either be based on the highest NPV or the highest IRR. It would make no difference to the firm, whichever the measure followed, simply because they reflect each other consistently. Having a positive value for the NPV means having an IRR that exceeds the firm's cost of capital, and having a negative value of the NPV refers to having an IRR lower than the firm's cost of capital (Table 12.5):

$$\text{If IRR} > \text{MCC} \rightarrow \text{NPV} > 0;$$

$$\text{IRR} < \text{MCC} \rightarrow \text{NPV} < 0.$$

TABLE 12.5

Year	Project I	Project II	
0	250,000	250,000	Initial Capital ($)
1	−25,000	87,500	
2	0	87,500	
3	125,000	87,500	Cash Inflows ($)
4	125,000	87,500	
5	350,000	87,500	
NPV ($)	131,653	85,973	Discount Rate
IRR	20.2%	22.1%	$9\frac{1}{2}\%$

Therefore, either measure would be fine if followed, but that is especially true if the firm is assessing only a single independent project. But if the firm wants to assess two or more projects that are mutually exclusive, then the measures of NPV and IRR may not mean the same(!) Mutually exclusive projects are those projects that compete to earn the decision of approval. In other words, the firm can only choose one project among the alternatives. Let us calculate both the NPV and IRR for the two projects whose 5-year cash inflows are shown in the last table, given that both are vying with each other for the $250,000 initial capital that is to be invested at least at the firm's $9\frac{1}{2}\%$ cost of capital (Figure 12.7):

$$NPCV = \sum_{i=1}^{n}\left[\frac{CF_i}{(1+r)^n}\right] - I_0,$$

$$NPV_I = \left[\frac{-25,000}{(1+0.095)^1} + \frac{0}{(1+0.095)^2} + \frac{125,000}{(1+0.095)^3} + \frac{125,000}{(1+0.095)^4} + \frac{350,000}{(1+0.095)^5}\right]$$

$$- 250,000,$$

$$NPV_I = [-22,831 + 0 + 95,207 + 86,947 + 222,330] - 250,000,$$

$$NPV_I = 131,653,$$

$$IRR_I = 20.2\% \text{ (obtained using a calculator)},$$

$$NPV_{II} = \left[\frac{87,500}{(1+0.095)^1} + \frac{87,500}{(1+0.095)^2} + \frac{87,500}{(1+0.095)^3} + \frac{87,500}{(1+0.095)^4} + \frac{87,500}{(1+0.095)^5}\right]$$

$$- 250,000,$$

$$NPV_{II} = [79,908 + 72,976 + 66,645 + 60,862 + 55,582] = -250,000,$$

$$NPV_{II} = 85,973,$$

$$IRR_{II} = 22.1\% \text{ (obtained using a calculator)}.$$

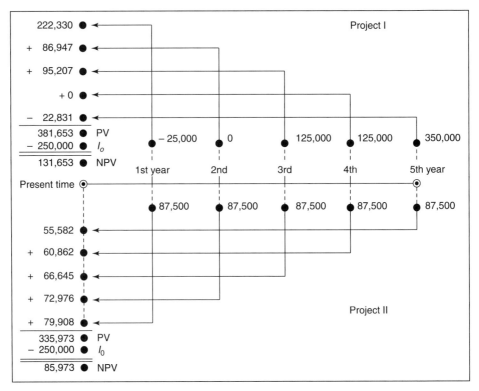

FIGURE 12.7

The calculation shows that the NPV and the IRR are inconsistent across the two projects. While project I has a higher NPV ($NPV_I = 131{,}653$ compared with $NPV_{II} = 85{,}973$), project II has a higher IRR ($IRR_{II} = 22.1$ compared with $IRR_I = 20.2$).

Therefore, the firm has to decide which would be the better project. Theoretically, it would be better for the firm to decide project acceptability on the basis of the higher NPV rather than the higher IRR. One of the justifications for that is the assumption that the earned cash inflows are to be reinvested at a reasonable cost of capital rate, and there would be no guarantee of reinvestment of the cash inflows earned by the other project at a higher rate of return. However, practically most financial managers in the business market tend to favor decisions based on the higher IRR. One interpretation for such a tendency is the common reliance on relative change than on absolute change, which makes the "rates" more preferable than the actual dollar as in the case of the NPV.

The relative measures can still remain reliable for comparison, especially when the firm faces many investment proposals but it cannot afford to fund all proposals except the most profitable one due to budgetary constraints. Let us consider a firm's six investment project proposals requiring different capitals and promising different NPVs as shown in Table 12.6. Suppose that the firm can only allocate a maximum of $800,000 and one of the proposals is asking for an initial capital of $800,000 and the rest of the proposals are asking for funds ranging from $150,000 to $400,000. In this case, it is better not to consider the absolute amounts of the NPV but to find the yield or the NPV per dollar by dividing the NPV by the amount invested or the initial capital allocated.

TABLE 12.6

Projects	I_0 ($)	NPV ($)	NPV/I_0	
I	800,000	2,560,000	3.2%	
II	290,000	725,000	2.5%	
III	250,000	850,000	3.4%	←
IV	350,000	770,000	2.2%	3.6125
V	400,000	1,440,000	3.6%	←
VI	150,000	600,000	4.0%	←
Firm's total funding capacity: $800,000				

The firm can invest in project I only by investing all it has and getting a return of $3.2 per dollar invested, but a combination of more than one project not only reduces the risk that arises by concentration but also increases the return. Therefore, the available capital of $800,000 can be shared by projects III, V, and VI generating a total of $2,890,000 (850,000 + 1,440,000 + 600,000) NPV, which would be translated into a 3.6125% earning per dollar invested ($\frac{2,890,000}{800,000}$). It is higher than the 3.2% from the first project that required the entire investment budget. Projects I, II, and IV would be dismissed.

12.4.4   NPV Profile, Crossover Rate, and the Ranking Reversal

A NPV profile is the relationship between a project's NPV and several alternative costs of capital rates. It is expressed in Table 12.7 and Figure 12.8 for projects I and II. The table and figure show how the NPV changes in response to changes in the firm's cost of capital rate.

TABLE 12.7

	Net Present Value ($)	
Cost of Capital (%)	I	II
0	20,000	25,000
2.5	15,972	20,656
4	12,270	15,662
6	10,527	12,498
7.5	9,057	10,775
8	8,765	8,765
10	5,695	4,307
11.5	2,772	240
13	60	−3,480
15	−2,462	−6,887
IRR	13.3%	11.7%

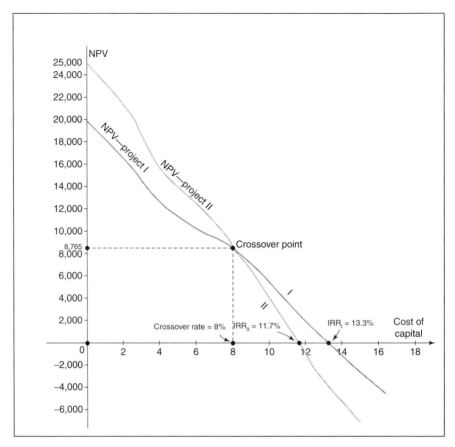

FIGURE 12.8

Looking at Table 12.7 and Figure 12.8, we can make the following observations:

1. Since the relationship between the NPV and the discount rate is negative, both curves, NPV_I and NPV_{II}, are sloping downwards from their initial values of $20,000 and $25,000 at zero rate, to negative values at the highest rate. It means that, as the firm's cost of capital increases, its NPV decreases.

2. The curve for project II is steeper than the curve for project I. This reflects that project II is more sensitive to the change in cost of capital rate than project I:

$$\frac{\partial NPV_{II}}{\partial r} > \frac{\partial NPV_I}{\partial r}.$$

We can observe, for example, that as the cost of capital rate goes up by 92% (from 6% to 11.5%), the NPV for project II goes down by 98% while the NPV for project I declines by 74%:

$$\frac{11.5 - 6}{6} = 92\%, \quad \frac{10,527 - 2772}{10,527} = 74\%, \quad \frac{12,498 - 240}{12,498} = 98\%.$$

The difference in the project sensitivity to changes in the cost of capital is due to the differences in the magnitude as well as the timing of the cash inflows. Because the discounting process is just the reverse of the compounding process, the present value of cash inflows in its later years would decrease at a higher rate than those inflows in its earlier years. This is the reason for the curves to intersect at the crossover point:

1. When the NPVs of the two projects are equal, their curves intersect at the crossover point. The cost of capital rate corresponding to that point is called the crossover rate. Therefore, the crossover rate is defined as the rate at which the NPVs of two projects become equal to each other and where their curves intersect.

2. The crossover rate serves as the turning point where the reversal of project ranking occurs. For any cost of capital below the crossover rate, project II would be preferred for its higher NPV. For any cost of capital above the crossover rate, project I would be preferred for its higher NPV.

3. The NPVs of both projects would decline to zero when they cross the x-axis at their firm's IRR. The graph shows that the IRR for project I is 13.3%, and for project II is 11.7%, and those where the two curves cross the x-axis, respectively.

12.5 PROFITABILITY INDEX AND CAPITAL RATIONING

We have briefly discussed the relative measure of NPV and the NPV per dollar invested. NPV, a relative measure can be considered as one of the criteria for project acceptability. It is the PI that is a ratio of the present value for cash inflows and outflows:

$$PI = \frac{\sum_{i=1}^{t}\left[\dfrac{CF_i}{(1+r)^n}\right]}{\sum_{i=1}^{t}\left[\dfrac{I_i}{(1+r)^n}\right]}.$$

It can also be expressed as a ratio between the present value of cash inflows and the initial investment:

$$PI = \frac{PV(CF_i)}{I_0} PI \geq 1.$$

The criterion for project acceptability is the value of PI, whether the value is equal to or larger than 1, since a value equal to 1 would indicate the equality between the cost and benefit.

In two of the projects mentioned previously, the NPV for one was $770,000, and the other was $600,000, but because the investment capital required for both were $350,000 and $150,000 respectively, their values for the firm would differ dramatically. Calculating the PI for both would reveal the difference. However, we need to restore the present value for cash flows by combining the NPV and the initial investment for both:

$$PV = NPV + I_0,$$

$$PV_1 = 770,000 + 350,000 = 1,120,000,$$

$$PV_2 = 600,000 + 150,000 = 750,000,$$

$$PI_1 = \frac{PV_1(CF_i)}{I_0}$$

$$= \frac{1,120,000}{350,000}$$

$$= 3.2,$$

$$PI_2 = \frac{750,000}{150,000}$$

$$= 5.$$

The conclusion is that while the NPV of the first project ($700,000) is 28% more than the NPV of the second project ($600,000), the PI of the second project (5) is 56% more than the PI of the first project (3.2). This would illustrate the benefits of the PI as a tool, especially when judgment by the NPV alone would not be conclusive. The relative measure of the NPV may rise again when the firm has some constraints on its capacity of investment. Usually, there is a certain limit to a firm's capacity for financing all its available feasible projects. The senior management of firms may fix a limit and determine the maximum capacity of capital investment, and decide whether project financing should be done by borrowing from banks and financial institutions or from the public in terms of corporate bonds and equity shares. Declaring and recognizing the limit on investment may mean recognizing some sort of capital scarcity which should most likely lead to seeking allocation efficiency and that is what is called capital rationing. Capital rationing is defined as the process of allocating scarce financial capital as efficiently as the firm's conditions and circumstances permit. It is obvious that capital rationing would be exercised when the total funds requested to finance all eligible projects exceeds the firm's affordability as set by the maximum level of funding. Capital rationing involves contemplating every possible combination of projects that can be funded, and choosing the best combination of projects where

1. their total required capital would not exceed the firm's maximum level of funding;
2. their total NPV per dollar is the largest among the alternative combinations.

Tables 12.8 and 12.9 show how capital rationing is done. Table 12.8 shows five competing projects all of which were considered worthy, but the firm cannot fund all because the required total capital is $300,000 and the firm's maximum level of funding is $200,000. Table 12.9 lists the possible combinations of projects with their combined capital and combined NPV. It also lists the remaining funds out of the available $200,000 (Column 4) and their compounded future values (Column 5). Column 6 shows the sum of NPV and the accumulated future value, and finally Column 7 shows the adjusted NPV per dollar of funded capital. This is the column that shows which combination of projects is the best based on the highest adjusted NPV per dollar, and that is the combination containing projects (1, 4, and 5) which shows 79% NPV for each dollar of initial investment.

TABLE 12.8

Project	Initial Capital ($)	NPV ($)
1	100,000	60,000
2	75,000	40,000
3	50,000	35,000
4	45,000	30,000
5	30,000	15,000
	300,000	180,000

TABLE 12.9

1	2	3	4	5	6	7
Project Combination	Combined Capital	Combined NPV	Remaining Fund (RM) $200 - (2)$	Value of Invested Remaining Funds $RM(1 + r)^n$	Final NPV $(3 + 5)$	NPV Per $ Invested $(6 \div 2)$
1, 2	175	100	25	33.45	133	0.75
1, 3, 5	195	125	5	6.70	132	0.68
1, 3, 5	180	110	20	26.76	137	0.76
1, 4, 5	175	105	25	33.45	138	0.79
2, 3, 4, 5	200	120	0	0	120	0.60

12.6   PAYBACK METHOD

Among the most common methods that were used to evaluate investment projects, especially during the precomputer age, was the payback method. It may still be in use in some business houses for its simplicity and straightforwardness. Payback period (PB) refers to the expected number of operational years during which the initial investment can be recovered. In particular, as a criterion for project selection, the shorter the PB the better the better the project. The short recovery time would be a crude measure of liquidity of the project. It can also be an indication of less potential risk. The fewer the number of years in which the initial capital can be fully recovered, the more the project can cut off the potential risk that may lie ahead.

The PB can be obtained by the following two techniques:

1. For projects yielding an equal amount of cash inflow during the project life time, PB is obtained by dividing the initial investment or the proposed capital (I) by the annual cash flow (CIF):

$$PB = \frac{I}{CIF}.$$

2. For projects yielding variable cash inflows throughout the years of the project operation. The PB can be obtained by

$$PB = (f - 1) + \left[\frac{I - \sum_{t=1}^{f-1} CIF_t}{CIF_f} \right],$$

where

f = year in which the initial investment can be fully recovered;

$f - 1$ = year before the year of full recovery of the initial investment;

I = initial investment or the capital proposed for allocation;

CIF_t = cash inflow during the period t up to the year before the year of full recovery of initial investment;

CIF_f = the cash inflow in the year of full recovery of the initial investment.

Let us calculate the PB for the following two proposed projects:

Sunshine Company is considering the following two projects for capital allocation. Project X is asking for $64,000 and project Y is asking for $68,000. Calculate the PB for both projects (Table 12.10).

TABLE 12.10

| | Project X ($64,000) | | Project Y ($68,000) | |
| | Expected Profits | | Expected Profits | |
Year	(After Taxes) ($)	Cash Inflows ($)	(After Taxes) ($)	Cash Inflows ($)
1	9,500	16,000	21,500	40,800
2	10,200	16,000	9,000	12,200
3	10,200	16,000	5,500	10,000
4	8,000	16,000	4,500	10,000
5	7,100	16,000	4,000	8,000
	9,000	16,000	8,900	16,000

For project X,

$$PB = \frac{I}{CIF}$$

$$= \frac{64,000}{16,000}$$

$$= 4 \text{ years.}$$

For project Y,

$$
PB = (f - 1) + \left[\frac{I - \sum_{t=1}^{f-1} CIF_f}{CIF_f} \right]
$$

$$
= 3 + \left[\frac{68,000 - (40,800 + 12,200 + 10,000)}{10,000} \right]
$$

$$
= 3.5 \text{ years,}
$$

where

> $f =$ the fourth year since the \$68,000 would be within the accumulated cash inflows by the end of the fourth year, that is (\$40,800 + \$12,200 + \$10,000 + \$10,000 = \$73,000);
>
> $f - 1 =$ the third year (the year before the fourth);
>
> $CIF_f =$ the annual cash inflow (\$10,000) in the fourth year as the year in which the initial investment would be fully recovered.

In addition to the major shortcoming of the payback method wherein the time value of money change is ignored, it has also been criticized for ignoring the dynamics of the cash inflows obtained during the years after the year of full recovery.

12.7 COST OF CAPITAL

Firms usually raise investment capital using either internal or external sources. The only internal source is the allocation of a growth fund out of the firm's own past profits. However, there are many external sources, for example borrowing money either from the public in terms of issuing corporate bonds or from commercial banks in terms of short- and long-term business loans. Another major external source of capital is equity finance wherein business is shared with investors by issuing common and preferred stocks. Generally speaking, firms usually fund their investment projects through a certain combination of debt and equity. Capital budgeting involves the business decisions on whether investment projects should be funded and whether they are worthwhile. It is, therefore, crucial for the management to assess the cost of its funded projects, and this is where the firm's cost of capital comes in the picture.

Cost of capital is defined as the rate of return which

1. the firm must earn on its investment in order to maintain a proper market value for its stock;
2. the investors require in order to make their capital attractive and be able to lead their funds to new investment opportunities.

Since the most common financing sources of capital for the majority of firms are debt and equity financing, we focus on the estimation of the cost of capital in these sources.

12.7.1   Cost of Debt Capital

Cost of debt capital is represented by the rate of return that the lending investors would require when they supply their funds to the firm for a new investment project. As for the borrowing firm, it would be the minimum rate possible that must be earned on the capital borrowed. Since the interests on debt finance are tax deductible, this rate on debt capital is measured on after tax basis. If (k_d^b) is the nominal interest rate (before taxes) that is paid on debt capital, and (T) is the marginal tax rate that the firm usually pays, then the after tax rate of debt capital (k_d^a) is

$$k_d^a = k_d^b(1 - T).$$

Suppose that a firm borrows a certain fund at $9\frac{3}{4}\%$ interest, but it pays 39% marginal tax rate on its earnings, the after tax rate on its debt capital would be

$$k_d^a = 0.0975(1 - 0.39),$$
$$k_d^a = 5.95\%.$$

This calculated rate of interest would be applied only on the additional capital borrowed by the firm. This would give the term "cost of capital" the meaning that it is actually measured in terms of the "marginal" cost of capital. If the firm borrows money from the public in terms of issuing corporate bonds, then its before tax cost of capital (k_{db}^b) in such a long-term debt would be calculated by

$$k_{db}^b = \frac{I + \left[\dfrac{M - NP}{n}\right]}{\left[\dfrac{NP + M}{2}\right]},$$

where I is the annual interest, M is the face value of bond, NP is the net proceeds (face value adjusted to flotation cost), and n is the number of years to redemption.

Suppose a firm is issuing its 20-year corporate bond of $1000 at a coupon rate of $9\frac{3}{4}\%$. The bond is sold at $3\frac{1}{2}\%$ discount and the firm pays a flotation cost of $1\frac{1}{2}\%$ per bond. The cost of capital for this bond can be calculated as

$$I = M(\text{cr}) \text{ cr: coupon rate}$$
$$= (1000)(0.0975) = 97.50.$$

Bond price at discount $(B_d) = 1000(1 - 0.035) = 965,$

$$NP = B_d(1 - 0.015) = 950.52,$$

$$k_{db}^b = \frac{I + \left[\dfrac{M - NP}{n}\right]}{\left[\dfrac{NP + M}{2}\right]}$$

$$= \frac{97.50 + \left[\dfrac{1000 - 950.52}{20}\right]}{\left[\dfrac{950.52 + 1000}{2}\right]}$$

$$= 10.2\%.$$

12.7.2 Cost of Equity Capital

Cost of equity capital is represented by the rate of return that the stockholders require when they share the firm's ownership, by buying its stocks. As for the firm issuing the stocks, it would be the cost of building the firm's equity and elevating its performance to achieve the maximum equity possible. Since dividends paid to stockholders is not tax deductible and it is not going to reduce the firm's taxable income in any form, this rate of return is measured on a before tax basis. The rate of return on equity capital (k_e) incorporates two elements into its estimation:

1. The opportunity cost to investors of forgoing current consumption when diverting some of their income to buy stocks. This element is represented by the interest rate on short-term US treasury bills. It is a **risk-free rate of return** on investment (R_f).
2. The cost of risk that investors take when they choose to invest in stocks as opposed to investing in other safer investment opportunities. This element is represented by the risk premium (R_p).

Therefore, the rate of return on equity capital (k_e) can be

$$k_e = R_f + R_p.$$

There are two common methods to estimate k_e. The **capital asset pricing model (CAPM)** and the dividend evaluation methods. The risk premium (R_p) for any stock in the market can be estimated using the financial index beta (β), and the risk-free interest rate.

The CAPM Estimation   The CAPM can estimate the value of risk premium (R_p) for any stock in the market using the financial index beta (β) that compares the risk associated with any stock to the overall risk of securities in the market. Therefore, the cost of equity capital (k_e) can be estimated as

$$k_e = R_f + R_p,$$
$$k_e = R_f + \beta_i[k_m - R_f],$$

where the risk premium (R_p) is obtained by multiplying the financial index β by the market risk premium, which is the difference between the market expected rate of return (k_m) and the risk-free rate (R_f). The risk premium and the CAPM will be explained in detail in the next chapter. For example, consider a stock that is riskier than the average stock with a beta of 1.3, an expected market return of $8\frac{1}{2}\%$, and a risk-free rate of 5%. The rate of return on equity capital for this particular stock would be

$$
\begin{aligned}
k_e &= R_f + \beta_i[k_m - R_f] \\
&= 0.05 + 1.3[0.085 - 0.05] \\
&= 9.5\%.
\end{aligned}
$$

Now consider a stock safer than the average stock in the market with beta equal to 0.4, and if we assume that the risk-free rate and the expected market rate stay the same, then the rate of return on equity capital would be

$$
\begin{aligned}
k_e &= 0.05 + 0.45[0.085 - 0.05] \\
&= 6.6\%,
\end{aligned}
$$

which makes perfect sense that the riskier stock would cost more than the safer stock.

The Dividend Valuation Estimation   Since the firm issues and sells common stocks and pays dividends to the stockholders, we can assume that the value of a common stock share (V_0) is the present value of all dividends (D_t) paid in the future for period t, discounted at the firm's cost of equity capital (k_e):

$$
\begin{aligned}
V_0 &= \sum_{t=1}^{\infty} \left[\frac{D_t}{(1 + k_e)^t} \right] \\
&= \frac{D_1}{(1 + k_e)^1} + \frac{D_2}{(1 + k_e)^2} + \cdots + \frac{D_t}{(1 + k_e)^t}
\end{aligned}
$$

under the assumption that those dividends will continue to be paid for an indefinite period of time, V_0 can be viewed as a perpetuity, and can therefore be expressed by

$$
V_0 = \frac{D}{k_e},
$$

where the dividend D remains constant throughout the future. But if the dividend increases by a certain annual rate of growth, for example (g), then

$$
V_0 = \frac{D}{k_e - g}.
$$

V_0 is the value of a common stock share and D is the dividend paid to stockholders. We can logically replace V_0 by the market price per share (MPS) and D by the dividend per share (DPS):

$$\text{MPS} = \frac{\text{DPS}}{k_e - g},$$

and therefore, we can express this equation in terms of k_e:

$$\text{MPS} \cdot k_e - \text{MPS} \cdot g = \text{DPS},$$

$$\text{MPS} \cdot k_e = \text{DPS} + \text{MPS} \cdot g,$$

$$k_e = \frac{\text{DPS}}{\text{MPS}} + g,$$

and if we want to use the net market price of a share, we can factor in the percentage of the flotation cost (F) so that the net price per share becomes $\text{MPS}(1 - F)$ and, therefore, the cost of equity capital (k_e) becomes

$$k_e = \frac{\text{DPS}}{\text{MPS}(1 - F)} + g,$$

since the ratio of DPS to the MPS is the dividend yield (DY), the cost of equity capital (k_e) would be equal to the DY plus the dividend growth rate (g):

$$k_e = \text{DY} + g,$$

which is the rate of return used to calculate equity cost while new stock is to be sold or even while using the firm's own retained earnings.

Suppose that the dividend per share for a firm is \$16 and this particular stock sells at \$104 in the market and is expected to increase by 4% every year. The cost of equity capital in this firm can be estimated after obtaining the DY as

$$\text{DY} = \tfrac{16}{104} = 16.6\%,$$

$$k_e = 0.166 + 0.04,$$

$$k_e = 20.6\%.$$

It is important here to say that (g) represents a constant annual rate of growth in the dividend per share. In reality, growth fluctuates over the years and also within the same year. The following formula presents an example of the value of share (V_0) for which the growth varies between nonconstant and constant periods. It is from such specific formulas that a more realistic cost of equity capital can be obtained:

$$V_0 = \sum_{t=1}^{n} \left[\frac{\text{DPS}_t}{(1 + k_e)^t} \right] + \left(\frac{\text{DPS}_{n+1}}{k_e - g} \right) \left[\frac{1}{(1 + k_e)} \right]^n,$$

where

DPS_t = dividend per share for a period t in which the growth rate is constant;

DPS_{n+1} = the first dividend per share obtained for a period in which the growth rate is variable;

k_e = cost of equity capital;

g = constant rate of growth in DPS.

12.7.3   The Weighted Marginal Cost of Capital

Firms use different types of capital to finance their new investment projects. Since each type has its own cost of capital and may pose a different level of risk to the firm, most firms try to maintain an optimal capital structure where they adopt a certain combination of debt and equity capital that would minimize the firm's overall cost of capital and maximize the market stock price. In this case, the MCC becomes a composite rate weighted by the proportion of each type of capital in the firm's capital structure. Let us assume that a firm is using four types of capital, where each has its own proportion (weight) in the firm's capital structure (w_1 through w_4) and each has its own cost of capital rate (k_1 through k_4). The MCC for the firm would be a composite measure represented by the weighted average cost of capital (k_w):

$$k_w = w_1 k_1 + w_2 k_2 + w_3 k_3 + w_4 k_4,$$

$$k_w = \sum_{i=1}^{n} w_i k_i.$$

Suppose that a firm's capital structure is made up of the following components:

1. Common stock—52%
2. Preferred stock—11%
3. Long-term debt—37%

and if the cost of capital for common stock is 13.5%, for preferred stock is 9.25%, and for debt is $7\frac{3}{4}$%, then the weighted average cost of capital for the firm is 10.9% as calculated according to Table 12.11 of the firm's capital structure:

TABLE 12.11

Type of Capital	Proportion (w_i)	Cost of Capital (k_i)	$w_i k_i$
Common stock	52%	13.5%	0.0702
Preferred stock	11%	9.25%	0.010175
Long-term debt	37%	7.75%	0.028675
	100%		$\sum w_i k_i = 0.10905$

Weighted average cost of capital can also be calculated for the industry. Table 12.12 and Figure 12.9 show five firms with their capital structures of debt and equity capitals and their own individual weighted average costs of capital which together form the industry's weighted average cost of capital.

TABLE 12.12

Firm	Debt Capital (w_d)	Cost of Debt Capital (k_d)	Equity Capital (w_e)	Cost of Equity Capital (k_e)	Firm's Weighted Cost of Capital (k_w)	Weight of Firm in Industry (v_i)	$k_w \, v_i$
1	5%	4%	95%	7%	6.85%	33%	2.3%
2	25%	4.25%	75%	7.5%	6.7%	25%	1.7%
3	50%	4.5%	50%	8.75%	6.6%	18%	1.2%
4	75%	4.75%	25%	10.75%	6.25%	15%	0.9%
5	90%	5.5%	10%	13%	6.25%	9%	0.5%

Industry's weighted average cost of capital = 6.6%

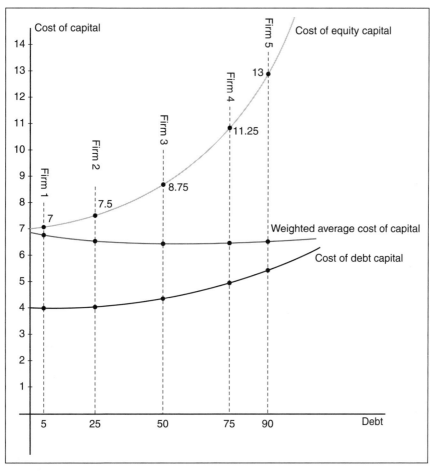

FIGURE 12.9

Generally, if any firm tries to fund new investment projects beyond its affordable limit, the MCC would start to increase right at that point. As we have seen before and as the graph in Figure 12.10 shows, the MCC curve would turn out to be a positively sloped curve at and beyond the point of maximum affordability of funding (the fifth project as shown in Figure 12.10).

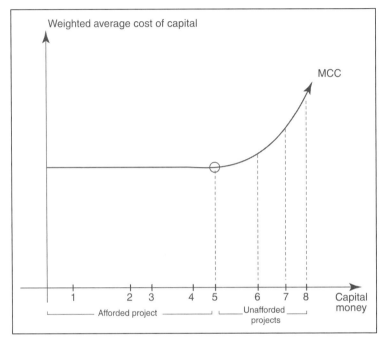

FIGURE 12.10

12.7.4   Capitalization and Capitalized Cost

In relation to capital budgeting, capitalized cost calculations are often used within the firm's decision-making process, especially on selecting the most economic alternative of assets and their uses.

Capitalization of a fund (asset or liability) refers to the present value or cash equivalent of its unlimited number of periodic payments. For example, if a certain fund is invested now at a certain interest rate, we can assume that we would continue to collect periodic interests on that fund forever. Therefore, if we reverse this logic, we can realize that the current fund is, in fact, the present value for all of its periodic payments that are held in perpetuity. Capitalization is used to evaluate the cash equivalent of assets and liabilities that have periodic payments.

From a successful business management perspective, a firm should not only allocate funds to buy capital assets, but also allocate additional funds to maintain them throughout their useful lives, and allocate investment to replace them after they give their due services. Therefore, the capitalized cost of an asset is the sum of its original cost, the present value of unlimited maintenance cost, and the present value of unlimited number of replacements:

$$K = C + \frac{C - S}{(1 + r)^n - 1} + \frac{M}{r},$$

where

K = capitalized cost of an asset;

C = original cost of the asset;

S = scrap value of the asset after its useful life;

M = annual maintenance cost of the asset.

Let us suppose that a construction company is contemplating the purchase of heavy equipment. The decision maker narrowed down the alternatives to two of the best machines (Table 12.13).

TABLE 12.13

	Machine I	Machine II
Initial cost ($)	35,000	39,000
Useful life (years)	10	15
Annual maintenance ($)	3,000	2,500
Scrap value ($)	5,000	4,000

Which of the two machines should be purchased if the interest rate is $9\frac{1}{2}\%$?

We calculate the capitalized cost for both machines individually and then choose the least costly as the better alternative:

$$K_1 = C_1 + \frac{C_1 - S_1}{(1 + r)^n - 1} + \frac{M_1}{r}$$

$$= \$35,000 + \frac{\$35,000 = \$5000}{(1 + 0.095)^{10} - 1} + \frac{\$3000}{0.095}$$

$$= \$86,873.52,$$

$$K_2 = C_2 + \frac{C_2 - S_2}{(1 + r)^n - 1} + \frac{M_2}{r}$$

$$= \$39,000 + \frac{\$39,000 = \$4000}{(1 + 0.095)^{15} - 1} + \frac{\$2500}{0.095}$$

$$= \$77,379.25.$$

Machine II should be purchased for having lesser capitalized cost.

Example 12.5

A town board was asked to estimate an endowment to build a children's playground. If the construction costs $50,000 and needs to be replaced every 10 years at an estimated cost of

$40,000, and the maintenance cost is $15,000, how much would the endowment be when the interest rate is 12%?

Solution:

The endowment total would be considered a capitalized cost and the replacement cost would be the $(C - S)$:

$$K = \$50,000 + \frac{\$40,000}{(1 + 0.12)^{10} - 1} + \frac{\$1500}{0.12}$$

$$K = \$193,994.72.$$

The board will ask the donor to allocate $194,000.

Another purpose of capitalized cost is to figure out the extent of improvement that can be made on asset performance or equipment productivity. Let us assume that we have a printing machine, the original cost of which was $65,000 and its scrap value is estimated at $5000 after 12 years. The productivity of the machine is 20,000 books a year and its maintenance cost is $3000. The firm's engineer figured that installing an additional part could raise the machine's productivity to 30,000 books a year without affecting its maintenance or its useful age. How much can the firm spend economically to achieve the boost in productivity if the investment rate is 8%?

Here, we can set an equation of ratios—the ratios of the capitalized costs of the machine to its productivity before and after the technological improvement. If K_b and K_a are the capitalized costs of the machine before and after the technological improvement, and P_b and P_a are the productivities of the machine before and after the technological improvement, then

$$\frac{K_b}{P_b} = \frac{K_a}{P_a}.$$

We set up the capitalized costs where the question (how much can we spend?) would be an addition (x) to the original cost in the calculation of the capitalized cost after the technological improvement. Then we would algebraically solve for x:

$$K_b = C_b + \frac{C_b - S_b}{(1 + r)^n - 1} + \frac{M_b}{r},$$

$$K_b = \$65,000 + \frac{\$65,000 - \$5000}{(1 + 0.08)^{12} - 1} + \frac{\$3000}{0.08},$$

$$K_b = \$142,021,$$

$$K_a = C_a + \frac{C_a - S_a}{(1 + r)^n - 1} + \frac{M_a}{r}.$$

Since $C_a = C_b + x$, where x is what should be spent on the technological improvement of the machine

and $S_a = S_b$

$M_a = M_b$, where there would be no change in the life of the machine and its residual value.

Then

$$K_a = (C_b + x) + \frac{C_b + x - S_b}{(1+r)^n - 1} + \frac{M_b}{r},$$

$$K_a = (\$65{,}000 + x) + \frac{\$65{,}000 + x - \$5000}{(1+0.08)^{12} - 1} + \frac{\$3000}{0.08},$$

$$K_a = \frac{\$227{,}271 + 3x}{1.5},$$

$$\frac{K_b}{P_b} = \frac{K_a}{P_a},$$

$$\frac{\$142{,}021}{20{,}000} = \frac{\dfrac{\$227{,}271 + 3x}{1.5}}{30{,}000,}$$

$$x = \$30{,}758.$$

The firm can spend \$30,758 to improve the machine and raise its productivity to 30,000 books a year.

12.7.5 Last Words on the Cost of Capital

- Throughout the discussion on the cost of capital, it was assumed that only the flotation cost would tell the difference between the new common stock and the retained earnings when it comes to the cost of capital for both. In reality, there could be other reasons for the difference. Among those reasons is the plausible investor's preference for capital gain (as represented by g) over the DY, that is, $\left(\frac{\text{DPS}}{\text{MPS}}\right)$. This preference can most likely be due to the fact that capital gains are taxed at a lower tax rate than the dividend income when it comes to the personal income tax for investors.

- In our explanation, the typical cost of capital did not include neither the firm's depreciation as a source of capital, which may be significant for some firms nor the firm's deferred taxes, which sometimes form a source of capital, and can, in reality, be collectively considered a source equal to an interest-free loan from the internal revenue service (**IRS**).

- The discussion focused on the publicly owned corporations but the same principles of the cost of capital should apply to private, nonpublicly owned trading firms, as well as to small businesses.

- Just like with many theoretical concepts, cost of capital calculations may prove to be difficult to be used in practice, especially for estimating the risk premium for different securities, as well as for correctly assessing risks and growth rates.

SUMMARY

- This is the first chapter in the last unit that addresses the managerial decisions in the long run. It discusses capital budgeting, which focuses on the strategic planning of all capital expenditures that are made to sustain a stable and more productive future for the firm. Specifically, capital budgeting is concerned about making decisions to replace, improve, and expand the firm's major existing resource base compared with only extracting performance out of the resources. The emphasis would primarily be placed on assessing the firm's investment opportunities in order to choose the most viable option.

- The underlying theoretical framework for capital budgeting is based on the economic equimarginal principle, which states that a firm would pursue and continue to engage in an activity until the marginal cost is equal to its marginal benefit. As for the firm's decisions on investment projects, the principle is applied in a way that capital would continue to be allocated for investment purposes to the point where marginal return on investment, as represented by the incremental cash flows, would equal the marginal cost as represented by the added expenditures and the new investment capitals.

- There are two groups of methods of evaluation for the capital budgeting projects. The first group, which is commonly employed, consists of value-adjusted methods because they use time value of money to establish reliable criteria for project worthiness. This group includes the net present value (NPV), the internal rate of return (IRR), and the profitability index (PI). The second group includes the value-unadjusted methods because they do not use any time value of money adjustment. This group includes the PB technique. The NPV refers to the estimated stream of net cash flows from a project as it is discounted to the current value at the firm's cost of capital. The criterion is that the NPV has to be positive in order to undertake a proposed investment project. As for the IRR, it refers to the rate of discount at which the present value of the project's future cash flows would be equal to the initial capital invested in the project. The IRR has to be higher than the firm's cost of capital in order that the firm to approve the allocation of any investment capital. The PI refers to the ratio of the present value of the future cash flows of a project to the initial investment in the project. It is a useful measure to make a comparison of the proposed projects. The firm would naturally prefer the project with the highest PI. As for the payback method, the period of payback refers to the expected number of operational years during which the initial investment can be recovered. The shorter the period, the higher the preference for the project.

- The firm's cost of capital is the rate of return required to be earned in order to maintain a proper market value for the firm's stocks and it is also the rate required by investors in order that their capital be attractive and rewarding. Firms use either internal sources of capital, for example, the portion of their own profits that are dedicated for growth, or external sources, for example, borrowing or issuing common and preferred stocks for sharing the business equity. Cost of debt capital is the rate of return required by lenders if they supply funds for investment. Cost of equity capital is the rate of return that stockholders require when they share the firm's ownership by buying stocks. This rate is formed by the risk-free rate on short-term treasury bills and the risk premium. The capital asset pricing model (CAPM) is used to estimate the value of risk premium for any stock in the market using the financial index beta, which compares the risk associated with any stock to the overall risk of securities in the market. Since most firms use different types of funding capital, each with its own cost of capital, the weighted marginal cost of capital can serve as a composite rate weighted by the proportions of each type of capital used.

- Capitalization of a fund refers to the present value or cash equivalent of its unlimited number of periodic payments. It is used to evaluate the cash equivalent of assets and liabilities that have periodic payments. The capitalized cost of an asset is the sum of its original cost, the present value of unlimited maintenance cost, and the present value of unlimited number of replacements. For example, in buying equipment, a firm would choose the one with least capitalized cost. Another purpose of capitalized cost is to figure out the extent of improvement that can be made on an asset's performance or equipment's productivity.

KEY TERMS

capital budgeting
net present value
    (NPV)
profitability index (PI)
payback
cost of debt capital
risk premium
    financial beta

dividend valuation
capitalization
composite cost of capital
project evaluation
internal rate of return (IRR)
capital rationing
cost of capital

cost of equity capital
risk-free rate of return
capital asset pricing
    model (CAPM)
weighted marginal
    cost of capital
capitalized cost

LIST OF FORMULAS

• Net present value:

$$NPV = \sum_{i=1}^{t} \left[\frac{CF_i}{(1+r)^n} \right] - I_0.$$

• NPV in terms of profit and adjusted for depreciation and taxes:

$$NPV = \sum_{i=1}^{t} \left\{ \frac{[TR_i - TC_i](1 - T) + D_i}{(1+r)^n} \right\} - I_0.$$

• Internal rate of return:

$$IRR = \left[\frac{\sum_{i=1}^{n} CF_i - I_0}{\sum_i CF_i} \right].$$

• Profitability index:

$$PI = \frac{\sum_{i=1}^{t} \left[\frac{CF_i}{(1+r)^n} \right]}{\sum_{i=1}^{t} \left[\frac{I_i}{(1+r)^n} \right]}$$

$$PI = \frac{PV(CF_i)}{I_0}.$$

- Payback:

$$PB = \frac{I}{CIF},$$

$$PB = (f - 1) + \left[\frac{I - \sum_{t=1}^{F-1} CIF}{CIF} \right].$$

- Before Tax cost of capital for corporate bonds:

$$K_{db}^b = \frac{I + \left[\dfrac{M - NP}{n} \right]}{\left[\dfrac{NP + M}{2} \right]}.$$

- Cost of equity capital:

$$k_e = R_f + R_p.$$

    (a) With dividend growth:

$$k_e = \frac{DPS}{MPS(1 - F)} + g.$$

    (b) In terms of dividend yield:

$$k_e = DY + g.$$

- Risk premium:

$$RP = \beta_i [K_m - R_f].$$

- Value of common stock share:

$$V_0 = \sum_{t=1}^{\infty} \left[\frac{D_t}{(1 + k_e)^t} \right].$$

- Value of common stock share in terms of dividend per share:

$$V_0 = \sum_{t=1}^{n} \left[\frac{DPS_t}{(1 + k_e)^t} \right] + \left(\frac{DPS_{n+1}}{k_e - g} \right) \left[\frac{1}{(1 + k_e)} \right]^n.$$

- Weighted marginal cost of capital:

$$k_w = \sum_{i=1}^{n} w_i k_i.$$

- Capitalized costs:

$$K = C + \frac{C - S}{(1 + r)^n - 1} + \frac{M}{r}.$$

EXERCISES

1. Explain the purpose and basic principle of capital budgeting and how it works to serve the business?

2. List, explain, and compare the capital budgeting technical tools by which the proposed investment projects are usually evaluated for acceptance and allocation.

3. What is capital rationing? When should a firm ration its capital and what are the criteria and the process for such rationing?

4. List and explain the ways by which firms usually finance their investment projects. Explain the rate of returns required by each method of financing. What are the implications of multiple ways of financing for a firm, each with its own rate of return?

5. What is CAPM? What is its importance and how does it work?

6. The following table shows information on two proposed projects. Which project is most likely to win a funding approval?

Year	Project A—Initial Investment: 20,000 Cash Outflow	Project B—Initial Investment: 20,000 Cash Outflow
1	4,000	8,000
2	16,000	8,000
3	2,000	8,000
4	2,000	8,000

7. Calculate the approximate IRR for a proposed project wherein its presenters are asking for an initial capital of:

Period	Cash Flow	Initial Investment
1	20,000	100,000
2	40,000	
3	60,000	
4	40,000	
5	10,000	

8. Use the information given in the table below to (a) calculate the NPV and the PI for all three proposed projects and (b) determine the best funding decision for the firm considering these proposals.

Project	Present Value of Net Cash Flow	Initial Investment
A	7,800,000	6,000,000
B	4,200,000	3,000,000
C	4,200,000	3,000,000

9. A 20-year corporate bond of $2000 is issued at $8\frac{1}{2}\%$ coupon rate and is sold at $2\frac{3}{4}\%$ discount with a flotation cost of $1\frac{3}{4}\%$. What would be the cost of capital?

10. If the price of a certain stock is $56.00 with a potential annual growth rate of $5\frac{3}{4}\%$, what would be the cost of equity capital if the DPS in this firm is $9.80?

13

RISK ANALYSIS AND MANAGERIAL DECISIONS UNDER UNCERTAINTY

13.1 RISK AND UNCERTAINTY

It is fortunate that some managerial decisions are made under a good degree of certainty. However, a considerable number of other decisions are still to be made under the conditions of risk and uncertainty. **Certainty** in this context refers to the condition of having one possible outcome that is known and confirmed to the decision maker. Contrary to that, whenever there is a possibility of having more than one outcome, the condition is considered either risky or uncertain. This leads us to the distinction between risk and uncertainty, the two terms that may be used interchangeably but have a thin, though crucial, line between them, especially in the context of financial and economic considerations.

Risk refers to the condition in which there are multiple possible outcomes and the probability of each alternative outcome either is known or can be estimated. **Uncertainty** shares the first element with risk—the existence of multiple possible outcomes—but differs in the second element, so that the probability of each outcome either is unknown or cannot be estimated.

Managerial decisions often follow a certain scheme when it comes to facing conditions of risk or uncertainty. The scheme includes the following steps:

- Predicting a set of possible future conditions that would affect any possible managerial decision. These are often called the states of nature.
- Estimating the **expected payoff** for each possible decision and each possible state of nature.

Organizing these elements for each managerial decision would form a payoff matrix.

Managerial Economics: A Mathematical Approach, First Edition. M. J. Alhabeeb and L. Joe Moffitt.
© 2013 John Wiley & Sons, Inc. Published 2013 by John Wiley & Sons, Inc.

Suppose that a manager has to choose among three possible decisions: opening a new branch for the company, expanding and updating the existing branch, or just keeping the current branch with no change. Also suppose that the company sees the possibility of the economy descending into a recession during the next period. If the company can estimate the alternative outcomes in terms of the amount of total profits that can be earned in each of the possibilities, a payoff matrix can be constructed like Table 13.1.

TABLE 13.1

Decision/State of Nature	Recession	No Recession
Opening a new branch	$290,000	$350,000
Expanding the current branch	$480,000	$400,000
Keeping the current branch as it is	$300,000	$320,000

Comparing the option of no change with that of building a new branch reveals that doing nothing would do slightly better in a recession and slightly worse in no recession. However, the picture is significantly different when considering an expansion and renovation project. It would do much better than keeping the current state of the company in both economic conditions. However, comparing the expansion and renovation to establishing a new branch seems much better in recession and slightly better in no recession. This concludes and confirms that going with the expansion and renovation project is the winning decision no matter where the economy is heading.

13.2 SOURCES OF RISK

Many possible sources can introduce certain conditions of risk to the managerial decision-making process. Most of these sources are external to the firm. We can group the most common sources into four categories.

13.2.1 Economic Sources

This category includes a variety of sources that are related to the economic environment of a country. The fluctuations in the financial market pose a credible risk to the value of assets in the current and future periods. Such a risk is known as "market risk." Major economic factors such as inflation and interest rate pose yet another significant impact on prices and the value of lending and borrowing and their impact on earnings. Changes in the credit obligation and in the state of liquidity can also introduce credit risk and liquidity risk, in addition to the currency risk that can stem from changes in the exchange rate between the domestic and foreign currencies. Also, the state of competition in the same industry or region poses another type of economic risk.

13.2.2 Political Sources

This type of risk is related to the government policies, domestically and internationally, that may introduce certain risks to an industry in particular or to the economy as a whole.

One specific risk is the change in tax policies. Another possible risk is the "expropriation risk," where a government abroad may seize the property, restrict the rights, or remove the privileges of the hosted firm. Terrorism nowadays constitutes a significant political risk on business activities of all firms, domestically and globally.

13.2.3   Social Sources

These sources include the type of risks related to cultural or religious reasons or to certain social norms or trends that affect consumer preferences and demand. For example, certain food or clothing items or weather-related products may not have any chance to be marketed in certain countries, which is a big reason to determine the orientation of business dealing with such products.

Even domestically, consumer taste and preferences are subject to change, and any business that cannot respond and keep up with those changes would face the risk of losing its market share.

13.2.4   International Sources

A variety of risks can arise from within a certain firm or from the entire industry for commercially competitive reasons or for power conflicts and political struggles among the leadership personnel. They can also be related to the firm's inability to cope with the rising cost of production, declining demand of its products, or its failure to keep up with the technological advances in its own industry.

13.3   MEASUREMENT OF RISK

As it involves calculable multiple outcomes, risk can be defined in terms of the variability of those outcomes and to what extent they are dispersed. The relationship between risk and variability and dispersion of outcomes is direct. Large variability and wide dispersion means higher risk, whereas small variability and tight distribution of outcomes indicate lower risk. For example, if an investment earns a 5% fixed and guaranteed rate of return in one opportunity and may earn anywhere between 10% and 30% on another opportunity, we can easily realize that it would be considered risk-free in the first opportunity and highly risky in the second opportunity. Such a realization of the higher risk is definitely based on the wide range of possibilities of the earned return in the second opportunity. Ironically, in considering this example, we can also vividly see that the only possibility of earning a very high return such as 30% is available only with the risky package, hence the other direct relationship between risk and return. Seeking higher returns means the willingness to deal with higher risk and seeking security means accepting a modest return.

Therefore, risk can be measured by the classic statistical measurement of dispersion; that is, variance or standard deviation. We can classify this measure as an absolute and a **relative measure of risk**.

13.3.1   The Absolute Measure

The objective here is to see how the actual outcome deviates from the expected value. Suppose that we are considering how risky some assets are on the basis of their returns. The most simple idea that may come to mind first is to contemplate the range of those returns as a hint to the dispersion of returns. If, for simplicity, we take assets X and Y with three returns for each, as in Table 13.2, we can see that the difference between the highest and lowest returns for each would refer to more dispersion for asset Y (range: $15 - 5 = 10$), than for asset X (range: $11 - 9 = 2$). This may indicate that asset Y is riskier than asset X for having higher variability of returns.

TABLE 13.2

Return	X	Y
k_1	9	5
k_2	11	10
k_3	11	15
Range: $k_3 - k_1$	2	10

This variability notion can be better represented by the probability distribution of returns. The tighter the probability distribution, the more likely it is to have the actual return close to the expected value, and therefore, the lower the risk for that asset. On the other hand, the wider the probability distribution, the higher the variability of returns, and the higher the risk.

Variance (σ^2) provides a measure of variability or dispersion, for it is the weighted average of the squared deviations from the mean:

$$\sigma^2 = \sum_{i=1}^{n} [x - \bar{x}]^2 P(x).$$

The mean $\bar{x}$ here is the expected value of outcomes, which is calculated as the summation of the actual outcomes x_i multiplied by the probabilities in which the actual outcomes may occur (Px_i):

$$\bar{x} = \text{Expected value} = \sum_{i=1}^{n} x_i P(x_i).$$

Risk as expressed by variability or dispersion of outcomes can also be measured by the standard deviation (σ), as it is the square root of variance (σ^2):

$$\sigma = \sqrt{\sum_{i=1}^{n} [x - \bar{x}]^2 P(x_i)}.$$

Let us calculate the standard deviations of assets X and Y in Table 13.3, given that the probabilities of their returns are 25%, 50%, and 25%, respectively, for their three returns.

$$\Sigma_x = \sqrt{0.5} = 0.71.$$

$$\Sigma_y = \sqrt{12.5} = 3.5.$$

TABLE 13.3

Asset X	x_i	$P(x_i)$	$x_i P(x_i)$	$x_i - \bar{x}$	$[x_i - \bar{x}]^2$	$[x_i - \bar{x}]P(x_i)$
	9	0.25	2.25	−1	1	0.25
	10	0.50	5.00	0	0	0
	11	0.25	2.75	1	1	0.25
Asset Y	$\bar{x} = \Sigma x_i P(x_i) = 10$				$\sigma^2 = \Sigma[x_i - \bar{x}]^2 P(x_i) = 0.5$	
	5	0.25	1.25	−5	25	6.25
	10	0.50	5	0	0	0
	15	0.25	3.75	5	25	6.25
	$\bar{x} = \Sigma x_i P(x_i) = 10$				$\sigma^2 = \Sigma[x_i - \bar{x}]^2 P(x_i) = 12.5$	

The standard deviation of 0.71 means that the returns on asset X are much closer to their own expected value than the returns on asset Y, which has a standard deviation of 3.5, indicating how wide the dispersion of returns is, as shown in Figure 13.1.

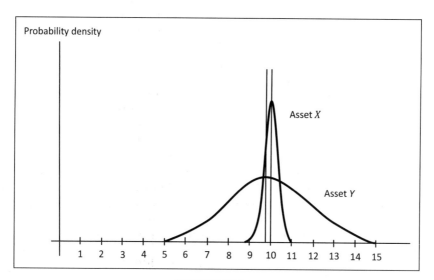

FIGURE 13.1

In the long run, asset risk would be an increasing function of time. The variability of returns gets wider and the risk gets greater as time goes by. Practically, this would be translated as that the longer the life of an investment asset, the higher the risk involved. Figure 13.2 shows how the dispersion of returns gets wider over 20 years.

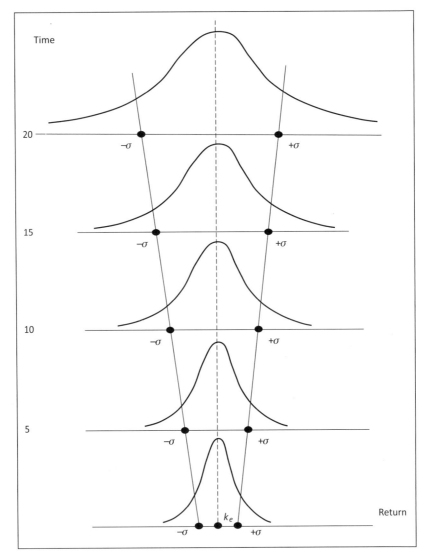

FIGURE 13.2

Example 13.1

Suppose that two investment project proposals were submitted to a firm for funding. The proposals came with their own estimations of the profits (in hundreds of thousands of dollars) that the two projects expect to earn in the next 5 years. How would the managers make their choice?

Solution:

First, we have to calculate the mean profit (expected value) for each project for 5 years, and second, we have to calculate the project's variances and standard deviations individually, as we arrange data in Tables 13.4 and 13.5.

TABLE 13.4

		Project I				
Years	Predicted Profits x_i	Probability $P(x_i)$	$x_iP(x_i)$	$[x_i - \bar{x}]$	$[x_i - \bar{x}]^2$	$[x_i - \bar{x}]^2 P(x_i)$
1	4375	0.10	437.5	−625	390,625	39,062.5
2	4450	0.25	1112.5	−550	302,500	75,625
3	4850	0.30	1455	−150	22,500	6,750
4	5300	0.25	1325	300	90,000	22,500
5	6700	0.10	670	1700	2,890,000	289,000

$$\bar{x} = \sum_{i=1}^{5} x_i P(x_i) = 5000 \qquad \sigma^2 = \sum_{i=1}^{5} [x_i - \bar{x}]^2 P(x_i) = 432,937$$

$$\sigma = \sqrt{432,937} = 658$$

TABLE 13.5

		Project II				
Years	Predicted Profits x_i	Probability $P(x_i)$	$x_iP(x_i)$	$[x_i - \bar{x}]$	$[x_i - \bar{x}]^2$	$[x_i - \bar{x}]^2 P(x_i)$
1	2000	0.10	200	−3000	9,000,000	900,000
2	3500	0.25	875	−1500	2,250,000	562,500
3	5000	0.30	1500	0	0	0
4	6500	0.25	1625	1500	2,250,000	562,500
5	8000	0.10	800	3000	9,000,000	900,000

$$\bar{x} = \sum_{i=1}^{5} x_i P(x_i) = 5000 \qquad \sigma^2 = \sum_{i=1}^{5} [x_i - \bar{x}]^2 P(x_i) = 2,925,000$$

$$\sigma = \sqrt{2,925,000} = 1710$$

Since the two projects yield the same expected value, the next crucial criterion would be which of them is safer or riskier than the other. The answer would be clear with the calculation of variance (σ^2) and standard deviation (σ). The calculated results show that project I had a smaller standard deviation (658) than project II (1710). Project I would win for being less risky than project II. It is clear in Figure 13.3 how data of project II are dispersed over horizontally, forming a widely spread curve, whereas they are much tighter in project I, showing how the outcomes are generally close to the expected value or mean.

As for the significance of standard deviation in expressing the dispersion of outcomes, and therefore reflecting the risk level, it means the following, under the assumption that the distribution is normal.

There is a 68.26% chance that the actual outcome is within one standard deviation from the expected value. Based on the symmetry of the normal distribution, this chance is divided equally between a negative 34.13% and a positive 34.13%. So, if the standard deviation is 1710, for example, there would be a 34.13% chance that the actual value is 5000 + 1710,

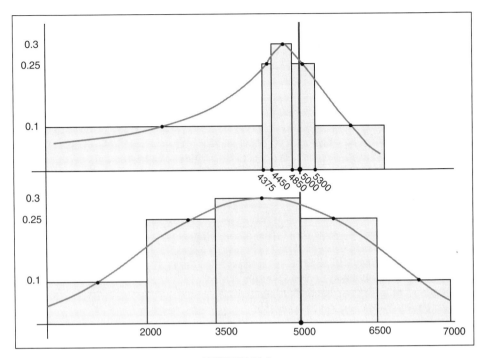

FIGURE 13.3

and a 34.13% chance that it is 5000 – 1710. So the general range would be from 3290 to 6710. The chance would increase to 95.44% within two standard deviations (2 × 1710), which is also split equally on both sides of the mean. In this case, the chance would be 47.7% that the range of the actual outcome would be between 1580 (i.e., 5000 – (2 × 1710)) and 8420 (i.e., 5000 + (2 × 1710)).

It is clear that if we deal with a smaller standard deviation such as 658, the ranges of the actual outcome would be closer to the expected value, rendering more security and less risk.

This interpretation is, of course, not limited to the discrete one, two, and three standard deviations from the mean. It would apply to any range in between. Therefore, we can find the probability of a specific outcome (x_i) such as 5500, for example. We can calculate how much of a standard deviation from the mean ($\bar{x}$) this value would reveal by calculating the value of Z and looking up the statistical table of the normal distribution (Table A.8):

$$Z = \frac{x_i - \bar{x}}{\sigma},$$

$$Z = \frac{5500 - 5000}{658} = 0.76.$$

This means that if we have an actual outcome of 5500, it would fall within a little more than three quarters of a standard deviation from the expected value. Looking at the table between 0.7 and 0.8 vertically (z-value) and under 2% horizontally, we can see that the area under the curve would be between 0.26 and 0.29.

13.3.2   The Relative Measure

The last example on the choice of two projects, as to which one of them was risky, depended on the comparison of their standard deviation as an **absolute measure of risk**. It was mainly because the two projects had the same expected value. However, when we have projects within different expected values, then the comparison of their standard deviations has to be first and foremost relative to their expected value. This is why we need to calculate the **coefficient of variation** (V), which better measures the outcome dispersion as it is related to each of the expected values individually:

$$V = \frac{\sigma}{\bar{x}}.$$

In this sense, the measure of risk would be translated into a measure of standard deviation per unit of the expected value. The relationship between the coefficient of variation and risk is still as positive. The lower the value of the coefficient, the lower the risk, whereas the higher the value, the riskier the outcome.

In our absolute measure in the last example, project II $(\sigma = 1710)$ was riskier than project I $(\sigma = 658)$, while both would yield the same expected value $(\bar{x} = 5000)$. Suppose now that project II has an expected value of $6000. It would still be riskier than project I if we compare their coefficient of variation (V):

$$V_{\text{I}} = \frac{\sigma_{\text{I}}}{\bar{x}_{\text{I}}} = \frac{658}{5000} = 0.13,$$

$$V_{\text{II}} = \frac{\sigma_{\text{II}}}{\bar{x}_{\text{II}}} = \frac{1710}{6000} = 0.28,$$

where project II reveals a higher coefficient of variation reflecting a higher risk.

13.4   RISK AVERSION

Risk aversion refers to people's general tendency to avoid, or at least minimize, risk and uncertainty in various decisions they make. There are three major attitudes that different decision makers exhibit toward risk. These attitudes reflect who these decision makers are:

- *Risk averter*: Given the choice between risk and no risk, a risk averter would choose the no-risk position. Among situations that all bear certain levels of risk, a risk averter would choose the lowest possible level of risk.
- *Risk-taker*: Risk-takers are those who prefer to venture and get involved in risky situations and in conditions that require a higher level of speculation in pursuit of the highest possible payoff.
- *Risk neutral*: A risk neutral is one who is indifferent to risk. A person who focuses on expected returns much more than to pay any attention to the way those returns are dispersed.

Although it has been very well established in the business world that the highest return is usually associated with the highest risk, most people, and specifically managers, are naturally risk averters, in particular when larger potential losses are involved. It has been observed that even risk neutrals would turn into risk averters when large amounts of money are at stake.

Suppose that a group of people in a club decide to play a coin gamble. Since many want to play, the following rules are put forward.

If it is heads, the player wins $200. If it is tails, the player loses $100. Because there is a competition to play, $10 is offered to the player who gives up his turn, basically pledges not to play. According to the definition of people's attitudes toward risk, a risk averter would have no problem leaving the game and take the sure $10 for doing nothing. For him, it would be pure and sure gain, although it is at the expense of foregoing a possibility of gaining $200. He would focus more on the equal possibility of losing $100, and therefore the $10 seems the best way to go. For a risk neutral, the focus would be on the weighted average that would come out of this game. He would make his decision based on the fact that in reality there would be an average gain since the amount of gain is higher than the amount of loss while both stand the same possibility. In this case, the risk neutral would calculate the expected value as follows:

$$x_1(p_1) + x_2(p_2) = \bar{x},$$

$$(200)(0.5) + (-100)(0.5) = 50.$$

A risk-taker would be the most enthusiastic to play, focusing on the highest win; he may not hesitate to play again in pursuit of $200.

13.5   RISK ATTITUDES AND UTILITY OF MONEY

The three types of attitudes taken by decision makers toward risk can be explained by the utility they derive from the money earned. Each attitude can be represented more accurately by the change in their total utility or what we call the marginal utility. This marginal utility is generally decreasing for the risk averter and increasing for the risk-taker and constant for the risk neutral. Tables 13.6, 13.7, and 13.8 contain data on five possible payoffs and both total utility and marginal utility derived from them, as it is subjectively determined by the three types of decision makers. Figure 13.4 uses these data and shows us a decreasing marginal utility (DMU) curve for the risk averter, an increasing marginal utility (IMU) curve for the risk-taker, and an upward straight line—constant marginal utility (CMU)—for the risk neutral.

TABLE 13.6

	Decreasing	
Payoff	Utility	Rate of Utility
−25,000	−6	
0	0	6
25,000	4	4
50,000	6	2
75,000	7.5	1.5
100,000	8.25	0.75

TABLE 13.7

| Payoff | Increasing | |
	Utility	Rate of Utility
−25,000	−1.75	
0	0	1.75
25,000	2	2
50,000	5	3
75,000	8.5	3.5
100,000	13.25	4.75

TABLE 13.8

| Payoff | Constant | |
	Utility	Rate of Utility
−25,000	−5	
0	0	5
25,000	5	5
50,000	10	5
75,000	15	5
100,000	20	5

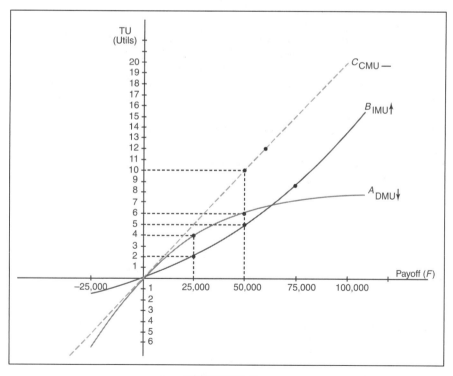

FIGURE 13.4

We can visually observe how three managers represented by their marginal utility curves *A*, *B*, and *C* perceive their money and assess its utility. For example, if we take a payoff of $50,000, it would provide a total utility (TU) of 6 utils for the risk averter represented by the diminishing marginal utility concave curve (*A*), provides 5 utils for the risk-taker represented by the increasing marginal utility convex curve (*B*), and provides 10 utils for the risk neutral represented by the constant marginal utility, straight line (*C*). We can observe further differences among these three managers based on their attitudes toward winning and losing money. If we consider an event that would increase the payoff from $50,000 to $75,000!, how would these managers respond? The risk averter's total utility would increase from 6 to 7.5 gaining 1.5 utils, the risk-taker's utility would increase from 5 to 8.5 gaining 3.5 utils, and the risk neutral's utility would increase from 10 to 15 gaining 5 utils, gaining 5 utils. The risk averter ultimately gained the least among the three from the same amount of money. Such a gain would get even less when we move them further in the payoff from $75,000 to $100,000. The risk averter would gain only 0.75 utils compared with 4.75 utils for the risk-taker and 5 utils for the risk neutral. This theoretical approximation means that only the risk neutral would respond proportionally to the change in the monetary payoff. He would take it dollar for dollar—or, a dollar gained would equal a dollar lost for him. It is an attitude of indifference toward risk. Table 13.9 shows that where the percentage change in the last column is identical in both cases with the percentage change in the payoff amounts in the second column. It also shows that the risk averter's utility responds less than proportionally compared with the change in the payoff where the third column shows 0.25 and 0.10 are less than their corresponding changes in the payoff amount, 0.50 and 0.30 respectively in the second column. As for the risk-taker's utility, it responds more than proportionally to the monetary change in the payoff amount. Note the percentage changes in the sixth column (0.70 and 0.56) and compare them with their corresponding changes of the payoff amounts in the second column (0.50 and 0.30), respectively. All the percentage changes were obtained by dividing the difference between the later and earlier amounts by the earlier amount:

$$\% \Delta x = \frac{x_2 - x_1}{x_1}.$$

TABLE 13.9

1	2	3	4	5	6	7	8
		Risk		Risk-		Risk	
	% Δ in	Averter's		Taker's		Neutral	
Payoff	Payoff	Utility	% Δ	Utility	% Δ	Utility	% Δ
$50,000		6		5		10	
$75,000	0.50	7.5	0.25	8.5	0.70	15	0.50
$100,000	0.30	8.25	0.10	13.25	0.56	20	0.30

13.6   EXPECTED UTILITY OF MONEY VERSUS EXPECTED MONETARY RETURN

Let us consider a fair game; according to statisticians, a fair game is one in which the expected value of the payoff is equal to zero. Let us consider the classic example of a firm's manager deciding on whether to invest in oil drilling in a certain area or not. He is considering the following possibilities if he decides to drill:

1. If no oil turns up, he would lose all the cost ($25,000). This outcome has 80% probability.
2. If there is oil, the payoff would be $100,000, but this case has only 20% probability.

The expected value of drilling would be

$$(100,000)(0.20) + (-25,000)(0.80) = 0,$$

and of course, if he decides not to drill, the expected value would already be zero. So, under this fair game, it would not matter what decision the manager takes. Both to drill and not to drill would eventually lead to a zero outcome. In this scenario, a decision based on the expected monetary value of the payoff would not help. What would help here is to make a decision based on the utility of money. Here, we would see three different assessments corresponding to three different managers and their attitudes about risk as we have seen earlier.

Using the previous table of utility, we can calculate the expected value of money utility for the three managers:

1. *For the risk averter*:

$$\text{Expected value of utility} = (Ut_1)(P_1) + (Ut_2)(P_2)$$
$$= (8.25)(0.20) + (-6)(0.80)$$
$$= -3.15.$$

2. *For the risk-taker*:

$$\text{Expected value of utility} = (13.25)(0.20) + (-1.75)(0.80)$$
$$= 1.25.$$

3. *For the risk neutral*:

$$\text{Expected value of utility} = (20)(0.20) + (-5)(0.80)$$
$$= 0.$$

Therefore, it is expected that the risk averter would decide not to drill because of the negative expected utility (−3.15) compared with the expected utility of zero in the case of no drilling. On the contrary, the risk-taker would decide to drill based on his positive expected utility of (1.25). The risk neutral would end up with no expected utility and, therefore, it is as good as no drilling.

Example 13.2

Suppose that a manager's utility of money has the following function:

$$U = 400 \, m^{0.25},$$

where U is the utility of money as a function of the initial amount of money (m). It is an increasing function of money since the first derivative is positive:

$$\frac{dU}{dm} = (0.25)(400) \, m^{-0.75}$$
$$= 100 \, m^{-0.75} > 0,$$

which is positive for any amount of money larger than zero. The second derivative of the function would determine the type of function for the marginal utility:

- For constant marginal utility,

$$\frac{d^2U}{dm^2} = 0,$$

    which indicates the risk neutral attitude.
- For the decreasing marginal utility,

$$\frac{d^2U}{dm^2} < 0,$$

    which refers to risk aversion.
- For the increasing marginal utility,

$$\frac{d^2U}{dm^2} > 0,$$

    which indicates the risk-taking attitude.

The second derivative for our function would be

$$\frac{d^2U}{dm^2} = (-0.75)(100)(m)^{-10.75},$$

and if $m = 1000$, then

$$\frac{d^2U}{dm^2} = (-0.75)(100)(1000)^{-10.75}$$
$$= -4.22,$$

which confirms that the marginal utility function is decreasing. The person of this function is a risk averter.

Now, let us consider the impact of winning $500 as well as losing $500 on an initial amount of money of $1000 ($m = 1000$):

$$U_1 = 400 \, m^{00.25}$$

$$= 400(1000)^{0.25}$$

$$= 2249.36.$$

If the person wins $500, m would be 1500:

$$U_2 = 400(1500)^{0.25}$$

$$= 2489.33.$$

If the person loses $500, m would be 500:

$$U_3 = 400(500)^{0.25}$$

$$= 1891.48,$$

$$\Delta U_{1-2} = U_2 - U_1$$

$$= 2489.33 - 2249.36$$

$$= 239.97,$$

$$\Delta U_{1-3} = U_3 - U_1$$

$$= 1891.48 - 2249.36$$

$$= -357.88.$$

Given that this is a coin-flipping game, the expected value of utility would be obtained by

$$E(U) = \Sigma \Delta UP_i$$

$$= \Delta U_1(P_1) + U_2(P_2)$$

$$= (239.97)(0.5) + (-357.88)(0.5)$$

$$= -58.95.$$

Since the expected value of utility turns out to be negative, the decision would be not to get into this gamble.

13.7 RISK DISCOUNT AND CERTAINTY EQUIVALENT

Let us recall the case (in the previous example) of receiving $10 only to leave the game. The person who receives this compensation for giving up the gamble is certainly a risk averter. This amount is called certainty equivalent (CE). It is defined as the compensation that renders the player indifferent to a risky gamble. In that example, the expected value of the game was 50 as the risk neutral player has considered it. The person who accepted a significantly lesser outcome ($10) is for sure a player with a definite risk-aversion attitude. This would further define the risk averter as one whose certainty-equivalent limit is less than the expected value of a certain risk. The difference between the expected value $E(v)$ and the certainty equivalent is called the risk discount (RD):

$$RD = E(v) - CE.$$

Risk discount shows the extent to which the expected value for a given risk is reduced in order to avoid such a risky prospect. In our previous example, risk discount was $40:

$$RD = E(v) - CE$$
$$= 50 - 10$$
$$= 40.$$

Figure 13.5 shows the certainty equivalent and risk discount as we recall the shapes of the curves for the risk averter (the DMU curve), and for the risk neutral (the CMU curve).

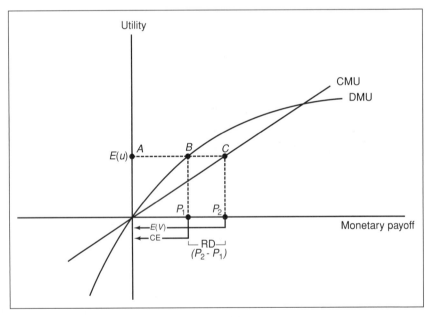

FIGURE 13.5

Point A represents the expected utility of the game; the level that would generate two points, B and C, on the risk-averter and risk neutral curves, respectively. From those points, we can drop verticals to see the amounts of payoff for both players. For the risk averter, point P_1 would represent the certainty equivalent, and for the risk neutral, point P_2 would represent the expected value. The difference $(P_2 - P_1)$ would be the risk discount.

13.8   RISK IMPACT ON THE VALUATION MODEL

When a firm wants to evaluate the worthiness of an investment project, the risk factor should be considered as it affects the actual net present value (NPV) of the project. There are two common ways to adjust the valuation model for risk:

13.8.1   Risk Premium Adjustment

Risk premium is defined as the difference between the expected rate of return on a risky investment and the risk-free rate. Let us consider three managers or investors with three different attitudes about risk, as represented by the three curves in Figure 13.6, where risk is on the x-axis as it is measured by the standard deviation (σ), and the rate of return is on the vertical axis.

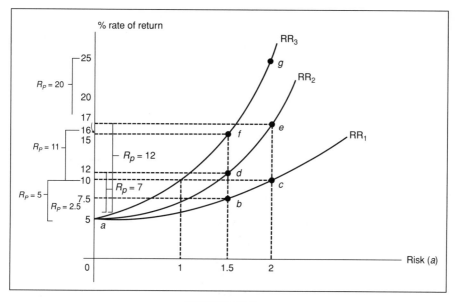

FIGURE 13.6

Let us think of these curves in a way similar to the indifference curves. They depict the tradeoff between risk and return from three different attitudes toward risk. The first, RR, represents the least risk averse among the three. The top, RR_3, represents the most risk averse, and RR_2 stands in between. Point a is on all curves and it shows a 5% risk-free rate (risk $= 0$). RR_1 shows a manager who is indifferent between accepting a 5% rate with no risk and taking a 1.5 σ risk to get a 7.5% return. In other words, for the added risk (from 0 to 1.5σ), his risk premium becomes 2.5% (7.5% − 5%). For the more risk-averse manager on RR_3, the move to accept the additional risk of 1.5σ would not be satisfactory unless there is a higher-risk premium of 11% so that the required rate of return becomes 16%. Not only that, but if the next opportunity happens to come with an additional risk of 0.5σ (such as moving from 1.5σ to 2σ), the risk-averse manager on RR_3 would want his return to be as high as 25% where his risk premium goes to 20% (25% – 5%). The same level of risk (2σ) would make the manager of RR_1 happy to accept only 10% return making his risk premium 5% this time (10% – 5%). As for the moderate manager on RR_2, he would accept moderate levels of risk for reasonable rates of return. He would be indifferent between risk-free rate of 5% and 10% rate with 1.5σ risk and 17% rate with 2σ risk. His risk premium would be 7% (12% – 5%) at point d, and 12% (17% – 5%) at point e. Table 13.10 shows a comparison between the three positions on risk and return, and risk premium.

TABLE 13.10   Risk Attitudes for Three Different Managers

Risk Attitude	Point	Rate of Return (%)	Risk Level (σ)	Risk Premium (%)
RR_1	a	5	0	
Least risk averse	a	7.5	1.5	2.5
	c	10	2	5
RR_2	a	5	0	
Moderately risk averse	d	12	1.5	7
	e	17	2	12
RR_3	a	5	0	
Most risk averse	p	16	1.5	11
	g	25	2	20

The different attitudes by managers toward risk would produce various risk premiums and that would be reflected on the valuation model of a firm as the risk-adjusted rate (k) would replace the risk-free rate (r) that is normally used in the evaluation model:

$$V = \sum_{t=1}^{n} \frac{\pi_i}{(1+r)^t},$$

where V is the value of the asset, π_i is the expected profit per year, r is the **risk-free rate of return** so that the value is equal to the present value of the future returns or cash flow. When the firm faces the prospect of a risky project, the valuation would be adjusted to the expected risk by incorporating the firm's risk premium (R_p). In this case, the NPV of the project would be

$$NPV = \sum_{t=1}^{n} \frac{\pi_i}{(1+k)^t} - C_0,$$

where k is the risk-adjusted rate of return, which is equal to the risk-free rate (r) used previously, plus the firm's risk premium R_p,

$$k = r + R_p,$$

and C_0 is the initial cost of the project. The criteria would remain as that an investment is worthwhile when the NPV is either equal or larger than zero:

$$NPV \geq 0.$$

Example 13.3
A managerial team has to decide on capital allocation for two proposed investment projects, each of which will yield profits for the next 5 years as shown in Table 13.11. They require initial investments of $420,000 and $500,000, respectively. Although the firm's cost of capital is 6%, further investigation revealed certain risk elements associated with both projects. The team found it necessary to adjust for risk by assigning risk premiums of $2\frac{1}{2}\%$ and $3\frac{1}{2}\%$ to both projects, respectively. On what criterion would the team decide granting a capital allocation approval?

TABLE 13.11

Time	Project A Cash Inflows	Project B Cash Inflows
Year 1	126,000	280,000
2	126,000	108,000
3	112,000	90,000
4	98,000	80,000
5	84,000	70,000
Initial Investment	420,000	500,000
r	6%	6%
R_p	$2\frac{1}{2}\%$	$3\frac{1}{2}\%$

Solution:
First, we calculate the NPV of the cash inflows for both projects for the time of their yields using the firm's interest rate ($r = 6\%$). Then, we calculate the same NPVs using the risk-adjusted rate (k):

$$k = r + R_p$$
$$= 0.06 + 0.025 = 0.085 \text{ for project } A$$
$$= 0.06 + 0.035 = 0.095 \text{ for project } B,$$

$$NPV_A = \sum_{t=1}^{5} \frac{\pi_i}{(1+r)^t} - C_0$$
$$= \frac{\pi_1}{(1+r)^1} + \frac{\pi_2}{(1+r)^2} + \frac{\pi_3}{(1+r)^3} + \frac{\pi_4}{(1+r)^4} + \frac{\pi_5}{(1+r)^5} - C_0$$
$$= \frac{126,000}{(1+0.06)^1} + \frac{126,000}{(1+0.06)^2} + \frac{112,000}{(1+0.06)^3} + \frac{98,000}{(1+0.06)^4} + \frac{84,000}{(1+0.06)^5}$$
$$- (420,000)$$
$$= 118,868 + 112,140 + 94,037 + 77,625 + 62,767 - 420,000$$
$$= 465,440 - 420,000$$
$$= 45,440,$$

$$NPV_B = \frac{280,000}{(1+0.06)^1} + \frac{108,000}{(1+0.06)^2} + \frac{90,000}{(1+0.06)^3} + \frac{80,000}{(1+0.06)^4} + \frac{70,000}{(1+0.06)^5}$$

$$-(500,000)$$

$$= 264,151 + 96,120 + 75,565 + 63,367 + 52,308 - 500,000$$

$$= 551,511 - 500,000$$

$$= 51,511,$$

$$NPV_A^{adj} = \frac{126,000}{(1+0.085)^1} + \frac{126,000}{(1+0.085)^2} + \frac{112,000}{(1+0.085)^3} + \frac{98,000}{(1+0.085)^4} + \frac{84,000}{(1+0.085)^5}$$

$$-(420,000)$$

$$= 116,129 + 107,031 + 87,685 + 70,714 + 55,864 - 420,000$$

$$= 17,423,$$

$$NPV_B^{adj} = \frac{280,000}{(1+0.095)^1} + \frac{108,000}{(1+0.095)^2} + \frac{90,000}{(1+0.095)^3} + \frac{80,000}{(1+0.095)^4} + \frac{70,000}{(1+0.095)^5}$$

$$-(500,000)$$

$$= 255,707 + 90,073 + 68,549 + 55,646 + 44,466 - (500,000)$$

$$= 514,440 - 500,000$$

$$= 14,440.$$

At the normal interest rate of 6%, project B would win the approval of the managerial team since its NPV ($51,511) is larger than that of project A ($45,440). However, after considering the expected risk involved in both projects, the team would give its approval to project A because to its larger adjusted NPV ($17,423) than that of project B ($14,440).

13.8.2 Certainty-Equivalent Adjustment

As it was explained before, certainty equivalent is the sure sum that is equal to the expected value of the risky project $E(v)$. The equivalency is in the utilities of both to the manager or investor, not necessarily in their monetary value. Let us assume that there is a proposal that requires the company to invest $30,000 in a project. The probability of its success and failure is 50/50 between earning $100,000 and zero, respectively. The expected value for such a project would be

$$E(v) = 100,000(0.5) + 0(0.50) = 50,000.$$

If the company approves the funding for such a project, it would mean that it is trading off the certainty of $30,000 for a risky expected return of $50,000. It, in fact, means that a sure or risk-free capital of $30,000 yields the same utility of a risky $50,000; hence, the term certainty equivalent to the amount of $30,000 that would make the decision maker indifferent between the two prospects. The **certainty-equivalent coefficient**, α, is the ratio between the certainty equivalent, CE, and its expected risky return, $E(v)$:

$$\alpha = \frac{CE}{E(v)}.$$

The certainty equivalent is subjectively determined by the decision maker, and therefore, it would be a product of how risk averse or risk-taker that decision maker is. Figure 13.7 shows that three different attitudes toward risk would produce three certainty-equivalent amounts for the same expected value of $1000 for a specific risky project: the most risk-averse manager on RR_3 would assign $870, the least risk-averse one would assign $220, and the moderate manager among the three would assign $460. These cases would produce three different certainty-equivalent coefficients:

$$\alpha_3 = \frac{870}{1,000} = 0.87,$$

$$\alpha_2 = \frac{460}{1,000} = 0.46,$$

$$\alpha_1 = \frac{220}{1,000} = 0.22.$$

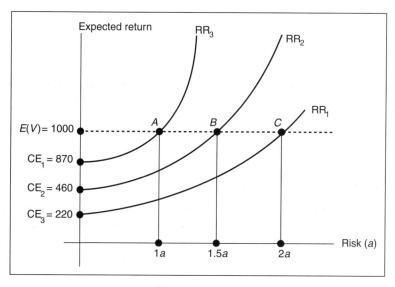

FIGURE 13.7

The risk-averse manager would value the sure and risk-free money more; that is why his alpha is highest. An alpha of 0.87 means that each dollar of the certain money would be worth 87¢, compared with the 22¢ for the risk-taker. This is one reason why the risk-taker dares to take a high risk. Alternatively, each dollar of the expected risky return is valued less ($1.15) for the risk averse than for the risk-taker, who values his expected dollar at $4.55.

Generally speaking, the criteria for alpha are as follows:

- When $\alpha = 0$, it is an indication that the probability of getting the expected return does not exist, and therefore, the project is too risky to be pursued.
- When $\alpha = 1$, it refers to the equality between the certainty equivalent and the expected value of return of the risky project. When the manager or investor gets his return equal to what he assigns as a certainty equivalent, the project is considered risk free.
- When $0 < \alpha < 1$, it is an indication that there is some level of risk. The project is riskier as α is closer to zero, and less risky if it is closer to 1. It would depend on how smaller the certainty equivalent is than the expected value of the risky return $(E(v))$.

The valuation model would be adjusted for risk by introducing α to the numerator of the formula as a multiplier to the expected return or profit or cash flow, while the denominator of the formula would keep the risk-free rate (r):

$$NPV = \sum_{t=1}^{n} \frac{\alpha \pi_i}{(1+r)^t} - C_0.$$

Let us assume that the manager assigned certainty-equivalent sums to each and every annual return of 5 years in both projects of the last example. Table 13.12 shows α values, as they are calculated by dividing the assigned certainty equivalent by the corresponding expected return.

TABLE 13.12

	A			B		
Time	Expected Return	Certainty Equivalent	α	Expected Return	Certainty Equivalent	α
Year 1	126,000	123,000	0.98	280,000	240,000	0.86
2	126,000	123,000	0.98	108,000	100,000	0.93
3	112,000	106,000	0.95	90,000	86,000	0.95
4	98,000	95,000	0.97	80,000	76,000	0.95
5	84,000	82,000	0.98	70,000	68,000	0.97
Initial Investment		420,000			500,000	
r		6%			6%	

Applying those calculated alphas, we get

$$
\begin{aligned}
NPV_A &= \sum_{t=1}^{n} \frac{\alpha \pi_i}{(1+r)^t} - C_0 \\
&= \frac{(0.98)(126,000)}{(1+0.06)^1} + \frac{(0.98)(126,000)}{(1+0.06)^2} + \frac{(0.95)(112,000)}{(1+0.06)^3} + \frac{(0.97)(98,000)}{(1+0.06)^4} \\
&\quad + \frac{(0.98)(84,000)}{(1+0.06)^5} - 420,000
\end{aligned}
$$

$$= (116{,}490 + 109{,}897 + 89{,}335 + 75{,}296 + 61{,}514) - 420{,}000$$

$$= 452{,}532 - 420{,}000$$

$$= 32{,}532,$$

$$\text{NPV}_B = \frac{(0.86)(280{,}000)}{(1+0.06)^1} + \frac{(0.93)(108{,}000)}{(1+0.06)^2} + \frac{(0.95)(90{,}000)}{(1+0.06)^3} + \frac{(0.95)(80{,}000)}{(1+0.06)^4}$$

$$+ \frac{(0.97)(70{,}000)}{(1+0.06)^5} - 500{,}000$$

$$= (227{,}170 + 89{,}391 + 71{,}787 + 60{,}199 + 50{,}739) - 500{,}000$$

$$= 499{,}286 - 500{,}000$$

$$= -714.$$

Considering the expected risk for both projects in terms of estimating the certainty equivalent and calculating α for each return in every year reveals that project A is more worthwhile, yielding a positive value of \$32,532, while project B goes into a negative net value.

13.9   DIVERSIFIABLE VERSUS NONDIVERSIFIABLE RISK

Diversifiable or **unsystematic risk** is the risk specific to an individual firm as it is related to its internal conditions and circumstances such as lawsuits against the firm, marketing or accounting problems, product defects, workers' strikes, problematic contracts, and so on. It is, therefore, the risk associated with a particular asset or project or the risk of an entire financial portfolio. This type of risk can be reduced or even eliminated by the classical remedy of the diversification of assets within the portfolios so that the no-risky or less-risky assets mitigate the risky ones.

The nondiversifiable or **systematic risk** is the general and market-related risk that affects all firms and all projects and assets, simultaneously and with no discrimination. It is associated with the state of the economy and structure of markets as well as with national and regional big events such as wars, political unrest, natural disasters, and severe weather. However, the most striking impact of such external factors relates to economic conditions such as recession, inflation, unemployment, and unusual interest rate fluctuations. Unlike the unsystematic risk, systematic risk cannot be reduced or eliminated by diversification of assets. In fact, there is no other way to minimize it or remove its impact. However, it can be assessed by monitoring how a particular asset tends to respond to the market state and its changes. This will be addressed by the **capital asset pricing model (CAPM)**, where the systematic risk is measured by beta (β). However, before that we should address the unsystematic risk at the portfolio level and how it can be reduced by diversification of assets within a specific portfolio.

Figure 13.8 shows how **portfolio risk** tends to decline as the financial portfolio includes more and more individual assets and securities. Its curve would asymptotically approach the line of the systematic nondiversifiable risk. The relationship between diversifiable and nondiversifiable risks is shown at any size of assets and securities in the portfolio such as a or d. Note that the nondiversifiable risk level stays constant at σ_m, while the **diversifiable risk** level gets smaller as the number of assets and securities increases in the portfolio.

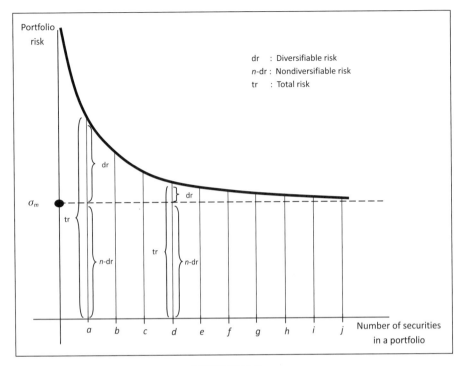

FIGURE 13.8

13.10 PORTFOLIO RISK

Since a financial portfolio contains many individual assets and securities, one may think that the total risk of the portfolio would be collective and can be measured as an additive value or as a weighted average, but that is not the case. Portfolio risk would be less as the portfolio includes more and different individual assets. Two factors play major roles in determining the risk level in a portfolio:

1. How diversified are the assets? Risk has a negative relationship with diversification. The higher the diversification, the lower the risk level.
2. How correlated are the assets? Risk has a positive relationship with correlation of assets. The higher the correlation, the higher the risk level.

However, more crucial is the degree and direction of correlation. Diversification of assets cannot reduce the risk level unless the assets are either negatively correlated or at least positively correlated, but to a much lower degree. If they are strongly positively correlated, risk cannot be eliminated or reduced by merely diversifying the portfolio. Let us take a look at two pairs of assets, X and Y on the one hand, while Z and W on the other. Table 13.13 shows the returns of asset X and asset Y where the variance of the two sets of return are individually calculated at the seventh and twelfth columns as

$$\sigma_X^2 = \sum_{i=1}^{5} \left(k_i^X - k_e^X \right)^2 \mathrm{Pr}_i = 0.046$$

TABLE 13.13

1	2	3	4	5	6	7	8	9	10	11	12	13
		Asset X						Asset Y				
	$\Pr_i$	k_i^X	k_e^X	$k_i^X - k_e^X$	$(k_i^X - k_e^X)^2$	$(k_i^X - k_e^X)^2 \Pr_i$	k_i^Y	k_e^Y	$(k_i^Y - k_e^Y)$	$(k_i^Y - k_e^Y)^2$	$(k_i^Y - k_e^Y)^2 \Pr_i$	$(k_i^X - k_e^X)(k_i^Y - k_e^Y)\Pr_i$
k_1	0.20	−0.12	0.155	−0.275	0.0756	0.015	−0.15	0.174	−0.324	0.105	0.021	0.0178
k_2	0.15	0.405	0.155	0.25	0.0625	0.0094	0.50	0.174	0.326	0.1063	0.016	0.0122
k_3	0.25	−0.07	0.155	−0.225	0.0506	0.0126	−0.08	0.174	−0.254	0.0645	0.016	0.0143
k_4	0.18	0.38	0.155	0.225	0.0506	0.0091	0.45	0.174	0.276	0.0762	0.014	0.0112
k_5	0.22	0.18	0.155	0.025	0.000625	0.00014	0.15	0.174	−0.024	0.00058	0.00013	−0.00013
						0.046					0.067	0.0554

and

$$\sigma_Y^2 = \sum_{i=1}^{5} \left(k_i^Y - k_e^Y\right)^2 \Pr_i = 0.067.$$

The standard deviations of the two sets of return have been calculated as

$$\sigma_X = \sqrt{\sum_{i=1}^{5} \left(k_i^X - k_e^X\right)^2 \Pr_i},$$

$$\sigma_X = \sqrt{0.046} = 0.214,$$

$$\sigma_Y = \sqrt{\sum_{i=1}^{5} \left(k_i^Y - k_e^Y\right)^2 \Pr_i},$$

$$\sigma_Y = \sqrt{0.067} = 0.259.$$

The covariance between the two sets of return $\text{cov}(X, Y)$ is also calculated at the thirteenth column as

$$\text{cov}(X, Y) = \sum_{i=1}^{5} \left(k_i^X - k_e^X\right)\left(k_i^Y - k_e^Y\right)\Pr_i,$$

$$\text{cov}(X, Y) = 0.0554,$$

and finally, the correlation coefficient (COR) between the two sets of return is calculated as

$$\text{COR}_{X,Y} = \frac{\text{cov}(X, Y)}{\sigma_X \sigma_Y},$$

$$\text{COR}_{X,Y} = \frac{0.0554}{(0.214)(0.259)},$$

$$\text{COR}_{X,Y} = 990.9\%.$$

A correlation coefficient, which is large enough to be close to a (+100) would be considered a solid indication of a perfectly positively correlated assets. It means that they exhibit a similar dynamics that makes them move together, up and down, in tandem. This kind of matching pattern would not benefit from diversification in risk reduction. The upper panel of Figure 13.9 shows such a synchronized movement of the returns of those assets.

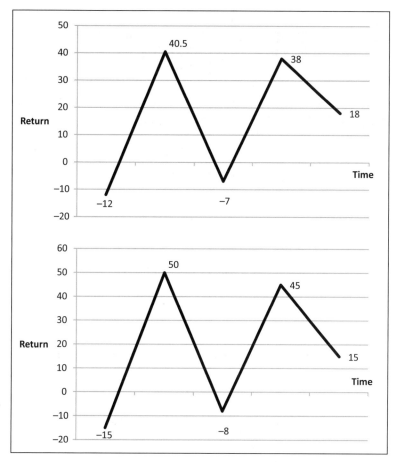

FIGURE 13.9

The second set of assets, Z and W, is presented in Table 13.14 and the same parameters are calculated in the same manner as they were calculated in Table 13.13.

The variances of the assets are in Columns 7 and 12:

$$\sigma_Z^2 = \sum_{i=1}^{5} \left(k_i^Z - k_e^Z \right)^2 \text{Pr}_i,$$

$$\sigma_Z^2 = 0.0339,$$

$$\sigma_W^2 = \sum_{i=1}^{5} \left(k_i^W - k_e^W \right)^2 \text{Pr}_i,$$

$$\sigma_W^2 = 0.0129.$$

TABLE 13.14

1	2	Asset Z					Asset W					
		3	4	5	6	7	8	9	10	11	12	13
	$\Pr_i$	k_i^Z	k_e^Z	$k_i^Z-k_e^Z$	$(k_i^Z-k_e^Z)^2$	$(k_i^Z-k_e^Z)^2\Pr_i$	k_i^W	k_e^W	$(k_i^W-k_e^W)$	$(k_i^W-k_e^W)^2$	$(k_i^W-k_e^W)^2\Pr_i$	$(k_i^Z-k_e^Z)(k_i^W-k_e^W)\Pr_i$
k_1	0.20	0.40	0.20	0.20	0.04	0.008	0.08	0.138	−0.058	0.0034	0.00068	−0.00232
k_2	0.15	0.10	0.20	−0.10	0.01	0.0015	0.35	0.138	0.212	0.045	0.00675	−0.00318
k_3	0.25	0.38	0.20	0.18	0.0324	0.0081	−0.05	0.138	−0.188	0.0077	0.001925	−0.00846
k_4	0.18	−0.10	0.20	0.30	0.09	0.0162	0.25	0.138	0.112	0.0125	0.00225	−0.00605
k_5	0.22	0.22	0.20	0.02	0.0004	0.000088	0.06	0.138	−0.078	0.0061	0.001342	−0.000343
						0.0339					0.0129	−0.020353

The standard deviations are

$$\sigma_Z = \sqrt{0.0339} = 0.1841.$$

$$\sigma_W = \sqrt{0.0129} = 0.1136.$$

The covariance is calculated in Column 13 as

$$\text{cov}(Z, W) = \sum_{i=1}^{5} \left(k_i^Z - k_e^Z \right) \left(k_i^W - k_e^W \right)^2 \text{Pr}_i,$$

$$\text{cov}(Z, W) = -0.020353.$$

The correlation coefficient (COR) is

$$\text{COR}_{Z,W} = \frac{\text{cov}(Z, W)}{\sigma_X \sigma_W},$$

$$\text{COR}_{Z,W} = \frac{-0.020353}{(0.1841)(0.1136)} = -97.3\%.$$

A correlation coefficient of –97.3% shows the opposite case of X and Y combination. It indicates that assets Z and W are almost perfectly negatively correlated, which means that the return changes of these assets go up and down, opposite to each other. This is the ideal case to offer the opportunity for these assets to cancel each other out. If one is down, the other is up to compensate for it. That is the beauty of diversification. The combination of such assets in a portfolio gives the opportunity to have an optimal impact of diversifying the risk away. The lower panel of Figure 13.10 shows how the return patterns act opposite to each other in a consistently contracting manner.

Combining assets into portfolios most likely reduces the risk even for those assets that are positively correlated. In Table 13.15, we combined asset X and asset Y and obtained an average vector of returns for the combination XY. Also, we combined asset Z and W and obtained an average vector of returns for the combination ZW (Table 13.16). The standard deviation test shows that the combination helps reduce risk even for combining X and Y, which are perfectly positively correlated as we have seen. The standard deviation of the combined set XY ($\sigma_{XY} = -195$) is still less than either of the asset taken individually, where $\sigma_X = 0.214$, and $s_Y = 0.259$. This means that the combined assets are not as risky as either of them individually. This standard deviation test showed much better results when we combined the negatively correlated assets Z and W. The standard deviation of the combined set ZW is ($\sigma_{ZW} = 0.056$), which is much less than either of the assets' standard deviation, where $\sigma_Z = 0.1841$ and $\sigma_W = 0.1136$. It is further proof that combining assets into portfolios increases diversification and reduces risk. However, the extent of risk reduction depends primarily on the degree and sign of the correlation between the assets. In reality, most of the assets are positively correlated. Studies show that, on average, randomly selected assets show a correlation coefficient of around 0.60. The lower the positive correlation, the better the results of the combination.

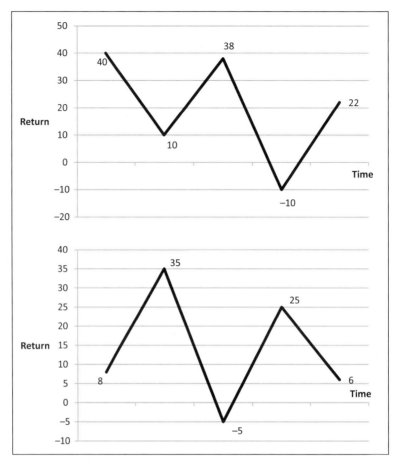

FIGURE 13.10

TABLE 13.15   Combined Assets *XY* with Average Returns

Return	Pr_i	k_i^{XY}	k_e^{XY}	$(k_i^{XY} - k_e^{XY})$	$(k_i^{XY} - k_e^{XY})^2$	$(k_i^{XY} - k_e^{XY})^2 Pr_i$
k_1	0.20	−0.135	0.164	0.029	0.00084	0.00017
k_2	0.15	0.452	0.164	0.288	0.083	0.0124
k_3	0.25	−0.075	0.164	−0.239	0.057	0.0142
k_4	0.18	0.415	0.164	0.251	0.063	0.0113
k_5	0.22	0.165	0.164	0.001	0.000001	0.00000022
	$\sum_{i=1}^{5} (k_i^{XY} - k_e^{XY})^2 Pr_i$					0.038

TABLE 13.16   Combined Assets ZW with Average Returns

Return	Pr_i	k_i^{ZW}	k_e^{ZW}	$(k_i^{ZW} - k_e^{ZW})$	$(k_i^{ZW} - k_e^{ZW})^2$	$(k_i^{ZW} - k_e^{ZW})^2 Pr_i$
k_1	0.20	0.24	0.169	0.071	0.00504	0.001
k_2	0.15	0.225	0.169	0.056	0.00314	0.00047
k_3	0.25	0.165	0.169	−0.004	0.000016	0.000004
k_4	0.18	0.075	0.169	−0.094	0.00884	0.00159
k_5	0.22	0.14	0.169	−0.029	0.00084	0.00018
	$\sum_{i=1}^{5}\left(k_i^{ZW} - k_e^{ZW}\right)^2 Pr_i$					0.0032

In yet another abstract presentation, Figure 13.11 shows three possible ways to combine two assets in a portfolio, two extreme combinations and one common combination. The assets are A with an expected return of k_A and k_B and risk level of σ_A, and B with an expected higher return of k_B and higher risk level σ_B:

- The first extreme case of combination occurs at any point along the straight line AB if assets A and B are perfectly positively correlated. This combination cannot benefit much from diversification.
- The second extreme case of combination occurs at any point along BCA where a zero risk can be achieved with a rate of return equal to k_C when the allocation of the two

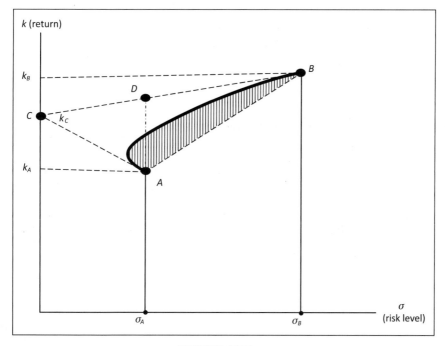

FIGURE 13.11

assets can be achieved in inverse proportion to their risk levels. This combination is the showcase for the benefit of diversification.

- The third case of combination occurs at any point along the curve *BA*. It is the most likely case to occur because assets are often neither negatively nor positively perfectly correlated. The correlation would often be in a moderate level and the combination of assets can enjoy a wide range of returns from k_A to k_B for a wide range of risk level from σ_A to σ_B. The curve would include all the possible combinations that are better alternatives to any point along the straight line *AB* but lower alternatives to most of the points along *BCA*, which would offer higher rates of return for the same level of risk, especially along the segment *BD*.

13.11   RISK OF TWO-ASSET PORTFOLIO

Among the major issues addressed by Markowitz (1952) in his pioneering study are portfolio diversification of assets and the positive outcome on portfolio's return and risk through the compensatory effect of the assets that move in different directions.

Figure 13.12 shows what happens if an investor decides to invest in two different choices of stocks: Stock I with an expected return of 8% and a low risk (represented by the standard deviation of return) of 15% and Stock II, which offers a higher return of 12% but at a higher risk of 22%.

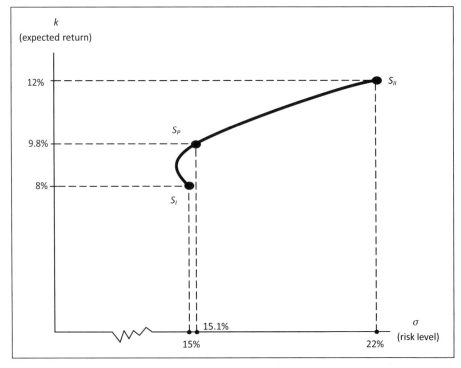

FIGURE 13.12

The logical expectation is to calculate the combined return and risk for the mix if we know how much investment the investor is willing to dedicate to each of the stocks. Let us assume that this investor, or this portfolio manager, is willing to dedicate 55% of investment to Stock I and 45% to Stock II. The portfolio rate of return would be calculated as the weighted average of two returns:

$$k_p = w_1 k_1 + w_2 k_2,$$

$$k_p = (0.55)(0.08) + (0.45)(0.12),$$

$$k_p = 9.8\%.$$

As for the portfolio risk, it would be determined by the standard deviation of the combined assets, given a correlation between the two assets of 0.38:

$$\sigma_{I,II} = \sqrt{\sigma_I^2 w_I^2 + \sigma_{II}^2 w_{II}^2 + 2COR_{I,II}(w_I \sigma_I)(w_{II} \sigma_{II})},$$

$$\sigma_{I,II} = \sqrt{(0.15)^2(0.55)^2 + (0.22)^2(0.45)^2 + 2(0.38)(0.55)(0.15)(0.45)(0.22)},$$

$$\sigma_{I,II} = \sqrt{0.0228} = 15.1\%.$$

So the risk level of the combined stocks in an asset is less than the weighted average risk of the two individual assets:

$$(0.55)(0.15) + (0.45)(0.22) = 18.2\%.$$

Therefore, a combination of assets at S_p would yield a 9.8% rate of return at a reasonable level of risk at 15.1%. If we move from this hypothetical example of only two assets in a portfolio to the reality of the investment in the market, we would find that there is a large number of assets forming a large number of combinations and producing a large number of portfolios. The broken-egg-shaped area in Figure 13.13 represents all the combinations of assets that are attainable to all investors with their different objectives and different risk and return preferences.

The following are some major observations regarding Figure 13.13:

- The shaded broken-egg-shaped area is a locus of portfolios with all possible combinations of assets representing a wide range of investor's preferences regarding risk and return.
- The solid-line curve represents the diversified portfolios with the highest returns for any given risk level between the lowest level of risk (CR) and the highest level of risk (DR). Markowitz called this curve the **"efficient portfolio curve."** It is also called the "frontier of risky portfolios."
- Point D is the portfolio that yields the highest return (k_D) but bears the DR.
- Point C is the portfolio that yields the lowest return (k_C) but enjoys the CR.
- Segment DB contains a collection of portfolios that enjoy a tradeoff between risk and return in favor of the risk side. For example, moving from D to B means getting a slightly less return than k_D but for more reduction in the risk level, from DR to BR. Similarly, moving from B to D means gaining a slightly more return than k_B but carrying more risk from BR to DR.

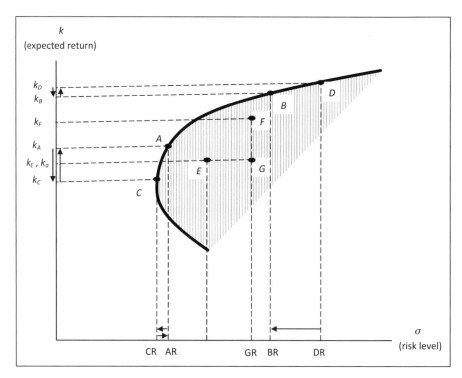

FIGURE 13.13

- Segment AC contains a collection of portfolios that enjoy a tradeoff between risk and return in favor of the return. For example, moving from A to C means accepting more reduction in return, from k_A to k_C for less reduction in risk, from AR to CR. Similarly, moving from C to A means getting a much higher return for accepting a little more risk, from CR to AR.

- Segment AB contains all the portfolios that exhibit an almost equal tradeoff between risk and return. In other words, gaining or losing a certain amount of return comes with gaining or losing a compatible amount of risk.

- Inside the shape, we can observe that moving toward the northeast means getting portfolios with higher return and higher risk. On the contrary, moving toward the southwest means getting portfolios with lower return and lower risk.

- Portfolio F is preferred to portfolio G because it yields more return for the same amount of risk.

- Portfolio E is preferred to portfolio G because it enjoys a much lower level of risk for the same rate of return.

13.12   LENDING AND BORROWING AT THE RISK-FREE RATE OF RETURN

Let us assume that an investor wants to split his initial investment between asset A on the efficient portfolio curve and treasury bills that offer a risk-free rate of return equal to 5%. Suppose that A yields 12% at a risk level of 15% (Figure 13.14). The investor would like to have 60% of his money invested in asset A and 40% invested in the treasury bills.

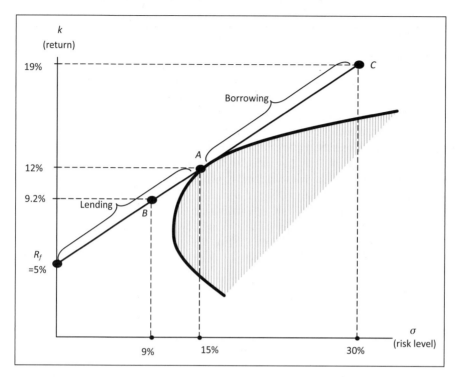

FIGURE 13.14

The investor in this case is lending 40% of his money to the treasury bills. His rate of return would be

$$(0.40)(0.05) + (0.60)(0.12) = 9.2\%,$$

and his level of risk would be

$$(0.40)(0) + (0.60)(0.15) = 9\%.$$

He would be at point B. This means that he could be at any point along the line A R_f depending on the proportions of his investment between asset A and the treasury bills.

Now, let us assume that he borrows at the risk free rate of 5% an amount of money equal to his own money and invest the total of his own and the borrowed money in asset A alone. His return would be

$$(2)(0.12) - (0.05) = 19\%,$$

and his risk would be

$$(2)(0.15) + (0.05)(0) = 30\%.$$

He would be at point C, which means that he could be at any point along CA depending on how much he borrows and how much risk he tolerates.

13.13   MEASURING THE SYSTEMATIC RISK BY BETA (β)

Beta (β) is a mathematical tool to measure the systematic undiversifiable market risk. It is, in this sense, an index of the extent to which a security return moves in response to the changes in the overall market. This makes it a measure of the securities volatility in relation to an average security represented by the state of the market. Market return is an aggregate measure of the return of all traded securities in the market at a specific time. The beta value can be positive or negative. Generally, it ranges between –2.5 and 2.5. The value of 1.00 denotes the full impact of market risk. Any individual security with a beta of 1.00 indicates that the return pattern of that security moves up and down perfectly with the market return. The value of zero refers to total independence from the market impact. A value of more than 1.00, such as 2.00, reveals that the security is twice as volatile as the average security in the market. A negative value says that the asset return pattern moves in the opposite direction to the market. Table 13.17 shows beta coefficients of selected American companies estimated at some point in time. The estimation changes for the same company from time to time.

TABLE 13.17   Beta Estimates for Selected American Companies

Company	Beta
AOL	2.46
Dell	2.23
Microsoft	1.82
Texas Instrument	1.75
Intel	1.70
GE	1.16
GM	1.10
Colgate-Palmolive	1.03
Family Dollar Store	0.99
K-Mart	0.98
ATT	0.98
McGraw Hill	0.81
Gillette	0.76
NY Times	0.71
JC Penny	0.52
Johnson & Johnson	0.49
Campbell	0.41
Exxon	0.36

Mathematically, beta is obtained by dividing the covariance between the individual security return (k_i) and the market return (k_m) by the variance of market return (k_m):

$$\beta = \frac{\text{COV}(k_i, k_m)}{\text{Var}(k_m)}.$$

In this sense, beta is a concept of correlation to assess how one security return is correlated with the rest in the market. From another perspective, beta measures the percentage change in one security return as it responds to the changes in the external market return. Therefore, it can be interpreted as the financial elasticity of the change in a given asset relative to market change. Accordingly, beta becomes the slope of the regression line between the changes in market return and the corresponding response of the asset return. In Figure 13.15, the changes in market return are tracked down on the horizontal axis and the responses to them by a given security are tracked down on the vertical axis. The result is the regression line $y = \alpha + \beta x + e$, where β denotes the slope, and is calculated by dividing the change in the vertical axis over the change in the horizontal axis:

$$\beta = \frac{\Delta y}{\Delta x}.$$

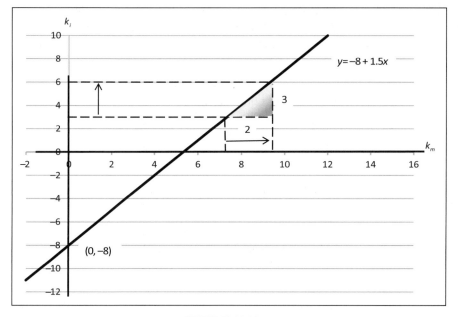

FIGURE 13.15

If we track down the change in the market rate when it increases from 7.3 to 9.3, the linear equation line of $y = -8 + 1.5x$ would allow the return of the asset k_i to increase from 3 to 6. Therefore, we can obtain the slope of the line:

$$\text{Slope} = \frac{\Delta y}{\Delta x} = \frac{6 - 3}{9.3 - 7.3} = \frac{3}{2} = 1.5,$$

which is the value of β in the equation of the line. It signifies that the asset rate of return follows the market return more robustly. Its volatility is one and a half times that of the market return. For example, if the market rate increases by 5%, the asset's rate would increase by 7.5%.

TABLE 13.18   Rates of Return for x-Corporation and the Market for 10 Periods

	x-Corporation			Market				
Period	k_i^x	k_e^x	$\left(k_i^x k_e^x\right)$	k_i^m	k_e^m	$\left(k_i^m k_e^m\right)$	$\left(k_i^m k_e^m\right)^2$	$\left(k_i^x k_e^x\right)\left(k_i^m k_e^m\right)$
1	−0.06	0.105	−0.165	0.027	0.082	−0.055	0.003	0.0091
2	0.27	0.105	0.165	0.095	0.082	0.013	0.00017	0.0021
3	0.065	0.105	−0.04	0.038	0.082	−0.044	0.0019	0.0018
4	0.13	0.105	0.025	0.055	0.082	−0.027	0.00073	−0.00067
5	0.055	0.105	−0.05	−0.017	0.082	−0.099	0.0098	0.0049
6	0.28	0.105	0.175	0.176	0.082	0.094	0.0088	0.0164
7	−0.045	0.105	−0.15	0.119	0.082	0.037	0.0014	−0.0055
8	0.03	0.105	−0.075	0.128	0.082	0.046	0.0021	−0.0034
9	0.35	0.105	0.245	0.156	0.082	0.074	0.0055	0.0181
10	−0.025	0.105	−0.13	0.044	0.082	−0.038	0.0014	0.0049
							0.0348	0.04773

We can also calculate the beta value by the formula. For example, we can calculate beta for x-corporation given 10 periodic rates of return $(k_i^m)$and market rates for the same period (k_i^m). In Table 13.18, we calculate the expected return of both as the averages (k_e^x) and (k_e^m), and we proceed to calculate the covariance between the two sets of rates and the variance of the market. Beta would be calculated by dividing the covariance by the market variance:

$$\mathrm{cov}(x, m) = \frac{\sum\limits_{i=1}^{10} \left(k_i^x - k_e^x\right)\left(k_i^m - k_e^m\right)}{N},$$

$$\mathrm{cov}(x, m) = \frac{0.04773}{10} = 0.0048,$$

$$\mathrm{var}(m) = \frac{\sum\limits_{i=1}^{10} \left(k_i^m - k_e^m\right)^2}{N},$$

$$\mathrm{var}(m) = \frac{0.0348}{10} = 0.0035,$$

$$\beta_x = \frac{\mathrm{cov}(x, m)}{\mathrm{var}(m)},$$

$$\beta_x = \frac{0.0048}{0.0035} = 1.37,$$

$$\beta_p = \sum_{i=1}^{n} \beta_i w_i.$$

Note that β_x is the beta of asset x. A portfolio beta would be the weighted average of betas for all individual assets within the portfolio, where β_p is the portfolio beta, β_i is the beta for any individual asset within the portfolio, w_i is the proportion of asset i out of the entire portfolio that contains n-assets.

13.14 THE CAPM MODEL

The Capital Asset Pricing Model (CAPM) is a technical tool for analyzing the relationship between the financial asset's expected return and the nondiversifiable market. We can write the central equation of the CAPM where beta is an essential factor to calculate the required rate of return on any asset (k_i), given the asset beta (β_i), the market's required rate of return (k_m), and the riskless rate of return, which is traditionally the rate of return on the US Treasury bond (R_f):

$$k_i = R_f + \beta_i[k_m - R_f].$$

This model means that the required rate of return for any asset would be obtained by adding the risk-free rate of return to the market risk premium (MRP), given that

1. it is the difference between the market required rate of return and the risk-free rate of return, $[k_m - R_f]$; and
2. it is adjusted to that asset's index of risk by being multiplied by beta:

$$\beta_i[k_m - R_f].$$

Example 13.4

What would be the required rate of return for y-corporation that has a beta of 1.85, given that the return on the market portfolio of assets is 12% and the risk-free rate is 6.5%?

Solution:

$$k_i = R_f + \beta_i[k_m - R_f]$$
$$= 0.065 + 1.85[0.12 - 0.065]$$
$$= 16.67\%.$$

So, the MRP is 5.5% ($0.12 - 0.065$), and it went to a little more than 10% when it was adjusted to the asset's index of risk, a beta of 1.85. When the result of the adjustment was added to the risk-free rate of 6.5%, we got the corp-required rate of 16.67%.

Algebraically, we can obtain any of β_i, R_f, and k_m if the other variables in the equation are available.

- Finding beta (β_i):

$$k_i = R_f + \beta_i[k_m - R_f],$$
$$k_i - R_f = \beta_i[k_m - R_f],$$
$$\beta_i = \frac{k_i - R_f}{k_m - R_f},$$
$$\beta_i = \frac{0.1667 - 0.065}{0.12 - 0.065} = 1.85.$$

- Finding the free-risk of return (R_f):

$$k_i = R_f + \beta_i [k_m - R_f],$$

$$k_i = R_f - \beta_i R_f + \beta_i k_m,$$

$$k_i - \beta_i k_m = R_f (1 - \beta_i),$$

$$R_f = \frac{k_i - \beta_i k_m}{1 - \beta_i},$$

$$R_f = \frac{0.1667 - (1.85)(0.12)}{1 - 1.85},$$

$$R_f = \frac{-0.0553}{-0.85} = 0.065.$$

- Finding the market rate of return (k_m):

$$k_i = R_f + \beta_i [k_m - R_f],$$

$$k_i = R_f + \beta_i k_m - \beta_i R_f,$$

$$k_i + R_f (\beta_i - 1) = \beta_i k_m,$$

$$k_m = \frac{k_i + R_f(\beta_i - 1)}{\beta_i},$$

$$k_m = \frac{0.1667 + 0.065(1.85 - 1)}{1.85},$$

$$k_m = 0.12.$$

13.15   THE SECURITY MARKET LINE (SML)

When we graph the CAPM equation, we get a straight line with a positive slope equal to beta (1.85). This line is called the **security market line** (SML). From the last example, we have all the points we need to draw the SML for this example. As shown in Figure 13.16, the level of risk, as measured by beta, is on the horizontal axis, and the required rates of return are on the vertical axis. The risk-free rate of 6.5% is associated with zero beta, the market rate of 12% is associated with beta value of 1.00, and the return k_i of 16.67% is associated with a beta of 1.85. The vertical line *BD* represents the MRP, which is obtained as (*BE* – *DE*) standing for [$k_m - R_f$] in the equation. All assets that have betas higher than 1.00 would have a risk premium higher than the MRP. Our beta is 1.85, which makes the risk premium much higher than the MRP, as depicted by the vertical line *CE*, which is (*CF* – *EF*) = 16.67 – 6.5 = 10.17. Similarly, all assets that have betas less than 1.00 will have risk premiums less than the MRP, e.g., firm *S* with a beta of 0.5. The risk premium for this firm would be represented by the line *GH*, which is (*GI* – *HI*), and it is lower than the MRP.

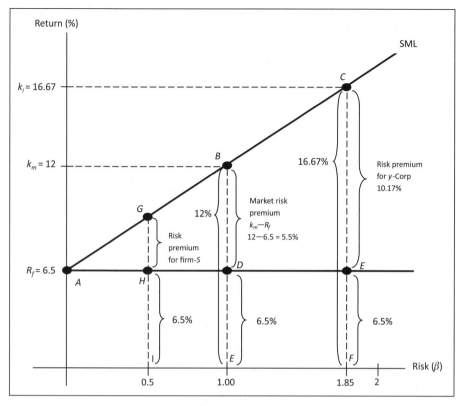

FIGURE 13.16

The slope of the SML stands for the degree of risk aversion. A steeper SML would reflect a higher degree of risk aversion, and a flatter SML would reflect a lower degree of risk aversion in the economy. Also, the steeper the SML, the higher the risk premium and the higher the required rate of return on the risky assets with higher betas.

13.15.1 SML Shift by Inflation

The risk-free rate of return (R_f) is considered the price of money to a riskless borrower. Therefore, it is affected by inflation like any other price. In fact, it includes a built-in component designed to absorb the impact of inflation. This component is called the inflation premium (IP), which is to protect the investor's purchasing power from declining as the prices rise. The second component is the real core (k^0) that is inflation free:

$$R_f = k^0 + \text{IP}.$$

Let us assume that the risk-free rate of the last example, which is 6.5%, is in fact a combination of the real rate k^0, which is 2.5%, and the IP, which is 4%.

Since the SML originates from the R_f point, any increase in inflation would lead to an increase in the IP component and in the R_f, and it would cause the point of SML origin to go up, shifting the entire line up. Figure 13.17 shows how the SML shifts to a higher position (SML$_2$) originating from the 8% rate if the inflation rises by 1.5 points from 4% to 5.5%,

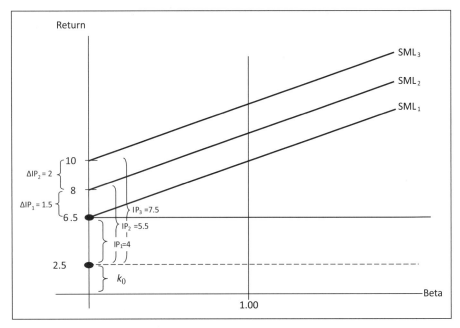

FIGURE 13.17

$$R_f^1 = k_0 + \text{IP}_1$$
$$= 2.5 + 4 = 6.5,$$
$$R_f^2 = k_0 + \text{IP}_2$$
$$= 2.5 + 5.5 = 8.00,$$

and if inflation continues to rise to, say, 7.5, the SML shifts again to SML$_3$ originating from

$$R_f = 10,$$
$$R_f^3 = k_0 + \text{IP}_3$$
$$= 2.5 + 7.5 = 10.0.$$

13.15.2   SML Swing by Risk Aversion

The slope of the SML represents how much risk aversion investors usually exhibit. Therefore, the line would swing up and down to reflect the change in investors' risk aversion. The slope would be equal to zero and the SML would be horizontal at the risk-free level of return (R_f). There would be no risk premium to the point that even risky assets would sell at the risk-free level of return. As the risk aversion starts to rise and the risk premium starts to grow, the SML would pivot at the R_f point and its other end starts to rise according to how much risk premium there is. From that point, the line would continue to swing up. Figure 13.18 shows that when risk aversion rises, the MRP would rise, in this example, from 4% to 9% (vertical FG to EG), and consequently the market required rate (k_m) would jump from 10% to 15% (vertical FK to EK), and our risky asset return (k_i) of the 1.75 beta would be up from 13% to 21.75%. This asset risk premium (ARP) would shoot from 7% to 15.75% (vertical CB to DB):

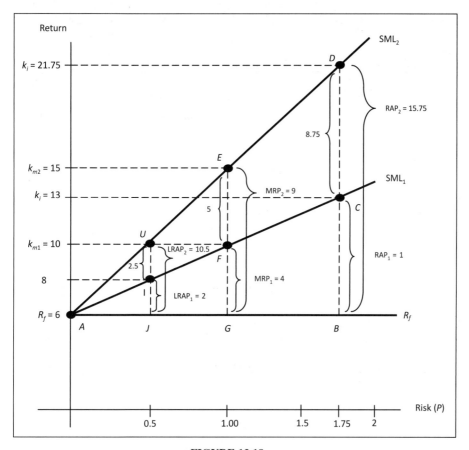

FIGURE 13.18

$$k_i^1 = R_f + \beta_i \left[k_m^1 - R_f \right]$$
$$= 0.06 + 1.75 \left[0.10 - 0.06 \right]$$
$$= 0.06 + 0.07$$
$$= 0.13,$$

where

$$k_i^2 = R_f + \beta_i \left[k_m^2 - R_f \right]$$
$$= 0.06 + 1.75 \, [0.15 - 0.06]$$
$$= 0.06 + 0.1575$$
$$= 0.2175,$$

where $1.75 \, [0.10 - 0.06] = 7\%$ and $1.75 \, [0.15 - 0.06] = 15.75\%$ are the risky ARPs during the change. This change would result in an increase in the slope of the line, and making it steeper. SML_1 would swing up to SML_2. It is clear that the impact of the change on the risk aversion level would be more pronounced on assets that are riskier with a higher beta compared with less risky assets that have betas less than 1.00. This is shown on the increase in the required rate of return between the two types of assets for the risky asset with 1.75 beta, the required rate of return increased by 8.75% (from 13% to 21.75%), while the required rate of return for the asset of 0.5 beta rose by 2.5% (from 8% to 10.5%). This means that such a risky asset of 1.75 beta faced an increase in the required return three and a half times more than what the less risky asset of 0.5 beta faced as an increase in its required return.

It is important to emphasize that the SML slope is not equal to beta as may be guessed by looking at the equation of the model:

$$k_i = R_f + \beta_i [k_m - R_f].$$

Beta, as we have seen before, is equal to the slope of the regression line that describes the response of the return of a certain asset to the change in the market return. Let us consider the difference among three assets as they respond to a certain change in the market return. Let us assume that the market return at some point is 8% and it goes up to 12%, which is an increase of 50%. Let us also assume that our three assets X, Y, and Z, all have 8% rates and they respond to such a change in the market return in the following manner (Figure 13.19):

Asset X: Return increases by the same percentage as the market, that is, 50%. Its return of 8% goes up to 12%.

Asset Y: Return increases by 100%. It goes up from 8% to 16%.

Asset Z: Return increases by 25%. It goes up from 8% to 10%.

- Asset X would have a 45° line going through the original point. Its slope is equal to 1 because the change in the asset return is the same as the change in the market return:

$$\text{slope}_X = \frac{\text{Rise}}{\text{Run}} = \frac{\Delta \text{Asset return}}{\Delta \text{Market return}}$$
$$= \frac{12 - 8}{12 - 8} = 1 = \text{Beta}.$$

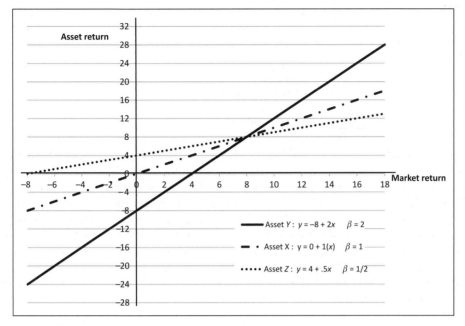

FIGURE 13.19

The line equation would be

$$y = a + bx,$$
$$y = 0 + (1)(x),$$
$$y = x.$$

- Asset Y would have a line with a slope of 2, an x-intercept at 4, and y-intercept at -8:

$$\text{Slope}_Y = \frac{16 - 8}{12 - 8} = \frac{8}{4} = 2.$$

The line equation would be

$$y = 8 + 2x.$$

- Asset Z would have a line with a slope of 0.5, and a y-intercept of 4, and x-intercept of -8:

$$\text{Slope}_Z = \frac{10 - 8}{12 - 8} = \frac{2}{4} = \frac{1}{2}.$$

The line equation would be

$$y = 4 + 0.5x.$$

Since all of these three equations are linear equations of regression lines, beta can be directly read off the equation as it corresponds to *b*-value in the standard format of the linear equation:

$$y = a + bx.$$

13.16   MANAGERIAL DECISION TREE

A decision tree is a graphical representation of the possible paths of alternative decisions and subsequent decisions according to their potential probabilities and values and under possible conditions. Figure 13.20 illustrates a decision tree for a firm that is facing the choice between launching a new product and just improving an existing product. This specific tree considers only one perspective to come up with the final value of the expected profit. Many other perspectives could be incorporated in such a tree or even creating a series of trees to illustrate different determinants of the decision such as the cost of alternative locations, markets, availability of material, labor, technology, and many other perspectives that may serve as keys in decision making. In this illustration, we have shown only two strategies: (*A*) launching a new product or (*B*) improving on an existing product. Each of these strategies is discussed from the possible position of the competitive firms and whether they respond by lowering or increasing the price of their competitive products. So we have the possibilities of A_1 and A_2 as well as B_1 and B_2. Each of these four possibilities has its own expected probability: 0.50, 0.50, 0.60, and 0.40, respectively. Each of these possible positions by competitors may be taken in a specific state of the economy. There are three

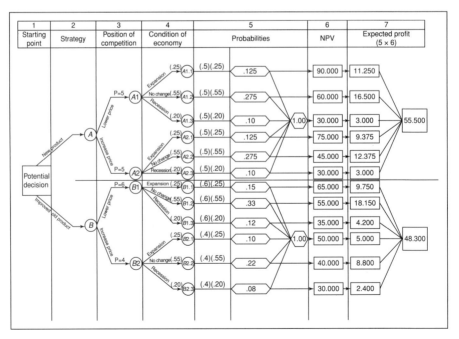

FIGURE 13.20

possibilities for that: An expansion, a recession, and a normal state of the economy in which conditions would experience no significant change. The probabilities of these three states of the economy are 0.25 for expansion, 0.20 for recession, and 0.55 for the continuation of the normal state. Applying these three possibilities on each of the four competitor's position would produce 12 probabilities, one for each state for each position. Each one of these probabilities is a product of the position probability and the state probability. For example, the chance of competitors deciding to lower the price of their product as a response to this firm introducing a new product would be 12.5% if the economy is in expansion, 27.5% if the economy is in normal state, and 10% if the economy is in recession. Incidentally, the chances for the competitors to respond by lowering the price of their own product are the same—12.5%, 27.5%, and 10%—so that these two sets of probabilities add up to 100% for each strategy. Note that the chances for B_1 and B_2 are not the same as it is for A_1 and A_2, but they still add up to 100. The final column of the expected profit is obtained by multiplying each probability by the corresponding NPV of profit in Column 6. The final six expected profit values for each strategy are added up to form the final total expected value of profit under each of the two strategies. Here, in this state, the final figures are compared for the final decision toward the strategy that yields the highest expected value of profit. It is strategy A here, which is to go ahead with the plan for producing a new product and introducing it in the market as an alternative to spend resources on trying to improve the old product.

13.17   MATHEMATICAL SIMULATION AND SENSITIVITY ANALYSIS

Similar to the iconic models in the physical world of design and engineering, which are made to reduce the potential risks, explore flaws and enhance the positive features, as well as estimate costs, mathematical simulation models are designed to mimic the realities of the business world and deal with their changes. They present yet another technique that assists the decision maker in exploring all the possibilities surrounding the problem at hand when it comes to dealing with risky and uncertain conditions. The essential features of the real world can be translated into a multivariable model complete with estimations of the probability distributions of the key variables. The model can be tested repeatedly with random values given to the variables in each test until a probability distribution and risk for the general model are estimated so that these can be used to calculate the expected outcome for any given variables.

Suppose that we want to estimate the NPV of a project and explore the risk involved. We can simulate the profit model and randomize the values of its variables many times, and calculate the probability distribution and the standard deviation so that they become the template for estimating the NPV in any risky circumstances. We can start with a mathematical formula to represent the profit as a net cash flow for the t-period (π_t) :

$$\pi_t = [R - C - D](1 - x) + D.$$

Here

R is the total revenue, which is equal to the amount of product sold (s) times the product unit price (p):

$$R = s(p).$$

C is the total cost, which is equal to the amount of product sold (s) times the unit cost, including production cost (c_1) and selling cost (c_2):

$$C = s(c_1 + c_2).$$

D is the annual depreciation, which is equal to the original depreciable cost and initial capital outlay divided by the lifetime of the physical capital asset:

$$D = \frac{d}{L}.$$

x is the marginal tax rate, where the profit is adjusted accordingly by $(1 - x)$:

$$\pi_t - \left[s(p) - s(c_1 + c_2) - \frac{d}{L} \right](1 - x) + \frac{d}{L}.$$

Now, let us give these variables their numerical values:

- Product sold (s) = 5000 units.
- Product unit price (p) = \$15.
- Production cost per unit (c_1) = \$2.50.
- Selling cost per unit (c_2) = \$0.50.
- Original equipment depreciation (d) = \$18,000.
- Equipment lifetime (L) = 10 years.
- Marginal tax rate (x) = 36%.

Profit π_t would be

$$\pi_t = \left[5000(15) - 5000(2.50 + 0.50) - \frac{8000}{10} \right](1 - 0.36) + \frac{8000}{10},$$

$$\pi_t = 38,688.$$

The \$38,688 is the profit earned for the period t. If we assume that it will be earned in every year of the project life for the next 4 years ($n = 4$), then the NPV for the cash flow during the entire period of n would be

$$\text{NPV}_n = \sum_{t=1}^{n} \frac{\pi_t}{(1 + k)^t} - C_0.$$

If the risk-free rate of interest (r) is 5% and the firm's risk premium (R_p) is 7%, then k would be

$$k = r + R_p$$

$$= 0.05 + 0.07 = 0.12.$$

If the initial cost of the project (C_0) is \$50,000, then

$$
\begin{aligned}
\text{NPV}_4 &= \left[\frac{\pi_1}{(1+k)^1} + \frac{\pi_2}{(1+k)^2} + \frac{\pi_3}{(1+k)^3} + \frac{\pi_4}{(1+k)^4} \right] - C_0 \\
&= \left[\frac{38{,}688}{(1+0.12)^1} + \frac{38{,}688}{(1+0.12)^2} + \frac{38{,}688}{(1+0.12)^3} + \frac{38{,}688}{(1+0.12)^4} \right] - 50{,}000 \\
&= [34{,}543 + 30{,}841 + 27{,}537 + 24{,}587] - 50{,}000 \\
&= 117{,}508 - 50{,}000 \\
&= 67{,}508.
\end{aligned}
$$

This is one estimate of the NPV of a project. If this type of estimation is repeated hundreds of times using different values of the variables taken from their probability distribution, we can eventually form the probability distribution of the general NPV of the project, and we can estimate its mean, as well as its standard deviation, as the level of risk. Suppose that repeated simulation ends up with an expected NPV of \$65,000 and a standard deviation of 24,000, we can calculate the x-value and obtain the table value that refers to the probability of having a negative NPV (Figure 13.21):

$$
\begin{aligned}
Z &= \frac{x - \bar{x}}{\sigma} \\
&= \frac{0 - 65{,}000}{24{,}000} \\
&= -2.7.
\end{aligned}
$$

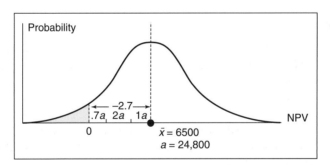

FIGURE 13.21

Looking this value up in the z-table reveals the value of 0.0035 in the zero column. It means that the zero value is 2.7 standard deviations below the mean and that the probability of the NPV being negative (less than zero) is 35%.

In addition to the full-fledged process of mathematical simulation, there are other related techniques to deal with risk, but to a lesser extent. Sensitivity analysis utilizes the same set of variables and their mathematical model, but it stops short of obtaining complete probability distribution of the whole set. It focuses on randomizing the value of one key variable in the model in order to test the impact of the single change on the rest and establish how sensitive the model is in its response. For example, a sensitivity analysis can be performed on the NPV model by changing the unit price of the product frequently and tracking down the impact of such change on the outcome. Another similar technique is the scenario analysis, which differs from the sensitivity analysis only by extending the random change into more than one variable to see the impact of changing a number of variables simultaneously. While sensitivity and scenario analyses are limited, they are more practical and more commonly used. Full simulation is comprehensive and powerful, but it is more expensive and time consuming, even in this computer age. For most managers, it can, be reserved for only the major cases.

13.18   ADVANCED CHOICE UNDER RISK, AMBIGUITY, AND UNCERTAINTY

This section focuses on management decisions that are characterized as a choice among a finite number of alternatives using advance choice techniques. It is often possible to quantify economic outcomes used in areas such as policy and cost–benefit analysis conditional on uncontrolled events. Uncontrolled events can include the value of unknown parameters in a response function, the effectiveness of a new technology, weather events, and so on. This section illustrates the decision criteria that are available, always assuming that, at the least, conditional economic outcomes can be determined. The notions of "rv" and "pdf" reviewed in Chapter 2 are used in this section along with some additional background on the **cumulative distribution function** (cdf).

The notion of the cdf is defined as the area under the pdf of an rv to the left of a particular value of the rv. Hence, it is the probability that an rv is less than or equal to that value. The cdf $F(x)$ of a random variable X is the probability that X has a value that is less than or equal to x; that is,

$$F(x) = \Pr[X \leq x].$$

Example

If the pdf of X is $f(x) = \dfrac{1}{\sqrt{2\pi\sigma^2}}\exp\left[-\dfrac{1}{2\sigma^2}(x-\mu)^2\right]$, then the cdf of X will be

$$F(x) = \int_{\infty}^{x} \frac{1}{\sqrt{2\sigma^2}}\exp\left[-\frac{1}{2\sigma^2}(1-\mu)^2\right]dt.$$

13.18.1   Stochastic Dominance

Stochastic dominance has been developed to identify conditions under which one risky alternative is preferred to another. The approach of stochastic dominance is to identify the preferred alternative while making the weakest possible assumptions. Generally, stochastic dominance assumes that an individual is an expected utility maximizer and then adds further assumptions relative to preference. In other words, stochastic dominance relies on the appropriateness of expected utility maximization and the underlying assumptions on preference. It should be mentioned that some experimental decision problems from the 1950s and 1960s, such as the Allais paradox and the Ellsberg paradox, have suggested that decision makers do not follow expected utility maximization. On the other hand, some econometric tests with real-world data have tended to support expected utility maximization.

Assumptions

1. Expected utility maximization.
2. Two, mutually exclusive, alternatives are to be compared.
3. Analysis is based on true (population) probability distributions.

Expected Utility   Suppose the two alternative decisions yield alternative probability density functions for benefit, x; namely, $f(x)$ and $g(x)$.

Expected utilities, $E[U(x)]$, corresponding to the different decisions are

$$\int_{-\infty}^{\infty} U(x)f(x)dx \quad \text{and} \quad \int_{-\infty}^{\infty} U(x)g(x)dx.$$

The difference in these expected utilities is

$$\int_{-\infty}^{\infty} U(x)f(x)dx - \int_{-\infty}^{\infty} U(x)g(x)dx,$$

$$\int_{-\infty}^{\infty} U(x)(f(x) - g(x))dx.$$

Note that the difference is positive when $f(x)$ yields higher expected utility than $g(x)$ and negative otherwise. If positive, $f(x)$ is a preferred gamble to $g(x)$, otherwise $g(x)$ is a preferred gamble to $f(x)$.

First-Degree Stochastic Dominance   Consider

$$\int_{-\infty}^{\infty} U(x)(f(x) - g(x))dx.$$

Using integration by parts, let $u = U(x)$ and $v = F(x) - G(x)$. Note that $du = U'(x)\,dx$ and $dv = (f(x) - g(x))\,dx$. So,

$$\int_{-\infty}^{\infty} U(x)[f(x) - g(x)]dx = U(x)[F(x) - G(x)]\Big|_{-\infty}^{\infty} - \Big|_{-\infty}^{\infty} U'(x)[F(x) - G(x)]dx$$

$$= U(\infty)[F(\infty) - G(\infty)] - U(-\infty)[F(-\infty) - G(-\infty)]$$

$$- \int_{-\infty}^{\infty} U'(x)[F(x) - G(x)]dx$$

$$= U(\infty)(1 - 1) - U(-\infty)(0 - 0) - \int_{-\infty}^{\infty} U'(x)[F(x)$$

$$- G(x)]dx$$

$$= \int_{-\infty}^{\infty} U'(x)[G(x) - F(x)]dx.$$

Observe that this term is nonnegative if $U'(x) > 0$ and $G(x) > F(x)$.

Probability density function f dominates probability density function g by *first-degree stochastic dominance* (FSD) when $U'(x) > 0$ if and only if the cdf associated with f is less than or equal to the cdf associated with g (i.e., $F(x) \le G(x)$ for all (x) and strict inequality holds for at least one x.

Interpretation of FSD Conditions   Two implications of FSD are that the mean of f is greater than the mean of g and that for every level of probability at least as much money is made under f as under g. This is what can be concluded from characterizing the choice between two alternatives for every expected utility maximizer that prefers more to less.

Second-Degree Stochastic Dominance   Consider

$$\int_{-\infty}^{\infty} U'(x)[G(x) - F(x)]dx.$$

Note that if this expression is positive, then f is preferred to g since the expected utility under f is greater than the expected utility under g.

Using integration by parts, let $u = U'(x)$ and let $dv = [G(x) - F(x)]\,dx$. Note that $du = U''(x)$ and $v = \int_{-\infty}^{\infty} [G(t) - F(t)]dt$. So,

$$\int_{-\infty}^{\infty} U(x)[G(x) - F(x)]dx = U'(x) \int_{-\infty}^{x} [G(t) - F(t)]dt \Big|_{-\infty}^{\infty} - \int_{-\infty}^{\infty} U(x) \int_{-\infty}^{x} [G(t)$$

$$- F(t)]dt \, dx \Big|_{-\infty}^{\infty}.$$

Focus on the first term:

$$U'(x) \int_{-\infty}^{x} [G(t) - F(t)]dt \Big|_{-\infty}^{\infty} = U(\infty) \int_{-\infty}^{x} [G(t) - F(t)]dt - U(\infty) \int_{-\infty}^{\infty} [G(t)$$

$$- F(t)]dt.$$

Assume that $U'(x) > 0$ and that $\int_{-\infty}^{x} [G(t) - F(t)]dt \geq 0$ with strict inequality for some x (the first assumption is from FSD; the second assumption is new and is used in signing the second term as well). This makes $\int_{-\infty}^{\infty} [G(t) - F(t)]dt \geq 0$ and, of course always, $\int_{-\infty}^{-\infty} [G(t) - F(t)]dt = 0$. This makes the first term positive.

Focus on the second term:

$$\int_{-\infty}^{\infty} U'(x) \int_{-\infty}^{x} [G(t) - F(t)]dt \, dx \Big|_{-\infty}^{\infty}.$$

In order to guarantee that f is preferred to g, the sign of this whole term must be negative (since the whole term is subtracted). Second-degree stochastic dominance (SSD) assumes that the second derivative of the utility function with respect to x is negative everywhere (assume $U''(x) < 0$). With this assumption, if $\int_{-\infty}^{x} [G(t) - F(t)]dt \geq 0$ with strict inequality for at least one x (this was already assumed in signing the first term) then this makes $\int_{-\infty}^{\infty} [G(t) - F(t)]dt \geq 0$ and, of course always, $\int_{-\infty}^{-\infty} [G(t) - F(t)]dt = 0$. These assumptions make the second term negative. The minus sign in front of the second term makes it positive.

Under the assumptions of positive marginal utility ($U'(x) > 0$) and DMU ($U''(x) < 0$), f dominates g by SSD if and only if $\int_{-\infty}^{x} [G(t) - F(t)]dt \geq 0$ for all x with strict inequality for at least one x.

Interpretation of FSD Conditions   Though the derivation is not given here, an interpretation of SSD is not difficult. The area under the cdf of X, i.e, F, up to x is the expected "shortfall" of X relative to x (here "shortfall" refers to the difference between a target return (or goal), x, and the outcome). f dominates g according to SSD if and only if the expected shortfall under g relative to target return x is greater than or equal to the expected shortfall under f relative to target return x for all possible target returns with "greater than" holding for at least one target return. This interpretation suggests that a risk-averse decision maker ranks gambles by how well the gamble is expected to meet a goal (in fact, any goal).

Applications of SSD Conditions   Recall that stochastic dominance analysis uses conditions on the cdfs associated with different decisions to derive the set of decisions that can be ruled out as inefficient relative to other decisions in terms of expected utility. The conditions provided by SSD, which is the workhorse among stochastic dominance criteria, are that decision A_i is superior to decision A_k if and only if $\int_{-\infty}^{x} [F_{A_k}(t) - F_{A_i}(t)] dt \geq 0$ for all x with strict inequality for at least one x where F_{A_i} the cdf associated with decision A_i. The left pane of Table 13.19 depicts a policy decision featuring decisions (A_i), events (E_j), event probabilities (P_j), and outcomes conditional on each decision and event $(V(A_i, E_j))$, where the latter are shown in the body of the table. Figure 13.21 shows the cdfs F_{A_3} and F_{A_2} in the left pane and F_{A_1} and F_{A_2} in the right pane. Visual inspection of the figures confirms that the stochastic dominance condition is satisfied by policy decision, A_2, which is unique (in this case) in maximizing expected utility.

13.18.2   Choice under Ambiguity

If the likelihood of uncontrolled events can be determined up to a convex set (e.g., ranges of probability values are known), then there is said to be ambiguity about the risks associated with decision; that is, decision making under ambiguity. This case represents a middle ground between the risk and uncertainty environments. For such cases, an emerging decision criterion known as maxmin expected utility (Gilboa and Schmeidler, 1989) suggests maximizing the minimum expected utility over the convex set; that is, with linear utility, decision A_i is superior to decision A_k. Suppose

$$\min_{(P \in S)} E[V(A_i, E_j)] > \min_{(P \in S)} E[V(A_k, E_j)],$$

where P is a vector of probabilities associated with uncontrolled events and S is a convex set. The right pane of Table 13.19 shows the decision problem under ambiguity. The maxmin expected utility optimal decision is given by $\frac{\text{Maximize}}{A_i} \frac{(\text{Min})}{(P)} \Sigma_j 9V(A_i, E_j) p_j)$; subject to $\Sigma_j p_j = 1$, $p_j = \in [a_j, b_j] \forall j$. The maxmin expected utility criterion generalizes both expected utility maximization and the maximin criterion in the sense that both criteria are special cases of maxmin expected utility. To see this, observe that the maxmin expected utility optimal decision corresponds to expected utility maximization when S consists of a single point and corresponds to the maximin criterion when S does not restrict the ranges of possible probabilities (S is a unit n-simplex). Application of maxmin expected utility to the right pane of Table 13.19 shows A_2 to be the optimal choice.

13.18.3   Choice under Uncertainty

We begin this section with some interesting observations made by economists:

> I am still puzzled at the insistence of many writers on treating the uncertainty of result in choice as if it were a gamble on a known mathematical chance.
>
> Frank Knight, 1933[1]

---

[1]Knight's 1921 book made perhaps the earliest distinction between risk and uncertainty; uncertainty is sometimes referred to as Knightian uncertainty.

TABLE 13.19

Event Probability Policy	E_1 0.2	E_2 0.5	E_3 0.3	Event Probability Policy	E_1 [0.15, 25]	E_2 [0.4, 0.6]	E_3 [0.25, 0.35]	Event Probability Policy	E_1?	E_2?	E_3?
A_1	0.8	0.9	1.0	A_1	0.8	0.9	1.0	A_1	0.8	0.9	1.0
A_2	0.8	1.1	1.3	A_2	0.8	1.1	1.3	A_2	0.8	1.1	1.3
A_3	0.8	0.95	1.4	A_2	0.8	0.95	1.4	A_3	0.8	0.95	1.4

[E]conomists have tinkered endlessly with the risk model, yet they appear to have largely ignored problems dominated by uncertainty. This is especially troubling to the extent that uncertainty is rapidly growing and perhaps dominant in the dynamic global economy.

C.R. Taylor, 2003

Predicting or determining the likelihood of uncontrolled events is often difficult and can involve significant time and expense. In the cases where the latter are prohibitive, often referred to as decision making under uncertainty, there are several approaches. Traditional decision criteria, including the maximin, maximax, Laplace, and Hurwicz criteria (Render et al., 2009), may be possible. While none of these criteria require knowledge of uncontrolled event probabilities for application, the first two represent polar extremes in terms of optimism and pessimism, while the latter two require information similar to probabilities in order to be applied.

The Laplace criterion has come under criticism in the philosophy literature owing to what has come to be known as the *paradox of the envelopes*. The decision problem, followed by three decision tables that apply the Laplace criterion to the problem and achieve three different optimal solutions, is given below (Tables 13.20, 13.21, and 13.22).

TABLE 13.20   **Envelopes Sealed**

Event →	E_1	E_2	Expected Payoff
Probability →	$\frac{1}{2}$	$\frac{1}{2}$	← By Laplace
Act↓	Payoff↓	Payoff↓	Optimal act: indifferent
Keep	x	$2x$	$\frac{3}{2}x$
Switch	$2x$	x	$\frac{3}{2}x$

TABLE 13.21   **Open Yours: Find $x**

Event →	E_1	E_2	Expected Payoff
Probability→	$\frac{1}{2}$	$\frac{1}{2}$	←By Laplace
Act↓	Payoff↓	Payoff↓	Optimal act: switch
Keep	x	x	x
Switch	$2x$	$\frac{3}{2}$	$\frac{5}{4}x$

TABLE 13.22   **Open Other: Find $x**

Event →	E_1	E_2	Expected Payoff
Probability→	$\frac{1}{2}$	$\frac{1}{2}$	←By Laplace
Act↓	Payoff↓	Payoff↓	Optimal act: eep
Keep	$2x$	$\frac{x}{2}$	$\frac{5}{4}x$
Switch	x	x	x

Situation: Two sealed envelopes (yours and theirs). One contains twice the money of the other. You can keep yours or switch. What should you do?

Putting aside the questions raised by the paradox of the envelopes, each of the criteria for decision making under uncertainty can be interpreted in the context of Table 13.19. The maximin optimal decision is found as the solution to $\frac{\text{Maximize}}{A_i} \frac{\text{Min}}{E_j} V(A_i, E_j)$; the maximax optimal decision is found as the solution to $\frac{\text{Maximize}}{A_i} \text{Max} E_j V(A_i, E_j)$;the Laplace optimal decision is found as the solution to $\frac{\text{Maximize}}{A_i} \Sigma_j V(A_i, E_j)$; the Hurwicz optimal decision (given a value for $w \in [0, 1]$) is found as the solution to $\frac{\text{Maximize}}{A_i} (\frac{w \text{ Max}}{E_j} V(A_i, E_j 0 + (1-w)$ $\text{Min} E_j V(A_i, E_j)0$. It is easily verified that application of these criteria to the information in the center pane of Table 13.19 gives the following optimal decisions: (maximin, A_1, A_2, A_3) (maximax, A_3); (Laplace, A_3), (Hurwicz ($w = 0.7$), A_3).

SUMMARY

- The majority of managerial decisions are taken under the conditions of risk and uncertainty. Risk is defined as the condition in which there are multiple possible outcomes and the probability of each alternative outcome either is known or can be estimated. Uncertainty, on the other hand, refers to the same possibilities of multiple outcomes, but the probability of each outcome is unknown or cannot be estimated. There are many sources of risk including economic sources such as fluctuation in the major economic determinants (e.g., inflation, interest rate, employment, and the like). The political sources of risk include tax policies, foreign trade policies, terrorism, etc. Social sources include all the factors related to cultures, religions, etc.

- Risk can be measured absolutely or relatively. The absolute measure of risk is represented by the standard deviation, which is a statistical tool to measure the dispersion of possible outcomes from the expected value of that outcome. The relative measure of risk is represented by another tool called the coefficient of variation, which is obtained by dividing the standard deviation by the expected value of outcome.

- People, business managers in particular, tend to deal with risk in three different ways: either to be a risk-taker, risk averter, or risk neutral. Most business managers are considered risk averters. Managerial decisions that are based on risk aversion strategies seek to maximize the expected utility rather than to maximize the mere monetary return. The expected utility is equal to the summation of all possible outcomes multiplied by their probabilities of occurrence.

- Risk is considered in the firm's evaluation of its investment. There are two ways to factor in risk in this evaluation process: the risk premium adjustment and the certainty-equivalent adjustment. In the first adjustment, a certain risk premium is added to the risk-free rate of return when finding the present value of the cash flow of investment. In the second adjustment, the net cash flow is multiplied by the certainty-equivalent coefficient, which is obtained as the ratio of the equivalent certain sum to the expected risky sum or net return from the investment.

- Risk is categorized into diversifiable and nondiversifiable risk depending on the extent to which risk can be minimized or not when assessing its impact on managerial decisions. Diversifiable or unsystematic risk is the risk specific to an individual firm as related to its internal conditions and circumstances such as lawsuits against the firm, marketing or accounting problems, product defects, workers' strikes, and problematic contracts. The nondiversifiable or systematic risk is the general and market-related risk that affects all firms and all projects and assets, simultaneously and with no discrimination.

- A portfolio risk is not collective. It would be less if the portfolio includes more and different individual assets. Its magnitude depends on two factors: diversification of the assets and their correlation. The higher the diversification of the assets in a portfolio, the lesser the risk, and the lesser the correlation among the different assets in a portfolio, the lesser the risk. As for the nondiversifiable or systematic risk, it can be approximated in the market by a mathematical tool called beta. It is a measure of securities' volatility in relation to an average security represented by the state of the market. It is, in this sense, an index of the extent to which a security return moves in response to the changes in the overall market. CAPM, discussed in Chapter 12, is a technical tool to analyze the relationship between the financial asset's expected return and the nondiversifiable risk in the market.

- Another way to address risk is to put into order the subsequent events and decisions visually on a decision tree. It is a graphical representation of the possible paths of alternative decisions and subsequent decisions according to their potential probabilities and values and under possible conditions. Mathematical simulation models are yet another way to mimic the realities of the business and deal with their changes. In this sense, the essential features of the real world can be translated into a multivariable model complete with estimations of the probability distributions of the key variables. Such models can be tested repeatedly with random values given to the variables in each test until a probability distribution and risk for the general model are estimated so that these can be used to calculate the expected outcome for any given variable. The last section of the chapter deals with advanced decision making under risk, ambiguity, and uncertainty. It focuses on management decisions that are characterized as a choice among the finite number of alternatives using advanced choice techniques. It is often possible to quantify economic outcomes used in areas such as policy and cost-benefit analysis, conditional on uncontrolled events that can include the value of unknown parameters in a response function. The section illustrates the decision criteria that are available, always assuming that, at the least, conditional economic outcomes can be determined.

KEY TERMS

risk	financial beta	risk premium
absolute measure of risk	security market line (SML)	nondiversifiable risk
coefficient of variation	mathematical simulation	efficient portfolio curve
risk averter	cumulative distribution	risk-free rate of return
risk neutral	function	unsystematic risk
expected monetary	choice under ambiguity	CAPM
return	uncertainty	decision tree
certainty equivalent	relative measure of risk	sensitivity analysis
diversifiable risk	risk aversion	stochastic dominance
portfolio risk	risk-taker	choice under uncertainty
Markowitz model	expected utility of money	expected payoff
systematic risk	risk discount	

LIST OF FORMULAS

- Standard deviation:

$$\sigma = \sqrt{\sum_{i=1}^{n} [x - \bar{x}]^2 P(x_i)}.$$

- Expected value (mean):

$$\bar{x} = \sum_{i=1}^{n} x_i P(x_i).$$

- Coefficient of variation:

$$v = \frac{\sigma}{\bar{x}}.$$

- Risk discount:

$$RD = E(v) - CE.$$

- Certainty-equivalent coefficient:

$$\alpha = \frac{CE}{E(v)}.$$

- Risk-adjusted net present value:

$$NPV = \sum_{t=1}^{n} \left[\frac{\alpha \pi_i}{(1 + r)^t} \right] - C_0.$$

- Portfolio risk:

$$\sigma = \sqrt{\sum_{i=1}^{n} (k_i - k_e)^n \text{Pr}_i},$$

$$\text{cov}(X, Y) = \sum_{i=1}^{n} \left(k_i^X - k_e^X \right)^n \left(k_i^Y - k_e^Y \right)^n \text{Pr}_i,$$

$$\text{cor}_{X,Y} = \frac{\text{cov}(X, Y)}{\sigma_X \sigma_Y}.$$

- Standard deviation of combined assets:

$$\sigma_{I,II} = \sqrt{\sigma_i^2 w_i^2 + \sigma_{II}^2 w_{II}^2 + 2\text{COR}_{I,II}(w_i \sigma_i)(w_{II} \sigma_{II})}.$$

- Beta:

$$\beta = \frac{\text{cov}(k_i, k_m)}{\text{var}(k_m)}.$$

- CAPM:

$$k_i = R_f + \beta_i[k_m - R_f],$$

$$\beta_i = \frac{k_i - R_f}{k_m - R_f},$$

$$R_f = \frac{k_i - \beta_i k_m}{1 - \beta_i},$$

$$k_m = \frac{k_i + R_f(\beta_i - 1)}{\beta_i}.$$

- Inflation adjusted risk-free rate of return:

$$R_f = k_0 + \text{IP}.$$

- Simulated profit:

$$\pi = \left[s(p) - s(c_1 + c_2) - \frac{d}{L} \right](1 - x) + \frac{d}{L}.$$

EXERCISES

1. What is risk and what is uncertainty? How would each and both affect the managerial decision making and what are the sources of risk?

2. How is risk measured? Explain the ways of measurement, the technical tools used, and how they work.

3. How do people generally deal with risk? What are the types of attitudes toward risk? What attitude do business managers usually exhibit toward business risk? Explain risk aversion, risk and utility of money, expected utility of money, expected monetary return, risk discount, and certainty equivalent.

4. Compare the diversifiable and nondiversifiable risks. How would each of them be measured? What is portfolio risk, CAPM, and market beta?

5. What is the managerial decision tree? Can you come up with your own example to illustrate how the decision tree works? Explain how mathematical simulation works to serve business decisions.

6. The following are data on predicted profits and their probabilities for two projects, A and B:

Project	Predicted Profits	Probability
	10,000	60%
A	15,000	40%
	7,500	40%
B	12,500	30%
	17,500	30%

Find out which project is riskier. Use both the absolute and relative measures of assessment.

7. The following table shows the money utility and the outcome probabilities of a risky project for three types of managers according to their risk attitudes.

		Utility		
Outcome	Probability	Manager 1	Manager 2	Manager 3
300,000	0.25	12.25	30.50	3.44
20,000	0.75	−3.5	1.2	−5.7

Which manager is most likely to undertake the project?

8. Consider the following function as a manager's utility of money function:

$$U = 370 \, m^{0.40},$$

where m is the initial capital required. Based on the expected value of utility, what would most likely be the manager's decision as to either undertake or pass on this project given that the initial capital is $20,000 and it could either earn or lose $10.000?

9. Consider the following two investment projects I and II.

Project	Required Capital	Cash Flow 1	Cash Flow 2	Cash Flow 3
I	50,000	19,000	35,000	20,000
II	40,000	16,000	35,000	30,000

Based on the net present value, which project is most likely to be approved given a risk-free discount rate of 7.5%? Also, would the choice of project remain the same if the risk premium for project I is 2.5% and for project II, 5.5%?

10. If the market return on a certain asset is 9.75% and the risk-free rate is 5.25%, what would be the required rate of return for the firm handling this asset if its beta is 1.66?

14

MANAGEMENT CONSULTANTS AND INFORMATION

Management consulting has expanded dramatically during the past 25 years with estimated growth rates exceeding 20% in many of those years. The consulting industry has grown to include a number of large firms with instantly recognizable names that serve a wide range of public- and private-sector clients and many highly specialized firms that serve the specific needs of very specific types of clients. The growth in the industry is, of course, a reflection of the growth in the demand for consultant services by private, public, and nonprofit firm managers. In fact, managers of both large- and medium-sized firms have increasingly come to rely on consultants for objective guidance and expertise. This brief chapter focuses on measuring information that may be gained from the employment of a management consultant, the notion of **perfect information**, and the willingness of a firm's management to pay to engage the services of a management consultant. The latter may be especially useful as a practical and timely tool for gauging the appropriateness of engaging a management consultant for a specific management problem.

14.1 MEASURING INFORMATION AND ITS IMPACT ON UNCERTAINTY

Managers seek the counsel of management consultants for many reasons. Often, consultants may provide expertise that would otherwise be absent from the organization. Other times, managers may need guidance from outside the organization to help resolve the problems that the organization is faced with. Managers may want to ensure that the advice received is objective and that it will ultimately resolve the problem(s). Consultants may also be needed to supplement the existing resources in a firm; that is, consultants may be employed to carry out tasks that managers could do for themselves but for which they simply do not have sufficient time.

Managerial Economics: A Mathematical Approach, First Edition. M. J. Alhabeeb and L. Joe Moffitt.
© 2013 John Wiley & Sons, Inc. Published 2013 by John Wiley & Sons, Inc.

Very often, contracting with a management consultant signifies, at its core, contracting for information. This raises the questions of how the information can be measured and valued, and what its impact can be. The answer to the first question is that information can be measured in bits, where a bit is counted as a correct answer to a question that can be answered as "yes" or "no." With this measure in mind, the information needed to answer a more complex management question can be described as the expected minimum number of "yes/no" type questions needed to determine the answer to the complex question with certainty. Eliminating uncertainty through information often results in improved decision making.

An abstract example can help understand the meaning of **measurement** of information more clearly. Suppose a number selector chooses a number from among the natural numbers less than or equal to 5, that is, a number has been chosen from among the set $\{1, 2, 3, 4, 5\}$, but the number chosen is kept secret. What is the minimum number of queries to the number selector, answerable by either a "yes" or a "no," that is required to determine the number that was chosen? The sequence of questions "Is the number 1? Is the number 2?" and so on will identify the number in no more than 4 questions. Hence, the amount of information needed to know the number selected is certainly no more than 4 bits. The actual number of questions needed to identify the number using this questioning scheme will, of course, depend on the number chosen. For example, if the number chosen were 1, then the first question asked in the sequence would find this out. If the number chosen were 2, then the number would be identified by the second question in the sequence, and so on. The probability that one question will be needed to identify the number is $1/5$, which is the probability that the number is 1. The probability that two questions will be needed to identify the number is also $1/5$, which is the probability that the number is 2. The probability that three questions will be needed to identify the number is also $1/5$, which is the probability that the number is 3. The probability that four questions will be needed to identify the number is $2/5$, which is the probability that the number is either 4 or 5. So again, if the probability that a number is chosen is the same for each of the five numbers (i.e., $1/5$), then the expected number of questions needed to identify the number through the use of this sequence of questions is

$$1 \times \left(\tfrac{1}{5}\right) + 2 \times \left(\tfrac{1}{5}\right) + 3 \times \left(\tfrac{1}{5}\right) + 4 \times \left(\tfrac{2}{5}\right) = \tfrac{14}{5}.$$

So the sequence of questions will reveal the true number with an expected sequence of questions just less than 3 in number. Of course, it is not hard to imagine other questioning schemes that could determine an expected number of bits of information needed to eliminate uncertainty, aside from this sequence of questions that inquires about each possible number seriatim.

With the knowledge that information can be measured in bits, it is not hard to imagine how uncertainty can be lessened with bits of information less in number than the bits expected to be needed in order to eliminate uncertainty entirely. Continuing with the example of identifying a number that has been selected from the set $\{1, 2, 3, 4, 5\}$, suppose that only one question can be asked and the question is "Is the number 1?" How can the impact of the answer to this one question, that is, this single bit of information, be measured? One way to measure the information is to compare the information needed to eliminate the residual uncertainty after the question is answered with the original number of bits of information needed to eliminate uncertainty. If the answer to the question is that the number is 1, then no additional information is needed since the uncertainty has been eliminated. There is a 1/5 probability that this will occur. If the answer to the question is that the number is not 1, then it is either 2, 3, 4, or 5 with each being equally likely. The probability of this occurrence is 4/5. Using the form of the calculation for the expected number of questions needed to eliminate uncertainty previously employed gives

$$0 \times \left(\tfrac{1}{5}\right) + \left(1 \times \left(\tfrac{1}{4}\right) + 2 \times \left(\tfrac{1}{4}\right) + 3 \times \left(\tfrac{1}{2}\right)\right) \left(\tfrac{4}{5}\right) = \tfrac{9}{5}$$

as the expected number of questions needed to eliminate uncertainty following acquisition of an answer to the question of whether or not the number chosen is 1 given the questioning scheme, which was based on a sequence of simple queries.

The measurement of information in terms of bits and the notion that a sufficient number of bits of information can help eliminate uncertainty or at least lessen it, to the benefit of decision making, provide a foundation for a quantitative approach to determining a firm's willingness to pay for a management consultant's services. If economic considerations were introduced to the example of determining the value of a number drawn from the set {1, 2, 3, 4, 5}, the marginal benefit of a bit of information could be compared with the cost of acquiring the bit (the cost of getting a question in the sequence answered) to determine the optimal amount of information. Conceptually, a comparison of a similar nature can guide the decision to engage the services of a management consultant.

14.2 PERFECT MANAGEMENT INFORMATION

From a firm's perspective, a management decision may often be regarded as a choice among a finite number of alternatives with uncertain outcomes. The uncertainty inherent in many decisions may spur the desire on the part of a firm's managers to acquire additional information such as may be obtained through engagement of a management consultant. Such management decisions are frequently represented analytically by a decision table similar to the decision tables utilized earlier. Table 14.1 serves as an example of a decision table associated with a management decision depicting three possible choices and two equally probable outcomes per choice. Perfect information related to the management decision depicted in the table would provide sufficient information to eliminate the uncertainty surrounding the decision and reveal which of the two columns of the table are applicable for a choice. If a management consultant provided such advice, the firm could then focus on the much simpler problem of making a choice among alternatives with certain outcomes.

TABLE 14.1 Management Decisions with Two Equally Likely Outcomes

Choice↓ Outcome→	Probability $= 1/2$	Probability $= 1/2$
Choice 1	80,000	−20,000
Choice 2	30,000	20,000
Choice 3	23,000	23,000

14.3   VALUING PERFECT MANAGEMENT INFORMATION

A manager's maximum willingness to pay for information provides an upper bound on the amount a firm might pay to engage a management consultant. Maximum willingness to pay is evaluated using the concept of **expected value of perfect information** (EVPI). The EVPI is found by subtracting the best expected outcome a firm can achieve without a management consultant from the best expected outcome a firm can achieve with sufficient expert advice to eliminate the uncertainty that surrounds the decision:

$$\text{EVPI} = \text{Best expected outcome with uncertainty eliminated}$$

$$-\text{Best expected outcome without a consultant.}$$

An important advantage of using EVPI to evaluate the willingness to pay to engage a management consultant is its simplicity. EVPI is evaluated using the management decision problem depicted in Table 14.1. If the firm does not engage a management consultant, then following the discussion in Chapter 12, the firm will evaluate the best choice under uncertainty and implement it. In this case, the evaluations are

Choice 1: $\left(\frac{1}{2}\right) \times 80,000 + \left(\frac{1}{2}\right) \times (-20,000) = 30,000,$

Choice 2: $\left(\frac{1}{2}\right) \times 30,000 + \left(\frac{1}{2}\right) \times 20,000 = 25,000,$

Choice 3: $\left(\frac{1}{2}\right) \times 23,000 + \left(\frac{1}{2}\right) \times 23,000 = 23,000.$

The firm's best choice and best expected outcome are Choice 1 and 30,000, respectively. With information sufficient to eliminate the uncertainty that the firm faces with respect to this management decision, the firm can make Choice 1 when the first column of outcomes is relevant, achieving outcome 80,000, and Choice 3 when the second column of outcomes applies based on the advice received, achieving outcome 23,000. Thus,

$$\left(\tfrac{1}{2}\right) \times 80,000 + \left(\tfrac{1}{2}\right) \times 23,000 = 51,500.$$

EVPI is then given by

$$51,500 - 30,000 = 21,500.$$

The maximum amount that the firm will be willing to pay a management consultant is 21,500. For the decision problem depicted in Table 14.1, the firm would need to compare the management consultant's rate and time required with this amount. Clearly, the firm may benefit from engaging a management consultant; however, the cost of the contract must never exceed the firm's EVPI in order for a possible benefit to be realized.

14.4   VALUING LESS-THAN-PERFECT MANAGEMENT INFORMATION

While the expected value of perfect advice from a management consultant on a management issue is very useful in providing an upper bound on how much it might make sense to pay a consultant, the more common case that firm managers face concerns the possible acquisition of **less-than-perfect information**. The situation is conceptually similar to that described in Section 14.3 where some bits of information could be obtained about a number selected from the set $\{1, 2, 3, 4, 5\}$; however, some uncertainty, albeit reduced uncertainty, remained after the information was acquired. In deciding whether to engage a management consultant, a manager needs to determine the expected value of the information that the consultant can provide and compare this amount with the cost of the consulting contract. This evaluation can (perhaps) best be described within the context of a decision problem, though highly simplified, that a manager might face, and this is the course we pursue.

We suppose that a manager is considering an addition to available production capacity in anticipation that additional output of the firm's primary product line can be marketed. The firm can add 100,000 square feet of production area or it can add only 50,000 square feet. The expansion to 100,000 square feet would be very desirable if the additional amount of product could be sold but disastrous for the firm if the hoped-for demand fails to materialize. An expansion of production area by 50,000 square feet incurs similar uncertainty about the firm's ability to market the product but incurs lessened risk and reward if the market turns out to be firmer or softer, respectively, than expected. The firm can, of course, choose not to undertake an expansion of production capacity at all. As is apparent from the discussion so far, the main source of uncertainty the manager faces is the ability of the firm to market the expanded output that would follow from additional capacity. Table 14.2 shows the basic information that is available for making a decision about the possible expansion of production capacity. The values in the table show the change in the firm's profit that would follow from the expansion possibilities and product demand realizations. Note that the firm can expect to earn a dollar per square foot in the cases where demand is high, but will lose 80 cents per square foot in case demand turns out to be low. In case the additional capacity expansion is not undertaken, there will be no impact on the firm. As indicated in the table, the two demand scenarios, high and low, are regarded as equally likely. Without engaging a management consultant, the firm will choose to maximize expected profit, by going forward with the larger expansion project, which will add $100,000 to the expected profit, but risks an $80,000 loss.

TABLE 14.2   Changes in Profit due to Capacity Expansion with Uncertain Demand

Choice↓ Outcome→	Pr[HD] = 1/2	Pr[LD] = 1/2
100,000 sq. ft. addition	100,000	−80,000
50,000 sq. ft. addition	50,000	−40,000
No addition	0	0

The firm's manager contacts a management consultant about acquiring better information on what the demand for its expanded output might be. It is determined that the consultant can provide a marketing study for $10,000 that will forecast a "high" or "low" future demand. The consultant's forecast will enable the probability of the demand levels to be revised depending critically on the consultant's reliability in demand forecasting as indicated by past work. In other words, the management consultant will provide a forecast of future demand that will fall into the category of either "high demand" or "low demand," but the firm's manager must require that the consultant also provide some information on past performance in order to make rational use of the consultant's prediction.

To see that this is indeed the case, recall the formula for the probability of an event A conditional on the occurrence of an event B from previous courses that you have taken:

$$Pr[A|B] = \frac{Pr[A \text{ and } B]}{Pr[B]},$$

where A and B are random events. Recall that the formula describes the conditional probability of an event A conditional on the occurrence of an event B as the joint probability of events A and B divided by the marginal probability of event B. It is a short step from the conditional probability formula to **Bayes formula**, that enables the probability of an event to be revised based on acquisition of information from a management consultant. Bayes formula is as follows:

$$Pr[A \mid B] = \frac{Pr[A \text{ and } B]}{Pr[B]} = \frac{Pr[B \mid A] Pr[A]}{Pr[B \mid A] Pr[A] + Pr[B \mid \neg A]]Pr]\neg A]},$$

where $\neg A$ is read as "not A" and means that the event A does not occur. Bayes formula describes the joint probability of events A and B in terms of reliabilities and prior probabilities. The numerator in Bayes formula ($Pr[B \mid A] Pr[A]$) is the product of the reliability or relative frequency with which the occurrence of event B will mirror the occurrence of event A ($Pr[B \mid A]$) and the prior probability that event A will occur ($Pr[A]$). The denominator in Bayes formula describes the marginal probability of event B in a similar manner. The denominator evaluates the probability of event B as the relative frequency with which the occurrence of event B will mirror the occurrence of event A ($Pr[B \mid A]$) times the prior probability that event A will occur ($Pr[A]$) *plus* the relative frequency with which the occurrence of event B will mirror the occurrence of any event other than event A ($Pr[B \mid \neg A]$) times the prior probability that event A will not occur ($Pr[\neg A]$).

Using Bayes formula, a manager can make rational use of the consultant's forecast provided that some essential information on the consultant's forecasting performance is also available. To see how this can be accomplished, we first introduce some notation related to Table 14.2 and the forecast provided by the management consultant. Let HD = high demand and LD = low demand. From the data shown in the table, we can see that the prior probabilities are $Pr[HD] = 0.5$ and $Pr[LD] = 0.5$. Let the 100,000 square foot addition be denoted by LA (for large addition), the 50,000 square foot addition be denoted by SA (for small addition), and let "no addition" choice be denoted by NA. We denote a consultant's forecast of high demand by CHD and a forecast of low demand by CLD. With this notation, we can describe the expected changes in profit shown in Table 14.2 as follows:

$$\text{Expected change in profit} \mid LA; HD = \$100,000,$$

$$\text{Expected change in profit} \mid LA; LD = -\$80,000,$$

$$\text{Expected change in profit} \mid SA; HD = \$50,000,$$

$$\text{Expected change in profit} \mid SA; LD = -\$40,000,$$

$$\text{Expected change in profit} \mid NA; HD = \$0,$$

$$\text{Expected change in profit} \mid NA; LD = \$0.$$

As already mentioned, if a consultant is engaged, the cost is \$10,000 and the demand forecast that will be received from the consultant is denoted by CHD and CLD for forecasts of high demand and low demand, respectively. However, in order to make rational use of the consultant's forecast, it is essential that the reliability of the consultant in past demand forecasting be obtained by the firm manager. The key information that must be obtained from the consultant is the relative frequencies with which similar forecasts have correctly reflected the true state of the market in the past; namely, Pr[CHD | HD] and Pr[CLD | HD] are needed from the consultant or from other information sources, for example, the consultant's past clients.

Let us suppose that this information has been obtained by the firm's manager and is as follows:

$$\Pr[CHD \,|\, HD] = 0.8,$$

and

$$\Pr[CLD \,|\, LD] = 0.7.$$

As can be seen from the probabilities, the consultant's forecasts have correctly predicted a high demand state of the market in 80% of past forecasting efforts. The consultant has been somewhat less reliable in forecasting a low demand state of the market with accurate forecasts in only 70% of past cases. Of course, a consultant could be equally good at forecasting a strong and weak product demand, but we do not require it in this example problem. The reliabilities enable other probabilities to be evaluated since the probabilities of different events conditional on a given event must add up to 1. Hence,

$$\Pr[CLD \,|\, HD] = 1 - \Pr[CHD \,|\, HD] = 1 - 0.8 = 0.2,$$

and

$$\Pr[CHD \,|\, LD] = 1 - \Pr[CLD \,|\, LD] = 1 - 0.7 = 0.3.$$

Now we can apply Bayes formula to revise prior probabilities. Bayes formula for arbitrary events A and B is

$$\Pr[A|B] = \frac{\Pr[A \text{ and } B]}{\Pr[B]} = \frac{\Pr[B \,|A]\,\Pr[A]}{\Pr[B \,|A\,]\,\Pr[A] + \Pr[\,B\,|\,\neg A\,]\,]\,\Pr]\,\neg A]}.$$

To obtain a revised prior probability, known as a posterior probability (Chapter 12), we need to substitute into the formula only the relevant events related to this problem. The posterior probability of a high demand (HD), given that the consultant predicts a high demand (CHD), is found by letting event A be HD and event B be CHD in the formula, namely,

$$\Pr[HD \,|\, CHD] = \frac{\Pr[CHD \,|\, HD]\,\Pr[HD]}{\Pr[CHD \,|\, HD]\,\Pr[HD] + \Pr[CHD \,|\, LD]\,\Pr[\,|\, LD]}$$

$$= \frac{0.8 \times 0.5}{0.8 \times 0.5 + 0.3 \times .05}$$

$$= 0.73.$$

Similarly,

$$Pr[LD \mid CLD] = \frac{Pr[CLD \mid LD] \, Pr[LD]}{Pr[CLD \mid LD] \, Pr[LD] + Pr[CLD \mid HD] \, Pr[HD]}$$

$$= \frac{0.7 \times 0.5}{0.7 \times 0.5 + 0.2 \times 0.5}$$

$$= 0.78.$$

Also note that event probabilities conditioned on the same event must add up to 1:

$$Pr[LD \mid CHD] = 1 - Pr[HD \mid CHD]$$

$$= 1 - 0.73$$

$$= 0.27$$

and

$$Pr[HD \mid CLD] = 1 - Pr[LD \mid CLD]$$

$$= 1 - 0.78$$

$$= 0.22.$$

We are now in a position to evaluate the expected profit change conditional on different expansion choices (LA, SA, and NA) and different forecasts from the consultant (HD and LD). We begin by considering the expected change in profit, depending on the choice of capacity expansion, when the consultant forecasts a high demand. Bear in mind that the following evaluations take into account the $10,000 charge for the consultant's advice:

Expected change in profit | LA; CHD $= 0.73 \times (100,000 - 10,000)$

$$+ 0.27 \times (-80,000 - 10,000)$$

$$= \$41,400,$$

Expected change in profit | SA; CHD $= 0.73 \times (50,000 - 10,000) + 0.27$

$$\times (-40,000 - 10,000)$$

$$= \$15,700,$$

Expected change in profit | NA; CHD $= 0 - 10,000 = -\$10,000$

$$= -\$10,000.$$

Note that in the case when a consultant's advice is contracted for and the consultant predicts a high demand, the expected profit-maximizing choice about expanding production capacity is to choose the 100,000 square foot expansion, which yields an expected profit change of $41,400 (compare to $15,700 with the 50,000 square foot expansion and –$10,000 for no change in capacity). Now we do a similar evaluation for the case when the consultant is engaged and forecasts a low demand:

$$\text{Expected change in profit} \,|\, \text{LA; CLD} = 0.22 \times (100{,}000 - 10{,}000) + 0.78$$
$$\times (-80{,}000 - 10{,}000)$$
$$= -\$50{,}400,$$

$$\text{Expected change in profit} \,|\, \text{SA; CLD} = 0.22 \times (50{,}000 - 10{,}000) + 0.78$$
$$\times (-40{,}000 - 10{,}000)$$
$$= -\$30{,}200,$$

$$\text{Expected change in profit} \,|\, \text{NA; CLD} = 0 - 10000$$
$$= -\$10{,}000.$$

Note that with the low demand forecast, the best choice is not to expand production that leads to an expected profit change of –$10,000 (the consultant's charge) but avoids the larger losses associated with the 100,000 square foot expansion (–$50,400) and the 50,000 square foot expansion (–$30,200).

Observe that the unconditional probability that the consultant predicts a high demand, Pr[CHD], is given by

$$\Pr\,[\text{CHD}] = \Pr\,[\text{CHD} \,|\, \text{HD}] \,\Pr[\text{HD}] + \Pr\,[\text{CHD} \,|\, \text{LD}] \,\Pr[\text{LD}]$$
$$= 0.8 \times 0.5 + 0.3 \times 0.5$$
$$= 0.55.$$

The unconditional probability that the consultant predicts a low demand, Pr[LD], is given by

$$\Pr\,[\text{CLD}] = \Pr[\text{CLD} \,|\, \text{LD}] \,\Pr\,[\text{LD}] + \Pr\,[\text{CLD} \,|\, \text{HD}] \,\Pr\,[\text{HD}]$$
$$= 0.7 \times 0.5 + 0.2 \times 0.5$$
$$= 0.45.$$

As we have already seen, if the firm selects capacity expansion to maximize the expected change in profit for each possible forecast by the consultant, it will choose the 100,000 square foot addition when the forecast is for a high demand yielding an expected change in profit of $41,400 and no addition when the consultant's forecast is for a low demand, yielding an expected change in profit of –$10,000. Combining these decisions with the probability of the consultant's predictions gives an expected change in profit when a consultant is engaged of

$$\text{Expected change in profit} \,|\, \text{Consultant} = 0.55 \times (41{,}400) + 0.45 \times (-10{,}000)$$
$$= \$18{,}270.$$

So engaging a management consultant with the reliability assumed in this problem will lead to an expected increase in profit of $18,270, assuming that the optimal decision about

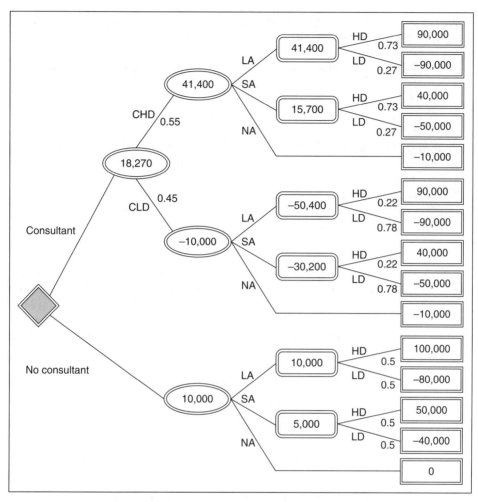

FIGURE 14.1   Decision tree analysis of capacity addition and management consultant engagement.

adding production capacity is made following consultation. This value can be compared with the expected change in profit that will occur if the decision about adding production capacity is made on the basis of the information in Table 14.2, that is, without engaging a management consultant. Comparisons of the different expansion choices (LA, SA, and NA) are made on the basis of the following evaluations. Note that there are no consultant charges since decisions are made without the consultant's advice:

$$\text{Expected change in profit} \,|\, \text{No consultant; LA} = 0.5 \times (100{,}000) + 0.5 \times (-80{,}000)$$

$$= \$10{,}000,$$

$$\text{Expected change in profit} \,|\, \text{No consultant; SA} = 0.5 \times (50{,}000) + 0.5 \times (-40{,}000)$$

$$= \$5{,}000,$$

$$\text{Expected change in profit} \,|\, \text{No consultant; NA} = \$0.$$

Note that without a management consultant's advice, the best choice is to expand production by choosing the 100,000 square foot addition, which leads to an expected profit change of $10,000. This expected profit change can be compared with the expected increase of $5,000 from the 50,000 square foot addition and, of course, no expected change in profit if no capacity is added.

Comparing the expected change in profit with a management consultant ($18,270) to the expected change in profit without a management consultant ($10,000) identifies the following optimal strategy for the firm's manager.

Optimal strategy: Hire the management consultant—if the consultant indicates a high demand, choose the 100,000 square foot addition; if the consultant indicates a low demand, choose "no addition."

All of the evaluations underlying identification of the optimal strategy in this problem can also be depicted with the aid of a decision tree. Figure 14.1 shows how the optimal strategy can be derived using the decision tree technique. Note that, as in the Chapter 12 examples, the strategy can be identified from the tree's branches that are not pruned with two short parallel lines as shown in the figure.

It cannot be overemphasized that the decision to engage a management consultant depends critically on a proper vetting of the consultant's record. In the example problem considered here, the consultant's experience and performance in demand forecasting were critical to rational use of the consultant's forecast through implementation of Bayes formula. Failing to properly vet a management consultant's record and incorporate that record into the decision process does not constitute rational engagement of a management consultant and can have disastrous consequences both in terms of the charges paid to the consultant and the decisions that follow.

SUMMARY

The management consulting industry has grown dramatically during recent decades as more medium- and large-sized firms have turned to consultants for counsel. Managers may be motivated to engage management consultants as a source of objective advice, special expertise, and/or to undertake specific projects for which the firms simply do not have sufficient time. Information theory has provided a measure of information corresponding to a "yes/no" type question, which is known as a bit. The information needed to adequately address complex questions can often be described as a sequence of bits of information. The concept of perfect information is associated with the expected number of bits of information sufficient in number to eliminate uncertainty about a particular question. Bits of information that are insufficient in number to eliminate uncertainty can nevertheless be informative and valuable and typify the character of information obtained from management consultants. In terms of a firm's management decision problem depicted as a decision table with a finite number of choices with uncertain outcomes, the firm's maximum willingness to pay to engage a management consultant is measured by the expected value of perfect information (EVPI). The EVPI may be especially useful as a practical and timely tool for analyzing the economic desirability of engaging a management consultant at all for a particular problem that the firm is concerned about. However, the more typical case involves engagement of a management consultant in order to reduce rather than eliminate uncertainty in decision making. Under these circumstances, rational use of a management consultant usually entails use of conditional probabilities through application of Bayes formula in evaluating the expected return to a management consultant's advice. The return to engaging a management consultant depends critically on the consultant's reliability as (perhaps) best measured by past performance. Hence, proper vetting of a management consultant is the key to rational use of the information provided by the consultant as well as the key to determining when it is best to engage a consultant and how best to apply the information that is acquired.

KEY TERMS

management consulting information	less-than-perfect information	expected value of perfect information (EVPI)
measurement	perfect information	Bayes formula

LIST OF FORMULAS

- Expected value of perfect information (EVPI):

$$\text{EVPI} = \text{Best expected outcome with uncertainty eliminated}$$
$$-\text{Best expected outcome without a consultant.}$$

- Prior probabilities:

$$\Pr[\text{HD}],$$
$$\Pr[\text{LD}].$$

- Conditional probability:

$$\Pr[A \mid B] = \frac{\Pr[A \text{ and } B]}{\Pr[B]}.$$

- Bayes formula:

$$\Pr[A \mid B] = \frac{\Pr[A \text{ and } B]}{\Pr[B]} = \frac{\Pr[B \mid A]\Pr[A]}{\Pr[B \mid A]\Pr[A] + \Pr[B \mid \neg A]]\Pr]\neg A]}.$$

- Reliabilities:

$$\Pr[\text{CHD} \mid \text{HD}],$$

$$\Pr[\text{CLD} \mid \text{LD}].$$

- Posterior probabilities based on Bayes formula:

$$Pr[HD \mid CHD] = \frac{Pr[CHD \mid HD] Pr[HD]}{Pr[CHD \mid HD] Pr[HD] + Pr[CHD \mid LD] Pr[LD]},$$

$$Pr[LD \mid CLD] = \frac{Pr[CLD \mid LD] Pr[LD]}{Pr[CLD \mid LD] Pr[LD] + Pr[CLD \mid HD] Pr[HD]}.$$

EXERCISES

1. Give reasons why a firm's management might seek the advice of a consultant.

2. Discuss how information can be measured as "bits."

3. Give an interpretation of the expected value of perfect information.

4. Explain what is meant by the prior and posterior probabilities of an event.

5. Using the concept of probability, explain what is meant by the reliability of a management consultant's advice about an uncertain event.

6. Suppose a coin has been flipped but you do not know the outcome (either heads or tails). How many bits of information are needed to eliminate the uncertainty about the outcome of this random event?

7. Evaluate the expected value of perfect information that might be obtained from a management consultant for the decision problem depicted in the table given below.

Event $\Rightarrow$	E_1	E_2	E_3
Probability $\Rightarrow$	0.2	0.4	0.4
Act $\Downarrow$			
A_1	160	150	350
A_2	100	400	200
A_3	75	50	500

8. Suppose you know the following probabilities that describe the reliability of a macroeconomic forecasting firm's past performance:

The probability of a positive forecast given a good macroeconomy is 0.60.

The probability of a negative forecast given a good macroeconomy is 0.40.

The probability of a positive forecast given a bad macroeconomy is 0.25.

The probability of a negative forecast given a bad macroeconomy is 0.75.

Suppose your prior probability of a good macroeconomy is 0.10. Find the probability of a good macroeconomy given that the forecast is for a good macroeconomy and the probability of a bad macroeconomy given that the forecast is for a bad macroeconomy.

9. Using the information in the last question, find the probability of a good macroeconomy given a negative forecast and the probability of a bad macroeconomy given a positive forecast.

10. Suppose that the probability of every uncertain event is the same so that uncertainty about what event will occur is in a real sense maximized. Use the information in exercise 7 to see if the expected value of perfect information necessarily increases with this uncertainty.

APPENDIX

TABLE A.1 The Greek Alphabet

Name	Greek Capital	Greek Lowercase	English
Alpha	A	α	A
Beta	B	β	B
Gamma	Γ	γ	G
Delta	Δ	δ	D
Epsilon	E	ε	E
Zeta	Z	ζ	Z
Eta	E	η	E
Theta	Θ	θ	Th
Iota	I	ι	I
Kappa	K	κ	K
Lambda	Λ	λ	L
Mu	M	μ	M
Nu	N	ν	N
Xi	Ξ	ξ	X
Omicron	O	o	O
Pi	Π	π	P
Rho	ρ	ρ	R
Sigma	Σ	σ	S
Tau	T	τ	T
Upsilon	υ	υ	U
Phi	Φ	φ	Ph
Chi	X	χ	Ch
Psi	Ψ	ψ	Ps
Omega	Ω	ω	$\bar{o}$

Managerial Economics: A Mathematical Approach, First Edition. M. J. Alhabeeb and L. Joe Moffitt.
© 2013 John Wiley & Sons, Inc. Published 2013 by John Wiley & Sons, Inc.

TABLE A.2 One- and Two-Tail *t*-Distribution

Two-Tail Probability:	0.20	0.10	0.95	0.02	0.01	
One-Tail Probability:	0.10	0.05	0.025	0.01	0.005	
df						df
1	3.078	6.314	12.706	31.821	63.657	1
2	1.886	2.920	4.303	6.965	9.925	2
3	1.638	3.353	3.182	4.541	5.841	3
4	1.533	2.132	2.776	3.747	4.604	4
5	1.476	2.015	2.571	3.365	4.032	5
6	1.440	1.943	2.447	3.143	3.707	6
7	1.415	1.895	2.365	2.998	3.499	7
8	1.397	1.860	2.306	2.896	3.355	8
9	1.383	1.833	2.262	2.821	3.250	9
10	1.372	1.812	2.228	2.764	3.169	10
11	1.363	1.796	2.201	2.718	3.106	11
12	1.356	1.782	2.179	2.681	3.055	12
13	1.350	1.771	2.160	2.650	3.012	13
14	1.345	1.761	2.145	2.624	2.977	14
15	1.341	1.753	2.131	2.602	2.947	15
16	1.337	1.746	2.120	2.583	2.921	16
17	1.333	1.740	2.110	2.567	2.898	17
18	1.330	1.734	2.101	2.552	2.878	18
19	1.328	1.729	2.093	2.539	2.861	19
20	1.325	1.725	2.086	2.528	2.845	20
21	1.323	1.721	2.080	2.518	2.831	21
22	1.321	1.717	2.074	2.508	2.819	22
23	1.319	1.714	2.069	2.500	2.807	23
24	1.318	1.711	2.064	2.492	2.797	24
25	1.316	1.708	2.060	2.485	2.787	25
26	1.315	1.706	2.056	2.479	2.779	26
27	1.314	1.703	2.052	2.473	2.771	27
28	1.313	1.701	2.048	2.467	2.763	28
29	1.311	1.699	2.045	2.462	2.756	29
30	1.310	1.697	2.042	2.457	2.750	30
32	1.309	1.694	2.037	2.449	2.738	32
35	1.306	1.690	2.030	2.438	2.725	35
40	1.303	1.684	2.021	2.423	2.704	40
45	1.301	1.679	2.014	2.412	2.690	45
50	1.299	1.676	2.009	2.403	2.678	50
60	1.296	1.671	2.000	2.390	2.660	60
75	1.293	1.665	1.992	2.377	2.643	75
100	1.290	1.660	1.984	2.364	2.626	100
120	1.289	1.658	1.980	2.358	2.617	120
140	1.288	1.656	1.977	2.353	2.611	140
180	1.286	1.653	1.973	2.347	2.603	180
250	1.285	1.651	1.969	2.341	2.596	250
400	1.284	1.649	1.966	2.336	2.588	400
1000	1.282	1.646	1.962	2.330	2.581	1000
∞	1.282	1.645	1.960	2.326	2.576	∞
Confidence levels:	80%	90%	95%	98%	99%	

TABLE A.3 *F*-Statistics with 5% Significance

Degrees of Freedom for Numerator $(k-1)$

	1	2	3	4	5	6	7	8	9	10	12	15	20	24	30	40	60	120
1	161	200	216	225	230	234	237	239	241	242	244	246	248	249	250	251	252	253
2	18.5	19.0	19.2	19.2	19.3	19.3	19.4	19.4	19.4	19.4	19.4	19.4	19.5	19.5	19.5	19.5	19.5	19.5
3	10.1	9.55	9.28	9.12	9.01	8.94	8.89	8.85	8.81	8.79	8.74	8.70	8.66	8.64	8.62	8.59	8.57	8.55
4	7.71	6.94	6.59	6.39	6.26	6.16	6.09	6.04	6.00	5.96	5.91	5.86	5.80	5.77	5.57	5.72	5.69	5.66
5	6.61	5.79	5.41	5.19	5.05	4.95	4.88	4.82	4.77	4.74	4.68	4.62	4.56	4.53	4.50	4.46	4.43	4.40
6	5.99	5.14	4.76	4.53	4.39	4.28	4.21	4.15	4.10	4.06	4.00	3.94	3.87	3.84	3.81	3.77	3.74	3.70
7	5.59	4.74	4.35	4.12	3.97	3.87	3.79	3.73	3.68	3.64	3.57	3.51	3.44	3.41	3.38	3.34	3.30	3.27
8	5.32	4.46	4.07	3.84	3.69	3.58	3.50	3.44	3.39	3.35	3.28	3.22	3.15	3.12	3.08	3.04	3.01	2.97
9	5.12	4.26	3.86	3.63	3.48	3.37	3.29	3.23	3.18	3.14	3.07	3.01	2.94	2.90	2.86	2.83	2.79	2.75
10	4.96	4.10	3.71	3.48	3.33	3.22	3.14	3.07	3.02	2.98	2.91	2.85	2.77	2.74	2.70	2.66	2.62	2.58
11	4.84	3.98	3.59	3.36	3.20	3.09	3.01	2.95	2.90	2.85	2.79	2.72	2.65	2.61	2.57	2.53	2.49	2.45
12	4.75	3.89	3.49	3.26	3.11	3.00	2.91	2.85	2.80	2.75	2.69	2.62	2.54	2.51	2.47	2.43	2.38	2.34
13	4.67	3.81	3.41	3.18	3.03	2.92	2.83	2.77	2.71	2.67	2.60	2.53	2.46	2.42	2.38	2.34	2.30	2.25
14	4.60	3.74	3.34	3.11	2.96	2.85	2.76	2.70	2.65	2.60	2.53	2.46	2.39	2.35	2.31	2.27	2.22	2.18
15	4.54	3.68	3.29	3.06	2.90	2.79	2.71	2.64	2.59	2.54	2.48	2.40	2.33	2.29	2.25	2.20	2.16	2.11
16	4.49	3.63	3.24	3.01	2.85	2.74	2.66	2.59	2.54	2.49	2.42	2.35	2.28	2.24	2.19	2.15	2.11	2.06
17	4.45	3.59	3.20	2.96	2.81	2.70	2.61	2.55	2.48	2.45	2.38	2.31	2.23	2.19	2.15	2.10	2.06	2.01
18	4.41	3.55	3.16	2.93	2.77	2.66	2.58	2.51	2.46	2.41	2.34	2.27	2.19	2.15	2.11	2.06	2.02	1.97
19	4.38	3.52	3.13	2.90	2.74	2.63	2.54	2.48	2.42	2.39	2.31	2.23	2.16	2.11	2.07	2.03	1.98	1.93
20	4.35	3.49	3.10	2.87	2.71	2.60	2.51	2.45	2.39	2.35	2.28	2.20	2.12	2.08	2.04	1.99	1.95	1.90
21	4.32	3.47	3.07	2.84	2.68	2.57	2.49	2.42	2.37	2.32	2.25	2.18	2.10	2.05	2.01	1.96	1.92	1.87
22	4.30	3.44	3.05	2.82	2.66	2.55	2.46	2.40	2.34	2.30	2.23	2.15	2.07	2.03	1.98	1.94	1.89	1.84
23	4.28	3.42	3.03	2.80	2.64	2.53	2.44	2.37	2.32	2.27	2.20	2.13	2.05	2.01	1.96	1.91	1.86	1.81
24	4.26	3.40	3.01	2.78	2.62	2.51	2.42	2.36	2.30	2.25	2.18	2.11	2.03	1.98	1.94	1.89	1.84	1.79
25	4.24	3.39	2.99	2.76	2.60	2.49	2.40	2.34	2.28	2.24	2.16	2.09	2.01	1.96	1.92	1.87	1.82	1.77
26	4.23	3.37	2.98	2.74	2.59	2.47	2.39	2.32	2.27	2.22	2.15	2.07	1.99	1.95	1.90	1.85	1.80	1.75
27	4.21	3.35	2.96	2.73	2.57	2.46	2.37	2.31	2.25	2.20	2.13	2.06	1.97	1.93	1.88	1.84	1.79	1.73
28	4.20	3.34	2.95	2.71	2.56	2.45	2.36	2.29	2.24	2.19	2.12	2.04	1.96	1.91	1.87	1.82	1.77	1.71
29	4.18	3.33	2.93	2.70	2.55	2.43	2.35	2.28	2.22	2.18	2.10	2.03	1.94	1.90	1.85	1.81	1.75	1.70
30	4.17	3.32	2.92	2.69	2.53	2.42	2.33	2.27	2.21	2.16	2.09	2.01	1.93	1.89	1.84	1.79	1.74	1.68
40	4.08	3.23	2.84	2.61	2.45	2.34	2.25	2.18	2.12	2.08	2.00	1.92	1.84	1.79	1.74	1.69	1.64	1.58
60	4.00	3.15	2.76	2.53	2.37	2.25	2.17	2.10	2.04	1.99	1.92	1.84	1.75	1.70	1.65	1.59	1.53	1.47
120	3.92	3.07	2.68	2.45	2.29	2.18	2.09	2.02	1.96	1.91	1.83	1.75	1.66	1.61	1.55	1.50	1.43	1.35

Source: Merrington and Thompson (1943).

TABLE A.4 *F*-Statistics with 1% Significance

Degrees of Freedom for Numerator (k − 1)

	1	2	3	4	5	6	7	8	9	10	12	15	20	24	30	40	60	120
1	4.052	5.000	5.403	5.625	5.746	5.859	5.928	5.982	6.023	6.056	6.106	6.157	6.209	6.235	6.261	6.287	6.313	6.339
2	98.5	99.0	99.2	99.2	99.3	99.3	99.4	99.4	99.4	99.4	99.4	99.4	99.4	99.5	99.5	99.5	99.5	99.5
3	34.1	30.8	29.5	28.7	28.2	27.9	27.7	27.5	27.3	27.2	27.1	26.9	26.7	26.6	26.5	26.4	26.3	26.2
4	21.2	18.0	16.7	16.0	15.5	15.2	15.0	14.8	14.7	14.5	14.4	14.2	14.0	13.9	13.8	13.7	13.7	13.6
5	16.3	13.3	12.1	11.4	11.0	10.7	10.5	10.3	10.2	10.1	9.89	9.72	9.55	9.47	9.38	9.29	9.20	9.11
6	13.7	10.9	9.78	9.15	8.75	8.47	8.26	8.10	7.98	7.87	7.72	7.56	7.40	7.31	7.23	7.14	7.06	6.97
7	12.2	9.55	8.45	7.85	7.46	7.19	6.99	6.84	6.72	6.62	6.47	6.31	6.16	6.07	5.99	5.91	5.82	5.74
8	11.3	8.65	7.59	7.01	6.63	6.37	6.18	6.03	5.91	5.81	5.67	5.52	5.36	5.28	5.20	5.12	5.03	4.95
9	10.6	8.02	6.99	6.42	5.99	5.80	5.61	5.47	5.35	5.26	5.11	4.96	4.81	4.73	4.65	4.57	4.48	4.40
10	10.0	7.56	6.55	5.99	5.64	5.39	5.20	5.06	4.94	4.85	4.71	4.56	4.41	4.33	4.25	4.17	4.08	4.00
11	9.65	7.21	6.22	5.67	5.32	5.07	4.89	4.74	4.63	4.54	4.40	4.25	4.10	4.02	3.94	3.86	3.78	3.69
12	9.33	6.93	5.95	5.41	5.06	4.82	4.64	4.50	4.39	4.30	4.16	4.01	3.86	3.78	3.70	3.62	3.54	3.45
13	9.07	6.70	5.74	5.21	4.86	4.62	4.44	4.30	4.19	4.10	3.96	3.82	3.66	3.59	3.51	3.43	3.34	3.25
14	8.86	6.51	5.56	5.04	4.70	4.46	4.28	4.14	4.03	3.94	3.80	3.66	3.51	3.43	3.35cv	3.27	3.18	3.09
15	8.68	6.36	5.42	4.89	4.56	4.32	4.14	4.00	3.89	3.80	3.67	3.52	3.37	3.29	3.21	3.13	3.05	2.96
16	8.53	6.23	5.29	4.77	4.44	4.20	4.03	3.89	3.78	3.69	3.55	3.41	3.26	3.18	3.10	3.02	2.93	2.84
17	8.40	6.11	5.19	4.67	4.34	4.10	3.93	3.79	3.68	3.59	3.46	3.31	3.16	3.08	3.00	2.92	2.83	2.75
18	8.29	6.01	5.09	4.58	4.25	4.01	3.84	3.71	3.60	3.51	3.37	3.23	3.08	3.00	2.92	2.84	2.75	2.66
19	8.18	5.93	5.01	4.50	4.17	3.94	3.77	3.63	3.52	3.43	3.30	3.15	3.00	2.92	2.84	2.76	2.67	2.58
20	8.10	5.85	4.94	4.43	4.10	3.87	3.70	3.56	3.46	3.37	3.23	3.09	2.94	2.86	2.78	2.68	2.61	2.52
21	8.02	5.78	4.87	4.37	4.04	3.81	3.64	3.51	3.40	3.31	3.17	3.03	2.88	2.80	2.72	2.64	2.55	2.46
22	7.95	5.72	4.82	4.31	3.99	3.76	3.59	3.45	3.35	3.26	3.12	2.98	2.83	2.75	2.67	2.58	2.50	2.40
23	7.88	5.66	4.76	4.26	3.94	3.71	3.54	3.41	3.30	3.21	3.07	2.93	2.78	2.70	2.62	2.54	2.45	2.35
24	7.82	5.61	4.72	4.22	3.90	3.67	3.50	3.36	3.26	3.17	3.03	2.89	2.74	2.66	2.58	2.49	2.40	2.31
25	7.77	5.57	4.68	4.18	3.86	3.63	3.46	3.32	3.22	3.13	2.99	2.85	2.70	2.62	2.53	2.45	2.36	2.27
26	7.72	5.53	4.64	4.14	3.82	3.59	3.42	3.29	3.18	3.09	2.96	2.81	2.66	2.58	2.50	2.42	2.33	2.23
27	7.68	5.49	4.60	4.11	3.78	3.56	3.39	3.26	3.15	3.06	2.93	2.78	2.63	2.55	2.47	2.38	2.29	2.20
28	7.64	5.45	4.57	4.07	3.75	3.53	3.36	3.23	3.12	3.03	2.90	2.75	2.60	2.52	2.44	2.35	2.26	2.17
29	7.60	5.42	4.54	4.04	3.73	3.50	3.33	3.20	3.09	3.00	2.87	2.73	2.57	2.49	2.41	2.33	2.23	2.14
30	7.56	5.39	4.51	4.02	3.70	3.47	3.30	3.17	3.07	2.98	2.84	2.70	2.55	2.47	2.30	2.30	2.21	2.11
40	7.31	5.18	4.31	3.83	3.51	3.29	3.12	2.99	2.89	2.80	2.66	2.52	2.37	2.29	2.20	2.11	2.02	1.92
60	7.08	4.98	4.13	3.65	3.34	3.12	2.95	2.82	2.72	2.63	2.50	2.35	2.20	2.12	2.03	1.94	1.84	1.73
120	6.85	4.79	3.95	3.48	3.17	2.96	2.79	2.66	2.56	2.47	2.34	2.19	2.03	1.94	1.86	1.76	1.66	1.53

TABLE A.5 Critical Values of the Durbin–Watson Test Statistic for 0.05 Significance

	$k = 1$		$k = 2$		$k = 3$		$k = 4$		$k = 5$	
n	d_L	d_U	d_L	d_U	d_L	d_U	d_L	d_U	d_L	d_U
15	1.08	1.36	0.95	1.54	0.82	1.75	0.69	1.97	0.56	2.21
16	1.10	1.37	0.98	1.54	0.86	1.73	0.74	1.93	0.62	2.15
17	1.13	1.38	1.02	1.54	0.90	1.71	0.78	1.90	0.67	2.10
18	1.16	1.39	1.05	1.53	0.93	1.69	0.82	1.87	0.71	2.06
19	1.18	1.40	1.08	1.53	0.97	1.68	0.86	1.85	0.75	2.02
20	1.20	1.41	1.10	1.54	1.00	1.68	0.90	1.83	0.79	1.99
21	1.22	1.42	1.13	1.54	1.03	1.67	0.93	1.81	0.83	1.96
22	1.24	1.43	1.15	1.54	1.05	1.66	0.96	1.80	0.86	1.94
23	1.26	1.44	1.17	1.54	1.08	1.66	0.99	1.79	0.90	1.92
24	1.27	1.45	1.19	1.55	1.10	1.66	1.01	1.78	0.93	1.90
25	1.29	1.45	1.21	1.55	1.12	1.66	1.04	1.77	0.95	1.89
26	1.30	1.46	1.22	1.55	1.14	1.65	1.06	1.76	0.98	1.88
27	1.32	1.47	1.24	1.56	1.16	1.65	1.08	1.76	1.01	1.86
28	1.33	1.48	1.26	1.56	1.18	1.65	1.10	1.75	1.03	1.85
29	1.34	1.48	1.27	1.56	1.20	1.65	1.12	1.74	1.05	1.84
30	1.35	1.49	1.28	1.57	1.21	1.65	1.14	1.74	1.07	1.83
31	1.36	1.50	1.30	1.57	1.23	1.65	1.16	1.74	1.09	1.83
32	1.37	1.50	1.31	1.57	1.24	1.65	1.18	1.73	1.11	1.82
33	1.38	1.51	1.32	1.58	1.26	1.65	1.19	1.73	1.13	1.81
34	1.39	1.51	1.33	1.58	1.27	1.65	1.21	1.73	1.15	1.81
35	1.40	1.52	1.34	1.58	1.28	1.65	1.22	1.73	1.16	1.80
36	1.41	1.52	1.35	1.59	1.29	1.65	1.24	1.73	1.18	1.80
37	1.42	1.53	1.36	1.59	1.31	1.66	1.25	1.72	1.19	1.80
38	1.43	1.54	1.37	1.59	1.32	1.66	1.26	1.72	1.21	1.79
39	1.43	1.54	1.38	1.60	1.33	1.66	1.27	1.72	1.22	1.79
40	1.44	1.54	1.39	1.60	1.34	1.66	1.29	1.72	1.23	1.79
45	1.48	1.57	1.43	1.62	1.38	1.67	1.34	1.72	1.29	1.78
50	1.50	1.59	1.46	1.63	1.42	1.67	1.38	1.72	1.34	1.77
55	1.53	1.60	1.49	1.64	1.45	1.68	1.41	1.72	1.38	1.77
60	1.55	1.62	1.51	1.65	1.48	1.69	1.44	1.73	1.41	1.77
65	1.57	1.63	1.54	1.66	1.50	1.70	1.47	1.73	1.44	1.77
70	1.58	1.64	1.55	1.67	1.52	1.70	1.49	1.74	1.46	1.77
75	1.60	1.65	1.57	1.68	1.54	1.71	1.51	1.74	1.49	1.77
80	1.61	1.66	1.59	1.69	1.56	1.72	1.53	1.74	1.51	1.77
85	1.62	1.67	1.60	1.70	1.57	1.72	1.55	1.75	1.52	1.77
90	1.63	1.68	1.61	1.70	1.59	1.73	1.57	1.75	1.54	1.78
95	1.64	1.69	1.62	1.71	1.60	1.73	1.58	1.75	1.56	1.78
100	1.65	1.69	1.63	1.72	1.61	1.74	1.59	1.76	1.57	1.78

TABLE A.6 Critical Values of the Durbin—Watson Test Statistic for 0.01 Significance

	$k = 1$		$k = 2$		$k = 3$		$k = 4$		$k = 5$	
n	d_L	d_U	d_L	d_U	d_L	d_U	d_L	d_U	d_L	d_U
15	0.81	1.07	0.70	1.25	0.59	1.46	0.49	1.70	0.39	1.96
16	0.84	1.09	0.74	1.25	0.63	1.44	0.53	1.66	0.44	1.90
17	0.87	1.10	0.77	1.25	0.67	1.43	0.57	1.63	0.48	1.85
18	0.90	1.12	0.80	1.26	0.71	1.42	0.61	1.60	0.52	1.80
19	0.93	1.13	0.83	1.26	0.74	1.41	0.65	1.58	0.56	1.77
20	0.95	1.15	0.86	1.27	0.77	1.41	0.68	1.57	0.60	1.74
21	0.97	1.16	0.89	1.27	0.80	1.41	0.72	1.55	0.63	1.71
22	1.00	1.17	0.91	1.28	0.83	1.40	0.75	1.54	0.66	1.69
23	1.02	1.19	0.94	1.29	0.86	1.40	0.77	1.53	0.70	1.67
24	1.05	1.20	0.96	1.30	0.88	1.41	0.80	1.53	0.72	1.66
25	1.05	1.21	0.98	1.30	0.90	1.41	0.83	1.52	0.75	1.65
26	1.07	1.22	1.00	1.31	0.93	1.41	0.85	1.52	0.78	1.64
27	1.09	1.23	1.02	1.32	0.95	1.41	0.88	1.51	0.81	1.63
28	1.10	1.24	1.04	1.32	0.97	1.41	0.90	1.51	0.83	1.62
29	1.12	1.25	1.05	1.33	0.99	1.42	0.92	1.51	0.85	1.61
30	1.13	1.26	1.07	1.34	1.01	1.42	0.94	1.51	0.88	1.61
31	1.15	1.27	1.08	1.34	1.02	1.42	0.96	1.51	0.90	1.60
32	1.16	1.28	1.10	1.35	1.04	1.43	0.98	1.51	0.92	1.60
33	1.17	1.29	1.11	1.36	1.05	1.43	1.00	1.51	0.94	1.59
34	1.18	1.30	1.13	1.36	1.07	1.43	1.01	1.51	0.95	1.59
35	1.19	1.31	1.14	1.37	1.08	1.44	1.03	1.51	0.97	1.59
36	1.21	1.32	1.15	1.38	1.10	1.44	1.04	1.51	0.99	1.59
37	1.22	1.32	1.16	1.38	1.11	1.45	1.06	1.51	1.00	1.59
38	1.23	1.33	1.18	1.39	1.12	1.45	1.07	1.52	1.02	1.58
39	1.24	1.34	1.19	1.39	1.14	1.45	1.09	1.52	1.03	1.58
40	1.25	1.34	1.20	1.40	1.15	1.46	1.10	1.52	1.05	1.58
45	1.29	1.38	1.24	1.42	1.20	1.48	1.16	1.53	1.11	1.58
50	1.32	1.40	1.28	1.45	1.24	1.49	1.20	1.54	1.16	1.59
55	1.36	1.43	1.32	1.47	1.28	1.51	1.25	1.55	1.21	1.59
60	1.38	1.45	1.35	1.48	1.32	1.52	1.28	1.56	1.25	1.60
65	1.41	1.47	1.38	1.50	1.35	1.53	1.31	1.57	1.28	1.61
70	1.43	1.49	1.40	1.52	1.37	1.55	1.34	1.58	1.31	1.61
75	1.45	1.50	1.42	1.53	1.39	1.56	1.37	1.59	1.34	1.62
80	1.47	1.52	1.44	1.54	1.42	1.57	1.39	1.60	1.36	1.62
85	1.48	1.53	1.46	1.55	1.43	1.58	1.41	1.60	1.39	1.63
90	1.50	1.54	1.17	1.56	1.45	1.59	1.43	1.61	1.41	1.64
95	1.51	1.55	1.49	1.57	1.47	1.60	1.45	1.62	1.42	1.64
100	1.52	1.56	1.50	1.58	1.48	1.60	1.46	1.63	1.44	1.65

Source: Durbin and Watson (1951).

TABLE A.7 Value of the Discount Factor for $1.00 under Many Discount Rates and Periods ($PVIF_{r,n}$) or (V^n) Value $= \dfrac{1}{(1+r)^{n}}$

Period	1%	2%	3%	4%	5%	6%	7%	8%	9%	10%	12%	14%	15%	16%	18%	20%	24%	28%	32%	36%
1	0.9901	0.9804	0.9709	0.9615	0.9524	0.9434	0.9346	0.9259	0.9174	0.9091	0.8929	0.8772	0.8696	0.8621	0.8475	0.8333	0.8065	0.7813	0.7576	0.7353
2	0.9803	0.9612	0.9426	0.9246	0.9070	0.8900	0.8734	0.8573	0.8417	0.8264	0.7972	0.7695	0.7561	0.7432	0.7182	0.6944	0.6504	0.6104	0.5739	0.5407
3	0.9706	0.9423	0.9151	0.8890	0.8638	0.8396	0.8163	0.7938	0.7722	0.7513	0.7118	0.6750	0.6575	0.6407	0.6086	0.5787	0.5245	0.4768	0.4348	0.3975
4	0.9610	0.9238	0.8885	0.8548	0.8227	0.7921	0.7629	0.7350	0.7084	0.6830	0.6355	0.5921	0.5718	0.5523	0.5158	0.4823	0.4230	0.3725	0.3294	0.2923
5	0.9515	0.9057	0.8626	0.8219	0.7835	0.7473	0.7130	0.6806	0.6499	0.6209	0.5674	0.5194	0.4972	0.4761	0.4371	0.4019	0.3411	0.2910	0.2495	0.2149
6	0.9420	0.8880	0.8375	0.7903	0.7462	0.7050	0.6663	0.6302	0.5963	0.5645	0.5066	0.4556	0.4323	0.4104	0.3704	0.3349	0.2751	0.2274	0.1890	0.1580
7	0.9327	0.8706	0.8131	0.7599	0.7107	0.6651	0.6227	0.5835	0.5470	0.5132	0.4523	0.3996	0.3759	0.3538	0.3139	0.2791	0.2218	0.1776	0.1432	0.1162
8	0.9235	0.8535	0.7894	0.7307	0.6768	0.6274	0.5820	0.5403	0.5019	0.4665	0.4039	0.3506	0.3269	0.3050	0.2660	0.2326	0.1789	0.1388	0.1085	0.0854
9	0.9143	0.8368	0.7664	0.7026	0.6446	0.5919	0.5439	0.5002	0.4604	0.4241	0.3606	0.3075	0.2843	0.2630	0.2255	0.1938	0.1443	0.1084	0.0822	0.0628
10	0.9053	0.8203	0.7441	0.6756	0.6139	0.5584	0.5083	0.4632	0.4224	0.3855	0.3220	0.2697	0.2472	0.2267	0.1911	0.1615	0.1164	0.0847	0.0623	0.0462
11	0.8963	0.8043	0.7224	0.6496	0.5847	0.5268	0.4751	0.4289	0.3875	0.3505	0.2875	0.2366	0.2149	0.1954	0.1619	0.1346	0.0938	0.0662	0.0472	0.0340
12	0.8874	0.7885	0.7014	0.6246	0.5568	0.4970	0.4440	0.3971	0.3555	0.3186	0.2567	0.2076	0.1869	0.1685	0.1372	0.1122	0.0757	0.0517	0.0357	0.0250
13	0.8787	0.7730	0.6810	0.6006	0.5303	0.4688	0.4150	0.3677	0.3262	0.2897	0.2292	0.1821	0.1625	0.1452	0.1163	0.0935	0.0610	0.0404	0.0271	0.0184
14	0.8700	0.7579	0.6611	0.5775	0.5051	0.4423	0.3878	0.3405	0.2992	0.2633	0.2046	0.1597	0.1413	0.1252	0.0985	0.0779	0.0492	0.0316	0.0205	0.0135
15	0.8613	0.7430	0.6419	0.5553	0.4810	0.4173	0.3624	0.3152	0.2745	0.2394	0.1827	0.1401	0.1229	0.1079	0.0835	0.0649	0.0397	0.0247	0.0155	0.0099
16	0.8528	0.7284	0.6232	0.5339	0.4581	0.3936	0.3387	0.2919	0.2519	0.2176	0.1631	0.1229	0.1069	0.0930	0.0708	0.0541	0.0320	0.0193	0.0118	0.0073
17	0.8444	0.7142	0.6050	0.5134	0.4363	0.3714	0.3166	0.2703	0.2311	0.1978	0.1456	0.1078	0.0929	0.0802	0.0600	0.0451	0.0258	0.0150	0.0089	0.0054
18	0.8360	0.7002	0.5874	0.4936	0.4155	0.3503	0.2959	0.2505	0.2120	0.1799	0.1300	0.0946	0.0808	0.0691	0.0508	0.0376	0.0208	0.0118	0.0068	0.0039
19	0.8277	0.6864	0.5703	0.4746	0.3957	0.3305	0.2765	0.2317	0.1945	0.1635	0.1161	0.0829	0.0703	0.0596	0.0431	0.0313	0.0168	0.0092	0.0051	0.0029
20	0.8195	0.6730	0.5537	0.4564	0.3769	0.3118	0.2584	0.2145	0.1784	0.1486	0.1037	0.0728	0.0611	0.0514	0.0365	0.0261	0.0135	0.0072	0.0039	0.0021
21	0.8114	0.6598	0.5375	0.4388	0.3589	0.2942	0.2415	0.1987	0.1637	0.1351	0.0926	0.0638	0.0531	0.0443	0.0309	0.0217	0.0109	0.0056	0.0029	0.0016
22	0.8034	0.6468	0.5219	0.4220	0.3418	0.2775	0.2257	0.1839	0.1502	0.1228	0.0826	0.0560	0.0462	0.0382	0.0262	0.0181	0.0088	0.0044	0.0022	0.0012
23	0.7954	0.6342	0.5067	0.4057	0.3256	0.2618	0.2109	0.1703	0.1378	0.1117	0.0738	0.0491	0.0402	0.0329	0.0222	0.0151	0.0071	0.0034	0.0017	0.0008
24	0.7876	0.6217	0.4919	0.3901	0.3101	0.2470	0.1971	0.1577	0.1264	0.1015	0.0659	0.0431	0.0349	0.0284	0.0188	0.0126	0.0057	0.0027	0.0013	0.0006
25	0.7798	0.6095	0.4776	0.3751	0.2953	0.2330	0.1842	0.1460	0.1160	0.0923	0.0588	0.0378	0.0304	0.0245	0.0160	0.0105	0.0046	0.0021	0.0010	0.0005
26	0.7720	0.5976	0.4637	0.3607	0.2812	0.2198	0.1722	0.1352	0.1064	0.0839	0.0525	0.0331	0.0264	0.0211	0.0135	0.0087	0.0037	0.0016	0.0007	0.0003
27	0.7644	0.5859	0.4502	0.3468	0.2678	0.2074	0.1609	0.1252	0.0976	0.0763	0.0469	0.0291	0.0230	0.0182	0.0115	0.0073	0.0030	0.0013	0.0006	0.0002
28	0.7568	0.5744	0.4371	0.3335	0.2551	0.1956	0.1504	0.1159	0.0895	0.0693	0.0419	0.0255	0.0200	0.0157	0.0097	0.0061	0.0024	0.0010	0.0004	0.0002
29	0.7493	0.5631	0.4243	0.3207	0.2429	0.1846	0.1406	0.1073	0.0822	0.0630	0.0374	0.0224	0.0174	0.0135	0.0082	0.0051	0.0020	0.0008	0.0003	0.0001
30	0.7419	0.5521	0.4120	0.3083	0.2314	0.1741	0.1314	0.0994	0.0754	0.0573	0.0334	0.0196	0.0151	0.0116	0.0070	0.0042	0.0016	0.0006	0.0002	0.0001
35	0.7059	0.5000	0.3554	0.2534	0.1813	0.1301	0.0937	0.0676	0.0490	0.0356	0.0189	0.0102	0.0075	0.0055	0.0030	0.0017	0.0005	0.0002	0.0001	*
40	0.6717	0.4529	0.3066	0.2083	0.1420	0.0972	0.0668	0.0460	0.0318	0.0221	0.0107	0.0053	0.0037	0.0026	0.0013	0.0007	0.0002	0.0001	*	*
45	0.6391	0.4102	0.2644	0.1712	0.1113	0.0727	0.0476	0.0313	0.0207	0.0137	0.0061	0.0027	0.0019	0.0013	0.0006	0.0003	0.0001	*	*	*
50	0.6080	0.3715	0.2281	0.1407	0.0872	0.0543	0.0339	0.0213	0.0134	0.0085	0.0035	0.0014	0.0009	0.0006	0.0003	0.0001	*	*	*	*
55	0.5785	0.3365	0.1968	0.1157	0.0683	0.0406	0.0242	0.0145	0.0087	0.0053	0.0020	0.0007	0.0005	0.0003	0.0001	*	*	*	*	*

TABLE A.8 Values of the Standard Normal Distribution Function

Z	0	1	2	3	4	5	6	7	8	9
−3.	0.0013	0.0010	0.0007	0.0005	0.0003	0.0002	0.0002	0.0001	0.0001	0.0000
−2.9	0.0019	0.0018	0.0017	0.0017	0.0016	0.0016	0.0015	0.0015	0.0014	0.0014
−2.8	0.0026	0.0025	0.0024	0.0023	0.0023	0.0022	0.0021	0.0021	0.0020	0.0019
−2.7	0.0035	0.0034	0.0033	0.0032	0.0031	0.0030	0.0029	0.0028	0.0027	0.0026
−2.6	0.0047	0.0045	0.0044	0.0043	0.0041	0.0040	0.0039	0.0038	0.0037	0.0036
−2.5	0.0062	0.0060	0.0059	0.0057	0.0055	0.0054	0.0052	0.0051	0.0049	0.0048
−2.4	0.0082	0.0080	0.0078	0.0075	0.0073	0.0071	0.0069	0.0068	0.0066	0.0064
−2.3	0.0107	0.0104	0.0102	0.0099	0.0096	0.0094	0.0091	0.0089	0.0087	0.0084
−2.2	0.0139	0.0136	0.0132	0.0129	0.0126	0.0122	0.0119	0.0116	0.0113	0.0110
−2.1	0.0179	0.0174	0.0170	0.0166	0.0162	0.0158	0.0154	0.0150	0.0146	0.0143
−2.0	0.0228	0.0222	0.0217	0.0212	0.0207	0.0202	0.0197	0.0192	0.0188	0.0183
−1.9	0.0287	0.0281	0.0274	0.0268	0.0262	0.0256	0.0250	0.0244	0.0238	0.0233
−1.8	0.0359	0.0352	0.0344	0.0336	0.0329	0.0322	0.0314	0.0307	0.0300	0.0294
−1.7	0.0446	0.0436	0.0427	0.0418	0.0409	0.0401	0.0392	0.0384	0.0375	0.0367
−1.6	0.0548	0.0537	0.0526	0.0516	0.0505	0.0495	0.0485	0.0475	0.0465	0.0455
−1.5	0.0668	0.0655	0.0643	0.0630	0.0618	0.0606	0.0594	0.0582	0.0570	0.0559
−1.4	0.0808	0.0793	0.0778	0.0764	0.0749	0.0735	0.0722	0.0708	0.0694	0.0681
−1.3	0.0968	0.0951	0.0934	0.0918	0.0901	0.0885	0.0869	0.0853	0.0838	0.0823
−1.2	0.1151	0.1131	0.1112	0.1093	0.1075	0.1056	0.1038	0.1020	0.1003	0.0985
−1.1	0.1357	0.1335	0.1314	0.1292	0.1271	0.1251	0.1230	0.1210	0.1190	0.1170
−1.0	0.1587	0.1562	0.1539	0.1515	0.1492	0.1469	0.1446	0.1423	0.1401	0.1379
−0.9	0.1841	0.1814	0.1788	0.1762	0.1736	0.1711	0.1685	0.1660	0.1635	0.1611
−0.8	0.2119	0.2090	0.2061	0.2033	0.2005	0.1977	0.1949	0.1922	0.1894	0.1867
−0.7	0.2420	0.2389	0.2358	0.2327	0.2297	0.2266	0.2236	0.2206	0.2177	0.2148
−0.6	0.2743	0.2709	0.2676	0.2643	0.2611	0.2578	0.2546	0.2514	0.2483	0.2451
−0.5	0.3085	0.3050	0.3015	0.2981	0.2946	0.2912	0.2877	0.2843	0.2810	0.2776
−0.4	0.3446	0.3409	0.3372	0.3336	0.3300	0.3264	0.3228	0.3192	0.3156	0.3121
−0.3	0.3821	0.3783	0.3745	0.3707	0.3669	0.3632	0.3594	0.3557	0.3520	0.3483
−0.2	0.4207	0.4168	0.4129	0.4090	0.4052	0.4013	0.3974	0.3936	0.3897	0.3859
−0.1	0.4602	0.4562	0.4522	0.4483	0.4443	0.4404	0.4364	0.4325	0.4286	0.4247
−0.0	0.5000	0.4960	0.4920	0.4880	0.4840	0.4801	0.4761	0.4721	0.4681	0.4641

(*Continued*)

TABLE A.8 (*Continued*)

Z	0	1	2	3	4	5	6	7	8	9
0.0	0.5000	0.5040	0.5080	0.5120	0.5160	0.5199	0.5239	0.5279	0.5319	0.5359
0.1	0.5398	0.5438	0.5478	0.5517	0.5557	0.5596	0.5636	0.5675	0.5714	0.5753
0.2	0.5793	0.5832	0.5871	0.5910	0.5948	0.5987	0.6026	0.6064	0.6103	0.6141
0.3	0.6179	0.6217	0.6255	0.6293	0.6331	0.6368	0.6406	0.6443	0.6480	0.6517
0.4	0.6554	0.6591	0.6628	0.6664	0.6700	0.6736	0.6772	0.6808	0.6844	0.6879
0.5	0.6915	0.6950	0.6985	0.7019	0.7054	0.7088	0.7123	0.7157	0.7190	0.7224
0.6	0.7257	0.7291	0.7324	0.7357	0.7389	0.7422	0.7454	0.7486	0.7517	0.7549
0.7	0.7580	0.7611	0.7642	0.7673	0.7703	0.7734	0.7764	0.7794	0.7823	0.7852
0.8	0.7881	0.7910	0.7939	0.7967	0.7995	0.8023	0.8051	0.8078	0.8106	0.8133
0.9	0.8159	0.8186	0.8212	0.8238	0.8264	0.8289	0.8315	0.8340	0.8365	0.8389
1.0	0.8413	0.8438	0.8461	0.8485	0.8508	0.8531	0.8554	0.8577	0.8599	0.8621
1.1	0.8643	0.8665	0.8686	0.8708	0.8729	0.8749	0.8770	0.8790	0.8810	0.8830
1.2	0.8849	0.8869	0.8888	0.8907	0.8925	0.8977	0.8962	0.8980	0.8997	0.9015
1.3	0.9032	0.9049	0.9066	0.9082	0.9099	0.9115	0.9131	0.9147	0.9162	0.9177
1.4	0.9192	0.9207	0.9222	0.9236	0.9251	0.9265	0.9278	0.9292	0.9306	0.9319
1.5	0.9332	0.9345	0.9357	0.9370	0.9382	0.9394	0.9406	0.9418	0.9430	0.9441
1.6	0.9452	0.9463	0.9474	0.9484	0.9495	0.9505	0.9515	0.9525	0.9535	0.9545
1.7	0.9554	0.9564	0.9573	0.9582	0.9591	0.9599	0.9608	0.9616	0.9625	0.9633
1.8	0.9641	0.9648	0.9656	0.9664	0.9671	0.9678	0.9686	0.9693	0.9700	0.9706
1.9	0.9713	0.9719	0.9726	0.9732	0.9738	0.9744	0.9750	0.9756	0.9762	0.9767
2.0	0.9772	0.9778	0.9783	0.9788	0.9793	0.9798	0.9803	0.9808	0.9812	0.9817
2.1	0.9821	0.9826	0.9830	0.9834	0.9838	0.9842	0.9846	0.9850	0.9854	0.9857
2.2	0.9861	0.9864	0.9868	0.9871	0.9874	0.9878	0.9881	0.9884	0.9887	0.9890
2.3	0.9893	0.9896	0.9898	0.9901	0.9904	0.9906	0.9909	0.9911	0.9913	0.9916
2.4	0.9918	0.9920	0.9922	0.9925	0.9927	0.9929	0.9931	0.9932	0.9934	0.9936
2.5	0.9938	0.9940	0.9941	0.9943	0.9945	0.9946	0.9948	0.9949	0.9951	0.9952
2.6	0.9953	0.9955	0.9956	0.9957	0.9959	0.9960	0.9961	0.9962	0.9963	0.9964
2.7	0.9965	0.9966	0.9967	0.9968	0.9969	0.9970	0.9971	0.9972	0.9973	0.9974
2.8	0.9974	0.9975	0.9976	0.9977	0.9977	0.9978	0.9979	0.9979	0.9980	0.9981
2.9	0.9981	0.9982	0.9982	0.9983	0.9984	0.9984	0.9985	0.9985	0.9986	0.9986
3.	0.9987	0.9990	0.9993	0.9995	0.9997	0.9998	0.9998	0.9999	0.9999	1.000

Source: Statistical Analysis: With Business and Economic Applications, 1969 by Holt, Rinehard and Winston, Inc.

FURTHER READING

Adams W, Brock J, editors. *The Structure of American Industry*. Upper Saddle River, NJ: Prentice Hall; 2001.

Adams W, Brock J, editors. *The Structure of American Industry*. Upper Saddle River, NJ: Prentice Hall; 2008.

Allen RGD. *Mathematical Analysis for Economists*. New York: MacMillan; 1976.

Argote L, Epple D. Learning curves in manufacturing. *Science* 1990;247: 920–924.

Baldani J, Bradfield J, Turner R. *Mathematical Economics*. New York: The Dryden Press; 1996.

Baumol W. *Economic Theory and Operations*. Englewood Cliffs, NJ: Prentice Hall; 1977.

Baye M. *Managerial Economics and Business Strategy*. McGraw-Hill; 2003.

Ben-Haim Y. *Info-Gap Decision Theory: Decisions under Severe Uncertainty*. 2nd ed. Amsterdam: Academic Press; 2006.

Bernheim B, Whinston M. *Microeconomics*. New York: McGraw-Hill; 2008.

Brennan M, Carroll T. *Preface to Quantitative Economics and Econometrics*. Estados Unidos: South-Western Publishing Co.; 1987.

Brigham E, Houston J. *Fundamentals of Financial Management*. New York: The Dryden Press; 1999.

Carlton DW, Perloff JM. *Modern Industrial Organization*. Reading, MA: Addison-Wesley; 2000.

Carlton DW, Perloff JM. *Modern Industrial Organization*. Reading, MA: Addison-Wesley; 2007.

Chiang A. *Fundamental Methods of Mathematical Economics*. 4th ed. New York: McGraw-Hill; 2005.

Colander D. New millennium economics: how did it get this way, and what way is it? *Journal of Economic Perspectives* 2000;14:121–132.

Cramer H. *Mathematical Methods of Statistics*. Princeton: Princeton University Press; 1999.

Douglas P. The Cobb-Douglas production function once again: its history, its testing, and some new empirical values. *Journal of Political Economy* 1984; 903–915.

Dowling ET. *Introduction to Mathematical Economics*. New York: McGraw-Hill; 2001.

Durbin J, Watson GS. Testing for serial correlation in least squares regression. *Biometrika* 1951;38:159–177.

Managerial Economics: A Mathematical Approach, First Edition. M. J. Alhabeeb and L. Joe Moffitt.
© 2013 John Wiley & Sons, Inc. Published 2013 by John Wiley & Sons, Inc.

Dukarat JR. Forecasting demand. Utility Business. May 2001.

Fama EF, Kenneth FR. The capital asset pricing model: theory and evidence. *Journal of Economic Perspectives* 2004; 25–46.

Friedman D. *Price Theory: An Intermediate Text*. Estados Unidos: South-Western Publishing Co; 1986.

Friedman J. Oligopoly pricing: old ideas and new tools. *Journal of Economic Literature* 2001; 573–575.

Gilboa I, Schmeidler D. Maximin expected utility with a non-unique prior. *Journal of Mathematical Economics* 1989;18:141–153.

Gitman L. *Principles of Managerial Finance*. 12th ed. Reading, MA: Addison-Wesley; 2008, Chap 5, pp. 8–9.

Glass J. *An Introduction to Mathematical Methods in Economics*. New York: McGraw-Hill; 1980.

Granger CW. *Forecasting in Economics and Business*. New York: Academic Press; 1989.

Green W. *Econometric Analysis*. Upper Saddle River, NJ: Prentice Hall; 2008.

Gujarati D. *Basic Econometrics*. New York: McGraw-Hill; 1995.

Hadar J. *Elementary Theory of Economic Behavior*. Reading, MA: Addison-Wesley; 1966.

Harris M, Raviv A. The theory of capital structure. *Journal of Finance* 1991; 297–355.

Henderson J, Quandt R. *Microeconomic Theory: A Mathematical Approach*. New York: McGraw-Hill; 1980.

Hirschey M. *Managerial Economics*. Australia: Thompson South-Western; 2006.

Hong H, Stein J, Yu J. Simple forecasts and paradigm shifts. *Journal of Finance* 2007; 1207–1242.

Honthakker H, Taylor L. *Consumer Demand in the United States: Analysis and Projections*. Cambridge, MA: Harvard University Press; 1970.

Jennings MM. Business schools' formula for irrelevance. *The Wall Street Journal—Manager's Journal*, November 28, 1994; A18.

Kahn AE. *The Economics of Regulation*. New York: John Wiley & Sons; 1971.

Katzner DW. *Time, Ignorance, and Uncertainty in Economic Models*. Ann Arbor, MI: University of Michigan Press; 1998.

Keat P, Young P. *Managerial Economics: Economic Tools for Today's Decision Makers*. Upper Saddle River, NJ: Pearson-Prentice Hall; 2006.

Knight FH. *Risk, Uncertainty, and Profit*. Houghton Mifflin Co. Re-issued by Chicago, IL: University of Chicago Press; 1921.

Lancaster K. *Consumer Demand: A New Approach*. New York: Columbia University Press; 1971.

Lancaster, K. Competition and product variety. *Journal of Business* 1980; S79–S105.

Landsbury S. *Price Theory and Applications*. Thompson South-Western; 2011.

Layard P, Walters A. *Microeconomic Theory*. McGraw-Hill; 1978.

Markowitz HM. Portfolio selection. *Journal of Finance* 1952;7: 77–91.

Mas-Colell A, Whinston MD, Green JR. *Microeconomic Theory*. New York: Oxford University Press; 1995.

Maxwell W. Production theory and cost curves. *Applied Economics* 1969; 211–224.

McGuigan J, Moyer R. *Managerial Economics*. West Publishing Company; 1979.

McMillan J. *Games, Strategies, and Managers*. New York: Oxford University Press; 1996.

Merrington M, Thompson CM. Tables of percentage points of the inverted beta (F) distribution. *Biometrica* 1943;33:73.

Modigliani F, Miller MH. The cost of capital, corporation finance and the theory of investment. *American Economic Review* 1958; 261–297.

Mukherjee TK, Henderson GV. The capital budgeting process: theory and practice. *Interfaces* 1987; 78–90.

Nechyba T. *Microeconomics: An Intuitive Approach.* South-Western Publishing; 2011.

Nevin JR. Laboratory experiments for establishing consumer demand: a validation study. *Journal of Marketing Research* 1974.

Nicholson W. *Microeconomic Theory.* Chicago, IL: The Dryden Press; 1985.

Oster SM. *Modern Competitive Analysis.* New York: Oxford University Press; 1999.

Pashigian B. *Price Theory and Applications.* Boston, MA: Irwin/McGraw-Hill; 1998.

Perloff J. *Microeconomics: Theory and Applications with Calculus.* Boston, MA: Pearson/Addison-Wesley; 2008.

Perold AF. The capital asset pricing model. *Journal of Economic Perspectives* 2004; 3–24.

Png I. *Managerial Economics.* Blackwell Publishers; 1998.

Porter M. *The Competitive Advantage of Nations.* New York: Free Press; 1990.

Porter M. *On Competition.* Cambridge, MA: Harvard University Press; 2008.

Posner R. Theories of economic regulation. *Bell Journal of Economics and Management Science* 1974; 335–358.

Ramanathan R. *Introductory Econometrics with Applications.* New York: The Dryden Press; 1998.

Render B, Stair RM Jr, Hanna ME. *Quantitative Analysis for Management.* 10th ed. Upper Saddle River, NJ: Pearson Education; 2009.

Robinson J. *The Economics of Imperfect Competition.* London: MacMillan; 1933.

Salvatore D. *Managerial Economies in a Global Economy.* New York: Oxford University Press; 2012.

Salvatore D. *Microeconomic Theory and Applications.* 5th ed. New York: Oxford University Press; 2009.

Salvatore D, Derrick R. *Theory and Problems of Statistics Econometrics.* 2nd ed. New York: McGraw-Hill; 2002.

Samuelson W, Marks S. *Managerial Economics.* New York: John Wiley & Sons; 2003.

Schelling TC. *The Strategy of Conflict.* Cambridge, MA: Harvard University Press; 1990.

Schultz H. *Theory and Measurement of Demand.* Chicago, IL: University of Chicago Press; 1964.

Shepherd WG. *The Economics of Industrial Organization.* Upper Saddle River, NJ: Prentice Hall; 2004.

Sick GA. A certainty-equivalent approach to capital budgeting. *Financial Management* 1986; 23–32.

Silberberg E. *The Structure of Economics: A Mathematical Analysis.* New York: McGraw-Hill; 1990.

Solomon D. Economic and accounting concepts of income. *The Accounting Review* 1961; 36.

Stigler G. *The Theory of Price.* New York: MacMillan; 1987.

Takayama A. *Mathematical Economics.* Cambridge: Cambridge University Press; 1985.

Teece DJ. Economies of scope and the scope of the enterprise. *Journal of Economic Behavior and Organization* 1980.

Truett L, Trueti D. *Managerial Economics: Analysis, Problems, and Cases.* South-Western College Publishing; 1998.

Varian H. *Intermediate Microeconomics: A Modern Approach.* W.W. Norton & Co; 1987.

Webster T. *Managerial Economics: Theory and Practice.* Amsterdam: Academic Press; 2003.

Weiss NA. *Introductory Statistics.* Reading, MA: Addison Wesley Longman; 2007.

Wetzstein M. *Microeconomic Theory.* Mason, OH: Thompson South-Western; 2005.

Wilson J, Keating B. *Managerial Economics.* Tokyo: Academic Press; 1986.

Wong RE. Profit maximization and alternative theories: a dynamic reconciliation. *American Economic Review* 1975; 65.

INDEX